ISOBEL DOOLE, ROBIN LOWE
AND ALEXANDRA KENYON

EIGHTH EDITION

# INTERNATIONAL MARKETING STRATEGY

## Analysis, Development and Implementation

Australia • Brazil • Mexico • Singapore • United Kingdom • United States

***International Marketing Strategy,***
**Eighth Edition**
**Doole, Lowe and Kenyon**

Publisher: Annabel Ainscow

List Manager: Virginia Thorp

Marketing Manager: Anna Reading

Content Project Manager: Melissa Beavis

Manufacturing Manager: Eyvett Davis

Typesetter: SPi Global

Text Design: SPi Global

Cover Design: Simon Levy Associates

Cover Image(s): ©nopporn/Shutterstock
.com, ©solarseven/Shutterstock.com,
©makc/Shutterstock.com

© 2019, Cengage Learning EMEA

For product information and technology assistance, contact us at
**emea.info@cengage.com**

For permission to use material from this text or product and for permission queries, email **emea.permissions@cengage.com**

*British Library Cataloguing-in-Publication Data*

A catalogue record for this book is available from the British Library.

ISBN: 978-1-4737-5874-2

**Cengage Learning, EMEA**
Cheriton House, North Way
Andover, Hampshire, SP10 5BE
United Kingdom

Cengage Learning is a leading provider of customized learning solutions with employees residing in nearly 40 different countries and sales in more than 125 countries around the world. Find your local representative at: **www.cengage.co.uk**.

Cengage Learning products are represented in Canada by Nelson Education, Ltd.

For your course and learning solutions, visit **www.cengage.co.uk**.

Purchase any of our products at your local college store or at our preferred online store **www.cengagebrain.com**.

Printed in China by RR Donnelley
Print Number: 01          Print Year: 2019

*To, Rob, Ash and Isla, Libby and Graham, Will, Rach and Margo.*

*Sylvia, Jonathan, Catherine, Simon, Ben and Edward*

*Steve, Peter, Sylvia and Tizzie*

# BRIEF CONTENTS

# CONTENTS

## PART I

## PART II

PART III

IMPLEMENTATION    301

# LIST OF FIGURES, TABLES, ILLUSTRATIONS AND MANAGEMENT CHALLENGES

## LIST OF FIGURES

## LIST OF ILLUSTRATIONS

## LIST OF MANAGEMENT CHALLENGES

# PREFACE

## Introduction

Markets and marketing are becoming ever more international in their nature, and managers around the world ignore this fact at their peril. To achieve sustainable growth in markets that are becoming increasingly global, or merely to survive in domestic markets that are increasingly attacked by international players, it is essential that organizations understand the complexity and diversity of international marketing. Their managers must develop the skills, aptitudes and knowledge necessary to compete effectively around the globe.

This new revised edition of *International Marketing Strategy* continues to meet the needs of the international marketing student and practitioner in an up-to-date and innovative manner. It recognizes the increasing time pressures of both students and managers and so strives to maintain the readability and clarity of the previous editions, as well as providing a straightforward and logical structure that will enable them to apply their learning to the tasks ahead.

The book continues to incorporate new, significant and relevant material with learning innovations that ensure its continued status as the best-selling UK text on international marketing strategy.

## Structure of the book

As in previous editions, the book is divided into three main subject areas – analysis, strategy development and implementation – each of which has four chapters. For each chapter the learning objectives for the reader are stated at the outset and these then lead to the key themes of the chapter which are explored in the text. Boxed 'Illustrations' throughout the text enable the reader to focus on the key issues and discuss the practical implications of these issues for international marketing strategy development. 'Management Challenges' in each of the chapters provide examples of the kind of practical dilemmas faced by international marketing managers in their everyday operations. Throughout the book we highlight a number of continuing and emerging themes in the management of international marketing. We provide the opportunity to explore the different mindsets of many types of businesses that depend on international markets for their survival and growth: from small poor farmers, to born global innovative technology businesses, to the global brand giants.

Success in international marketing is achieved through being able to integrate and appreciate the interaction between the various elements of the international marketing strategy development process, and this is addressed in two ways. First, at the end of each chapter two case studies are included. While the main focus of the chapter 'Case Studies' is on integrating a number of the chapter themes, the reader should also draw on his/her learning from the chapters that have gone before to give a complete answer. Second, at the end of each part there is a more comprehensive 'Directed Study Activity' for the reader that focuses on international marketing strategy development. At the end of Part I this activity is concerned with analysis, at the end of Part II with strategy development and at the end of Part III with implementation. The format for these study activities is similar so that the three Directed Study Activities, when added together, integrate all the learning from the book and provide a practical and comprehensive exercise in international marketing strategy development for the reader.

# New for this edition

All the chapters have been revised and updated to ensure the inclusion of the latest developments in international marketing and in response to the changing focus of international marketing and the new challenges posed by the new patterns of developments in global markets. For this reason, we provide many examples of international marketing and innovation in the newly emerging economies of Africa, particularly South Africa, and the Middle East, adding to the examples of development in Asian markets that we also include and build further on the website. We also explain the increasingly global risks, such as natural disasters and the increasing use of the Internet as a purchasing and process tool by consumers, and the changing development and implementation plans that international organizations, large or small, are making

In Chapter 1 we have included a full section introducing sustainability in an adapted SLEPTS approach to examining the environmental influences on international marketing. Sustainability is about considering the environmental impact of everything we do and ensuring there is longevity. This means encouraging a holistic way of thinking in our responses to the global marketing challenges we identify, together with the opportunities that technology and 'being responsible' bring for businesses engaging in the international arena.

The global economic crisis sparked a contraction in the volume of global trade; however, environmental disasters and cybercrime are shaping the agenda for both governments and business. The implications of these risks and political changes have altered the business landscape. These are discussed in Chapters 2 and 3 where we examine the world trading environment and discuss the institutions that aim to influence world trade. Chapters 5 and 6 on international marketing in SMEs and global firms have been expanded to include a section examining the skills base needed by global managers, the implications of the strategy development issues, how some companies are born global rather than grow internationally, and the age-old mantra that marketers must understand their target market and not assume all consumers, or workforces, are the same. Further examples of international companies from emerging markets provide the basis for discussion of the different contexts faced and the alternative growth strategies.

Customers around the world are more comfortable with the use of technology, and are becoming daily, if not hourly, users of social media, mobile commerce and cloud computing. We also highlight online/Internet engagement of different business-to-business and business-to-consumer situations throughout the chapters, particularly recognizing how new social media and the technology that drives this has impacted upon different geographic, economic, social and cultural contexts. This is examined particularly in the chapters in Part III where we focus on implementation issues. Chapter 12 focuses on this further when we examine how technology not only supports but drives invention and re-interpretation of international marketing communication strategies and delivery mechanisms. It examines how these enable individuals and businesses to use the Internet of Things, Artificial Intelligence and robots to their advantage.

The majority of the Case Studies, Illustrations and Management Challenges are new or updated. We have endeavoured to ensure the material we use reflects a global perspective and have included practical examples from across the world. For this edition we have included a number of our new Case Studies, Illustrations and Management Challenges from north and south Africa and the Middle East, and other emerging countries, in response to the advice and suggestions from reviewers, tutors and students. The authors have focused on responding to the needs of readers who are developing their international marketing skills in Europe, the Americas, Asia and Africa or other parts of the world. Moreover, we believe that organizations operating in these countries face some of the most significant and interesting international marketing challenges today and are developing the most novel solutions. Each Illustration and Management Challenge has questions highlighting specific issues that should be considered in the context of both the industry it focuses on and the area of the world it is spotlighting.

The Directed Study Activity (DSA) is an innovative section at the end of each part with the objective of encouraging readers to integrate their learning from the chapters and the parts. The DSA at the end of Part I highlights the rapid development of the mobile phone services market in Africa and uses this scenario as a backdrop for examining trading infrastructure issues, consumer behaviour issues and the development of a latent and exciting market. We focus in DSA 2 on the companies from emerging markets that are challenging the more established players and encourage readers to explore the alternative strategies adopted by these companies to expand their activity. We also encourage readers to consider those companies from emerging markets that have made substantial progress towards becoming global players during the last few years.

In DSA 3 we focus on the opportunities for growth for ISS World, which is a large international B2B outsourcing organization. They typically grow by spotting opportunities for their services such as contract cleaning, catering and security in emerging markets, due to the growth in businesses outsourcing, particularly for professional services.

By obtaining and analyzing data through secondary sources, typically through the Internet, the reader is able to proceed through the steps of the international marketing strategy process, thus acquiring further knowledge and using this opportunity to practise a number of their international marketing skills.

## How to study using this book

The aim of the book is for readers to have an accessible and readable resource for use both as a course book and for revision. The text is also recommended reading for students of the CIM qualifications.

It has a clear structure which is easy for the reader to follow, thus making it ideal for incorporation into a course delivered in a 12-week teaching semester. Its geocentric view of international marketing, with examples of good practice in competing internationally from around the globe, makes it ideal for use with courses with multicultural students.

*International Marketing Strategy* has been developed to help the reader learn, understand and practise a number of elements of the international marketing strategy process. The process involves the analysis of a situation, development of a strategy against a background of a number of strategic options, and the implementation of the chosen option. It is important to recognize that there is not one 'right' strategy, because success is ultimately determined by many factors. Besides, it will usually take a number of years before the strategy can be seen finally as a success or failure. Therefore, this book provides a framework, within the parts and chapter structure, in which to understand and evaluate the factors that should be taken into account (and which should be dismissed too) in building an international marketing strategy.

## Structure

### Parts

The three parts focus on the topics of analysis, strategy development and implementation. Each part contains an introduction to the four chapters that have been grouped together.

Readers should realize that these groupings of chapter topics within parts are primarily to provide a clear structure and layout for the book. In practice, however, there is considerable overlap between analysis, strategy development and implementation topics. For example, product strategy and market entry are considered by organizations in some situations to be implementation issues, and technology might be used to support analysis, set the overall international marketing strategy or support implementation.

**Part I Analysis** Part I focuses on analyzing the international marketing environment. It provides an introduction to how the international marketing environment influences how firms operate. It explores the changing nature of the environment and explains the structures that support and control international trade. Also considered are the social and cultural influences on customer buying behaviour in international markets.

Frameworks and processes that provide the means to systematically identify and evaluate marketing opportunities and carry out market research across the world are explained.

**PART II Strategy Development**   Part II explains the international marketing strategy options available for small- and medium-sized firms and also the largest organizations that will enable them to compete effectively in global markets. The factors that affect the choice of strategy are considered as well as the challenges that are posed to the managers of these strategies.

A key decision for most organizations is which market entry method to use to exploit the market opportunities from the many options available. This is then followed by the selection and development of the products and service strategy that determine the portfolio that will be offered to customers.

**PART III Implementation**   Part III deals with the international communication, distribution and pricing strategies that support the introduction and development of the business in the various worldwide markets. The different local market factors that affect implementation are considered. These factors may allow the associated implementation programmes and processes to be standardized across different markets but, frequently, it is necessary to adapt the strategies to suit local needs.

Technology plays a key enabling role in international marketing strategy implementation. It supports the programme and process delivery and also provides opportunities for creativity that allow innovative firms to gain competitive advantage.

## CASE STUDIES AT THE END OF EACH CHAPTER

### PART I ANALYSIS

#### Chapter 1

**Fast food: the healthy option goes global** Rising health awareness among consumers is impacting on the traditional fast food industry. Together with growth in online ordering and app-based companies offering delivery services, new opportunities are opening up for alternatives giving easily accessible healthy fast food to a health-conscious populace. This case looks at a fledgling company which has global ambitions to build an international base.

**Going international? You need a language strategy** Marketing internationally means communicating with customers, employees, investors and supply chain operators in a common language, but this inevitably means communicating in many different languages. This case explains the need for developing a language strategy and how it can be implemented.

#### Chapter 2

**Export tourism increases the host country's GDP** Exporting tourism can make a significant contribution to GDP both for developed and less developed countries. This case explores the tourism value chain and

how domestic companies can benefit from promotion and mega events targeted at international tourism.

**The mobile phone services market in Africa** Penetration of mobile phones is high in many but not all African countries. This case explores the economic and political factors driving the market growth. However, as well as identifying significant consumer benefits and attractive opportunities for firms in the market, this case also looks at the associated risks.

#### Chapter 3

**Building an international ethical brand: coffee** Large, multinational companies overwhelmingly dominate the global coffee drinking industry. Such companies have come under increasing scrutiny on ethical standards. The guidance by ethical consumer watchdogs has been to drink coffee sourced by Fairtrade suppliers. Yet, recently, they too have been criticized. This case presents a discussion about using ethical trading as a business strategy.

**Cultural challenges of the Brazilian market** Many organizations have tried to enter Brazil, but failed. The Brazilians have strong cultural and social behaviours that international organizations have found difficult to understand and embrace. This case examines the cultural challenges of establishing a presence in Brazil.

#### Chapter 4

**Global brands use of big data** Companies across the globe use huge data sets to mine information to their advantage: automating processes, gaining insight into their target markets and improving overall performance. This case looks at several companies that use such data in investigating international markets.

**Cultural segmentation map** Despite the ever-expanding global marketplace, consumers are not homogeneous. Differing values by country are presented in this case study. Differences are mapped showing which countries have traditional values and self-expression values, and which have secular rational values and survival values.

## Directed Study Activity 1 – International marketing planning: analysis

In this DSA we spotlight the rapid development of the mobile phone services market in Africa and use this scenario as a backdrop for examining trading infrastructure issues, consumer behaviour issues and the development of a latent and exciting market.

## PART II STRATEGY DEVELOPMENT

## Chapter 5

**Telensa: a shining light in smart cities** A streetlight technology firm demonstrates the innovative use of the Internet of Things in a city planning environment and rapid international sales growth.

**Pin it, share it, desire it, sell it** Pinterest is a fast-growing social media platform where SME e-tailers have the opportunity to provide a shop window to promote their products. This case looks at the benefits Pinterest offers to SMEs and how they should plan their presence on the platform to reach a global audience.

## Chapter 6

**Huawei: overcoming market obstacles** Huawei is an information and communication technology (ICT) company in China. It started making switches for up and coming technology businesses and went on to become an international company by investing in and creating cloud technology. Huawei is successful in a number of international markets, and this case study will prompt discussions around strategies that can be used to break into the US market.

**Re-shoring: rethinking global reach** Outsourcing of manufacturing and services offshore has been common practice for many firms, largely based on reasons of cost saving. However, many organizations have

been rethinking this strategy. This case considers the pros and cons of re-shoring and when it is an appropriate strategy.

## Chapter 7

**Wagamama's international expansion** Wagamama has company-owned outlets and franchises. The market entry strategy it uses has been successful, and it is keen to expand in new markets over the coming years. The success of Wagamama is down to a range of marketing mix activities, and these are outlined in this case study.

**IKEA in China: market entry flat packed?** IKEA wanted to engage with the Chinese market. Cultural traditions, existing home brands and other international competitive brands provide challenges for IKEA which are explored in this case study.

## Chapter 8

**Autonomous cars: looking for a driver!** Technology can make things happen that were deemed impossible. One of these things is the driverless car. This case study provides details of the benefits of an autonomous car, highlighting in particular Tesla's driverless vehicles.

**Accor inseparable services: online and face-to-face** Around the world the Accor brand has developed an excellent reputation for service in the hospitality sector. This case explores the importance of all the elements of the marketing mix of hospitality services and looks at how other organizations might learn from studying Accor's integrated approach.

## Directed Study Activity 2 – International marketing planning: strategy development

**Future global players** examines the different starting points and means used by newcomers from developing economies to build the global competitive capability necessary for them to compete with the more established competitive firms from developed countries.

## PART III IMPLEMENTATION

## Chapter 9

**UNiDAYS: a good deal for students worldwide** UNiDAYS is a case study that shows how tapping into the psyche of Generation Z through digital platforms can help global brands reach 10 million consumers worldwide, all of whom have one thing in common – they are students.

**Greenpeace: global campaigner** Greenpeace must balance the need to create awareness, which often requires shock tactics, with the need to raise funds and best leverage its resources, which are limited when compared to corporates and governments. This case explores how it must communicate effectively by adopting and integrating a variety of traditional offline and online media to appeal to its various target audiences.

## Chapter 10

**Bulk wine shifts the global wine market** The growth of the bulk wine sector has led to major changes in the way wine is distributed internationally. Bulk wine, which was once seen as the commodity low end of the market, has now become a major player in the distribution of wine globally. This case looks at how this trend has shifted the competitive nature of the market.

**Poor packaging = lost profits** This case looks at how the use of inappropriate packaging by the smallest rural farmer to the largest multinational can prove costly in terms of financial loss, waste of resources and environmental impact, and what can be done to specify more sustainable materials.

## Chapter 11

**The impact of cryptocurrencies** Cryptocurrency is a digital asset which has many capabilities, but one thing it is known for is being the functioning tool that distributes bitcoin. Technology of this kind has its advantages and disadvantages, and some are highlighted in this case study.

**Torque Developments International plc** Torque, a supplier of car components, faces a number of challenges in costing and pricing its products for global markets. This case considers the alternative costing and pricing models it is using and their relative merits in addressing these challenges.

## Chapter 12

**Heart problems? Wearable tech could save your life** Enabling consumers to be technology connected through the Internet of Things offers huge potential benefits. This case looks at the use of Wireless Body Area Network (WBAN) to monitor patients and rapidly provide information and alerts to medical staff. The case also looks at sharing personal information and the concerns of many people about privacy.

**Yum! brands: eating into international markets** Yum! Restaurants International (YRI), which holds brands such as KFC and Taco Bell, continues to grow. But despite its growth, YRI is still learning how to provide an international brand that adapts the marketing mix to ensure local culture and traditions are present.

## Directed Study Activity 3 – International marketing planning.

In this DSA we outline how a small business grew into an international provider of services including security, cleaning and catering. ISS World has grown organically but has made great strides in becoming a global player by identifying growth opportunities in different countries, by forming excellent B2B relationships which encourage repeat business, and because more businesses worldwide are choosing to outsource services.

# Chapters

After a brief introduction to each chapter the learning objectives are set out, which should provide the focus for study. To help to reinforce the learning and encourage the reader to explore the issues more fully, the chapters contain a number of additional aids to learning.

# Illustrations

The Illustrations that have been provided are not present just to reinforce a key issue or learning point that has been discussed within the chapter. The questions that have been added are intended to enable the reader to reflect upon the deeper and broader implications too and thus provide further opportunity for discussion. Our aim is that the settings for the Illustrations be as diverse as possible, geographically, culturally, by business sector, size and type of organization, in order to try to help the reader consider the situations described from alternative perspectives.

# Management Challenges

The Management Challenges emphasize the point that there are few simple and straightforward management decisions in international marketing. Organizations and managers often face difficult problems that require a decision. The Management Challenges within a chapter provide the opportunity for the reader to identify those factors that should be taken into account in coming to the decision and, hopefully, consider rather more creative ideas that lead to decisions and solutions that add greater value.

# Case Studies

The Case Studies provide the opportunity for the reader to carry out more comprehensive analysis of key chapter topics before deciding what strategic decisions or plans should be made. These Case Studies can also be used in the classroom so that analysis and discussions can take place following further research into the topic under investigation. These short cases provide only limited information and, where possible, readers should obtain more information on the Case Study subject from appropriate websites in order to complete the tasks. The reader should start with the questions that have been supplied in order to help guide the analysis or discussion. After this, however, the reader should think more broadly around the issues raised and decide whether these are indeed the right questions to ask and answer. International markets change fast and continuously, and new factors that have recently emerged may completely alter the situation.

# Directed Study Activities

At the end of each of the three parts of the book we have included a Directed Study Activity (DSA). Their purpose is to integrate the four chapters that make up each of the parts. More importantly, however, is that as a whole the three activities provide a framework for planning an international marketing strategy and give the opportunity for readers to consider the practical issues involved in developing, planning and implementing an outline international marketing strategy. The objective of these activities is to provide a vehicle through which the reader is able to develop practical skills in research, analysis, evaluation and strategy development. In completing these activities, you will need to synthesize the various strands and themes explored throughout the book and apply them to a practical situation.

*ID, RL, AK*

# ABOUT THE AUTHORS

## Isobel Doole

Isobel is an Emeritus Professor of International Marketing at Sheffield Hallam University and previously Dean of Sheffield Business School. She is an experienced marketing professional and senior academic in international marketing and in the international competitiveness of small firms. She has built an international reputation through her academic research and a number of highly successful textbooks. In her career she has worked with a range of companies from those with major international operations to small local exporters. She has also acted as an expert adviser on governmental committees.

## Robin Lowe

Robin is a Marketing and Management Consultant. Through his research, consultancy and policy development work in international trade, innovation and entrepreneurship, Robin has made a major contribution to government policy and business support. He also has considerable experience of consulting and training with multinationals around the world, including IBM, Microsoft, AstraZeneca, Renault Nissan, Huawei and Batelco. He is the joint author of several bestselling texts in international marketing, innovation and entrepreneurship.

## Alexandra Kenyon

Alexandra is a Course Director in Hospitality Management in the School of Events, Tourism and Hospitality at Leeds Beckett University. Alexandra was an FP7 European Commission Expert Evaluator and is on the Editorial Review Board for the *Journal of Advertising Research*. Alexandra also has knowledge and experience of empirical research and evaluation of matter congruent with the meetings and events industry and social media marketing for MPI Dallas, US, economic impact studies for the Tour de Yorkshire and social policy research for Leeds City Council of problem and at-risk gamblers following the opening of a large casino in Leeds City Centre.

# ACKNOWLEDGEMENTS

Inevitably, in the task of writing this textbook, we have had help, support and valuable contributions from many people. We would especially like to thank our colleagues from Sheffield Hallam University, Leeds Beckett University and other universities who have contributed a number of Case Studies and Illustrations. We would also like to thank Case Study contributors for their invaluable contributions to the digital support resources which accompany this book.

We are indebted to our students from many countries and the managers of many businesses who have freely given their time to share their expert knowledge of international niche marketing. Also, the managers in many larger companies who have discussed with us the challenges they face in global marketing. Over the years they have all helped to shape and influence our view of international marketing strategy.

The team at Cengage Learning have always encouraged us and we are grateful for their professionalism in turning the manuscript into its finished form.

The publisher would like to thank the following reviewers for their insightful feedback:

Edward Collins, University of Reading, UK

Nikolina Fuduric, University of Applied Sciences Northwestern Switzerland

Nima Heirati, Queen Mary University of London, UK

Jaan Ketts, Hanze University of Applied Sciences, The Netherlands

Wendy Tabrizi, Aston University, UK

## AIMS AND OBJECTIVES

Knowledge and an understanding of the markets in which companies operate are important for all business activities. In international markets, because of geographical distances and the complexities of operating in a number of disparate markets where risk and uncertainty are high, the need for knowledge and understanding becomes of paramount importance. It is this issue that is central to Part I of this book. The chapters in this section concentrate on helping the reader generate a greater understanding of the concepts of the international marketing process and the international environment within which companies operate. It aims to extend the range of understanding in order to enable the reader to deal with international marketing situations and to develop the skills to analyze and evaluate non-domestic markets, which in turn will enable their firms to compete effectively in world markets.

In Chapter 1 we focus on the international marketing environment. The book uses the SLEPTS approach to understand the complexities of external influences on international marketing, thus enabling the reader to acquire an appreciation of marketing on an international basis. We examine what is meant by international marketing and introduce the reader to the international market planning process. We also examine the reasons for success and failure in international marketing strategies and the characteristics of best international marketing practice.

In Chapter 2 the focus is on gaining an understanding of the world trading environment. We first examine, at a macro level, the development of international trading structures and the changes in trading patterns, as well as reviewing the major international bodies formed to foster world trade. The evolution of trading regions is analyzed and the implications for international marketing companies assessed.

In Chapter 3 we take a fairly detailed look at the social and cultural influences in international marketing. The components of culture are examined, together with the impact of these components on international marketing. We then look at how cultural influences impact on buyer behaviour across the globe both in consumer markets and in business-to-business markets and discuss methods that can be used to analyze cultures both within and across countries.

In Chapter 4 the focus is on the identification and evaluation of marketing opportunities internationally. Segmentation of international markets and how to prioritize international opportunities are discussed. The marketing research process and the role it plays in the development of international marketing strategies are also examined. The different stages in the marketing research process are discussed, with particular attention being paid to the problems in carrying out international marketing research in foreign markets and coordinating multi-country studies.

## CHAPTER 1

# AN INTRODUCTION TO INTERNATIONAL MARKETING

## LEARNING OBJECTIVES

After reading this chapter you should be able to:

- Explain and use the SLEPTS factors to assess international markets
- Discuss the differences between export marketing, international and global marketing
- Understand the criteria required to evaluate a company's international marketing strategy
- Appreciate the key steps in the international marketing planning process

## INTRODUCTION

Managers around the globe are recognizing the necessity for their companies and organizations to develop the skills, aptitudes and knowledge to compete effectively in international markets.

The fact that the world economy is open and interdependent, plus the globalization of consumer tastes and the unabated expansion of mobile Internet applications, which can be downloaded to smartphones to perform all kind of feats from social networking to online banking, all increase the interdependency and interconnections of country economies across the globe. The need for managers to develop the skills to maximize the opportunities such technological developments bring, impacts on companies of all shapes, sizes and sectors.

In this chapter, readers will be introduced to the concepts of international marketing, enabling them to acquire an appreciation of the complexities of marketing on an international basis and how this activity differs from operating purely in domestic home markets. In the following sections we will define international marketing, examine the important trends in the global marketing environment, and introduce the reader to the international marketing strategy development and international marketing planning process.

# The strategic importance of international marketing

The dollar value of world trade in merchandise exports is up based on 2017 data and now stands at US$17.2 trillion, an annual increase of 11 per cent. Similarly, world trade in commercial services exports has also increased and now stands at US$5.25 trillion, an increase of 7 per cent, again based on data from 2017 (World Trade Organization 2018). It is almost impossible to visualize such large amounts of money; however, it does serve as an indication of the scale of international trade today.

The world's population consisted of 7.6 billion people in 2017. The population is expected to rise to 9.8 billion by 2050 and could rise to 11.2 billion by 2100 (United Nations 2017). The population rate is not growing as fast as it used to. In fact, in 2007 the global population was growing around 1.24 per cent per year. Today's level (2017) is slightly lower with the population growing at a rate of around 1.10 per cent per year. However, the population is still growing, in part because in some countries, large families are still customary and people are living longer. Having said that, the United Nations predicts that by 2100 the population of the world might begin to plateau and possibly start to decline (see Figure 1.1).

Figure 1.1 shows that overall the global population will continue to rise but at a slower pace; populations in some countries will continue to grow while declining in others. For example, it is expected that 47 of the least developed countries, such as Burundi, Somalia and Zambia, will continue to have high growth in their populations. However, around 51 countries around the world, including Bulgaria, Croatia and Romania, will see their population reducing by around 15 per cent by 2050. What is interesting is by 2050 just nine countries will accommodate 50 per cent of the world's population.

The last few years have also seen a worldwide increase in personal wealth. Personal wealth means the total value of an adult's non-financial (usually land and housing) and financial assets less the debts that a person owes. Wealth per adult rose by 4.9 per cent, suggesting that an average adult's wealth is US$56 540, with United Kingdom (UK) adults being a high income country, enjoying US$278 038. Yet for low income countries such as Gambia, adult wealth is US$898 and in Ethiopia US$153. Despite the differences all regions have shown an increase in wealth per adult since 2000 when records of this nature began (Credit Suisse 2017). Within regions there are differences in wealth. This can be seen when comparing the UK average adult wealth of US$278 038 with the European average wealth, which is US$135 163. Similarly, the percentage share of the world's total wealth is not equally distributed, with North America accounting for 36.0 per cent and Europe 28.4 per cent. China, the country whose adult population is the

FIGURE 1.1   Population of the world 1950–2100, according to different projections and variants

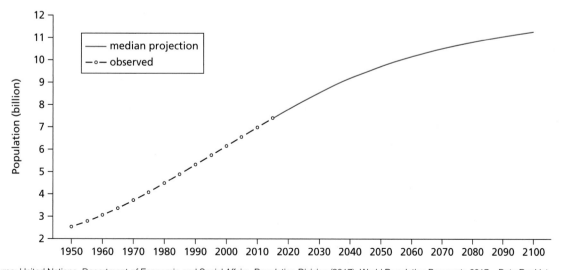

Source: United Nations, Department of Economic and Social Affairs, Population Division (2017). World Population Prospects 2017 – Data Booklet (ST/ESA/SER.A/401). Copyright © [2017] United Nations. Reprinted with the permission of the United Nations.

highest, accounts for 10.3 per cent of the world's total wealth. The increase in worldwide adult wealth suggests to the marketer that there is a general increase in demand for goods and services. Increasing affluence and commercial dynamism from nations such as China, Brazil and countries across Eastern Europe, means that consumers actively seek choice, with the result that globally competition is intensifying as companies compete to win the battle for disposable income.

Population growth and increased affluence together have helped create a global youth culture which accounts for approximately 30 per cent of the population globally. In many countries, more than half the population is pre-adult, creating one of the world's biggest single markets, the youth market. Everywhere adolescents project worldwide cultural icons: Coca-Cola, Apple, YouTube and Nike. Social networking in the forms of Facebook, Instagram and SnapChat are all now commonplace, creating a one-world youth culture market that potentially can exceed all others as a premier global market segment. Parochial, local and ethnic products may not satisfy the international culture and identity young people seek.

Older consumers are also increasingly transnational in their consumer identity. They drive globally produced cars, take worldwide holidays, watch programmes from across the globe on television, use globally developed technology and are increasingly plugged into the online digital media technology previously only used by the younger generation. On the supply side, transnational corporations are increasing in size and embracing more global power. The top 500 companies in the world account for 70 per cent of world trade and 80 per cent of international investment. Total sales for multinationals are now in excess of world trade, which gives them a combined gross product of more than some national economies.

To strategically position themselves for global competitiveness, companies are consolidating through mergers, acquisitions and alliances to reach the scale considered necessary to compete in the global arena. At the same time, there is a trend towards global standardization as companies strive for world standards for efficiency and productivity. With over a third of businesses worldwide considering growing their businesses through M&A, there will be many international marketing opportunities riding on the back of that (Consultancy.uk 2015). In 2017 the mergers and acquisitions total volume of dealmaking peaked at $3.5 trillion, trending upwards for the fourth year in a row (*FT* 2018). Some of the interesting deals made in 2017 included giant brands such as Facebook buying Instagram, the sale of the 21st Century Fox empire to Disney and the acquisition of Whole Foods by Amazon. It is anticipated that big brand M&As will increase in the coming years suggesting businesses are looking outside country borders and diversifying into multiple product portfolios.

In the telecommunication market, the French company Altice is an example of an organization growing its business both locally and cross-border. In 2015, Altice acquired SFR, a domestic French-based mobile communication company. Other organizations look further afield, with some seeing Turkey as a good place in which to do business. The Commercial Bank of Qatar looked to Turkey as part of their international strategy and joined forces with Alternatifbank AS in Turkey with an acquisition of over 70 per cent. The Japanese company Panasonic also entered Turkey when they acquired Viko, an organization that supplies electrical wiring equipment. Panasonic was not only interested in acquiring a local company to make and supply wires for its household electronic equipment, it sees this strategic move as an opportunity to break into the Russian and African markets. Panasonic is not the only Japanese organization to expand internationally. During 2016 China looked outward and bought many global assets including Syngenta, the producer of agrochemicals and seeds, and more 'trophy' assets such as football clubs, film productions companies, hotels and tourist resorts. In fact, for the first time, Chinese companies overtook US ones in terms of buying global assets (by value). However, it is expected that from 2018, Chinese companies will invest more heavily domestically and encourage two-way investment with companies with whom they currently do business.

The global marketplace is no longer the summation of a large number of independent country markets but much more multilateral and interdependent: economically, culturally and technically. Money, information and corporate ownership move seamlessly throughout the world. The ease of doing transactions and transmissions are facilitated by the convergence of long distance telecoms, cuts in the cost of electronic processing and the exponential growth in Internet access.

The combination of these forces has meant that all companies need to develop a marketing orientation which is global in nature. Companies also need managers who have the skills to analyze, plan and implement strategies across the world. It is for these reasons that international marketing has become such a critical area of study for managers and an important component of the marketing syllabus of business faculties in universities.

So perhaps now we should turn our attention to examining exactly what we mean by international marketing.

## What is international marketing?

Many readers of this textbook will have already followed a programme of study in marketing. But, before explaining what we mean by international marketing, let us reflect for a few moments on our understanding of what is meant by marketing itself. The Chartered Institute of Marketing defines marketing as the 'Management process responsible for identifying, anticipating and satisfying customer requirements profitably'. Thus, marketing involves:

- focusing on the needs and wants of customers
- identifying the best method of satisfying those needs and wants
- orienting the company towards the process of providing that satisfaction
- meeting organizational objectives.

In this way, it is argued, the company or organization best prepares itself to achieve competitive advantage in the marketplace. It then needs to work to maintain this advantage by manipulating the controllable functions of marketing within the largely uncontrollable, external marketing environment made up of the SLEPTS factors, i.e. Social, Legal, Economic, Political, Technological and Sustainable.

How does the process of international marketing differ? Within the international marketing process the key elements of this framework still apply. The conceptual framework is not going to change to any marked degree when a company moves from a domestic to an international market; however, there are two main differences. First, there are different levels at which international marketing can be approached. Second, the uncontrollable elements of the marketing environment are more complex and multidimensional, given the multiplicity of markets that constitute the global marketplace. This means managers have to acquire new skills and abilities to add to the tools and techniques they have developed in marketing to domestic markets.

## International marketing defined

At its simplest level, international marketing involves the organization making one or more marketing mix decisions across national boundaries. At its most complex, it involves the organization in establishing manufacturing/processing facilities and coordinating marketing strategies across the world. At the one extreme, there are organizations that opt for 'international marketing' simply by signing a distribution agreement with a foreign agent who then takes on the responsibility for pricing, promotion, distribution and market development. At the other, there are huge global companies, such as Ford and Ben and Jerry's, with an integrated network of manufacturing plants worldwide who operate in around 150 and 40 country markets, respectively. Thus, at its most complex, international marketing becomes a process of managing on a global scale. These different levels of marketing can be expressed in the following terms:

- *Domestic marketing*, which involves the company manipulating a series of controllable variables. These include price, advertising, distribution and the product/service attributes in a largely uncontrollable external environment. This environment is made up of different economic structures, competitors, cultural values and legal infrastructures within specific political or geographic country boundaries.

- *International marketing*, which involves operating across a number of foreign country markets. Here, uncontrollable variables differ significantly between one market and another, but the controllable factors in the form of cost and price structures, opportunities for advertising and distributive infrastructure, are also likely to differ significantly. It is these sorts of differences that lead to the complexities of international marketing.
- *Global marketing management*, which is a larger and more complex international operation. Here a company coordinates, integrates and controls a whole series of marketing programmes into a substantial global effort. The primary objective of the company is to achieve a degree of synergy in the overall operation. By so doing, it can take advantage of different exchange rates, tax rates, labour rates, skill levels and market opportunities. As a result, the organization as a whole will be greater than the sum of its parts.

This type of strategy calls for managers who are capable of operating as international marketing managers in the truest sense, a task which is far broader and more complex than that of operating either in a specific foreign country or in the domestic market. In discussing this, Doyle (2017) suggests international marketing managers have dual responsibilities to the parent brand and the local needs of consumers in a foreign country. She says, 'You can carry on with the same global architecture of your idea [brand], but you need to bring this . . . [brand] . . . into the local market with relevance. You need to make sure to offer the ideas differently for each market.' She therefore emphasizes that international brands must be managed by staying true to their values and goals. So, international marketing managers must coordinate marketing efforts in multiple countries, combining domestic and foreign markets, and standing out . . . in a highly competitive marketplace.

Thus, how international marketing is defined and interpreted depends on the level of involvement of the company in the international marketplace. International marketing could therefore be:

- Export marketing, in which case the firm markets its goods and/or services across national/political boundaries, often without any adaptations to the goods and/or services. Generally, exporting begins with neighbouring countries that have similar laws, regulations and consumer culture.
- International marketing, where the marketing activities of an organization include activities, interests or operations in more than one country. There is usually some kind of influence or control of marketing activities from outside the country in which the goods or services will actually be sold. Sometimes markets are typically perceived to be independent and a profit centre in their own right, in which case the term multinational or multi-domestic marketing is often used.
- Global marketing, in which the whole organization focuses on the selection and exploitation of global marketing opportunities. It marshals its resources around the globe with the objective of achieving a global competitive advantage.

The first of these definitions describes relatively straightforward exporting activities, numerous examples of which exist. However, the subsequent definitions are more complex and more formal. They indicate not only a revised attitude to marketing but also a very different underlying philosophy. Here the world is seen as a market segmented by social, legal, economic, political, technological and sustainable (SLEPTS) groupings.

In this textbook, we will incorporate the international marketing issues faced by firms, be they involved in export, international or global marketing.

For all these levels, the key to successful international marketing is being able to identify and understand the complexities of each of these SLEPTS dimensions of the international environment and how they impact on a firm's marketing strategies across their international markets. As in domestic marketing, the successful marketing company will be the one that is best able to manipulate the controllable tools of the marketing mix within the uncontrollable, external environment. It follows that the key problem faced by the international marketing manager is that of coming to terms with the details and complexities of the international environment. It is these complexities that we will examine in the following sections.

At this point it is also useful to refer to the concept of the internationalization of an organization, widely discussed in the academic literature. There are a number of definitions of internationalization, much research and many different theories on the subject, which are too extensive to cover here. Moreover, the sheer complexity of international marketing suggests that all the theories have limitations. We have introduced some, but by no means all, theories in Table 1.1 and invite discussion.

Table 1.1   Theories of internationalization

**Definition of internationalization**  The method of adapting an organization's operations to foreign environments.

**Internationalization process theories**  From the brief introduction in this chapter, the reader should undertake research to gain an understanding of the key aspects and limitations of the theories. The theories that probably (but not always) work best with multinational enterprises (MNEs) are the economic and behavioural approaches. Smaller firms, on the other hand, often adopt a network/relationship approach or a 'born global' approach.

**Economic model**  With a base in the economics of organizations and markets, Transaction Cost Theory focuses on the cost of taking part in a market (from start to finish). It is based on whether the external transactions are greater than the internal transactions. For example, an MNE internationalizes due to economies of scale and efficiencies. These result from better knowledge and technology and enable them to compete successfully against local organizations that have traditionally supplied the market. Dunning's (1988) Eclectic Theory provides a framework to explain the factors, incentives and configurations that drive MNEs in international markets. The theory seeks to answer the questions: should the firm enter foreign markets; in which markets should it invest; and how should it organize for the markets? An international version of the product life cycle might propose that after saturating the domestic market, further growth for the organization would require participation in foreign markets.

**Behavioural model**  The Uppsala model proposes that firms build their knowledge in the domestic market, then start overseas operations in nations that are close culturally, geographically and in terms of religion. They should start with export-type approaches before progressing to more involvement in countries.

**Network or relationship model**  This theory proposes that a network of long-term relationships among suppliers, customers, competitors, extended family, friends and other stakeholders provide the opportunity, support and motivation for internationalization. The relationships are dependent on technical, market knowledge, and economic interdependence, but maintaining personal relationships is key.

**Born global model**  Organizations based on an innovation that appeals to global customers, use web-based communications technology to market their products and services to customers, anywhere in the world, from day one. They believe that it is necessary to build their global market before competition emerges. Born global firms tend to have leaders that create and transform companies through a clear, shared vision for the business. The leader is strong with an envisioning style that communicates and demonstrates a team spirit culture. He/she is someone who also empowers their team to take responsibility and collectively drive the business forward.

# The international marketing environment

The key difference between domestic marketing and marketing on an international scale is the multidimensionality and complexity of the many foreign country markets a company may operate in. An international manager needs a knowledge and awareness of these complexities and the implications they have for international marketing management.

There are many environmental analysis models which the reader may have come across. For the purposes of this textbook, we will use the SLEPTS approach and examine the various aspects and trends in the international marketing environment through the social/cultural, legal, economic, political, technological and sustainability dimensions, as depicted in Figure 1.2. In this edition, we have added a sustainability dimension. Sustainability is about considering the impact of everything we do, be it sympathy for the biodiversity of a region in which we want to construct a factory, or the human rights of the workforce. This means encouraging a holistic way of thinking in our responses to the global marketing challenges we identify and assessing the impact of our marketing strategies – socially, economically and environmentally – in our approach to ensuring sustainability over the longer term.

**FIGURE 1.2**   Factors influencing international markets

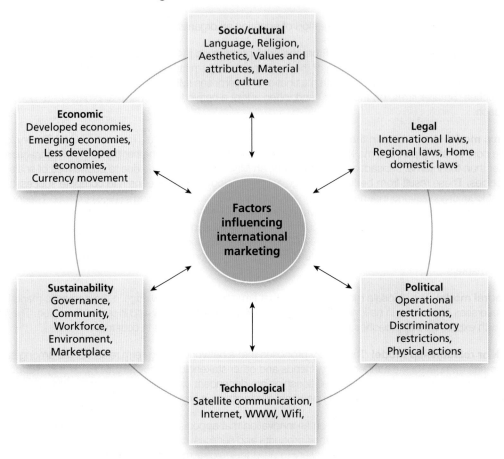

## Social/cultural factors

The social and cultural influences on international marketing are immense. Differences in social conditions, religion and material culture all affect consumers' perceptions and patterns of buying behaviour. It is this area that determines the extent to which consumers across the globe are either similar or different and so determines the potential for global branding and standardization.

A failure to understand the social/cultural dimensions of a market are complex to manage, as McDonald's found in India. It had to deal with a market that is 40 per cent vegetarian and where the population does not eat either beef or pork. They also have a hostility to frozen meat and fish, but with the general Indian fondness for spice. To satisfy such tastes, McDonald's discovered it needed to do more than provide the right burgers. Customers buying vegetarian burgers wanted to be sure that these were cooked in a separate area in the kitchen using separate utensils. Sauces such as McMasala and McImli were developed to satisfy the Indian taste for spice. Interestingly, however, these are now innovations they have introduced into other markets.

## Cultural factors

Cultural differences and especially language differences have a significant impact on the way a product may be used in a market, its brand name and the advertising campaign, for example, Yong Fang Pearl Cream is a moisturising cream produced for Chinese women. The word Fang 芳 conjures up images of beauty in China; however, Western women would associate the word fang with the teeth of a wolf or a poisonous snake. So, they would shy away from products associated with possible danger. Images associated with words are just one element the international marketer must consider in terms of product management. Another cultural factor is the pronunciation of words. For example, Coca-Cola had enormous problems in China, as Coca-Cola sounded like 'Kooke Koula', which translates into 'A thirsty mouthful of candle wax'. The company managed to find a new pronunciation 'Kee Kou Keele' which means 'joyful tastes and happiness'. Companies that have experienced similar problems in Germany include Irish Mist, which introduced its drink brand, and Estée Lauder, who exported liquid make-up called Country Mist. The problem word was 'Mist', which is a slang word for 'manure' in Germany.

Pepsi Cola had to change its campaign 'Come Alive with Pepsi' in Germany as, literally translated, it means 'Come Alive Out of the Grave'. In Japan, McDonald's character Ronald McDonald failed because his white face was seen as a death mask. Products launched in France have not always been successful. When Apple launched the iMac in France it discovered the brand name mimicked the name of a well-established brand of baby laxative – hardly the image they were trying to project. An actual baby product by Gerber is sold in many countries, but not in France, as Gerber means 'vomit' in French.

Operating effectively in different countries requires recognition that there may be considerable differences in different regions. Consider northern Europe versus Latin Europe, the northwest of the USA versus the south, or Beijing versus Taipei. At the stage of early internationalization, it is not unusual for firms to experience what appear to be cultural gaps with their counterparts in the countries they are expanding into. This can be for West going East or the East going West. A campaign by Camay soap which showed a husband washing his wife's back in the bath was a huge success in France. It failed in Japan, however, not because it caused offence but because Japanese women viewed the prospect of a husband sharing such time as a huge invasion of privacy.

On the other hand, some commentators argue there are visible signs that social and cultural differences are becoming less of a barrier. The dominance of a number of world brands such as Apple, Burberry, Facebook, Mini Cooper, McDonald's, Holiday Inn and Google etc., all competing in global markets that generally transcend national and political boundaries, are testimony to the convergence of consumer needs and international acceptance of new words worldwide. However, it is important not to confuse globalization of brands with the homogenization of cultures. There are a large number of global brands but even these have to manage cultural differences between and within national country boundaries.

There are also a number of cultural paradoxes which exist. For example, in Asia, the Middle East, Africa and Latin America, there is evidence both for the westernization of tastes and the assertion of ethnic, religious and cultural differences. Companies such as Avon Cosmetics who sell directly through their own distributors are well placed to exploit such paradoxes in emerging markets. In Thailand, Buddhist monks are often seen in full traditional dress doing their online mobile banking with an app downloaded to their mobile phone, or taking selfies in front of one of the many historical statues. Thus, there is a vast and sometimes turbulent mosaic of cultural differences when buying, sharing experiences and giving product advice through the online global village or in cafes and tea shops around the world. Indeed, the social and commercial online borderless village enables organizations to promote their goods and services to consumers in different regions of the world simultaneously. In fact, 'born global' organizations, mostly niche small- and medium-sized enterprises, begin with a vision to *be* international from the moment they launch their brand. In 2016 Jean-François Gagné, an established entrepreneur, and Yoshua Bengioir, whose background is in artificial intelligence research, joined forces to form Element AI (Artificial Intelligence). Their goal is to 'push the limits of AI to make it much more flexible'. They do this with a team of scientists and engineers that works together with a worldwide client network. Element AI has the characteristics of growing fast, providing cutting edge AI solutions to businesses and debating the future of AI in journals and at conferences around the globe.

The social/cultural environment is an important area for international marketing managers. We will return to this subject in a number of chapters where we examine the various aspects of its strategic implications. Chapter 3 is devoted to a full examination of the social and cultural influences in international marketing. In Chapter 5 we will examine the forces driving the global village and its strategic implication for companies across the world.

## Social factors

Growth and movement in populations around the world are important factors heralding social changes. Currently, of the world's population, 60 per cent live in Asia (notably 4.5 billion of the world's population of 7.6 billion), with 17 per cent living in Africa. In terms of countries, China and India have the highest populations with 1.4 billion and 1.3 billion, respectively, which accounts for 36 per cent of the world's population (United Nations 2017). This means nearly two out of every five people live in China and India. However, while world population is growing dramatically, the growth patterns are not consistent around the world. Examples of inconsistency are due to life expectancy and number of births.

Worldwide, the life expectancy at birth has changed in recent years, increasing from 65 years for men in 2000–2005 to 69 years in 2010–2015. For women, the life expectancy at birth has risen from 69 years to 73 years. Population life expectancy in some countries such as Australia, Hong Kong SAR (China) Island, Italy, Japan, Macao SAR (China), Singapore, Spain and Switzerland at present is around 82 years for both men and women. However, it is as low as 55 years for those living in other countries such as the Central African Republic, Chad, Côte d'Ivoire, Lesotho, Nigeria, Sierra Leone, Somalia and Swaziland.

It is also useful to note that continents have differing age densities. Some have a relatively young population and others an older population. Take for example Africa and Europe. In Africa 60 per cent of the population is under the age of 24 years old, whereas in Europe the average is 27 per cent. At the other end of the population scale 25 per cent of the population in Europe is 60 years and over, whereas in Africa it is 5 per cent. Globally, life expectancy for both sexes combined is projected to rise from 71 years in 2010–2015 to 77 years in 2045–2050 and around 83 years in 2095–2100.

The number of births per woman is another indicator that can help predict changes in the world's population. As shown in Figure 1.1 and indicated in Table 1.2, the population by 2095–2100 may stabilize or even fall. One of the reasons for this is the number of births per woman. In 2005–2010 the number of births per woman in the world was 2.57. This is predicted to fall to 1.97 by 2095–2100. The only continents where there is predicted to be an increase in the number of births per woman are Europe and North America. It is worth noting that the number of births per woman for the replacement of the population in the long term is around 2.1 births per woman.

It had been predicted that India would surpass China's population by 2028. However, the latest projections (United Nations 2017) show that in 2024, both India and China will have populations of 1.44 billion, with India exceeding China's population in 2030. China's population is predicted to decline slowly after the 2030s.

There are also visible moves in the population within many countries, leading to the formation of huge urban areas where consumers have a growing similarity of needs across the globe. In 2016, an

Table 1.2　Births per woman 2005–2010 to predicted 2095–2100

| Region, country or area | Total fertility (live births per woman) | | |
|---|---|---|---|
| | 2005–2010 | 2025–2030 | 2095–2100 |
| **World** | 2.57 | 2.39 | 1.97 |
| **Africa** | 4.89 | 3.90 | 2.14 |
| **Asia** | 2.30 | 2.06 | 1.81 |
| **Europe** | 1.55 | 1.69 | 1.84 |
| **Latin America and the Caribbean** | 2.26 | 1.89 | 1.78 |
| **Northern America** | 2.01 | 1.87 | 1.91 |
| **Oceania** | 2.53 | 2.23 | 1.86 |

Source: United Nations, Department of Economic and Social Affairs, Population Division (2017). World Population Prospects: The 2017 Revision, Key Findings and Advance Tables. Working Paper No. ESA/P/WP/248. Copyright © [2017] United Nations. Reprinted with the permission of the United Nations.

estimated 54.5 per cent of the world's population lived in urban settlements. By 2030, urban areas are projected to house 60 per cent of people globally, and one in every three people will live in cities with at least half a million inhabitants.

What is even more interesting is the number of people living in *megacities*. Megacities are those with more than 10 million inhabitants. Currently there are 31 megacities, with Tokyo being home to 38 million people. Tokyo is predicted to have the highest population of residents in 2030 but with a slightly lower population of 37.2 million. New York, once one of the top megacities, is being overtaken by cities in India and China (United Nations 2016). Table 1.3 shows the 20 megacities of the world and the projections for the future. This has powerful implications for international marketing as these cities will provide a new type of consumer, particularly the urban dweller who requires faster, more convenient services and products, is highly connected online, tends to live in an apartment and seeks convenient transportation. The urban

**Table 1.3**   Top 20 megacities of the world and projections for the future

| Rank | City, Country | Population in 2016 (thousands) | City, Country | Population in 2030 (thousands) |
|---|---|---|---|---|
| 1 | Tokyo, Japan | 38 140 | Tokyo, Japan | 37 190 |
| 2 | Delhi, India | 26 454 | Delhi, India | 36 060 |
| 3 | Shanghai, China | 24 484 | Shanghai, China | 30 751 |
| 4 | Mumbai (Bombay), India | 21 357 | Mumbai (Bombay), India | 27 797 |
| 5 | São Paulo, Brazil | 21 297 | Beijing, China | 27 706 |
| 6 | Beijing, China | 21 240 | Dhaka, Bangladesh | 27 374 |
| 7 | Ciudad de México (Mexico City), Mexico | 21 157 | Karachi, Pakistan | 24 838 |
| 8 | Kinki M.M.A. (Osaka), Japan | 20 337 | Al-Qahirah (Cairo), Egypt | 24 502 |
| 9 | Al-Qahirah (Cairo), Egypt | 19 128 | Lagos, Nigeria | 24 239 |
| 10 | New York-Newark, USA | 18 604 | Ciudad de México (Mexico City), Mexico | 23 865 |
| 11 | Dhaka, Bangladesh | 18 237 | São Paulo, Brazil | 23 444 |
| 12 | Karachi, Pakistan | 17 121 | Kinshasa, Democratic Republic of the Congo | 19 996 |
| 13 | Buenos Aires, Argentina | 15 334 | Kinki M,M.A. (Osaka), Japan | 19 976 |
| 14 | Kolkata (Calcutta), India | 14 980 | New York-Newark, USA | 19 885 |
| 15 | Istanbul, Turkey | 14 365 | Kolkata (Calcutta), India | 19 092 |
| 16 | Chongqing, China | 13 744 | Cuangzhou, Guangdong, China | 17 574 |
| 17 | Lagos, Nigeria | 13 661 | Chongqing, China | 17 380 |
| 18 | Manila, Philippines | 13 131 | Buenos Aires, Argentina | 16 956 |
| 19 | Guangzhou, Guangdong, China | 13 070 | Manila, Philippines | 16 756 |
| 20 | Rio de Janeiro, Brazil | 12 981 | Istanbul, Turkey | 16 694 |

Source: United Nations, Department of Economic and Social Affairs, Population Division (2016). The World's Cities in 2016 – Data Booklet (ST/ESA/ SER.A/392). Copyright © [2016] United Nations. Reprinted with the permission of the United Nations.

dweller also wants to engage in many leisure and lifestyle experiences. For businesses, urban city dwellers are easily identifiable. Firms can communicate with them efficiently via advertising and communication tools on electronic billboards, social media and through geo-tracking technology.

Therefore, megacities are an attractive place to do business and to seek and attract new consumers. And with the likelihood of ten new megacities emerging by 2030 – Lahore (Pakistan), Hyderabad (India), Bogotá (Colombia), Johannesburg (South Africa), Bangkok (Thailand), Dar es Salaam (Tanzania), Ahmadabad (India), Luanda (Angola), Ho Chi Minh City (Vietnam) and Chengdu (China) – such cities are fertile ground for marketers. Some cities such as Paris (France) and London (UK) were once in the top ten megacities in the world. However, they are currently 25th and 29th respectively and are projected to fall further down the worldwide list of megacities by 2030 to 33rd and 36th.

## Legal factors

Legal systems vary both in content and interpretation. A company is not just bound by the laws of its home country but also by those of its host country and by the growing body of international law. This can affect many aspects of a marketing strategy – for instance advertising – in the form of media

**ILLUSTRATION 1.1**

# Megacities or mega digital: which will dominate in the future?

Market analysts and business models favoured the development of megacities. And it has long been expected that megacities will continue to grow to unimaginable sizes. It has been acknowledged that there are downsides to megacities such as:

- the huge displacement of millions of people
- unsustainable infrastructure
- large areas of inadequate slum-like housing
- poor air quality, and
- high numbers of socially fragmented citizens.

However, the opportunities for people who live and work in megacities are endless in terms of the different cultural experiences available, the variety of night and day-time entertainment, uber-modern technology and, of course, potential job opportunities.

In terms of economics, whether a developing or a developed country, those with cities populated with over 10 million citizens account for around one-third to one-half of the country's Gross Domestic Product. Megacities, therefore, are hubs that boost innovative ideas, growth and productivity. Indeed, clustering workforces within cities not only provides vibrant workspaces but leads to excellent economies of scale.

Despite the expected growth in megacities' businesses, workers and consumers are turning away from the megacities' professional services, manufacturing and retail spaces, and looking instead at digital opportunities. Digital opportunities for the manufacturing industry include 3-D printing to create anything from cars to sports training shoes and no longer need to cluster a large workforce. Shopping centres have always been located near cities, yet visits by consumers have declined by around 50 per cent as they prefer to browse and buy using smartphones and tablets.

## Questions

**1** In addition to 3-D printing and shopping online, what other digital activities will affect manufacturing and retail?

**2** How should professional services such as doctors, dentists, banks or offices adapt and move from megacities to digital?

**Reference:** Lim, C.H. and Mack, V. (2017) Can the world's megacities survive the digital age? Available from: www.smithsonianmag.com/innovation/can-worlds-megacities-survive-digital-age-180964967/ (accessed 21 January 2018).

restrictions and the acceptability of particular creative appeals (see Illustration 1.2). Product acceptability in a country can be affected by minor regulations on such things as packaging and by more major changes in legislation. In the USA, for example, the MG sports car was withdrawn when the increasing difficulty of complying with safety legislation changes made exporting to that market unprofitable. Kraft Foods sells a product called Lifesavers, which is very similar to the Nestlé Polo brand, in many countries. Using EU law, Nestlé attempted to stop the sale of Lifesavers in the EU purely to protect their market share.

## ILLUSTRATION 1.2

# Product placement laws in films

Young people often look to film stars to be their role models. They know that film stars set trends in fashion and behaviour. Film stars, and the characters they depict, reach out from the screen and form 'para social' relationships with the audience. So close is this relationship that audiences, especially adolescents, suspend their everyday life to join the glamorous party, hang out with the rebels or join the space crew to explore the galaxy and save the world.

Many highly sought after branded products are placed, for a fee, within the film set to stimulate awareness and desirability, particularly when linked, even for a fleeting moment, with film heroes and villains. Viewers, therefore, associate products with behaviours they see in films. Sometimes in a film the character reaches for a cigarette to show they are being defiant, have had a hard day or just to be part of the crowd.

It is the depiction of smoking behaviour that worries organizations such as the World Health Organization, World Lung Foundation and the National Cancer Institute. It is declared, especially by cigarette companies, that smoking in films is not advertising. However, there are many that disagree and go on to say that the fact smoking is in films normalizes behaviour and influences young people to smoke.

Currently around 50 per cent of films contain smoking behaviour (this includes old and new films). Some governments have put sanctions in place to reduce and remove smoking behaviour and links to cigarette brands from films. In India, any film that includes scenes of characters smoking has to include a written health warning. Additionally, a 20-second video outlining the side effects that smoking has must appear at the beginning and in the middle of the film. In China, the State Administration of Radio, Film and Television (SARFT) has advised film and television drama producers to reduce the number of excessive smoking scenes. The Chinese authority also stated that young people (minors) cannot be seen buying cigarettes or being with people who are smoking.

## Questions

**1** What would be the benefits of having one set of laws and regulations for all countries to implement regarding smoking in films?

**2** What would be the downside of having one set of laws and regulations for all countries to implement regarding smoking in films?

**3** What other products that are placed in films should be governed by laws and regulations?

It is important, therefore, for the firm to know the legal environment in each of its markets. These laws constitute the 'rules of the game' for business activity. The legal environment in international marketing is more complicated than in domestic markets since it has three dimensions: (1) local domestic law; (2) international law; (3) domestic laws in the firm's home base.

■ *Local domestic laws*: These are all different! The only way to find a route through the legal maze in overseas markets is to use experts on the separate legal systems and laws pertaining in each market targeted.

■ *International law*: There are a number of international laws that can affect the organization's activity. Some are international laws covering piracy and hi-jacking. Others are more international conventions and agreements and cover items such as the International Monetary Fund (IMF) and World Trade Organization (WTO) treaties, patents and trademarks legislation and organizations such as the United Nations which developed the Universal Declaration of Human Rights that belongs to all people worldwide.

■ *Domestic laws in the home country*: The organization's domestic (home market) legal system is important for two reasons. First, there are often export controls which limit the free export of certain goods (e.g. military items) and services to particular marketplaces. Second, there is the duty of the organization to act and abide by its national laws in all its activities, whether domestic or international.

It is easy to understand how domestic, international and local legal systems can have a major impact upon the organization's ability to market into particular overseas countries. Laws will affect the marketing mix in terms of products, price, distribution and promotional activities quite dramatically. For many firms, the legal challenges they face in international markets are almost a double-edged sword. Often firms operating internationally face ethical challenges in deciding how to deal with differing cultural perceptions of legal practices.

In many mature markets, they face quite specific and, sometimes, burdensome regulations. Following the Paris Climate Convention 2012, many countries are striving to implement environmental regulations and laws. These regulations and laws require a firm to be responsible for the retrieval and disposal of the packaging waste it creates and produce packaging which is recyclable. In many emerging markets there may be limited patent and trademark protection, judicial systems that are still being developed, non-tariff barriers and instability through an ever-evolving reform programme.

China earned notoriety in the past for allowing copyright infringements and blatant piracy. However, this is now changing. Some governments are reluctant to develop and enforce laws protecting intellectual property, partly because they believe such actions favour large, rich multinationals. Anheuser Busch (USA) and Budvar (Czech Republic) have been in constant litigation over the right to use the name Budweiser in the European Union, and both companies have recently been given the legal right to use it.

Piracy in markets with limited trademark and patent protection is another issue. One of the biggest challenges faced internationally is the use of unlicensed, therefore pirated, online streaming. The English Premier League was triumphant when it won an anti-piracy court order to block illegal access and streaming of football matches ahead of the 2017/18 football league. UK Internet Service Providers (ISPs) will receive a 'blocking order' to prevent illegal access and streaming of Premier League matches. So far over 5000 server IP addresses have been blocked together with associated and non-associated apps and add-ons being closed down. Broadcasting channel BBC 5 Live investigated the issue with sports fans and found that around half of the participants stated they had streamed a football match from an unofficial provider. Therefore, the anti-piracy court order and 'blocking order' will be of great benefit to BT Sports and Sky, who may see the return of paid subscribers to their sports channels. This, in turn, will contribute to the £5.136 billion (for three years) they pay for the rights to show football matches live (*BBC News* 2017).

India is regarded by many firms as an attractive emerging market beset with many legal difficulties, bureaucratic delay and lots of red tape. For example, pairs of shoes cannot be imported, which causes huge problems for shoe manufacturers who need to import shoes as production samples. By separating the pairs and importing each shoe to a different port, importers of shoes are using a loophole in the law and trying to overcome this problem. Coca-Cola has found the vast potential of India's market somewhat hard to break into. In 2014 one of Coca-Cola's bottling factories in the north of India, Uttar Pradesh, was ordered to close after local activists and farmers accused Coca-Cola of building the factory on land that belonged to the local council. They also claimed that Coca-Cola was taking too much water from the underground water table, making it difficult for agricultural farmers to grow their crops, and depositing polluted water which damaged the environment (*RT News* 2014). Similar battles began during 2017 in Tamil Nadu (south India) with retailers boycotting Coca-Cola, favouring local beverage products and accusing Coca-Cola of taking scarce water. At the same time Maharashtra's food and drink administration (western India) banned Coke Zero from McDonald's fast food outlets because there were growing concerns over the artificial sweetener contained in the drink and, more importantly, that there was no legal warning displayed on product packaging (*The National* 2017). When marketers research different countries to add to their international portfolio, the political squabbles, legal battles, bureaucratic delays and infrastructure headaches may be obstacles that need to be considered.

## Economic factors

It is important that the international marketer has an understanding of economic developments and how they impinge on the marketing strategy. This understanding is important at a world level in terms of the world trading infrastructure. Such infrastructure includes world institutions and trade agreements developed to foster international trade, regional trade integration and at a country/market level. Firms need to be aware of the economic policies of countries and the direction in which a particular market is developing economically. In this way they can make an assessment as to whether they can profitably satisfy market demand and compete with firms already in the market.

Gross national income in the world is around US$70 trillion (2017). However, the gross national income of a nation is not shared equitably across the world, and the range across the globe is enormous. Among the 209 countries of the world, there are varying economic conditions, levels of economic development and gross national income per capita (GNIpc) at purchasing power parity, or PPP). For example, Qatar, with the highest figure, has a GNIpc (PPP) of US$125 000 and Macao SAR, China is second with US$65 650. The lowest figures are for Liberia at US$710 and the Central African Republic at US$700.

Another key challenge facing companies is the question as to how they can develop an integrated strategy across a number of international markets when there are divergent levels of economic development. Such disparities often make it difficult to have a cohesive strategy, especially in pricing.

*The Economist* 'Big Mac' Index (Figure 1.3) is a useful tool which illustrates the difficulties global companies have in trying to achieve a consistent pricing strategy across the world. It provides a rough measure of the purchasing power of a currency. UBS, a bank in the USA, uses the price of the Big Mac burger to measure the purchasing power of local wages worldwide. It divides the price of a Big Mac by the average

**FIGURE 1.3**   An alternative Big Mac index: how many minutes to earn the price of a Big Mac?

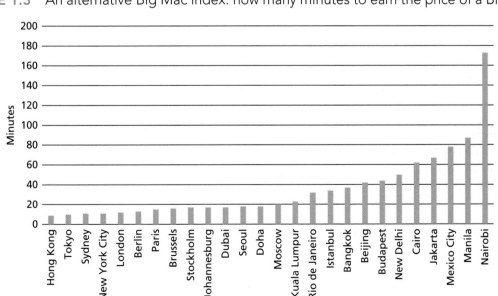

Source: Adapted from *The Economist*, Big Mac Index 2018; UBS Prices & Earnings, Working Time Edition 2015.

net hourly wage in cities around the world. Fast food junkies are best off in Hong Kong where it takes a mere nine minutes at work to afford a Big Mac. By contrast, employees must toil for almost three hours to earn enough for a burger in Nairobi. This causes problems for McDonald's in trying to pursue a standard product image across markets. Priced in US dollars, a Big Mac in Sweden would cost US$6.12, in China US$3.17, whereas in South Africa it would be US$2.45.

In order to examine these challenges further we divide the economies into developed economies and least developed economies.

## The developed economies

In developed economies, the top five traders for merchandise exports and imports (in terms of value) are China, the USA, Germany, Japan and France. In terms of world merchandise trade, when added together, these five countries account for just over 38 per cent of all countries' merchandise trade. Merchandise trade as a term is the average of exports and imports. There are some countries that are more inclined to be strong in imports or exports. For example, the Netherlands is ranked fourth in the world when just considering exports and the UK ranked fifth in the world when just considering imports. Table 1.4 highlights the import/export situation of three regions. As shown, Europe is both the highest importer of merchandise trade and the highest exporter.

For many firms, this action of importing and exporting constitutes much of what is termed the global market. Even though many companies call themselves global, most of their revenues and profits will be earned from these markets. This leads some commentators to argue that most competition, even in today's global marketplace, is more active at a regional level than a global level.

Table 1.4   Merchandise regions: exports and imports

|               | Imports US$ trillion | Exports US$ trillion |
|---------------|----------------------|----------------------|
| Asia          | 3.07                 | 5.75                 |
| Europe        | 5.92                 | 5.94                 |
| North America | 5.21                 | 2.22                 |

Source: Adapted from World Trade Organization (2017) World trade statistical review 2017.

## The emerging economies

Brazil, Russia, India and China (the BRIC economies) are no longer considered to be the only emerging economies. Mexico, Indonesia, Nigeria and Turkey, known as the MINT economies, are countries that marketing managers of global brands have started doing business with. In these countries, there is a huge and growing demand for everything from automobiles to mobile phones. All are viewed as key growth markets where there is an evolving pattern of government-directed economic reforms, lowering of restrictions on foreign investment and increasing privatization of state-owned monopolies. All these rapidly developing economies herald significant opportunities for the international marketing firm.

Such markets often have what is termed a 'dual economy'. Usually there tends to be a wealthy urban professional class alongside a poorer rural population. Income distribution tends to be much more skewed between the 'haves' and the 'have nots' than in developed countries. The number of Chinese and Indonesian people that earn less than US$2 per day has reduced dramatically with a general increase in the middle earners.

## Least developed countries

This group includes underdeveloped countries and less developed countries. The main features are a low gross domestic product (GDP) per capita, a limited amount of manufacturing activity and a very poor and fragmented infrastructure. Typical infrastructure weaknesses are in transport, communications, education and healthcare. In addition, the public sector is often slow-moving and bureaucratic. Having said that,

Ethiopia's GDP is forecast to be around 8.3 per cent, which is higher than the global growth rate forecast at around 2.7 per cent. Ethiopia is a low-income country, and it is expected that its GDP will continue to grow. This growth is due in part to the government of Ethiopia accelerating its spending on infrastructure. Ethiopia's prospects are good; however, the infrastructure costs are high and thus public debt now exceeds 50 per cent of GDP.

It is common to find that least developed countries (LDCs) are heavily reliant on exporting raw materials, and these products are the main export earners. In the Democratic Republic of Congo, for instance, their exports comprise copper (over 50 per cent), cobalt (over 21 per cent) and petroleum (around 15 per cent). In addition, three-quarters of LDCs depend on their main trading partner for more than one-quarter of their export revenue. The risks posed to the LDC by changing patterns of supply and demand are great. Falling commodity prices can result in large decreases in earnings for the whole country. The resultant economic and political adjustments may affect exporters to that country through possible changes in tariff and non-tariff barriers, changes in the level of company taxation and through restrictions on the convertibility of currency and the repatriation of profits. In addition, substantial decreases in market sizes within the country are probable.

A wide range of economic circumstances influence the development of the less developed countries in the world. Some countries are small with few natural resources. For these countries it is difficult to start the process of substantial economic growth. Poor health and education standards need money on a large scale, yet the pay-off in terms of a healthier, better-educated population takes time to achieve. At the same time, there are demands for public expenditure on transport systems, communication systems and water control systems. Without real prospects for rapid economic development, private sources of capital are reluctant to invest in such countries. This is particularly the case for long-term infrastructure projects. As a result, important capital spending projects rely heavily on world aid programmes. Marketing to such countries can be problematic.

## MANAGEMENT CHALLENGE 1.1

## How SMEs internationalize

Small and medium enterprises (SMEs) are motivated to expand internationally for a number of reasons. These include gaining access to a new customer base with different viewpoints on their products that they can capitalize on, or because there are too many competitors in the home market. The speed at which SMEs internationalize varies and is one of the decisions that needs to be made. Fast SME internationalizers are those that enter many countries in quick succession. Slow SME internationalizers, on the other hand, only enter one new country every 20 years or so.

There are a number of stages that SMEs go through once they have thoroughly investigated their expansion options and feel there is nothing more they can do within the domestic market.

Stage one is the expansion stage when SMEs develop export activities. Exporting activities often happen with neighbouring countries to the SME's home country.

Stage two is the internationalization stage, which means exports may continue but SMEs then decide to invest in another country through acquisition of a similar SME, hiring a salesforce or purchasing/building a production centre.

Stage three is the internationalization review stage when SMEs decide to increase, decrease or withdraw from internationalization activities. Stage three is an activity that occurs year on year as SMEs constantly review their success and the external opportunities.

### Question

1 Why do SMEs usually expand into neighbouring countries first?

## Currency risks

While we have examined economic factors within markets, we also need to bear in mind that in international marketing, transactions invariably take place between countries, so exchange rates and currency movements are an important aspect of the international economic environment. On top of all the normal vagaries of markets, customer demands, competitive actions and economic infrastructures, foreign exchange parities are likely to change on a regular if unpredictable basis. World currency movements, stimulated by worldwide trading and foreign exchange dealing, are an additional complication in the international environment. Companies that guess wrongly as to which way a currency will move can see their international business deals rendered unprofitable overnight. Businesses that need to swap currencies to pay for imported goods, or because they have received foreign currency for products they have exported, can find themselves squeezed to the point where they watch their profits disappear.

In Europe, the formation of the European Monetary Union (EMU) and the establishment of the Single European Payments Area (SEPA) led to greater stability for firms operating in the market. The formation of the EMU and the introduction of a single currency (the euro) in many countries in the European Union had important implications for company strategies. We will discuss these in Chapter 2 when we examine regional trading agreements, and in Chapter 11 when we look at pricing issues in international marketing.

## Political factors

The political environment of international marketing includes any national or international political factors that can affect the organization's operations or its decision making. Politics has come to be recognized as the major factor in many international business decisions, especially in terms of whether to invest and how to develop markets.

Politics is intrinsically linked to a government's attitude to business and the freedom within which it allows firms to operate. Unstable political regimes expose foreign businesses to a variety of risks that they would generally not face in the home market. This often means that the political arena is the most volatile area of international marketing. The tendencies of governments to change regulations can have a profound effect on international strategy, providing both opportunities and threats. One threat that has been in the news over recent years is terrorism. There is an economic cost due to acts of terrorism, and this was calculated at US$84 billion (Statista 2016). In some cases, this has an effect on world peace and political relations. In others it brings nations together. The Global Peace Index 2018 shows Syria, Afghanistan, South Sudan, Iraq and Somalia as places of instability and unrest. The instability in the Middle East and the continued threat of global terrorism have served to heighten firms' awareness of the importance of monitoring political risk factors in the international markets in which they operate. Lesser developed countries and emerging markets pose particularly high political risks, even when they are following reforms to solve the political problems they have. The stringency of such reforms can itself lead to civil disorder and rising opposition to government. Political risk is defined as a risk due to a sudden or gradual change in a local political environment that is disadvantageous or counter-productive to foreign firms and markets.

The types of action that governments may take which constitute potential political risks to firms fall into three main areas:

- *Operational restrictions.* These could be exchange controls, employment policies, insistence on locally shared ownership and particular product requirements.
- *Discriminatory restrictions.* These tend to be imposed on purely foreign firms and, sometimes, only firms from a particular country. Economic sanctions were put in place during the crisis in Ukraine. During that time Russia responded by banning food imports from several European Union countries, the USA, Norway, Canada and Australia. They have also imposed bans on imports from Libya and Iran in the past. Such barriers tend to be special taxes and tariffs, compulsory subcontracting or loss of financial freedom.
- *Physical actions.* These actions are direct government interventions such as confiscation without any payment of indemnity, a forced takeover by the government, expropriation, nationalization or even damage to property or personnel through riots and war. The Argentine government seized Spanish oil company Repsol's assets in the country in 2012, claiming it had failed to invest to meet internal demand. Two years later Repsol agreed compensation of US$5 billion, half of the initial claim, and withdrew from the country (*BBC News* 2014).

Investment restrictions are a common way governments interfere politically in international markets by restricting levels of investment, location of facilities, choice of local partners and ownership percentage.

Recent decisions by certain Latin American countries to compel foreign investors to renegotiate their investment contracts on sanction of expulsion, introduced considerable uncertainty for companies operating in the region. One of the most difficult countries to operate in is Venezuela, despite it being a country with a large economy. Signing agreements, getting land deals, paying taxes and simply withdrawing money from the bank takes an inordinate amount of time. For example, as a general rule, worldwide, there are around nine procedures to complete when a business decides to register and begin the process of starting a business. However, in Venezuela, there are 17, which take around 144 days to complete due to the extensive bureaucratic process. Permits and approvals, with associated fees and certificates, are required from the Ministry of Labour and the National Bank for Housing and Habitat, plus from the banks, road, fire and telecoms agencies. And just to get electricity connected to a new business is very costly and takes around 150 days to complete.

The World Trade Organization (WTO) has led negotiations on a series of worldwide agreements to expand quotas, reduce tariffs and introduce a number of innovative measures to encourage trade among countries. Together with the formation of regional trading agreements in the European Union, North and South America, and Asia, these reforms constitute a move to a more politically stable world trading environment. An understanding of these issues is critical to the international marketing manager. In Chapter 2 we examine in some detail the patterns of world trade, the regional trading agreements and the development of world trading institutions intended to foster international trade. In Chapter 4 we will examine in some detail the procedures, tools and techniques which can help the analysis and evaluation of opportunities across such markets.

The political and economic environments are greatly intertwined and, sometimes, difficult to categorize. It is important, however, that a firm operating in international markets assess the countries in which it operates to gauge the economic and political risk and to ensure it understands the peculiarities and characteristics of the market it wishes to develop (see Illustration 1.3).

## ILLUSTRATION 1.3

## Sproxil born global to help us live longer

Counterfeiting is a global problem. Consumers are extremely disappointed when they buy a high-end luxury item via the Internet only to find they have bought a fake. Losing money on a handbag or watch is one thing, but buying fake medicine can cost lives. Counterfeit medicine is dangerous for patients as up to 700 000 people die each year from buying fake anti-malaria medicine and tuberculosis drugs. The multi-million dollar problem is worldwide. It is worse in emerging countries and is a drain on businesses and international regulatory bodies. Sproxil is a brand protection service organization in emerging markets with headquarters in the USA. Born global is at the very heart of Sproxil. They saw an important niche in the market and developed technology to solve an international problem. Sproxil opened their first local office in Nigeria 12 months after they launched their business and now have offices in Ghana, Pakistan and India. They help businesses, be they global or local, to protect their brands and to help consumers ensure they are buying legitimate medicines and drugs. Consumers at point of purchase text (free of charge) the product's on-pack ID number and an immediate reply shows if the product is legitimate or fake. Sproxil has branched out into verifying branded cosmetics, fast moving consumer goods (FMCGs) and electrical goods.

### Question

**1** Many organizations are born global. What factors enable them to do this?

**Reference:** www.sproxil.com.

## Technological factors

Technology is a major driving force both in international marketing and in the move towards a more global marketplace. The impact of technological advances can be seen in all aspects of the marketing process. The ability to gather data on markets, management control capabilities and the practicalities of carrying out the business function internationally have been revolutionized in recent years with the advances in electronic communications.

Satellite communications, the Internet and local wifi means that in the international marketplace, information and connectivity is power. At the touch of a button we can access information on the key factors that determine our business. Multiple channels supply news 24 hours a day, 7 days a week. Manufacturers wanting to know the price of coffee beans or the relevant position of competitors in terms of their share price or new product activity have it at the touch of a button, often through a mobile app.

As mobile technology renders landline cables and telephone lines redundant, developing countries have abandoned plans to invest in land-based communication and go straight to mobile. They have bypassed terrestrial communication systems, enabling them to catch up with and, in some cases overtake, developed countries in the marketplace. In emerging economies consumers are jumping from no telephone to the latest in global communications technology. Wireless application protocol (WAP) technology allows online services to be available to mobile phone users on the move, wherever they happen to be in the world. The use of Global System for Mobile Communications (GSM) technology enables mobile phone operators to determine the location of a customer globally to send them relevant and timely advertising messages.

British Airways operates its worldwide online operations from Mumbai: everything from ticketing to making an 'exceptional request' facility, such as wheelchair assistance needed for a passenger, can be managed from the centre in India. The ease of hiring computer-literate graduates by the hundred, who are intelligent, capable, keen and inexpensive to hire, as is local property to rent, has enabled India to build a global advantage in this rapidly developing industry.

# The Internet

The Internet has revolutionized international marketing practices. Airlines such as easyJet and Ryanair have helped completely change the way we book our airline reservations with more airline operators abandoning many face-to-face operations. Consumers flying with easyJet book, check-in and choose their seat online. Upon arrival at the airport there is no representative to take the consumer through check-in. Now check-in is done by using kiosks to scan tickets and consumers load their own luggage onto a conveyor belt aptly entitled 'bag-drop'. Alibaba Group with headquarters in China set up an online only business-to-business (B2B) facility to enable small Chinese exporters and manufacturers to sell their goods internationally. Firms ranging in size from a few employees to large multinationals have realized the potential of marketing globally online and developed the facility to buy and sell their products and services online to the world.

Around 46 per cent of the world's population are Internet users. In 2000, the penetration of Internet users was 6.8 per cent. This has had a major effect on the retail high street in that e-commerce sales worldwide account for $2.29 trillion. This means that of all retail sales worldwide one-tenth of those sales are through e-commerce.

Another major growth area is B2B sales due to the fact that many multinational and international businesses are completing more transactions with their own supply chain online as well as with consumers. Nevertheless, at this stage, the amount of business completed online far outstrips business-to-consumer (B2C). However, more consumers than ever before are using smartphones, tablets and PCs to browse and shop for goods and services online.

The Internet has meant huge opportunities for SMEs and rapid internationalization for many. It has enabled them to substantially reduce the costs of reaching international customers, reduce global advertising costs and made it much easier for small niche products to find a critical mass of customers. Because of the low entry costs of operating as an online business, it has permitted firms with low capital resources to become global marketers, in some cases overnight. There are, therefore, quite significant implications for

SMEs, which will be examined further in Chapter 5 where we discuss in some detail the issues in international marketing pertinent to SMEs.

For all companies, the implications of being able to market goods and services online have been far reaching. The Internet has led to an explosion of information to consumers, giving them the potential to source products from the cheapest supplier in the world. This has led to the increasing standardization of prices across borders or, at least, to the narrowing of price differentials as consumers become more aware of prices in different countries and buy a whole range of products via social media such as Facebook and Twitter. In B2C marketing this has been most dramatically seen in the purchase of such items as financial services, flights, holidays, music downloads and books. Social media communication activities connect end-users and producers directly, reducing the importance of traditional intermediaries in international marketing (i.e. agents and distributors) as more companies have built the online capability to deal direct with their customers, particularly in B2B marketing. To survive, such intermediaries have begun offering a whole range of new services. The value added element of their offering is no longer principally in the physical distribution of goods, but rather in the collection, collation, interpretation and dissemination of vast amounts of information. The critical resource possessed by this new breed of 'cybermediary' is information rather than inventory. The Internet has also become a powerful tool for supporting networks both internal and external to the firm. Many global firms have developed supplier intranets through which they source products and services from preferred suppliers who have met the criteria to gain access to their supplier intranets. It has become the efficient new medium for conducting worldwide market research and gaining feedback from customers.

Thus, the Internet produces a fundamentally different environment for international marketing and requires a radically different strategic approach affecting all aspects of the marketing process. Not all forays into Internet marketing have been successful.

## The dual technological/cultural paradox

On the one hand, commentators view technological advancement and shrinking communications as the most important driving force in the building of the global village where there are global consumers who have similar needs. On the other, to access this global village a person invariably needs a command of the English language and access to the latest technology. In many markets, we stumble against the paradox that while in some countries there is a market of well-educated and computer-literate people, in other countries the global electronic highway has completely bypassed them.

Despite all that has been said in previous sections, many developing and emerging markets are characterized by poor, inadequate or deteriorating infrastructures. Essential services required for commercial activity, ranging from electric power to water supplies, from highways to air transportation, and from phone lines to banking services, are often in short supply or unreliable. In the least developed countries the number of Internet users is low with Eritrea having only 1.1 per cent of the population using the Internet, Burundi 1.5 per cent, Sierra Leone 2.4 per cent and Cambodia 11.1 per cent.

The huge population shifts discussed earlier have also aggravated the technical infrastructure problems in many of the major cities in emerging markets. This often results in widespread production and distribution bottlenecks, which in turn raises costs. 'Brown outs', for instance, are not uncommon in the Philippines, even in the capital city Manila. Here, companies and offices regularly lose electric power and either shut down in those periods or revert to generators. Fragmented and circuitous channels of distribution are a result of a lack of adequate infrastructure. This makes market entry more complicated and the efficient distribution of a product very difficult. Pepsi Cola in Eastern Europe has a large number of decentralized satellite bottling plants in an attempt to overcome the lack of a distribution infrastructure.

The reader will find that we examine the impact of the Internet on the relevant marketing practices and processes as we move through the chapters of the book. Another major change in products and services, enabled by the Internet, is the ability to use the Internet to manage and operate 'things'. The Internet of Things was considered a very hi-tech phenomena, but has more recently become commonplace. CGI, Microsoft and Thyssenkrupp Elevator have got together to make the perfect elevator. The everyday elevator used in hotels, office blocks and shopping centres can now be linked to the Internet, the Thing being the elevator.

As with all things mechanical, an elevator will need to be maintained. Linking the elevator to the Internet, predictive data showing the 'wellness' of the elevator is streamed to Thyssenkrupp so that they can understand if the elevator is healthy or if maintenance is needed.

## Sustainability factors

In considering the environmental challenges to international marketing we also need to take heed of numerous reports that warn of the danger to future prosperity if current overconsumption of natural resources is left unchecked. More than three-quarters of the world's people live in countries where national consumption has outstripped biological capacity. Human demands, sometimes created by marketers, measure nearly a third more than the Earth can sustain over time. There is increasing proof of sea levels rising, temperatures warming and uncertain effects on forest and agricultural systems. There is growing evidence of increased variability and volatility in weather patterns which are expected to have a significant and disproportionate impact in the developing world. This is where the world's poor remain most susceptible to the potential damages and uncertainties inherent in a changing climate.

It is feared by some that as global economic wealth increases, global natural wealth and diversity will continue to decline. There is concern that indigenous and national culture and languages could be eroded by the strength of globalized brands. It is also argued by some analysts that globalized markets leave many behind economically. Some countries have been unable to take advantage of globalization of markets. Their standards of living are seen to be dropping further behind the richest countries. The gap in income within countries also gives an indication of the state of the nation. South America and the Caribbean region have narrowed the inequality earnings gap by increased investment in education. In China, due to so many people moving from rural to urban areas, the inequality earnings gap has widened creating a poorer rural population and a wealthier urban population. Generally, inequality in both developed and developing countries has widened because the wealthier minorities have just got richer.

As responsible global marketers, we need to ensure in our strategic thinking that we respond to all the issues we have raised in the previous sections. In particular, using ethical and socially responsible business practices that are sustainable in terms of their environmental, societal and economic impact (see Figure 1.4). This involves ensuring in any global marketing action plan that we maximize the positive impacts of global marketing while minimizing the negative ones. These include social or environmental impacts on a local, regional or global basis.

Sustainability interfaces with global marketing through the social and ecological consequences of marketing activities. Sustainability involves ensuring the social, cultural, economic, political and environmental aspects of a global marketing strategy are integrated.

**FIGURE 1.4**   Holistic model of sustainability in global marketing

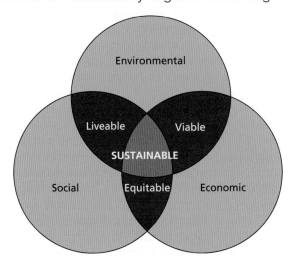

The rise in ethical consumerism and green brands that identify themselves as ethical, has led to a rise in ethic-based decisions across global markets. They have been enabled by increased understanding and information about business practices across the globe. Large corporations now see it as a priority that they are regarded as socially responsible global citizens who are working ethically and improving the ethical standards of their industry.

Sustainability is about considering the environmental impact of everything we do. This means encouraging a holistic way of thinking in our responses to the global marketing challenges we identify and assessing the impact of our global marketing strategies – socially, economically and environmentally – in our approach to ensuring sustainability. This is central to the values of responsible international marketing strategies. We will return to this theme at various points as we go through the different stages of strategy development in the chapters of this book.

The greatest legacy for the future that we can create is in the perspectives we take and the skills we use as marketing practitioners. While our global marketing strategies need to be innovative and build global competitiveness, we need also to make sure any strategies we develop are grounded in socially and environmentally sustainable business practices. Global marketing strategies should promote sustainable growth, balance prosperity across the world economies and protect our shared global environment. We hope readers of this book developing international marketing strategies will also make sure we all protect our world environmental capital and manage our global market growth creatively, responsibly and ethically.

# Differences between international and domestic marketing

As we have seen in the previous sections, there are many factors within the international environment which substantially increase the challenge of international marketing. These can be summarized as follows:

1 *Culture*: often diverse and multicultural markets.
2 *Markets*: widespread and sometimes fragmented.
3 *Data*: difficult to obtain and often expensive.
4 *Politics*: regimes vary in stability – political risk becomes an important variable.
5 *Governments*: can be a strong influence in regulating importers and foreign business ventures.
6 *Economies*: varying levels of development and varying and sometimes unstable currencies.
7 *Finance*: many differing finance systems and regulatory bodies.
8 *Stakeholders*: commercial, home country and host country.
9 *Business*: diverse rules, culturally influenced.
10 *Control*: difficult to control and coordinate across markets.

## The international competitive landscape

A major difference for managers operating on international markets is the impact all these currents and cross-currents have on the competitive landscape. In fact, Nyaga (2014, p. 685) stated 'a company's long-term success is driven largely by its ability to maintain sustainable competitive advantage and keep it'. The task of achieving this in a competitive environment where firms are subject to local, regional and global competition can be immensely challenging. This is especially so if indigenous local competitors are supported by the government of the country.

Across international markets, advanced countries are seeing significant competition from both emerging markets and less developed countries which are exploiting modern technology and their own low labour costs to compete in markets no longer so protected by tariff walls. The birth of global brand names is no longer the domain of the West.

The complexity of competition is also heightened by the strategic use of international sourcing of components by multinationals and global firms to achieve competitive advantage.

## ILLUSTRATION 1.4

# Four Seasons Hotel Amman embracing the traditions of Jordan

To embrace the traditions and culture of a country is often the reason travellers seek destinations which are not blighted by mass tourism. The Four Seasons Amman prides itself on the excellent customer service that permeates from the local culture of Jordan.

The hospitality experience enjoyed by guests at the Four Seasons is taken from that of Jordanian society and reaches back to the philosophy of the Bedouins. 'No traveller, even an enemy, is turned away or denied food or shelter'.

Jordanians are joyous in giving, receiving and being hospitable. And as hoteliers, the Four Seasons wants to be an excellent hospitality venue and it feels it has done that by bringing the country's culture into the hotel. In fact, the Four Seasons has many customer service excellence awards and promotes these alongside images and comments on its website, Facebook and Instagram pages. Similarly, it proudly promotes the comments made on Trip Advisor sharing the excellent customer posts it has received from its guests.

Another way the Four Seasons Hotel Amman has brought the Jordanian culture into its hotel is through art. The hotel partnered with a local art gallery Foresight32 and together they showcase the work of local artists. This further enables the guests of the Four Seasons hotel to enjoy the culture, traditions and history of Jordan through the artworks hanging within the hotel. And of course, the Four Seasons Hotel provides an extensive range of traditional local dishes in its restaurants. One of the restaurants, the Oleă, is particularly interesting in that the kitchen doors are open and the chefs welcome guests to their workstation where a range of local Middle Eastern food is available. Guests can choose their own foods and see them being prepared in a traditional manner.

### Question

**1** What examples of local traditions and culture are promoted by other international businesses?

**Reference:** Four Seasons Hotel, www.fourseasons.com/amman.

Given the nature of the challenges and opportunities identified earlier and the speed of change within the international environment, this means that substantially different pressures are being placed upon management than if they were purely operating in domestic markets. It follows from this that the manager of international marketing needs a detailed knowledge and understanding of how traditions and social behaviour impact on a firm's international marketing operations (see Illustration 1.4).

Perlmutter (1995) identified nine cross-cultural management incompetences which lead to failure across a spread of country markets. He defined these core incompetences as: 'the bundle of activities and managerial skills that are mismatched in a great variety of countries where firms do business'.

The first three are interrelated and relate to the failure to be market driven.

1 Inability to find the right market niches.

2 Unwillingness to adapt and update products to local needs.

3 Not having unique products that are viewed as sufficiently higher added value by customers in local markets.

4 A vacillating commitment. It takes time to learn how to function in countries such as Japan.

5 Assigning the wrong people. Picking the wrong people or the wrong top team in an affiliate.

6 Picking the wrong partners. There is a list of difficulties in building alliances: a main limitation is picking partners who do not have the right bundle of capabilities to help reach the local market.

7 Inability to manage local stakeholders. This includes incompetence in developing a satisfactory partnership relationship with unions and governments.

8  Developing mutual distrust and lack of respect between HQ and the affiliates at different levels of management.

9  Inability to leverage ideas developed in one country to other countries worldwide.

If mistakes are not to be made in your marketing strategies it is essential to ensure that the company has a robust and rigorous approach to its international marketing planning processes. Approaches to achieving this will be discussed in the following sections.

# The international market planning process

In international marketing, the very complexity of handling the diverse range of factors that must be considered make planning and control difficult activities to carry out satisfactorily. For large global companies, the problem becomes one of how to structure the organization so that its increasingly complex and diverse activities around the world can be planned and managed effectively, its goals can be achieved and its stakeholders' expectations satisfied.

In this section, we look at the international marketing planning and control process. We also consider how managers can respond to the challenges posed in the previous sections by ensuring they have robust strategy development and market planning processes.

## The planning process

The planning process is the method used by the management of the firm to define in detail how it will achieve its current and future strategic aims and objectives. In doing this, it must evaluate the current and future market opportunities, assess its own current and potential capabilities, and attempt to forecast how those changes over which it has no control might help or hinder its efforts to reach those objectives.

The international planning process must allow the company to answer the following three marketing questions:

1  Where is the company now?

2  Where does it want to go?

3  How might it get there?

These questions are fundamental for the majority of businesses whether they are large or small, simple or complex. They emphasize the firm's need to prepare for the future to ensure its own survival and growth within the increasingly competitive international environment. There is an implication in these questions that the future is likely to be significantly different from the past. Planning is therefore inevitably about forecasting and implementing change which determines the very nature and future direction of the organization.

The starting point of the planning process for any company is to set long-term goals and objectives which reflect its overall aspirations. These goals cannot be set in isolation, however, as the company's history and current levels of success in its different country markets are usually major determinants of its future. Other factors over which the company has little control in international markets all have a major impact upon the company's operations and will have a significant effect on determining whether or not it will meet its goals. Such factors include the economic and political situation of the countries in which it is operating, the response of the competition, and the diverse background, behaviour and expectations of its customers.

Too many firms, particularly smaller ones, fail to prepare contingency plans to cope with the unexpected and, in some cases, even the predictable events in international markets. They are often surprised and unprepared for success too. When unexpected events occur, many companies too easily ignore the plan and develop new strategies as they go along. While it may be possible to survive in a relatively uncomplicated domestic environment by reacting rapidly to new situations as they arise, it is impossible to grow significantly in international markets. This is because an overly reactive management style is usually wasteful of opportunities and resources.

In international markets, planning and control are essential for both day-to-day operations and the development of long-term strategies. This is because of the need to manage the differences of attitudes, standards and values in the extended parts of the organization and avoid the problems of poor coordination and integration of the diverse activities. The plans being developed must be sufficiently flexible to cope with unfamiliar cultures, rapidly changing political, economic and competitive environments, and the effects of unexpected events. All of these can affect global companies in one way or another throughout the world on an almost daily basis.

As a company moves into international markets, having previously been marketing solely to domestic markets, the processes of planning and control remain largely the same; however, the complexity of the process increases dramatically. In a domestic situation, misunderstandings between different departmental managers can be relatively quickly sorted out with a face-to-face discussion. In the international situation, however, this is much harder and often impractical. More impersonal communications, along with longer lead times, different cultures and the use of different languages, result in seemingly inconsistent and often negative attitudes in international managers.

## Major evolutionary stages of planning

As most companies move gradually into international markets, they go through the major evolutionary stages of planning: the unplanned stage, the budgeting stage, the annual business planning stage and the strategic planning stage.

**The unplanned stage**: In its early stages of international marketing, the company is likely to be preoccupied with finding new export customers and money to finance its activities. Frequently, business is very unpredictable and is consequently unplanned, so that a short-term 'crisis management' culture emerges.

**The budgeting stage**: As the business develops, a system for annual budgeting of sales, costs and cash flow is devised, often because of pressure from external stakeholders such as banks. Being largely financial in nature, budgets often take little account of marketing research, product development or the longer-term potential of international markets.

**Annual business planning**: Companies begin to adopt a more formalized annual approach to planning by including the whole of the business in the planning review process. One of three approaches to the process of international market planning generally emerge at this stage:

1 *Top-down planning*: This is by far the simplest approach, with senior managers setting goals and developing quite detailed plans for middle and senior staff to implement. To be successful, this clearly requires the senior managers to be closely in touch with all their international markets and for the business to be relatively uncomplicated in the range of products or services offered. It has the advantage of ensuring that there is little opportunity for misinterpretation by local managers, but the disadvantage of giving little opportunity for local initiative. Most of the strategic decisions at Google are taken in the USA, Alibaba Group in China, Samsung in the Republic of Korea and Vodafone in the UK.

2 *Bottom-up planning*: In this approach, the different parts of the company around the globe prepare their own goals and plans and submit them to headquarters for approval. This can encourage local initiative and innovation. However, it can be difficult to manage as the sum of the individual parts that make different demands on resources, financial returns and marketing profiles rarely add up to a feasible international development plan.

3 *Goals down, plans up*: In an attempt to benefit from the positive elements of the first two approaches, this third approach is based upon senior management assessing the firm's opportunities and needs, setting corporate global objectives and developing broad international strategies. Financial goals are then set for each part of the company, which has the responsibility for developing individual strategies and plans to achieve these targets. For this approach to work effectively, the senior management generally allows considerable flexibility in the way that the goals are achieved by the component parts of the firm around the globe. This approach is adopted particularly by companies that have a very diverse portfolio of businesses and products.

**The strategic planning stage**: So far, the stages discussed have been concerned with relatively short-term planning (one to two years). For many aspects of international marketing such as new market entry, growth strategies and brand management, however, much longer-term planning is essential. By developing strategies for a five-year timescale, it is possible to avoid short-term, highly reactive and frequently contradictory and wasteful activity. The annual marketing plan then becomes a more detailed version of the five-year strategic plan which can be rolled forward year on year.

The obvious benefits of strategic planning are that all staff can be better motivated and encouraged to work more effectively by sharing a vision of the future. There are, however, potential dangers too. Long-term strategic plans often fail to cope with the consequences of unexpected events, either environmental or political. There is often confusion between managers over what are strategic issues and what are operational tactics. A manager in a foreign subsidiary might consider something to be a strategic issue, such as achieving a substantial market share increase in the country. This might, however, be regarded as an operational matter by a senior manager at the headquarters, which does not consider success in that particular country a priority for the company.

## The international marketing planning process

There are a number of elements in the international marketing plan, as detailed in Figure 1.5.

**FIGURE 1.5**  Aspects of international marketing planning

**Stakeholder expections**
- Shareholders, customer, host government, employees in each country, pressure groups

**Situation analysis**
- Evaluation of the environment and individual markets

**Resources and capabilities**
- Individual small business unit strengths and weaknesses analysis
- Capability to deal with threats and opportunities

**Corporate aims and objectives**
- Financial, market, area, brand and mix objectives

**Marketing strategies**
- Growth strategies
- Standardization and adaptation

**Implementation of the plan**
- Individual SBU and marketing mix plans
- Regional, global or multidomestic integration

**Control and feedback**
- Setting relevant standards, measuring performance, correcting deviations

**Stakeholder expectations**  The complexities of the international marketing environment mean companies competing on international markets have many more organizations and people who have a stake in how they conduct their business. Consequently, many more stakeholders with differing expectations have to be managed. The ability of a company to pursue its chosen marketing strategy is determined to a large degree by the aims and expectations of the stakeholders, who directly or indirectly provide the resources and support needed to implement the strategies and plans. It is important to clearly identify the different stakeholder groups, understand their expectations and evaluate their power. This is because it is the stakeholders who provide the broad guidelines within which the firm operates. Figure 1.6 identifies the typical stakeholders of a multinational enterprise (MNE). The Body Shop, the environmentally conscious UK toiletries retailer, is always likely to have problems balancing the widely differing pricing and profit expectations and environmental concerns of its franchisees, customers and shareholders.

Senior management usually aim to develop and adopt strategies which do not directly oppose these stakeholder expectations. Frequently, however, they widen or alter the firm's activities due to changes in the market and competition. Moreover, a wide range of stakeholders influence what MNEs do by giving greater attention to the political, commercial and ethical behaviour of the organizations. They might also take more interest in the actual operation of the business and the performance and safety of the products. As a result

**FIGURE 1.6** Some typical stakeholders of multinational enterprises

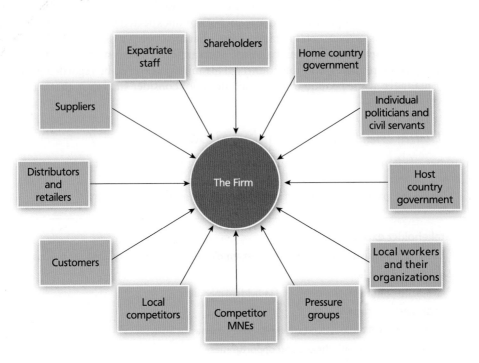

of this, companies need to explain their strategies and plans to shareholders through more detailed annual reports. They also need to explain these to staff through a variety of briefing methods and to pressure groups and the community in general through various public relations activities. This is particularly important when their activities have an impact on the local environment or economy. In international marketing it is vital that the firm addresses the concerns of its host country stakeholders, who may be physically and culturally very distant from the headquarters.

Particular attention should be paid to the different expectations of the stakeholders and their power to influence the firm's strategic direction. Given the different expectations of the firm's stakeholders, it is inevitable that conflicts will occur. For example, shareholders usually want a high return on their investment and may expect the firm to find countries with low production costs. The workers in these countries, however, want an adequate wage on which to live. It is often the firm's ability to manage these potential conflicts that leads to success or failure in international marketing (see Figure 1.6).

International pressure groups are another important stakeholder MNEs have to manage. Global communications and the ability of the Internet to draw together geographically dispersed people with shared interests have led to the growing power of globally based pressure groups. Such has been the success of a number of these, it is now the case that pressure groups are seen by many global operators as one of the key stakeholders to be considered in international strategy decision-making. The role of pressure groups in global markets tends to raise awareness of issues of concern. Among those that have received wide press coverage affecting international marketing strategies are:

- the Greenpeace efforts to raise awareness to threats on the environment
- the anti-globalization lobby demonstrating against the perceived dark global forces they see manifested in the World Trade Organization
- the anti-child labour movement
- exploitation of factory workers.

Retailers including Gap and H&M have been accused of exploiting workers in factories in Bangladesh (Paige 2013). Workers often started work at 7 a.m. and continued until 10.30 p.m. Other retailers, including Lidl, were also reported to pay Bangladeshi workers around $19 for a ten-hour day. More recently,

Emmanuel Bani, sole director, was fined $227 300 for exploiting seasonal workers picking fruit and vegetables in Queensland. The seasonal workers were not paid fairly and were working in appalling conditions (Mckillop 2017).

One of the main roles of international public relations is to try to manage the expectations and aspirations of pressure groups and all the stakeholders of a company. In international marketing one of the key responsibilities is to establish good practice to respond to publicity generated by pressure groups on issues where they have not been seen to meet stakeholder expectations.

## Situation analysis

Situation analysis is the process by which the company develops a clear understanding of each individual market and then evaluates its significance for the company and for other markets in which the business operates. As the international business environment becomes more competitive, dynamic and complex, there is a greater need for individual managers to be aware of their immediate situation. They also need to be aware of the possible impact of changes taking place in surrounding areas. Individual national markets can be both surprisingly similar and surprisingly dissimilar in nature. It is important to understand these linkages and the implications of the changes which take place. Chapters 2 and 3 give the reader a detailed insight into the factors to consider in carrying out a situational analysis of the international marketing environment.

The processes and procedures for segmenting international markets and carrying out the necessary research to build the situational analysis are examined in some depth in Chapter 4.

A detailed analysis of each of these factors as they affect both the local and international market environments is necessary in order to forecast future changes. The most frequently adopted approach by firms is to extrapolate past trends. However, with so many factors to consider and the increasing frequency with which unexpected events seem to occur, it may be extremely difficult and misleading to build up one all-embracing vision of the future. Firms are responding to this uncertainty by developing a series of alternative scenarios as the basis of the planning process. An effective and robust strategy needs to contain contingency plans to deal with a variety of situations in which the company might find itself.

## Resources and capabilities

In stressing the need to analyze and respond to external forces over which even global companies have little control, there can be a temptation among some managers to believe that the current capabilities of the organization are inadequate when facing the future. A more thorough analysis of the firm's situation is needed. The SWOT framework (analyzing the firm's strengths, weaknesses, opportunities and threats) is appropriate for this purpose. It is important to audit the most obvious company weaknesses. The strengths of the company, which are often taken for granted but which are really its source of competitive advantage, should also be audited. This is particularly important in international markets as, for example, customer and brand loyalty may be much stronger in certain markets than others. Products which may be at the end of their life in the domestic market may be ideal for less sophisticated markets. SWOT analysis should, therefore, be carried out separately on each area of the business by function, product or market. It should focus on what action should be taken to exploit the opportunities and minimize the threats that are identified in the analysis. This will lead to a clearer evaluation of the resources that are available or which must be acquired to ensure the necessary actions are carried out.

## Knowledge management

The increasing globalization of business, particularly because it is being driven by information technology, has led many firms to re-examine what contributes to their global competitive advantage. They have recognized that it is the pool of personal knowledge, skills and competences of the firms' staff that provides its development potential. They have therefore redefined themselves as 'knowledge-based' organizations. Moreover, these firms have acknowledged that they must retain, nurture and apply the knowledge and skills across their business if they wish to be effective in global markets. The growth potential can only be exploited if the firm becomes a learning organization in which the good practice learned by individual members of staff can be 'leveraged', transferred and built upon throughout its global activity.

## Corporate objectives

Having identified stakeholder expectations, carried out a detailed situation analysis and made an evaluation of the capabilities of the company, the overall goals to be pursued can be set. It is important to stress that there is a need for realism in this. Too frequently, corporate plans are determined more by the desire for short-term credibility with shareholders than with the likelihood that they will be achieved. The objectives must be based on realistic performance expectations rather than on a best case scenario. Consideration must also be given to developing alternative scenarios so that realistic objectives can be set and accompanied by contingency plans in case the chosen scenario does not materialize.

The process adopted for determining long-term and short-term objectives is important and varies significantly depending on the size of the business, the nature of the market and the abilities and motivation of managers in different markets. At an operational level, the national managers need to have an achievable and detailed plan for each country. This should take account of the local situation, explain what is expected and how performance will be measured. For most companies, the most obvious international strategic development opportunities are either in increasing geographical coverage and/or building global product strength. This is discussed in much further detail in Chapter 5 from the viewpoint of the SME and in Chapter 6 from the viewpoint of globally based organizations. Management Challenge 1.2 helps you consider this question from the viewpoint of fast food firms trying to grow their global business.

---

### MANAGEMENT CHALLENGE 1.2

## The Silk Road reopens as the China-Pakistan Economic Corridor

In 2017 the China-Pakistan Economic Corridor (CPEC) gathered pace following the 'belt and road' forum held in Beijing. The purpose of the corridor (the road) is to improve the economy not just in Pakistan and China but along the route that will connect Asia with Europe and Africa. Therefore, CPEC is similar in nature to the ancient Silk Road where networks of travellers traded in many items from silk and spices to exotic fruits.

The corridor itself will be a major feat of engineering. It will provide jobs in Pakistan and boost its economy. At the same time, there will be many projects that will need the expertise of China's heavy machinery, thus presenting opportunities for China.

As did the ancient Silk Road, this corridor will be of great benefit to countries along the route. This is already evidenced as US$50 billion has been invested by Chinese entrepreneurs into countries along the route. Such a huge project could be considered to have major environmental issues. However, huge investments have been made to include solar, wind and hydro plants along the corridor that support the worldwide renewable energy agenda.

### Question

1 In addition to engineering and manufacturing, what other trades and businesses will benefit from the China-Pakistan Economic Corridor?

---

## Marketing strategies

Having set the objectives for the company, both at the corporate and subsidiary level, the company will develop detailed programmes of the marketing strategies and activities which will achieve the objectives. Decisions will need to be made as to how the company will segment and target its international markets. How will it position itself in different international markets? How will it add value to its efforts through its product portfolio, communications, distribution and pricing strategies? It is this that is at the heart of the following chapters of this book as we take the reader through the detailed considerations in developing an international marketing strategy. A central concern in marketing strategy development for international markets is the dilemma facing all international managers as to how far they can standardize marketing strategies in different country markets. This essential question will be examined as we go through different aspects of international marketing strategy development and implementation.

## Implementation of the marketing plan

Having agreed the overall marketing strategy, plans for implementation are required at a central and local subsidiary level. Firms usually allocate resources to individual subsidiaries on a top-down basis. This will need to be modified to include the special allocations made to enable foreign subsidiaries to resource specific market opportunities or difficulties encountered in particular markets. Agreement is reached through a process of discussion between the operating department and management levels. Detailed budgets and timescales can then be set for all areas of marketing including those outside agencies (such as marketing researchers, designers and advertising agencies), in order to ensure that their contributions are delivered on time and within the budget. Some allowance must be made for those activities which might be more difficult to estimate in terms of cost or time, such as research and development of new products.

We have, so far, emphasized the need for careful, detailed and thorough preparation of the plan. However, it is essential that the plan be action oriented and contain programmes designed to give clear direction for the implementation, continuous evaluation and control of all the firm's marketing activity. The plan must, therefore, be: *strategic*, by fulfilling the corporate and marketing objectives and coordinating the individual strategic business unit (SBU) plans; *tactical*, by focusing upon individual SBU marketing activities in each country; and *implementable*, by detailing the individual activities of each department within the SBU.

## The control process

The final stage of the planning process is setting up an effective system for obtaining feedback and controlling the business. Feedback and control systems should be regarded as an integrated part of the whole planning process. They are essential in ensuring that the marketing plans are not only being implemented but are still appropriate for the changing international environment.

There are three essential elements of the control process:

1  *Setting standards*: The standards that are set need to be relevant to the corporate goals such as growth and profits reported by financial measures, return on capital employed and on sales, and non-financial indicators, e.g. market share. Intermediate goals and individual targets can be set by breaking the plan down into measurable parts which when successfully completed will lead to the overall objectives being achieved. The standards must be understandable, achievable and relevant to each local country situation.

2  *Measuring performance against standards*: To obtain measurements and ensure rapid feedback of information, firms use a variety of techniques. These include reports, meetings and special measurements of specific parts of the marketing programme, such as cost–benefit analysis on customers, product lines and territories. They also include marketing audits for a thorough examination of every aspect of marketing in a particular country. In addition, another technique a firm might use is benchmarking, which allows comparisons of various aspects of the business, such as efficiency of distribution, customer response times, service levels and complaints. Benchmarking might also be with other companies that are not necessarily from the same business sector.

3  *Correcting deviations from the plan*: Perhaps the most difficult decisions that must be made are to determine when performance has deviated sufficiently from the plan to require corrective action to be taken. This might be by way of changing either the plan or the management team charged with the responsibility of carrying out the plan.

A checklist of the essential elements of the international marketing plan is summarized in Figure 1.7.

## Reasons for success

Firms operating in the international environment succeed when they research, learn, are pro-active and have the foresight to understand what is beyond the horizon that will affect the global marketplace at micro and macro levels. Gathering and analyzing crucial information enables firms to respond and develop strategies. Firms that do well will base their success largely on the early identification and even pre-emptive expectation of changes in boundaries of markets and industries in their analysis of their international marketing environment. Management foresight and organizational learning are, therefore, the basis of a sustainable competitive advantage in global markets.

**FIGURE 1.7**   Essential elements of the international marketing plan

**Does the plan contain:**

**International analysis**

- assumptions about the world economy and the environment trends in the principal markets?
- details of historical performance (sales, cost, profitability)?
- forecast of future performance based on (a) an extrapolation of the past (b) alternative scenarios?
- identified opportunities and threats?

**Company capability assessment**

- analysis of the company strengths, weaknesses and future capabilities in comparison with local and international competition?

**International mission statement with:**

- long-term aims and objectives and the strategies to achieve them?
- one year marketing objectives and individual strategies (for example, budgets, brand objectives and development of personnel)?

**Operational plans**

- detailed country by country forecasts and targets?
- detailed country by country plans for all marketing activities and coordination with other functions (for example, manufacturing)?
- an explanation of how country plans will be integrated regionally or globally if appropriate?

**Contingencies and controls**

- a summary of the critical factors for success?
- an assessment of the likely competitor response?
- a contingency component for when things do not go to plan?
- a control process for feedback, evaluation and taking corrective action?

Firms are increasingly vulnerable to losing valuable personal assets because of the greater mobility of staff, prevalence of industrial espionage and the security risks and abuse associated with the Internet. Moreover, with the increase in communications, it is becoming more difficult to store, access and apply the valuable knowledge that exists among the huge volume of relatively worthless data that the company deals with. Consequently, effective knowledge management is now critical for success. This means having online database systems that facilitate effective data collection, a cloud computing capability, storage in data warehouses and data mining (the identification of opportunities from patterns that emerge from detailed analysis of the data held).

Successful global operators use the knowledge gained to assess their strengths and weaknesses in light of their organizational learning. This ensures they have the company capability and resources to respond to their learning in order to sustain their competitive advantage. This is particularly important in international markets as, for example, customer and brand loyalty may be much stronger in certain markets than others, and products that may be at the end of their life in the domestic market may be ideal for less sophisticated markets. In the dynamic international markets, therefore, if a firm is to succeed, it must develop the ability to think, analyze and develop strategic and innovative responses on an international, if not global, scale.

## Characteristics of best practice in international marketing

It is apparent, therefore, that firms and organizations planning to compete effectively in world markets need a clear and well-focused international marketing strategy. This strategy should be based on a thorough understanding of the markets which the company is targeting or in which it is operating. International markets are dynamic entities that require constant monitoring and evaluation. As we have discussed, as markets change so must marketing techniques. Innovation is an important competitive variable, not only in terms of the product or service but throughout the marketing process. Countertrading, financial innovations, networking and value-based marketing are all important concepts in the implementation of a successful international strategy.

The challenge then of international marketing is to ensure that any international strategy has the discipline of thorough research and an understanding and accurate evaluation of what is required to achieve the competitive advantage. Doole (2000) identified three major components to the strategies of firms successfully competing in international markets:

- A clear international competitive focus achieved through a thorough knowledge of the international markets, a strong competitive positioning and a strategic perspective which is truly international.
- An effective relationship strategy achieved through strong customer relations, a commitment to quality products and service and a dedication to customer service throughout international markets.
- Well-managed organizations with a culture of learning. Firms are innovative and willing to learn, show high levels of energy and commitment to international markets and have effective monitoring and control procedures for all their international markets.

## SUMMARY

- In this chapter, we have discussed the growing strategic importance of international marketing and examined the issues associated with successfully competing in international markets. The chapter examines the main differences between domestic and international marketing, the different levels at which international marketing can be approached and the more complex and multidimensional uncontrollable elements of the international marketing environment.
- We have examined the major aspects of the SLEPTS factors in the international marketing environment. The environments in which international companies must operate is typically characterized by uncertainty and change – factors which, taken together, increase the element of risk for international marketing managers.
- It has been suggested that marketing managers need to have a properly planned approach to any international activity because, without this, the costs and likelihood of failure will probably increase. We examined the international marketing planning and control process. We considered how managers can respond to the challenges posed in the international marketing environment by ensuring they have robust strategy development and market planning processes.
- The reasons for success and failure on international markets were examined. It was suggested the firms operating globally that succeed are those that perceive the changes in the international environment and are able to develop strategies which enable them to respond accordingly. Management foresight and organizational learning are, therefore, the bases for a sustainable competitive advantage in global markets.
- The reader has been introduced to many of the concepts that are important to the international marketing management process and will have gained an understanding of the issues to be addressed. All the various aspects of the international marketing strategy process introduced in this chapter will be examined in more detail in the following chapters. In Chapter 2 the world trading environment and the trends and developments in trading patterns will be examined.

## KEYWORDS

| | | |
|---|---|---|
| world trade | cultural paradoxes | least developed economies |
| international trade | European Union | World Trade Organization |
| global youth culture | piracy | emerging economies |
| export marketing | gross national income | multinational enterprise |
| international marketing | gross national income per capita | globalization |
| global marketing | purchasing power parity | |

## CASE STUDY 1

# Fast food: the healthy option goes global

According to a recent report by US firm, Zion Market Research, the global fast food industry is currently worth approximately US$600 billion and is growing at a rate of over 4 per cent per annum. It is expected to reach above US$691 billion by 2022. Hectic lifestyles and a reluctance to cook on a daily basis have led people to prefer quickly accessible food, which has fuelled a higher demand for fast food

Traditionally, fast food has been considered as 'empty calorie food' of little nutritional value. Many people living in towns and cities, however, prefer a cheap and fast way to acquire meals as they lead busy lives and don't want to spend their limited free time cooking. This has also led to growth in the fast food industry.

However, an emerging opinion is that increased health awareness among consumers will impact the traditional fast food industry. Ordering food online has become more popular in recent years leading to an increase in app-based food delivery companies. This could open the market to healthy option fast food companies. It is believed a lot of new growth in the industry could come from such companies in the future.

Leon was set up in 2004 by John Vincent, Henry Dimbleby and chef Allegra McEvedy who say they opened it because: 'we wanted to prove that it was possible to serve food that both tastes good and does you good. We want to make it easy for people to eat well on the high street. We want to do this in every major city in the world'. Leon is using this change in the market to produce healthy fast food such as salads, sandwiches, wraps and bowls of fresh ingredients. Its menu is full of low calorie and healthy options for reasonable prices, allowing it to compete against the biggest global names in fast food.

Leon now has almost 50 restaurants in the UK and the Netherlands and is currently expanding into the US market. It is also building a presence in Scandinavia and major cities in Europe. Leon has been described by its supporters as 'a disruptive fast-food model that was born in the UK but has immense potential to become global'. The company recently secured £25 million from a private equity backer to help it expand into the USA as well as new European partners to bolster its European growth plans.

Leon has stated its aim is 'to become the world's leading natural fast food company' and has set a long-term goal to become a more valuable global brand than McDonald's. The brand has been pioneering in its business proposition and its business model but as yet has engaged with little global above-the-line marketing activity. To date, the company has focused on the use of social media platforms as a way of building in-depth relationships with its consumers in the locality of the cities in which they operate. It believes this will be a central component of its marketing strategy as it expands across international markets.

## Questions

**1** What are the strengths and weaknesses of Leon's current operations in light of its vision?

**2** What are the challenges and risks Leon faces as it develops into new international markets?

**3** How would you advise Leon in its international strategy development to ensure the achievement of its vision?

**Sources:** www.zionmarketresearch.com/report/fast-food-market (accessed 3 March 2018); http://uk.businessinsider.com/new-healthy-fast-food-chains-better-than-mcdonalds (accessed 4 March 2018); https://leon.co/ (accessed 4 March 2018);https://globenewswire.com/news-release/2017/12/26/1274575/0/en/At-CAGR-4-20-Global-Fast-Food-Industry-Share-Will-Reach-690-80-Billion-by-2022.html (accessed 5 June 2018).

## CASE STUDY 2

# Going international? You need a language strategy

One of the ways to ensure an organization is successful when it enters the international arena is to have a language strategy. The marketing manager provides a common language with customers, employees, investors and supply chain operators. He or she promotes issues including the organization's brand values, its sustainability credentials and promotional offers. Additionally, the marketing manager will be communicating with multiple international marketing agencies to ensure advertisements on television, websites and Twitter are interesting and compelling to their respective local consumer market. To do all this successfully, organizations need a language strategy; yet at the moment not many global brands have a cohesive language strategy.

To engage in a cohesive international language strategy, an organization must engage with the following four elements:

1 Choose a lingua franca, also known as the trade language. The lingua franca is the chosen adopted language by organizations which work within a community that does not have a shared language. Therefore, a lingua franca is used when organizations have international teams working in countries outside the business's home country and also with traders along the supply chain. The most used lingua franca languages are English, Spanish, Arabic, Chinese and Swahili.
2 Have a policy to provide foreign language training and/or hire expatriates that can speak the lingua franca and also another language in countries where the organization does business.
3 Provide all employees with cultural awareness training, specifically highlighting differences and similarities in countries where the organization does business.
4 Have a communication strategy so that consumers see and can engage with the organization in their preferred language.

Multinational companies that do not engage in a cohesive language strategy can be inefficient. The reason inefficiencies occur is because unrestricted multilingualism, with no common language or cultural understanding, causes confusion, misinterpretation, alienation and friction. These inefficiencies occur between employees and traders, particularly when working across borders. They also cause tension which leads to a disjointed, disorganized business. Having said that, not all businesses have the funds or expertise to develop and engage with a language strategy.

This can be problematic when launching new marketing communications in a new market. Every bit of a communication plan needs to adapt to the language and culture as the message will need to resonate locally. This includes advertising, packaging, online and verbal communication from the sales team and customer service. An international marketing strategy should take into consideration not only the primary language of a new target market but also their idiomatic expressions, culturally acceptable methods of communication, etc.

For example, Lays Potato Chips uses the brand name 'Smiths' in Australia because it resonates better with the local consumers. They keep their logo the same to remain consistent globally, but their messaging changes with the local culture and language.

Marketing managers of international brands such as IBM know their consumer markets. They know they do business in many consumer markets outside their home country's borders, so the lingua franca they choose is English. However, IBM also does business in many other countries. Therefore, they have a policy of hiring someone that knows at least one of the languages native to the country in which they do business, as well as the lingua franca. Other members of staff at IBM are also trained in foreign languages and cultural awareness so they can engage with overseas colleagues and markets. A coherent language strategy is not only crucial for organizations that have international teams in cross-border trade, it also permits successful mergers and acquisitions and standardization of processes/regulations under a shared vision. It also enables employees to work closely with local markets and traders where a local language is best suited.

The Accor hotel brand clearly has a language strategy. Accor communicates with its customers, who incidentally come from 92 countries across the world. It translates over 20 million words per year to communicate effectively with its consumers in their preferred language. Communications take place on many traditional advertising channels as well as on social media platforms.

## Questions

**1** What are the benefits and weaknesses of a language strategy to an organization?

**2** What are the benefits of a language strategy to the consumer?

**3** If an organization cannot engage in all of the four elements of the language strategy immediately, which of the elements should they develop first?

**References:** Forbes Community Voice, How to build an international marketing strategy that adopts the 'mother tongue'. Available from www.forbes.com/sites/theyec/2017/11/02/how-to-build-an-international-marketing-strategy-that-adopts-the-mother-tongue/#5d098a356cb0 (accessed 3 March 2018); Neeley, T. and Kaplan, R.S. (2014) What's your language strategy. *Harvard Business Review*, 92(9), 70–76; Wakefield, M.A. (2014) 'SDL millennial study reveals language strategy is critical to enhancing customer experience success', published in SDL on 23 June 2014. Available from www.sdl.com/about/news-media/press/2014/sdl-millennial-study-reveals-language-strategy-is-critical-to-enhancing-customer-experience-success.html (accessed 21 June 2015).

# DISCUSSION QUESTIONS

**1** What are the major environmental influences which impact on international marketing? Show how they can affect international marketing strategies.

**2** Using examples, examine the reasons why marketing strategies fail in international markets.

**3** Identify three major global pressure groups. Examine how they have influenced the international marketing strategies of particular firms.

**4** What skills and abilities are necessary requirements for an effective international marketing manager? Justify your choices.

**5** How can marketing managers accommodate the multiplicity of international markets in a cohesive international marketing strategy and plan?

# REFERENCES

1.  *BBC News* (2014) Spanish oil company Repsol ends operations in Argentina. BBC News online 23 May. Available from www.bbc.co.uk/news/world-latin-america-27549309 (accessed 13 June 2018).
2.  *BBC News* (2017) Premier League wins anti-piracy court order. Available from www.bbc.co.uk/news/business-40727972 (accessed 13 November 2017).
3.  Consultancy.uk (2015) Grant Thornton: One third of firms plan to grow via M&A, published 16 April 2015. Available from www.consultancy.uk/news/1827/grant-thornton-one-third-of-firms-plan-to-grow-via-ma (accessed 13 August 2015).
4.  Credit Suisse (2017) *Global Wealth Report 2017*. Available from: www.credit-suisse.com/corporate/en/research/research-institute/global-wealth-report.html (accessed 5 January 2018).
5.  Doole, I. (2000) How SMEs learn to compete effectively on international markets. PhD paper.
6.  Doyle, L. (2017) By thinking local, brands can capture growth in newer, dynamic markets. Beauty Breakthroughs. Available from: www.gcimagazine.com/ (accessed 3 January 2018).
7.  Dunning, J.H. (1988) The eclectic paradigm of international production: A restatement and some possible extensions. *Journal of International Business Studies*, 19(1), 1–31.
8.  *The Economist* (2018) The Big Mac index, published 17 January 2018. Available from www.economist.com/content/big-mac-index (accessed 2 May 2018).
9.  Forbes Community Voice, How to build an international marketing strategy that adopts the 'mother tongue'. Available from https://www.forbes.com/sites/theyec/2017/11/02/how-to-build-an-international-marketing-strategy-that-adopts-the-mother-tongue/ (accessed 3 March 2018).
10.  *FT* (2018) Global M&A exceeds $3tn for fourth straight year. Available from www.ft.com/content/9f0270aa-eabf-11e7-bd17-521324c81e23 (accessed 4 January 2018).
11.  Lim, C.H. and Mack, V. (2017) Can the world's megacities survive the digital age? Available from:

www.smithsonianmag.com/innovation/can-worlds-megacities-survive-digital-age-180964967/ (accessed 21 January 2018).

12. Institute for Economics and Peace (2018) The Global Peace Index 2018 Available from: http://visionofhumanity.org/app/uploads/2018/06/Global-Peace-Index-2018-2.pdf Accessed 29th August 2018

13. Mckillop, C. (2017) Shocking exploitation of workers prompts renewed calls for national crackdown on dodgy labour hire companies. Available from: www.abc.net.au/news/rural/2017-03-28/growers-call-for-national-crackdown-on-worker-exploitation/8394252 (accessed 28 December 2017).

14. *The National* (2017) Coca-Cola losing its fizz in India. Available from www.thenational.ae/business/coca-cola-losing-its-fizz-in-india-1.72443 (accessed 3 January 2018).

15. Neeley, T. and Kaplan, R.S. (2014) What's your language strategy. *Harvard Business Review*, 92(9), 70–76.

16. Nyaga, M.N. (2014) The role of lending design on sustainable competitive advantage among deposit taking sacco's in Kenya. *Strategic Journal of Business & Change Management*, 1(2), 685.

17. Paige, J. (2013) Bangladesh clothing workers still exploited, five months after factory fire, Panorama investigation finds, published in *The Independent*, 23 September 2013. Available from www.independent.co.uk/news/world/asia/bangladesh-clothing-workers- still-exploited-five-months-after-factory-fire-panorama-investigation-finds-8833102.html (accessed 3 February 2015).

18. Perlmutter, M.V. (1995) Becoming globally civilised, managing across culture. Mastering Management Part 6, *Financial Times*, 1 December.

19. *RT News* (2014) Coca-Cola forced to close India bottling factory over excessive water use, pollution. Available from www.rt.com/news/167012-coca-cola-factory-closed-india/ (accessed 3 January 2018).

20. Statista (2016) Global economic costs of terrorism from 2000 to 2016 (in billion 2016 U.S. dollars). Available from www.statista.com/statistics/489649/global-economic-costs-of-terrorism/ (accessed 10 January 2018).

21. UBS Prices&Earnings, Working Time Edition 2015, www.ubs.com/microsites/prices-earnings/edition-2015.html (accessed 5 June 2018).

22. United Nations (2016). The World's Cities in 2016: Data Booklet (ST/ESA/ SER.A/392). United Nations: Department of Economic and Social Affairs, Population Division.

23. United Nations (2017) World Population Prospects Data Booklet. Available from: https://esa.un.org/unpd/wpp/Publications/Files/WPP2017_DataBooklet.pdf (accessed 5 January 2018).

24. Wakefield, M.A. (2014) 'SDL millennial study reveals language strategy is critical to enhancing customer experience success', published in SDL on 23 June 2014. Available from www.sdl.com/about/news-media/press/2014/sdl-millennial-study-reveals-language-strategy-is-critical-to-enhancing-customer-experience-success.html (accessed 21 June 2015).

25. World Trade Organization (2017) World Trade Statistical Review. Available from https://www.wto.org/english/res_e/statis_e/wts2017_e/WTO_Chapter_05_e.pdf (accessed 13 June 2018).

26. World Trade Organization (2018) Strong Trade Growth in 2018 rests on policy choices. Available from https://www.wto.org/english/news_e/pres18_e/pr820_e.htm (accessed 7 June 2018).

## CHAPTER 2

# THE WORLD TRADING ENVIRONMENT

## LEARNING OBJECTIVES

After reading this chapter you should be able to:

- Discuss the effects and implications of the risks and factors impacting on world trade
- Explain the key trends in the major regional trading blocs around the globe
- Understand the role of the major world institutions that foster the development of multilateral free trade across the world

## INTRODUCTION

International marketing takes place within the framework of the world trading environment. If the reader is to have the skills necessary to develop international marketing strategies, some understanding of the parameters of the world trading environment in which they operate is needed.

In this chapter we examine the development of world trade in recent years and the world trading environment in the context following the global financial crisis in 2008–09. We also look at how recent events provide opportunities and risks for marketing managers around the world. We will analyze the growth and changing patterns of world trade and discuss the institutions that aim to influence world trade.

We will also look at the changing regional trading blocs and the implications these have on trading structures around the globe.

# External factors impacting governments and business

There are many factors that both governments and businesses consider when making proactive long-term strategic decisions and reacting to global opportunities and risks that occur unexpectedly. There is a lot of optimism regarding technology, with many consumers happily embracing the Internet of Things technology. Voice-activated Alexa or Amazon Echo can order a Uber taxi, suggest wine and food pairings or instruct the robot lawn mower to cut the grass. Yet millions of people and businesses are reeling from cyber-attacks. Recent floods in Rwanda and Argentina have caused general devastation, yet the crops failed on farms in Western Australia due to lack of rainfall. In January each year, the World Economic Forum presents expectations of future events, such as risks that governments, multinational and small businesses may face in that same year. The list below presents the main risks; each risk has several sub-sections:

- economic risk
- environmental risk
- geopolitical risk
- societal risk
- technological risk

Risks change each year, as demonstrated in Figure 2.1. The most likely global risk expected in 2008 was an 'Asset Price Collapse', a sub-set of economic risk. The 'Asset Price Collapse' occurred and its aftermath

FIGURE 2.1   Top 5 global risks in terms of likelihood

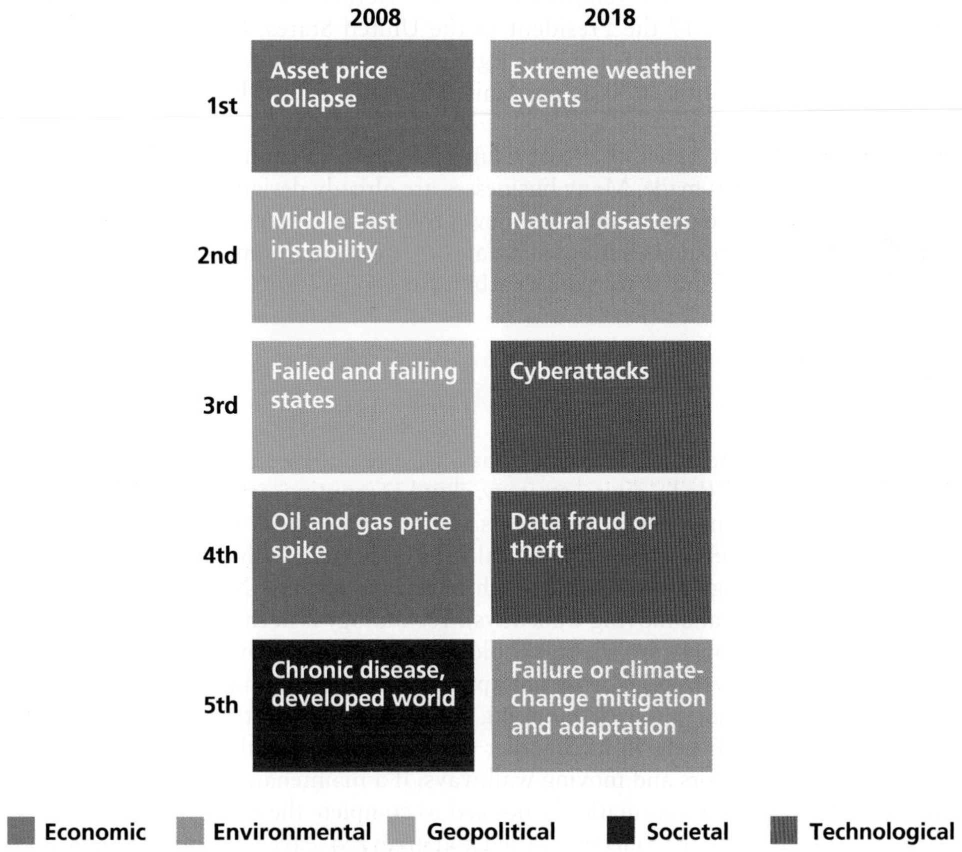

Source: World Economic Forum® (2018) *The Global Risks Report 2018*, 13th edition: Switzerland.

was felt around the world. 'Asset Price Collapse' was expected as the number one risk for 2009 and 2010. As financial crises cast a long shadow, businesses and markets were affected for a number of years. In 2008 two geopolitical risks were highlighted as potential risks for the year ahead. These manifested themselves as difficulties in the Middle East and instability in other states. The third risk expected in 2008 was global disease, which later in the year presented itself as Avian flu. Figure 2.1 shows the expected risks for 2008 and 2018. The top five risks for 2018 were not in the same categories as the risks of 2008; in 2018 the risks expected were environmental and technological.

## Environmental risks

Environmental risks can come in many forms. The three environmental risk sub-sections (Figure 2.1) expected in 2018 were extreme weather events, natural disasters and climate change. These were borne out in 2018. First, 2018 was heralded as one of the hottest years on record with mini heatwaves in the UK and Australia at unexpected times of the year. Second, the Arctic had such hot weather that it stunned scientists. Third, there was some risk that not all nations and businesses would commit to climate change initiatives.

It is expected that environmental risks are on the agenda of all nations as pollutants from one country can affect the air, land and sea quality around the world. The Paris Convention, 12 December 2015, a monumental gathering of representatives of 195 countries, drew up the first ever universal, legally binding global climate agreement. Not only were there representatives of governments present in Paris, but also NGOs (Non-Government Organizations) and agencies from the United Nations. All countries that signed the Paris Climate Agreement showed they were committed to reducing greenhouse gases and to helping to slow the increase in global temperature. On 5 October 2016 the Paris Climate Agreement was ratified in New York. In 2017 the President of the United States, Donald Trump, stated that the USA was no longer involved in the Paris Climate Agreement (note: the withdrawal of the USA from the Agreement cannot take place until 2020 as per United Nations rules). In 2017, Syria signed the Paris Climate Agreement.

Each of the governments that signed the Paris Climate Agreement cannot act alone. Businesses need to be involved to fulfil the promises made. Many businesses are already designing environmental policies into their strategy. Many are also seeking to innovate new products and services. Throughout the rest of this text there will be examples of businesses innovating and creating environmental solutions. Illustration 2.1 shows how McDonald's has set targets to reduce carbon emissions.

## Technology risks

The World Economic Forum presented Technology as an expected risk in 2018 (see Figure 2.1). With the advent of the Internet of Things (IoT), digital strategy, cloud computing, artificial intelligence (AI) and augmented reality (AR), to name but a few, governments and businesses need to be conscious that despite the benefits they bring there are likely to be technological risks associated with them.

Positive benefits of technology are shown through businesses such as Nordstrom and Shindler Group (makers of elevators, escalators and moving walkways). Technology is at the forefront of their business and they leverage it as the main proposition for stakeholders. Nordstrom provides excellent customer service whether the shopper visits its website, Nordstrom apps or through shop tags on Instagram. Data analytics instantly know each consumer and their shopping habits across all platforms. AI recommendations are sent to consumers based on their behaviour. Shindler Group uses data analytics to pre-exempt mechanical problems in its elevators, escalators and moving walkways. If a maintenance issue or problem is identified, parts are ordered and an engineer automatically booked to complete the task.

The vast amounts of data that are collected, stored and analyzed leave consumers and businesses at risk. In 2018, there were many cyberattacks. The city of Atlanta was a victim of a ransomware attack where city employee computers were locked and employees asked for a ransom of $6800 to be paid online to unlock

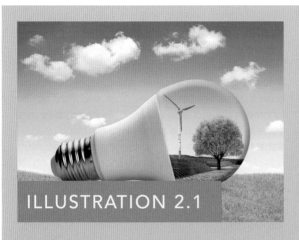

ILLUSTRATION 2.1

## McDonald's reducing environmental risk

Steve Easterbrook, President and CEO of McDonald's Restaurants, has made a bold move. McDonald's (the company) and its franchisees will reduce greenhouse gas emissions in restaurants and associated offices by 36 per cent by 2030. Not only does McDonald's need the cooperation of its 37 000 restaurants in 120 markets, it also needs to work in partnership with organizations along its supply chain. Therefore, this is a global project. If McDonald's achieves its greenhouse gas reduction target it has been calculated to be the equivalent of:

■ taking 32 million cars off the road for a year, or

■ planting 3.8 billion trees and growing them for 10 years

McDonald's is taking its inspiration of reducing environment risks from three of the United Nation's Sustainability Development goals, namely:

1   Goal 7: Affordable and clean energy

2   Goal 13: Climate action

3   Goal 17: Partnership for good

In terms of Goal 13: Climate action, McDonald's is working with its restaurant chain to make each one energy efficient. Already it has implemented greenhouse gas reduction actions by ensuring 100 per cent of new restaurants have LED lighting in the UK. LED lighting uses 50 per cent less energy. McDonald's also wants to remove and replace lightbulbs from its existing restaurants and has allocated a $5 million budget to do that. Once complete, the reduction in greenhouse gas emissions amounts to 100 587 metric tonnes. To put that into context, 100 587 metric tonnes is equivalent to removing 21 539 automobiles from the road for a year.

### Questions

1 McDonald's is helping to reduce greenhouse gas emissions. What other activities could it undertake to help reduce environment risks?

2 What may stop McDonald's achieving its target of reducing greenhouse gas emissions by 2030?

**Source:** McDonald's (2018). www.mcdonalds.

each computer. In the UK the National Lottery was hacked, and because of this breach the National Lottery recommended that all 10.5 million online account holders change their passwords. Chapter 12 develops the use of technology further as something which businesses need to embrace. Also, see Management Challenge 2.1 for details of a recent cybercrime and the fallout from it.

## World trading patterns

The world economy consists of 195 nations (193 countries being members of the United Nations and two that are not) with a population of 7.6 billion (United Nations 2017) and a gross domestic product (GDP) output of around US$75.9 trillion. **Gross domestic product** is a term used to describe the market value in monetary terms of goods and services produced in a period of time. Each year, since the early 2000s, global GDP has grown. However, there was a fall in global GDP in 2009 due to the financial crisis, but it has grown every year since 2009. The World Trade Organization (WTO) estimates world export trade for merchandise, which includes all exports including oil, automotive products and electronic components, to total almost US$16 trillion. Trade in commercial services is currently estimated to be about US$4.77 trillion (WTO 2018).

# Cybercrime affects businesses globally

At a low estimate, global revenue from cybercrime totals US$1.5 trillion. If cybercrime were a country, it would be ranked 13th in the world by GDP, placing it between Russia and Italy. Cybercriminals are profiting from businesses and organizations large and small.

There are different ways cybercriminals make profit:

- Earnings from illicit/illegal online transactions                  US$860bn
- Intellectual property theft              US$500bn
- Data trading                            US$160bn
- Crimeware-as-a-service                   US$1.6bn
- Ransomware                              US$1.0bn

The 'Web of Profit' is a term coined by researcher Michael McGuire (UK). It states that the interconnectedness of illegal businesses and the web platforms used to spread malware, sell illegal goods and services, steal personal data or set-up an e-commerce retail business that is actually trafficking human slaves, is a phenomenon that cannot be ignored. What also must not be ignored is the fact that legal and illegal activities take place side by side. The same platforms being used by illegal businesses are also those used by consumers completing their weekly grocery shop or searching for a life-long partner on dating sites.

## Question

1 What should an online retailer do to ensure its own, its customers' and its suppliers' data are safe? And what marketing messages should be communicated to stakeholders that the online retailer is passionate about online security?

**Sources:** Ismail, N. (2018) Global 'Cybercrime economy generates over $1.5TN, according to new study', https://www. information-age.com/global-cybercrime-economy-generates-over-1-5tn-according-to-new-study-123471631/

Figure 2.2 shows the most recent data from 2017 for international *export trade* for merchandise for ten countries.

The **Next Eleven** (or N-11) are 11 countries – Bangladesh, Egypt, Indonesia, Iran, Mexico, Nigeria, Pakistan, the Philippines, South Korea, Turkey and Vietnam – identified by Goldman Sachs investment bank as having a high potential of becoming the world's largest economies in the 21st century. The list includes both the BRIC (Brazil, Russia, India and China) and more recently introduced MINT (Mexico, Indonesia, Nigeria and Turkey) countries. The bank chose these states due to their promising outlooks for investment and future growth. This of course is a much longer-term prediction; time itself will tell how accurate that prediction turns out to be. Organizations could certainly include these countries in their long-term plans, particularly if they wanted to enter the country and start doing business. Organizations can consult The World Bank's Doing Business economy ranking regarding the N-11 countries. See Table 2.1 to see how the N-11 countries rank out of a total of 190 countries analyzed.

As Table 2.1 shows, the N-11 economies are ranked starting from which countries are easy to do business with down to the countries which are difficult, such as Pakistan and Bangladesh. There are many indicators that construct the ranking, such as an analysis of the country's economic status, access to finance, taxes, quality of legal structures, rights of employees, obtaining permits for a building and so on. The more difficulties with these factors makes for a higher score and the lower their ranking becomes. The lower a country's ranking is, the more businesses will find it frustrating to set up a business and continue working in that country. Currently New Zealand's 'Doing Business Rank' is 1, scoring well in the indicators outlined above. Eritrea and Somalia rank 189 and 190 respectively, meaning it would be more difficult to set up and do business there.

In global trade, emerging economies are now major players in comparison with the way businesses used to trade. In the mid-1990s, 63 per cent of trade took place between advanced economies, 32 per cent between the advanced economies and emerging economies, and just 5 per cent between emerging economies. Now trade between advanced countries has fallen to 38 per cent, trade between advanced economies and emerging economies has grown to 45 per cent and between emerging economies it has grown to 17 per cent (Currie 2018).

## FIGURE 2.2   International merchandise trade: exports

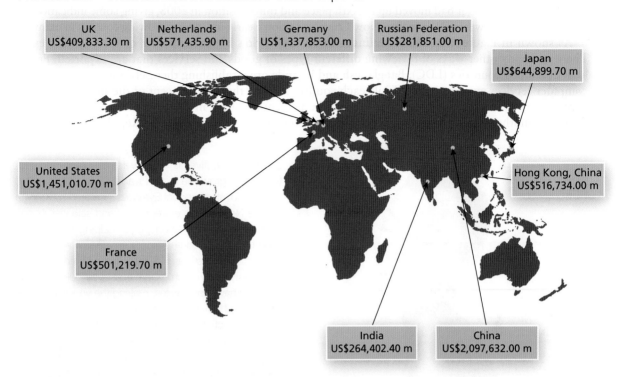

UK
US$409,833.30 m

Netherlands
US$571,435.90 m

Germany
US$1,337,853.00 m

Russian Federation
US$281,851.00 m

Japan
US$644,899.70 m

United States
US$1,451,010.70 m

Hong Kong, China
US$516,734.00 m

France
US$501,219.70 m

India
US$264,402.40 m

China
US$2,097,632.00 m

- World merchandise Export Trade is US$19 trillion
- CIS = Commonwealth of Independent States

Source: Adapted from https://www.wto.org/english/res_e/statis_e/statis_bis_e.htm (accessed 13 June 2018).

### Table 2.1   Countries: Ease of doing business rank

| Country | Doing Business Rank (out of 190 countries) |
|---|---|
| Republic of Korea (South Korea) | 4 |
| Mexico | 49 |
| Turkey | 60 |
| Vietnam | 68 |
| Indonesia | 72 |
| Philippines | 113 |
| Iran | 124 |
| Egypt | 128 |
| Nigeria | 145 |
| Pakistan | 147 |
| Bangladesh | 177 |

Source: World Bank (2018). www.doingbusiness.org (accessed 5 June 2018).
Note: A high ease of doing business ranking (e.g. 1) means that the country is easier to do business in.

This is a huge development. China did not even warrant a place in this top ten table in the 2001 edition of this textbook; by 2003 it had moved up to sixth place and third position in 2008, giving some indication of the trajectory of the growth of its economy. Now China's position clearly indicates a growing country in many ways.

As shown in Figure 2.2, China continues to be the world's biggest exporter of merchandise exports. There are many other ways of reviewing different types of goods and services that are exported. From the least developed countries (LDC), Bangladesh and Uganda are establishing themselves as competitors in the computer services export market. While each country has less than 0.1 per cent of the share of the world's export market, it will be interesting to review the percentage share in the future. See Illustration 2.2 for details of another way of reviewing exports from a company exporting from the Republic of South Africa.

## ILLUSTRATION 2.2

## South Africa's manufacturing export for busy people

The Republic of South Africa's vision for the future is to enable its citizens to reach their full potential through employment. The Department of Trade and Industry is marketing South Africa's globally competitive economy and the excellent skills base of its citizens to aid the export market. Currently, its exports amount to US$69.1 billion and its imports are US$73.76 billion. This means it has a negative balance of trade. Therefore, one of South Africa's

strategic objectives is to grow its manufacturing sector to help grow the export trade.

An innovative product Eyeslices® created by Kerryne Krause-Neufeldt, an entrepreneur and scientist, is one manufacturing innovation that is helping to grow the export market of South Africa. Kerryne saw a gap in the market. Eyeslices® are for men and women who lead busy lifestyles so much so that their eyes look red, over-tired and have dark circles, making the young business professional look older and more stressed than they are. Using products from Mother Nature, the traditional remedy for 'overtired' eyes was to lie down and put cucumber slices over the eyes. Now with 21st-century science and a lot of innovative flair, Kerryne Krause-Neufeldt produces Eyeslices® to reduce hectic lifestyle eye problems. The Cyrogel technology for the product was licensed and the product was marketed, launched and sold out in two hours. Eyeslices® are now available in many high class Spa and Wellness Clinics worldwide including Maha Desert Resort Dubai, Malinowy Zdroj Wellness Clinics in Poland and TRUMP Towers, New York. Eyeslices® continue to be manufactured in South Africa and are exported to 20 countries worldwide. Consumers can also buy direct through the Eyeslices® Facebook page.

### Question

**1** South Africa has manufacturing know-how and creative skills such as crafts, fashion and textiles. What are the opportunities and challenges that face South Africa's strategic objective to boost manufacturing exports?

**Reference:** Eyeslices.com; Department of Trade and Industry, South Africa; World Trade Organization

## Future prospects

The global economic crisis sparked a 12.2 per cent contraction in the volume of global trade in 2008–09. World trade volume suffered the sharpest decline in more than 70 years. However, world trade has begun to grow and is expected to continue growing year on year in the next decade to 2028, with forecasts expecting GDP to grow from US$74.5 trillion to US$103.2 trillion by 2022 (Statista 2018).

Table 2.2 provides details of the GDP growth and inflation changes from 2016 to 2017 for 27 countries across the world. The data for each country tells a story and five mini stories are given connected to the data shown.

Table 2.2    Percentage change on previous year in real GDP growth rate and inflation

| Country | GDP growth rate (%) | | Inflation rate (%) | |
|---|---|---|---|---|
| | 2016 | 2017 | 2016 | 2017 |
| Angola | −0.7 | 1.5 | 32.4 | 30.9 |
| Argentina | −2.2 | 2.5 | 26.5* | 26.9 |
| Australia | 2.5 | 2.2 | 1.3 | 2.0 |
| Brazil | −3.6 | 0.7 | 8.7 | 3.7 |
| China | 6.7 | 6.8 | 2.0 | 1.8 |
| Egypt | 4.3 | 4.1 | 10.2 | 23.5 |
| France | 1.2 | 1.6 | 0.3 | 1.2 |
| Germany | 1.9 | 2.1 | 0.4 | 1.6 |
| Greece | 0.0 | 1.8 | 0.0 | 1.2 |
| India | 7.1 | 6.7 | 4.5 | 3.8 |
| Indonesia | 5.0 | 5.2 | 3.5 | 4.0 |
| Japan | 1.0 | 1.5 | −0.1 | 0.4 |
| Libya | −3.0 | 55.1 | 27.1 | 32.8 |
| Mexico | 2.3 | 2.1 | 2.8 | 5.9 |
| Netherlands | 2.2 | 3.1 | 0.1 | 1.3 |
| Nigeria | −1.6 | 0.8 | 15.7 | 16.3 |
| Poland | 2.6 | 3.8 | −0.6 | 1.9 |
| Russia | −0.2 | 1.8 | 7.0 | 4.2 |
| Saudi Arabia | 1.7 | 0.1 | 3.5 | −0.2 |
| Sweden | 3.2 | 3.1 | 1.1 | 1.6 |
| South Sudan | −13.8 | −6.3 | 379.8 | 182.2 |
| Sudan | 3.1 | 3.7 | 17.8 | 26.9 |
| Turkey | 3.2 | 5.1 | 7.8 | 10.9 |
| UK | 1.8 | 1.7 | 0.7 | 2.6 |
| USA | 1.5 | 2.2 | 1.3 | 2.1 |
| United Arab Emirates | 3.0 | 1.3 | 1.8 | 2.1 |
| Venezuela | −16.5 | −12.0 | 254.4 | 652.7 |

Source: World Facts 2018. www.CIA.org.
GDP – real growth rate compares GDP growth on an annual basis
* 2015 rates provided not 2016

The first story is about Japan with GDP growth of 1.0 per cent (2016) and 1.5 per cent (2017) and inflation of –0.1 per cent (2016) and 0.47 per cent (2017), reflecting the steady, clear and focused reputation Japan has internationally. Its work ethic helps it develop as an advanced country. It is Japan's keiretsu system that interlocks manufacturers, suppliers and distributors. In addition, the guaranteed 'job for life', which a high proportion of the labour force enjoys, keeps growth modest.

Egypt has experienced difficulties in terms of living conditions and job opportunities for its citizens. In 2016 Egypt asked for a loan from the IMF of US$12 million. At the same time Egypt floated its currency on the stock market. The effects of these events showed in its high inflation rate of 23.5 per cent in 2017.

Greece has had a number of setbacks, particularly as the country stayed in recession for quite some time and had austerity measures put in place. Two bailouts took place – one from the Eurozone governments and the second from European leaders. The bailouts were given to help Greece reduce its debt burden. During 2014 Greece began to recover and has seen recent decreases in unemployment. The figures in Table 2.2 show GDP growth from 0 per cent in 2016 to 1.2 per cent in 2017.

Nigeria is one of the MINT countries (Mexico, Indonesia, Nigeria and Turkey) and it relies on oil as its main export. The economic crisis and volatile exchange rates have affected Nigeria's economy. The infrastructure in Nigeria is poor and government reform is slow to take shape, both of which slowed down the amount of oil exported over recent years. With the recent increase in oil prices, Nigeria's GDP growth has increased from –1.6 per cent to 0.8 per cent.

South Sudan is the final mini story linked to Table 2.2. It is a difficult place to research as there is a lot of corruption, a large black market and it is a poor, underdeveloped country. Its infrastructure is a major drawback to growth. There are approximately 700 km of road, but only around 200 are paved (World Bank 2016). South Sudan does export oil but not via its road network; oil is passed through a pipeline. South Sudan is actually an oil-dependent country. Over 50 per cent of the population earns just US$2 per day, electricity and water are scarce, and the majority of goods and consumables are imported. The figure of 379.8 per cent inflation during 2016 was a 'year average'. During 2016 there were periods of inflation as high as 800 per cent.

It is not just a country's GDP that is important to consider. It is also important to view a country's trade deficit. According to Table 2.3, firms are likely to have difficulties in such markets as Egypt, Venezuela and Argentina, as each has a high trade deficit.

Table 2.3   Balance of Trade

| Country | US$ |
| --- | --- |
| Argentina ** | 611 million Deficit |
| Brazil** | 6 280 million Surplus |
| China ** | 4 980 million Deficit |
| Egypt * | 3 626 million Deficit |
| India** | 13 690 million Deficit |
| Indonesia** | 1 092 million Surplus |
| Mexico** | 1 918 million Surplus |
| Russia* | 12 192 million Surplus |
| Thailand** | 1 270 million Surplus |
| Taiwan** | 6 001 million Surplus |
| USA* | 57 591 million Deficit |
| Venezuela * | 782 million Deficit |

Source: Trading Economics www.tradingconomics.com as reported 2018.
* as of February 2018
** as of March 2018

# The reasons countries trade

International trade is a vital part of world economic activity, but it is not a new phenomenon. While the growth of international trade has accelerated since the late 1970s, it goes back far beyond then and has been developing throughout the ages since the time when barter was used.

The great growth period for trade was in the 18th and 19th centuries when many of today's important trading links were forged and developed.

A major source of many of the conflicts in the 19th century was the desire by nations to win the right to trade in foreign markets. One of the reasons why Great Britain went to war with Napoleon was to open the French markets to our newly industrialized nation. The colony of Hong Kong and the associated New Territories returned to China in 1997 were acquired by the UK in the early 19th century for trading purposes.

The reasons nations trade are many and varied. Two key explanations of why nations trade, however, are based on the theory of comparative advantage and the international product life cycle.

## The theory of comparative advantage

The rationale for world trade is based largely upon Ricardo's theory of comparative advantage. At its simplest level, the theory suggests that trade between countries takes place because one country is able to produce a product at a lower price than is possible elsewhere. An example of this is the way in which Japanese companies such as Sony and Hitachi came to dominate the European television market. Their strategy was based upon higher product quality, better design and, more importantly for our purposes here, the lower prices that were made possible by far greater economies of scale and better manufacturing technology than was currently being achieved by the European producers.

It is this notion of relative cost that underpins world trade; in other words, countries concentrating upon producing products in which they have a comparative advantage over their foreign competitor countries.

## How comparative advantage is achieved

A comparative advantage can be achieved in a variety of ways:

- *Sustained period of investment*: This may well lead to significantly lower operating costs.
- *Lower labour cost*: A firm operating internationally may locate a manufacturing plant in an emerging economy to take advantage of the lower labour costs there.

  Here is a comparison of average annual wages:

  | | |
  |---|---|
  | Denmark | US$64 900 |
  | United States | US$60 109 |
  | United Kingdom | US$46 219 |
  | Greece | US$19 165 |
  | Taiwan | US$18 147 |
  | Estonia | US$15 615 |
  | Venezuela | US$  1 145 |

  Source: MarketLine (2018).

  This clearly shows that labour costs are much higher in some countries than others, suggesting that manufacturing in low-income countries could be of benefit to the bottom line. Many developed countries complain of the disadvantage this creates for them in trying to compete in international markets because their wage bill can be substantially higher. This competitive disadvantage is further compounded by the government subsidies and support given in such countries.
- *Proximity to raw materials*: This is another way to achieve comparative advantage as has been the case with Australia's reserves of coal and mineral ores.
- *Subsidies to help native industries*: When the USA announced increased wheat subsidies to US farmers, they outraged the Australian and Canadian wheat farmers who saw it as a direct attack

on their international markets. Without comparable government support, they felt they were unable to compete with US wheat in these markets. Controversy in Europe flared recently when it was discovered by Greenpeace that the EU farming subsidiaries, which are given to all regardless of size of farm, were being distributed to farmers who are billionaires.

■ *Building expertise in certain key areas*: This is another way to achieve comparative advantage. Countries that have the highest number of organizations investing in biotechnology research and development include the USA, France, Switzerland, South Korea, Japan, Germany and Denmark. By specifically targeting the research field of innovation and development of biotechnology, it has become a key area where these countries have comparative strength, and their reputations have grown as a result.

Some countries use international trade to buy in a comparative advantage, buying in highly developed products and so speeding up their development. There are, however, some fundamental requirements to gain competitive status. Schwab (2018) states that to be competitive within the world's marketplace, countries need to be stable, productive and sustainable, supported by basic foundations. With that in mind he, together with the World Economic Forum, provides a Global Competitive Index based on 12 Pillars of Competitiveness. The 12 Pillars of Competitiveness are split into three stages.

## Stage 1. Basic Requirements

The Factor Driven Pillars are the foundations; without these a country cannot be a major competitor in the international market. The pillars are:

1 *Institutions*: honest and fair interconnected public and private administrative legal networks, working with government to improve the economy.
2 *Infrastructure*: developed telecommunications, uninterrupted power supplies and transport systems.
3 *Macro-environment*: stable macro-environment.
4 *Health and Primary Education*: healthy citizens contributing to the business and skills economy; primary education for all.

Countries engaging in the Basic Requirements of Stage 1 include Bangladesh, Nicaragua and Tanzania. Once the Basic Requirements are in place, a country can start to become more effective through efficiency-driven activities; in doing so they become more competitive within the world marketplace.

## Stage 2. Efficiency Driven

5 *Higher Education and Training*: Secondary and tertiary (undergraduate degree to Doctor of Philosophy) education, together with continuous work-based training.
6 *Goods Market Efficiency*: A range of services and goods enabling a balance between supply and demand; open market to encourage foreign investment.
7 *Labour Market Efficiency*: Equal gender and age opportunities together with potential for promotion or movement within and/or across economic activities.
8 *Financial Market Efficiency*: Solid banking sector; efficient risk and investment activities.
9 *Technology Readiness*: Communication and information technology enabling cross-border and/or national research and business opportunities.
10 *Market Size*: Includes both domestic and international market size/potential.

Countries engaging in the efficiency dimensions of Stage 2 include Albania, Indonesia and Peru.

## Stage 3. Innovation Driven Stage

11 *Business Sophistication*: Countries known to create quality, brand leading products and services with modern, unique production and distribution mechanisms.
12 *Innovation*: Research and Development, design and creation of technological and scientific products and services.

Countries at Stage 3 which are high in innovation with complex businesses include China, Qatar and the UK.

## The international product life cycle

The theory of comparative advantage is often used as the classic explanation of world trade. Other observers, however, believe that world trade and investment patterns are based upon the product life cycle concept. Writing from a US perspective, Vernon and Wells (1968) suggested that on an international level, products move through four distinct phases:

1  US firms manufacture for the home market and begin exporting.
2  Foreign production starts.
3  Foreign products become increasingly competitive in world markets.
4  Imports to the USA begin providing significant competition.

These distinct phases are still used today to outline the International Product Cycle. This cycle begins with the product being developed and manufactured, for example, in the USA for high-income markets. It is subsequently introduced into other markets in the form of exports. The second phase begins to emerge as the technology is developed further and becomes more easily transferable. Companies in other countries then begin manufacturing and, because of lower transportation and labour costs, are able to undercut the US manufacturers in certain markets.

The third phase is characterized by foreign companies competing against US exports which, in turn, leads to a further decline in the market for US exports. Typically, it is at this stage that US companies either begin to withdraw from selected markets or, in an attempt to compete more effectively, begin investing in manufacturing capacity overseas to regain sales.

The fourth and final stage begins when foreign companies, having established a strong presence in their home and export markets, start the process of exporting to the US and begin competing against the products produced domestically.

It is these four stages, Vernon suggests, that illustrate graphically how US automobile firms have found themselves being squeezed out of their domestic markets, having enjoyed a monopoly in the US car market originally.

Although the product life cycle provides an interesting insight into the evolution of multinational operations, it should be recognized that it provides only a partial explanation of world trade, as products do not inevitably follow this pattern. First, competition today is international rather than domestic for all goods and services. Consequently, there is a reduced time lag between product research, development and production, leading to the simultaneous appearance of a standardized product in major world markets. Second, it is not production in the highly labour-intensive industries that is moving to the low labour-cost countries, but the capital-intensive industries such as electronics. This creates the anomalous situation of basing production for high-value, hi-tech goods in the countries least able to afford them. Neither does the model go very far in explaining the rapid development of companies' networking production and marketing facilities across many countries. Thus, global business integration and sharing of R&D technological and business resources are seen as a more relevant explanation of today's world trade.

# Barriers to world trade

## Marketing barriers

While countries have many reasons for wishing to trade with each other, it is also true to say that all too frequently an importing nation will take steps to frustrate negotiations, and inhibit or change regulations that disrupt the inward flow of goods and services. Illustration 2.3 provides an example of how India's new food and drink regulations frustrated many brands importing alcoholic drinks into India.

One of the reasons international trade is different from domestic trade is that it is carried on between different political units, each one a sovereign nation exercising control over its own trade. Although all nations control their foreign trade, they vary in terms of the degree of control. Each nation or trading bloc invariably establishes trade laws that favour their indigenous companies and discriminate against foreign ones.

Thus, at the same time as trade has been developing worldwide, so has the body of regulations and barriers to trade. The WTO lists the technical barriers to trade that countries use in their attempts to protect their economy from imports. The main protagonists are seen as the USA, Italy, France and Germany.

However, the major barriers to trade are becoming increasingly covert, i.e. non-tariff barriers which are often closely associated with the cultural heritage of a country and very difficult to overcome. The complex distribution patterns in Japan are one such example. Thus, while Japan is seen not to have many overt barriers, many businesses experience great difficulties when trying to enter the Japanese market. In Russia recently, 167 500 Motorola handsets were seized at a Moscow airport. They were alleged to have been smuggled, to be counterfeit, to violate a Russian patent and to be a danger to public health. As a result, some 50 000, it was claimed, were destroyed by the Interior Ministry, but surprisingly, a large number of Motorola phones appeared on the Russian black market. Whatever the rights and wrongs of the intentions, trade distortion practices can provide nightmare scenarios for the international marketer. It is thus important to be aware of the practices of the countries being targeted and the types of barriers companies face. Trade distortion practices can be grouped into two basic categories: **tariff** and **non-tariff barriers**, as illustrated in Figure 2.3.

ILLUSTRATION 2.3

# Regulations frustrate importers of alcohol

The Food Safety Authority of India has recently regulated all imports of alcoholic drinks. The import regulation was set into law in 2011 but it was not until 2018 that the law was put into force. The new regulations are intricate, and many consider them to be tedious and unhelpful. Two regulations in particular are causing irritation:

1  Labels on each bottle of wine or spirit must be in Hindi or English.

2  Labels need to include all ingredients contained within the product.

Due to these regulations, there are millions of bottles of wine and spirits piled high at Indian ports. Without the correct labelling, no products can pass through Indian customs. Many bottles of wine have landed in India with labelling stating the 'country of origin'. Therefore, bottles of wine that state 'Producto de España' are deemed unacceptable: the label should have read 'Product of Spain' (English) or स्पेन का उत्पाद (Hindi). Many millions of bottles of spirits cannot pass through customs because the bottles do not have a list of all the ingredients contained in the product. A spokesman, Aashish Kasbekar, from an alcohol clearing house in India, advised it is relatively easy to list the ingredients for vodka as it is mainly just one ingredient. He went on to say that 90 per cent of alcoholic drinks have many ingredients. So for a blended Scotch whisky this would mean including a list of the different types of whiskies that have been blended to make the brand of whisky, as well as the malted grains, yeast, colourings and flavourings. There is confusion if any further details are needed and in what format. Whisky manufacturers seem reluctant to start labelling, particularly as it has not yet been decided if the bottles of alcohol have to be labelled as vegetarian or non-vegetarian.

In terms of wine, a certified sommelier advised that it is important ingredients are provided so that consumers can make decisions. Red wine often contains fish bladders to keep the wine bright and clear; without them red wine can become cloudy. Vegetarians and vegans need to be aware of this so that they can read the ingredients' label and choose accordingly.

One additional thing that frustratates importers of alcohol into India is that in each shipment that passes through, the labelling regulation is tested. Testing means that two bottles per shipment are opened and tested. This stage is considered time-consuming and expensive and it further delays the alcohol reaching stores and restaurants.

## Questions

**1** What difficulties are the new regulations causing importers of alcohol to India?

**2** You have three shipments of wine each containing 100 cases of wine stacked in the warehouse at a port in India. The labelling is incorrect as there are no ingredients listed on the label. What will your next move be with these shipments of wine to ensure they 'get to market' as soon as possible?

**Source:** *The Guardian* (2018) India's new alcohol labelling laws leave importers needing a drink. Available from: www.theguardian.com/world/2014/jul/11/india-labelling-laws-wine-wallahs-importers-running-dry (accessed 5 June 2018).

**Tariff barriers**   Tariffs are direct taxes and charges imposed on imports. They are generally simple, straightforward and easy for the country to administer. While they are a barrier to trade, they are a visible and known quantity and so can be accounted for by companies when developing their marketing strategies.

Tariffs are used by poorer nations as the easiest means of collecting revenue. The Bahamas, for example, has a minimum import tariff of 85 per cent on vehicles/trucks over 20 tonnes, 75 per cent on motorcycles, 60 per cent on batteries and plastic shopping bags, 45 per cent on pineapples and 30 per cent on energy drinks, to name but a few.

Tariffs are often imposed to simply protect the home producer, as in the USA and Australia. Both of these countries have high tariff walls for certain industries they wish to protect – for example, agricultural products. The trend towards the lowering of tariff barriers across the globe in recent years (the average tariff is now 5 per cent whereas in 1945 it was 45 per cent) together with the opening up of new markets to foreign investment, notably Asia and South America, has greatly complicated the decision for many companies as to where to place manufacturing facilities.

These trends have made global production much more possible, but it has also reduced the need for many overseas plants. Markets that previously demanded local production facilities because tariff levels made importing prohibitive can now be supplied from non-domestic sources.

A good example of these dynamics can be seen in Australia's automotive sector. Tariffs on imported cars have fallen from 57.5 per cent to 5 per cent. Recent discussions have been held in Australia to abandon import tariffs on cars. The reason for this is to encourage Australians to own a new, cleaner (energy-wise), safer car. Japanese manufacturers, therefore, found they no longer needed to have plants in Australia to serve the market.

Tariffs can take many forms, as can be seen in Figure 2.3. The most common, however, are:

■ *Specific*: charges are imposed on particular products either by weight or volume and usually stated in the local currency.

■ *Ad valorem*: a straight percentage of the import price.

■ *Discriminatory*: in this case the tariff is charged against goods coming from a particular country, either where there is a trade imbalance or for political purposes.

## Non-tariff barriers

Since the late 1970s, the world has seen a gradual reduction in tariff barriers in most developed nations. However, in parallel with this, non-tariff barriers have substantially increased. Non-tariff barriers are much more elusive and can be more easily disguised. The effect can, however, be more devastating because they are an unknown quantity and are much less predictable.

**Figure 2.3**   Market entry barriers

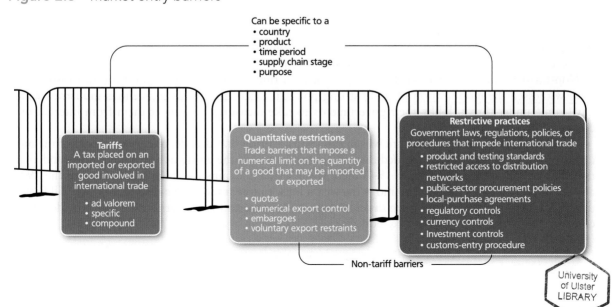

Non-tariff barriers take many different forms:

■ Increased government participation in trade is one that is gaining more dominance and which is used by nations to gain competitive advantage, as in the case of the US wheat subsidy previously discussed.

■ Customs entry procedures can also impede trade. These take many forms: administrative hold-ups, safety regulations, subsidies and differing technical standards are just a few. To import goods into some economic regions, businesses experience 'bloated border bureaucracy'. To import goods into high income countries, on average, 7 documents are required, which are all signed by 3 administrative departments, which means border delays are around 14 days. However, when importing goods into sub-Saharan Africa it is much more bureaucratic as, on average, 13 documents are required, each signed by 30 administrative departments, which means border delays last around 60 days.

■ Therefore, the need for customs modernization and harmonization has become a priority for companies who find their operations severely hampered by 'bloated bureaucratic' requirements and administrative delays at borders and which are likely to get worse as economic globalization gathers pace.

■ Clearly the extent of customs delays and bureaucratic red tape varies enormously from country to country but everywhere there is a need for governments to take account of business needs for simple, transparent, coordinated and harmonized customs procedures.

■ Quantitative restrictions such as quotas are another barrier. These are limits on the amount of goods that may enter a country. An import quota can be more restrictive than a tariff as there is less flexibility in responding to it. The Japanese car industry faced quotas both in Europe and the USA and so developed manufacturing capacity in these markets as a means of overcoming the barriers. The USA also imposes quotas on imports from China. However, China, according to the USA, has been transhipping products through other ports such as Hong Kong in order to circumvent the quotas.

■ Financial controls were last seen in the UK in the mid-1970s but have been used recently in Mexico and South America where high inflation and lack of hard currency required stringent monetary controls. This is probably the most complete tool for the regulation of foreign trade as it gives the government a monopoly in all dealings in foreign exchange. A domestic company earning foreign exchange from exporting must sell it to the national bank and, if goods from abroad need to be bought, a company has to apply for foreign exchange. Thus, foreign currency is scarce. The International Monetary Fund has placed stringent controls on several countries, in particular Indonesia, Brazil and Argentina. The latter countries especially have huge external debts which are viewed as unsustainable.

Countries practising exchange controls tend to favour the import of capital goods rather than consumer goods. The other major implication to companies operating in foreign markets is the restrictions on repatriating profits in foreign currency. This requires either countertrade dealings or the use of distorted transfer prices to get profits home (see Chapter 11 on pricing issues).

Non-tariff barriers become much more prevalent in times of recession. In the USA and Europe, we have witnessed the mobilization of quite strong political lobby groups, as indigenous industries which have come under threat, lobby their governments to take measures to protect them from international competition.

The last major era of protectionism was in the 1930s. During that decade, under the impact of the most disastrous trade depression in recorded history, countries around the world adopted high tariffs and abandoned their policies of free trade. In 1944 there was a reaction against the high tariff policy of the 1930s and significant efforts were made to move the world back to free trade. In the next section we will look at the global institutions that have been developed since that time to foster world trade and provide a trade climate in which such barriers can be reduced.

In the 1930s world trade was at a low ebb, protectionism was rife and economies were strangling themselves. Several initiatives were born, primarily out of the 1944 Bretton Woods conference, to create an infrastructure that fostered trading relations. These initiatives fell into three areas:

- *Need for international capital*: The International Bank for Reconstruction and Development (IBRD).
- *International liquidity*: International Monetary Fund.
- *Liberalization of international trade and tariffs*: General Agreement on Tariffs and Trade, which became the World Trade Organization.

## International Bank for Reconstruction and Development (IBRD)

The World Bank, officially called the International Bank for Reconstruction and Development, was founded together with the International Monetary Fund (IMF) in 1944. The World Bank began operating in June 1946. Membership of the Bank is open to all members of the IMF. Currently, there are 189 member countries. The Bank is owned and controlled by its member governments. Each member country subscribes to shares for an amount relative to its economic strength. The largest shareholder in the World Bank at the moment is the USA.

The World Bank is a vital source of financial and technical assistance to developing countries around the world. It helps governments in developing countries to reduce poverty by providing them with the money and technical expertise they need for a wide range of projects, such as education, health, infrastructure, communications, government reforms, as well as many other purposes. Most recent bank lending to developing countries has been by the IBRD and its sister organization the International Development Association (IDA), overseen by 173 shareholder nations. The IDA focuses particularly on the 75 poorest nations around the world. Established in 1960, the IDA aims to reduce poverty by providing interest-free credits and grants for programmes that boost economic growth, reduce inequalities and improve people's living conditions. To date it has provided US$345 billion for investment in 113 countries. Approximately US$18 billion is committed to helping the poorer countries each year. The IDA complements the IBRD, which serves middle-income countries with capital investment and advisory services.

The scope of the Bank's operations has increased phenomenally since the late 1990s. The Bank provides support for a wide variety of projects related to agriculture, education, industry, electricity, rural development, tourism, transportation, population planning, urban development, water supply and telecommunications. The Bank lends money only for productive purposes and gives serious consideration to the prospects of repayment before granting the loan.

While the countries who are members subscribe to the share capital of the World Bank, it relies mainly on private investors for its financial resources through borrowing in various capital markets. In this way, private investors become involved in the development efforts of developing countries. Since the IBRD obtains most of its funds on commercial terms, it charges its borrowers a commercial rate of interest. Loans are usually repayable over a 20-year period.

This has led to what has been euphemistically termed the 'debt crisis'. Many of the poor developing countries, recipients of large capital loans, are finding it impossible to meet the burden of debt facing them. Some of this debt is unpayable when the interest on the debt is greater than what the country produces. However, in some cases, this is what is known as 'odious debt', debt incurred by undemocratic countries and misspent. Spokespersons often request rich countries to 'write off' the debt of poorer countries; yet this still has not happened. The World Bank Group provides debt relief to the poorest countries through the HIPC Initiative and the Multilateral Debt Relief Initiative (MDRI). The Initiative calls for the voluntary provision of debt relief by all creditors, whether multilateral, bilateral or commercial, and aims to provide a fresh start to countries with a foreign debt that places too great a burden on export earnings or fiscal revenues.

However, since the global banking crisis, the level of debt has become a heavy burden to a number of major exporting countries as well as developing countries. It was expected following the banking crises that some of the major, developed economies would strategically choose to reduce their debt over the last few years. This did not occur. Indeed, no major economy has reduced its debt. To further show the effect that the banking crisis has had on the world's economy, 14 countries have actually increased their debt-to-GDP%, including Japan, Portugal and Greece. See Table 2.4 for information regarding the 20 highest debt-to-GDP% countries.

Following the Great Depression in the 1930s and the accumulating years of monetary devaluation and exchange rate difficulties, the United Nations realized that there was a need to help poorer countries obtain fair loans and opportunities for growth. The IDA was established to help meet this need. It was made an affiliate of the World Bank and was to be administered in accordance with the Bank's established methods. The IDA makes soft loans of about US$7 billion annually. Almost all are granted for a period of 15 years without interest, except for a small charge to cover administrative overheads. Repayment of loans does not start until after a ten-year period of grace. Both the IDA and the IBRD lay down stringent requirements that

Table 2.4   Debt-to-GDP ratio

| Countries with the highest public debt 2017 | |
| --- | --- |
| Country | Public debt in relation to GDP (%) |
| Japan | 240.3% |
| Greece | 180.18% |
| Lebanon | 152.29% |
| Italy | 133.02% |
| Cabo Verde | 128.75% |
| Eritrea | 127.42% |
| Portugal | 125.72% |
| Republic of Congo | 117.71% |
| Bhutan | 112.83% |
| Gambia | 112.68% |
| Singapore | 110.58% |
| United States | 108.14% |
| Jamaica | 107.04% |
| Cyprus | 105.54% |
| Belgium | 104.29% |
| Egypt | 101.24% |
| Spain | 93.69% |
| Barbados | 97.92% |
| France | 96.84% |
| Jordan | 95.56% |

**Source:** Statista (2018) The 20 countries with the highest public debt in 2017 in relation to the gross domestic product. www.statista.com.

## MANAGEMENT CHALLENGE 2.2

# Do high debts mean high risk?

Following the world banking crisis, some governments had to reassure the world that their country was economically viable. Table 2.4 provides a ranking of the top 12 Debt-to-GDP% by country.

Singapore and Greece have high Debt-to-GDP% ratios. Underlying the Debt-to-GDP% are three main sources of debt which show the real economy debt change (2007–14) by per cent: government debt, corporate debt and household debt. An increase in real economy debt change provides the underlying notion of whether a high Debt-to-GDP% means the country is at risk or is not at risk. Take for example, Singapore and Greece. Both have a high Debt-to-GDP%. However, how Singapore and Greece's debt changed between 2007 and 2014 helps to determine if the relevant country is at risk or not:

Singapore's government debt is 22 per cent. This debt is low and is mainly money put aside for their citizens' pensions. Singaporean's household debt is at 15 per cent. The Singaporean government recently capped the amount of money its citizens can borrow, either through loans or credit cards. Singapore's corporate debt is high for two specific reasons. First, many foreign banks and other financial organizations have chosen Singapore in which to set up a regional headquarters. Second, many of these and businesses in the Asia region raise debt in Singapore and use the money to expand internationally.

Greece's government debt is high as public spending has soared since the late 2000s. Additionally, government employees, of which there are many in Greece, received a large salary increase (almost double). Greece has low household and corporate debt.

## Questions

**1** Compare and contrast the different types of debt that make up the total real economy debt change, 2007–14 by percentage.

**2** Compare and contrast the real economy debt charge of Singapore and Greece.

**3** Which country has a high debt but is of low risk?

| Sources of debt | Debt-to-GDP % | Total | Real economy debt change, 2007–14 by % | | |
| | | | Government | Corporate | Household |
|---|---|---|---|---|---|
| Singapore | 382 | 129 | 22 | 92 | 15 |
| Greece | 317 | 103 | 70 | 13 | 20 |

**Sources:** IMF.org; McKinsey Global Institute (2015) Debt and (Not Much) Deleveraging. McKinsey &Company.

have to be met before any loans are granted. In many cases this has meant that countries have had to make quite hard political decisions in order to achieve the balanced budget required. In some cases, this has led to severe hardship and social disorder, for which the institutions have been severely criticized.

## International Monetary Fund (IMF)

The objective of the IMF was to regain the stability in international exchange rates that had existed under the gold standard. Although the system of pegged rates failed to keep up with the growth in international trade, the functions of the IMF have continued to develop.

The main function was to provide short-term international liquidity to countries with balance of payments deficit problems, enabling them to continue to trade internationally. Now its purpose is to ensure stability within the international monetary system, make sure exchange rates between countries are fair and further enable countries to transact with each other through multilateral systems of payment that again are fair for all. The IMF, with its 189 members, provides a forum for international monetary cooperation enabling the making of reciprocal agreements. Thus, it serves to lessen the risk of nations taking arbitrary actions against each other, as happened before it came into being. It can also sound a warning bell for nations with potential liquidity problems.

The IMF's seal of approval is, for emerging markets, essential to attract foreign investment and finance. It is also a precondition of financial assistance from the Fund. Recently Portugal, Greece, Ukraine and Pakistan have borrowed money to support and restore financial stability in their country and, over time, enhance growth within the country. Mexico, Poland, Colombia and Morocco also requested funds from the IMF. However, for these countries the *precautionary loan* will be used to prevent a crisis. The IMF experienced a sharp decline in its lending business following the financial crisis but has more recently seen a resurgence in requests for lending.

Lending via borrowing or loans is not done in isolation. The IMF expect details from the country that would like funds to show 'corrective policy actions' that will help underpin prosperity for that country. The Group of 20 (G20) empowered the IMF by making it the key lending institution for crisis-affected countries in need of balance of payments support. As a result, the IMF's lending portfolio increased during 2018 and the cumulative amount of money pledged was US\$1.0 trillion (IMF 2018).

## The World Trade Organization

The predecessor of the WTO was the General Agreement on Tariffs and Trade (GATT). Established in January 1948, it was a treaty not an organization, with the signatories being contracting parties. The WTO began and continued with eight trade liberalization 'rounds'. These entailed tens of thousands of tariff concessions on industrial goods and covered trade flows worth hundreds of billions of dollars. In all, 23 countries participated in the 1948 opening round when 45 000 tariff concessions were agreed covering US\$10 billion worth of trade. Under the first eight GATT rounds, the average tariff on manufactured products in the industrial world fell from around 45 per cent in 1947 to under 5 per cent. This has been an important engine of world economic growth which, in turn, has stimulated further increases in world trade. Signatories to these treaties account for well over 90 per cent of world trade.

More recently the WTO has increased its focus to adapt to current worldwide issues. The Fourth Global Review of Aid for Trade provided an agenda for future discussions 'post 2015'. The WTO now engages members to discuss value chains between countries, particularly how developed countries can engage with the LDCs (Least Developing Countries) in goods and services and share knowledge and help with infrastructure and skills. The WTO currently has 164 members.

The WTO generally encourages discussion and participation in multilateral trade and most-favoured-nation status, which obliges each signatory to the treaties to grant the same treatment to all other members on a non-discriminatory basis. It has evolved regulations which it has tried to enforce through its adjudicatory disputes panels and complaints procedures. Since its start in 1995, over 400 disputes have been through the dispute settlement mechanism of the WTO. China approached the WTO to join a consultation regarding the increased duties that the USA had imposed on China's steel and aluminium product imports that were bound for the USA. China stated the increased duties were inconsistent with trading agreements.

The main aim of the WTO is to promote a free market international trade system. It promotes trade by:

■ working to reduce tariffs

■ prohibiting import/export bans and quotas

■ eliminating discrimination against foreign products and services

■ eliminating other impediments to trade, commonly known as non-tariff barriers.

The WTO continues to liberalize trading rules and labour equalities in a number of areas, including agricultural subsidies, textiles and clothing, services, technical barriers to trade, trade-related investments and rules of origin.

Progress towards the WTO's objectives has been seriously stalled several times. One of the main problems is the USA's unease due to developing countries' refusal to open up markets to the extent demanded. Of equal concern to developing countries is the refusal by the USA to reduce the trade-distorting subsidies which developing countries view as leading to the unlawful dumping of produce from the USA onto global markets. Of equal concern is the EU's refusal to reduce the agricultural tariffs which block developing countries from EU markets. However, the WTO continues to be the voice of fairness and flexibility and one that encourages trade and discussions between countries to lower barriers. It also stands for cooperation between countries and, recently, has called upon the whole community to help countries recover from any natural disasters that may occur.

It is believed by some that during the 50 years of global economic expansion under the auspices of GATT, despite the long-term commitments to multilateral trade and all the work to develop a free multilateral trading system across the world, what we have in reality is a series of giant trading blocs. We will explore some of the more important ones in the next section.

## The development of world trading groups

The formation of the EMU in 1999 was, perhaps, the most significant trading bloc to be formed. When the Single European Market was formed in 1993, the United States effectively became the second largest market in the world. Given the rise of the economies of China and India, the question that interests many observers of the global competitive battles now being fought is who will dominate the global markets of the future? There is a fear that the world economy may divide into three enormous trading blocs dominated by the world's major trading regions, the EU, NAFTA and China/East Asia, rather than a world of multilateral free trade, particularly if the implementation of the DOHA Declaration does not fully succeed. Some commentators argue that national economies are becoming vulnerable to the needs of the trading blocs within which trade is free, currencies are convertible, access to banking is open and contracts are enforceable by law. While this scenario may be a long way from the present position, we are already seeing the growing strength of trading blocs such as the North American Free Trade Association (NAFTA), Association of South East Asian Nations (ASEAN) and the formation of the EMU.

In this section we will examine in detail the regional trading blocs that are emerging, but first let us examine different forms of trade agreements.

### Forms of market agreement

There are nine levels of market association ranging from limited trade cooperation to full-blown political union (see Table 2.5). At the lower level of association, agreements can be purely for economic cooperation in some form, perhaps a decision to consult on or coordinate trade policies. At the next level of cooperation, there will be the development of trade agreements between countries on either a bilateral or multilateral basis. Often these are for a particular sector – for example the multi-fibre agreement on textiles. Sometimes such agreements, especially trade preference ones, will act as a forerunner to closer ties. As far as formal trade groupings are concerned, there are five major forms: free trade areas, customs unions, common markets, economic unions and political unions.

### Free trade area

The free trade area type of agreement requires different countries to remove all tariffs among the agreement's members. Let us assume that there are three countries – A, B and C – that agree to a free trade area agreement and abolish all tariffs among themselves to permit free trade. Beyond the free trade area, A, B and C

Table 2.5   Main types of trade associations

| Type | Description | Degree of policy harmonization among members | Common external tariff | Free movement of capital and people | Example |
|---|---|---|---|---|---|
| Economic cooperation | Broad agreement for consultations on and possible coordination of economic trade policies | None/very low | No | No | Canada–EC framework agreement, APEC |
| Bilateral or multilateral trade treaty | Trade regulation and often, but not necessarily, liberalization in one or more specified sector(s) | Low | No | No | The Peru, Chile Accord |
| Sectoral free trade agreement | Removal of internal tariffs in a specified sector may include non-tariff barrier reduction | Medium (within specified sector(s)) | No | No | The multi-fibre agreement |
| Trade preference agreement | Preferred trade terms (often including tariff reduction) in all or most sectors, possibly leading to free trade area | Low/medium | No | No | South African Development Cone (SADC) |
| Free trade area (or agreement) | Removal of internal tariffs and some reduction of non-tariff barriers in all or most sectors | Medium | No | No | ASEAN, NAFTA |
| Customs union | Free trade area but with a common external tariff, harmonization of trade policy towards third countries | Medium/high | Yes | Possibly | **ECOWAS &EECSA, ECOWAS** COMESA, ANCOM, CACM Mercosur |
| Common market | Provisions for the free movement of capital and people, removal of all trade barriers, elaborate supranational institutions, significant harmonization of internal market structure and external policies | High | Yes | Yes | European single market |
| Economic union | Common market, but with integration of monetary policies, possibly common currency, significant weakening of national powers of member states | Very high | Yes | Yes | European Monetary Union, CEMAC |
| Political | Full or partial federalism, including sharing of powers between supranational institutions and national governments | Highest | Yes | Yes | Would resemble federal states (e.g. US, Canada, Germany) |

may impose tariffs as they choose. The EEA (European Economic Area) formed between the EU and EFTA (European Free Trade Area), and the LAFTA (Latin American Free Trade Area) illustrate the free trade area type of agreement, as does NAFTA, the agreement between the USA, Canada and Mexico, and the **Asian Free Trade Area (AFTA)**.

## Customs union

In addition to requiring abolition of internal tariffs among the members, a customs union further requires the members to establish common external tariffs. To continue with the example (countries A, B and C), under a customs union agreement, B would not be permitted to have a special relationship with country X – A, B and C would have a common tariff policy towards X. Prior to 1993, the EC was, in reality, a customs union. Both the Economic Community of Central African States (ECCAS) and the Economic Community of West African States (ECOWAS) have the objective of being a customs union. **Global System of Trade Preferences Among Developing Countries (GSTP)** is a system allowing for preferential trade between developing countries. The main purpose of the GSTP is to help developing countries cooperate economically and discuss ways to develop trade through open and fair negotiations to the benefit of all.

## Common market

In a common market type of agreement, not only do members abolish internal tariffs among themselves and levy common external tariffs, they also permit free flow of all factors of production among themselves. Under such an agreement, countries A, B and C would not only remove all tariffs and quotas among themselves and impose common tariffs against other countries such as country X, but would also allow capital and labour to move freely within their boundaries as if they were one country. This means that, for example, a resident of country A is free to accept a position in country C without a work permit.

The European Union is essentially a common market, with full freedom of movement of all factors of production. Similarly, the Andean nations in South America have formed ANCOM, the Central American nations have grouped themselves as CACM, the Caribbean community has formed CARICOM and Southern Africa has formed the Common Market for Eastern and Southern Africa (COMESA).

## Economic union

Under an economic union agreement, common market characteristics are combined with the harmonization of economic policy. Member countries are expected to pursue common fiscal and monetary policies. Ordinarily this means a synchronization of money supply, interest rates, regulation of capital market and taxes. The Economic and Monetary Community of Central African States (CEMAC) has the objective of being an economic union. In effect, an economic union calls for a supranational authority to design an economic policy for an entire group of nations. This is the objective of the EMU.

## Political union

This is the ultimate market agreement among nations. It includes the characteristics of economic union and requires, additionally, political harmony among the members. Essentially, it means nations merging to form a new political entity: Germany and the USA are perhaps the closest examples historically. Yugoslavia, which was created after the First World War, was a political union, as was the Soviet Union, although neither of these still exist.

Figure 2.4 shows the major trading regions to have developed significantly in the past decade, together with their member countries. In the following sections we will examine these major trading groups and the developments they have undergone.

Figure 2.4   Regional trading areas of the world

**APEC**

| | | | |
|---|---|---|---|
| Australia | United States | Taiwan, China | Peru |
| Brunei | Malaysia | China | Russia |
| Canada | New Zealand | Mexico | Vietnam |
| Indonesia | Philippines | Chile | |
| Japan | Singapore | Hong Kong, China | |
| Thailand | Rep. of Korea | Papua New Guinea | |

**NAFTA**
Canada
Mexico
United States

**OBSERVER STATUS**
Mexico
New Zealand

**EU**
Austria
Belguim
Britain (Brexit 2019, transition period)
Bulgaria

**MERCOSUR**
Argentina
Brazil
Paraguay
Uruguay
Venezuela (suspended 2016)
*associate members*
Peru
Bolivia
Chile
Equador
Columbia

| | | |
|---|---|---|
| Croatia | Lithuania | |
| Cyprus | Luxembourg | |
| Czech Republic | Malta | |
| Denmark | Netherlands | |
| Estonia | Poland | |
| Finland | Portugal | |
| France | Romania | |
| Germany | Slovakia | |
| Greece | Slovenia | |
| Hungary | Spain | |
| Ireland | Sweden | |
| Italy | | |
| Latvia | | |

**ASEAN FTA**
Brunei
Cambodia
Indonesia
Laos
Malasyia
Myanmar
Philippines
Singapore
Thailand
Vietnam

**ASEAN existing free trade agreements**
Australia
China
India
Japan
South Korea
New Zealand

# The European Union

Since 1987 and the signing of the Single European Act, Europe has undergone momentous changes, the key among these being:

- the creation of the European Union and its single market
- formation of the European Monetary Union
- the expansion of the European Union to include members of the European Economic Area (EEA) and central, eastern and southern Europe
- In 2018 there were 28 countries in the EU; Croatia was the latest to join, in 2013. Following Brexit, the number of countries in the EU is 27, as the UK left the European Union in 2019.

# The Single European Market

The formation of the European Union meant that it became the largest trading bloc in the world with an estimated population of over 445 million people (2019), making it a powerful competitive force in global markets. This, of course, was the key objective of the moves towards unification and the formation of the single market across the union. In the early 1980s it was recognized that if European companies were to compete successfully in the increasingly interdependent and global economy, a free and unbridled large internal market was necessary. This would enable companies to develop the critical mass needed to compete globally. The highly fragmented and restricted European market was seen as a major barrier to the ability to compete in global markets.

The European Union was formed as a result of the signing of the Single European Act in 1986 which created, within Europe, 'an area without internal priorities in which the free movement of goods, personal services and capital is ensured in accordance with the provision of the Treaty of Rome'.

The key changes were:

- *Removal of tariff barriers*: a single customs check at all intra-EU borders enabling goods and services to move freely across Europe.

- *Removal of technical barriers*: a major impediment to trade was the differing and complex standards required in each country. Harmonization of these standards has paved the way for product standardization throughout Europe.

- *Public procurement*: public procurement amounts to 17 per cent of the European Union's GNP; in the past only 2 per cent went to foreign suppliers. By opening up the market to all European suppliers and by ensuring its enforcement, it is estimated that €17.5 billion are saved per annum.

- *Free movement of labour and workers' rights*: nationals of member states now have the right to work in other member states.

- *Opening up of professions*: through mutual recognition of qualifications, professionals in certain categories have their qualifications recognized by other member states.

- *Financial services*: the opening up of banking, insurance and investment services through the introduction of a single banking licence and the harmonization of banking conditions.

- *Transport, haulage and coastal cabotage*: road haulage permits and quotas have been abolished. A more competitive air transport industry is also being pursued, as is unlimited cabotage for transport through the EU. Trucks are now allowed to pick up goods in any EU country and drop them off where required without the bureaucracy of permits and border documentation.

- *Company law*: several European developments in the area of company law are taking place in the fields of takeover bids, health and safety, cross-border merger, etc. The road to greater control from Brussels is now becoming especially apparent in this area.

- *Fiscal barriers*: there are many EU variations of fiscal policies, VAT rates vary across the EU from 7 per cent in the Canary Islands to 27 per cent in Hungary. Moves are being made to reduce these disparities.

- *The environment*: the European Environment Agency was established to try to provide an integrated and Europe-wide policy for environmental protection.

Most analysts agree that the formation of the European Union has greatly enhanced market opportunities for European companies. Intra-regional trading among European Union members accounts for 75 per cent of all trade. With such interdependency, it is little wonder that so much effort has been put into completing the unification. However, since the early 2000s, while most goods are now crossing Europe's national borders with little or no hindrance, the liberalization of trade in services has not made the same progress. Europe's service providers are hindered by all sorts of petty bureaucratic rules, often justified on health, safety or consumer protection grounds, which discourage them from entering new European markets. In some cases, the European Commission has itself hampered progress by granting certain industries exemptions from the normal rules of fair competition, although these exemptions are starting to be undone.

Before and following Brexit, the UK strengthened its trading links with Commonwealth countries such as Australia and India, as well as the US and China. European Union countries have been making strategies for Brexit for several years, with some such as Norway expecting to trade with the UK 'as normal' during a transition period.

## European Monetary Union

The idea of a single European currency had been around since the early 1960s. As trade between member countries increased, various attempts were made to stabilize exchange rates. Previous systems such as the **Exchange Rate Mechanism (ERM)** attempted to create monetary stability through a system of fixed and floating exchange rates. This proved, however, to be incapable of coping with capital flows, which resulted in problems for sterling and the lira in September 1992. The remaining currencies also faced problems the following year. Pressure for further integration in the Community resulted in the move to monetary union and a single European currency. This created the Economic and Monetary Union (EMU), sometimes called the Eurozone as countries within the zone all use the euro as a domestic currency. The UK never joined the Eurozone, and countries such as Sweden and some recent members to the European Union are also not members of the Eurozone. Firms from these countries, however, trading in the European Union, are affected by the euro and economic activity in the Eurozone. Companies not in the Eurozone have to convert their customer invoices and accounts, credit notes and prices into euros. Company computer systems for customer and/or supplier accounts have had to be adapted to deal with euros as many companies who operate across Europe follow a strategy of pricing all products in euros.

## Strategic implications

The EMU was not just a monetary event, but one that has had a serious impact on the real economy. Prices and wages became transparent, consumers now shop around for the best deals, middlemen try to exploit any prevailing regional price differences and margins everywhere are now coming under pressure.

The competitive environment is viewed by many as being tougher under the EMU. The development of the EMU in Europe affected companies both inside and outside the Eurozone, but companies operating inside the Eurozone have had to adjust more quickly than companies operating outside it.

Companies that have concentrated on their national markets have been particularly vulnerable to take-over or extinction at the hands of their more far-sighted European competitors. Those businesses already used to competing internationally have had a strong advantage. As sources of supply widen, specializations based on national talents have developed further. French and German companies, for example, run call centres from Dublin, where multilingual Irish operators (or continental expatriates) provide advice or take orders over the telephone more cheaply and flexibly than would be possible in the companies' home countries. Another effect of the single currency has been to open the European market for those small and medium-sized companies who have previously concentrated on their domestic customers. It has been estimated that currency fluctuations and the costs of dealing with them previously deterred a third of small and medium-sized German companies from venturing abroad. Many who did export concentrated exclusively on countries where currencies were informally linked to the old deutschmark, such as Austria and the Netherlands.

## Widening European membership

Enlargement of the European Union has happened at several stages of its development, and there have been four previous enlargements.

In 1993 the European Council adopted the Copenhagen Criteria for admission to the European Union. These require that member countries attain the following:

■ Stable institutions guaranteeing democracy and the rule of law

■ A functioning market economy, as well as the capacity to cope with the competitive pressure and market forces within the EU

■ The ability to fulfil membership obligations, including adherence to the aims of political, economic and monetary union.

The 12 new member states of central and eastern Europe have enjoyed a higher average percentage growth rate than their western European counterparts since joining the European Union. The reasons for this include government commitments to stable monetary policy, export-oriented trade policies, low flat-tax rates and the utilization of relatively cheap labour. It is reasonable to expect such a differential to continue in the medium term and as such the member states of central and eastern Europe may be where the exciting market opportunities are in Europe. Croatia is one of the newest countries to join the European Union. Illustration 2.4 discusses one such example.

**ILLUSTRATION 2.4**

# Škoda: from shameful to stardom

The Czech word Škoda means pity or shame, so on seeing a passing Škoda car, Czechs used to say 'there goes a shame' – and nobody would argue much. Today Škoda Autos (of the Czech Republic) has now completely overhauled its image and is one of the star businesses in the Czech Republic. Škoda's mantra is to be innovative but ensure new ideas, technology and production are for the benefit of the customer under the 'Simply Clever' aim.

Škoda is unique in the Czech Republic as it is the only car manufacturer that produces and develops cars. And the investment, and of course international sales, make Škoda the largest production company in central and eastern Europe, according to Deloitte CEE TOP 500.

But it is not just about building cars that makes Škoda so popular. The brand image has won the 'Rhodos – Award for Image – in non-food manufacturing'.

Prof. Dr H.C. Winfried Vahland, Chairman of the Board of Management, states that one of the key elements that make Škoda successful is Škoda's hardworking team, all 25 000 of them, from engineers to marketers, and patternmakers to designers. The proof in that statement shows in their impressive list of awards:

1st in the CZECH TOP 100

Best Industry Employer

Top Automobile Industry Employer

Best Career Website

Škoda is also keen to invest time and money in graduates from domestic universities, where they gained second place on the Czech Republic Graduate Barometer and the Best Presentation at Job Fairs.

Behind all the glitz and positive news, unfortunately, there are disruptions. Wages in some areas of Škoda are low and workers and their unions are calling for higher pay rises – or strike action. Further job layoffs and movement of some jobs to external organizations are also fuelling strike action.

## Question

**1** Evaluate the reasons for Škoda's success and imminent problems.

**References:** www.praguepost.com; www.deloitte.com; Škoda's Report and Accounts.

# The North American Free Trade Area

The North American Free Trade Area (NAFTA) consisting of the USA, Canada and Mexico, is regarded as the world's richest single market, with a combined population of 444 million people and a combined economy of over US$17 trillion. Together, the NAFTA members account for 34 per cent of world GDP.

The main provisions of the NAFTA agreement aimed to:

- Eliminate tariffs on manufactured goods
- Harmonize and streamline customs procedures and bureaucracy
- Liberalize telecommunications, transport, textiles, banking and finance
- Establish a NAFTA trade commission to settle trade disputes.

The attractive feature of NAFTA is that by virtue of the fact that Mexico is at a different stage of economic development from the USA and Canada, the gains through specialization have been relatively large, allowing the USA to specialize in more complex products that are intensive in their use of knowledge, technology and capital equipment.

The available evidence suggests that this is precisely what has happened. US exports to Mexico of electronic goods, transport equipment and services have increased substantially. Meanwhile, most of the anecdotal evidence about US workers harmed by NAFTA comes from light manufacturing industries and agriculture.

However, it must be said that the scale of change induced by NAFTA is probably quite small relative to other factors impinging on the US economy since the late 2000s, such as technological change and its foreign policy initiatives.

For many, the creation of NAFTA was a US response to the formation of the single market in Europe.

# The Asian Pacific Trading Region

## Asia Pacific Economic Cooperation

The Asia Pacific Economic Cooperation (APEC) is essentially a forum among 21 member economies which border the Pacific. Thus, it includes the NAFTA member states, Russia, China and Japan, as well as the founding father Australia, New Zealand, ASEAN nations and Peru and Chile in South America. APEC members account for approximately 40.5 per cent of the world's population, 54.2 per cent of world GDP and 43.7 per cent of world trade.

The APEC forum has worked to reduce tariffs and other trade barriers across the Asia Pacific region, with the aim of creating efficient domestic economies and increasing exports. Key to achieving APEC's vision are what are referred to as the 'Bogor Goals' of free and open trade and investment in the Asia Pacific region. It has three key objectives:

■ to develop and strengthen the multilateral trading system across APEC
■ to increase the interdependence and prosperity of member economies
■ to promote sustainable economic growth in the region.

Some members of the group would like an Asia Pacific trading bloc to emerge because they fear being excluded from traditional US markets.

## ILLUSTRATION 2.5

# North Korea: open or closed?

During 2018, two monumental events occurred. First, North and South Korean athletes joined together as a unified team, namely Korea, for the 2018 Winter Olympics. While North Korean athletes have competed in the Olympics before, this was the first time North and South Koreans competed as a unified team. Second, North Korea's leader Kim Jong-un stepped across the border to meet South Korea's President Moon Jae-in. Kim Jong-un is the first leader of North Korea to set foot on South Korean soil since 1953. They met at the Peace House. In the guestbook Kim wrote 'New history starts from now, at the historic starting point of an era of peace'.

Despite the fact that North Korea is a closed country it exports products around the world. Its biggest export market is its neighboring Asian countries which account for around 96 per cent of foreign trade. However, other regions such as Europe and Africa import goods from North Korea, indeed these exports amounted to US$1.8 billion in 2017. Just ten export products account for 88 per cent of exports. The "Number 1" export is clothing and accessories (not knitted or crocheted) at US$499.8 million (27.1% of total exports). Despite mineral fuels (including oil) being the "Number 2" exported product group, this category has retreated by -66 per cent due to the low international price of coal. Fruits and nuts have been the fastest growing export; which increased 54.9 per cent between 2016 and 2017.

### Question

**1** Considering Kim Jong-un's first step to peace in 2018, what internal and external factors may improve exports and what may reduce them?

**Source:** Workman, D. (2018) North Korea's Top 10 Exports, http://www.worldstopexports.com/north-koreas-top-10-exports/, published 13 June2018.

Combining Free Trade Area of the Americas (FTAA), East Asian and Australasian countries into one Asia Pacific bloc would mean that nearly 70 per cent of their trade would be intra-regional. However, there is marked resistance among Asian members of APEC to an enhanced role of the group. The USA is giving a high priority to the APEC grouping and intends to forge closer trade and investment ties across the Pacific.

The Asia Pacific region has the fastest growth in the world. Asia is the principal export region for US products. Transpacific trade is 50 per cent greater than its transatlantic trade, and more than 40 per cent of US trade is now in the Asian region. To foster this growth, the USA supports a more active APEC.

The members of the Association of South East Asian Nations (ASEAN) – Thailand, Indonesia, Singapore, Brunei, Malaysia, the Philippines, Vietnam, Myanmar, Cambodia and Laos – completed the formation of the ASEAN free trade zone (AFTA) in 2015 and plan to form an Asian Economic Region by 2020.

ASEAN is already well on the way to creating a largely tariff-free market of 580 million people, nearly one-tenth of the global population. The goal is to increase 'the region's competitive advantage as a production base geared for the world market'. The primary mechanism for achieving this is the Common Effective Preferential Tariff (CEPT) scheme, which established a schedule for phased tariff reductions to a rate between 0–5 per cent. The combined GDP of ASEAN members is US$2.4 trillion, and the group is now the third-largest growing economy.

However, some observers are sceptical about the potential development of AFTA. Geographical distances and cultural and political disparities have meant that previous attempts at closer economic integration have failed. These nations are keenly competitive, and some members have not kept to agreements to lower trading restrictions. ASEAN has also failed to support action against its rogue state of Myanmar, thus making many doubt the political will of the group. Where EU and NAFTA integration has been based on treaties, in Asia so far it has been based on market forces, the chief of these being the region's fast rate of growth. Asia accounts for about a third of the world's production. Increasingly, growth is also coming from intra-Asian trade, which recent estimates have put as high as 45 per cent.

## ILLUSTRATION 2.6

# China and India: the technology challenge

China is now the third-biggest buyer of hi-tech goods and services in the world, behind the USA and Japan. China and India make an interesting contrast in their technological development. They have roughly the same population, but China spends 2.5 times as much on technology as India. China is the world's largest mobile phone market with some 800 million mobile/cell phone users. It has the second-largest market for PCs. India has some 545 million mobile/cell phones, enough to serve about 45 per cent of the population. Only about 366 million people or 31 per cent of the population, however, have access to improved sanitation. China has around 384 million Internet users compared with 51 million in India. The two countries are adopting technology at different paces and in different ways.

A further difference is that China's manufacturing strength means hi-tech gear is available locally at low cost, whereas India must import it. India has focused more on software and services which can be delivered via networks without bureaucratic interference. China has focused on competing in physical goods. However, India is seen as playing an invaluable role in the global innovation chain. Motorola, Hewlett-Packard, Cisco Systems, Google and other tech giants now rely on their Indian teams to devise software platforms and the tech hubs in such places as Bangalore. These companies are spawning companies producing their own chip designs, software and pharmaceuticals at an exhilarating pace of innovation.

## Question

**1** Compare and contrast the opportunities and challenges of competing in the market for a hi-tech product in India and China.

**Source:** Economy Watch. www.economywatch.com.

## ASEAN-China Free Trade Area (ACFTA)

A significant development in the progress of ASEAN has been the formation of the ASEAN-China Free Trade Area in 2010. The new free trade area brought together the ASEAN countries and China to create a trading bloc with a combined population of 1.9 billion, a combined GDP of up to US$6 trillion and total trade volume of US$4.5 trillion.

**Barriers to developing a cohesive trading region**   While an Asian trading bloc may never have the cohesion of either Europe or America as the fastest-growing economic region in the world, any move towards integration will be watched closely by international competitors. There are particular barriers to developing a liberalized Asian trading bloc. First, there is a huge diversity among the nation states, not just culturally but in historical, religious and economic terms. Japan currently has a GDP per capita of US$39 400 and Myanmar just US$462. Politically, the countries embrace very different systems. Vietnam and Laos have communist dictatorships, Myanmar and Thailand have military juntas and Brunei is an absolute monarchy. In a number of countries, the institutions are either non-existent or too weak to ensure the economic fairness necessary to sustain the progress to regulation of markets and trust in the rule of law which is crucial to any commercial relationship. Furthermore, the geographical area is huge and there are no natural groupings of nation states. Management Challenge 2.3 focuses on the opportunities and challenges that Rwanda poses to companies trying to develop a presence in east Africa.

### MANAGEMENT CHALLENGE 2.3

## Small businesses help Rwanda recover

Rwanda has received considerable international attention due to its 1994 genocide in which an estimated 800 000 people were killed. Since then the country has recovered and is now considered as a model for developing countries. For example the growth in Rwanda is expected to accelerate to 7.2% in 2018 and to 7.5% in 2019.

However, political oppression, lack of free speech and poverty often seem to tarnish the country's positive growth data. Following elections in 2017, more women are now in government roles. But citizens of Rwanda are growing in confidence and are taking care of themselves and their communities. Green activists have persuaded the population that plastic bags damage the environment – so much so they are banned from shops and confiscated at airports. Community Action Groups are forming to ensure local citizens clean their streets and make their parks and green spaces beautiful. More importantly, the business dreams of citizens are becoming a reality.

Christine Mbabazi began her fashion business in her bedroom in Rwanda's capital city of Kigali. She wanted to promote the beautiful African fabric, demonstrating one of the cultural influences of 'what is Africa'. So, Christine began designing and sewing for her Christine Creative Collection. Now, through determination she has a boutique on the high street selling both formal and fun clothes. NafassiNews Africa caught up with Christine in her store to ask her what drives her passion for fashion. Christine stated she is selling to local people who want tailor-made clothes as that is the tradition. She employs local tailors to enable her customers to buy custom-made clothes. She also has expatriates coming to the store who do not want to wait for clothes to be made. Therefore, Christine provides a range of 'off the peg' clothes for those who want something fashionable with Rwandan prints. The fashion industry in Rwanda is slowly growing. Christine is glad there is competition as it means more people are employed and more people can spend money. And when her store is visited by someone from outside Rwanda, she is delighted, as sales of her clothes are contributing to the growth of Rwanda's economy.

### Question

1 How is Christine's business helping Rwanda grow economically?

**Source:** World Bank (2018) World Bank Rwanda Economic. Update Published 21st June 2018, https://www.worldbank.org/en/news/pressrelease/2018/06/21/world-bank-rwanda-economic-update CNN (2014) 'From Bedroom To Boutique Handmade Fashion With A Rwandan Heart', http://edition.cnn.com/2014/11/27/world/africa/christine-creative-collections-rwanda-fashion/ Accessed 25th March 2018.

# SUMMARY

- In this chapter we have discussed the major developments in international trade. The world economy consists of 195 nations with a population of 7.6 billion and an output (GDP) of approximately US$75.9 trillion. World trade in merchandise totals US$16 trillion and trade in services is currently estimated by the WTO to be about US$4.77 trillion.

- Since the late 1960s, multilateral trade has flourished, and a number of institutions have been developed to foster international trade. The World Bank, the IMF and the WTO all play important roles in ensuring a multilateral and fair world trading environment. It is important for the reader to have an understanding of how they may impact on the international marketing strategy of a company.

- The major trading regions around the globe are at different stages and their continuing development has been discussed. The creation of the European Union and the formation of the Economic and Monetary Union (EMU) have radically changed the competitive landscape across the globe. Other areas are now formally developing as trading regions with free trade areas are emerging in Asia, the Pacific and the Americas. Some commentators believe this is moving world trade to a more regionally focused trading pattern.

- In recent years there have been substantive changes in the global competitive structures as emerging markets strengthen their economic foundations and regional trading areas become more cohesive. The BRIC economies, Brazil, Russia, India and China, are viewed as the star performers in emerging economies.

- The centre of gravity and dynamism of the Asia Pacific economy in the past decade has been China. China is developing the potential to dwarf most countries as it continues its rapid development and speedy economic growth. Commentators are interested to see whether it is China or India that will dominate the global trading structures of the 21st century.

# KEYWORDS

Next Eleven (or N-11)

trade deficit

international product life cycle

comparative advantage

tariff barriers

non-tariff barriers

hard currency

International Monetary Fund

World Bank

International Development Association (IDA)

balance of payments

Doha Round

trading blocs

Single European Market

Association of South East Asian Nations (ASEAN)

Asian Free Trade Area

Global System of Trade Preferences Among Developing Countries (GSTP)

Mercosur

Exchange Rate Mechanism

Economic and Monetary Union

The North American Free Trade Area (NAFTA)

## CASE STUDY 1

# Export tourism increases host country's GDP

Exporting a country's historic culture, beautiful beaches or amazing city museums through advertising encourages tourists to visit and spend their money. Both the tourists and the money they spend while visiting, indirectly help increase the country's GDP. To encourage tourists, it is also important for governments to invest in the tourism infrastructure to ensure tourists can travel easily and safely while enjoying a variety of experiences, attractions and cultures.

Australia recently invested in the tourism infrastructure and this has assisted in increasing the number of tourists from New Zealand, the USA, China, Singapore, Malaysia, Hong Kong, India and Germany. Australia has 'Approved Destination Status' for the benefit of Chinese tourists. Approved Destination Status provides Chinese people with the advantage of choosing government certificated guided tours around the host country of Australia. The benefit of marketing and investing in Approved Destination Status for the Chinese market has paid off. In Australia over AUD$10 billion was spent by Chinese tourists in 2017 (SBS 2017). This was double the figure a few years previously. In the same year, over 1.3 million Chinese tourists visited Australia. Exporting Australia and increasing the number of tourists visiting Australia is of significant indirect benefit to its GDP because

tourists contribute to the tourism value chain. The tourism value chain includes five key areas where tourists spend money and indirectly contribute to a country's GDP (see Figure 2.5).

As Figure 2.5 shows, exporting a country as a tourism destination indirectly affects many different businesses. Boutique hotels or bed and breakfast owners will provide accommodation for tourists, small businesses such as taxi firms will transport tourists around the city and pubs or restaurants will feed hungry tourists. The tourist expenditure will, therefore, indirectly contribute to the host country's GDP.

The UK is forecast to have a tourism industry worth over £257 billion by 2025 – just under 10 per cent of UK GDP, which is estimated to potentially support 3.8 million jobs, which is around 11 per cent of the total UK workforce. In employment terms, when more tourists arrive in the host country, they spend money on accommodation, transport, entertainment, or indeed any area within the tourism value chain. They also help increase the number of people who are directly or indirectly employed in the tourism trade. For example, tourists that eat in hotels, restaurants, cafés or pubs contribute to the number of people employed in agriculture as the more tourists there are, the more food needs to be harvested by the UK farmer. The more tourists that visit the UK's football museums, the more tour guides are needed.

Exporting tourism is definitely not a marketing or business strategy for developed countries only. Developing countries are also experiencing benefits from tourism expenditure. Uganda historically had coffee as its highest exported product. However, tourism is now Uganda's single highest foreign exchange earner, contributing 23.5 per cent of total exports.

It is estimated that the tourism sector employs 6 per cent of Uganda's labour force. This includes employment by hotels, travel agents, airlines and other passenger transportation services. It is because of this that tourism is seen by the government as a major weapon in fighting poverty in Uganda. Tourism companies employ people directly as drivers, guides, secretaries, accountants, etc. It also provides opportunities to sell local products. These include art and crafts and

**Figure 2.5   Tourism value chain**

traditional attire. Tourist attractions in Uganda include national game parks, game reserves, traditional sites and natural tropical forests.

The Uganda Tourism Board has consulted with three public relations firms to increase its tourism appeal to large international markets. PHG advises on North America, Kamageo knows the market in the UK and KPRN consults on Germany. This has led to increased investment in Ugandan tourism and increased interest in it as a 'preferred destination'.

Visitors arriving in Uganda increased to 1.3 million in 2016 compared to 0.8 million in 2008.

## Questions

**1** What are the benefits of the tourism value chain?

**2** For a developing country of your choice, what areas of the tourism value chain could you promote to the international tourist?

**3** From your findings from question 2, what businesses would benefit and how?

**Sources:** Adapted from: www.austrade.gov.au; www.ons.gov.uk; www.visitbritain.org; www.ugandatravelguide.com/growth-of-ugandas-tourism.html (accessed 5 June 2018).

## CASE STUDY 2

# The mobile/cell phone services market in Africa

The average penetration of mobile/cell phones in Africa is almost 66 per cent. Gabon, the Seychelles and South Africa now boast almost 100 per cent penetration. Only five African countries – Burundi, Djibouti, Eritrea, Ethiopia and Somalia – still have a penetration of less than 10 per 100 inhabitants.

Popular mobile services include money transfers which allow people without bank accounts to send money by text message. Many farmers use mobiles to trade and check market prices. Besides sending money and paying for goods, they check balances, buy mobile airtime and settle utility bills.

In most of Africa, only a fraction of people have bank accounts – but there is huge demand for cheap and convenient ways to send money and buy prepaid services such as airtime. In Kenya, a pilot scheme called

M-Pesa is being used to disburse and pay microloans by phone. Meanwhile, Celpay is offering platforms for banks and phone companies in Zambia and Congo. Interestingly, it has inspired a shift in banking services across the world. Operators in other countries have been doing their best to catch up.

However, not all potential consumers are ready to make the leap. Many think banking is too expensive and complicated, and helping new customers become financially literate takes time. The technology remains a problem in some cases, with downloads requiring dozens of text messages. Several rival platforms are still in the fight, but so far those that emphasize simplicity and ease-of-use over state-of-the-art technology and security have made the greatest strides. A lot also hangs on putting the right laws and regulations in place. They need to be tight enough to protect vulnerable users and discourage money laundering, but open enough to allow innovative mobile banking to grow.

However, the main barrier to further expansion remains the cumbersome regulatory frameworks. Taxes can also act as a barrier, particularly import duties on handsets or special mobile communications surcharges. The mobile industry has been seen as a cash cow by governments in some countries who have used its popularity to generate tax revenues but have not invested in the infrastructure for its growth. To expand coverage into rural and remote areas, government support will be required.

Rural areas in some countries are also often economically unattractive for operators to invest in. This is usually not due to a lack of demand but rather to lack of basic infrastructure. The roads in Africa can be notorious, the infrastructure underdeveloped and the continent has more than its fair share of conflicts and crises.

The cost of making calls and sending texts in Africa is also relatively high and many of its countries are poor. A 'digital divide' also persists in terms of Internet access and broadband speed. Governments need to address this situation and bring the continent more meaningfully online if the industry is to expand.

## Questions

**1** Analyze and evaluate the economic and political influences that will impact on the growth of the mobile/cell phone services market in Africa.

**2** What do you see as the major risks to an international company wishing to compete in this industry sector in the African market?

**References:** www.reuters.com; www.bbc.co.uk; www.economist.com; www.guardian.co.uk.

## REFERENCES

1.  Currie M. (2018) How emerging markets are transforming global trade. Available from www.martincurrie.com (accessed 13 June 2018).
2.  *The Guardian* (2018) India's new alcohol labelling laws leave importers needing a drink. Available from: www.theguardian.com/world/2014/jul/11/india-labelling-laws-wine-wallahs-importers-running-dry (accessed 5 June 2018).
3.  IMF (2018) www.IMF.org.
4.  MarketLine (2018) Country Statistics.
5.  McDonald's (2018) www.mcdonalds.com
6.  SBS (2017) Spending by Chinese tourists reaches $10 billion in Australia. Available from www.sbs.com.au/news/spending-by-chinese-tourists-reaches-record-10-billion-in-australia (accessed 5 June 2018).
7.  Schwab, K. (2018) *The Global Competitiveness Report 2017–2018*, Geneva. World Economic Forum.
8.  Statista (2018) Global gross domestic product (GDP) at current prices from 2012 to 2022.
9.  United Nations (2017) World Population Prospects Data Booklet. Available from: https://esa.un.org/unpd/wpp/
    Publications/Files/WPP2017_DataBooklet.pdf (accessed 5 January 2018).
10. Vernon, R. and Wells, L. T. (1968) International Trade and International Investment in the Product Life Cycle. *Quarterly Journal of Economics*, May.
11. World Bank (2016) A triumph over long odds: Building rural roads in South Sudan. Available from www.worldbank.org/en/news/feature/2016/02/09/a-triumph-over-long-odds-building-rural-roads-in-south-sudan (accessed 13 June 2018).
12. World Bank (2018). www.doingbusiness.org (accessed 5 June 2018).
13. World Facts (2018) CIA. www.cia.gov/library/publications/the-world-factbook/rankorder/2003rank.html#ch (accessed 5 June 2018).
14. World Economic Forum (2018) *The Global Risks Report 2018*, 13th edition. Switzerland.
15. WTO (2018) *World Trade Statistical Review 2017*. Available from www.wto.com.

## USEFUL WEBSITES

www.economist.co.uk

http://news.ft.com/

www.imf.org

www.wto.org

www.oecd.org

www.cia.gov/library/publications/the-world

www.google.com/publicdata/directory

www.un.org

www.worldbank.org

## CHAPTER 3

# SOCIAL AND CULTURAL CONSIDERATIONS IN INTERNATIONAL MARKETING

## LEARNING OBJECTIVES

After reading this chapter you should be able to:

- Discuss and evaluate social and cultural factors impacting on an international marketing strategy
- Understand the cross-cultural complexities of buying behaviour in different international markets
- Assess the impact of social and cultural factors on the international marketing process
- Carry out a cross-cultural analysis of specified international markets

## INTRODUCTION

Markets in countries around the world are subject to many influences, as we saw in Chapter 1. While it is possible to identify those influences common to many country markets, the real difficulty lies in understanding their specific nature and importance.

The development of successful international marketing strategies is based on a sound understanding of the similarities and differences that exist in the countries and cultures around the world. The sheer complexity of the market considerations that impinge on the analysis, strategic development and implementation of international marketing planning is a major challenge.

In this chapter we will examine the social and cultural issues in international marketing and the implications they have for strategy development.

# Social and cultural factors

Social and cultural factors influence all aspects of consumer and buyer behaviour. The variation between these factors in different parts of the world can be a central consideration in developing and implementing international marketing strategies. Social and cultural forces are often linked together. While meaningful distinctions between social and cultural factors can be made, in many ways the two interact and the distinction between the various factors is not clear-cut. Differences in language can alter the intended meaning of a promotional campaign. Differences in the way a culture organizes itself socially may affect the way a product is positioned in the market and the benefits a consumer may seek from that product. A sewing machine in one culture may be seen as a useful hobby; in another it may be necessary to the survival of a family.

Babin and Harris (2018) stated there are many reference groups that impact consumers in the way they conform, think and behave. Reference groups include family, friends and colleagues as well as online groups such as brand communities and aspirational groups such as film stars or sports men and women. While these are useful distinctions from the broader forces of culture or social class, behavioural factors are clearly influenced by cultural factors. Take the example of the family, which is an important medium of transmitting cultural values. Children learn about their society and imbibe its culture through many means, but the family influence is strong, particularly during the early formative years of a child's life. Furthermore, the way in which family life is arranged varies considerably from one culture to another. In some cultures, the family is a large extended group encompassing several generations and including aunts and uncles. In other cultures, the family is limited more precisely to the immediate family of procreation. Even then the unit might not be permanent and the father and mother of the children might not remain together for the entirety of the child-rearing process. Thus, social and cultural influences intertwine and have a great impact on the personal and psychological processes in consumer and buyer behaviour. As such, they play an integral part in the understanding of the consumer in international markets.

Barbie is an international brand that appeals to children worldwide. Mattel which owns the Barbie brand has developed Barbie over the years by launching new dolls depicting Barbie in a new career. Barbie has had 150 careers from president to ballerina, chef to airline pilot. However, the Barbie doll is accused of being over-produced standardized white, blond and skinny with perfectly pointed toes that are ideal for high heels. The accusations cried out that Barbie was not representing the body shape and look of international women. Recently Mattel saw Barbie doll sales decline, four years in a row. Mattel got to work on 'body diversity' creating 10 skin tones, 4 body types and 16 hairstyles. Sales in the second quarter of 2017 showed that the number of Barbie dolls increased. Barbie dolls represent many nationalities and cultures. Mattel has tried to appeal to a wider audience as it attempts to reflect the changing roles and look of women.

It is not feasible to examine all the social or cultural influences on consumer and buyer behaviour in one chapter. Neither is it possible to describe all the differences between cultures across the world. In the first section we will highlight the more important sociocultural influences which are relevant to buyer behaviour in international markets. In the following section we will focus on developing an understanding of the components of culture, its impact on consumer behaviour and the implications for international marketing strategies. We will then discuss the methodologies which can be used to carry out cross-cultural analysis to enable comparisons to be made across cultures. Finally, we will examine business-to-business (B2B) marketing and the impact of culture in these types of markets.

# What is culture?

Perhaps the most comprehensive definition of culture is that of Matsumoto and Van de Vijver (2010) who said culture: 'is a unique meaning and information system, shared by a group and transmitted across generations that allow the group to meet the basic needs of survival by coordinating social behaviour to achieve a viable existence and to transmit successful social behaviours' (p. 5). Or perhaps, more appropriately: 'it's just the way we do things around here'. In relation to international marketing, culture can be summed up as: 'The sum total of learned beliefs, values and customs that serve to direct consumer behaviour in a particular country market'.

Thus, culture is made up of three essential components:

Beliefs: A large number of mental and verbal processes which reflect our knowledge and assessment of products and services.

Values: The indicators consumers use to serve as guides for what is appropriate behaviour. They tend to be relatively enduring and stable over time and widely accepted by members of a particular market.

Customs: Overt modes of behaviour that constitute culturally approved or acceptable ways of behaving in specific situations. Customs are evident at major events in one's life, e.g. birth, marriage, death, and at key events in the year, e.g. Christmas, Ramadan, Hanukkah, Chinese New Year, etc.

Such components as values, beliefs and customs are often ingrained in a society. Many of us only fully realize what is special about our own culture – its beliefs, values and customs – when we come into contact with other cultures.

When it comes to organizations, particularly for those who want to trade internationally or have chosen a strategy to grow internationally through mergers and acquisitions, cultural values, beliefs and customs are important. In fact, culture and strategy are intertwined. Groysberg *et al.* (2018) state that 'Strategy offers a formal logic for the company's goals and orients people around them. Culture expresses goals through values and beliefs and guides activity through shared assumptions and group norms'. Consumer culture and the culture embedded within an organization with roots in a different country can lead to misunderstandings and failure. Misunderstandings occur when firms expand internationally and build up a market presence in foreign markets. Often the problems and misunderstandings they face are a result of their mistaken assumption that foreign markets will be similar to their home market and that they can operate overseas as they do at home. Frequently in international markets the toughest competition a firm may face is not another supplier but the different customs or beliefs as a result of cultural differences. This means that for a company to succeed in that market they often have to change ingrained attitudes about the way they do business. The beliefs and values of a culture satisfy a need within that society for order, direction and guidance. Thus, culture sets the standards shared by significant portions of that society, which in turn sets the rules for operating in that market.

Hofstede Insights (2018) identifies a number of layers within a national culture.

## Layers of culture

- A national level according to one's country which determines our basic cultural assumptions
- A regional/ethnic/religious/linguistic affiliation level determining basic cultural beliefs
- A gender level according to whether a person was born as a girl or as a boy
- A generation level which separates grandparents, parents and children
- A social class level associated with educational opportunities, a person's occupation or profession.

All of these determine attitudes and values and everyday behavioural standards in individuals and organizations.

Given such complexities, market analysts have often used the 'country' as a surrogate for 'culture'. Moreover, culture is not something granted only to citizens of a country or something we are born with. It is what older generations set in place for us and what popular culture, through advertisements and television, helps us to learn and grow in our environment. Similar environments provide similar experiences and opportunities and hence tend to shape similar behaviours.

Terpstra *et al.* (2012) identify eight components of culture which form a convenient framework for examining a culture from a marketing perspective.

## The components of culture

**Education**   The level of formal primary and secondary education in a foreign market will have a direct impact upon the sophistication of the target customers. A simple example will be the degree of literacy. Providing product instructions is especially important when dealing with prescriptions and medication. Alburikan *et al.* (2017) found that the patients from the Kingdom of Saudi Arabia with a low education and low monthly income were unable to read and understand the labels and instructions on medicine bottles. This of course could ultimately cause great damage – at best, patient dissatisfaction and at worst, harm.

**Social organization**   This relates to the way in which a society organizes itself: how the culture considers kinship, social institutions, interest groups and status systems. The role of women and caste systems are easily identifiable examples – if the firm has a history of successfully marketing to 'the housewife/ homemaker', life is more difficult in a culture where women have no social status at all. House ownership is another example. In Switzerland and Germany, just 43 per cent and 52 per cent respectively own their own homes. However, in Romania and Lithuania, 96 per cent and 91 per cent respectively own their homes. This has a knock-on effect as to who may or may not rent or own domestic appliances, fitted kitchens or bathroom suites as the attitude to property ownership is very distinctive for people living in different European cultures.

**Technology and material culture**   This aspect relates not to materialism but to the local market's ability to handle and deal with modern technology. Some cultures are using natural sources, such as solar panels and wind turbines, to provide heating and lighting for their homes. This technology is not just for advanced western countries. Some families in Africa who have never had electricity before are using solar technology. Some cultures find servicing cars and trucks on a yearly basis astounding as they only pay attention to their cars when they are broken. In instances such as these the international organizations are often faced with the choice of either educating the population (expensive and time-consuming) or de-engineering the product or service (difficult if you have invested heavily in product development).

**Law and politics**   The legal and political environments in a foreign market are usually regarded as consequences of the cultural traditions of that market. Islamic law such as Sharia law is generally based on the traditions and guiding principles from the Muslim holy book, the Qur'an. The guidance known as the Hadith is provided by the prophet Muhammad and the Islamic scholars' judgments known as fatwas. Legal and political systems are often a simple codification of the norms of behaviour deemed acceptable by the local culture. Laws and regulation were dealt with in some detail in Chapter 1. Cultural sensitivity to political issues in international markets is of the utmost importance. Thus, an advertisement for the Orange mobile phone network in Ireland with the strapline 'The future's bright, the future's orange', clearly did not have any awareness of political and sectarian sensitivities surrounding the 'Orange Order' marches that take place in Northern Ireland.

**Aesthetics**   This covers the local culture's perception of things such as beauty, good taste and design, and dictates what is acceptable or appealing to the local eye. A firm needs to ensure that use of colour, music, architecture or brand names in their product and communications strategies is sympathetic and acceptable to the local culture. For the unwary, there are many, many traps in this area. Pepsodent tried to sell its toothpaste in the far reaches of East Asia by emphasizing that it 'whitens your teeth'. Unfortunately, they did not realize there was a practice among local natives in some areas of chewing betel nuts to blacken their teeth to make them attractive. Businesses selling body adornments are often culture-specific as we can see in Illustration 3.1.

**Values and attitudes**   The values consumers from different countries place on things such as time, achievement, work, wealth and risk-taking will seriously affect not only the products offered but also the packaging and communication activities. The methods used by a firm to motivate its personnel are also strongly influenced by the local culture and practice. Encouraging local sales forces to sell more by offering cars and more money, for example, may not work in all cultures.

**Religion**   Religion is a major cultural variable and has significant if not always apparent effects on marketing strategy. For example, the identification of sacred objects and philosophical systems, beliefs and

## ILLUSTRATION 3.1

# Nose piercing and culture

Body adornments, such as ear and nose piercings, together with face and body tattoos, have a long history. Nose piercings have often been considered as status symbols or suggestions of a person belonging to a certain group.

Through the ages there have predominately been two favoured places for nose piercings, the first being nostril piercings which are on the side of the nose above the natural crease of the nostril or higher along the bridge of the nose. The other favoured place is at the underside of the nose through the cartilage known as the septum.

Piercings for men have had a tradition of being through the septum. Australian aboriginals for example have had this as a cultural symbol for over 1000 years. The nose adornment is often a ring, but some examples showing bones, considered to represent the bones of enemies killed in battle, have also been worn by men in Tibet, Nepal and by North American Indian tribes. The adornments associated with tribal battles were worn to make men look fierce.

Piercings for women are often historically associated with Indian culture. Some Indian women had nostril piercings that contained a simple jewel. Others had highly jewelled chains reaching from their nostril piercing to their ear. The left nostril was favoured by many Indian women in consideration of teaching from Ayurvedic medicine. The left side is associated with female organs and thus can aid fertility and reduce menstrual pain. Hindu women often pierce their nostril at the age of 16 to signify they are of marriable age. A nose piercing is reference to the Hindu Goddess of Marriage. Interestingly, other female observers of Indian culture remove nose rings when they are married.

Nose piercings through the ages moved into popular culture with celebrities wearing jewels and rings in nostrils and the septum. Film and music artists create social media storms when they post Instagram pictures or are photographed by the paparazzi showing their first piercing or adding to their existing piercings. Bollywood star Ranveer Singh recently wore a nose ring with a chain attached to his left ear. It was claimed this was a way he could show his metrosexual personality through fashion.

## Questions

**1** What mistakes could marketing managers make if they use models with nose or other body piercings in advertisements?

**2** What cultural and traditional research should marketing managers do prior to choosing models for internal/external communications, be they online or offline in print media?

**3** Why is cultural and traditional research important?

norms as well as taboos, holidays and rituals is critical for an understanding of a foreign market. Religion, for example, will affect the food that people eat and when they eat it, as well as their attitudes to a whole range of products from deodorants to alcoholic drink. Therefore, products such as Laughing Cow, a cheese spread made in Kentucky as part of Bel Brands USA, cannot be exported to India under that brand name, as the cow is a sacred animal.

In some countries religion is the most dominant cultural force. For instance, in Islamic markets such as Saudi Arabia, no violation of religion by advertising and other promotional practices, no matter how insignificant, will go unnoticed or unpunished either by the government or the consumer. This can cause problems for advertisers. It is important, therefore, that brands carefully research cultural differences. For example, some brands may wish to use the same promotional materials across Europe to save advertising and production costs. But the brand manager must take into account that if the product is aimed at married women, a married woman wears her wedding ring on her left hand in many European countries but on the right hand in Norway, Austria, Poland, the Netherlands and some parts of Denmark. Therefore, advertisements showing a mother and her baby must ensure the wedding ring is worn on the correct hand, as in some European cultures it would show that the baby is born to an unmarried mother which, for them, is taboo.

Comparative ads are banned as, according to the laws of Islam, comparing one product against another diminishes the sense of unity and social community. Companies operating in these markets need to understand the difference between three key terms: *Haraam*, *Halal* and *Makruh*.

*Haraam* are subjects or things that are absolutely unlawful and strongly prohibited in Islam, such as alcohol and cheating. These taboo subjects are banned in advertising and other promotional activities in countries such as Saudi Arabia, Kuwait and Iran. *Halal* is the opposite to *Haraam* and is a term designating any object or an action which is permissible to use or engage in, according to Islamic law. The term is commonly used to designate food seen as permissible according to Islamic law. *Makruh* are subjects which are seen as distasteful; they are discouraged in Islam but are not banned.

**Language**   Language can be divided into two major elements: the spoken language of vocal sounds in patterns that have meaning, and silent **language**, which is the communication through body language, silences and social distance. This is less obvious but is a powerful communication tool. To many commentators, language interlinks all the components of culture and is the key to understanding and gaining empathy with a different culture. In the following section we will examine the different components of language.

---

## MANAGEMENT CHALLENGE 3.1

# Walking the talk: researching body language

Communication in business is essential to keep all stakeholders – be they employees, investors or consumers – abreast of company values and performance. Annual reports, websites and job descriptions are written in a manner generally accepted by all. However, when a manager is discussing the values of the business, its performance or indeed future plans of the organization, the audience interprets the manager's body language and tone of voice as much as what is actually being said. This is because audiences tend to interpret the speaker's body language within the first ten seconds and that impression may stick for a long time.

Interpretations of verbal communications by managers are based on three main aspects, of which 7 per cent is from what is being said, 38 per cent from the tone of voice and around 55 per cent from the body language of the speaker. Therefore, the manager needs to understand that the following ten parts of the body will influence how the audience interprets what is being communicated:

- **eye contact**: whether to make eye contact or not
- general **posture**
- tilting and movement of the **head**
- **arms** outstretched or folded
- **legs** open or crossed
- the **angle of the body** to lean forward or away
- **hand** gestures such as friendly palms up or dominating palms down
- **proxemics**: knowing personal space
- **ears**: notably using both and demonstrating active listening, and
- the **mouth**: the lips give away clues of displeasure and joy.

Different cultures interpret body language in all kinds of ways. A UK person makes eye contact and holds it for around 60 per cent of the time when talking to others. However, Nigerians may not make eye contact with people and this is a sign of respect. Similarly, they will only make direct eye contact with people with whom they have had a long relationship.

## Question

**1** Why should marketing managers research the interpretation of body language in different cultures?

**Source:** Kar, A.K. and Kar, A.K. (2017) How to walk your talk: Effective use of body language for business professionals. *IUP Journal of Soft Skills*, 11(1), 16.

## *Language and culture*

**Spoken language**   Spoken language is an important means of communication. In various forms, e.g. plays and poetry, the written word is regarded as part of the culture of a group of people. In the spoken form the actual words spoken and the ways in which the words are pronounced provide clues to the receiver about the type of person who is speaking.

Chinese is spoken as the mother tongue (or first language) by three times more people than the next largest language, English. However, Chinese is overtaken by English when official language population numbers are taken into account. The official language is not always spoken by the whole population of a country. For example, French is an official language in Canada, but in some areas Canadians have little or no fluency in French. English is often, but by no means always, the common language between business people of different nationalities.

Speaking or writing in another language can be a risky activity (see Illustration 3.2). In any communication message, particular attention needs to be paid when translating from one language to another.

ILLUSTRATION 3.2

# Language and meaning: lost in translation

The English language is often used in communication signs around the world. However, many signs produce funny or unusual translations.

Visitors to a zoo in Budapest were asked 'Not to feed the animals. If you have any suitable food, give it to the guard on duty'.

At a Kenyan zoo, visitors were asked 'Please do not put your hand in orphan's mouth or risk losing a finger'.

In cities, retailers often produce interesting advertisements.

A Bangkok dry cleaner to potential customers: 'Drop your trousers here for best results'.

Pee Cola available in Ghana does not necessarily sound appetizing.

A Hong Kong dentist claims to extract teeth 'By the latest Methodists'.

Airports often present some interesting communication messages to international travellers.

'Delayed due to some reasons'.

For mothers and babies 'Baby diaper exchange'.

And for emergencies 'If you are stolen, call the police at once'.

To encourage travellers to recycle their plastic water bottles there are waste bins provided: 'Liquid abandoned place'.

And for all other waste use the bin entitled: 'Poisonous and evil rubbish'.

And finally, to encourage kindness, international travellers are requested to:

'Please look after oldster and child'.

And give foreign currencies in the charity box 'for especially difficult children'.

## *Question*

**1** Consider any communications signs or advertisements that you have seen. What 'meaning' have you seen that has been lost in translation?

**References:** *Daily Mail*, Lonely Planet and *The Sunday Times*.

The creative use of copy to gain attention and to influence comprehension of the target audience can result in a clever use of words. However, inadequate translation often results in clumsy errors. In Germany, a General Motors' advertisement mentioned a 'body by Fischer', which became 'corpse by Fischer'. This is clearly a straightforward translation error, directly resulting from the mistranslating of the word 'body'. The Hertz company's strapline, 'Let Hertz put you in the driving seat', became 'Let Hertz make you a chauffeur'. Instead of communicating liberation and action as intended, this translation provided an entirely different meaning, implying a change of occupation and status. In India, an advertisement for the milky drink Horlicks was translated into Tamil as '20 men asleep under the tree'.

## Language of social media marketing

The choice of language to use for company websites, Facebook pages and mobile apps is also problematic for companies operating across many borders. Should it be multilingual, thus incurring greater costs in ensuring its sustainability, or should it be in one language? The top four languages used on the internet are English with around 25 per cent, Chinese 20 per cent, Spanish 8 per cent and Arabic 5 per cent. English is a widely spoken language throughout the world.

Many marketing managers ensure that, where necessary, their organization's website offers multilingual translations. There are many businesses around the world that offer to translate website content into several languages. The websites that have most multilingual translations are the Jehovah's Witnesses' website (780 languages including dialects) and Wikipedia with 287 languages. It is predicted that more Chinese, Russian and Indonesian internet sites will be created thus changing the dominant social media marketing language.

A preferred solution for many companies is to build the main website capability to offer a multilingual website, localized to the language and cultural sensitivities of the market. A global brand then needs to centralize the message, translate it and colloquialize it. Another reason for localization is to ensure a company is compliant with local regulations. In France, for instance, consumers enjoy a one-week grace period after they receive an online purchase. In Germany, comparative advertising is banned on the Internet. In China, clients' companies may find their websites are monitored by the Chinese government.

## Silent language

Silent language is a powerful means of communication and the importance of non-verbal communication is greater in some countries than others. In these cultures, people are more sensitive to a variety of different message systems. Silent language examines the many influences we face each day, influences that are silent in that they are not verbal but are quite loud in terms of the effects they have on our development, our relationships and so on. Many of these influences are cultural, attitudes and behaviours we inherit from our cultural heritage and learning. Understanding the cultural similarities and differences is essential when leading a new workforce in a different country or persuading new consumers to try a different brand (Goman 2011). As different cultures speak different verbal languages, so our cultures give rise to differences in the silent languages used to communicate. The silent language factors that are important in international marketing include attitudes to time, which influences the importance of being on time, and attitudes to space, which impacts on the conversational distance between people. What is universal, however, is that silent language provides subliminal messages. These give people a clear way to analyze whether or not the person they are working with or speaking to is credible and trustworthy, likeable or nervous. And when trusted friends are a social insurance, it is very important for international marketers to be able to interpret the very varied silent language.

Silent languages are particularly important in sales negotiations and other forms of business meetings. They will, in addition, influence internal communications in companies employing people from different countries and cultures.

Difficulties can arise even between cultures which are geographically close to each other but have different perceptions of language. The word concept in English translates into 'an abstract idea; a general notion', whereas *konzept* in German translates more into a 'plan or programme'. German and English executives could meet with hugely varying expectations if a conceptual discussion was on the agenda.

## ILLUSTRATION 3.3

# Who is speaking your language?

Many hospitality and tourism organizations have a language policy. And with the advancements in technology many websites can now be programmed to be multilingual. This is an excellent development for organizations whose target markets are spread across the globe. Taj Hotels recently added four languages to its website and booking systems. Established in India in 1903, Taj Hotels has grown and has 99 luxurious palaces, safari-based hotels and fully serviced resorts in 61 locations. The main locations are India, the UK, North America, Africa, Middle East, Malaysia, Sri Lanka, Maldives, Bhutan and Nepal. Clearly Taj Hotels will appeal to a worldwide audience.

The four languages added to its website (which was only available in English previously) are German, Spanish, Chinese and French. It also added language and location specific domains www.tajhotels.de, www.tajhotels.es, www.tajhotels.cn and www.tajhotels.fr. This enables existing and potential guests to complete online searches for the Taj Hotel specifically or organically and be directed to a Taj Hotel website in the appropriate language. Taj Hotels feels this implementation will enhance the consumer experience. Consumers can access detailed information on prices, room choices, the hotel's location and surrounding areas, search through the 10 000 glorious images and, of course, complete their booking in a language and currency they feel more comfortable with.

Translations.com is just one of the many privately owned language services that innovatively as well as pragmatically have translation-related technology. It provides these to international organizations like Taj Hotels to enable them to develop their consumer experience. Translation is big business as Translations.com demonstrates with its impressive annual revenue of over $500 million and through its offices in 90 cities across 6 continents. Its international client base amounts to 3000 organizations and Translations.com has built a database of over 170 languages.

Bangkok Airport has employed the skills of Translations.com to add Chinese to its website which was previously available in only Thai and English. Bangkok Airport feels this addition will attract more travellers from the Asian market. Translations.com not only has the expertise to provide web translations but it also uses OneLink software that recognizes text changes from Bangkok Airlines' main website and any associated 'click through' pages such as Destination Guides, Company Values or Job Opportunities, and automatically routes the new content into English and Chinese.

## Questions

**1** Why should organizations whose target markets spread around the globe have a language policy?

**2** Organizations may not be able to provide webpages in every language throughout the world. Which languages should they choose and why?

**References:** Taj Hotels www.tajhotels.com; www.translations.com; Bangkok Air www.bangkokair.com.

**Cultural learning**   The process of enculturation, i.e. learning about their own culture by members of a society, can be through three types of mechanism:

- *formally*, through the family and the social institutions to which people belong
- *technically*, through the educational processes, through schools or religious institutions, and
- *informally*, through peer groups, advertising and various other marketing-related vehicles.

This enculturation process influences consumer behaviour by providing the learning we use to shape the toolkit of labels, skills and styles from which people construct strategies of action, e.g. persistent ways of going through the buying process.

The process of acculturation is the process international companies need to go through to obtain an understanding of another culture's beliefs, values and attitudes in order to gain an empathy with that market. As we have seen, culture is pervasive and complex. It is not always easy for someone outside a given culture to gain an empathy with that market.

Having examined the main components of culture and the various important dimensions, we will now look at how culture impacts on consumer behaviour.

## Culture and consumer behaviour

There are several important ways in which the various components of culture influence a consumer's perception, attitude and understanding of a given product or communication and so affect the way a consumer behaves in the buying process. Jeannet and Hennessey (2006) identify three major processes through which culture influences consumer behaviour – cultural forces, including religion, history, family and language; cultural messages, including symbols, morals and knowledge; and consumer decision processes, including selecting, prioritizing wants and decision making.

Culture is seen as being embedded in elements of society such as religion, language, history and education (cultural forces). These elements send direct and indirect messages to consumers regarding the selection of goods and services (cultural messages). The culture we live in determines the answers to such questions as: do we drink coffee or juice at breakfast? Do we shop daily or on a weekly basis? In doing so, the consumer's decision processes are affected.

The body of theory on which our understanding of consumer behaviour is based comes predominantly from the USA. Therefore, Usunier and Lee (2012) argue that the means by which international marketing managers understand consumer behaviour is flawed. The theoretical principles on which we base our understanding do not necessarily hold true across different cultures. There are some important assumptions which international marketers need to question when applying western theoretical principles to consumer behaviour across international markets, such as:

1  Does Maslow's hierarchy of needs remain consistent across all cultures?
2  Is the buying process in all countries an individualistic activity?
3  Are social institutions and local conventions the same across all cultures?
4  Who, within the family, does the consumer buying process include? And is this consistent across cultures?

### Does Maslow's hierarchy of needs remain consistent across all cultures?

Culture influences the hierarchy of needs (Maslow 1970) on two levels. First, the axiom that one need must be satisfied before the next appears, is not true for every culture. Second, similar kinds of needs may be satisfied by different products and consumption types.

For example, in some less developed countries, a consumer may go without food in order to buy a refrigerator and, therefore, satisfy the dominant need of social status before physical satisfaction. A study identified that self-esteem needs were most important to Chinese consumers, and physiological needs the least important. Physiological needs include food, water and shelter; self-esteem needs include prestige and success.

In building a presence in the Chinese market, companies would need to target consumers with high self-esteem needs by linking a product such as credit cards to success in business, or beer to success in sporting activities.

Likewise, similar kinds of needs may be satisfied in very different ways. For example, to a Hindu the need for self-realization does not necessarily imply material consumption, as in western cultures, but in fact suggests abandoning all worldly possessions.

## Is the buying process in all countries an individualistic activity?

Many western buying behaviour models are primarily based on individual purchases with reference to family decision making in the context of husband and wife decisions. They assume buying decisions are focused on an individual's decision-making process. In Asian or Arabian cultures, a family may be a complex structure. An individual would need to take into account all members of the family in making major purchase decisions, so the decision making is generally of a more collectivist nature. See Illustration 3.4 for more details regarding shopping behaviour in collectivist cultures.

## Are social institutions and local conventions the same across all cultures?

Institutions such as the state, religious institutions, trade unions and the education system also influence consumer behaviour.

The UK company Rompa©, which serves the market for people with learning disabilities, found enormous cultural differences across their European market due to the varying influences the national institutions had on how charities and social institutions should be organized. In Germany, the market was highly organized and strongly supported financially by the state. In Spain, the state lottery was the prime benefactor of major national charities. In Italy, the church was the major benefactor, with very little involvement by the state.

## Who, within the family, does the consumer buying process include? And is this consistent across cultures?

There are many inconsistencies in the buying processes across cultures around the globe. Three aspects which are particularly pertinent to our discussion are the differences in the level of consumer involvement, the perception of risk in a purchase and the cognitive processes of consumers.

**Consumer involvement**   The Chinese are seen as having a low level of involvement when purchases are for private consumption, but a high level of involvement when they are buying products for their social or symbolic value. Since the Chinese greatly value social harmony and smoothness of relationships within the extended family, the social significance of products is highly important, be it to express status, gratitude, approval or even disapproval.

**Perceived risk**   The level of risk consumers associate with a purchase varies enormously across cultures. As such it is an important variable in consumer behaviour. It will determine whether a consumer will go for the comfortable purchase or is willing to try new products and services. Risk incorporates three components: physical, financial and social.

Whereas in some countries *physical risk* may be important (e.g. the fear of Ebola or AIDS), others may be more sensitive to *social risk* and the loss of social status if a wrong buying decision is made (i.e. the Chinese fear of losing face). *Financial risk* closely relates to the level of economic development in a country. It is likely to be less in the more affluent economies where if an incorrect purchase decision is made the financial hardship suffered may not be so profound.

The level of brand loyalty found in a market is also closely related to the perception of risk. There are huge variations in attitudes to brand loyalty across different cultures. In the USA, the standard buyer behaviour is that of disloyalty. A consumer will shift from one brand to another because it is standard behaviour to test several competitive products and so foster price competition. Thus, in the USA, it is relatively easy for a new entrant to persuade Americans to try their product, but much harder to get them to keep buying it. Similarly, in Poland, consumers are not loyal to supermarkets. They will collect leaflets and coupons providing details of special offers and shop at the store which provides the best value.

# ILLUSTRATION 3.4

# Cultural dimensions for international sport advertising

Getting marketing communications understood and enjoyed by the target audience is crucial. This is particularly important when a brand has an international audience. Discussions continue as to whether international brands should devise localized advertisements when marketing products and services to audiences in different countries. Seo *et al.* (2017) investigated this issue for sportswear advertising and decided to investigate if US students and South Korean international students had different preferences for the communication styles shown in advertisements for athletic footwear.

Hofstede's cultural dimensions are often used as part of an advertising manager's toolkit when briefing the creative team to produce advertising campaigns. It has been established by Hofstede that US citizens are highly individualistic and are likely to prefer low context communication styles (see Table 3.1) that include simple, direct textual content and clear visual images associated with the product being promoted. On the other hand, South Korean citizens from a collectivist society enjoy high, complex communications styles. Therefore, South Koreans enjoy advertisements that play highly on metaphoric visuals. They also prefer symbolic messages in the textual content of advertisement, which means the textual content does not have to be explicitly associated with the product being promoted.

Seo *et al.*'s investigations included a survey with US and South Korean international students. As expected, the findings showed that South Korean students reacted favourably to the high, complex communications styles in advertisements for athletic footwear and also reacted less favourably to the low, simple advertisements. It was expected that US students would not react favourably to high, complex communications and they would react favourably to the low, simple communications. However, the US students enjoyed both low, simple and high complex communications styles.

To investigate this unexpected phenomenon, one-to-one interviews were conducted and an investigation undertaken into external and internal factors that intertwine with US society. US society, while individualistic generally, is a society that is multicultural. This means the US population has become accustomed to decoding cultural meanings as they integrate with both individualistic and collectivist groups on a regular basis. Additionally, US students advised that they enjoyed the high, complex communications because they were familiar with the 'symbolic sports schema' they had grown up with. The 'symbolic sports schema' is a general perception guide used by sports fans to understand images, taglines and slogans used around the world. Therefore, it is suggested that US students have been highly exposed to high, complex communications and have become accustomed to them and found the symbolism actually motivated them to concentrate and interpret the brands being advertised.

## Questions

**1** Hofstede's cultural dimensions help marketing managers in many ways. In addition to considering advertising content, on what other occasions should marketing managers investigate cultural dimensions?

**2** What circumstances could change the cultural dimension of a country?

**References:** Seo, W.J., Sung, Y. and Park, S.H. (2017) 'Cultural preferences for visual and verbal communication styles in sport advertisements'. South African Journal for Research in Sport, Physical Education and Recreation, 39(2) 99–215.

In other cultures, consumers are more fundamentally loyal, less brand-conscious and not so used to cross-product comparisons. In Australia and South East Asia, buyers have a greater need for brand security, are less confident with regard to trying unknown products and so are less willing to take risks. See Management Challenge 3.2, which shows consumer strategies to limit perception risks.

MANAGEMENT CHALLENGE 3.2

## What's the risk?

When purchasing a family skiing holiday, choosing a birthday present for a 6-year-old child or deciding which university to attend, consumers are often worried about the potential financial, social and physical risks involved. When purchasing products or services, consumers have strategies to reduce the potential risks, such as staying loyal to a brand or reading expert reviews and searching through magazines. Another strategy that consumers use is to simply ask advice and recommendations from friends and family members. Consumers use Word of Mouth (WOM) recommendations on a regular basis because it helps to decrease the fear of risk. To further lower the perceived risks, consumers turn to Facebook, Twitter, Trip Advisor and other online community sites where 'friends' can provide WOM advice and recommendations.

Organizations such as the Belgian fashion brand Kipling, or Just Eat, the world's leading online takeaway ordering service, recognize the value of word of mouth, so much so, that they reward happy customers. Happy customers that endorse products and services are worth more than messages in print magazines. Viewing photographs and reading online reviews provides consumers with sufficient WOM information to reduce many perceived financial, social and physical risks.

### Question

**1** What online photographs and reviews have you used and how did this help reduce your perceived risks?

**Reference:** *Marketing Week*, 'How to get fans to cheer your brand on', 10/09/2014.

**Cognitive style**   Western consumer behaviour models assume a logical buying process with rational steps, including the formation of awareness, the search for information, reviewing the information, evaluating alternatives and finally making a choice. Sometimes by attacking traditional cognitive styles advertisers have had surprising success.

Many authors argue that internationally there are many different models of the buying process. Asian consumers tend to have a quite different cognitive style to western consumers. The Chinese as well as the Japanese have a more synthetic, concrete and contextual orientation in their thought patterns, as opposed to the Americans who tend to have a more analytical and abstract decision-making process. Thus, culture not only impacts on how we behave as consumers but on the whole decision-making process.

## Analyzing cultures and the implications for consumer behaviour

As we have seen in previous sections, there are many social and cultural influences which determine our values, beliefs and customs. These combine to form a cultural identity which, in turn, influences the process of decision making when buying products. All these aspects need to be examined to understand the consumer in any international market.

Blackwell *et al.* (2006) suggest the following steps should be undertaken when analyzing consumer behaviour in international markets. They propose that if a company is to fully empathize with a culture, they must pose a series of questions about buyer behaviour, culture and the suitability of various marketing communications approaches for that culture. These steps consist of:

■ *Determine relevant motivations in the culture.* What needs are fulfilled with this product in the minds of members of the culture? How are these needs presently fulfilled? Do members of this culture readily recognize these needs?

- *Determine characteristic behaviour patterns.* What patterns are characteristic of purchasing behaviour? What forms of division of labour exist within the family structure? How frequently are products of this type purchased? Do any of these characteristic behaviours conflict with behaviour expected for this product? How strongly ingrained are the behaviour patterns that conflict with those needed for distribution of this product?

- *Determine what broad cultural values are relevant to this product.* Are there strong values about work, morality, religion, family relations and so on that relate to this product? Does this product denote attributes that are in conflict with these cultural values? Can conflicts with values be avoided by changing the product? Are there positive values in this culture with which the product might be identified?

- *Determine characteristic forms of decision making.* Do members of the culture display a studied approach to decisions concerning innovations, or an impulsive approach? What is the form of the decision process? Upon which information sources do members of the culture rely? Do members of the culture tend to be rigid or flexible in the acceptance of new ideas? What criteria do they use in evaluating alternatives?

- *Evaluate promotion methods appropriate to the culture.* What role does advertising occupy in the culture? What themes, words or illustrations are taboo? What language problems exist in present markets that cannot be translated into this culture? What types of sales staff are accepted by members of the culture? Are such sales staff available?

- *Determine appropriate institutions for this product in the minds of consumers.* What types of retailers and intermediary institutions are available? What services do these institutions offer that are expected by the consumer? What alternatives are available for obtaining services needed for the product but not offered by existing institutions? How are various types of retailers regarded by consumers? Will changes in the distribution structure be readily accepted?

## Self-reference criterion

As we have discussed, it is of crucial importance when examining foreign markets that the culture of the country is seen in the context of that country. It is better to regard the culture as different from, rather than better or worse than, the home culture. In this way, differences and similarities can be explored and the reasons for differences can be sought and explained. The differences approach avoids the evaluative and often superior approach based on one's own self-reference criterion.

Self-reference criterion (SRC) characterizes our unconscious reference to our own cultural values when examining other cultures. Usunier and Lee (2012) suggest a four-step approach to eliminate SRC:

1 Define the problem or goal in terms of home country cultural traits, habits and norms.
2 Define the problems or goals in terms of the foreign culture, traits, habits and norms.
3 Isolate the SRC influence in the problem and examine it carefully to see how it complicates the problem.
4 Redefine the problem without the SRC influence and solve for the foreign market situation.

The process of enculturation to gain empathy with a foreign country market is not an easy one. It requires:

- *Cultural empathy*: the ability to place yourself in the position of the buyer from another culture. In this way a strong attempt is made to understand the thinking approaches, the decision-making process and the interactions between this and the cultural and other forces influencing the buyer.

- *Neutrality*: the ability to identify the differences that exist without making value judgements about 'better' or 'worse' cultures. Inevitably, self-reference will exist. If the focus is placed on differences rather than superiority, the chances of achieving accurate cross-cultural analysis are increased.

To ensure they achieve this, companies follow a number of policies. They may recruit foreign staff at their head office, collaborate with local firms when entering a new market or they may put managers through acculturation programmes. Guinness, the makers of Ireland's famous stout, understood the importance of avoiding SRC in developing their knowledge base of the new international markets in which they were operating. They ensured they had a management team in each market which was truly multinational, as well as including managers with a local knowledge of Ireland, its landmarks and the history of Guinness stout.

# Cross-cultural analysis

So far, our discussions have been concerned primarily with understanding what is meant by culture, examining its components and surveying its influence on consumer behaviour and how that differs across cultures.

However, strategists and students of international marketing need to move beyond this and endeavour to develop ways to compare and contrast consumers, market segments and buyers across cultures. In today's global environment where culture is becoming increasingly deterritorialized, and each culture is penetrated by the influences of other cultures, this is becoming increasingly complex as a research task. Cultural influences are much more diffuse and opaque than previously. This means that cultural analysis does not necessarily equate to country analysis. Any research design must account for such complexities.

International marketers must decide the relevant cultural segments/grouping for analysis. They then need appropriate frameworks or conceptual schemata to enable comparisons to be made and contrasts and similarities to be drawn across cross-cultural groupings.

For the most part, cross-cultural classification approaches tend to be either mere lists or incredibly theoretical complex structures. There is a recognized lack of a universal, broadly generalizable framework within which to visualize cross-cultural analysis. The contextual approach and the work of Hofstede *et al.* (2010) is used by many researchers as the basis for methodologies of cross-cultural analysis. A further framework has been developed through the GLOBE programme which focuses on cross-cultural leadership attributes. In the following sections we will examine how these concepts can be used by firms in attempting to analyze consumer behaviour across cultures. We will then highlight some further frameworks which readers may find useful.

## *The high/low context approach*

The main thesis of the contextual approach to analyzing culture is that one culture will be different from another if it understands and communicates in different ways. Languages are therefore seen as the most important component of culture.

The language differences between some cultures will be large. Therefore, there will be marked differences in their cultures. Language and value differences between the German and Japanese cultures, for instance, are considerable. There are also differences between the Spanish and Italian cultures, but they are much less; both have languages based on Latin, they use the same written form of communication and have similar although not identical values and norms.

In different cultures the use of communication techniques varies. In some languages communication is based on the words that are said or written (spoken language). In others, the more ambiguous elements such as surroundings or social status of the message-giver are important variables in the transmission of understanding (silent language). Hall and Hall (1987) used cultural dimensions to classify cultures into what they referred to as low context cultures and high context cultures.

- *Low context cultures* rely on spoken and written language for meaning. These are cultures where people tend to have many connections but of short duration or for some specific reason. In these societies, cultural behaviour and beliefs may need to be spelled out explicitly so that those coming into the cultural environment know how to behave. Senders of messages in low context cultures encode their messages expecting that the receivers will accurately decode the words used to gain a good understanding of the intended message. Germany, Switzerland, the UK and the USA are viewed as low context cultures. These cultures have a high explicit content in their communications.

- *High context cultures* are those cultures where people have close connections over a long period of time. Many aspects of cultural behaviour are not made explicit because most members know what to do and what to think from years of interaction with each other. High context cultures use and interpret more of the elements surrounding the message to develop their understanding of the message. In high context cultures the social importance, knowledge of the person and the social setting add extra information and will be perceived by the message receivers. Saudi Arabia, Japan, Asia and South America are seen as high context cultures. These cultures have subtle and complex ways of communicating with people according to their age, sex and the relative and actual social positions of the people conversing.

The greater the contextual difference between those trying to communicate, the greater the difficulty firms will have in achieving accurate communications. Table 3.1 outlines the communication differences between low and high context cultures.

## Hofstede's cultural dimensions

Hofstede (2010) was primarily interested in uncovering differences in work-related values across countries. He identified five dimensions of culture: individualism, power distance, uncertainty avoidance, masculinity and Confucianism. These dimensions, he argued, largely account for cross-cultural differences in people's belief systems and behaviour patterns around the globe.

Table 3.1  Communication styles in low and high context cultures

| Factor | High context culture | Low context culture |
| --- | --- | --- |
| Overtness of messages | Many covert and implicit messages, with use of metaphor and reading between the lines. | Many overt and explicit messages that are simple and clear. |
| Locus of control and attribution for failure | Inner locus of control and personal acceptance for failure. | Outer locus of control and blame of others for failure. |
| Use of non-verbal communication | Much non-verbal communication. | More focus on verbal communication than body language. |
| Expression of reaction | Reserved, inward reactions. | Visible, external, outward reaction. |
| Cohesion and separation of groups | Strong distinction between ingroup and outgroup. Strong sense of family. | Flexible and open grouping patterns, changing as needed. |
| People bonds | Strong people bonds with affiliation to family and community. | Fragile bonds between people with little sense of loyalty. |
| Level of commitment to relationships | High commitment to long-term relationships. Relationship more important than task. | Low commitment to relationship. Task more important than relationships. |
| Flexibility of time | Time is open and flexible. Process is more important than product. | Time is highly organized. Product is more important than process. |

Source: Straker, D. (2008) *Changing Minds: In Detail*. Syque Press.

**Individualism**    Individualism (IDV) describes the relationship between an individual and his or her fellow individuals in society. It manifests itself in the way people live together, for example in nuclear families, extended families or tribes, and has a great variety of value implications. At one end of the spectrum are societies with very loose ties between individuals. Such societies allow a large degree of freedom and everybody is expected to look after his or her own self-interest and possibly that of the immediate family. Societies of this type exemplify high individualism (high IDV) and display loose integration. At the other end are societies with very strong ties between individuals. Everybody is expected to look after the interests of their ingroup and to hold only those opinions and beliefs sanctioned by the ingroup which, in turn, protects the individual. These 'collective' (low IDV) societies show tight integration. Hofstede identified highly individualistic countries as the USA, the UK and the Netherlands. Collectivist countries were Colombia, Pakistan and Taiwan. The mid-range contains countries such as Japan, India, Austria and Spain.

## Power distance

Power distance (PDI) involves the way societies deal with human inequality. People possess unequal physical and intellectual capacities which some societies allow to grow into inequalities in power and wealth. However, some other societies de-emphasize such inequalities. All societies are unequal, but some are more unequal than others. The Philippines, India and France score relatively high in power distance. Austria, Israel, Denmark and Sweden show relatively low PDI scores, while the USA ranks slightly below midpoint.

Combining power distance and individualism reveals some interesting relationships (see Figure 3.1). Collectivist countries seem to show large power distance, but individualist countries do not necessarily display small power distance. For example, the Latin European countries combine large power distance with high individualism. Other wealthy western countries combine smaller power distance with high individualism. It is interesting to observe that in Hofstede's sample, almost all developing countries tend to rate high on both collectivism (low individualism) and power distance. Of the countries Hofstede studied, only Costa Rica combined small power distance with high collectivism (low individualism).

## Uncertainty avoidance

Uncertainty avoidance (UA) reflects how a society deals with uncertainty about the future, a fundamental fact of human existence. At one extreme, weak UA cultures socialize members to accept and handle uncertainty. People in such cultures tend to accept each day as it comes, take risks rather easily, do not work too hard and tolerate opinions and behaviour different from their own. Denmark, Sweden and Hong Kong all rated low in UA. The other extreme – strong UA societies – fosters the need to try to beat the future, resulting in greater nervousness, aggressiveness and emotional stress. Belgium, Japan and France ranked relatively high in UA while the USA scored somewhat below midpoint.

## Masculinity

Masculinity (MAS) deals with the degree to which societies subscribe to the typical stereotypes associated with males and females. Masculine values stress making money and the pursuit of visible achievements. Such societies admire individual brilliance and idolize the successful achiever, the superman. These traditional masculine social values permeate the thinking of the entire society, women as well as men. Hofstede's research indicated that within his sample, Japan, Austria, Venezuela and Italy ranked highest in MAS.

In more feminine societies, both men and women exhibit values associated with traditionally feminine roles such as endurance and an emphasis on people rather than money. Societal sympathy lies with the underdog, the anti-hero rather than the individually brilliant. Sweden, Norway, the Netherlands and Denmark rank as some of the most feminine societies studied by Hofstede. The USA scored fairly high on the MAS dimension, placing it near the top one-third.

An assertive salesperson would be better accepted in a highly masculine culture such as Austria than in Denmark's more feminine culture. The level of MAS also explains part of the perception that business people have of each other. In feminine countries where relationships are more highly valued, the supplier–client relationship is seen much more as a partnership than in more masculine cultures. Thus, the affective aspects of the business relationship are seen as of vital importance, particularly in negotiations, as we will see in the section on cross-cultural negotiating later in this chapter.

**FIGURE 3.1**   Power distance/individualism dimensions across culture

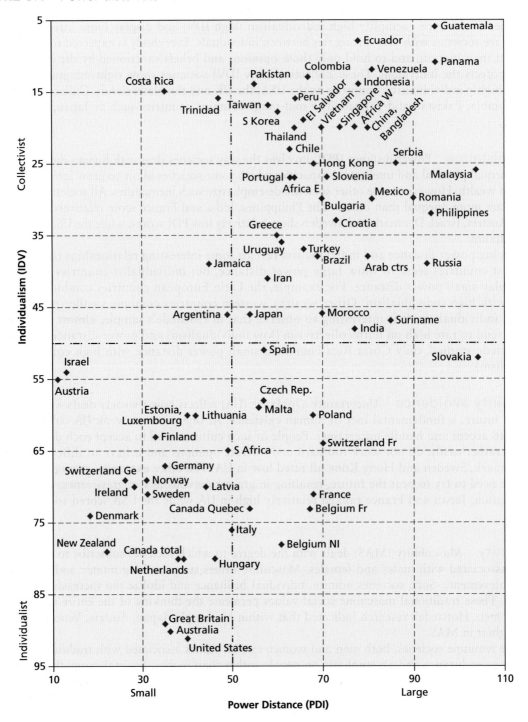

**Confucian dynamism**   The Confucian dynamism dimension assesses cultures on the degree they are universalistic or particularistic. Universalistic cultures believe that what is true and good can be determined and defined and can be applied everywhere. Particularistic cultures evolve where 'unique circumstances and relationships are more important considerations in determining what is right and good rather than abstract rules' (Hofstede 2010). Confucian philosophy traditionally pervades Chinese culture. Its major characteristics include a strong bias towards obedience, the importance of rank and hierarchies, and the need for smooth social relations. Within Confucian ethics, four basic relations were: between ruler and those ruled, father and son, husband and wife, and friend and friend. Everyone is expected to know where they stand in the hierarchy of human relations. One's place carries with it fixed standards of how one behaves towards others.

## Culture/communication typologies

A number of writers have developed frameworks that can be utilized for cross-cultural analysis which have built on the above work. In this section we will discuss the communication typologies and the relationship between the cultural dimensions identified by Hofstede and the adoption of new products.

**Communication typologies**   Four verbal communication typologies were suggested by Gudykunst (2005) which can be used as a basis for cross-cultural analysis. These are as follows:

1  *Direct vs indirect* refers to the degree of explicitness of the verbal message of a culture. The Chinese use the indirect style, often hiding their real feelings and being more concerned with group harmony and the feelings of others. The use of the indirect style refers to the high context culture and Hofstede's collective dimension.

2  *Elaborative vs succinct* reflects the quantity of talk that people feel comfortable with in a particular culture. The succinct style is where quantity of talk is relatively low. This reflects high uncertainty avoidance and a high context culture. Elaborative styles may be used more in low context cultures where the spoken language is of greater importance, as in the USA.

3  *Personal vs contextual* style focuses on the role of the speaker and the role of relationships. The role and hierarchical relationship of the parties in conversation will be reflected in the form of address and words that are used. This type of communication reflects high power distance, collectivism and high context cultures, such as Japan.

4  *Instrumental vs affective* defines the orientation of the speaker. In the affective verbal style the speaker is process oriented. There is concern that neither the speaker nor the receiver will be put in an uncomfortable position. The speaker also listens to and closely observes the receiver in order to interpret how the message is being taken. This is a reflection of a high context collective culture, such as South East Asia.

Such typologies may influence the receptiveness of consumers across cultures to humour in advertising. We explore this in Illustration 3.5.

**Hofstede's cultural dimensions vs rate of product adoption**   Moon and Song (2015) suggest that international retailers should realize that consumers may not like products and services from another culture. This is because they feel disconnected to the product as it does not seem relevant to them. However, consumers are more likely to accept products from other cultures that they value or find to be aspirational, suggesting that Hofstede's cultural dimensions play a part in product decision making. It is also important to understand that specific dimensions can move consumers to behave in a certain way. For example, individualistic cultures are more likely to be swayed by more impersonal channels, whereas collectivist cultures are more likely to be swayed by interpersonal communications. Heineken tapped into the need for social acceptance to avoid uncertainty in collectivist cultures in their innovative campaign in Asia. They built a perception of popularity by asking staff in bars selling Heineken to leave bottles on tables by

ILLUSTRATION 3.5

# What does the international language of emojis tell us?

Text messaging between brands and consumers and of course, consumers to consumers, has increased exponentially over the last few years as Smartphones have become a 'must have' for many. The style and message content of text messages can be personalized in numerous ways such as using fun letter colours, emojis and GIFs.

Emojis provide a ubiquitous language for users of Smartphones with the KiKa emoji keyboard. The emojis from KiKa enable consumers and marketing managers of brands to share emotion-laden messages via text messages, Facebook, Twitter and Instagram, to name just a few. Emotion-laden messages include text and emojis such as smiley faces, hand gestures, body parts, food, drinks and hearts. The question that Lu *et al.* (2016) asked was: Do users that message friends and family from different countries use the same emojis? Or is emoji use country specific?

To answer these questions, research took place collecting data from 3.88 million active text message users across 212 countries around the world. In total 427 million text messages that included text only and text with emojis were analyzed. Twice as many women text message users than men included emojis when communicating via Smartphones. What was discovered by country was that users from France, Russia, the USA, Mexico, Turkey, Brazil, Columbia, Spain, Indonesia and Argentina, were in the top ten when monitoring the number of users that included emojis within their text messages. In fact, 19.8 per cent of text messages from citizens in France included an emoji in their text message. For Russia, this was 10.9 per cent, the USA 9.2 per cent, Mexico 7.9 per cent, Turkey 5.8 per cent, Brazil 5.1 per cent, Colombia 3.7 per cent, Spain 3.4 per cent, Indonesia 3.2 per cent and Argentina 3.1 per cent.

What was equally fascinating was the type of emoji used. The emoji entitled 'face with tears of joy' 😂 from the smileys and people emoji category, was very popular. In fact, seven out of the top ten countries that use emojis regularly include 😂 in their text messages. Despite France being a texting nation full of emojis, the 😂 was not their favourite emoji. The French prefer hearts. In fact nine out of the top ten emojis used by the French were hearts: including 'red heart' 🖤 as the most used emoji as well as six pink hearts from 'growing heart' to 'arrow in heart' 💜🖤🖤💗💞💘 and 'smiley face with heart eyes' 😍 and 'face blowing a kiss' 😘.

The citizens of the top ten countries whose citizens included emojis included the 'red heart' 🖤 in their top ten emojis.

## Question

**1** Does this study suggest that emojis represent an international silent language? Based on this study what would you recommend international brands should investigate?

**Source:** Lu, X., Ai, W., Liu, X., Li, Q., Wang, N., Huang, G. and Mei, Q. (2016) September. Learning from the ubiquitous language: An empirical analysis of emoji usage of smartphone users. In *Proceedings of the 2016 ACM International Joint Conference on Pervasive and Ubiquitous Computing* (pp. 770–780). ACM.

not pouring full beers into glasses and not collecting the empties. Suddenly little green bottles were seen everywhere, and it didn't take long for customers to start asking for that particular brand.

## Globe programme

The GLOBE (Global Leadership and Organizational Behaviour Effectiveness) programme is an extensive research project which has built on previous studies of cultural divergences and patterns. It is working to integrate previous research to develop one single platform to carry out cross-cultural analysis on leadership attributes. Across 62 countries, the GLOBE programme investigates how cultural values are related to organizational practices, conceptions of leadership, the economic competitiveness of societies and the human condition of its members. The programme identifies the following nine cultural dimensions:

- uncertainty avoidance
- power distance
- collectivism – ingroup (family and organization)
- collectivism – society (societal and organizational institutions)
- gender egalitarianism
- assertiveness
- future orientation
- performance orientation
- humane orientation.

# Social and cultural influences in B2B marketing

Much of the discussion relating to the influences of social cultural factors on international marketing assumes a market for predominantly fast-moving consumer goods where decisions are made on either a family or individual basis. Yet a considerable proportion of exports relates to industrial goods and services where companies are primarily concerned with company-to-company (C2C) or B2B marketing and dealing. In other words, they are concerned with primarily organizational or even government buyers. The question we now need to address is how relevant the social/cultural factors we have been discussing are to these types of markets.

In B2B marketing there are essentially two types of buyers: organizations and governments. In this section we will highlight some of the social/cultural influences on these types of buyers which are particularly relevant to international marketing. Following this we will discuss the impact of culture on cross-cultural negotiating styles and the practice of gift-giving in international business relationships.

## *Organizational buyers*

Business buying decisions are influenced by decisions about technology, the objectives and tasks of the company, the organizational structure of the buying company and the motivations of people in the company. The technology decision is an interesting area. Some companies rely on their own internal capability to produce solutions to problems they need to solve in the areas of technology and how to manufacture the product. However, Japanese companies have encouraged their suppliers to help them by providing technological improvements. This approach is now influencing business practices across the world. The US adversarial approach of developing a precise buying specification and then challenging supplying firms to win the contract by providing the best deal is now less common.

Culture at the organizational level can play a significant part in the way in which the various roles are enacted. When it comes to international encounters, humour for instance can be a double-edged sword. The dangers of a joke backfiring are increased when the parties concerned do not share a common culture. Different cultures have different beliefs and assumptions which determine when humour is considered appropriate, what can be joked about and even who can be joked with. Attitudes to uncertainty, status and the sanctity of business influence the extent to which humour is allowed to intrude on proceedings.

There are a number of different corporate cultural characteristics in European countries which influence buyer behaviour. The French have a hierarchical system of management with a strong tendency to centralism. Consequently, it is often difficult for sales people to reach the top manager as that individual may well be buffered behind half a dozen assistants. Spanish and Italian decision making tends to be highly autocratic and based on the model of the family; decision making is shared with systems that tend to be informal. The German position is influenced by earned respect for formal qualifications and technical competence. Leadership depends upon respect rather than subservience.

## Government buyer behaviour

In many countries, the government is the biggest buyer, far larger than any individual consumer or business buyer. Governments buy a wide range of goods and services: roads, education, military, health and welfare. The way in which governments buy is influenced by the extent to which public accountability in the expenditure of public money is thought important.

It has been estimated that 20 per cent of the GDP of the European Union is controlled through the value of purchases and contracts awarded by the public sector. In the USA, approximately 30 per cent of the GNP is accounted for by the purchases of US governmental units. For some companies their international business comprises government buyers in different countries. It is important, therefore, to understand the government buying processes.

Usual forms of buying procedure are the open tender and selective tender. In open bid contracts, tenders are invited against a tight specification, and contracts are usually awarded to the lowest-price bid. Selective tender contracts are offered to companies who have already demonstrated their ability in the area appropriate to the tender. Only those companies on the selective tender list will be invited to tender. As with open tender, the lowest price is often used to adjudicate the bids.

In the European Union specific rules have been drawn up in an attempt to remove the barriers between potential suppliers of government contracts from different countries of the European Union. Suppliers from all European Union member states should have an equal opportunity to bid for public authority contracts, and public works contracts must be advertised throughout the European Union.

## The B2B buying process

In the B2B buying processes the various types of buying are classified into three different classes of buying: straight re-buy, modified re-buy and new task.

A straight re-buy represents the bulk of the business buying. The buy signal is often triggered through information systems when stock levels reach a predetermined replenishment point. The modified re-buy indicates a certain level of information search and re-evaluation of products/services and supplies before the purchase is made. The new task represents an area of considerable uncertainty in which the company needs to make decisions about what it wants, about performance standards and about supplier capabilities. The new task, particularly if the purchase is of major importance to the company, will involve senior management and might take a long time to complete.

The way in which a company manages each of the buy classes will be influenced by cultural factors. Companies with a strong ethnocentric orientation may limit their search to suppliers from their own country. For more internationally oriented companies, the country of origin effect will distort information collection and appraisal. The influence of established relationships in cultures in which personal contacts and relationships are important will act as a barrier to companies which operate in a more formal way.

Relationship marketing is very important in B2B marketing, where companies may gain competitive advantage not necessarily from the product but through the added value they have built because of their relationship. This is especially important in markets such as China. The Chinese rely heavily on personal relationships in business dealings. It is important for foreign companies to understand the dynamics of these relationships (known as *guanxi*). There is a saying in Chinese, 'If you do not have a relationship you do not exist'.

Personal selling and negotiation between the buyer and seller as they go through the interaction process to build a business relationship which is mutually beneficial is an important part of international marketing. It is in this process of negotiation and relationship building that cultural factors have their greatest impact.

## The role of culture in negotiation styles

Culture can be a major determinant in the success or failure of business negotiations. In Saudi Arabia business may look informal and slow paced, but in negotiations a businessman would be grossly insulted if they were expected to negotiate with a representative rather than the top person. Indian negotiators bargain much longer and tend to be much more competitive and persistent in trying to maximize their gains.

Some commentators suggest that a lack of understanding of the cultural differences in negotiation styles may be a major cause of negotiation failure. However, awareness of cultural differences may not be a major factor in negotiation success, unless that awareness is accompanied by a deeper understanding of how culture impacts on the whole negotiation process. A negotiation process (Graham and Sano 1989) can be broken down into four stages:

1 Non-task discussion
2 Task-related exchange of information
3 Persuasion
4 Concession and agreement.

The first stage, *non-task discussion*, describes the process of establishing rapport between members of the negotiation teams. Japanese negotiators will spend considerable time and money entertaining foreign negotiating teams in order to establish a rapport, whereas US executives see the delays as frustrating and the money spent as wasteful. GEC Alsthom sales executives found karaoke sessions very useful when negotiating with the North Koreans for a contract for high-speed trains between Seoul and Pusan. The firm understood from the outset that the first stage of negotiations needed to include a broad range of activities, such as singing, to help establish a rapport on which the relationship could be built.

The *task-related exchange of information stage* describes the exchange of information that defines the participants' needs and expectations. Well over 90 per cent of all large Japanese companies and most of the smaller ones use a decision-making process called *ringi*. The system is based on the principle that decisions are made only when a consensus is reached by the negotiating team. Proposals are circulated among the negotiating team for each to affix their own personal seal of approval. Without the group's approval, which takes a long time to acquire, no proposal will be accepted. What may appear to US negotiators as stalling tactics is often simply the different process by which the Japanese reach a decision.

The *persuasion stage* for US executives is the one that consumes time, whereas for Japanese negotiators who have previously taken the time to understand each other's expectations, it is seen as unnecessary. Japanese negotiators may, as a result, remain silent. This is not because they do not agree with the proposal. It is because they are either waiting for more information or, for them, agreement has been reached and therefore negotiations are complete.

This often leads to misunderstanding at the *concession and agreement stage*. An extension of the Japanese preference for establishing strong personal relationships is their dislike for the formal western-style contract. A loosely worded statement expressing mutual cooperation and trust developed between negotiating parties is much preferred. The advantage of these agreements is that they allow a great deal of flexibility in the solution of unforeseen problems. For western negotiators, however, they may feel the need to bargain to the end and do not see their job as complete until they have actually obtained a signature. Table 3.2 gives an interesting summary of differences in buyer–seller negotiating styles in selected countries.

Usunier and Lee (2012) suggest a number of ways to minimize cultural impact in negotiations in order to build effective transcultural relationships:

■ *Adaptation*. In international business meetings, people who do not appear to feel the need to adapt may be considered indolent. 'Those who adapt are aware of differences, whereas those to whom others adapt remain unaware' Usunier and Lee (2012).

■ *Interpreters*. Be aware that interpreters influence meaning. They may translate better from one language into another than in the opposite direction. The loyalty of interpreters needs to be considered. Are they more in favour of one party than the other? Should you use your own interpreter? Should you use several interpreters to reduce stress errors and bias?

■ *Cultural blocks*. Not everything will translate – it is not possible to translate meaning exactly for all elements in an interpretation. Culture-specific elements will block some attempts at translation.

■ *The stereotype*. Avoid negative stereotyping which is likely to increase negotiation conflicts and difficulties.

■ *Intercultural preparation*. Good prior preparation in intercultural understanding is a necessary investment to improve international business effectiveness.

## Table 3.2   Differences in buyer–seller relationships styles

| International market | Climate | Importance of relationships | Process | Decision making |
|---|---|---|---|---|
| United States | Sometimes viewed as an aggressive or confrontational climate. | Of less importance. Focus is on achieving desired results. | Ordered process where each point is discussed in sequence. | Can be either an individual or group decision process. |
| Canada | Positive, polite climate. Hard sell will not work here. | Of less importance. Focus is on achieving desired results. | Ordered process where each point is discussed in sequence. | Can be either an individual or group decision process. |
| Latin America | Positive and hospitable climate. | Personal, one-on-one relationships very important. | Relationship building through socialization will precede negotiations. | Decisions are usually made by a high-level individual. |
| United Kingdom | Traditional, polite climate. Hard sell will not work here. | Of less importance. Focus is on achieving desired results. | Ordered process where each point is discussed in sequence. | Can be either an individual or group decision process. |
| Germany/Austria | Rigid, sober climate. | Low. Germans remain aloof until negotiations conclude. | Systematic process with emphasis on contractual detail. | Even the most routine decisions are made by top-level officials. |
| France/Belgium | Formal, bureaucratic climate. Hard sell will not work here. | Formal, arm's-length relationships with attention to etiquette. | French teams use argument to generate discussion. | Usually a group process headed by a senior negotiator. |
| Japan | Formal polite climate with many idiosyncratic nuances. | Great importance. Long-term relationships are what matter most. | First, all general items are agreed on, then details are discussed. | A total group process with all levels involved in the final decision. |
| China | Bureaucratic climate with an abundance of 'red tape'. | Very important. Traditional, cultural courtesies are expected. | Discussions are long and repetitive. Agreements must be in writing. | Usually a group process headed by a senior negotiator. |
| Russia | Bureaucratic climate with an abundance of 'red tape'. | Low. Russians will remain reserved until negotiations conclude. | Cumbersome process due to bureaucratic constraints. | Usually a group process headed by a senior negotiator. |

Source: Lewin, J.E. and Johnston, W.L. (1997) Managing the international salesforce. *Journal of Business and Industrial Marketing* 12 (3/4), Emerald Insight

## *Ethical issues in cross-cultural marketing*

Cultural sensitivity is often at the heart of the ethical dilemmas that managers face when operating in international markets. There are few, if any, moral absolutes and few actions for which no one can provide reasonable justification. Almost every action can be justified on the basis that it is acceptable in one particular culture. In thinking about ethics managers need to be aware that simply defining what is ethical by the standards, values and actions from their own culture may be insufficient in satisfying all the stakeholders of a multinational enterprise. What is often seen as an acceptable business practice in one culture can be seen as ethically questionable in another. The SRC effect discussed earlier is particularly relevant to the discussion of how cultural sensitivities impact on what is an ethical business practice. Managers from different cultures will always be able to challenge, for instance, the US, African or Japanese perspective of what is ethical.

The ethical challenges facing international marketing managers are many. In recent years such issues as environmental abuse, the use of child labour, poor working conditions and the low levels of pay in developing country factories have received particular attention. Western consumers choosing brands look for reassurance that the product has been produced in what they see as a socially responsible manner. Some clothing brands such as Primark, Nike and Gap have suffered adverse publicity when it became known that child labour had been used to produce their products. Some brands have made valiant attempts to ensure ethical standards in their international operations. But often it is not the brand that is wholly to blame but their supply chain (see Illustration 3.6). This means international businesses must not only act responsibly themselves but ensure all parts of their supply chain do so too.

Consumers globally are becoming well informed through better education and faster and more effective communications. Increasingly, therefore, they are able to question the actions of multinational enterprises, as we saw in the discussion of the role of pressure groups in Chapter 1. For their part, while the largest multinationals are extending their influence within the global markets, they are becoming more vulnerable to criticism. Over the past few years, quality and service have improved considerably. But now firms are

ILLUSTRATION 3.6

# Blockchain: pure ethically sourced diamonds

Transactions between people and organizations have been recorded on tablets of stone, chalk boards, page ledgers and digital cloud-based accounting systems. When goods and services are exchanged internationally, ensuring the recording of transactions is done in a safe, secure and transparent manner is of paramount importance. This is especially so for an industry that has a poor record when it comes to unethical trading, diamond pillaging and the enslavement of workers to mine diamonds to fund wars.

The diamond industry, as a whole, has suffered. Legitimate traders have worked hard to provide solutions that enable them to distance themselves from corrupt regimes. One of the ways they are doing this is to use blockchain. Blockchain is being championed by De Beers so that anyone can track each of its gems from when and where it was mined to each point along the supply chain to the final consumer.

During the journey from the mine to the consumer, a diamond moves from one country to another. All countries have different legal systems, financial regulations, tax and exchange rates, manufacturing protocols, as well as the diamonds passing through the hands of numerous dealerships. The journey of a diamond, therefore, is long and complex. However, there are many diamonds that take a different journey through the hands of smugglers and counterfeiters that avoid paying the expected taxes and are mined and manufactured using unethical working practices.

Blockchain will track each diamond along its journey so that dealers and consumers know the diamond they have in front of them has been mined from reputable and ethical organizations and thus is pure. Blockchain provides a synchronized and secure list of transactions from beginning to end. This often means there are over 100 transactions recorded in the blockchain ledger. What appears at the end is a unique fingerprint of connected transactions showing the journey of each diamond.

## Questions

**1** What benefits could marketing managers gain by working with organizations that use blockchain?

**2** What countries and organizations outside the diamond industry could benefit from blockchain?

increasingly expected to ensure that their behaviour is ethical and in the interests of the global community which makes up their market.

However, international marketing executives operating across cultures will find themselves facing moral and ethical dilemmas on a daily basis on a wide range of issues when faced with the ethical dilemmas operating in countries where bribery and corruption are endemic.

## Bribery and corruption

An integral part of conducting business internationally is the practice of gift-giving. However, in many western countries such practice is seen as bribery/corruption and is tightly regulated and controlled. Business gift-giving – or bribery, depending on your point of view – if improperly executed, could stop sensitive negotiations and ruin new and potential business relationships. German and Swiss executives tend to feel uncomfortable accepting gifts, which they view as bribes, as they will not want to be seen as being under an obligation to the other party. However, business gift-giving in many cultures is an important part of persuasion. In cultures where a business gift is expected but not given, it is an insult to the host.

Cultures that view bribery as an acceptable business practice tend to fall into the high context category. In such a culture the communication style is more implicit, non-verbal and more reliant on hidden cues in the context of personal relationships. In Japan, for example, a highly developed and affluent society, gift-giving practices are widespread in the business culture. Refusing to participate in gift-giving in such cultures can cause bad feeling and misunderstandings between business clients. In high context cultures, financial inducements are often seen as an important step in bringing a person into the inner circle of a business relationship or to strengthen the relationship between a buyer and a seller.

---

### MANAGEMENT CHALLENGE 3.3

## Pirates roaming the high seas

Transportation of goods can be smooth or fraught with danger. Indonesia is well aware of the dangers found on the high seas. Indonesia exports vast amounts of liquified natural gas, along with shipping containers full of electrical appliances, electronic equipment and textiles. Danger on the high seas can be brought on by extreme weather fronts. However, the danger that the Indonesian government has had to deal with recently is piracy. Indonesian goods travel on huge merchant ships that go through a narrow enclosure along the Strait of Malacca. This waterway is a busy trading route, not just because of Indonesian merchants but because it is also used by merchants from China, Japan and South Korea. These waterways are full of modern-day pirates. Also around Indonesia's Sumatra area, pirates lie in wait for high volume, high value cargo ships.

Robbery on the high seas is not a one-off occurrence. Indonesian trading ships had 108 actual and attempted piracy attacks in 2015, 49 in 2016 and 43 in 2017. Numerous reports about the dangers from The International Chamber of Commerce (ICC) and International Maritime Bureau (IMB) state that waters around Southeast Asia are the world's sea 'piracy capital'. Arie Soedewo, Chief of The Indonesian Maritime Security Agency, has taken this seriously and all ASEAN nations (Association of Southeast Asian Nations) have joined forces and created the Strait of Malacca Sea Patrol.

### Question

1 What should the marketing manager consider when choosing suppliers that use merchant ships for transportation?

**Sources:** Jensen, F. (2018) 'Indonesia pushes for Southeast Asian patrols of disputed waters', https://uk.reuters.com/article/uk-australia-indonesia-politics/indonesia-pushes-for-southeast-asian-patrols-of-disputed-waters-idUKKCN1G-S0CR. Accessed 29th March 2018.

---

By contrast, people in low context cultures rely on explicit contracts, communication is more formal and explicit, and negotiations are based on a more legalistic orientation. Laws applying to bribery tend to be very well laid out. In some cultures, all business gifts will be viewed as illegal bribes; conversely, other cultures view gifts, pay-offs and even bribes merely as a cost of business. Bribery and corruption are part of the commercial traditions of many parts of Asia, Africa and the Middle East. Transparency International, a global counter-corruption watchdog, ranks Somalia as the most corrupt country, followed closely by Afghanistan and Myanmar. To many international marketing managers operating in those markets, how to respond to the demand for a bribe could be a problematic ethical dilemma. It can sometimes be very difficult to empathize with the cultural values of another country if they challenge your own personal morals.

## Piracy

Piracy has been a particular problem to the global music and software industry.

Different cultures have varying perspectives on piracy. The US courts take a very stringent view and prosecute offenders that are caught. In China and India views on intellectual property rights are much more difficult to define. The International Intellectual Property Alliance claims that despite now being members of the WTO, piracy is still a big problem in China.

In China, Havoscope estimates at least US$26 billion of goods sold each year inside the country are counterfeit. However, according to Fox News, the Chinese authorities are now cracking down on product piracy. In just three months in 2011 they arrested 3001 people, confiscated huge amounts of pirated products and closed some 300 websites selling counterfeit and fake goods.

Worldwide sales of counterfeit goods are estimated by Havoscope to be in the region of US$532.93 billion. Over 5.5 billion cigarettes, or 20 per cent of all cigarettes sold in South Africa, are either smuggled or counterfeit cigarettes. Procter and Gamble estimates that 10–15 per cent of its revenues are lost each year to counterfeit products. The Ukraine now exports counterfeit optical discs, Russia markets counterfeit software and Paraguay markets imitation cigarettes. Counterfeit pharmaceuticals are routinely marketed to countries unable to afford the expensive products of the authentic drug companies; often these are substandard, or have fake labels. It is estimated by the World Health Organization that between 5 and 7 per cent of drugs sold are counterfeits, with potentially fatal consequences.

US industries lose US$200–250 billion a year to counterfeiting. The fact that many global manufacturers have moved their production to low-cost bases around the world is seen by some to have opened the floodgates to counterfeiting. The global brands have been able to take advantage of low labour costs but have given insufficient attention to securing intellectual property rights in such countries. In today's markets, where so much of the added value of a product is in its brand identity, counterfeiters have been able to exploit consumers' expectations of quality and service with counterfeit products. Brands such as Louis Vuitton, Nike, Microsoft, Gucci and Prada are among the most counterfeited of global brands.

Much of the problem stems from cultural attitudes to the rights of anyone to own intellectual property. The Chinese have argued that if all ideas were copyrighted they should be able to patent the compass, ice-cream, noodles and many other products they have given to the world. Recently, Starbucks won a high profile case against a Chinese company using the Chinese version of its name, the court ruling that the company had the sole right to its name in both English and Chinese. The French cognac company Hennessey also won a piracy case in China against two companies copying its brand and selling it as French cognac brandy, even though it was produced and bottled in China. In Europe, the European Commission has proposed new rules to harmonize member states' legislation on IPR enforcement. This has been particularly important since the European Union embraced new members from eastern Europe, where counterfeiting is a serious problem in some countries.

Although nations and organizations often provide ethical guidelines on bribery, counterfeiting, etc., ultimately international managers have to make decisions based on their own personal views of what is and is not ethical. Managers need to form a view when operating across different cultures as to what constitutes ethical decision making within an organization. Managers need to reflect on what constitutes ethical behaviour, how decisions will be viewed by stakeholders and the perceived and real impact upon the organization of making a decision that breaches ethical standards. Central is the importance the company places on the need for an ethically responsible approach to their operations in the global markets.

Companies are increasingly of the view that organizational behaviour considered to be unethical can decrease a firm's wealth. Behaviour considered by stakeholders to be ethical, on the other hand, can enhance a company's competitive advantage on global markets. Attempting to take an ethically responsible decision, though, could mean the loss of perhaps an efficient and cheap source of supply or in some cases the loss of a potential deal. Any decision would need very careful consideration.

The consequence of an ethically responsible approach would involve increased resources and attention being applied to a number of areas, such as:

- The increased need for accurate and timely information
- Increased attention to press, public reaction and global pressure groups
- Closer relationships with stakeholders and members of the supply chain to ensure all interests are taken into consideration
- Being prepared, when serious risks are identified, to take positive and constructive action.

## SUMMARY

- The influence of social and cultural factors in international marketing is complex and often extremely difficult for a firm operating in foreign markets to analyze and understand. In today's global environment, where culture is becoming increasingly deterritorialized and each culture is penetrated by the influences of other cultures, the issue of examining and understanding cultural sensitivities is becoming increasingly complex.
- If the firm is operating across a number of markets, finding consistent methods of analyzing their cross-cultural markets poses particular challenges. The cultural dimensions of Hofstede, the contextual classification of cultures and the GLOBE programme dimensions are three frameworks that can be used.
- This chapter has focused on developing an understanding of the components of culture and how these components impact on consumer beliefs, values, attitudes and purchasing behaviour.
- Culture also affects the way that business is carried out in different markets. Culture underpins the legal structure of a country and ethical attitudes to decision making and the acceptability of bribes, etc. Managers need to form a view when operating across different cultures as to what constitutes ethical decision making within an organization and what constitutes ethical behaviour.
- Culture has a significant impact, therefore, on the international marketing strategies of firms, both in consumer and B2B markets. In this chapter the reader should have acquired an awareness of the possible methods that can be used to categorize differences across cultures to enable a cross-cultural analysis to be carried out. In Chapter 4 we go on to look at the methods of analyzing and researching international markets.

## KEYWORDS

| | | |
|---|---|---|
| social and cultural factors | non-verbal communication | cross-cultural |
| beliefs | enculturation | low context cultures |
| values | attitude | high context cultures |
| customs | consumer behaviour | individualism |
| cultural sensitivity | perception of risk | ethical challenges |
| silent language | cultural identity | piracy |
| spoken language | self-reference criterion | |

## CASE STUDY 1

# Building an international ethical brand: coffee

Large multinational companies overwhelmingly dominate the global coffee industry. Such companies have come under increasing scrutiny over the last few years when they have been perceived to operate under poor ethical standards. An outcome of this has been that customers have been urged by consumerist lobbies to switch to independent coffee shops and away from major brands such as Costa, Caffè Nero and Starbucks who scored poorly in an assessment of their social and environmental impacts.

Caffè Nero was found to have little evidence of environmental or ethical sourcing, while Costa's policies were described as 'weak' in the ratings scorecard produced by the *Ethical Consumer* magazine. As well as being penalized for its well-publicized tax avoidance, Starbucks has been criticized for trade union violations, removing paid lunch breaks, political lobbying and a lack of commitment to sourcing sustainable palm oil. And yet at the same time Starbucks has been named one of the world's most ethical companies according to the Ethisphere Institute.

The guidance for many consumers by ethical consumer watchdogs has been to drink coffee sourced by Fairtrade suppliers. Yet recently they too have been criticized. Research found that the Fairtrade Foundation was unable to ensure that all its workers are paid a living wage. Many producers of Fairtrade coffee work out of small farms and are poor themselves. They then employ a few workers who are paid even more poorly. If they have less than 20 workers the farmers do not legally have to pay the minimum wage set by the government. As thousands of these farms exist in multiple countries it is difficult for the Fairtrade Foundation to regulate and police, especially as the farmers are not breaking the law by underpaying their workers. Unfortunately, despite the ethical stance the Fairtrade Foundation has aspired to, this practice has led to the tarnishing of the brand among consumers.

Companies with a focus on ethical marketing do evaluate their decisions from a business perspective. They also evaluate their marketing decisions from a moral perspective which, in a long international supply chain, is exceedingly difficult.

The problem for an international company taking such a stand is that from a consumer's perspective, ethical marketing is not a strategy; it is an overarching philosophy. This means if a company is building an international brand on an ethical stance, every part of its operation has to stand up to scrutiny. It needs to ensure its marketing platform in all countries in which it operates is honest and trustworthy so it is able to build strong relationships with consumers through a set of shared values across the globe.

## Questions

**1** Discuss the challenges to building a brand internationally on an ethical stance.

**2** Compare and contrast the marketing strategies of Fairtrade with that of a global coffee brand.

**3** How would you advise Fairtrade to build an international brand on an ethical stance?

**References:** www.theguardian.com; www.Ethicalunicorn.com; www.ethicalconsumer.org/buyersguides/drink/coffee-shops (accessed 5 March 2018).

## CASE STUDY 2

# Cultural challenges of the Brazilian market

With a population of nearly 210 million, Brazil is the world's fifth largest country. It is also the fifth largest in terms of land area. However, 90 per cent of the overall population lives on just 10 per cent of the available land, specifically along the country's 200 miles of coastline. The two largest cities are Sao Paulo and Rio de Janeiro, where roughly 15 million of Brazil's population reside. The largest ethnic group is of European descent at 55 per cent of the population, most of whom are Portuguese.

Portuguese is unsurprisingly the prevailing language, although a variety of others are spoken such as Spanish and Italian as well as some Amerindian languages. The rest of the population is made up of a mixture of various ethnicities. Thirty-eight per cent are German and Japanese, while only a small percentage is African or Amerindian. The prevailing religion is Roman Catholic despite the lack of an official religion. Among this mixture of cultures almost half of the Brazilian population is under 20 years old.

The Hofstede analysis reveals much of the population is risk adverse and not quick to accept change. There is much concern with rules and regulations as well as work security indicated by 'uncertainty avoidance' ranking the highest. Unsurprisingly, it also has a high 'long-term oriented' ranking making the population more traditionalist and willing to work towards long-term goals despite the high 'power distance' pointing towards inequality in society.

Brazil's culture is based on a national sense of collectivism following the same pattern as other South American countries. The group becomes more important than the individual in this type of culture. The bonds to family, extended family and other human relationships are of more concern to people. In such cultures, loyalty can be placed above the normal rules of society. Belonging to the team is paramount despite this requiring more tolerance and little complaint from those involved. Independence in the workplace, for example, working by yourself or not taking part in company gatherings or lunches, is frowned upon, attaching a stigma to the individual.

Many companies have seen Brazil as a new market opportunity only to be unsuccessful in their attempts to conquer it. Such companies assume the market in Brazil will be similar to those in other countries where they have succeeded. But they fail to negate the challenges of a completely different culture. 'They tend to underestimate the cultural challenges and fail to understand the "local way" of doing business and so lose opportunities for building relationships with potential partners, local suppliers and customers' (Cyborlink.com).

Xiaomi, the Chinese electronics company, and Lenovo have found Brazil a challenging market. Xiaomi has ceased its local manufacturing activity and moved many of its staff from areas including marketing back to China, leaving only a small support base in Brazil to handle areas such as customer care and technical support.

Recently, Lenovo reorganized its operations in Brazil as part of a cost-cutting strategy and reduced the workforce originally of 5000 staff down to 800 employees. In a bid to re-establish its earlier success, it hired a new head for Brazil and invested heavily in strengthening its channel presence in the country.

## Questions

**1** Evaluate the social and cultural considerations for a foreign company entering the Brazilian market.

**2** What advice would you give to a company attempting to build a competitive position in this market?

**Sources:** Brazilian Etiquette and Culture. Available from www.cyborlink.com/besite/brazil (accessed 5 March 2018); ZDNet.com: Angelica Mari: 'Lenovo bounces back in Brazil', 17/9/2017; www.zdnet.com, Angelica Mari, 'Xiaomi downsizes Brazil operations', 31/5/2016 (accessed 5 June 2018).

# DISCUSSION QUESTIONS

**1** Discuss the view that culture lies at the heart of all problems connected with international marketing.

**2** What is culture? Is it important for international marketers to take account of it or is globalization going to make it a thing of the past?

**3** Given the cultural sensitivities to ethical dilemmas, can there ever be a global harmonization of ethical business practices in international marketing?

**4** How do social and cultural influences impact on international business negotiations? Using examples, advise a company preparing for cross-cultural negotiations.

**5** It has been suggested that firms from developed countries should market to developing countries by establishing partnerships in a neighbouring developing country. Explain the reasons behind such a proposition and the implications for a firm developing a globalization strategy.

# REFERENCES

1. Alburikan, K.A., AbuAlreesh, A., Alenazi, M., Albabtain, H., Alqouzi, M., Alawaji, M. and Aljadhey, H.S. (2017) Patients' understanding of prescription drug label instructions in developing nations: The case of Saudi Arabia. *Research in Social and Administrative Pharmacy*.

2. Babin, B.J. and Harris, E. (2018) *CB*, 8th edition. Cengage.

3. Blackwell, R.D., Miniard, P.W. and Engel, J.L. (2006) *Consumer Behaviour*, 9th edition. The Dryden Press.

4. Goman, C.K. (2011) *The Silent Language of Leaders: How Body Language Can Help – or Hurt – How You Lead*. John Wiley & Sons.

5. Graham, J.L. and Sano, Y. (1989) *Smart Bargaining: Doing Business with the Japanese*. Harper Business.

6. Groysberg, B., Lee, J., Price, J. and Chung, Y.J. (2018) The leader's guide to corporate culture. *Harvard Business Review* 96(1), 44–52.

7. Gudykunst, W.B. (2005) *Cross-Cultural and Intercultural Communication*. Sage Publications.

8. Hall, E.T. and Hall, M.R. (1987) *Hidden Differences: Doing Business with the Japanese* (Vol. 94). Anchor Press/Doubleday.

9. Hofstede, G. (2010) The GLOBE debate: Back to relevance. *Journal of International Business Studies* 41(8), 1339–1346.

10. Hofstede, G., Hofstede, G.J. and Minkov, M. (2010) *Cultures and Organizations: Software for the Mind: Intercultural Cooperation and Its Importance for Survival*, 3rd edition. McGraw-Hill.

11. Hofstede Insights (2018) www.hofstede-insights.com/.

12. Jeannet, J.-P. and Hennessey, H.O. (2006) *Global Marketing Strategies*, 2nd edition. Houghton Mifflin.

13. Kar, A.K. and Kar, A.K. (2017) How to walk your talk: Effective use of body language for business professionals. *IUP Journal of Soft Skills* 11(1), 16.

14. Lewin, J.E. and Johnston, W.L. (1997) Managing the international salesforce. *Journal of Business and Industrial Marketing* 12 (3/4).

15. Lu, X., Ai, W., Liu, X., Li, Q., Wang, N., Huang, G. and Mei, Q. (2016) September. Learning from the ubiquitous language: an empirical analysis of emoji usage of smartphone users. In *Proceedings of the 2016 ACM International Joint Conference on Pervasive and Ubiquitous Computing* (pp. 770–780). ACM.

16. Maslow, A.H. (1970) *Motivation and Personality*, 2nd edition. Harper and Row.

17. Matsumoto, D. and Van de Vijver, F.J.R. (2010) *Cross Cultural Research Methods in Psychology (Culture & Psychology)*. Cambridge.

18. Moon, S. and Song, R. (2015) The roles of cultural elements in international retailing of cultural products: An application to the motion picture industry. *Journal of Retailing* 91(1), 154–170.

19. Seo, W.J., Sung, Y. and Park, S.H. (2017) Cultural preferences for visual and verbal communication styles in sport advertisements. *South African Journal for Research in Sport, Physical Education and Recreation* 39(2), 199–215.

20. Straker, D. (2008) *Changing Minds: In Detail*. Syque Press.

21. Terpstra, V., Foley, J. and Sarathy, R. (2012) *International Marketing*. Naper Press.

22. Usunier, J.-C. and Lee, J.A. (2012) *Marketing Across Cultures*. Pearson Education.

## CHAPTER 4

# INTERNATIONAL MARKETING RESEARCH AND OPPORTUNITY ANALYSIS

## LEARNING OBJECTIVES

After reading this chapter you should be able to:

- Appreciate the key roles of marketing research in international marketing
- Understand the concepts and techniques to identify and evaluate opportunities internationally
- Build a market profile analysis of a foreign country market
- Discuss the difficulties and issues that arise in developing multi-country primary research studies

## INTRODUCTION

Discussions in previous chapters have illustrated the highly risky and complex environment in which the international marketing manager operates. If a company is to survive in the international marketplace, it is important that it searches for methods to reduce the risk of making a wrong decision as far as possible.

This is why **marketing research** is so fundamentally important to the international marketing process. It cannot help a manager reduce risk to the point of zero, but it can ensure that the starting point for decision making is knowledge, rather than guesswork. Lack of knowledge of foreign markets is one of the first major barriers an international marketing manager will encounter. An effective marketing research strategy is the first step in overcoming that barrier.

The purpose of this chapter is to examine the place of marketing research in international strategy and the contribution it makes to the decision-making process. We will, therefore, be examining such concepts as the role of marketing research and opportunity analysis in international markets and the building of an international marketing information system. We will also examine some of the aspects of primary marketing research in international markets and discuss the practicalities and problems in implementing multi-country studies.

# The role of marketing research and opportunity analysis

Marketing research can be defined as the systematic gathering, recording, analysis and interpretation of data on problems relating to the marketing of goods and services.

The role of research is primarily to act as an aid to the decision maker. It is a tool that can help to reduce the risk in decision making caused by the environmental uncertainties and lack of knowledge in international markets. It ensures that the manager bases a decision on the solid foundation of knowledge and focuses strategic thinking on the needs of the marketplace, rather than the product. Such a role is, of course, necessary in all types of marketing.

In international marketing, because of the increased uncertainties and complexities in world markets, the capacity to ensure a systematic planned process in the research and the use of secondary information, prior to field research, is of paramount importance if quality information is to be obtained. The research process (Gravetter and Forzano 2019; Malhotra *et al.* 2013) consists of a number of key stages. These steps are the logical process for any research study to go through in its implementation and will be relevant for all research studies:

1  *Selecting a research problem.* It is important to decide what information is needed and set the objectives of the research, ensuring it is both theoretically and commercially worthwhile and that the objectives are feasible and achievable. Discussions with key stakeholders, decision makers and reviewing current secondary data is also fundamental in defining the problem. From the discussions the research question evolves.

2  *Developing the approach to be taken.* The planning phase will concern itself with timescales, resources to carry out the work, the expertise required to meet the objectives and the decision as to whether a qualitative or quantitative approach is to be taken.

3  *Selecting research strategy and designing the research.* In designing the research, strategy consideration will be given to the different action steps that need to be taken. Ensuring full use of secondary data sources will be important, as will the use of a pilot study.

4  *Identifying the participants and planning the ethical process.* It is important to ensure that the sample of people who will take part in the research is accessible and appropriate for the study. Similarly, a research ethics protocol, ensuring anonymity and confidentiality for example, is in place.

5  *Completing a pilot study.* Completing a pilot study only provides a snap shot but it helps the research design process, further enabling the researcher to test the questionnaire or ensure participants understand the questions contained in the semi-structured interview guide.

6  *Carrying out the fieldwork.* Decisions as to how the questionnaires will be administered (telephone, mail, online, personal interviews) or where focus groups will take place will be made. In addition, decisions will be made as to who will do the work and what resources, including mobile devices or recording equipment, are required.

7  *Analyzing the data.* The data analysis stage will need to take full account of the objectives of the research and the client's needs. Many researchers will argue that the methodology to be used should be decided in the first stages of the research planning as it will impact on the questionnaire design and how the interviews are administered. Completing data analysis includes rigour in coding and transcription.

8  *Preparing the report and presentation.* The report and presentation are the researcher's outputs. These are vital in establishing the credibility of the research methods used and the validity of the findings of the research.

## The role of international marketing research

The ability for research to deliver fast and yet sensitively analyzed results across a range of different countries in today's global markets is crucial for competitive success. Since the late 2000s, we have seen the speed of business increase substantively with the global diffusion of computers, digital technologies and instant global telecommunication. Instant communication has become the standard across global markets. This means that marketing research has a critical role in feeding into decision makers' time-sensitive insights and changes in market behaviours around the globe. As such, the Internet has transformed the way we find information on our customers and track our markets worldwide. Social media analysts can provide selective, dynamic and up-to-date information to a larger number of users or individuals. This enables marketers to save on the expensive research costs of collecting data from different countries. Companies worldwide are able to get information that was previously impossible or too expensive to come by if they have access to the Web. This is now available 24 hours a day, often at a reasonable cost and sometimes free of charge. This is hugely beneficial to smaller companies for whom accessing up-to-date information used to be a huge barrier to competing internationally. Now SMEs have the power of information, giving them access to new markets worldwide.

## What big data is telling us

It is also important to recognize the impact big data is having on market research activities. So many things we do are recorded. Our personal data is stored in databases belonging to governments, NGOs, organizations, researchers, schools, universities and online communities. Our data is collected, researched and analyzed to understand the world, make predictions and help marketers recommend changes to products and services. The data that are collected include: purchase transactions, clicks made online, mobile connections, geo-location data and posts made on Facebook or other online communities.

These, together with analyzing what we search for on Google, facial recognition at airports, hospitals and supermarkets, bio-metric sensors in our bodies that monitor our heart-rate or glucose levels, to name just a few, are gathered and form big data. Big data is known by the 4Vs, see Table 4.1 below.

Table 4.1   The 4Vs of big data

| **Volume**: from **gigabytes** to **terabytes**, **exabytes** and **zettabytes** | **Velocity**: the speed at which data can be collected and analyzed |
|---|---|
| **Variety**: numeric or alpha, text, voices, music, images, film, videos | **Veracity**: accuracy of data |

Source: Adapted from Goes (2014). Big data and IS research. MIS Quartley, 38(3), iii–viii.

Big data is still at the innovative stage of its evolution. Marketing managers are constantly searching for new ways to understand consumer behaviour and predict or anticipate and identify their needs. It will be necessary for the marketing manager to embrace this opportunity, train a workforce to access and manage real-time big data and deliver real-time, location aware communications that are perfectly relevant to each consumer (Lichy et al. 2017). An example of analyzing global data is shown in Illustration 4.1.

The development of better decision tools and decision support systems and of globally based research supplier networks has in turn led to an increase in the usage of continent-wide and worldwide online surveys which often transcend national boundaries. The development of specialist global niche marketing research strategies and a rapid increase in the rate and spread of product innovation have all meant that the old days of slow-moving local or national marketing research studies are long gone. But businesses need to keep up with product innovations to maintain their markets. In just a short time span the Internet has transformed all areas of marketing research simply because it allows the researcher to make instant connections to multiple sources of competitive and customer information. This enables the researcher to mine for customer information and competitor information, and permits marketers to monitor customer activity across the globe with great ease. The use of social network sites to carry out global marketing research is also expanding rapidly.

Worldwide retail e-commerce sales in 2017 increased by a staggering 24.8 per cent over the previous year. The total amount in sales reached $2.304 trillion (eMarketer 2018). Mobile commerce or mCommerce

## ILLUSTRATION 4.1

# Worldwide online shopping behaviour

More consumers worldwide have joined the online shopping revolution. The advances in technology, shipping, logistics, secure payment platforms and, of course, the willingness of consumers to trust online businesses has enabled US$1.9 trillion of transactions to take place.

Clearly there are millions of consumers sharing the online centric experience. What is not clear is if all consumers use online shopping spaces for the same reason. Therefore, KPMG put a 'shout out' online requesting anyone who had shopped online at least once in the last year to complete a survey of their shopping experiences. A total of 18 430 consumers from 51 countries responded.

Findings show that the average number of online transactions per person, per year varies.

- Generation X (born 1966 to 1981) complete on average 18.6 transactions
- Millennials (born 1982 to 2001) complete an average of 15.6 transactions, and
- Baby Boomers (1946 to 1965) slightly less at 15.1 transactions per person per year.

While Baby Boomers transact slightly less often than Generation X and Millennials, they do spend, on average, slightly more. For example, Baby Boomers spend on average $203 per transaction, Generation X $190 and Millennials $173.

What consumers buy online is different when viewed from a country perspective. Findings show that in Australia and Belgium, when analyzing the top five online purchases, wine is a popular purchase. In the USA, Indonesia and Turkey, accessories are the top purchases; in Brazil and Greece it is pharmacy and healthcare products; and in the UK and China it is groceries. Crunching online big data also tells us that Millennials are 50 per cent more likely than Baby Boomers to visit high-street stores and talk to their friends and family before making their purchases. Despite the physical visit to the store and consultations with their friends and family, when it comes to sharing feedback Millennials choose Facebook (34 per cent) more often than Baby Boomers (25 per cent).

It is always interesting for marketers to understand what motivates consumers to shop online. KPMG's findings showed that consumers from China, Singapore and India do so to 'avoid crowds'. Nevertheless, the top reason worldwide as to why consumers shop in stores is because the want to 'see/touch the item first'.

## Questions

**1** Based on these findings, what should marketing managers promote to consumers to encourage them to shop online?

**2** How should marketing managers encourage consumers to make more visits to retail stores?

**3** Consumers seem to trust businesses to deliver the goods and services purchased. What attributes do online businesses have in common that makes consumers trust them?

**Source:** KPMG (2017) The truth about online consumers 2017 Global Online Consumer Report https://home.kpmg.com/xx/en/home/insights/2017/01/the-truth-about-online-consumers.html (accessed 5 June 2018).

from China, Japan, South Korea and the UK was a major factor in the staggering increase in worldwide retail commerce. Together, consumer and B2B behaviour have created an information explosion ready to be explored to identify trends and opportunities. The availability of online databases and social media analytics has transformed the nature of international marketing research and the role it plays in the marketing process. Global internet networks enable companies across the globe to build the ultimate in customization strategies or 'one-to-one' marketing plans. It is estimated that over three-quarters of revenue for marketing research agencies is derived from online research. Equally, the role of the marketing researcher has become much more closely aligned with the decision-making processes of organizations.

Research into international market issues can incorporate three major roles:

- *Cross-cultural research*: The conducting of a research project across nation or culture groups.
- *Foreign research*: Research conducted in a country other than the country of the commissioning company.
- *Multi-country research*: Research conducted in all countries where a company is represented.

This does not in any way convey the enormity of the task involved in developing an international market intelligence system which would be sufficient to provide the information necessary to make sound international marketing decisions. Such an information system would have to identify and analyze potential markets. It would also have to have the capacity to generate an understanding of the many external factors discussed in the previous three chapters. Many external factors will affect international marketing decisions, from macro-level economic factors to political–legal factors, as well as the micro-market structures and cultural factors affecting the consumer. It is a truism of international marketing that by competing in countries around the world uncertainty is generally greater, as are the difficulties in getting standardized information. The lack of market knowledge is the greatest obstacle to companies; those that do not engage in market research to understand the macro and micro factors will fail. Therefore, access to such knowledge makes it possible for the internationally experienced company to extend its activities to new markets and succeed.

As such, the role of the international market researcher is to provide an assessment of market demand globally and an evaluation of potential markets. The researcher would also provide an analysis of the risks and costs involved in market entries, as well as detailed information on which to base effective marketing strategies.

To achieve this, the researcher has three primary functions to carry out:

1 **Scanning international markets** to identify and analyze the opportunities.
2 Building marketing information systems to monitor environmental trends.
3 Carrying out **primary marketing research studies** for input into the development of marketing strategies and to test the feasibility of the possible marketing mix options, both in foreign country markets and across a range of international markets.

In the next three sections we will examine each of these in some detail.

## Opportunity identification and analysis

### Scanning international markets

There are 193 countries in the world that are member states of the United Nations. Even a large multinational corporation would find it difficult to resource market development in all these countries. Thus, the first task for the researcher is to scan markets to identify which countries have the potential for growth. International markets are scanned primarily at this stage to identify countries that warrant further research and analysis; hence the researcher will look for countries that meet three qualifying criteria:

1 *Accessibility*. If a company is barred from entering the market, it would be an ineffective use of resources to take research further. The scanning unit would assess such things as tariffs, non-tariff barriers, government regulation and import regulations to evaluate the accessibility of the market. Japan is still seen as a highly profitable market, but it is viewed by some as inaccessible due to the perception of the difficulties involved in overcoming trade barriers.

2 *Profitability*. There are many countries, often less-developed, that have high import tariffs. This means market researchers may feel it is less profitable to import into Gabon and Chad which have applied tariff rates of 16.93 per cent and 16.36 per cent respectively (World Bank 2018). At a macro-level, the researcher may consider the market unprofitable for other reasons, such as the availability of currency, the existence of exchange regulations, government subsidies to local competition, price controls and substitute products. Many countries in Africa are fully accessible, but companies

question the ability of trade partners in some of these countries to pay. The extra risk of non-payment reduces the profit return calculations of those markets.

3 *Market size*. An assessment is made of the potential market size to evaluate whether future investment is likely to bear fruit.

The specific indicators a company will look for tend to be very product- and market-specific. Thus, a hand tool manufacturer in the north of England specializing in tools for woodworking craftsmen would look for evidence of a hobby market (accessibility), high levels of disposable income (profitability) and large numbers of educated, middle-aged people with leisure time (market size).

In Management Challenge 4.1 the reader is asked to consider what Pokémon Company do to ensure their country growth portfolio goes from strength to strength.

## MANAGEMENT CHALLENGE 4.1

# Pokémon Company goes worldwide

The Pokémon Company launched its first Pokémon game in February 1996. Millions of 'humans' of all ages were swept up with the idea of capturing a Pokémon and training it to be their very own competitor in sporting battles.

Over the years the Pokémon Company has enticed its worldwide audience with regular new and fascinating updates. To broaden its fan-base further there are Pokémon stores in hundreds of cities. Pokémon fans can visit the stores, hang out with other Pokémon fans and, when on holiday in another country, visit stores to see new merchandise. Pokémon merchandise is available in stores and online. Pokémon also has concessions to sell its products via Amazon, Argos and other supermarkets around the world. The merchandise includes fun soft toys, jigsaw puzzles, Pokémon Alpha Sapphire 3DS and the Pokémon Trading Card Game.

Pokémon's longevity is also down to its global online reach on many social media platforms. These enable Pokémon to keep in touch with its fan-base. Pokémon Company also shows its caring side to children in need. It set up Pokémon and You which is a relief fund providing much needed funds donated to charities following, for example, the Great East Japan Earthquake. Further, Pokémon Company provides a wide range of tools to enable parents to use technology to help their children learn.

On top of all that, Pokémon has done something amazing with their Pokémon Go App. The app recognizes which continent the gamer is in and introduces a continent specific character. For example, Pokémon has a character named Farfetch'd: the character is a wild duck. In Japan Farfetch'd is called 'Kamongi' and the duck has a leek strapped to its back. 'Kamongi' which is a shortened version of "Kamo ga negi o shotte kuru', which translated to English means 'A duck has come along carrying a leek on its back'. Duck soup, made with leeks, is a favourite dish in Japan. And it is a tradition in Japan to say 'Kamongi', suggesting someone is going to receive a 'stroke of good luck'.

## Question

1 What has Pokémon Company done to ensure its brand grows from strength to strength?

**Reference:** Pokémon Company www.Pokémon.co.jp/corporate/en/business/#international (accessed 5 June 2018).

Having identified those opportunities, the researcher will need to make an assessment of their viability for further investigation. In principle, there are three types of market opportunities:

1 Existing markets. Here, customers' needs are already serviced by existing suppliers; therefore, market entry would be difficult unless the company has a superior product or an entirely new concept to offer the market.

2 Latent markets. In this type of market there are recognized potential customers, but no company has yet offered a product to fulfil the latent need. As there is little or no direct competition, market entry would be easier than in existing markets as long as the company could convey the benefits of its

product to the market. There is a growing movement of socially responsible consumers who choose to purchase locally sourced food, fair trade clothing and fly with airlines that offset carbon emissions. There is also a latent market for consumers that would like to be socially responsible investors. Rossi *et al.* (2018) suggest banks and investment companies should extend their product portfolios. They should guarantee consumer money is not invested in tobacco, gambling and weapons industries, and is only invested in companies that are already dedicated to being environmentally responsible.

3  Incipient markets. Incipient markets are ones that do not exist at present, but conditions and trends can be identified that indicate the future emergence of needs that, under present circumstances, would be unfulfilled. It may be, of course, that existing companies in the market are positioning themselves to take advantage of emerging markets, but at present there is no direct competition. Management Challenge 4.2 asks you to think about the Grameen Foundation that enables men and women in poverty stricken areas to fulfil their dream of creating a small business.

## MANAGEMENT CHALLENGE 4.2

## Grameen Foundation: micro-funding helps incipient markets develop and grow

The Grameen Foundation has supported over 23 million men and women through the provision of micro-funding, financial services support and guidance, manpower in terms of volunteers and pro-bono advice. This has enabled many people to raise themselves out of poverty, open a new business and have the confidence to grow and develop their business. Micro-entrepreneurs from 40 counties in Asia, Latin America, Middle East, North Africa and sub-Saharan Africa have engaged with the Grameen Foundation.

Angeline from the Philippines recognized an incipient market and sought a loan from Grameen Foundation's partner ASHI. Angeline's mother had a Sari-Sari store (convenience store) and Angeline recognized the store could do more if there was a freezer. Together,

Angeline and her mother extended their product range to include meat and fresh vegetables. The success gave Angeline the confidence to negotiate credit payments with her customers which engenders trust between them and provides benefits on both sides. There are over 500 000 Sari-Sari stores in the Philippines' many islands, and there are many remote villages similar to where Angeline and her mother live. Often, those villages do not have a bank. Banks are needed to enable farmers or store holders to trade. The Grameen Foundation is helping Sari-Sari store operators to be the village's digital financial hub. The store holders act as agents to help farmers and other store holders buy and sell produce.

It is hoped more micro-entrepreneurs will take advantage of the micro-loans, build confidence and grow their own business, and help others in their village to do the same.

### Question

1 What are the pros and cons that the Grameen Foundation had to consider before it offered the micro-finance loans to entrepreneurs in poverty stricken places?

**References:** The Grameen Foundation www.grameenfoundation. org/ (accessed 5 June 2018); www.business.org/finance/loans/ pros-cons-microloans/ (accessed 5 June 2018).

The nature of competitive products can be analyzed in a broadly similar way, with three distinct product types: competitive products, improved products and breakthrough products. A competitive product is one that has no significant advantages over those already on offer. Brands often promote specific, but minor, elements of the product as their USP (unique selling point or proposition) to try to differentiate products that are essentially very similar. An improved product is one that, while not unique, represents an improvement upon those currently available. Improvements often come with pricing offers or new technological advances. A breakthrough product, by way of contrast, represents an innovation and, as such, is likely to have a significant competitive advantage.

FIGURE 4.1    Nature of competition and level of market development

| Types of market | | | | | |
|---|---|---|---|---|---|
| **Product** | **Existing** | **Latent** | **Incipient** | | |
| Competitive | 'Me too' little advantage | Classic market gap | Possible long-term advantage | | Low |
| Distinctive | Ease of market entry | No direct competition | Market development needed | | Cost |
| Truly innovative | High competitive advantage | First mover advantage | Markets need to be identified | | High |

Low                                                                          High

Risk

The level and nature of competition that a firm will encounter can, therefore, be analyzed by relating the three types of market demand to the three types of competitive products. This is illustrated in Figure 4.1 and can be used as a basis for determining first, whether market entry is likely to succeed, and second, whether the company possesses any degree of competitive advantage. This, in turn, provides an insight into the nature of the marketing task needed. In saying this, however, it needs to be emphasized that this sort of insight provides an initial framework for analysis and nothing more. What is then needed is a far more detailed assessment of the degree of competitive advantage that the company possesses.

Obviously, the greatest opportunities, together with the greatest risk and potential for profit, are in the identification of incipient markets. The problem is that because markets do not yet exist, there is no market data. Researchers, therefore, use analytical techniques to make sure they identify and recognize conditions in incipient markets, thus enabling their companies to develop strategies by which to be first into the market. Reflect back to Management Challenge 4.2 and the benefits and risks that had to be considered by Grameen Bank's founder when choosing to put his money into micro companies where there is accessibility to a market. He did not always know if the market would engage in the products and services offered in the Sari-Sari stores. In the research techniques used, the basic principle is to compare, contrast or correlate various factors in the market under study. External variants identify similarities within the market or with other markets, thus assessing whether the right conditions exist for a market to emerge.

Some of the key techniques used are now discussed.

## Demand pattern analysis

In this technique, it is assumed that countries at different levels of economic development have differing patterns of demand and consumption. By comparing the pattern of demand in the country under study with the pattern of demand in an established market when the product was first introduced, a broad estimate of an incipient market can be achieved.

## Multiple factor indices

This assumes that the demand for a product correlates with demand for other products. By measuring demand for the correlated product, estimates of potential demand can be made. For example, a manufacturer of frozen foods may make an assessment by measuring the number of houses with freezers. Not all market potential indexes are developed from a single comparison; some are combinations of several factors, occasionally as many as 20. Many of these indexes are developed by particular companies or industries to measure market potentials for their products in a given country where the market is seen as incipient. Multiple market indexes are designed to measure the relative potentials of different markets for a particular product. Such indexes have the advantage of taking into account several factors that influence the sales of the given product and so help the company identify potential markets.

## Analogy estimation

Analogy estimation is used where there is a lack of market data in a particular country. Analogies are made with existing markets comparing and contrasting certain ratios to test for market potential. This technique is based on the theory of diffusion of innovation. It assumes that the innovation in the new market will diffuse and develop in much the same manner in all other markets around the world. This technique arouses mixed levels of enthusiasm, since experiences of using it across international markets have been variable. In addition, it is an expensive technique to implement. Also, doubts have been expressed about the accuracy of its forecasts in a world of instant communication and global launches, and failures, of new products. Those who have used it typically adopt one of two approaches:

- A cross-section approach, where the product market size for one country is related to some appropriate gross economic indicator in order to establish a ratio. This ratio is then applied to potential countries under analysis to estimate the potential for the product's market size in those countries.

- A time-series approach based on the belief that product usage moves through a cycle. Thus, one assumes that the potential countries under analysis will follow the same pattern of consumption as a more advanced economy, albeit with a predetermined time lag.

## Macro-survey technique

This method is essentially anthropological in approach and can help companies to establish themselves early in emerging countries with obvious long-term marketing benefits. The technique is based on the notion that as communities grow and develop, more specialized institutions come into being. Thus, one can construct a scale of successively more differentiated institutions against which any particular country can be evaluated to assess its level of growth and development and its market potential.

These techniques highlight the importance of comparative research and regular market screening if incipient demand is to be identified at an early stage. However, the value of several of the techniques does rest upon the assumption that all countries and their consumption patterns will develop along broadly common lines. If firms are to make effective use of many of these techniques, the assumption of common economic development patterns must stand. Increasingly, however, evidence is emerging to suggest that global commonality does not exist to this degree. There are strong arguments for companies grouping country markets for the purposes of this sort of comparative analysis.

## Risk evaluation

As previously stated, incipient markets offer the greatest opportunity for profit potential, but, as Figure 4.1 shows, risks are high.

The risk factor in opportunity analysis cannot be over-estimated. Sometimes political risk itself can be the most important determining factor to the success or failure of an international marketing campaign. In the markets where opportunities have been identified, researchers need to make an assessment first as to the type of risk apparent in that market (political, commercial, industrial or financial), and second as to the degree of that risk. Matrices such as the one identified in Figure 4.2 can be useful in carrying out such assessments.

Over recent years marketers have developed various indices to help assess the risk factor in the evaluation of potential market opportunities. Nowadays a number of such indices are readily available online. The Knaepen package, an OECD sponsored classification, and the Business Environment Risk Index (BERI), are perhaps two of the most well-known ones.

FIGURE 4.2 The four-risk matrix

| Country | | | | | | |
|---|---|---|---|---|---|---|
| Risk level | A | B | C | D | E | F |
| Risk type | Low | Moderate | Some | Risky | Very risky | Dangerous |
| Political | | | | | | |
| Commercial | | | | | | |
| Industrial | | | | | | |
| Financial | | | | | | |

## World Economic Forum

The World Economic Forum provides an annual indication report of the competitiveness of countries. Their report ranks the competitiveness performance of 144 economies based on the 12 competitiveness factors (see Table 4.2).

There are many factors used in calculating the competitiveness of each country. The pillars in Table 4.2 show the 12 pillars of competitiveness. Pillars 1–4 indicate factor-driven competitive elements, pillars 5–8 provide factors demonstrating a country's competitiveness in efficiency, and the final 9–12 pillars show how innovative a country is. Countries that are ranked high in all pillars, such as Switzerland and Singapore, show they are a highly competitive country, advanced in research and development, have an excellent infrastructure and present themselves on the world stage as having an efficient financial market. Countries ranked low in competitiveness include Guinea, Chad and Yemen as they are not highly innovative, and do not have a high proportion of their population engaged in higher education and training. The interesting information provided in this report for marketers and businesses is the change in rankings. Countries that move up the rankings in efficiency and innovation are clearly showing they have the potential for international organizations to consider them as future growth opportunities.

Table 4.2 Competitiveness factors

| 12 Pillars of competitiveness | | |
|---|---|---|
| 1. Institutions | 5. Higher education and training | 9. Technology readiness |
| 2. Infrastructure | 6. Labour market efficiency | 10. Market size |
| 3. Macro-economic environment | 7. Goods market efficiency | 11. Business sophistication |
| 4. Health and primary education | 8. Financial market efficiency | 12. Research and development innovation |

Source: World Economic Forum (2014).

## The Knaepen Package

The Knaepen Package is a system for assessing country credit risk and classifying countries into eight country risk categories (0–7). It measures the country credit risk, i.e. the likelihood that a country will service its external debt. The classification of countries has two basic components:

1 the Country Risk Assessment Model (CRAM), which produces a quantitative assessment of country credit risk, and

2 a qualitative assessment, which considers political risk, commercial and other risk factors not taken into account in the CRAM model.

The final classification is a consensus decision of country risk experts who meet several times a year. These meetings are organized so as to guarantee that every country is reviewed whenever a fundamental change is observed and at least once a year. The list of country risk classifications is published after each meeting.

## Business Environment Risk Index (BERI)

The BERI provides country risk forecasts for 140 countries throughout the world and is updated three times a year. This index assesses 15 environment factors, including political stability, balance of payments volatility, inflation, labour productivity, local management skills, bureaucratic delays, etc. Each factor is rated on a scale of 0–4 ranging from unacceptable conditions (0) to superior conditions (4). The key factors are individually weighted to take account of their importance. For example, political stability is weighted by a factor of 2.5. The final score is out of 100 and scores of over 80 indicate a favourable environment for investors and an advanced economy. Scores of less than 40 indicate very high risk for companies committing capital.

The main value of subscribing to such indices is to give companies an appreciation of the risk involved in opportunities identified. There are a number of organizations around the globe who publish country risk ratings – Standard and Poor's, the OECD, *The Economist* and Moody's – so information on risk evaluation is readily available to the Internet researcher.

Major global corporations such as IBM, Microsoft and ICI have specialist political risk analysts monitoring environmental trends to alert senior managers to changes and developments which may affect their markets.

# International marketing segmentation

At the scanning stage, the manager researching international markets is identifying and then analyzing opportunities to evaluate which markets to prioritize for further research and development. Some framework is then needed to evaluate those opportunities and try to reduce the plethora of countries to a more manageable number. To do this, managers need to divide markets into groups so they can decide which markets to prioritize or even to target.

Market segmentation is the strategy by which a firm partitions a market into submarkets or segments likely to manifest similar responses to marketing inputs. The aim is to identify the markets on which a company can concentrate its resources and efforts so that they can achieve maximum penetration of that market. This is instead of going for a market-spreading strategy where they aim to achieve a presence, however small, in as many markets as possible.

The Pareto law usually applies to international marketing strategies with its full vigour. The most broad-based and well-established international firms find that 20 per cent of the countries they serve generate at least 80 per cent of the results. Obviously, these countries must receive greater managerial attention and allocation of resources. The two main bases for segmenting international markets are by geographical criteria (i.e. countries) and transnational criteria (i.e. individual decision makers).

## Geographical criteria

The traditional practice is to use a country-based classification system as a basis for categorizing international markets. The business portfolio matrix (Figure 4.3) is indicative of the approach taken by many companies. In this, markets are classified in three categories.

## The business portfolio matrix

**Primary opportunity**   These markets indicate the best opportunities for long-term strategic development. Companies may want to establish a permanent presence and so embark on a thorough research programme.

**Secondary opportunity**   These are the markets where opportunities are identified but political or economic risk is perceived as being too high to make long-term irrevocable commitments. These markets would be handled in a more pragmatic way due to the potential risks identified. A comprehensive marketing information system would be needed.

FIGURE 4.3  Business portfolio matrix

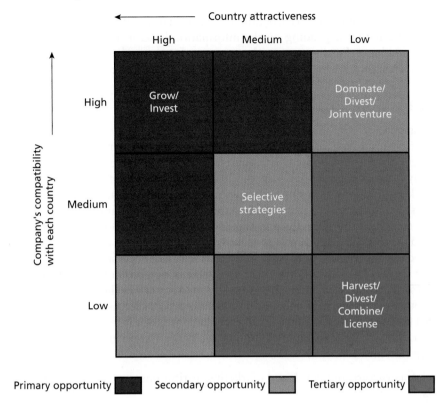

Sources: Harrell, G.D. and Keifer, R.D. (1993) 'Multinational market portfolio in global strategy development', International Marketing Review 10(1), Emerald Insight.

**Tertiary opportunity**   These are the catch-what-you-can markets. They will be perceived as high risk and so the allocation of resources will be minimal. Objectives in such countries would be short term and opportunistic and some companies would give no real commitment. No significant research would be carried out.

Figure 4.3 illustrates the business portfolio matrix. The horizontal axis evaluates the attractiveness of each country on objective and measurable criteria (e.g. size, stability and wealth). The vertical axis evaluates the firm's compatibility with each country on a more subjective and judgemental basis. Primary markets would score high on both axes.

This is a particularly useful device for companies operating in a portfolio of markets to prioritize market opportunity. Ford Tractor carried out such an analysis of key markets. In assessing market attractiveness it explored four basic elements:

1  market size
2  market growth rate
3  government regulations
4  economic and political stability.

Competitive strength and compatibility were defined in the international context. Factors such as market share, market representation, contribution margin and market support were examined. Using this analysis, they identified Kenya, Pakistan and Venezuela as primary markets.

The nature of competition and levels of risk (see Figure 4.1) and the business portfolio matrix (Figure 4.3) have a lot in common regarding risk, need for research and ways to identify countries in which to do business.

Equally, a company may use the BERI index, Hofstede's cultural dimensions or the Knaepen package as a basis for classifying countries. Whatever measurement base is used, once the primary markets have been identified companies then normally use standard methods to segment the markets within countries. To do this they use such variables as demographic/economic factors, lifestyles, consumer motivations, geography, buyer behaviour, psychographics, etc.

Thus, the primary segmentation base is geographic (by country) and the secondary bases are within countries. The problem here is that depending on the information base, it may be difficult to fully formulate secondary segmentation bases. Furthermore, such an approach can run the risk of leading to a differentiated marketing approach. This can leave the company with a very fragmented or concentrated international strategy.

## Infrastructure/marketing institution matrix

Countries are in competition with one another for two reasons. First, they want to keep businesses that are investing and trading within their country. Second, countries want to attract businesses that are investing and trading in other countries to choose their country. As shown in Table 4.2, countries look attractive to businesses for many reasons. Howard-Jones *et al.* (2018) and Gabrisch *et al.* (2016) have investigated the West Balkans' market position in terms of how it is ranked on the international stage. Their research has shown that the West Balkans needs to improve its standing on the international stage.

Gabrisch *et al.* researched the strengths and weaknesses of Albania, Bosnia and Herzegovina, Kosovo, Croatia, Macedonia, Montenegro and Serbia to identify what makes these countries attractive to businesses. They also researched the barriers and from these investigations made suggestions for improvements. Gabrisch *et al.* identified that the West Balkan countries need to engage in two promotion strategies. One of these is to advertise themselves as a group of countries that wants businesses, such as those in hospitality and tourism, to invest in them. Another is that the West Balkans has much to export such as hi-technology.

Sheth and Arma (2005) classified countries using research into their infrastructure and marketing institutional development. Infrastructure includes communications, legislation and open and free justice systems. The countries were classified as:

1  Developed infrastructure and developed marketing institutions, e.g. the US, the UK and Scandinavia.

2  Developed infrastructure but restricted marketing development, e.g. Japan and Germany. Examples of marketing development restrictions are countries that have time restrictions on when the store can be open (e.g. Germany) or restrictions on the size of stores (e.g. Japan).

3  Low levels of infrastructure development but have developed marketing institutions such as retailers and media, e.g. India and Mexico. The last category has low infrastructure development and low marketing institutional development. Typically, these are countries that have not developed efficient and effective distribution systems due to geography (e.g. Indonesia) or legal restrictions (e.g. Vietnam). (see Table 4.3).

**Table 4.3**   Infrastructure/marketing institution matrix

| | | Infrastructure | |
| --- | --- | --- | --- |
| | | Developed | Restricted |
| **Marketing institutions** | Developed | e.g. the UK, Scandinavia, the US | e.g. India, Mexico |
| | Restricted | e.g. Japan, Germany | e.g. Indonesia, Vietnam |

A major drawback with the country-based approach is that countries do not buy products, consumers do. Global markets, therefore, need to be understood in terms of groups of buyers who share the need and desire for a product and the ability to pay for it, not just those who share a national border. Companies may wish to establish brand positions across a number of international markets, as this is an increasingly common strategic goal. To do this they need to use a segmentation strategy that enables them to build a consistent brand position across those markets. If a company is to try to achieve a consistent and controlled marketing strategy across all its international markets, it needs a transnational approach to its segmentation strategy. If the basis for global market segmentation is one that cuts across national boundaries, then marketing strategies can be developed that will work for similar segments around the globe.

## Transnational segmentation

Buyers in any particular segment seek similar benefits from and exhibit similar behaviour in buying a product. According to Hassan and Stephen (2005), although these consumers may live in different areas of the world and come from very different backgrounds and value systems, they have commonalities in association with a given global brand. To achieve a transnational approach to segmentation therefore, a country as a unit of analysis is too large to be of operational use. An alternative approach is to examine the individual decision maker (*ibid*. 2005). Key bases for segmentation would include such variables as value systems, and demographic, psychographic and behavioural criteria.

Demographic variables have obvious potential as cross-national segmentation criteria. The most commonly used variables include sex, age, income level, social class and educational achievement. Frequently use is made of a battery of demographic variables when delineating transnational market segments.

Psychographic segmentation involves using lifestyle factors in the segmentation process. Appropriate criteria are usually of an inferred nature and concern consumer interests and perceptions of 'a way of living' in regard to work and leisure habits. Critical dimensions of lifestyle thus include activities, interests and opinions. Objective criteria, normally of a demographic nature, may also be helpful when defining lifestyle segments. Research International, when researching the transnational segments of young adults globally, divided them into four broad categories. 'Enthusiastic materialists' are optimistic and aspirational and to be found in developing countries and emerging markets like India and Latin America. 'Swimmers against the tide', on the other hand, demonstrate a degree of underlying pessimism, tend to live for the moment and are likely to be found in Southern Europe. In Northern Europe, the USA and Australasia consumers are the 'new realists', looking for a balance between work and leisure with some underlying pessimism in outlook and, finally, the 'complacent materialists' are defined as passively optimistic and located in Japan.

Behavioural variables also have a lot of potential as a basis for global market segmentation. In particular, attention to patterns of consumption and loyalty in respect of product category and brand can be useful, along with a focus on the context for usage. Variables such as the benefit sought or the buying motivations may be used. Behaviourally defined segments may be identified in terms of a specific aspect of behaviour which is not broad enough to be defined as a lifestyle. Papadopoulos and Martín Martín (2011) recommend behavioural elements of consumers be included in segmenting the market. Therefore, it may be more useful to include International Marketing Selection (IMSel) by behaviours such as 18- to 24-year-olds from Scandinavian countries who like skiing, or 24- to 35-year-olds from the sub-continent who take a pilgrimage to Mecca.

## Mosaic Global

One of the trends enabling segmentation using individualistic characteristics to become a feasible strategy for many companies, is the development of geo-demographic databases. One such database is the Mosaic Global from Experian. Mosaic Global is a single, consistent classification providing insight and understanding on the demographics, lifestyles and behaviour of 880 million people from the world's most prosperous economies including North America, Europe and Asia Pacific.

It is based on the idea that the world's cities share common patterns of residential segregation. Each have their enclaves of metropolitan strugglers, suburbs of career and family, and communities of sophisticated singles. Each of these can be characterized into neighbourhoods that display strong similarities in terms of their demographics, lifestyles and behaviour, regardless of where they are found. The result is a classification that identifies ten distinct neighbourhood types, each with a set of distinctive demographic and lifestyle characteristics that can be found in every country covered by the classification.

## ILLUSTRATION 4.2

# Global and glocal segmentation research

PSA Peugeot Citroën, the French car manufacturer, operates around the world, currently concentrating on China, Brazil, Argentina, Chile, Mexico and Russia. For these markets minor specification changes are needed for their classic Peugeot 508, together with full transformations of the Peugeot 207, which for the South American market is part car, part pick-up truck.

However, PSA Peugeot Citroën does not just sell cars – it sells emotions and feelings that surround the cars, such as French style, chic and *joie de vivre*. As outlined in Chapter 3, culture and traditions influence people in different countries when making purchasing decisions. Therefore, PSA Peugeot Citroën investigated global and glocal segmentation trends.

Consumers the world over have a bond with their car. Universally strong bonds occur if the car satisfies the following needs:

*Usage*: Does this car provide the functionality and suitability for the driver's needs, e.g. boot/trunk that fits golf clubs/shopping, fuel economy?

*Experience*: Will this car satisfy individual and/or family needs?

*Image*: Do the values and qualities of this car's brand match and demonstrate the personality and identity of the people that purchase this car?

Consumer bonds such as these are global. However, PSA Peugeot Citroën and other international brands need to identify specific characteristics of people in different countries and segment them in order to be successful. And this is *glocalization*, where a *global* brand understands the characteristics of the local consumer.

China is a country that PSA Peugeot Citroën is investing in. After considerable research, particularly qualitative research, it was discovered there are six dominant consumer segments in China:

1 *The Conservatives*: these people are older, rural citizens.

2 *The Solos*: intellectual people whose Chinese traditions and culture remain strong and China's open market and economy changes do not affect their own activities.

3 *The Followers*: as the name implies they follow the current economic trends and behavioural changes.

4 *The Bad Boys*: these are people who have dual lives – part with the dominant Chinese culture applied to them externally and from their parents, and part libertarian, where they enjoy the image and culture of a relaxed and fun modern society.

5 *The Social Creepers*: this category identifies people who continue to better themselves and to achieve the norms of those people at the next level of society's hierarchy.

6 *The Pioneers*: confident people who admire and stay embraced to China for its grand past and culture and are full of pride to see the opportunities for personal as well as country growth in the new China.

## Questions

1 Do you think the six consumer segments would be similar in other countries?

2 How can PSA Peugeot Citroën use these customer segments in its marketing strategy?

**Source:** Merza, A., Laetitia, R., Becker, C. and Zheng, X. (2014) Working on socio-cultural dynamics and customers' segmentation from local to global: An application case on well-being, health and Generation Z. *ESOMAR Asia Pacific*, Jakarta, May 2014.

The ten Mosaic Global types are:

- sophisticated singles
- bourgeois prosperity
- career and family
- comfortable retirement
- routine service workers
- hard working blue collar
- metropolitan strugglers
- low income elders
- post-industrial survivors
- rural inheritance.

The distribution of these typologies can be mapped by country and across the 29 countries in which it operates. Using the addresses of a company's customers, the system gives the researcher the ability to identify the type of people using certain products and services. It allows them to identify at a local level where the similar geo-demographic types are, thus acting as an aid to the segmentation of markets and the identification of primary and secondary markets. Retailers are among the biggest users of geo-segmentation, not only when deciding on the location of new stores but by generating a better understanding of their customer profiles. All they need is the address of their customers. Then, by adding the cluster codes to every customer address, they are able to define, group and describe the types or segments of their customers, assess their products' performance, decide site location and measure market performance by segments.

In Europe, with an ageing population, there is a growing interest by companies in senior retirees with disposable income and differing service requirements to the younger population. Financial services, health care providers as well as mobility equipment suppliers and housing developers, all use geo-segmentation to aid their segmentation and targeting strategies. Mosaic Global will also be of use in identifying the sample in a research survey and for building lists in a direct marketing exercise.

Despite the attractiveness of using individualistic characteristics, it is apparent there is strong potential for significant differences in the patterns of consumer behaviour within global segments derived using this method. Also, international similarities in lifestyle and behaviour do tend to be specific and relevant primarily to specialist products and niche markets.

## Hierarchical country: consumer segmentation

To overcome some of these problems, a compromise approach would be to implement a procedure for global segmentation which integrated features of both processes.

Hassan and Stephen (2005) propose a hierarchical approach to global market segmentation that takes into account country factors. It also incorporates individual behaviourist characteristics into a segmentation strategy that helps companies develop cross-national segments to allow for a global positioning strategy.

On this basis, the marketing strategy would build on the premise that world markets consist of both similarities and differences and that the most effective strategies reflect a full recognition of similarities and differences across, rather than within, markets. Thus, companies competing internationally should segment markets on the basis of consumers, not countries. Segmentation by purely geographical factors leads to national stereotyping. It ignores the differences between customers within a nation and ignores similarities across boundaries. Colgate and Palmolive reached such a conclusion when carrying out an analytical review of their own segmentation strategies, and now use the hierarchical approach.

Any global segmentation strategy needs to be carried out in stages:

1 Identify those countries that have the infrastructure to support the product and are accessible to the company.

2 Screen those countries to arrive at a shorter list of countries with the characteristics that make the market attractive, e.g. a frozen dessert manufacturer may say that for a market to be attractive they need to have at least 5 million refrigerators per market.

3   Develop mini-segments within these countries based on factors such as:
    ■ information search behaviour
    ■ product characteristics required.
    The outcome of this process would be a series of mini-segments within qualified countries.

4   The development of transnational segments begins by looking for similarities across segments. Factor analysis of the behavioural patterns of these segments would enable managers to understand the characteristics of the demand of each segment as regards marketing mix issues. Each mini-segment would, therefore, be rated on several strategic factors in terms of potential response.

5   Cluster analysis is then used to identify meaningful cross-national segments, each of which, it is thought, would evoke a similar response to any marketing mix strategy.

It is argued that this approach would enable marketers to design strategies for cross-national segments and so take a more consumer-oriented approach to international marketing. In prioritizing markets, companies would use consumers as their primary base. Some writers argue that companies still need a secondary segmentation stage to identify the key countries where these transnational segments can be found.

## The market profile analysis

### Analyzing foreign country markets

Having completed the scanning stage, the researcher will have reduced the number of potential countries to a feasible list requiring further research. The researcher needs then to systematically evaluate the markets identified and to build an analytical picture of the foreign country markets. This is primarily the role of the market profile analysis.

In building a market profile, the objective of the company is first, to develop a cost-effective information flow between the environment in which the company operates and the head office decision makers. Second, is to use a consistent approach to facilitate cross-country comparisons.

Using the 12C environmental analysis model in Table 4.4, this can help the researcher achieve these two objectives. The information input into the 12C analysis will help the researcher to draw up a market profile analysis, as shown in Figure 4.4.

The objective of a market profile analysis is to enable the company to use the environmental information to identify opportunities and problems in the potential marketing strategies. For example, the fact that television advertising is prohibited in a country will have major implications for a promotional strategy.

It is this type of detailed assessment that helps companies determine the degree of competitive advantage they may possess and the most appropriate method of market entry. Using consistent frameworks also enables the researcher to make cross-country comparisons much more easily.

### Sources of information

In building an MIS (marketing information system; also marketing intelligence system), companies would utilize a variety of information services and sources. The starting point for most international researchers in the UK is UK Trade and Investment. This government department helps businesses export and grow overseas, and provides a variety of support services to such organizations. The majority of western nations have similar government-sponsored organizations helping exporters to develop information on international markets.

Some reports have been critical of the deficiencies in the provision of market intelligence by government departments and of firms' abilities to use this information. The main criticisms are:

■ Information is non-specific to particular industries.
■ Firms experience problems with the bureaucratic nature of some government services.
■ Data is often in a form which is unsuitable for the company's needs, or too general to be of use.
■ Services have been available only in the capital city.
■ Inadequate publicity about the information and services available.

**Table 4.4**   The 12C framework for analyzing international markets

**Country**
- general country information
- basic SLEPTS data
- impact of environmental dimensions

**Concentration**
- structure of the market segments
- geographical spread

**Culture/consumer behaviour**
- characteristics of the country
- diversity of cultural groupings
- nature of decision making
- major influences of purchasing behaviour

**Choices**
- analysis of supply
- international and external competition
- characteristics of competitors
- import analysis
- competitive strengths and weaknesses

**Consumption**
- demand and end use analysis of economic sectors that use the product
- market share by demand sector
- growth patterns of sectors
- evaluation of the threat of substitute products

**Contractual obligations**
- business practices
- insurance
- legal obligations

**Commitment**
- access to market
- trade incentives and barriers
- custom tariffs

**Channels**
- purchasing behaviour
- capabilities of intermediaries
- coverage of distribution costs
- physical distribution
- infrastructure
- size and grade of products purchased

**Communication**
- promotion
- media infrastructure and availability
- which marketing approaches are effective
- cost of promotion
- common selling practices
- media information

**Capacity to pay**
- pricing
- extrapolation of pricing to examine trends
- culture of pricing
- conditions of payment
- insurance terms

**Currency**
- stability
- restrictions
- exchange controls

**Caveats**
- factors to be aware of

**FIGURE 4.4**   Market profile analysis

Other institutions that offer advice and information to companies researching international markets include:

- business libraries
- university libraries
- international chambers of commerce
- UK Trade and Investment: national and regional international marketing intelligence centres
- local business links
- embassies
- banks
- trade associations
- export councils
- overseas distributors
- overseas sales subsidiaries
- foreign brokerage houses
- foreign trade organizations.

## Online databases

As stated earlier, one of the main developments in the availability of secondary information for international markets is the plethora of web-based information sites, online databases, company customer response management (CRM) databases and online research services.

Online databases are systems which hold computerized information which can be accessed through the Internet, making a wide range of information available from an online database to a manager in a matter of seconds. Information can be transmitted from anywhere in the world instantaneously, bringing obvious benefits.

There are numerous advantages in using online databases. They are regularly updated – two or three times per day – and are therefore much more current than traditional printed sources. Retrieving information online is much more cost-effective than manual searching and is considerably faster. Online databases can be accessed 24 hours a day, 7 days a week. You also retrieve – and consequently pay for – only the information you want.

Online data sources can also be a solution for carrying out cross-cultural marketing research when primary data collection is prohibitive due to its cost. Marketing information globally is now becoming much more consolidated as global organizations develop databases that are excellent for cross-country comparisons and for accessing global market information. Table 4.5 gives examples of some of the globally based online databases that managers wishing to carry out comparative studies or globally based marketing research may find useful.

Organizations in developing countries are increasingly using online computerized databases for their market research work as they become better equipped with telecommunication facilities. The type and volume of trade information available through online databases has expanded dramatically over recent years, with new databases of interest to business and trade organizations continuously being introduced to the market.

The use of the Internet for marketing intelligence, therefore, is one of the most important ways in which connectivity can improve a firm's ability to develop international markets. Buying or commissioning market research reports can be a prohibitively expensive business. For a fraction of the cost, and in some cases free of charge, much of the same information can be gathered electronically. Given the time and expense associated with the collection of primary data, the use of web-based online databases is now central to building marketing information on international markets. However, researchers do need to be wary when using such databases and ensure they fully evaluate the credibility and worthiness of the data they obtain from such sources to ensure their accuracy and validity. The volume of relevant international marketing information available on the Internet is too extensive to describe in detail in this chapter. It includes: numerous online newspapers and journals; an extensive list of individual country and industry market research reports; trade

**Table 4.5**   Online databases

| Company information | |
| --- | --- |
| Companies House: | Company details of all registered companies in the UK |
| Kompass Global B2B Portal: | 11.6 million companies and 13 million executive contacts from international data in 70 countries |
| Extel: | 19 000 investment professionals provide a dataset of company and market information worldwide |
| Hoovers: | A commercial database providing 85 million companies, 100 million professionals and 1000 industry segments |
| **Trade data** | |
| Google public data: | Large global publicly available data sets |
| WTO gateway: | World Trade Organization data sets |
| Reuters: | Global market data |
| UN Comtrade: | Global merchandise trade statistics |
| Global Trade Information Services: | International merchandise trade data |
| Croners: | Comprehensive guide to exporting goods in over 200 export markets |
| Eurostat: | Detailed statistics on the EU countries |
| IMF/World Bank/UN: | World trade statistics |
| **Market information** | |
| MINTEL: | Global market and consumer data |
| Business Monitor International: | Analysis, ratings, rankings and forecasts covering 200 global marketing companies across 24 different industries |
| CIA World Factbook: | Profiles of countries and territories around the world |
| Euromonitor: | International market intelligence |
| Profound/MAID: | Commercial organization providing full text market research reports |

lists of suppliers, agents, distributors and government contacts in a large number of countries; details on host country legislation covering imports, agency agreements, joint ventures, etc.

Some of the best sites for undertaking general country screening and international marketing research include (all accessed 5 June 2018):

- Brand data: www.brandchannel.com; www.gbrands.com; www.globalstrategies.com
- BusinessWeek: www.businessweek.com
- *The Economist*: www.economist.com
- European Union: www.europa.eu
- Google: www.google.com/publicdata
- UK Trade and Investment: www.uktradeinvest.gov.uk

- UK Chambers of Commerce: www.britishchambers.org.uk
- United Nations: www.un.org
- World Bank: www.worldbank.org
- World Fact Book: www.cia.gov/cia/publications/factbook
- World Trade Organization: www.wto.org

These are just a few examples of the large number of websites which provide access to sources of international trade and marketing data as well as other useful services.

## Problems in using secondary data

In carrying out marketing research internationally, problems arise by virtue of the very nature of the number and complexities of the markets being investigated. While the use of secondary data is essential in international marketing research, the reader needs to be aware of its limitations and some of the problems that occur in using secondary data.

Perhaps the most frequently discussed issue is the availability and accessibility of quality secondary information in international markets. The collection of secondary data concerning the economy and the business infrastructure in some countries varies in quality and consistency, and evaluation of secondary data is critical for international marketing research. Different countries, even for internationally based statistics, may report different values for a given statistic, such as GDP, because of differences in the way the unit is defined. Measurement units may not be equivalent across countries, and the accuracy of secondary data may also vary from country to country. Business and income statistics are affected by the taxation structures and the extent of tax evasion. Population censuses may vary in frequency and year in which the data is collected.

One of the reasons for the distortion of data in some countries is the political considerations of governments. The International Labour Organization found the actual unemployment rate in Russia was 10 per cent rather than the officially reported 2 per cent. The Indian government estimates that India's middle class numbers 250 million. But, according to a recent survey of consumer patterns conducted by the National Council of Applied Economic Research in Delhi, the Indian middle class probably totals 100 million at best, and there is much stratification among them. This problem might be solved by obtaining authentic data from international organizations such as the OECD, European Union, World Bank, etc.

The inconsistencies which can be found in the classification of various types of data in various countries are also a problem when carrying out any comparative analysis across markets. Terpstra *et al.* (2012) say that the most significant problem associated with the secondary data, especially in developing countries, is its scarcity. A further problem which can be quite misleading is the timeliness of the collected secondary data: it might have been collected several years earlier and never updated and is therefore outdated and of little value for future planning. Thus, it can be a problem when accessing online databases where the year the data actually refer to may be a few years before the actual publication date. This may result in the researcher being misled into thinking they are viewing current data.

Many countries attempt to attract foreign investment by overstating certain factors that make the economic picture look better. On the other hand, some countries understate certain factors, making the economic situation appear worse in order to attract foreign aid.

The Asia Pacific market is an important market and so obtaining reliable information in this region is of crucial importance for many companies. INSEAD surveyed 1000 managers of European companies operating in the Asia Pacific region and found that only in Japan and Singapore were companies able to easily access data that was viewed as being of a reliable quality. In China, Taiwan and Vietnam data was not trusted by researchers. Even though Japanese data was relatively accessible, there were still difficulties due to the fact that the information was over-abundant. So it was difficult to select and interpret the relevant data or to give it any practical application.

None of the limitations discussed above should devalue the importance of secondary data in international marketing research. For many smaller companies lacking the resources to carry out primary research in markets which are geographically distant, it may be the only information to which there is relative ease of access. However, despite investing a great deal of time and money in both primary and secondary research, giant international organizations, such as McDonald's and KFC, have not been able to conquer the Indian market. See Illustration 4.3.

## ILLUSTRATION 4.3

## Research suggested India was full of potential. But sometimes reaping returns is slow business

India is one of the most exciting developing countries. There are 1.3 billion people in India and it is one of the fastest growing economies with a demographic of young, active and enthusiastic people. What is interesting though is that while many Indians are now above the poverty line, there are only a few million people (out of the 1.3 billion) that are considered rich or middle class. This could be why some of the expectations of giant brands have not been fulfilled.

Take for example McDonald's which has invested heavily in India and has been in the country for 12 years. It has not really broken into India and grown rapidly as it had projected would happen. Currently, it has around 300 outlets. Compare this to Poland: a smaller country with a shrinking population, where there are around 380 outlets.

Data on Indian online behaviour shows 'likely behaviour' sometimes changes abruptly. E-commerce boomed in India during 2014 and 2015 with sales growing by 100 per cent during both years. However, in 2016 growth in e-commerce was around only 10 per cent. During 2017 e-commerce sales in India improved to around 28 per cent. This shows there was improvement during 2017 but analysts may be nervous about predicting growth rates for the next ten years.

Despite that, many businesses including Amazon, Ikea and Starbucks have chosen to invest in India. Amazon had already invested $2 billion in India creating 45 000 jobs and has recently invested a further $3 billion. Ikea is also keen to engage in India by promising to open around 25 stores between now and 2025. Starbucks may have viewed India and China as comparable places in which to do business. However, in India, Starbucks opens only one coffee shop per month. In China a new Starbucks opens every 15 hours or so. In India, there are around 100 Starbuck coffee shops; in China there are 3000. A spokesman for Starbucks India has said that store openings, from start to finish, take around 6 to 9 months in the USA, whereas, in India the process takes 12–18 months.

### Questions

**1** Why might analysts be nervous about predicting consumer behaviour in India?

**2** What primary and secondary research would you recommend McDonald's engage in to understand why its predictions of fast growth in India have not been fulfilled?

**Sources:** McDonald's (2018). www.mcdonaldsindia.net; *The Economist* (2018) India's Missing Middle Classes. www.economist.com.

## Primary research in international markets

We have discussed scanning international markets to identify potential market opportunities and the building of market information systems from which the market profile analysis is formulated. So far, we have only discussed obtaining information from secondary sources. It is unlikely that a researcher will be able to obtain the information for input into a marketing information system from secondary sources alone. Having exhausted these sources, the researcher will need to embark on the collection of primary data to obtain the information required.

In the following sections we will discuss the issues facing the researcher which should be considered when endeavouring to carry out primary research studies. To do this we use the six-step framework (Malhotra *et al.* 2013) depicted in Figure 4.5.

FIGURE 4.5   Flowchart of the marketing research process

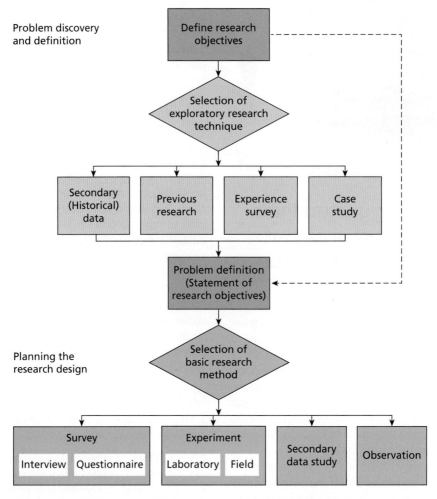

Source: Babin, B.J. and Zikmund, W.G. (2016) *Essentials of Marketing Research*, 6th edition. Cengage Learning.

## Problem discovery and definition report

The precise definition of the marketing research problem is more difficult and more important in international marketing research than in domestic marketing research. Unfamiliarity with the cultures and environmental factors of the countries where the research is being conducted can greatly increase the difficulty of obtaining accurate findings. Often there are no clear geographical boundaries to the market you are trying to investigate, which can make the design of the research problematic. Other issues occur when developing markets push in front of developed markets. Once again, showing the time-series approach assuming developing countries will follow the same pattern cannot always be observed.

On a practical level, the differences in climate and infrastructure create problems. A survey on floor cleaning products across Europe would have to take account of the fact that Scandinavians have wooden floors, there are lots of tiled and stone floors in the Mediterranean, and in the UK many houses have carpets, wood, tile and stone floors!

Many international marketing efforts fail not because research was not conducted but because the issue of comparability was not adequately addressed in defining the marketing research problem. This is why, as we saw in Chapter 3, it is so important to isolate the impact of self-reference criteria (SRC) and the unconscious reference to our own cultural values when defining the problem we are attempting to research in international markets.

## Developing an innovative approach

It is important in international marketing research to maintain flexibility in the approach you may have in the initial stages of the research. In the first stage of primary research, companies often use informal means to gather preliminary information. Extensive use is made of the network of contacts available to the company both at home and abroad. It is unlikely that a full understanding of the foreign market will be obtained without visiting that market to gain information first hand. The first steps in doing this would be by networking and obtaining information through relatively informal means such as networking consortia or multi-client studies. Advanced Apparel in Management Challenge 4.3 used networking in an innovative way to stand out from the crowd.

---

### MANAGEMENT CHALLENGE 4.3

## Networking helps you stand out in a crowd

Networking is an activity all marketers and business people know they should get involved in. This is particularly important for entrepreneurs who are often so focused on their business that they forget the 'time out' networking can provide and the enormous psychological and financial returns. The question people often ask, however, is: what networking should be done and how?

Stacy Johnson realized she needed to network. In 2000, she moved from Southern California to Utah. Suddenly, her network of friends, clients and businesses along with her supply chain vanished. Almost 20 years later Stacy feels she has fulfilled her dreams for Advanced Apparel, her screen-printing and embroidery business. She has her own premises, a fully operational warehouse with her own printing equipment and over 1000 clients. Looking back to the early days in Utah, Stacy reflects her business succeeded because she became a networking ninja. At first Stacy networked everything and everywhere. She joined the local Chamber of Commerce, other city-based networks, and went to every local event passing her business card to everyone, thinking . . . 'something will happen'. Stacy realized she needed to be more strategic. She joined fewer networks; granted some had a premium price-tag. But she felt she was immersed in spaces with like-minded people. At these networking events, she did not just hand over her business card but discussed ways in which her business could help other businesses fulfil a need.

Stacy also made new friends while networking. People began to trust her and like her business acumen. And soon Stacy noticed that her friends became her advocates and spread the word about her business. Together they made her business grow. Business networking and relationship building, Stacy muses, takes time, honesty and persistence, just like a loving relationship.

### Questions

1 Why are some people reluctant to network?

2 What are the benefits of networking?

**Reference:** Madison, R. (2017). Standing out in a Crowd: How Innovating and Networking Helped Grow a Small Business. *Utah Business* 10, 38.

---

## Networking

The use of contact networks to build information is vitally important because of the sometimes prohibitive cost of carrying out detailed market research studies overseas. Before any detailed studies are undertaken, trade contacts need to be fully explored.

In order to find solutions to the many international marketing research problems, improvisation in international research is essential.

Most companies will make extensive use of their existing networks to build the market profiles and develop information bases. These could be agents, distributors, licensees, joint venture partners or other companies operating in the country under investigation.

## Consortia

Marketing research consortia enable the comparison of data across different cultures and aid international marketing research efforts. Consortia are used by companies as a way of overcoming the difficulties involved in gathering data and establishing contacts in foreign markets. Essentially, a group of companies will come together to research a particular market area in which they have a common interest. The advantages are:

■ The consortium is more visible in the foreign market.

■ It is more likely to enjoy the support of the home export promotion organization.

■ It achieves economies through the joint use of export facilities both at home and in foreign markets.

■ It increases the resources available to support the research operation.

However, if a company is to join a consortium, then it has to be prepared to have its autonomy reduced. This fact alone is the major reason most consortia fail. There also has to be a strong reason to join together for the relationship to develop. Nevertheless, by the pooling of resources, consortia are very useful in giving companies the resources needed to acquire knowledge on markets. Often agencies will offer omnibus studies which have much the same benefits (see Illustration 4.4).

Due to the problems and considerations we have already discussed, it may be that detailed research studies will only be carried out in markets where the market viability is seen to be positive and when detailed consumer/market information is required to develop marketing strategy. The cost of primary field research can be high. So it will only be carried out after all other sources have been investigated.

A survey carried out by INSEAD of European companies operating in the Asia Pacific region showed that companies perceived the most significant sources of information as being personal contacts of the companies themselves, whether these were customers, other business relationships or their own market surveys.

A second tier of usefulness was then identified as consisting of other direct sources such as government contacts and contacts with competitors or trade associations. Finally, there was a third tier comprising publicly available information such as newspapers and magazines. This information may be widely read but relatively little weight seems to be given to its strategic value. The importance of directly collected information seems to confirm the view that business in Asia depends more heavily on the creation of a network of relationships than on analysis of hard data collected through surveys or other published information.

## The collection of primary data

The cost and effort of collecting primary data in new markets is far higher than that of collecting such data in the domestic market. This is particularly the case in developing countries where no marketing research infrastructure or experience is available. Primary research in these circumstances would entail substantial investment costs in developing basic information relating, for example, to sampling frames or trained qualified interviewers. This, of course, reinforces the importance of secondary data for research purposes and the need for a systematic planning process when embarking on a primary research project.

## Organizing the research study

There are two major organizational questions which the international marketing manager will need to address:

■ Should the research be carried out by foreign local subsidiaries or should all marketing research be centralized at headquarters?

■ Should the fieldwork be carried out in-house or by an agency?

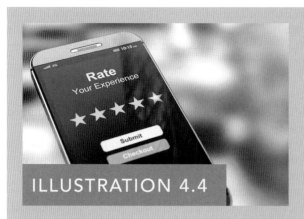

## ILLUSTRATION 4.4

# Omnibus telephone survey: what do you want to ask the experts?

IFF is a market research company that provides omnibus research. It is a long-established company with 50 years of primary research behind it. The primary research is done via telephone where 500 senior managers and directors – the experts – are telephoned and asked questions from a wide range of subjects including:

- the economic outlook
- purchasing patterns
- political perspectives
- financial confidence
- boardroom policies
- commercial issues

IFF telephones the 500 experts, establishes their opinions and provides a Business Spotlight report. For an **omnibus survey**, the questions asked are agreed in cooperation with the organization that IFF is working for. What is different about an omnibus survey is that several organizations pay to have their questions answered and all questions are submitted on one survey. Take for example three organizations: Organization 1 would like to ask experts ten questions about changes in purchasing patterns, Organization 2 has ten questions about the economic outlook, and Organization 3 has ten questions as to whether the experts agree on export trends and forecasts. IFF gathers the questions together and produces a 30-question survey. Each organization only gets a report on the answers to their specific questions. This is a cost-effective and efficient way to gather primary research as there are no individual set-up costs and no minimum fee.

IFF provides an excellent service and reassures its potential clients by promoting its Five Step Process:

1 Needs and goals consultation

2 Survey design, preparation and approval

3 Telephone fieldwork completed over a two-week period

4 Results are available via a basic report, a super report and a super, premium report

5 Follow-up telephone call to discuss results.

The research company collects and analyzes primary research for the public sector, private sector, not-for-profit organizations, membership organizations and regulatory bodies. The market research reports from IFF enable each organization to understand trends, opinions, track attitude changes and consumer/staff or supply chain behaviour.

## Questions

1 What are the advantages of using telephone-based surveys?

2 What are the benefits and weaknesses of joining a survey with other organizations?

**Reference:** IFF Research. www.iffresearch.com.

## Centralization vs decentralization

If a centralized approach is adopted, then decisions have to be made regarding the specific responsibilities of the operating unit and what managerial arrangements should exist between the unit and headquarters staff. Further to this, decisions have to be taken as to what relationship is to exist between the local research staff who are ultimately responsible to headquarters and the local line management.

If a decentralized approach is chosen, then arrangements have to be made for research findings to be transferred from one operating unit to another. There is also the question of who has the overall responsibility for administering and overseeing the market research budget to ensure that resources are not wasted by a possible duplication of research effort.

Such issues are complex and are also related to overall organizational issues. These are examined in some depth in Chapter 5. In this chapter we will concentrate our discussion on the decision as to whether the company should carry out international research itself, or involve independent research agencies.

## In-house or agency

Whether a company chooses to do all the research in-house or to use an agency will largely be determined by factors such as company resources, market expertise and product complexity.

If a company operates in a specialist B2B market with highly technological and complex products and has significant experience in the market, it may have no choice but to carry out research itself as it may be difficult to find an agency with the necessary competence.

However, if the company is operating in the consumer markets then a different scenario applies. Consumer research may require an established field force. The size of the markets may mean that a research company with fieldwork resources is needed. A priority could well be to obtain an independent objective assessment of a foreign country. This could require specialist interviewing skills which a company alone might not be able to resource and thus would require the services of an agency. If the company is carrying out a multi-country study and needs a consistent research approach across all markets, then an international agency with resources across markets may be much more able to handle the research programme. Often, however, research in foreign markets may require a local firm to do the fieldwork, gather data and provide some analysis and interpretation. The selection and use of a foreign firm may be extremely important to the success of the whole project.

In choosing an agency, a company has six basic options:

1  A local agency in the market under investigation.
2  A domestic agency with overseas offices.
3  A domestic agency with overseas associate companies.
4  A domestic agency which subcontracts fieldwork to an agency in the market under investigation.
5  A domestic agency with competent foreign staff.
6  A global agency with offices around the world.

Which solution is best for the researcher will depend on a number of factors: the ease of briefing the agency; supervising and coordinating the project; the probability of language problems arising; the requirements of specialist market knowledge; the standard of competence required; and the budget available.

Thus, no single option is universally the best to select. It is primarily dependent on the budget available, the requirements of the research, the expertise within the company and, of course, the market under investigation. In a research study in Saudi Arabia the UK agency wished to maintain control and coordination of the project. However, western interviewers would have had little success in eliciting meaningful information from Saudi businessmen. Therefore, it was decided to employ a Cypriot fieldwork agency to translate the questionnaire into Arabic and carry out the interviews. This led to certain control and communication problems, but it was the only realistic methodology to obtain the required information.

It may often be the case that in a multi-country study a combination of agencies are used. A typical multi-country study will go through the following steps:

1  The project is discussed at length with the client.
2  The fieldwork agencies in each country are selected.
3  The questionnaire is designed centrally.
4  The questionnaire is translated locally, and the translation is checked centrally.
5  The questionnaire is piloted locally.
6  The questionnaire is finalized centrally.
7  The interviewers are briefed locally by an executive of the central company.
8  The fieldwork is carried out locally.
9  The coding and editing plan is provided for the local agencies.

10　The edited and coded questionnaires are returned to head office.

11　A coding and editing check is carried out centrally.

12　Computing and analysis are carried out centrally.

## Research design

In formulating a research design, considerable effort is needed to ensure that the methods used will ensure comparability of data. In order to handle problems such as cultural bias in research design and interpretation of data etc., perspectives of researchers from different countries and cultures could be incorporated in the process so that the bias is minimal. However, this method will only work if there are no major problems of communication between researchers from different environments. If this is not the case, there is a possibility that some other kind of unknown bias might be introduced into the research process which could be even more harmful. A study of the cultural and social values and the method of conducting research in the host country could play an important role in facilitating the process of international marketing research.

One of the first factors to consider in developing a research design is the reliability and validity of the secondary data used. As we have previously discussed, the accuracy of secondary data varies enormously across countries. This means that the database being used to develop primary research may be inaccurate or highly biased, or lack the capability to make multi-country comparisons.

Further to this, the research design needs to incorporate methods which will be feasible in the foreign country markets, as well as allowing the international researcher to obtain meaningful and relevant findings.

For example, a researcher visiting different areas in India will find there is a highly variable literacy rate across the country and across genders and may not be able to ask participants to self-complete a questionnaire. According to www.india.gov, the literacy rate in the country is 65 per cent: 75 per cent for males and 54 per cent for females. However, in some rural areas it is much lower. In Bihar there is a literacy rate of 47 per cent; in Jammu and Kashmir it is 55 per cent. Therefore, the researcher may have to read the questionnaire to some participants. Further, there are hundreds of languages in India. In some rural areas, there can be very real fears that the interviewer is a government inspector in disguise. In such a scenario, a researcher would have problems throughout the research process in establishing the basic sample, designing the questionnaire, translation and data collection techniques.

Social and cultural factors are one of the most important issues which affect the process of international marketing research. In collecting primary data, the researcher needs to consider the issues facing them in evaluating the possible methods under consideration.

In this context, qualitative research, survey methods, questionnaire design and sampling considerations are particularly important.

## Qualitative research

Because the researcher is often unfamiliar with the foreign market to be examined, qualitative research is crucial in international marketing research. In the initial stages, qualitative research can provide insights into the problem and help in developing an approach by generating relevant research questions and hypotheses, models and characteristics which influence the research design. Thus, qualitative research may reveal the differences between foreign and domestic markets. It may also help to reduce the psychological distance between the researcher and the respondent. In some cases, the researcher must rely on qualitative research because secondary data may not be available. Some problems associated with qualitative techniques in developing countries include accessibility (different concept of time), sampling (extended demographic factors such as religion and tribal membership), shorter span of attention and less familiarity with abstract thinking.

Focus groups can be used in many settings, particularly in newly emerging markets where there is scant data and companies are trying to establish the cultural sensitivities in the market to their products and services. In some cultures, such as in the Middle or Far East, people are hesitant to discuss their feelings in a group setting. In these cases, in-depth interviews can be used.

The use of projective techniques is sometimes appropriate. Association techniques (word association), completion techniques (sentence completion, story completion) and expressive techniques (role playing, third-person technique) involve the use of verbal cues and so are all good cross-cultural research techniques.

## Survey methods

There are several issues to consider in evaluating the various interviewing methods available.

### Online surveys
As the Internet achieves greater penetration even in less developed markets, online surveys are now becoming predominant globally. Speed of execution, the obtaining of timely responses, ease of interview and speed of analysis are all major benefits to international marketing researchers. Globally, access to the Internet is still scarce in some countries and in others subject to government controls. This could mean potential bias in both the sampling and in the answers given by respondents.

### Telephone interviewing
With the setting up of global call centres, Internet telephony and the collapse in the price of international telephone calls, multi-country studies are now often conducted from a single global location and are much cheaper and easier to control. Most telephone data collection is conducted through CATI (Computer aided telephone interviews) which are cost-effective as well as reliable. CATI/telephone surveys are the most effective method of collecting data from global customers as they can be organized from one location and administered globally. In the USA, Canada and Europe, the telephone has achieved almost total penetration of households. In most developing nations, such as across Africa, however, mobile/cell phones are more prevalent than landlines and it could be that only a few households have telephones. Even in countries like Saudi Arabia, where telephone ownership is extensive, telephone directories can be incomplete and out of date.

Therefore, telephone interviews are most useful when employed with relatively upscale consumers who are accustomed to business transactions by phone, be it mobile/cell or landline, or consumers who can be reached by phone and can express themselves easily.

### Mail interviewing
Because of the rise of the online survey, the use of mail interviews internationally has declined dramatically. However, in countries where literacy is high and the postal system is well developed and where there are still problems in terms of access to the Internet, mail surveys still continue to be used. In Africa, Asia and South America, however, the use of mail surveys and mail panels is low because of illiteracy and the large proportion of population living in rural areas.

No questionnaire administration method is superior in all situations. Table 4.6 presents a comparative evaluation of the major modes of collecting primary data in the context of international marketing research.

## Questionnaire design

The questionnaire or research instrument should be adapted to the specific cultural environment and should not be biased in terms of any one culture. This requires careful attention to each step of the questionnaire design process. It is important to take into account any differences in underlying consumer behaviour, decision-making processes, psychographics, lifestyles and demographic variables.

The use of unstructured or open-ended questions may be desirable if the researcher lacks knowledge of the possible responses in other cultures. Unstructured questions also reduce cultural bias because they do not impose any response alternatives. However, unstructured questions are more affected by differences in educational levels than structured questions. They should be used with caution in countries with high illiteracy rates.

The questions may have to be translated for administration in different cultures. A set of guidelines has been proposed by Brislin (2001) for writing questionnaires in English so that they can be easily translated. These include:

- use short and simple sentences
- repeat nouns rather than using pronouns
- avoid metaphors
- avoid adverbs and prepositions related to place and time
- avoid possessive forms
- use specific rather than general terms
- avoid vague words
- avoid sentences with two different verbs if the verbs suggest different actions.

**TABLE 4.6**   Advantages and disadvantages of different survey approaches

| Characteristic | Door-to-Door Personal Interview | Mall Intercept Personal Interview | Telephone Interview | Snail Mail Survey | Email/Internet/ Smartphone Survey |
|---|---|---|---|---|---|
| Speed of data collection | Moderate | Fast | Very fast | Slow | Fastest |
| Geographic flexibility | Limited to moderate | Confined mostly to urban and suburban areas | High | High | High (worldwide) |
| Respondent cooperation | Moderate in getting an answer. Excellent once respondent agrees to participate | Good in agreement to respond. Moderate cooperation thereafter | Difficult to get an answer. Good cooperation thereafter. Varies landline versus cell | Moderate all the way around | Low from general population but high when hot button issue presented or sample is a computer panel |
| Versatility of questioning | Quite versatile | Extremely versatile | Limited versatility, particularly for cell calls | Not versatile; requires highly standardized format | Good versatility for logical branching and respondent assignment |
| Questionnaire length | Long | Moderate | Moderate for landline and short for cell | Moderate but varies depending on incentive | Moderate but varies depending on incentive |
| Item non-response rate | Low | Medium | Medium | High | Software can assure none |
| Possibility for respondent misunderstanding | Low | Low | Average | High | High |
| Degree of researcher or interviewer influence on responses | High | High | Moderate | Lowest | Low with exceptions depending on data source |

*(Continued)*

Table 4.6  Continued

| Characteristic | Door-to-Door Personal Interview | Mall Intercept Personal Interview | Telephone Interview | Snail Mail Survey | Email/Internet/Smartphone Survey |
|---|---|---|---|---|---|
| Supervision of interviewers | Moderate | Moderate to high | High, especially with central location interviewing | Not applicable | Not applicable |
| Anonymity of respondent | Lowest | Moderate | Low | Highest | Moderate |
| Ease of callback or follow-up | Difficult | Most difficult | Easy | Easy, but takes time | Difficult if respondents are unknown. Easy if sample drawn from email list |
| Cost | Highest | Moderate to high | Low to moderate | Low | Low to moderate depending on potential cost of access to sample |
| Special features | Visual materials may be shown or demonstrated; extended probing possible | Taste tests, product trials, viewing of marketing materials possible. Ideal for representing population of mall/shopping centre shoppers | Fieldwork and supervision of data collection are simplified. Distinction must be made between landline and mobile/cell phone calls | Respondent may answer questions at own convenience; has time to reflect on answers | Streaming media software allows use of graphics and animation as well as random assignment to experimental conditions |

Source: Babin, B.J. and Zikmund, W.G. (2016) *Essentials of Marketing Research*, 6th edition, Cengage Learning.

The problems of language and translation were discussed in Chapter 3 and equally apply in marketing research. A translation of a questionnaire might be grammatically correct, but this does not necessarily mean that it is conveying the appropriate message. For example: value for money is not a common phrase in Spain; the equivalent phrase is 'price for product'. In the Middle East 'payment' is a transactional word; it refers to repaying a debt and so would be inappropriate in the context of purchasing a product.

Another problem is that countries sometimes have more than one official language: a decision must then be made as to what the most appropriate language is. In Malaysia and Singapore, for instance, consumer surveys regularly employ three languages (English, Malay and Chinese). An interviewer may need a command of several languages or dialects to undertake fieldwork. In Pakistan, the official language is Urdu, but most of the official work in government departments is done in English. However, most local nationals who understand English also usually understand Urdu. There is also a particular segment of social class in the country which prefers English to Urdu in their daily routines. Should the researcher use English or Urdu?

The literal translation of a questionnaire can pose problems. A different language is not just a matter of different spellings but of different linguistic concepts. This is why translation agencies recommend back translation into the original language. This identifies and corrects many of the problems faced in simple translation. The technique of 'decentring' in translation, where the material is translated and retranslated each time by a different translator, also minimizes mistakes being made.

## Sample frame

The problems of obtaining valid sampling frames tend to be more complicated in researching international markets. It might be difficult or even impossible to obtain a reliable sampling frame. Due to problems associated with the validity and reliability of secondary data in some countries, experience and judgement need to play an important part in constructing the sample where there is no reliable database. It may mean that accepted techniques of marketing research in developed countries cannot always be directly transferred, even to other developed countries where data might have to be collected through less formalized methods. This applies especially in countries lacking a marketing infrastructure where, unless sufficient care is taken in selecting the sampling frame, the sample chosen will invariably be distorted.

## Fieldwork

**Interviewee bias**   The major problems in fieldwork are errors caused through bias in the interviewing stage of the process. These can mean that reliable multi-country studies where results can be compared and contrasted across different countries are sometimes difficult to achieve.

Different cultures will produce a varied response to interviews or questionnaires. For example, purchase intentions for new products frequently peak in Italy because Italians have a propensity to over-claim their likelihood to buy, whereas German results are much closer to reality. If Germans say they will buy a product they probably will.

Another problem is that in some countries it is not possible for the female members of a household to respond personally to a survey. In such countries, mail or online surveys for researching the female market might obtain a much better rate of response.

In some countries, the rate of response of a particular segment of society might be quite low due to tax evasion problems, with respondents unwilling to provide any information which gives an idea of their economic status. Even within the same country, different social classes of customers could have differing responses to marketing research techniques. In some cultures, the respondent may cause bias by attempting to please the interviewer and give the answers they think they want to hear. This happened to BSN in Japan. The BSN French conglomerate carried out a study in Japan to find out people's attitudes to yogurt. The results indicated that the Japanese were becoming much more westernized in their food and eating habits and that there was a potential market for yogurts. BSN launched their products, set up distribution and invested heavily in promotion. However, the sales were disappointing. Follow-up research showed that the questions used in the original research were too simplistic to elicit accurate responses. The Japanese were far too polite to reply NO to a question. Therefore the responses to yes/no questions were highly misleading. Likewise, they did not wish to offend westerners by criticizing the usage of a spoon as an eating implement.

**Interviewer bias**   Interviewer biases are often due to communication problems between the interviewer and respondents. Several biases have been identified in multicultural research, including rudeness bias, 'I can answer any question' bias, courtesy bias, sucker bias, hidden premises bias, reticence–loquaciousness bias, social desirability bias, status difference bias, racial difference bias and individual group opinion bias (Malhotra *et al.* 2013).

Extensive training and close supervision of the interviewers and other field staff may be required to minimize these biases.

The selection, training, supervision and evaluation of fieldworkers are critical in multi-country research. Local fieldwork agencies are unavailable in many countries. It may be necessary, therefore, to recruit and train local fieldworkers or import trained foreign workers. The use of local fieldworkers is desirable as they are familiar with the local language and culture. They can thus create an appropriate climate for the interview and be sensitive to the concerns of the respondents.

**Data analysis**   A number of issues need to be considered at the data analysis stage. First, in preparing data for analysis in multi-country or cross-cultural studies, how do you deal with 'outliers'? These are countries where the data is quite obviously different from the bulk of the data. It may not be a problem at all but, likewise, it could be due to some cultural bias, a problem in the sampling or a problem of translation in the questionnaire.

Second is the issue of how to ensure comparability of data across cultures. Some researchers prefer to standardize data to ensure comparability. In contrast, others prefer statistics based on non-standardized data on the basis that this allows a truer comparative analysis.

Consumers share personal information online through sites like Facebook, Pinterest and LinkedIn. Companies are using these networking sites as a means of promoting to their customer base but also comparing how different consumers respond, reply and engage across cultures. This gives organizations the opportunity to analyze consumption patterns, examine behavioural targeting, do cost-effective online product testing and build direct contact with the consumer to access a plethora of information. Illustration 4.5 shows how organizations gather research data with fans across the world.

## Report preparation and presentation

In any research study there is the chance of cultural bias in the research findings. International research often involves researchers from one cultural environment conducting research in another cultural environment, or communicating with researchers from another cultural environment. In international research situations, effective communication between the respondents and the researcher is essential to avoid problems of misinterpretation of the data. The phenomenon of cultural self-reference criteria is cited as a possible cause of the misinterpretation of data and can lead to a systematic bias in the findings. The reader is referred to the discussion in Chapter 3 on the steps that can be taken to remedy self-reference criteria.

Some agencies follow the practice of always ensuring foreign market studies are written in the local language and include interpretation as well as analysis. The nuance can then be discussed with the translator.

Face-to-face debriefings with agencies and researchers are also a good way to synthesize the results from multi-country surveys. In this way, they can form coherent conclusions through open discussions with representatives who have participated in the research across a range of countries.

**Continuous research**   In this chapter, in order to discuss the relevant issues in a logical manner, we have used the six-step research design framework. It is perhaps important to stress, however, that international market research, while expensive, is by no means a 'one-off' activity. In today's dynamic environment where changes occur almost on a daily basis in some rapidly growing markets (e.g. India and China), it is important that research be on a continuous basis to ensure a company keeps ahead of its competition.

## ILLUSTRATION 4.5

# The use of social networks to understand global consumer opinion

It is clear that businesses are encouraging consumers to spread positive messages about their business when on Facebook, Twitter, Instagram and, of course, through blogs. What international businesses often do not do is engage directly with consumers and ask for feedback and opinions. In fact, many organizations do not have a social media space specifically allocated for customer feedback. Even fewer businesses have strategic aims and objectives to gather feedback and opinions from their online community. This is despite thousands of dollars or euros being spent on focus groups and discussions with their 'offline' community.

One global organization that does understand the value of their consumer feedback and opinions is Starbucks. With over 38 million likes on Facebook, they must be doing something that is working.

MyStarbucksIdea.force.com is a dedicated web-based feedback, share and vote page. Starbucks' global community is encouraged to suggest new ideas and share opinions that are not only read by 'other fans' but are regarded as valuable, insightful and timely feedback from consumers. The suggestions include ideas and opinions such as 'free gift cards' for loyal Facebook likers to opinions about gluten-free food or recommendations for more recycling ideas. New product development ideas about coffee and espresso account for over 44 500 suggestions. Over 14 000 experience ideas are posted encouraging Starbucks to enable local artists to display their paintings, and thousands of involvement ideas suggest loyalty cards should 'go global' for use by frequent, overseas travellers.

## Question

1 Identify the main advantages and disadvantages of using social networks to understand consumers in global markets.

**Reference:** IFF Research, http://www.iffresearch.com

## SUMMARY

- In this chapter we have examined the three main roles of the international marketing researcher: scanning international markets, building up market profiles and carrying out primary research across global markets. The rise of the Internet has impacted critically on the role of international market research. It has led to the development of better decision tools and globally-based research supplier networks and global databases.

- International research is, in many cases, a complex, expensive and time-consuming task. Evidence suggests that for these reasons many international firms fail to research markets to the extent that is really necessary. The consequences of this are significant in terms of both missed opportunities and the failure to meet existing and developing market demand.

- The issues relevant to the identifying and analyzing of opportunities across the globe were discussed. The problems involved in categorizing and segmenting international markets were identified. Several models used in the segmentation process of international markets were presented.

- Within this chapter, we illustrated the strategic importance of opportunity analysis and the contribution that market research can make to the decision-making process.

- In examining the international marketing research process the six-step research design framework was used. It was suggested that many international marketing efforts fail not because research was not conducted, but because the issue of comparability was not adequately addressed in defining the marketing research problem. The importance of self-reference criteria (SRC) was discussed and at each of the six stages the relevant issues for the international marketer highlighted.

## KEYWORDS

| | | |
|---|---|---|
| marketing research | latent markets | online databases |
| research process | incipient markets | websites |
| research question | comparative research | secondary data |
| gigabyte | market segmentation | primary data |
| terabyte | Pareto law | omnibus studies |
| exabyte | differentiated marketing | omnibus surveys |
| zettabyte | transnational segmentation | multi-country study |
| marketing information | global segments | qualitative research |
| existing markets | market profile analysis | cross-cultural research |

CASE STUDY 1

## Global brands use of big data

The term 'big data' refers to 'extremely large sets of digital data that may be analyzed to reveal patterns, trends and associations relating to human behaviour and interactions' (icas.com).

Worldwide companies use big data to gain competitive advantage by acquiring a higher understanding of the market through this information.

According to Ajit Sivadasanod of Lenovo, 'Some of the clear and straightforward application of Data and Social Digital Marketing concepts that are becoming mainstream include concepts like Segmentation and Predictive selling, Behavioral Marketing, Social Monitoring for large scale trends and pulling out specific messages and insights. Leveraging machine level data helps to optimize marketing spend in real time to ensure better efficiency and efficacy for brand campaigns, establishing and working through concepts like

Life Time Value of Customers, Real time analysis of 4P execution (Place, Promotion, Price and Product) in a dynamic environment, Brand Benchmarking across Social platforms to name a few.'

There are a number of examples of companies leveraging machine level data to build a competitive position in international markets.

One of these companies is Vodafone, which uses big data to gain a global picture of the market through social media posts and internet history. It hopes to use this information to create more relevant marketing strategies for its customers and become more successful as a global wireless carrier.

Computer maker Dell is trying to create more personally relevant offers and deals for its customers by connecting transaction records with social media data such as user names and email addresses. It has doubled the accuracy with which it can identify respondents to its promotions from 33 to 66 per cent through using big data.

Amazon, the online retailer, has used the large volumes of data it accesses through its customers' accounts to improve customer relations, which has led to a strong customer service record. Other big companies often do not realize the potential of big data by using it in this way, focusing on the creation of advertising algorithms instead.

Netflix has branched out into producing original films and TV series for its own streaming service by using the data it collects through its customers. It also uses customers' preferences to buy the rights to box sets of certain series and films which will be popular among certain groups of customers. Its use of big data has allowed it to be internationally successful.

An example of this tactic is Netflix's recent commissioning of four new Adam Sandler films. Despite the actor's lack of popularity among US and UK audiences, his films have proven very popular among viewers from Latin America. Netflix only knows this through its extensive use of data and analytics.

## Questions

**1** Critically evaluate the impact of the use of big data in researching international markets.

**2** How can a company researching global opportunities best use big data to better understand its international markets?

**3** What are the risks to a company being over-reliant on the use of big data to search out opportunities?

**Sources:** Ajit Sivadasanod, VP/GM, Lenovo Corporation, Big Data Lessons for Global Brands: www.juniper-networks; www.teradata.com/data-points/; www.icas.com/ca-today-news (accessed 5 March 2018).

## CASE STUDY 2

# Cultural segmentation map

We have been exploring the social and cultural considerations that organizations who want to grow internationally must research. We have also reviewed databases that supply a wealth of information about the business world, be it B2B, global or international. Further, there are many secondary research databases which show the complex range of influences that guide consumers to behave, purchase and express themselves. A constant, year-on-year review of these databases is essential as the world has changed dramatically over the last 30 years and continues to change at a rapid rate. This change is brought on by social, legal, economic, political, technological and sustainability (SLEPTS) transformations which, in turn, provide new opportunities for businesses.

At the heart of any business is the consumer. Therefore, to research the growth in populations, merging cultures, migration and the fact that millions of consumers may all be viewing one social media space – at the same time – makes it a top priority for marketers. Therefore, it is crucial that marketers review existing research databases that show how consumers' behavioural, cultural priorities and aspirations can change over time.

One database, the World Values Survey (WVS), enables marketers to review a cultural map of people's views and beliefs from 100 countries. Such a high number of countries researched means countries from the very poor to the very rich are included. The map shows there are two cross-cultural variations that are distinguished by different deep-set values. The values shown vertically are **Traditional values** versus **Secular rational values** and on the horizontal axis there are **Survival values** versus **Self-expression values**.

**Traditional values** are shown where citizens consider religion and the family to be important. The parent/child relationship is very strong and there is great respect for authority figures.

Citizens from **secular-rational value** countries have very different beliefs and values to the traditional value dimensions. Citizens in secular-rational values tend to be less religious, live on a more level basis with authority figures and accept that civil partnerships, divorce and abortion are part of their society's way. Data collected through the WVS shows that 84 per cent of Zimbabwean citizens consider religion to be a very important aspect in their life. In Romania, 51 per cent of people think that religion is very important, whereas only 8 per cent of Swedish people think that way. This shows that citizens of Zimbabwe have high traditional values and Sweden has high secular-rational values.

The values shown on the horizontal axis consider the different dimensions of **survival values** against **self-expression values**. As the name implies, people who think survival values are important need personal physical security, money and economic survival. However, self-expression values needs go beyond survival and include equal rights for men and women and the protection of environments so that future generations can enjoy them. The WVS collects data asking citizens from Jordan and the Netherlands to consider the following scenario: 'If jobs were scarce would they agree that a man should have the job rather than a woman?' Just 7 per cent of citizens from the Netherlands agreed with this scenario; however, 81 per cent of people from

FIGURE 4.6   Cultural segmentation map

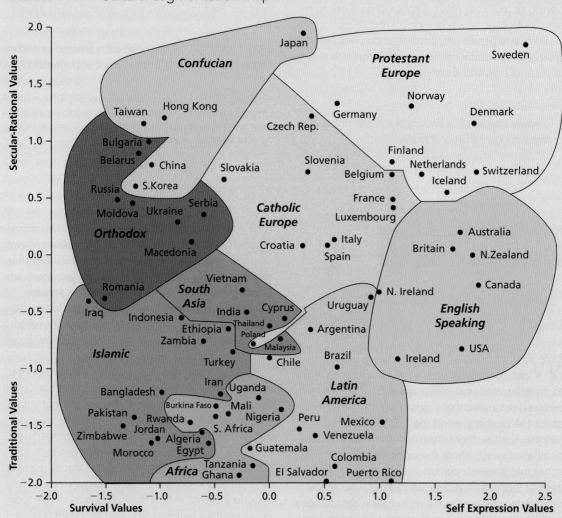

Jordan agreed that men should have more rights to a job if jobs were scarce. Self-expression countries such as the Netherlands believe in equal rights, whereas people from Jordan or other survival countries are less inclined to believe in equal rights for men and women.

These are just some examples of the data collected from thousands of people around the world. To understand the beliefs and values of people the world over, WVS asks many questions. These range from those about leisure time to politics, membership of charitable organizations to confidence in their government, and whether they are a nervous or imaginative person. WVS even asks people questions about the quality of air and roads in their hometown.

## Questions

1 In what ways can knowing the beliefs, values and motivations of people throughout the world help marketers?

2 How could marketers use the knowledge gained from the WVS to decide which country their organization should develop business relations with?

3 There are many reasons why it is important for marketers to know whether citizens of a country have traditional values or secular rational values. What are they?

**Source:** World Values Survey, www.worldvaluessurvey.org

# DISCUSSION QUESTIONS

**1** What are the problems in carrying out multi-country studies? As an international market researcher, how would you avoid these dangers?

**2** Many companies are looking to emerging markets in their internationalization programmes. What are the problems in researching these markets? How, if at all, may they be overcome?

**3** Identify the principal methods that companies might use in assessing and reviewing opportunities across international markets. Suggest the

alternative means by which firms can prioritize and segment international markets.

**4** As firms become more global so does their requirement to gather global information. Outline the key categories of a global information system and explain their relevance.

**5** Citing specific examples, show how the spread of the Internet has impacted on international market research. What are the problems and limitations of using web-based research?

# REFERENCES

1. Babin, B.J. and Zikmund, W.G. (2016) *Essentials of Marketing Research*, 6th edition. Cengage Learning.
2. Brislin, R.W. (2001) *Understanding Cultures' Influence on Behaviour*, 2nd edition. Harcourt.
3. Campbell, D., Edgar, D. and Stonehouse, G. (2011) *Business Strategy: An Introduction*. Palgrave.
4. *The Economist* (2018) India's Missing Middle Classes. www.economist.com.
5. eMarketer (2018) Worldwide Retail and Ecommerce Sales: eMarketer's Updated Forecast and New Mcommerce Estimates for 2016–2021 Available from: www.emarketer.com/Report/Worldwide-Retail-Ecommerce-Sales-eMarketers-Updated-Forecast-New-Mcommerce-Estimates-20162021/2002182 (accessed 15 February 2018).
6. Gabrisch, H., Hanzl-Weiss, D., Holzner, M., Landesmann, M., Pöschl, J. and Vidovic, H. (2016) *Improving Competitiveness in the Balkan Region–Opportunities and Limits*. Available from https://wiiw.ac.at/improving-competitiveness-in-the-balkan-region--opportunities-and-limits-dlp-3917.pdf (accessed 14 February 2018).
7. Goes, P.B. (2014) Big Data and IS Research. *MIS Quarterly* 38(3), iii–viii.
8. The Grameen Foundation www.grameenfoundation.org/ (accessed 5 June 2018).
9. Gravetter, F.J. and Forzano, L.-A.B. (2019) *Research Methods for the Behavioral Sciences*, 6th edition. Cengage.
10. GSMA (2014) The Mobile Economy Sub-Saharan Africa 2014. Accessed at www.gsmamobileeconomyafrica.com/GSMA_ME_SubSaharanAfrica_Web_Singles.pdf (accessed 7 October 2015).
11. Harrell, G.D. and Keifer, R.D. (1993) Multinational market portfolio in global strategy development. *International Marketing Review* 10(1).
12. Hassan, S.S. and Stephen, H.C.T. (2005) Linking global market segmentation decisions with strategic positioning options. *Journal of Consumer Marketing* 22(2), 81–89.
13. Howard-Jones, P., Holscher, J. and Radicic, D. (2018) Firm productivity in the Western Balkans: The impact of European Union membership and access to finance. *Economic Annals* 62(215), 7–51.
14. KPMG (2017) The truth about online consumers 2017 Global Online Consumer Report. Available from https://home.kpmg.com/xx/en/home/insights/2017/01/the-truth-about-online-consumers.html (accessed 5 June 2018).
15. Lichy, J., Kachour, M. and Khvatova, T. (2017) Big Data is watching YOU: Opportunities and challenges from the perspective of young adult consumers in Russia. *Journal of Marketing Management* 33(9–10), 719–741.
16. Madison, R. (2017) Standing out in a crowd: How innovating and networking helped grow a small business. *Utah Business* 10, 38.
17. Malhotra, N.K., Birks, D.F. and Wills, P. (2013) *Essentials of Marketing Research*. Pearson.
18. Merza, A., Laetitia, R., Becker, C. and Zheng, X. (2014) Working on socio-cultural dynamics and customers' segmentation from local to global: An application case on well-being, health and Generation Z. *ESOMAR Asia Pacific*, Jakarta, May 2014.
19. Papadopoulos, N. and Martín Martín, O. (2011) International market selection and segmentation: Perspectives and challenges. *International Marketing Review* 28(2), 132–149.
20. Rossi, M.C., Sansone, D., Torricelli, C. and van Soest, A. (2018) *Household Preferences for Socially Responsible Investments* (No. 18021). Universita di Modena e Reggio Emilia, Dipartimento di Economia' Marco Biagi'.
21. Sheth, J. and Arma, A. (2005) International e-marketing: Opportunities and issues. *International Marketing Review* 22(6), 611–622.
22. Sivadasanod, A. VP/GM, Lenovo Corporation, Big Data Lessons for Global Brands: www.juniper-networks.
23. Terpstra, V., Foley, J. and Sarathy, R. (2012) *International Marketing*. Naper Press.
24. World Bank (2018) Tariff rate, applied, weighted mean, all products (per cent). Available from: https://data.worldbank.org/indicator/TM.TAX.MRCH.WM.AR.ZS (accessed 13 February 2018).
25. World Economic Forum (2014) *The Global Competitiveness Report 2014–2015*. Available from www3.weforum.org /docs/WEF_GlobalCompetitivenessReport_2014-15.pdf (accessed 2 February 2015).

# DIRECTED STUDY ACTIVITIES

## An introduction

Successful international marketing is about taking a planned approach to analysis, strategy development and implementation. The chapters of this book focus upon providing the underpinning knowledge to support the process of planning an international marketing strategy. The purpose of the three directed study activities at the end of each of the three parts of the book is to integrate the four chapters that make up each of the parts. More importantly, however, is that as a whole, the three activities provide a framework for planning an international marketing strategy and give the opportunity for readers to consider the practical issues involved in developing, planning and implementing an outline international marketing strategy.

## Learning objectives

On completing the three integrated learning activities you should be able to:

- Analyze critically the international marketing environment of a given company situation.

- Apply relevant concepts and models to each of the development stages of an international marketing strategy.

- Make clear links between analysis and the chosen response. The issues identified in the analysis should lead directly to the development and implementation of a strategy.

- Develop a realistic and cohesive international marketing strategy.

The aims of the directed study activities (DSAs) therefore are much wider in scope than the short case studies found at the end of each chapter. The objective is to provide a vehicle through which the reader is able to develop practical skills in research, analysis, evaluation and strategy development. In completing these activities you will need to synthesize the various strands and themes explored throughout the book and apply them to a practical situation. To complete each of the activities you must move well beyond the boundaries of the textbook, researching new material and exploring the interplay of the concepts discussed in the text and possible solutions to the practical problems identified in each activity.

Each DSA depicts very different scenarios.

*Part 1*: We spotlight the rapid development of the mobile/cell phone services market in Africa and use this scenario as a backdrop for examining trading infrastructure issues, consumer behaviour and cultural issues and examine the development of a latent and exciting market.

*Part 2*: We identify a number of companies from emerging markets that are developing as global brands competing against entrenched western global players. How do such companies compete effectively against existing global competitors, and how can they ensure they build a sustainable competitive advantage?

*Part 3*: In each of the activities a series of questions is posed, together with suggestions on how to get started, a framework depicting the key factors to consider in completing the task, and suggested websites you may find useful.

Additional observations are also made that will assist you in addressing the key issues and how you could develop the activity further.

In all the activities we have provided only outline information on the scenarios. A key skill in international marketing is *finding* information about international markets, analyzing it, deciding what is most important and preparing a structured, logical rationale for the decisions that must ultimately be made. In each activity, therefore, you will need to seek information outside of the case to complete the task. Much of the information you can use is available online. You should not have to approach staff in the organizations depicted for further information to complete the task.

# INTERNATIONAL MARKETING PLANNING: ANALYSIS

## Introduction

In this activity we explore the development of the mobile/cell phone services' market in Africa and the attendant challenges and opportunities faced in its development by companies trying to undertake a marketing strategy across the region to enable them to become globally competitive. We explore the international marketing opportunities and challenges companies face in this market.

The mobile/cell phone services' market in Africa, especially southern Africa, can be defined as a latent market with huge growth potential. However, there are huge challenges in terms of lack of infrastructure and the ability of many in the market to pay, which mean it is a highly challenging market. Anyone entering the market needs to develop a thorough understanding of the complexities of the African marketing environment in which they are competing and decide how to segment the market, which segment to target and how to develop a positioning strategy to achieve competitive leverage. Increasing global competition in this market necessitates greater innovation, not just in products and services, but in all aspects of the operation. To understand such issues we need to build the skills to research, analyze and evaluate how such factors impact international strategy development. We hope the reader will develop these skills in this activity.

## Learning objectives

On completing this activity you should be able to:

- Identify and analyze international market opportunities and challenges
- Use appropriate conceptual frameworks to develop a market profile analysis
- Identify sources of information, methods of information collection and methods of information

analysis suitable for international marketing operations
- Understand the complexities of researching international markets and be able to identify possible solutions

## The scenario: market information

In a world where more people have access to mobile/cell phones than to flushing toilets, telecommunications operators in search of growth are naturally drawn to countries where phone usage is still low. Yet fixating on so-called penetration rates – the number of mobile/cell subscribers as a percentage of the population – can be a mistake. For example, the Egyptian operator Orascom entered what, on that measure, was the ultimate growth market, North Korea. Two years later, the mobile/cell penetration rate there was still barely above 0 per cent.

Operators have had better luck in Africa. Penetration across the continent will reach 50 per cent of subscribers by 2020 from 2 per cent in the late 2000s. Africa is in the grip of a mobile/cell phone revolution. In the past 15 years, subscribers in sub-Saharan Africa have risen from 72 000 to 329 million (GSMA 2014). While many rural villagers huddle around paraffin lamps as darkness falls, neon lights come to life as they illuminate the mobile/cell phone masts proliferating across the African landscape.

According to Mobile Africa, the number of mobile/cell phone subscriptions far exceeds fixed-line subscriptions. The International Telecommunication Union reckons that more Africans have begun using phones since the late 2000s than in the whole of the previous century! Use of mobile/cell phones is increasing at an annual rate of 7 per cent, more than twice the global average.

At the end of the 2000s, Africa was dubbed 'the hopeless continent'. Since then its progress has been remarkably hopeful. Thanks to rising living standards, the middle class in Africa has tripled since the late 1980s, and the continent's working-age population will double from 500 million today to 1.1 billion in 2040.

Africa's annual output is growing by approximately 5 per cent (adjusted for purchasing power parity), twice as fast as in the period from the mid-2000s and faster than the global average. Foreign direct investment to the region increased from US$10 billion to US$88 billion – more than India (US$42 billion) and, even more remarkably, catching up with China (US$108 billion). The Boston Consulting Group notes that the revenues of Africa's 500 largest companies (excluding banks) have grown at an average of 8.3 per cent a year since the late 2000s.

Consumer goods companies ranging from western giants such as Procter & Gamble to emerging market car companies such as China's Great Wall and India's Tata Motors are pouring into Africa. Foreign firms are starting to use Africa as a base for manufacturing as well, as labour costs in India and China rise.

The mobile/cell phone market has been an integral part of this growth.

In Africa, average penetration of mobile/cell phones stands at nearly half the population, and in North Africa it is almost two-thirds. Gabon, the Seychelles and South Africa now boast almost 100 per cent penetration. Only five African countries – Burundi, Djibouti, Eritrea, Ethiopia and Somalia – still have a penetration rate of less than 25 per 100 inhabitants.

Uganda, the first African country to have more mobiles/cells than fixed telephones, is cited as an example of cultural and economic transformation. Penetration has risen from 0.2 per cent in the late 2000s to 30 per cent now, with operators making huge investments in infrastructure, particularly in rural areas. Given their low incomes, only about a quarter of Ugandans have a mobile/cell subscription, but street vendors offer mobile/cell access on a per-call basis. They also invite those without access to electricity to charge their phones using car batteries.

Popular mobile services include money transfers, allowing people without bank accounts to send money by text message. Many farmers use mobiles/cells to trade and check market prices.

## Company information

Companies continue to invest heavily in this market. Forecasts suggest around US$100 billion will be invested by companies such as France Telecom and Bharti Airtel who paid US$10 billion for a group of African mobile/cell companies and recently acquired Zain Africa. Bharti, India's largest mobile/cell phone company, is aiming to more than double the number of mobile/cell phone users in Africa. In Africa it intends to pursue the low-cost outsourced business model of operations that has served it so well at home.

The Indian operator segments Africa by language and has divided its operations in Africa into three separate divisions to meet their needs. These divisions include Bharti Anglophone (comprising the English-speaking nations – Ghana, Kenya, Malawi, Sierra Leone, Tanzania, Uganda, Zambia), Bharti Francophone (comprising the French speaking nations – Burkina Faso, DRC, Chad, Congo B, Madagascar, Niger, Gabon), while Nigeria, the continent's largest market, will be a separate unit.

There are also a number of strong more local brands such as Essar Telecom, which offers services under the 'Yu' brand in Kenya. However, others such as Warid have been acquired by Bharti Airtel as industry consolidation takes place.

## Internet technologies

Mobile Internet technologies play a very important role in making Internet services available to many in Africa. Africans are using them for more than calling their friends and family. Many are using them to do their banking. About half a million South Africans now use their mobile/cell phones as a bank. For these new banking customers both the mobile/cell phone and the whole system of banking are new to them.

Besides sending money to relatives and paying for goods, they check balances, buy mobile/cell airtime and settle utility bills. Traditional banks offer mobile banking as an added service to existing customers, most of whom are quite well off. Wizzit, and to some extent First National Bank (FNB) and MTN Banking, are chasing another market: the 16 million South Africans, over half of the adult population, with no bank account. Significantly, 30 per cent of these people do have mobile/cell phones. Previously ignored as the bottom of the pyramid and of little commercial importance to the large corporations, such customers are now being courted. Wizzit hired and trained over 2000 unemployed people, known as Wizzkids, to drum up business. It worked: eight out of ten Wizzit customers previously had no bank account and had never used an ATM.

People using advanced technology to manage their finances had until now depended on the archaic system of barter. They have leapfrogged telephony technology and jumped from dealing only in cash or barter to the world of cellular finance. A simplified kind of account called Mzansi has been launched to reach the non-banking customers, and portable banks and ATMs have been rolled out in townships and in the countryside.

In most of Africa, only a fraction of people have bank accounts – but there is huge demand for cheap and convenient ways to send money and buy prepaid services such as airtime. In Kenya, a pilot scheme called M-Pesa is being used to disburse and pay micro-loans by phone. Meanwhile Celpay is offering platforms for banks and phone companies in Zambia and Congo. In countries like Somalia, with chaotic conditions, cash transfers by phone will be a bonus.

By clicking a few keys on a mobile/cell phone, money can be zapped from one part of Kenya to another in seconds. For urban migrants sending money home to their villages, and for people used to queuing at banks for hours to pay bills or school fees, the M-Pesa money-transfer service, operated by Safaricom, Kenya's largest mobile/cell operator, is a godsend. It is used by 17 million people, or over half the population, and transfers the equivalent of almost 50 per cent of Kenya's GDP each year. The most ambitious is Africa's biggest operator, MTN, which is rolling out mobile-money schemes in several African countries. Together with five other providers, it has opened up the Ugandan market where users of the service have increased from 10 000 in the late 2000s to 19 million now.

## Market challenges

There are many difficulties on the way. Not all potential consumers are ready to make the leap. Many think banking is too expensive and complicated, and helping new customers become financially literate takes time. The technology remains a problem in some cases, with downloads requiring dozens of text messages. Several rival platforms are still in the fight. But so far those that emphasize simplicity and ease-of-use over state-of-the-art technology and security have made the greatest strides. A lot also hangs on putting the right laws and regulations in place. They need to be tight enough to protect vulnerable users and discourage money laundering, but open enough to allow innovative mobile banking to grow.

However, the main barrier to further expansion remains the cumbersome regulatory frameworks. Countries with similar economic circumstances but with a liberalized market generally show higher penetration rates. Taxes can also act as a barrier, particularly import duties on handsets or special mobile communications surcharges. The mobile industry has been seen as a cash cow by governments in some countries who have used its popularity to generate tax revenues but have not invested in the infrastructure for its growth. To expand coverage into rural and remote areas, government support will be required.

Rural areas in some countries are also often economically unattractive for operators to invest in. This is usually not due to a lack of demand but rather to a lack of basic infrastructure. The roads in Africa can be notorious, the infrastructure underdeveloped and the continent has more than its fair share of conflicts and crises.

The cost of making calls and sending texts in Africa is also relatively high and many of its countries are poor. In South Africa and Kenya, running a mobile/cell phone costs the average user 5 per cent of a monthly income. Yet in countries such as Malawi and Central African Republic, average monthly mobile/cell costs are as much as 50 per cent of average monthly earnings. Big chunks of some markets remain unreachable because of this.

A 'digital divide' also persists in terms of Internet access, but this is changing too as Internet penetration has passed 20 per cent in Africa. Because of the lack of availability of fixed lines, mobile broadband accounts for 90 per cent of Internet subscriptions and so Internet access in Africa is much more dependent on the penetration of smartphones.

## References

www.reuters.com

www.bbc.co.uk/news

www.timesofindia.indiatimes.com

www.economist.com

www.guardian.co.uk

GSMA (2014) The Mobile Economy Sub-Saharan Africa 2014. Accessed at www.gsmamobileeconomyafrica.com/GSMA_ME_SubSaharanAfrica_Web_Singles.pdf (accessed 7 October 2015).

## The task

1 Analyze and evaluate the major environmental influences that will impact on the growth of the mobile/cell phone services market.

2 Building on the results of your analysis from Question 1, and with reference to a company of your choice, draw up a market profile analysis for the area.

3 Propose and justify an effective segmentation strategy of the African market that will form the basis on which a company of your choice can build a regional marketing strategy. This should form the basis on which the company you have chosen can enter and develop the market.

**4** For the company referred to in Question 2, show how the company should develop some of the segments identified. In doing so, you will need to fully appraise them of the challenges and problems they will face and how they should respond to these challenges.

## Useful websites

www.southafrica.net

www.allafrica.com

www.gamos.org

www.bbc.co.uk/news

www.globaldashboard.org

www.wto.org

www.ita.doc.gov/tradestats

www.worldbank.com

www.foreign-trade.com

## Getting started

In international markets it is exceedingly difficult to obtain a comprehensive understanding of the relevant market environment. Africa is particularly difficult due to the scarcity of reliable data. In tackling the task it is useful to categorize the elements of the environment into social and cultural, legal, economic, political and technological forces (SLEPT).

In the increasingly global marketplace, companies are trying to identify methodologies for segmenting and evaluating international markets that transcend national and cultural boundaries. You are asked to develop a segmentation strategy. It is important here to remember that simply segmenting the market on a geographical basis will be too simplistic and not form a basis on which the company can build a regional strategy. You will need a hierarchical approach where your segmentation strategy has several steps and can incorporate the multidimensional aspects of a global niche segment.

It is important in building a market profile analysis to develop a systematic method for building up market information on the markets you have prioritized. The 12C framework is a useful tool when developing profiles of international markets. Finally, you need to think through the implications of your research and consider the issues the analysis has highlighted and the implications for developing a strategy. Of particular importance, examine these issues in the light of possible resources/cultural/management constraints that the company you choose may face.

In summary, therefore, the framework shown in Table I provides a guide to the key factors that need to be considered in tackling the task identified.

## The way forward

After reading Part II of this textbook you may wish to return to plan the next stage of your strategy. The most important issue is deciding how quickly the firm should develop internationally and how – country by country, concentrating on a particular segment or seeking a regional presence distribution. You should define a strategy that builds upon the firm's competitive advantage, identifying a positioning strategy that meets the needs of the target segment you have chosen. Then you should identify the criteria that will determine the choice of market entry.

After reading Part III you will be in a position to define the implementation plan and make decisions on the marketing mix elements, relationship building and supply chain management. You can identify how management and technology systems might support the international expansion. Finally, you will be able to identify the monitoring and control systems that will be used.

Table I   Key factors to consider

| The element of the plan | Some concepts, models and issues to be addressed |
| --- | --- |
| Environment | • The global SLEPT factors, including political and economic issues and socio-cultural factors affecting the opportunities for the firm<br><br>• The changing global trends in competition and customer expectations that impact on business<br><br>• The international challenges to be met |
| Home and possible international markets | • The level of market development and competitive structures<br><br>• Prioritization of markets using country attractiveness and latent assessment of markets<br><br>• Commercial, home, host country stakeholder expectations and ethical issues |
| Company capability | • SWOT, competitive advantage<br><br>• Products: international product life cycle, knowledge and capability |
| Segmentation | • Basis of segmentation/criteria for global segmentation/global niche possibilities<br><br>• Hierarchy of segmentation |
| Market information | • Market profile analysis and the information systems, data collection and management to support it<br><br>• Market and environmental risk and potential commercial opportunity using the 12C framework |
| Strategic options | • Potential strategic alternatives for the company<br><br>• The challenges faced and potential responses to the issues identified in the analysis<br><br>• The resource constraints |

## AIMS AND OBJECTIVES

Having identified and analyzed the opportunities that exist within international markets in the first section of the book, we now turn our attention to the ways in which firms can use international marketing to develop their international business in order to exploit these opportunities profitably. The focus in Part II is on developing an international marketing strategy that is appropriate for the firm, given the environment and market context in which it is working, the firm's capability and the ambition of its management. Throughout the section we emphasize the importance of the mindset of the management of the firm in planning their international marketing. We also take decisive action to deal with the challenges posed by the business and market context, analyzed in section 1.

The first chapter in Part II, Chapter 5, concentrates on the international marketing strategies of small- and medium-sized enterprises. The discussion ranges from firms taking their first steps into international markets or marketing, to international customers from their home base, to those dynamic small firms that have the ambition and capability to grow quickly to become the major global players of the future.

When we think of globalization it is the very largest firms in the world that come to mind. Chapter 6 is concerned with the global strategies of the firms that operate within a global context and build brands that are instantly recognizable. Their global strategies aim to appeal to customers worldwide and ensure that as many customers as possible choose their products and services.

For any firm moving into a new international market the key step is to decide which market entry method should be chosen in order to achieve the best outcome from the investment that is made.

In Chapter 7 we discuss the factors that firms must consider in selecting an appropriate market entry method.

In Chapter 8 we consider the product and service management strategy and focus upon the need to have a constantly evolving portfolio of products and services that meet the current and future needs of global customers.

# INTERNATIONAL NICHE MARKETING STRATEGIES FOR SMALL- AND MEDIUM-SIZED ENTERPRISES

## LEARNING OBJECTIVES

After reading this chapter you should be able to:

- Appreciate the nature and types of international marketing undertaken in the SME sector
- Compare the different strategic approaches and mindsets of SMEs in international marketing
- Understand the factors affecting SME international strategic management
- Identify the characteristics of the different stages of international development of SMEs
- Evaluate the factors for success and failure in SME international marketing

## INTRODUCTION

Small- and medium-sized enterprises (SMEs) have always been significant creators of wealth and employment in domestic economies, but are a less powerful force outside their home territory, usually because of their limited resources. Indeed, many SMEs, despite what may be obvious business capability, never move into international markets at all. However, for reasons which will be explored in this chapter, SMEs have growth potential, both in fast-growing business sectors that involve applying new technology, and in market niches where innovation in mature industry sectors can lead to new opportunities. In less developed markets entrepreneurs can play a vital role in countering poverty by creating new businesses to employ local people. The impact of these SMEs in regenerating the economy can increase considerably if they can gain access to international markets.

In this chapter we discuss the factors which influence the patterns of international development of SMEs, including the strategic options available to them and the particular problems they face in implementing their strategy. We also emphasize the different mindsets of SMEs needed to exploit their business situation.

The traditional model of SME internationalization is exporting, in which goods are manufactured in one country and transferred to buyers in other countries. But many SMEs are involved in a broader range of international marketing activity. It is for this reason we observe many international niche marketing companies. Small service providers generate revenue from customers in foreign markets by providing services from the home country which customers can access wherever they are situated (for example, information and advice supplied via the Internet). They can also provide services in the firm's home country and require the customers to visit (for example, tourism, training and education residential courses).

Increasingly, large firms are finding that operating on a global scale often makes them inflexible and unresponsive to fast-changing markets. This results in smaller, more entrepreneurial firms with an innovative idea competing globally in their chosen niche market. These types of organizations are known as *born globals*. To be successful, all these international market approaches require an understanding of the factors affecting international marketing and what capabilities are needed to grow the business internationally.

# The SME sector and its role within the global economy

A number of definitions of the SME sector exist, but the most commonly used terms relate to the number of employees in the company. The European Union (EU), for example, defines SMEs as those firms employing fewer than 250 staff. (Note: in the USA SME is defined as having fewer than 500 employees.) The EU's SME definition can be broken down further into small firms with fewer than 50 employees but more than 10 employees, and medium firms that equate to between 50 and 249 employees. These organizations are collectively known as SMEs. From time to time it is useful to include an even smaller unit enterprise – a micro-SME – that has fewer than 10 employees. Therefore, when discussing micro, small and medium enterprises – from fewer than 10 employees up to 249 – this chapter will use the acronym MSMEs.

This characterization effectively includes over 99 per cent of all SME enterprises in the EU 28 (as of 2017), which equates to around 67 per cent (or 93 million people) of the total number of people employed in EU countries. The percentage in total employment between European countries varies quite markedly. For example, in Greece it is 87 per cent, Cyprus 83 per cent, Finland 65 per cent and the UK 54 per cent (Muller *et al.* 2017) (Figures include the UK that left the EU in March 2019).

In this chapter, therefore, the review of smaller firm international strategies is not restricted to firms with a specific number of employees, but instead focuses on those issues that apply to businesses in general which have the mindset to think and act like SMEs. The reason for adopting this stance is that a garment-making firm with 250 employees has a very restricted capacity to internationalize. A 250-employee financial services or computer software company could be a significant international player. Many quite large companies take business decisions within a small group of major shareholders or senior managers in much the same way that the family owners of small firms take decisions. Many of the fastest-growing international firms grow rapidly through the 250 employee ceiling without making significant changes to their international strategic approach or management style. Our discussion, therefore, relates to issues affecting firms which could not be described as large multinational enterprises (MNEs) with the global power to dominate their sector. We do, however, consider some of the implications for firms growing from being SMEs to global players. Additionally, as outlined in Chapter 1, there are many SMEs that are born global, see Illustration 5.1. Yet while having a small number of employees, they are in fact micro-multinationals.

SMEs can be vulnerable to changes in the competitive environment and there are high failure rates. Because of globalization, the liberalization of trade policies and removal of protectionism and most trade barriers, virtually all firms are part of the global market. This is simply because their suppliers, customers and competitors are likely to be global players. In practice, however, many SMEs do remain focused on the domestic market, which may soon become over-supplied. This may be one reason why many firms fail to grow. Only a small percentage of SMEs, perhaps less than 5 per cent, grow significantly. An even smaller percentage have the ambition to become international traders.

Despite this, the SME sector is increasingly recognized as a creator of wealth and employment. In the last 20 years many large firms, conglomerates even, have periodically downsized by reducing their workforce, rationalizing their operations, returning to their core products and outsourcing their activities, often to smaller firms. Public sector organizations have also increased their outsourcing. In many countries this has left the SME sector as the only significant growing source of wealth and employment.

## ILLUSTRATION 5.1

# Born in Berlin, raised globally

**Born global** is a business concept where from inception an organization internationalizes from day one of operation. Born global businesses come in many shapes and sizes, from health care suppliers to music-downloading platforms. Technology and e-commerce have been the driving forces that have made 'born global' happen.

The phenomenon began in the 1990s as the Internet began to flourish. Already born global businesses can be subdivided into four distinct categories:

1. Import–export start
2. Multinational trader
3. Geographically focused start
4. Global start

The type of business that has always flourished in the born global world is the technology-driven company. Indeed, it is considered that Skype was one of the most well-known and well-used born global companies. Though now owned by Microsoft, Skype provided Internet access to millions of people that wanted to communicate face-to-face with family and friends around the world.

Another born global business that also wants to bring communities together is eyeem.com. It began in 2010 with four friends that say their company was 'Born in Berlin but raised all over the world'. The four co-founders had a passion and a drive. Their passion is photography and their desire is to share their photographs with brands and advertising agencies around the world. To do this they provide a platform where Creators upload their photographs to eyeem.com's photograph library. Creators can be passionate artists who are full-time photographers that want to showcase their photograph to brands and advertising agencies and receive an income from the photographs that are chosen. Eyeem.com was a global community from the start. Its platform brings together a community of like-minded Creators and brands or advertising agencies that need the best, most avant-garde and/or thought-provoking photographs. The community now has over 20 million Creators and it is growing and thriving. One of the reasons the community is growing is because eyeem.com provides regular tutorials on photographic styles, from using black and white to creating mood portraits, to 25 tips on taking photographs at night and landscapes. Another is the cutting-edge advice that Creatives receive regarding keywords, tags and captions. Each photograph uploaded to eyeem.com's library needs to be indexed with keywords and tags so that brands and advertising agencies can search the library for photographs specific to their needs.

Another exciting feature from eyeem.com is its Missions which are a way of directly connecting Creators to brands and advertising agencies. Brands and advertising agencies create a Mission to inspire an exciting and stimulating photography competition. Recently eyeem.com teamed up with Allianz, an insurance company. The Mission was to visualize the contrast between the old and the new in Italy's ancient capital and provide photographs of traditional Italy with the most modern technology, such as hover boards as transport or jetpacks used as elevators. The number of Creators that enter Mission competitions exceed thousands, often up to around 70 000 people.

## Questions

1 Eyeem.com is attempting to make a fantastic online library of stock photographs for brands and advertising agencies. What are the benefits of this library for Creatives?

2 Think of a brand that you like. Create a mission for www.eyeem.com's Creatives.

**Reference:** www.eyeem.com.

## The role of SME internationalization in economic regeneration

Encouraging entrepreneurship is seen by many experts and the European Commission as the route to future prosperity for emerging markets. It can be argued that growing the private business sector helps put money in people's pockets, increases domestic demand, generates tax revenues and reduces dependency on international aid. Indeed, there is considerable debate about the proportion of international aid that should be used for alleviating hunger, addressing basic health care and education, and improving a country's infrastructure, as opposed to supporting and promoting business creation and development.

In practice, however, it can be argued that it is those SMEs that trade internationally which are most important. SMEs that market their products and services in the domestic economy often grow at the expense of other domestic SMEs because of the relatively limited home market. However, export markets offer seemingly unlimited scope for SMEs to grow and have the effect of importing jobs and foreign currency, so creating wealth in the domestic economy. Of particular significance in less developed countries (LDCs), as we shall see in Chapter 7, SMEs exporting goods can be the first 'level' of international market entry strategies. This includes domestic purchasing in which the international customer purchases products from the emerging market SME in its home country. Examples would include a supermarket sourcing fruit or coffee, and shop chains sourcing coffee beans from African farmers. In Chapter 7 we discuss this in more detail.

## The challenges for SMEs from LDCs

Small organizations from emerging markets are often severely disadvantaged in international marketing. For example, small farmers from poor countries are frequently exploited by aggressive multinational retailers who ruthlessly use the global competition among small organizations. The poor negotiating position of the farmers and the perceived demand from consumers for low prices forces down the price paid to farmers. The price can be so low that it results in workers living below the poverty line. Although the multinational retailers sign up to ethical social corporate responsibility principles, many fail to behave ethically in their everyday transactions. There are many stories of unacceptable behaviour.

### Fairtrade and the protection of the interests of farmers
The Fairtrade organization (www.fairtrade.org) was developed to promote ethical consumption to both businesses that buy products from farmers and for consumers who choose brands that include the Fairtrade label. It is an independent consumer label which appears on products as an independent guarantee that disadvantaged producers in the developing world are getting a better deal, fair prices for their products and decent working conditions.

For a product to display the Fairtrade mark it must meet international Fairtrade standards. These standards are set by the international certification body Fairtrade Labelling Organizations International (FLO), which inspects and certifies them. They receive a minimum price that covers the cost of sustainable production and an extra premium that is invested in social or economic development projects. Fairtrade principles include:

- direct purchasing from producers
- transparent and long-term trading partnerships
- cooperation not competition
- agreed minimum prices to cover the costs of production, usually set higher than market minimums
- focus on development and technical assistance via the payment to suppliers of an agreed social premium (often 10 per cent or more of the cost price of goods)
- provision of market information, and
- sustainable and environmentally responsible production.

There are 1.65 million farmers and workers spread across more than 74 countries participating in Fairtrade (Fairtrade Foundation 2018). It is also good to see that the revenue generated from Fairtrade International products worldwide amounted to about €7.88 billion and is up year on year (Statista 2018).

There are arguments for and against the Fairtrade principles. The major argument against Fairtrade is that it acts as a kind of subsidy and creates artificially high prices which can then encourage the creation of surpluses. In practice, the key step is connecting the farmers with their distant markets, helping them to develop their market knowledge, build their export or processing capability, or to diversify to meet newly identified demand. Fairtrade provides examples including coffee growers developing citrus or macadamia nuts, banana farmers moving into other premium tropical produce, or investment in alternative income-generation projects such as ecotourism, as well as support for community health and education programmes. Illustration 5.2 presents a story of a Fairtrade cooperative to inspire others to reinvest in their local community.

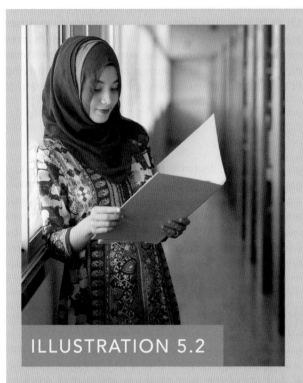

## ILLUSTRATION 5.2

## Women and food: production, control and collaboration

The women of Aceh, a rural part of Indonesia, have big dreams. Naturally, they want Fairtrade coffee farms to flourish and grow; what they also want is to be in charge of the decisions that are made for that to happen. In fact, many women, not just in Aceh, work on the land and produce around half the world's food. Often, however, the land they work on is controlled and owned by men, some of whom are their husbands.

The women of Aceh have got together and are beginning to disrupt this inequality. They felt they could not only produce coffee from the land but they had the confidence to grow the business further, despite the coffee business being a male-dominated environment. So they took action and formed the Aceh Fairtrade Cooperative, a group known as Koperasi Kopi Wanita Gayo (KKWG). Like many other women working on farms, they had to overcome the historic hurdle – could they own the land on which they wanted to grow their coffee beans? This meant the women had to approach their husbands and ask them to legally pass land ownership from husband to wife. Once this hurdle was overcome, the women gained more confidence. They were invited to training sessions exclusively for landowners, obviously something they had never been invited to before.

The training sessions further increased the KKWG members' enthusiasm and determination to become successful businesswomen. The Chair of KKWG went on to become an inspirational voice for many women in the region. At the same time, the women of the KKWG cooperative have not forgotten their caring and empathic organization. Therefore, they re-invested some of the money earned from the sale of their coffee beans into their local community. The KKWG cooperative invested in reproductive health and an ear, nose and throat clinic. It was noted that working alongside their husbands, as competitors, brought the community closer together through dialogue, as all parties shared ideas and inspired others.

### Questions

**1** How can the KKWG's story inspire others?

**2** KKWG would like to re-invest further in their local community. What would you recommend KKWG should re-invest in next year?

**Reference:** Fairtrade (2017) *Monitoring Report*. Available from: https://monitoringreport2016.fairtrade.net/en/ (accessed 5 June 2018).

**Infrastructure weaknesses**   The challenges for international marketers from emerging markets are huge. Many of the emerging countries have difficult geography and terrain with remote areas and an inhospitable climate. Many have a poorly developed infrastructure and suffer unreliable and often poor quality supplies of utilities, such as energy, water and power. Fixed line telecommunications and transport are slow and unreliable. Usually there is an overly bureaucratic and inefficient financial and business support infrastructure. The informal economy is huge in LDCs and, in addition, bribery and corruption are rife at all levels. War and terrorism can also have a devastating long-term effect on trade.

However, organizations from emerging markets can and do succeed in building their businesses despite these challenges if they can connect with their market and thus build the knowledge and capabilities to compete. For example, simply knowing what the actual international market price is for their products, rather than relying for price information on a buyer or a third party, is crucial. It can have a huge impact on the viability of a small organization. By enabling a real-time connection with international market information that bypasses incomplete, unreliable and out-of-date infrastructure, mobile computing could bring about the next 'industrial revolution'. It is also important for these SMEs to understand the value contributions of the supply chain. They also need to be able to identify changing customer demands and expectations, market trends, understand what quality standards are required and know how to meet them, and appreciate the power of branding to raise the perception of the products.

In countries that have a small, unsophisticated domestic market these issues may not be so significant. In international markets, however, the goods and services must compete with those from other countries, even though they may be cheaper or unique. This poses the problem of the customers' perceptions of the quality of their goods and service. What is acceptable in a local emerging market may not be acceptable to consumers in a developed country. While the obvious route to the international market is by becoming a contract manufacturer or grower, the Internet offers further potential. To address the imbalance in power between the supplier and major international customers, improved networking of small growers and manufacturers can help.

## Government support

We have explained the potential contribution of entrepreneurs and SMEs to the regeneration of national economies in terms of jobs and wealth creation through internationalization and the challenges they face. It is hardly surprising, therefore, that governments in developed and developing countries encourage SMEs to internationalize by running export promotion programmes providing support and advice.

Governments often provide support in the form of resources and advice but at significantly different levels. These range from help with documentation, comprehensive country market information, export credit guarantees, trade missions and, in some cases, target country representative offices. The Organization for Economic Cooperation and Development (OECD) is no longer just asking policymakers to determine what assistance might be useful in helping firms to become more marketing- and customer-focused (Cusmano *et al.* 2018). It also promotes policies that will improve not only the economic but also the social wellbeing of people around the world.

The OECD is a central forum to support government policymakers and help facilitate agreement over a range of issues, including reducing bribery and corruption, improving corporate social responsibility and forging ahead with ways to improve international standards and ways of doing business. The OECD is also committed to improving the lives of all by ensuring governments recognize their actions drive economic, social and environmental change. By monitoring market trends, the OECD can also make recommendations to policymakers. In 2018 the OECD's priorities are researching digital transformations, migration, international cooperation and 'Better Life Initiatives'. Of these priorities, the digital transformation is particularly of interest to SMEs. See Management Challenge 1 for an example of an organizing using digital technology to crowd source funds as opposed to borrowing funds from a bank.

MSMEs account for the majority of firms in most countries; around 95 per cent on average around the world (WTO 2016). Therefore, MSMEs provide many employment opportunities. For example, in Brazil 63 per cent of workers are employed in MSME enterprises.

Despite the opportunities, the OECD states that digital transformations are still in their early stages, with many countries facing interconnectivity challenges, one being that different digital tools are used in different countries (OECD 2017). Inconsistencies also occur with some countries, like Estonia, embracing blockchain technology, while other countries have not. Likewise, cities such as Paris and London enable consumers to use Smartphone-enabled platforms to rent cars or bikes within the city. But this is not available in all cities in France and the UK. The OECD is providing governments with data suggesting how they can connect better internationally, how governments should re-skill their workforce to embrace the digital age and also how SMEs can help in the development of the digital transformation.

During talks in 2018, the OECD and governments stated they would encourage SMEs to not only adopt digital technologies but stimulate innovation in this field. All governments know that SMEs play an important role in the employment and productively of their country, therefore, encouraging SMEs to embrace and improve digital technology can therefore be of benefit to all.

## MANAGEMENT CHALLENGE 5.1

### SMEs and crowdfunding

SMEs still use banks to help them finance projects. Increasingly, however, SMEs are using crowdfunding. Crowdfunding has been around for 20 years. It is a way to raise money for organizations from charities to SMEs as well as for individuals and international brands.

Berrywhite is a socially responsible drinks company that gives back to communities via donations from profits. The brand of ethical drinks began producing and selling non-carbonated, organic and sugar-free drinks in 2012 that 'do good, taste good and look good'. In 2014 the founder Andrew Jennings turned to Crowdcube to raise money and expand the business. His Crowdcube post encouraged a huge 'crowd' to invest – 170 investors in total. The crowd collectively invested over £378 000. Following this, Berrywhite is now sold in 30 countries and includes supermarkets such as Asda. Andrew Jennings is also showcasing his socially responsible mantra through the Foundation that donates 10 per cent of profits to help educate underprivileged children around the world.

Crowdfunding has grown rapidly worldwide, particularly in Europe and the USA. SMEs simply post their business idea and the money that is needed, and why, to a crowdfunding platform such as Kickstarter, Gofundme or Crowdcube. The funds asked for can be donations to acquire shares in the company.

| Funding type | Example |
|---|---|
| 1. Donations | Usually for charities |
| 2. Reward-based funding | Reward for investing, such as receiving a pot of honey each season from a beekeeping business to two nights' free stay at a Homestay in Thailand |
| 3. Lending-based funding | Lending from investors who receive a share in the business they are investing in |
| 4. Equity-based funding | Lending to investors who hold shares in the business they are investing in and have voting rights |

### Questions

Consider you want to crowdfund and you wish to offer the 'crowd investor' a rewards-based funding. What rewards could be given to your 'crowd investors' for:

1 An app-based SME promoting locally sourced home-delivered meat and vegetables throughout the UK?

2 An online language school?

**Sources:** Berrywhite (2018). www.berrywhite.com/our-story/ (accessed 5 June 2018); OECD (2017) www.oecd.org/cfe/smes/New-Approaches-SME-full-report.pdf (accessed 5 June 2018).

# The nature of SME international marketing strategies

In exploiting these opportunities to generate revenue from international markets, SMEs have a number of alternative strategies which provide a useful method of categorization of SME internationalization.

- *Exporting* is primarily concerned with selling abroad domestically developed and produced goods and services.
- *International niche marketing* is concerned with marketing a differentiated product or service overseas, usually to a single customer segment, using the full range of market entry and marketing mix options available.
- *Domestically delivered or developed niche services* can be marketed or delivered internationally to potential visitors.
- *Direct marketing including e-commerce* allows firms to market products and services globally from a domestic location.
- *Participation in the international supply chain* of an MNE can lead to SMEs piggybacking on the MNE's international development. This may involve either domestic production or establishing a facility close to where the MNE's new locations are established in other countries.

## Exporting

The emergence of global competition and the opening up of international markets has stimulated many firms to embark on the internationalization process. For many of them, exporting is the first significant stage. Exporting has been the most popular approach adopted by firms to enter and penetrate foreign markets. It requires less commitment of resources, has little effect on the firm's existing operations and involves low investment and financial risks. However, exporting, when defined as the marketing of goods and/or services across national and political boundaries, is not solely the preserve of SMEs. Neither is it a temporary stage in the process of internationalization for many firms. Many companies – both MSMEs and large – do not progress beyond the stage of relatively limited involvement in international markets. Data show that the size of a business is an indication as to whether a business will export outside its country's border or not (see Table 5.1).

Interestingly, the data is very different when it comes to singling out internet-enabled small businesses, where 97 per cent export through online networks. Those that do export must complete detailed research to learn the basics of exporting. These include identifying the needs of new customers, ensuring they are familiar with laws and bylaws, possibly learning a new language, becoming familiar with local culture and customs, and training local staff along the supply chain (Fraudmann 2017).

Table 5.1   Enterprise size and exporting activity

| Enterprise Size | Exporting Activity |
|---|---|
| Micro | 9% |
| Small | 38% |
| Medium | 50% |

Source: World Trade Report, 'Levelling the trading field for SMEs', (2016).
© World Trade Organization 2016, reprinted with permission.

## Motivation

In the OECD Working Party Report on SMEs and Entrepreneurship (2009) there are references to a large volume of literature covering exporting, including export stimuli, barriers to exporting and promotion programmes. Despite the wide variation in the contexts in which the research was carried out, some broad conclusions can be reached.

The research primarily focuses on proactive stimuli but it is also important to recognize that motivations to export can be reactive too. Two examples of reactive strategies are:

1  If a product has reached maturity or is in decline in the home market, the company may find new foreign markets where the product has not reached the same life cycle stage and which, therefore, offers potential for further growth.

2  Companies may seek new markets abroad to utilize their production facilities to their full capacity.

In these circumstances companies may well embark on marginal pricing and sell at lower prices on the export markets, seeking only a contribution to their overall cost for their home base market.

The following are reactive stimuli:

- adverse domestic market conditions
- an opportunity to reduce inventories
- the availability of production capacity
- favourable currency movements
- the opportunity to increase the number of country markets and reduce the market-related risk
- unsolicited orders from overseas customers.

To reduce risk, OECD (2009) identifies proactive stimuli for exporting as growth motives, including profits, an increased market size, a stronger market position and market diversification. If a company sees only limited growth opportunities in the home market for a proven product, it may well see market diversification as a means of expansion. This could lead to the identification of new market segments within a domestic market, but it may well lead to geographic expansion in foreign markets. Thus, companies try to spread risks and reduce their dependence on any one market. Equally the firm may identify market gaps.

The proactive company with knowledge assets will use these to identify foreign market opportunities. Knowledge assets include management's previous international experience and capability, innovation capability, unique products or services, resources, and a well-managed marketing information system. It could also include undertaking formal structured research. Proactive companies highlight the importance of networks, supply chain links and social ties, through immigrant communities in global markets.

The following are proactive stimuli:

- attractive profit and growth opportunities
- the ability to easily modify products for export markets
- public policy programmes for export promotion
- foreign country regulations
- the possession of unique products
- economies resulting from additional orders.

And certain managerial elements include:

- the presence of an export-minded manager
- the opportunity to better utilize management talent and skills
- management beliefs about the value of exporting.

## Barriers to internationalization

Many companies with export potential never become involved in international marketing. A series of export studies have found that it is often a great deal easier to encourage existing exporters to increase their involvement in international markets than it is to encourage those who are not exporting to begin the process. The reasons given by companies for not exporting are numerous. The biggest barrier to entry into export markets for these companies is the fear that their products are not marketable overseas. Consequently, they become preoccupied with the domestic market. Other SMEs believe that because of the particular nature of their business sector, their domestic market continues to offer the best potential for market growth or market share growth. They also believe that their sector is not so vulnerable to international competition, so a domestically focused strategy makes the best use of their resources.

The OECD (2009) has summarized a large number of recent research studies into the SME internationalization barriers. The following are the areas which are identified:

- Shortage of working capital to finance exports
- Inadequate knowledge of overseas markets and lack of information to find and analyze markets
- Inability to contact overseas customers, including finding the right partner, the right representation and suitable distribution channels
- Lack of managerial time, skills and knowledge, including differences in managers' perceptions and psychological barriers to internationalization.

There is significant risk too because SMEs have little influence over environmental change and recessions, which often lead to many business casualties, such as those experienced between 2007 and 2011. Sometimes SMEs can over-extend themselves financially by growing internationally too quickly. If there is a downturn

## ILLUSTRATION 5.3

# Win–win through DHL knowledge exchange with Botswana SMEs

Over 95 per cent of businesses in Africa are SMEs (Cull and Beck 2014). Africa is progressing well in terms of its exports from some Chinese direct investors and from its own SMEs. In fact, its exports to countries around the world grew faster than those of some other regions. Unfortunately, the exports are mainly dominated by primary commodities, such as oil, iron and gas, which account for the majority of exports from African countries (IMF 2015). However, one country that is gaining positive ground within the African region is Botswana. Botswana has three key exports: diamonds, beef and tourism. And with two recently introduced items on the political agenda, namely Botswana's Economic Diversification Drive and The National Export Strategy (OECD 2014) it will be interesting to see if the country will increase its merchandise exports in the next few years.

One major growth area within the Botswana economy is SMEs. Botswana's SMEs have a considerable number of employees in many regions across the country, which in turn contribute between 30 to 45 per cent of Botswana's GDP. Yet SME exports are limited due to lack of knowledge, financial resources, unclear distribution channels and few intermediaries. However, DHL Worldwide has stepped in to fill those gaps.

SMEs can discover the export opportunities available to them through DHL, either online, through books or face-to-face with local DHL employees. SMEs are encouraged to contact Mokgethi Magapa, DHL Express Botswana country manager, who will help them understand their potential and go global.

This is a win–win situation for SMEs, Botswana and DHL. It is beneficial for SMEs to improve and grow their business; it will also help the SMEs to expand into international markets which in turn will help Botswana's GDP and merchandise exports. And for DHL? Charles Brewer, managing director for DHL Express sub-Saharan Africa explains the benefits for DHL best by saying: 'In facilitating trade in and out of Botswana with the rest of the world, we intend to contribute meaningfully in making the country more successful and assist in the economic diversification drive, focused on international express delivery' (*Botswana Gazette* 2015).

## Questions

**1** What steps can small firms take to increase their international export opportunities?

**2** How can other countries and SMEs benefit from knowledge exchange?

**Sources:** *Botswana Gazette* (2015) DHL realising increasing demand in retail sector. Available from www.thegazette.news/dhl-realising-increasing-demand-in-retail-sector/ (accessed 20 March 2018); OECD (2014) Economic Outlook Africa 2014, www.oecd-ilibrary.org.

in demand, they may not be able to generate sufficient cash and profits to service their debt and often end up being taken over or going bankrupt.

Illustration 5.3 shows how a global company shares its knowledge of exporting with SMEs in Africa, which increases motivation and sustainability, resulting in a win–win situation for all.

Non-exporters tend to worry most about issues such as excessive bureaucracy associated with international markets and government-imposed trade barriers that in turn lead to 'non-activity'. Experienced exporters that are active tend to believe that these problems should be addressed through managerial proactivity, for example, by training staff and seeking expert assistance. A number of studies suggest other factors that might be specific in some contexts. For example, studies in Nigeria by DHL (2014) stated that other barriers such as poor infrastructure, limited utilities, poor payment systems, corruption and bureaucratic bottlenecks, particularly at customs, are more likely to prevent SMEs from going global.

**Niche marketing**   Having identified the motivations and barriers to exporting it is tempting to conclude that many exporters are characterized by being product-oriented – selling abroad the products and services that are successful in the domestic market. Moreover, exporters often seem to throw away their successful domestic marketing strategies in international markets, preferring instead to delegate their marketing to agents and distributors. In doing this they seem to overlook the alternative market entry and marketing mix strategies that are available to them, opting instead for a strategy of least involvement. In many cases this approach may meet the exporting firm's immediate objectives, especially if, for example, they are simply seeking to offload excess production capacity. But it does not provide them with a sound basis for substantially increasing their international market presence.

Table 5.2 sets out the differences between basic exporting and international niche marketing, together with a simple strategy that SMEs can engage in and how an SME can flourish by understanding the needs of consumers and relationships with stakeholders.

**Table 5.2**   The difference between exporting and international niche marketing

| Marketing strategy | Exporting selling production capacity | International niche marketing meeting customer needs |
| --- | --- | --- |
| *Financial objective* | To amortize overheads | To add value |
| *Segmentation* | Usually by country and consumer characteristics | By identifying common international customer benefit |
| *Pricing* | Cost based | Market or customer based |
| *Management focus* | Efficiency in operations | Meeting market requirements |
| *Distribution* | Using existing agents or distributor | Managing the supply chain |
| *Market information* | Relying on agent or distributor feedback | Analyzing the market situation and customer needs |
| *Customer relationship* | Working through intermediaries | Building multiple level relationships |

Source: www.unctad.org © UNCTAD, © United Nations 2000–2011.

By contrast, international niche marketing occurs where firms become a strong force in a narrow specialized market of one or two segments across a number of country markets. Having a customer-focused niche strategy, SMEs target specific markets that have a specific need. SMEs of this kind often use networks to gain new target markets and satisfy existing ones. It is the commitment and regular communication that enables customer-focused niche SMEs to specialize internationally (Hagen *et al*. 2012). They also confirm some of the issues that Brown and McDonald (1994) explain when considering the development opportunities listed in Table 5.3.

Table 5.3   International niche marketing: development opportunities

To sustain and develop the niche the firm must:

- Have good information about the segment needs

- Have a clear understanding of the important segmentation criteria

- Specialize based on customer-focused needs

- Understand the value of the product niche to the targeted segment(s)

- Provide high levels of service

- Demonstrate commitment and communication

- Carry out small scale innovations

- Seek cost efficiency in the supply chain

- Maintain a separate focus, perhaps by being content to remain relatively small

- Concentrate on profit rather than market share

- Evaluate and apply appropriate market entry and marketing mix strategies to build market share in each country in which they wish to become involved

Sources: Hagen *et al*. 2012; Brown and McDonald 1994.

As outlined in Table 5.3, international niche marketing is ideal for SMEs as segments are often very small or too specialized to attract large competitors. True niche marketing does not include well-known brands or companies that are minor players in a mass market offering undifferentiated products. Therefore, for the international niche player to be successful, the product or service must be distinctive (highly differentiated), be recognized by consumers and other participants in the international supply chain and have clear positioning. International niche marketing is vastly different from SMEs exporting internationally on a more standardized/undifferentiated approach.

## Niche marketing of domestically delivered services

In the travel industry domestic firms such as hotels, tour operators and leisure attractions generate foreign earnings for the country by attracting visitors. International destination marketing of cities such as Prague, the wildlife reserves of Botswana and countries such as Vietnam is increasingly important for economic success in certain areas. It is usually undertaken by relatively small organizations such as tourist boards that represent a huge network of dependent providers of accommodation, catering, leisure activities and experiences. Their role is becoming increasingly important as the economies of the destinations become ever more dependent on tourism, and competition between destinations and the number of potential visitors increase.

With increased international travel and improved access to worldwide communications, a much wider range of services is being offered to visiting customers. Examples include the provision of education, specialized training, medical treatment, sports, cultural and leisure events, and specialist retailing such as luxury goods. For example, over 442 000 students (UK Council for International Student Affairs 2018) from outside the UK come to study at higher education institutions in the UK. Many more study at colleges and private language schools. The British Council supports the international marketing efforts of what are largely independent institutions.

Clearly these activities lead to wealth and jobs being generated in the local economy in much the same way as with exporting and niche marketing. The international marketing strategy processes and programmes are similar too, in that the products and services must meet the requirements of, and be promoted to, international customers. Consequently, issues of standardization and adaptation of the marketing mix elements are equally important. The additional challenge is that the benefits obtained from the service provided must be unique and superior. Thus they outweigh the benefits to the consumer of their locally available services, as well as the cost of travel that the customers will incur in the purchasing and consumption process.

In addition to the services designed to be offered to individuals in both consumer and B2B markets, a whole range of additional services which fall into this category of being domestically delivered are concerned with developing solutions for opportunities or problems identified abroad. These might include technology developments, such as research into new drugs, trial and testing facilities, software development, and product and packaging design services.

There are many examples of research and development companies, such as Imagination Technologies and ARM in computer microchip design that licence their new technologies to customers around the world.

## Importing and reciprocal trading

Importing is clearly the opposite process to international marketing and as such might be seen by governments as 'exporting' jobs and potential wealth. However, the purpose of considering importing here is to highlight the nature of international trade as it is today. Rarely do supply chains for products and services involve solely domestic production and delivery. There has been a substantial increase in outsourcing, not only by large firms but by SMEs too.

Exporting and importing have become inextricably linked so that the challenge is one of adding value to imported components and services, no matter where they are sourced, so that they can then be re-exported in order to meet the international customers' needs effectively and profitably.

Importing activity can also considerably enhance a company's potential to network, leading ultimately, perhaps, to reciprocal trading in which, as a result, the supplier might take other products or services in return from the customer.

**Foreign direct investment**   It might be concluded from this that raising the level of value-adding supply chain activity in a particular country is the ultimate aim of governments. Most governments take this further by encouraging foreign direct investment (FDI) by multinationals in the belief that as well as aiding the economy through increasing employment and tax revenues, the MNEs' operations will benefit the indigenous SME supply sector by:

- providing additional B2B sales opportunities for the SME suppliers to provide components, subcontracted fabrication work and non-core services as part of the MNE's supply chain,
- setting and establishing higher international quality standards among the suppliers, which will then enable them to better compete in international markets.

The danger with FDI is that MNEs will only maintain their operations in a particular country while it is financially advantageous. When the MNE finds a lower labour cost country location for its operations it will move on. Many countries have found that low-cost assembly-type manufacturing or call centre operations can be easily relocated with the associated loss of jobs and tax revenues. While the government can take action to encourage continuing high levels of FDI through financial incentives, ensuring a well-educated and flexible workforce, an efficient, responsive and flexible SME supply chain will also be a significant factor in MNE location decisions. Illustration 5.4 highlights how SMEs can demonstrate how they are an excellent organization along the supply chain.

## Direct marketing and electronic commerce

Cross-border direct marketing and, in particular, electronic commerce continues to grow as customers become more confident in buying goods from abroad. Direct marketing offers the benefits of cutting out other distribution channel members such as importers, agents, distributors, wholesalers and retailers, by using a variety of communications media, including post, telephone, television and the Internet. For SMEs' suppliers these allow borders to be crossed relatively easily with limited investment and risk, and without the SMEs having to face many of the barriers already highlighted in this chapter.

## ILLUSTRATION 5.4

# Who is best and what makes them best?

Best Companies is an organization that wants to award organizations that do their best and are the best in class. The different award classes are:

Best Company to Work For

Best Big Company to Work For

Best Not-For-Profit Company to Work For

Best Small Company to Work For

Being the best is not about turnover, profits or growth. From the titles of the different award classes, it is clear that best means best for the employees that work there. Best Companies devised a methodology in which to ask employees about their organization and have the opportunity to speak up as to what is fantastic and what is not about a wide variety of issues. Questions put to employees, therefore, evolved around the following categories:

1  Leadership: Questions were asked to gain information about how employees felt about the head of their organization, not only the head, but other senior management who were involved in key decisions. They were also asked what they felt about the values and principles of the organization that underpin the kind of business they are working for.

2  My Manager: The employees were also asked about the relationship between 'me and my manager' to establish if communications between the two were open and direct.

3  My Company: The questions in this category were to establish how all employees felt about their own commitment and engagement to the company; to gain a feeling that perhaps their engagement with the company went beyond 'I am here and it's just a job'.

4  Personal Growth: Employees often have thoughts on whether their organization gives them an opportunity to grow; therefore, questions in this category are there to ascertain if the employee feels that training and development gained at their company will help improve their future prospects.

5  My Team: The questions in this section were included to establish how each person within the company felt towards their colleagues and if they worked together in a cohesive and productive manner.

6  Wellbeing: Organizations need to consider the wellbeing of their employees; therefore, questions in this category were designed to understand how employees feel about the work–life balance ratio of their organization and general opinions about how the stresses and pressures placed on employees are managed.

7  Fair Deal: All employers and employees consider it fair to receive pay and benefits equivalent to what is being asked. Questions in this category explore those issues for parity.

8  Giving Something Back: The final category asked employees if they felt their organization 'gives back' to society in some form or another, from enabling employees to take part in community activities to implementing a waste-management system.

## Question

1 Pick three of the eight categories above and consider what an SME would need to implement if it wanted to win an award for 'Best Small Company to Work For'.

**Source:** Best Companies. www.b.co.uk/factors/.

Direct marketing also has a number of disadvantages. Despite the range of media available, communicating can still be problematic as personalization of the communication is essential for direct marketing success. In cross-border direct marketing there is always the danger of cultural insensitivity and language mistakes in the communications. Many of the following comments apply to both traditional direct marketing using physical media and electronic commerce, but we have focused on online trading as it is this method that has had the most impact on SME internationalization.

If customers speak different languages then it may be necessary for online retailers to have multilingual websites. This can add cost in setting up and servicing the website. The continued growth of online retailers may depend on selling to international customers who do not speak the home country language. Moreover, because of the need to manage large numbers of customers, it is necessary to use databases which must be up-to-date, accurate and capable of dealing with foreign languages. Even an incorrectly spelt name can be insulting to the recipient.

The Internet provides smaller firms with a shop window and also the means of obtaining payment, organizing and tracking shipment, and delivery. For some products and services, it can provide the means by which market information can be accumulated and new ideas collected, developed and modified by customers and other stakeholders.

Electronic commerce has led firms to redefine their business and it can also be a business in its own right. For example, many electronic commerce services take the form of information transfer. This can become the basis of the product or service itself; for example, specialist advice on personal finance, travel and hobbies.

As well as being a route to market in its own right in the form of direct commerce, the Internet as an interactive marketing information provider has an increasingly important role in each of the above international niche marketing strategies.

The Internet offers the benefits to SMEs of real-time communications across distances and the levelling of the corporate playing field. This leads to more rapid internationalization as well as achieving competitive advantage by:

- creating new opportunities
- erecting barriers to entry (e.g. managing intellectual property)
- making cost savings from online communications
- providing online support for inter-firm collaboration, especially in R&D, as an information search and retrieval tool
- the establishment of company websites for marketing and sales promotion, and
- the transmission of any type of data including manuscripts, financial information and computer-aided design/computer-aided manufacture (CAD/CAM) files.

There are some disadvantages, especially the relative ease with which it is possible to become flooded with electronic messages (spam) and orders. While this may be manageable for certain products and services where production volumes can easily be increased or decreased, sales feasts and famines can cause havoc where production capacity is less flexible.

As advanced search engines become more sophisticated it is essential (and expensive) to make sure that the firm's offer is listed on the first page of search results for key words. The implications of this are that instead of marketing being essentially passive in electronic commerce, the marketing input required in designing websites needs to become increasingly sophisticated in promoting the products, providing interactive product design, development and safe payment arrangements. Technical and customer service support, and initial customer segmentation and targeting, are increasingly important to the delivery of an effective, focused business. Thus, while many SMEs see the Internet as a low-cost distribution channel, the greater competition and more sophisticated versions of electronic commerce make it more difficult for SMEs to compete. SMEs frequently face the dilemma of how to cope with powerful competitors. For example, dealing with niche markets used to be problematic for MNEs because of the difficulty of managing millions of small transactions, so SMEs could operate with more freedom in their chosen niche. Now, however, information and communications technology (ICT) allows MNEs to more cost-effectively manage relatively small volumes and values, making them more competitive in niche markets.

The advent of e-business and the Internet appears, therefore, to offer the benefits to SMEs of being able to ignore borders and make more direct interaction possible between international SMEs and their customers. However, Servais *et al.* (2007) explain that even 'born global' SMEs use the Internet only to a limited extent to sell their products and as a tool to support existing relationships. Considerable opportunities exist therefore for more creative direct marketing by SMEs.

# The nature of international development

The internationalization process differs enormously depending on whether the company first serves the domestic market and later develops into foreign markets (adaptive exporter), or is expressly established from its inception to enter foreign markets (born global). Adaptive and born global exporters differ in a variety of ways, including their respective market assessment processes, reasons for international market involvement, managerial attitudes and the propensity to take risks. Successful born globals are seen to overcome their distinctive challenges with flexible managerial attitudes and practices (Solhei 2012).

Many exporting firms, especially in hi-tech or industrial markets, internationalize through their network of relationships. Firms in any market establish and develop relationships through interactions with other individuals and firms, leading the parties to build mutual trust, respect and knowledge. Kulmeier and Knight (2010) explain that it is the quality of the relationships in four dimensions that are critical:

- communication
- cooperation
- trust, and
- commitment.

Internationalization of the firm, therefore, becomes a consequence of the interaction between the firms in the network they have formed. The network of business relationships comprises a number of different stakeholders – customers, customers' customers, competitors, supplementary suppliers, suppliers, distributors, agents and consultants – as well as regulatory and other public agencies. In any specific country, different networks can be distinguished. Any or all of these relationships may become the conduit for the internationalization of a company. In these cases, the internationalization process of a company is more aptly visualized as a series of multilateral cycles rather than a linear process (see Figure 5.1).

Thus, the internationalization process manifests itself by the development of business relationships in other countries through:

- the establishment of relationships in country networks that are new to the firm, i.e. international extension
- the development of relationships in those networks, i.e. penetration
- connecting networks in different countries, i.e. international integration.

FIGURE 5.1   The multilateral aspects of the internationalization process

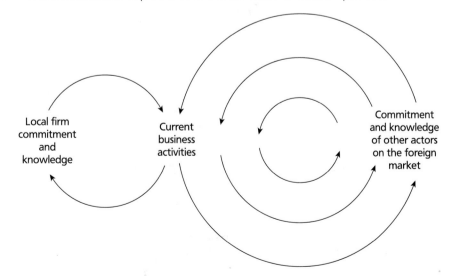

Source: Johannson, J. and Vahlne, J.E. (1992) The Mechanism of Internationalization. *International Marketing Review*, Emerald Insight.

Relationship and network building are especially important in the fast changing, global environment, but particularly in hi-tech industries. Studies of the internationalization process of small hi-tech firms indicate that some of these companies follow the traditional internationalization patterns, while others behave differently. They go directly to more distant markets and rapidly set up their own subsidiaries. One reason seems to be that the entrepreneurs behind those companies have networks of colleagues dealing with the new technology. Internationalization, in these cases, is an exploitation of the advantage created by networking and may benefit from external facilitation.

Crick and Crick (2014) found that internationalization strategy formation for high performing SMEs is not always planned. In fact, due to the managers' networks, closeness to consumers and experiences, opportunities are often seen but not expected. Therefore, the nature of SME niche business can often seem unplanned. But it is the very nature of being able to react to consumer needs that makes SMEs successful in niche businesses. In addition, SMEs with an entrepreneurial orientation are proactive, innovative and risk-takers. As recently pointed out, they are equally involved in the environment, their workforce and the international communities in which they engage (Ayuso and Navarrete-Báez, 2018).

## Geographic development of SMEs

For SMEs, country market selection and development of market share within each country are particularly important for growth. Given their limited resources and narrow margin for failure, it is vital that their method of country market development is effective. The various patterns of SME international development are shown in Figure 5.2.

**FIGURE 5.2**  Geographic development of SMEs

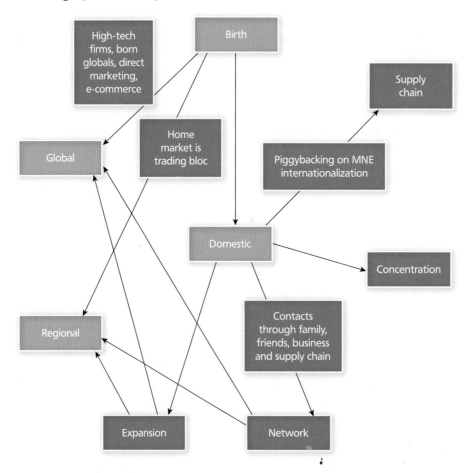

The conventional approach is for new companies to test the viability of their products in the domestic market before spreading internationally. But we have already indicated that a number of firms become international players almost immediately after they have been formed, either because they are born global or they operate within a common regional market. The different patterns of international spreading are now discussed.

## Market concentration and expansion

The conventional view of country selection is that from a sound domestic base SMEs develop either by choosing between expanding into many markets, gaining a superficial presence and accepting a low overall market share, or concentrating their marketing activities in a small number of markets in which they can build a significant market share. The research in this area is inconclusive about the precise reasons why firms adopt one strategy over another.

Katsikeas and Leonidou (1996) found that **market concentrators** tend, in general, to be smaller firms because of their greater interest in export profitability and lesser concern with export sales objectives. Typically, they make regular visits overseas and this appears to play a key role in their strategy for penetrating the market. Concentrators experience more problems associated with product adaptation to the needs of their customers, but pricing and their marketing organization needs present less of a problem.

**Market expanders** tend to be larger firms who are more concerned with export sales objectives, do more export marketing research and have greater overall market share expectations. They place less emphasis on profitability, personal visits are less important and they perceive fewer product adaptation-related problems. E-commerce businesses are typical market expanders.

## Where the domestic market is redefined

The lowering or removal of barriers between countries and the move, for example, in the EU to the harmonization of standards, the removal of tariff barriers, reduction of non-tariff barriers and the introduction of a common currency within a regional trading bloc, mean that SMEs are more likely to be active in more than one country market. This can also be because the regional market is considered to be their domestic market. In mainland Europe, for example, this is the case because there are no additional costs in travelling to a neighbouring country and, often, a common language may be used.

## Where the SME international development is the result of networking

Many SMEs adopt what appears to be a rather unsystematic approach to country market selection. Their patterns of development tend to be the result of a network approach. The selection of the market is not merely made on the relative attractiveness of the markets and their match with the company capability, but rather on the reduction of the risk of entering unknown markets by working with individuals or companies they know. International development through using existing networks of contacts is more typical of Asian firms than SMEs from western countries.

Internationalizing through networking using a small business management model still provides entrepreneurs with the means of achieving security, often because it allows fast adaptation in a rapidly changing world. Through a global network many small units can come up with a variety of solutions at an acceptable level of risk.

# Entrepreneur and family networks

Globally there is a need to move away from a managed economic system to a more international entrepreneurial society. The move has already started and SMEs and entrepreneurs are creating economic growth for developed as well as developing countries. The developed countries fared very well in the Global Entrepreneurial Index 2018. Currently, for investors in technology, the top five entrepreneurial countries are, in order: the USA, Switzerland, Canada, the UK and Australia.

Another network that needs to be included here is entrepreneurial family networks. Nueno (2000) explains that the Chinese can be effective entrepreneurs. While 1 per cent of the population of the Philippines is ethnic Chinese, they control 40 per cent of the economy. Half the economies of Indonesia and Thailand are controlled by 4 per cent and 10 per cent ethnic Chinese, respectively. In Malaysia two-thirds of the economy is controlled by ethnic Chinese.

They operate effectively within a family network and, because the Chinese are spread throughout the world, they can lay the foundations for stronger links among businesses across borders as a network of entrepreneurial relationships. In practice, most SMEs operate within a network of personal contacts, but this is much more formalized in some cultures, such as the Chinese, because it is based on *guanxi* and the obligation to return favours. The Confucian tradition of hard work, thrift and respect for one's social network provides continuity, and the small network-based enterprises bound by strong cultural links are well suited to fast-changing markets. Illustration 5.5 explains the impact of family groups on international trade and gives an example of the effect of family feuds.

## ILLUSTRATION 5.5

# Family networking

Success in Asia still runs on power, prestige, influence, favours given and received, family fortune and connections. Without these even the simplest deal can come unstuck for no obvious reasons. For example, the Chinese, Japanese, Koreans and Indians have their own special connections, and their business styles come down to trust and credibility – who vouches for whom.

There are six big economic groups in Asia that are growing fast as a result of networking. These are:

- Japanese *keiretsu* company connections
- Koreans with *chaebol* conglomerates
- Mainland Chinese with party and military links
- Ethnic or overseas Chinese with their stored wealth, extended family, dialect and guild connections
- The emerging *pribumi* and *bumiputera* (indigenous) business leaders of Indonesia
- Malaysians with their political connections; the Indians with their family dynasties.

It is networking on a grand scale that provides the basis of the international operations as there are an estimated 57 million Chinese and 18 million Indians that are living abroad. A Singaporean Chinese trader may have family connections in Taiwan, Hong Kong, Guandong, Fujian or Vietnam that can provide legal, banking and support services when moving across borders.

A small group of families also control the Indian economy and are successfully developing their global businesses. However, it is internal family disagreements that are their major concern. For example, the giant conglomerate, Reliance Industries, was built as a rags-to-riches story over decades by Dhirubhai Ambani. After he died his sons, Anil and Mukesh, fell out over the direction of the company. By 2005 they could no longer work together and their mother brokered a demerger into two groups. But the feud continued with Mukesh blocking Anil's telecom group's efforts to merge with South Africa's MTN. A dispute followed regarding gas prices and ended in court. Anil won and Mukesh appealed the ruling, but the oil ministry stepped in when it realized how damaging it was for the government when two wealthy men were seen to be fighting over the resources that should belong to the country.

The traditional power of the mainland Chinese dynasties was disrupted during the communist era and new dynasties will be created.

In the west many of the old, great family business dynasties have declined in importance and given way to the new entrepreneurs who have exploited new technologies, such as Rupert Murdoch of News International, which includes Sky. Perhaps such organizations are creating new family dynasties.

## Question

**1** To what extent do you expect the old family groups to be the future successes and to what extent do you expect the new groups that have created their wealth through new technologies to succeed them?

Networking and relationship marketing are now emphasized as key components of most SME internationalization strategies.

## Where the SME is born global

Some SMEs market their products and services globally from birth or soon after because the customer segment or competition is global (especially in hi-tech, breakthrough products) or because the distribution method is global, for example, direct marketing and telecommunications-based international marketing (e.g. the Internet). A survey for the Global Entrepreneurship Monitor (2014) found that many of the developed countries (the USA, the UK, Spain, Germany, Norway, Latvia) are innovation-driven economies, confirming the finding of the Global Entrepreneurial Index. Countries such as Botswana, Bolivia and the Philippines are factor-driven economies, showing that these countries are identified as being 'early stage entrepreneurs'. Therefore, they have not yet fully embraced an international orientation. Further, these countries have low export sales and limited experience of selling online to international consumers. As a consequence, this also identifies them as being in the early stages of entrepreneurialism. Few US entrepreneurs, for example, have a higher international orientation than 25 per cent of their customers, whereas three-quarters have a small percentage of international customers. Interestingly, eastern European countries tend to have high international orientation.

A number of studies of born global firms have been made in different country contexts. Kalinic and Forza (2012) examine the differences between born global firms/international new ventures (INVs), SMEs and those SMEs that *gradually* develop into international markets. They conclude that they do exhibit different characteristics. Born globals/INVs have a managerial vision from the start of their business, whereas SMEs that gradually move to international markets do so when they have a significant, well-developed, home base. Furthermore, born global/INV businesses have a clear niche-focus, are highly innovative and proactive in their strategic international development from inception. This is a more dynamic approach than the SMEs that react to opportunities internationally as time goes on and are less innovative because of that. Born Global Managers view the world as its marketplace from the outset, whereas INVs' management sees foreign markets as adjuncts to the domestic market and hence typically focuses on regional markets. The majority of born globals are formed by active entrepreneurs and tend to emerge as a result of a significant breakthrough in some process or technology. They may apply cutting-edge technology to developing a unique product idea or to a new way of doing business. The products and services that born globals sell directly involve substantial value added, and the majority of such products may be intended for industrial use. They do not compete on price.

Several trends have given rise to the emergence of born global firms:

- The increasing role of niche markets, especially in the developed world. As markets mature, products increasingly become commodities, and SMEs respond by identifying sub segments of customers that require a more specialized or customized product or service.

- To compete with large, powerful MNEs smaller firms must specialize. However, while the demand from a domestic niche market may be very small, the global demand can sustain an SME that is prepared to supply the niche on a worldwide basis.

- Recent advances in process technology mean low-scale batch production can be economical, and new technologies mean that SMEs can compete with large firms to produce sophisticated products.

- Communications technologies allow SMEs to manage across borders, and information is more readily accessible to everyone. It is now much less expensive to go international than it was just 20 years ago.

- Quicker response time, flexibility and adaptability to foreign tastes and specific customer requirements give these firms an immediate competitive edge.

- SMEs can gain access to funding and support, benefit from joint research programmes and technology transfer, and employ cross-border educated managers more easily than ever before.

- Increasingly, international business is facilitated through partnership with foreign businesses – distributors, trading companies, subcontractors and alliances – allowing new specialist firms to participate in global networks more easily than before.

Investigations by Efrat *et al.* (2017) suggest born globals need an internal structure based on three principles embraced by the whole team so that they work together and coordinate their efforts. The three principles are: (1) market intelligence, (2) team coherence and (3) marketing mix adaptation (product, place, price, promotion, process, people and physical environment – often the online environment).

1   Market intelligence is imperative for born globals. Naturally, the R&D team collects intelligence to understand the marketplace in which they are working, understands the global and local consumer, and investigates the competitive arena. The R&D team will do this through the life of the business, constantly keeping abreast of the fast-moving international environment and supporting the need for change in their own business, making their business unique and filling in the gaps not provided for by other competitors, and anticipating market needs.

2   The R&D team will not work alone as the second principle is team coherence. Not only will the R&D team be enjoining the sales team to share their findings. The production, distribution, HR and marketing teams will also have been collecting intelligence regarding new technology and new sales platforms. Cohesively the teams will discuss their data and make strategic and tactical moves.

3   Marketing mix adaptation. The third principal team within born global organizations will need to ensure it researches the marketplace but also that the R&D team meets with the production team, sales team and marketing team to ensure all parties can have their say and influence change together. The R&D team must also discuss the advantages and disadvantages of their strategic and tactical moves and adapt the marketing mix accordingly. Born global organizations are innovative and risk-takers; however, the above principles will ensure the organization adapts quickly but only through intelligence and as a collective.

## Supply chain internationalization

The pattern of internationalization of firms that are part of the supply chain of an MNE is usually determined by the international strategy adopted by the MNE. In a continual effort to achieve focus and operational efficiency, firms constantly think about what are their core competences and answer the question: what business are we in? The response to this question leads MNEs to identify those components and services that were part of the overall product offer but which they regarded as being peripheral to their business. As a result of this, many decide to outsource more of their supplies, either from MNE specialist component makers and service providers, or from SMEs that have exploited these new opportunities to grow.

The reasons for MNEs to outsource can be summarized as follows:

■   It reduces the capital requirements of the business (the supplier rather than the MNE invests in new processes and facilities).

■   It overcomes the difficulty of developing quickly and maintaining in-house knowledge in many different specialist knowledge areas.

■   It improves flexibility, as some firms are better equipped and can carry out small production runs, special designs and development tasks more quickly.

■   The MNE can take risks in more peripheral activities where their expertise is weak, stopping the firm from falling behind in the effectiveness of its non-core operations.

■   The economies of scale of suppliers may make components much cheaper through outsourcing rather than from in-house supplies.

■   The expertise of business support service providers, for example in transport and delivery systems, cannot be matched.

■   Downsizing without outsourcing can lead to management resources becoming too stretched and unfocused.

The disadvantages of outsourcing are:

■   *Loss of know-how*: western businesses in many sectors have outsourced manufacturing to Asian firms who have subsequently opened up as competitors.

■   *The costs of managing the outsourced supplies*: managing outsourced components and services does require time and technical expertise and, particularly in the case of IT, there have been some difficulties of integrating the service with the firm's primary strategic objectives.

Both large and smaller firms have been the beneficiaries of this increased outsourcing, but for smaller firms there are particular challenges. These include:

- The need to become closely linked with one or two major customers, upon which the SME is almost entirely dependent for survival and success.

- Internationalization being driven by the demands of the MNE. Failure to follow their product or market development demands may result in the loss of all the business as the MNE will seek alternative suppliers.

- Being under continual pressure to make operational efficiencies and design improvements in order to offer even better value for money.

- Concentrating on developing the relationship with the MNE may lead to the firm becoming relatively weaker in external marketing, putting the firm at a disadvantage if it needs to find new customers when difficulties occur.

Management Challenge 5.2 suggests another way of rethinking which country would be best when outsourcing the production side of the business.

---

## MANAGEMENT CHALLENGE 5.2

### SMEs in India: outsourcing human resource management

There are 51 million SMEs in India. This equates to the employment of 120 million people. As already mentioned in this chapter, management teams in SMEs have many roles and responsibilities. One of the roles is to decide how to invest in the human resources (HR) department. The HR department is often considered instrumental to any business, large or small. The reason for this is that the HR department recruits and selects the workforce, it is responsible for training and re-training, and ensures each member of the workforce is compensated for the work they do in a fair manner. However, the HR department brings a number of challenges for SMEs, such as finding the right talent, providing a schedule of training and development for all of the workforce and dealing with the many rules and regulations regarding compliance.

In India there is a steady growth in SMEs outsourcing their HR department. One of the reasons for this is

to save up to 35 per cent of their total business costs and bring a plethora of benefits. Indian SMEs state that using outsourced, experienced HR recruitment managers ensures the right mechanisms and tools are used to hire talent. Training schedules can be planned in advance. When needed, ad hoc re-skilling by expert trainers knowledgeable in the latest techniques and resources can be brought in. With planned and ad hoc training for an SME's workforce a great motivator, staff see that investment is being made in their development. The HR department also has to deal with other workforce health and safety regulations as well as conditions of employment, statutory benefits, leaves of absence and termination of employment, all of which are complex. Therefore, SMEs in India take comfort by outsourcing these complex arrangements to experts.

#### Questions

**1** What are the main benefits of outsourcing HR?

**2** Would there be any benefits for SMEs of having a small HR department and outsourcing the majority of roles?

**References:** *Economic Times* (2017) Why SMEs on growth trajectory should consider outsourcing HR requirements Available from: https://economictimes.indiatimes.com/small-biz/hr-leadership/people/why-smes-on-growth-trajectory-should-consider-outsourcing-hr-requirements/articleshow/61078889.cms (accessed 23 March 2017).

---

The advantages for SMEs are:

- The opportunities to learn from working with the MNE. This is likely to improve the smaller firms' strategic and operational management systems, communications and purchasing efficiency, particularly if they can join the MNE's existing global networks.

- They have greater business security through reliable and predictable ordering while the customer is successful.
- The opportunity to focus on production and technical issues rather than being diverted by the need to analyze changes to the market, customer and competition to the same degree.

## Developing relationships

The key to success in working within the supply chain of an MNE is developing an effective relationship. This can build upon the advantages and minimize the disadvantages of cooperative working between firms which may have some business objectives in common, but also may have a number of differences. As more SMEs become involved in international supply chains, the ways in which relationships between smaller suppliers and the MNE differ between western and Asian styles of management become particularly significant.

The western way of arranging sourcing is a competition-based approach and has the advantage of a much sharper focus on cost reduction, profit and individual creativity. The Asian approach is more cooperative-based and includes ensuring that more than one strong supplier is available, expertise is shared and built upon, and the competitive focus is always on the much larger market opportunity.

Over the past few years the number of cooperative arrangements between western and Asian styles within one supply chain has increased. As a result, arrangements which could be described as a combination of the two have been developed. Longer-term contracts have been agreed in order to maximize the cooperation between the MNE and supplier, but without the insistence on sharing information with the losing contractor, which was often a feature of the Asian approach.

# International strategic marketing management in SMEs

Having considered the various categories of SME internationalization and the nature of SME international development, we now turn to the factors which influence the international marketing management of SMEs. The McKinsey 7S framework, shown in Figure 5.3, is useful for discussing the elements.

## The McKinsey 7S framework

The first three elements – strategy, structure and systems – are considered to be the hardware of successful management and as such can be implemented across international markets without the need for significant adaptation. The other four – management style, staff, skills and shared values – are the software and are

**FIGURE 5.3**   McKinsey 7S framework

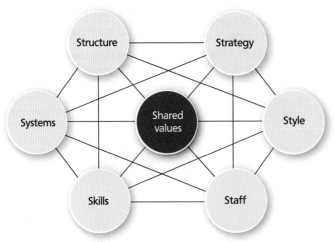

affected by cultural differences. Often it is the management of these aspects of the business that highlights good management in the best firms and relatively unimpressive management in poorer performing firms. It is quite obvious too that it is these elements of the framework which can vary considerably from country to country. They provide the most significant challenges for SMEs developing from their home base into an organization with involvement in a number of different countries.

The characteristics of these four software elements are:

1  *Style*: In organizations such as McDonald's, it is the consistency across the world of the management and their operational style that is one of the distinguishing features of the companies. For SMEs the management and operational style frequently reflects the personality, standards and values of the owner, and is often maintained as the firm matures, as in the case of Kiran Mazumdar-Shaw, one of the world's top-rated female entrepreneurs. She is known as a leader, global thinker and influencer across the globe as well as for her pioneering biotechnology industry in India that is committed to providing affordable healthcare medicines.

2  *Skills*: The sorts of skills that are needed to carry out the strategy vary considerably between countries and also over time as the firm grows rapidly and new strategies and systems are introduced. As the levels and quality of education of staff may vary considerably too, an effective human resource development strategy can be important to identify and build the necessary skills.

3  *Staff*: The people that are recruited around the world need to be capable, well trained, and given the jobs that will best allow them to make use of their talents. Recognition of the contributions of the staff, the criteria for advancement, acceptance of appraisal and disciplinary processes vary considerably between countries.

4  *Shared values*: Despite the fact that staff come from different cultural backgrounds there is a need for employees to understand what the organization stands for, where it is going and to share the same organizational values.

The first part of the next section on international strategic management focuses broadly upon the 'hardware' and the second part on the 'software' of the McKinsey 7S framework.

## The generic marketing strategies for SME internationalization

While there are an infinite number of individual implementation strategies that an SME might adopt, the generic marketing strategies provide a useful starting point.

**Segmentation, targeting and positioning**    The principal approach to marketing strategy development follows three stages, normally referred to as segmentation, targeting and positioning (STP marketing):

1  Identification of the various segments that exist within the sector, using the various segmentation methods which we discussed in Chapter 4. It is important for the SME to define cross-border segments with clearly identifiable requirements that it is able to serve.

2  The firm must then target the segments which appear to be most attractive in terms of their size, growth potential, the ease with which they can be reached and their likely purchasing power.

3  In seeking to defend and develop its business the firm needs to position its products or services in a way that will distinguish them from those of its local and international competitors and build up barriers which will prevent those competitors taking its business.

**Competitive strategies**    In order to create the competitive advantage necessary to achieve growth, Porter (1990) suggests that firms should adopt one of the following three generic competitive strategies. However, each poses particular challenges for SMEs in international markets:

1  *Cost leadership* requires the firm to establish a lower cost base than its local or international competitors. This strategy has typically been adopted by companies that are located in countries that are component or service providers and have lower labour costs. As a result of their limited financial resources, however, SMEs that adopt a low-cost strategy spend little on marketing activity and are vulnerable to either local firms or larger multinationals temporarily cutting prices to force the

firm out of the market. Alternatively, changes in currency exchange rates or other instability in the economic climate can result in newer, lower-priced competitors emerging.

2  *Focus*, in which the firm concentrates on one or more narrow segments and thus builds up a specialist knowledge of each segment. Such segments in the international marketplace are transnational in nature and companies work to dominate one particular segment across a number of country markets. Typically, this strategy necessitates the SME providing high levels of customer and technical service support, which can be resource intensive. Moreover, unless the SME has created a highly specialized niche, it may be difficult to defend against local and international competition.

3  *Differentiation* is achieved through emphasizing particular benefits in the product, service or marketing mix which customers think are important and a significant improvement over competitive offers. Differentiation typically requires systematic incremental innovation to continually add customer value. While SMEs are capable of the flexibility, adaptability and responsiveness to customer needs necessary with this strategy, the cost of maintaining high levels of differentiation over competitors in a number of international markets can be demanding of management time and financial resources.

Many SMEs base their international plans on the generic strategy which has given them competitive advantage in domestic markets and then attempt to apply this same successful strategy in international markets. US and Chinese firms benefit from having a huge domestic market. By contrast, SMEs from emerging markets and from countries with smaller domestic markets often have to export merely to find enough customers to enable them to survive.

**Growth strategies**   Typically, SMEs have limited resources and so need to make difficult decisions about how to use these resources to grow the business. As long ago as 1957, Ansoff identified four growth strategies – product penetration, market development, product development and diversification – that still guide marketers today. Growth strategies are shown in Figure 5.4. Following a product penetration strategy is appropriate if a company has an existing portfolio of products and a presence in its target markets, which offer considerable potential expansion of sales. The resources available to the company under these circumstances can be best used in concentrating on doing more of what is already being done well.

Diversification, on the other hand, is a strategy used in international markets in situations where demand for the company's existing products is falling rapidly (for example, in recent years in the defence industry), where resources are available but would not generate an acceptable return if used on existing activities. Also, in the case of firms run by entrepreneurs, the owner can often become bored with the firm's current activities and seeks out new challenges by developing a new product for a new market.

For most companies the most obvious strategic development opportunities are in increasing geographical coverage (market development), which is discussed in Chapter 7, and product development, which is discussed in Chapter 8, perhaps by further differentiating a current product or applying their current technology to a new application. However, these options compete for resources, and firms have to choose which approach will generate a greater return on investment.

**FIGURE 5.4**   Ansoff growth matrix

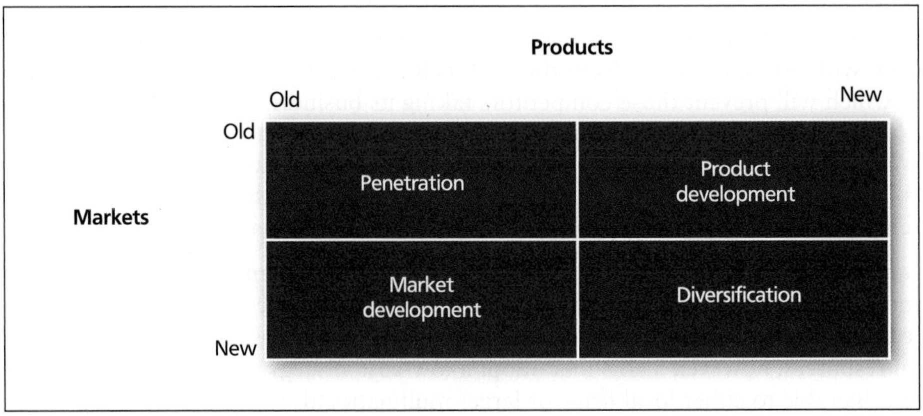

## The factors which affect the choice of an SME's international marketing strategy

Figure 5.5 indicates a number of the factors which influence the choice and development of an SME's international strategy. Particular issues include environmental trends, the market and industry structure, the customer requirements from different countries, the nature and intensity of local and international competition, and the degree to which the SME can defend its niche. In SMEs, however, specific company factors are particularly important in the decision. These include the resources available, the products and services that have been developed and the firm's attitudes to international development and management of risk. These will result in the firm adopting a specific approach to individual country selection as the strategy develops.

### Market factors

The most significant factor inherent in SMEs is their relatively small size and lack of power in most international markets in which they wish to be active. This puts them at a disadvantage with local competitors and MNEs. They often lack the management resources to spend on researching new markets, the contacts necessary to quickly develop effective distribution of their products and sufficient financial resources to enable them to compete with the promotional spend of their competitors. This can be vital to ensure they are strong enough to withstand a 'price war'.

At the same time, smaller size means that SMEs can offer customers the benefits of a more personal service from the firm's owners or senior managers, faster decision making and, usually, a greater willingness to listen. Of course, the SME must work out how to profit from international market developments by building on these potential strengths.

**FIGURE 5.5**   Factors affecting SME internationalization

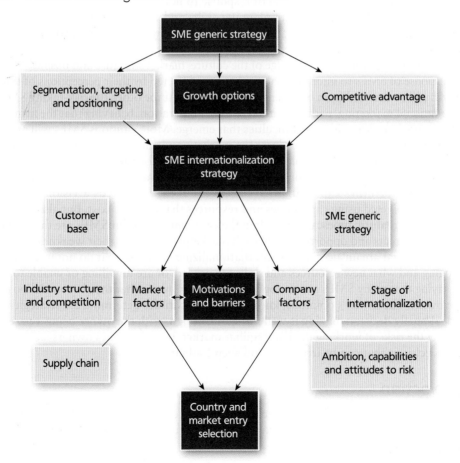

The SMEs' challenge is to communicate some unique selling propositions to their customers and create other competitive advantage dimensions, thus building barriers to entry around the niche that they have identified in order to stop attacks by competitors. There are a number of ways that this can be done.

First, underpinning any product/service offer must be a significant improvement in customer added value – there is little point in SMEs trying to market 'me-too' products internationally.

Second, if the product is a technical or design breakthrough, it should be protected wherever possible by patent or copyright. It is worth saying, however, that if the patent is challenged, the costs of fighting a court case, particularly in a foreign country, can be prohibitive for an SME with limited resources.

Third, the firm must exploit any creative way of shortcutting the route to market. It can do this by convincing experts or influential participants in the supply chain of the value of the product offer so they might recommend it, or by gaining exposure for the product at important events or in highly visible places. Some SMEs are using e-commerce to achieve some of these objectives: as a direct route to their international customers, to improve their efficiency in an international supply chain and to achieve greater effectiveness through collaboration with other SMEs.

Fourth, instead of using the traditional exporting routes to market such as agents and distributors, alternative methods of market entry, for example using licensing, franchising or joint ventures, can increase the diffusion of the product or service into the market more cost-effectively. Finally, more SMEs are now cooperating with other firms – a customer, competitor or a firm engaged in a complementary activity.

## Company factors

Only a minute proportion of the world's SMEs can be characterized as fast growth organizations and become the MNEs of the future. The sole objective of many businesses, such as the corner shop, the market trader and the car mechanic is to look for sufficient business from the domestic market to survive.

The smaller size and entrepreneurial approach of SMEs offer the advantages of flexibility and adaptability to new demands placed on them, speed of response to new opportunities and, usually, very focused management. However, SMEs lack adequate planning skills and are often unwilling or unable to devote sufficient time and finances to the research and development of new business opportunities. This can result in wasted effort and some expensive failures.

Frequently, SMEs have insufficient knowledge of the culture, market structure and business practices of new markets. The response of SMEs to international marketing is affected by their perceptions of this risk. At one extreme the SME will be deterred from becoming involved at all. At the other, the risk-taking SME will experiment with international marketing, perhaps with very little preparation, believing that the firm will be able to respond quickly enough to deal with any difficulties that emerge. More cautious SMEs will attempt to assess and manage the risks involved. They will evaluate the market opportunity and plan their use of management operations and financial resources to enable a cost-effective internationalization approach to be developed.

Underlying the diversity in the range of a firm's attitudes to risk are the owners' ambitions for the firm and how this fits with the firm's capabilities. To be successful the firm needs a vision of its international future which can be delivered using capabilities and resources that already exist. But also include those that can be acquired over a realistic timescale. It is often the case that successful SMEs are those that are able to clearly recognize the threats and opportunities in each marketplace, correct their weaknesses and build upon their strengths. SMEs that are unsuccessful in internationalizing are those that do not understand how their market is changing and what new resources and skills are needed, or are unwilling or unable to acquire them.

It is worth saying that many SMEs are so dominated by their owner that they become almost the personification of the owner. The owner's opinions, knowledge and attitudes determine the strategies adopted and decisions made. Usually decision making is well thought through, with the owner being aware, understanding and managing the risks of working in an unfamiliar market. But sometimes owners lacking international expertise make decisions that can be irrational and even foolhardy.

## Country selection

High levels of existing competition in developed countries make market entry challenging for SMEs. At the same time, the new high growth emerging markets offer opportunities for SMEs to develop their specialized niche products and services.

Increasing amounts of investment are now focused on the new emerging markets. The most adventurous SMEs recognize the need to be an early market entrant. Thus, for some, the most promising markets for their specialized products and services are in Africa and South America. At the same time, however, they are also the riskiest.

Cui *et al.* (2014) suggest SMEs that choose to develop and grow internationally select countries based on whether they are using an *exploitation* strategy or an *exploration* strategy. Essentially SMEs that choose the exploitation strategy choose new host countries that are similar to their home country in terms of the legal framework and the way organizations do business with one another. Additionally, SMEs will choose host countries where the general culture and behaviours of citizens are similar to those of their home country. Overall, there is familiarity between the home country and the new host country. This strategy gives the SMEs the opportunity to exploit and draw upon their existing success, extend the product life cycle of their products and benefit from economies of scale. If all these elements are equal, the marketing mix can remain standardized between the home country and the host country. However, if there is a great deal of unfamiliarity between an SME's home country and the new host country it has chosen to develop and grow, then the SME will have used the exploration strategy. Unfamiliarity between home and new host countries will mean there are different political issues, economic development structures may not be congruent, the way to conduct business and formalize agreements will have unfamiliar processes and timeframes, and so on. Nevertheless, many SMEs choose the exploration route if they wish to research, evolve and develop their products and services with new consumer markets. During the research and development stage in the new host country it is likely that through gaining knowledge of the host country's needs and wants, products and services will need to be adapted to accommodate different needs and wants. One of the benefits of choosing the exploration strategy is that it gives opportunities to gain competitive advantage by adapting current practice to the demands/requests of a new target market.

Figure 5.6 shows the differences between the two strategies and likens them to Ansoff's growth matrix (see Figure 5.4).

As shown in the table in Figure 5.6, there are two strategies that SMEs could take when considering which country to enter into as part of their growth plans. Figure 5.7 shows the different international country selection strategy visually, considering an SME from the UK.

**FIGURE 5.6**   SME: international country selection strategy

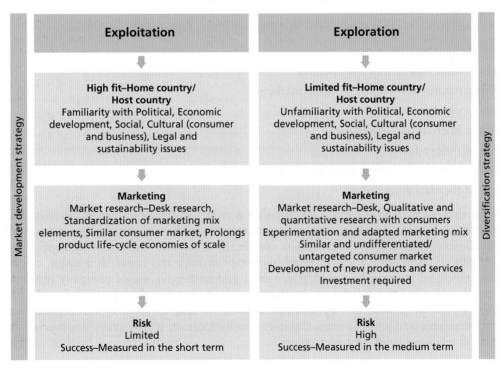

FIGURE 5.7   Exploration and exploitation strategy

————▶ Shows exploitation strategy
----▶ Shows exploration strategy

**Systems and support networks**   Typically, SMEs tend not to have sophisticated systems and support networks for managing their international operations, as is the case for large firms. Of course, advances in technology and the lower cost of IT systems, discussed in Chapter 12, are enabling SMEs to develop more advanced systems than they have had in the past. However, SMEs tend to rely on more informal, 'soft' systems and support networks that are based on personal contacts with family, friends, other business managers and officials for support, advice, information and knowledge.

## Organization structure

As an SME increases its involvement in international markets, so it needs to set up an organization structure that will enable the leadership and management to support, direct and control its often widespread and growing organization effectively.

Sarathy *et al*. (2006) identify some of the variables which might influence the decision:

- size of the business
- number of markets in which it operates
- level and nature of involvement in the markets
- company objectives
- company international experience
- nature of the products
- width and diversity of the product range, and
- nature of the marketing task.

For a firm starting out in export markets, the decision is relatively simple. Either its international business is integrated within the domestic business or separated as a specialist activity. Setting up a separate export department allows greater independence to look specifically at international marketing opportunities.

However, this could indicate a less or more important activity and could, as a result, create conflicts between domestic and international market demands and ineffective use of company resources. As the company develops further, it is faced with deciding how its international operations should be organized, for example by area, by product and by function. Figures 5.8 and 5.9 show typical organizational structures along geographic and product lines. Organization by function is only really appropriate for smaller companies with relatively simple product ranges.

FIGURE 5.8   Product structure

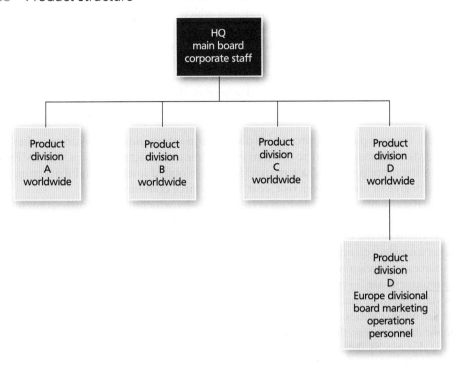

FIGURE 5.9   Geographic structure

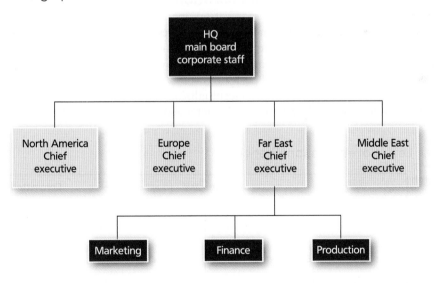

As the firm grows it may decide to establish control in different ways. For example, it may wish to control branding and corporate identity issues centrally through the use of international product managers. At the same time, it might wish to control the profitability of the business by having a senior executive in each individual country. In this way, the firm operates as a matrix structure within which individual managers might be responsible to different senior managers for different activities.

**Skills, capability and the stages of internationalization**   Having discussed the alternative categories of international marketing and the strategies which SMEs adopt, we now turn to the process of SME internationalization and the factors which lead to success and failure. In looking at a cross-section of firms it is possible to find some firms with different mindsets regarding international trade. These include those that are taking the major step from being a solely domestic company to generating their first revenue from foreign country sales. Others that are moving from the early stages of internationalization to a point where international marketing is totally integrated as part of the firm's activities are also looked at, as are a limited number of firms which are still small but have become confident world-class marketing companies.

**The first step**   Firms typically approach involvement in international marketing rather cautiously, as the first step towards what may appear to them to be a rather unpredictable future. For SMEs in particular, exporting remains the more promising alternative to a full-blooded international marketing effort, since it appears to offer a degree of control over risk, cost and resource commitment.

The further internationalization of the firm is the process by which the enterprise gradually increases its international involvement. This evolves in an interplay between the development of knowledge about foreign markets and operations on the one hand, and an increasing commitment of resources to foreign markets on the other. Market knowledge and market commitment are assumed to affect decisions regarding the commitment of resources to foreign markets and the way current activities are performed. Market knowledge and market commitment are, in turn, affected by current activities and operational decisions.

Thus, firms start internationalization by going to those markets that they can most easily understand. There they will see opportunities, perceive low market uncertainty and gain experience. As they go through the internationalization process, they will enter new more challenging markets where there is greater psychic distance. Psychic distance is defined in terms of factors such as differences in language, culture, political systems, etc., which disturb the flow of information between the firm and the market. This means that as the companies' market knowledge grows so does their commitment, which in turn affects the type of strategy they use.

**More advanced stages of internationalization**   As companies increase their international involvement so improvements occur in the organization, management and attitudes of those companies. Longer-term resources are committed and international business becomes part of the strategy rather than a tactical opportunity. Greater involvement in export marketing leads to better training and development, higher R&D expenditures, improvements in quality control, lower perceptions of risk and reduced costs of doing business, all of which lead to increased performance.

Figure 5.10 provides a staged approach to conceptualizing the internationalization process based on a composite of various writers' ideas. Firms can be characterized as being at one of the stages shown.

FIGURE 5.10   Levels of internationalization

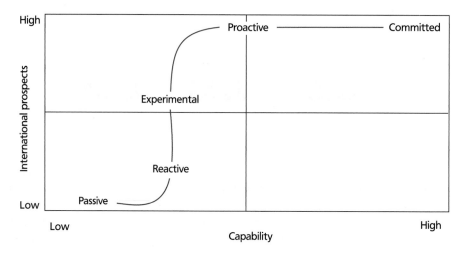

For many firms the internationalization process of companies is not a gradual incremental process but a series of step changes. There may be a number of factors which might initiate a step change. These include: an unexpected product or market success, the recruitment of a new chief executive, serious failure leading to a reassessment of the business, loss of markets, the changing expectations of stakeholders, owners impatient for a more substantial return on their investment, or business or family connections keen to share in the SME's success.

Grimes *et al.* (2007) developed profiles of the internationalizing firms and it is possible to use this to characterize firms at each stage of internationalization.

## The passive exporter
The passive exporter tends to lack any international focus and perceives export markets as having a high hassle factor. Many passive exporters are relatively new to the export business, often reacting to unsolicited orders, and tend to see their market as essentially home based.

Such firms do not carry out research or invest in export promotion campaigns and have little direct contact with foreign companies. Firms at this stage perceive little real need to export and have no plans to do so in the future.

## The reactive exporter
The reactive exporter sees export markets as secondary to the domestic markets but will put effort into dealing with key export accounts. Although they do not invest heavily in attracting export orders, once they have done business with a foreign customer they will follow up for repeat orders.

Such firms may have started to promote their export capacity and be starting to visit overseas clients. However, they have only a basic knowledge of their markets and are still undecided about their future role as an exporter.

## The experimental exporter
The experimental exporter is beginning to develop a commitment to exporting and starting to structure the organization around international activities. They are in regular contact with key accounts and are beginning to develop alliances with export partners to build better products and services by using information from their successful markets.

Although they would prefer not to, such firms are prepared to make product adaptations to suit overseas customer needs and may have appointed dedicated export staff to look after this part of the business.

## The proactive exporter
The proactive exporter is focused on key export markets and devotes substantial amounts of time and resources to entering and developing new markets. Regular market assessment in the form of desk research and using partners' information is carried out, and promotional materials are produced in a number of foreign languages.

Senior management regularly visit key accounts to maintain healthy relationships with clients. Exporting may account for up to 50 per cent of turnover. Exporting opportunities are welcomed and seen as crucial to the business.

## The well-established exporter
The committed exporter knows that exporting is integral to the business and sees the domestic market as just another market. The majority of the turnover is generated through international trade. Significant amounts of time are spent on this activity, with senior and middle managers frequently visiting customers.

Investment in training is substantial as skills are needed in-house. Thinking on export markets is both short-term tactical and longer-term strategic, with regular reviews of the overall mission and plan of action. Networks abroad provide excellent information and quality assured partners deliver on time, every time.

The firm's movement from one stage to the next, for example from reactive to experimental, experimental to proactive, and proactive to world class, therefore, is not gradual. Each of these step changes requires a coordinated strategy to improve the performance of the firm. Doole *et al.* (2006) explore the management practices and processes most closely associated with high levels of export capability. From this they identify ten benchmarks of international marketing practice (Figure 5.11) which indicate the most critical areas of the firms' management skills. Closer examination of the nature of these benchmarks reinforces the idea that

FIGURE 5.11   Characteristics of successful international business-to-business marketers

| Successful international business-to-business marketers: |
| --- |
| 1 Have a clear competitive focus in international marketplaces and a specific directional policy as to where the top management intend taking the firm. |
| 2 Have high levels of repeat business and operate tight financial controls in export markets. |
| 3 Have the tenacity and the resilience to face challenges and drive through change. |
| 4 Have a perception that risk indicates a problem to be solved, not an insurmountable barrier. |
| 5 View themselves as international niche marketers, not necessarily as good exporters. |
| 6 Fully invest in ensuring they have thorough knowledge of the international markets in which they operate. |
| 7 Are able to exploit distinctive product advantages in international markets. |
| 8 Are strongly committed to supplying quality products and services to all their customers wherever they are in the world. |
| 9 Build close relationships throughout the supply chain and invest in maintaining regular communications with their overseas partners. |
| 10 Have a well-defined communications strategy and invest in good quality promotional materials. |

Source: Isobel Doole's PhD thesis (2000).

successful international marketing is a predictor of fast growth. Further analysis suggests three key areas that SME international marketers need to focus on to ensure success:

1  Developing the characteristics of a learning organization.
2  Developing effective relationships.
3  Having a clear international competitive focus.

## Learning organization   A culture of innovation and learning throughout the firm is a common feature of successful firms that compete internationally. There is clear commitment from the top with senior management intent on building knowledge assets, and time and resources are invested in learning at all levels.

Investment in skills development enables the firms to be flexible in overcoming barriers and to be persistent in the face of difficulties. High levels of emotional energy are invested in the firm, and staff are innovative and willing to learn. A shared vision and a sharing of experiences among internal partners are also key elements of the successful organizations' commitment to learning. Tight financial measurement and performance are seen as crucial.

## Effective relationships   Firms who compete successfully in international markets build close relationships, not only with customers but with others throughout the supply chain. Effective relationships are crucial and sometimes the focus of successful organizations. Competitive advantage may not be the product itself, but rather the added value given to the product and the ability to exploit opportunities by the close, meaningful and regular communication with customers, increasingly through e-commerce.

A commitment to quality procedures, a quality mission and the use of quality-assured intermediaries are seen as vital. Service reliability is key to the firm's relationships and underpins its contribution to the supply chain.

## Clear competitive focus   Firms establish a clear and truly international focus, demonstrating a strong competitive position in a precisely identified market. Many successful firms adopt niche marketing strategies based on a clear mission statement and a planned development strategy.

Other features usually include clearly differentiated products, strong brand positioning and high levels of flexibility in adapting products to suit particular markets.

A thorough knowledge of markets is built up through innovative and informal means of collecting information and through focused research capability, concentrating resources where they are of most use. Most successful companies have primary markets which account for at least 30 per cent of their export turnover.

# International entrepreneurship and fast growth

There are a small number of firms which achieve hypergrowth through commercially exploiting a revolutionary idea, innovative business method or adopting a marketing strategy which simply leaves all the competitors behind. While some of these firms succeed as a result of a new technical or scientific invention, more important is the entrepreneurial flair needed to exploit the idea commercially. Some of the greatest successes are, therefore, associated with individual entrepreneurs who have the vision, determination, ability and ambition to succeed.

---

## MANAGEMENT CHALLENGE 5.3

### PayPal: is it trying to tell Malaysian SMEs something?

PayPal is the most well-known and well-used online payment platform. Consumers use PayPal for many online purchases including items from ebay.com, bookings from Hotels.com, Jet2.com and Trainline.com. Consumers can even load up their Starbucks card on the move using PayPal.

PayPal is a fantastic payment device for SMEs, particularly those that do business internationally. Alex Cheong, founder of web2ship.com is a B2B merchant from Malaysia who states he is very happy with PayPal. Like many merchants, fraud and security of monetary transactions are high on the list when trading internationally. PayPal's secure mechanisms make Alex and his consumers feel safe. But using PayPal is not just a payment tool, it is a research tool. The recent Cross Border Insights report from PayPal showed that online exports year-on-year (YoY) have increased dramatically.

Take, for example, Malaysian overland exports to Singapore and China. Exports have increased to Singapore by 5.1 per cent YoY and China by 9.2 per cent YoY. Contrast those figures with online exports and a different picture emerges. Singapore online exports increased 38 per cent YoY and China 58 per cent YoY. It is clear online export sales are growing at a much faster rate than overland export sales. This is good news for SMEs who are considering international growth and for existing businesses who should cement relations with their current stock of consumers. The boom is also steered by the government of Malaysia's initiatives which support local businesses. That mixed with consumer confidence in shopping directly from merchants internationally adds to the boom. With 143 million active PayPal accounts worldwide Malaysian SMEs could certainly benefit from this boom.

### Questions

**1** What are the benefits of comparing export sales by overland and online segments?

**2** How could SMEs in other countries benefit from the online export boom experienced in Malaysia?

**Reference:** *SME Magazine Asia* (2014) Export data is showing e-commerce is heating up export trade, 2 April 2014, www.smemagazine.asia (accessed 3 April 2014).

---

## The secret of high growth

For many firms, high growth in revenue and profits is the ultimate goal. But this challenge is set against a global background of ever-greater competition and the increasing expectations of customers. During times of recession or more intense competition some firms still manage to grow at a spectacular rate. It is by studying these firms that the drivers of fast growth in SMEs can be identified.

Kim and Mauborgne (2005) explain that it is necessary to find market areas that are uncontested (like the blue ocean of uncontested waters). Slower growth firms typically focus upon the competition by benchmarking and seeking to meet the customers' (slightly) increased expectations. Their goal is to outperform their rivals, usually by offering a little more value for a little less cost. The competitive response from the rivals is to do the same and, inevitably, this leads to a cycle of small-scale leapfrogging. A lot of blood is spilled (red ocean) as rivals try to damage each other!

Becoming embroiled within this competitive scenario initiates a pattern of strategic behaviour which is, in fact, the opposite of that which is associated with growth. Firms become reactive, drawing in resources to respond to the short-term competitive actions. They have no time or resources to think about the sorts of products and services that are needed for the future on a worldwide basis. Without this creativity the firms fall back on imitating competitors, believing the competitors' actions to be right for the market, rather than really exploiting the changes taking place in their customers' needs and wants.

By contrast, high growth firms leave the competitors to fight among themselves and, instead, seek to offer customers a quantum leap in value. The question that they need to pose is not what is needed to beat the competition, but rather what is needed to win over the mass of customers. The implications of this are that it is necessary to challenge the conventional wisdom and assumptions of the industry about the basis on which firms compete and what customers value. An additional bonus from challenging the way the industry does things is that if the firm thinks on an international scale it can also lead to large cost savings as unnecessary operations are eliminated. If the benefits really lead to a step change in value they will be perceived as such by customers all round the world.

Cirque du Soleil was a small organization that challenged the ideas that circuses are for children and should have animals, which are expensive to keep. For many it is also unethical to keep animals in captivity. Instead they created a spectacular show for adults which focuses on a combination of performance, art and music and has quickly become a worldwide phenomenon with 4000 employees.

In starting to change the way the firm thinks about its competitive strategy, it should address the following questions:

- What factors that your industry takes for granted should be eliminated?
- What factors that your industry competes on should be reduced well below the standard?
- What factors that your industry competes on should be raised well above the standard?
- What factors should be created that your industry has never offered?

By finding answers to these questions the firm can create new markets and new expectations for customers in existing markets. The Apple iPod, low-cost airlines (South West Airlines, easyJet and Ryanair), online communities (YouTube and Twitter) and mobile/cell phones (Nokia) show how providing a quantum leap in value to customers can reward the innovators. Typically, it is smaller firms that are not weighed down by the industry traditions and standards that challenge conventional wisdom. If the ideas are sufficiently innovative and appealing they will create new international niche opportunities.

**Shared values**   The core advantages of SMEs and the main factors for success are their innovative capability, responsiveness, adaptability and flexibility. These enable them to avoid direct competition from larger competitors. These values, which must come from senior management, must be shared and encouraged throughout the organization. They must also be underpinned by good strategic planning and management.

Due to the small scale of operations of SMEs, staff around the world often relate closely to and communicate regularly with the owner or senior manager of the SME. So it is often the personal values of the owner and their view of how the products and services should be marketed that become the shared values of the organization. See Illustration 5.6 for findings from research with SMEs that demonstrate corporate citizenship.

**The reasons for failure**   Many SMEs fail to reach their full potential because they do not manage effectively the international marketing and operational activities that are critical for international success. According to CBInsights (2018), the top 20 reasons for failure are shown in Figure 5.12.

SMEs entering the international market must not be complacent. It is important they research the market and their competitors. Similarly, they must be confident in their abilities and try to build barriers to entry to prevent the entry of potential competitors. Larger competitors can often gain business with an inferior product simply because of their greater promotional power or their control over the distribution channels. Therefore, SMEs must be proactive and keep their products up-to-date and be responsive to the needs of their consumers. Further, because of the often ad hoc, unplanned way that SMEs develop internationally, they can sometimes underestimate the level of resourcing needed. This can be in terms of time and money,

**FIGURE 5.12**    Reasons for failure of start-up businesses

Source: CBInsights (2018) www.cbinsights.com/research/startup-failure-reasons-top/ (accessed 5 June 2018).

## ILLUSTRATION 5.6

# SMEs and corporate citizenship: sharing harmony

It may be considered that only multinational organizations such as Pepsi, Burberry or Singapore Airlines can engage in corporate social responsibility for the good of global and local communities. However, it is not just big businesses that can make a difference within their communities. SMEs also have the opportunity to impact their communities through corporate citizenship. SMEs demonstrating corporate citizenship is a way of enhancing their reputation not just with their employees, but also with their customers and other businesses along the supply chain, which in turn boosts their competitive advantage.

Being a corporate citizen comes from the ethical and philanthropic influences of the SME owner/managers. First, SME owner/managers often seek employees from the local community, which improves the local community in terms of job opportunities which then enhances the local economy. Being an SME corporate citizen is more than just providing jobs, as Park and Campbell (2017) found. SME owner/managers embed the culture of the business. It is their influence and goals that drive an SME forward. Therefore, those that act on ethical and philanthropic goals often benefit more within their community than SME owner/managers who want personal gain through profit. SMEs who demonstrate corporate citizenship have a desire to form personal relationships with employees, customers and businesses along the supply chain. Through these relationships, cooperation, commitment and loyalty are formed, which in turn bring harmony and foster a feeling of community. This approach also reduces staff turnover as staff feel valued.

### Questions

**1** Why do SMEs that form relationships with employees, customers and businesses along the supply chain benefit?

**2** How could SMEs form other relationships that demonstrate corporate citizenship to boost their local community?

**Reference:** Park, J. and Campbell, J.M. (2017) US SMEs' corporate citizenship: collectivism, market orientation, and reciprocity. *Journal of Small Business&Entrepreneurship*, 29(2), 120–139.

difficulties and delays that may arise, and consequently the length of time it takes to reach profitability in new foreign markets. The investment that is needed is frequently greater than the firms expect. They often fail to negotiate a suitable arrangement with their bank or other funders before difficulties emerge.

The main danger associated with international niche marketing is that the income stream is often dependent upon one single product or service idea, or a very limited product portfolio. Given the capacity of competitors to copy product ideas, the firm must be absolutely sure that it has built in some unique competitive advantage such as a strong brand, unique technology or reliable business contacts to sustain it against the competition.

Creative SMEs find alternative ways to strengthen their international position, perhaps by finding a different way of expanding. This can be achieved by forming a joint venture or alliance with another firm, contracting out production to a firm with spare capacity, licensing the product or process, or even agreeing to be taken over.

## The future of SME internationalization

There are many pitfalls for an SME that is active in international markets. For some SMEs the greatest risk is internationalizing at all, particularly if they have no definable source of competitive advantage and little understanding of international marketing. However, with increasing globalization, firms such as these are no longer able to hide their inefficiency or lack of creativity in the domestic market as they will come under attack from international competitors. The global environment and the changing dynamics in markets can be equally challenging.

Almost as risky is operating as a traditional exporter – selling excess capacity into markets about which the SME has little or no information and with which its managers have little cultural empathy. Manufacturing SME exporters from developed countries struggle to compete with companies from emerging markets which have lower labour costs. However, small low-cost manufacturers in emerging markets are coming under pressure from manufacturers from less developed countries that can undercut their prices. For SMEs that are innovative and ambitious, are prepared to embrace new technology, use new routes to market and find new innovative ways of doing business, there are opportunities for success on a scale never before envisaged. But only if they are willing to learn, have a clear competitive focus and a strong network of connections. For the most successful there is often an alternative opportunity to sell out, for example, Innocent Smoothies by Coca-Cola, Pret à Manger by McDonald's, Ben and Jerry's by Unilever, and Seeds of Change by Mars.

## SUMMARY

- SMEs have always been involved in international marketing but now have greater opportunities to develop internationally and create wealth and employment for their domestic economy. New technology allows smaller firms to access information and communicate internationally in a way that was not possible before.

- Successful SME international marketers are those that build relationships with individuals and organizations that can help them understand the nature and value of the competitive advantage that they possess, and learn from their own experiences and those of others.

- The principles of international marketing can be applied to all categories of SME international activity, ranging from exporting manufactured goods, through e-commerce to marketing domestic attractions to tourists. However, SMEs use different ways of internationalizing and selecting countries for market entry from an incremental selection of countries, based on market potential or a network of contacts, through to hi-tech businesses that are 'born global'. This depends upon the context in which the firm is internationalizing.

- The chosen SME internationalization strategies are underpinned by generic marketing strategies but are often also affected by the management's perception of the barriers in the environment, the support that is provided in the domestic country and the specific market factors that affect their business sector.

- The stage of international development that the SME has reached reflects the company's capability, and the confidence and attitude of the senior management to internationalization. It usually shows how the SMEs have utilized their inherent strengths of flexibility, adaptability, innovative capability and speed of response in developing their markets.

- There are a number of factors that lead to success and failure for SME international development, but the most significant factor is the ability of SMEs to offer customers a quantum leap in value by innovating throughout the marketing process.

## KEYWORDS

small- and medium-sized enterprises

born global

micro-multinationals

domestically delivered or developed niche services

barrier to entry

international niche marketing

reciprocal trading

electronic commerce

network

market concentrators

market expanders

internationalization

supply chain

outsource

7S framework

generic marketing strategies

organization structure

stages of internationalization

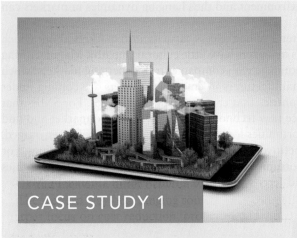

## CASE STUDY 1

# Telensa: a shining light in smart cities

Telensa, based in Cambridge, UK, claims to be the global leader in connected street lighting and Smart City applications. In February 2018 it was placed fourth in the Sunday Times SME Export Track 100, a league table of the UK's SMEs with the fastest-growing international sales. The firm's products were already in use in 80 cities worldwide, including Atlanta, Dubai and Wellington.

Telensa was founded in 2005 by Will Gibson and Tim Jackson. It was spun out from an electronics design consultancy Plextek in 2010. In 2017, £10.3 million of its £22.8 million sales were international sales, and growth had averaged almost 190 per cent per annum over two years as its expansion into the Middle East, Asia Pacific and Latin America followed success in Europe and the USA. The company had 100 staff and had opened offices in Atlanta and Melbourne. It uses lights manufactured by Sony UK Technology Centre in South Wales.

Telensa PLANet is the most used streetlight solution with 1.5 million lights worldwide. The system reduces energy use and maintenance costs. Its automatic fault reporting helps to improve service quality and the LED streetlight output can be dynamically controlled. These features enable city managers to continually make decisions about street lighting as conditions change.

Due to the fact that it is based around street poles, it is relatively easy to create a mounted wireless network with sensors distributed across the city. This means that it has the potential to provide a low-cost platform on which the data-driven Smart City can be created using multiple sensor application. For example, by working with partners that make sensors, the network can be used to track weather changes, traffic frequency, people movements and to monitor pollution.

The network can be enlarged through integration with third-party applications. Examples are to support car parking and charging, tracking of city and third-party assets and enabling sharing of data with and between them. This is a city application of the 'Internet of Things'.

In city planning and management, city leaders and managers are increasingly required to justify and prioritize the use of precious physical and financial resources. Increasing transparency of data and providing evidence of operational efficiency is essential to support strategic development and planning by the city leaders.

## Questions

**1** Who are likely to be the main targets for Telensa's Smart City marketing?

**2** What are Telensa's key selling propositions to them?

**3** How might these propositions need to be adapted in different regions of the world?

**4** How can Telensa ensure it remains a key player in Smart Cities as new applications are developed?

**References:** www.Telensa.com; Britain's SMEs with the fastest-growing international sales, The Sunday Times SME Export Track 100, February 2018. Available from www.fast-track.co.uk/league-tables/sme-export-track-100/league-table/ (accessed 5 June 2018).

## CASE STUDY 2

## Pin it, share it, desire it, sell it

Worldwide consumers are engaging with many social media platforms, and retailers must ensure they are active where their consumers are present. Pinterest is one of those platforms where SME e-tailers have the opportunity to provide another shop window, 'free of charge', promoting their products. Pinterest is in addition to the SME e-tailers website, Instagram, Facebook page and Twitter feed. What is crucial for business is that Pinterest boards and pins give SME e-tailers the opportunity to become part of their consumer's personal life. Enid Hwang, Pinterest's company community manager, states Pinterest is a very personal and intimate virtual platform where consumers choose what they want to view, pin and repin.

Pinterest was formed in 2010 in Silicon Valley and already has over 175 million monthly users (100 million monthly users outside the USA) and the numbers are expected to keep growing. Research suggests that 81 per cent of the shoppers are female. More importantly for businesses, 55 per cent of users are shopping for products, whereas only 12 per cent of other social media are shoppers. There are over 50 billion picture pins with personal pinboards entitled 'Shoes I Want' to 'Woodwork DIY' and 'Things to do in Montenegro'. Generally, pins are categorized into shopping and leisure categories called, for example, 'Wedding Cakes' or 'Clothes to Buy for Holidays'. E-tailers categorize folders and populate the folder with Pin It pictures that provide a visual bookmark for the consumer and a promotional tool for the e-tailer.

We Make Websites is a London-based company that is hugely successful in the Shopify e-commerce world. Two of their top tips for SME e-tailers provide an insight into how to communicate a brand, its values and ethos through Pinterest.

The example SME e-tailer used in this case study is Up Knörth based in Vancouver, British Columbia. Up Knörth provides high-quality, rugged outdoor, sustainable and durable clothes and accessories for men and women who have a keen environmental conscience.

### Tip 1. Tell a story

It is recommended that SME e-tailers like Up Knörth tell a story on Pinterest through pictures that encompass the brand's values, lifestyle, desirable products and places. The story-telling objective is to ensure pinners understand how the Up Knörth brand fits with the pinners' lifestyle. Up Knörth does this with PinBoards. PinBoards include items of their own products together with PinBoards entitled Cabin Design, Camping, Adventuremobile and Growing. Each PinBoard shows pins of how their products and values fit the values of pinners that also enjoy rugged, outdoor adventures and care for the environment.

### Tip 2. Contribute and get discovered

Pinterest is all about providing appealing pictures of products and lifestyles. Pin It pictures on Up Knörth's PinBoards are beautiful, inspiring and desirable. The products for sale are included. There are also 1287 pins of log cabins either taken by the Up Knörth team or Pin Its of cabins in Norway pinned from fantasticnorway. no and of a rustic cabin pinned from lostonabacroad. tumblr.com. All their log cabin pictures were repinned or liked by Up Knörth's 144 000 followers. Contributing beyond Up Knörth's own products attracts and engages followers and helps them understand the brand and what its values are.

These tips help a business such as Up Knörth stay connected and build further networks. More importantly, Pinterest Boards stimulate enquiries and click-throughs to the e-tailers' websites, blogs, Facebook and other social media platforms. Up Knörth blogs about environmental issues, produces video diaries of travel adventures in wild and wonderful places, as well as suggesting minimalistic DIY ideas (using recycled materials of course) and Nordic recipes including dill and salt-cured salmon.

### Questions

**1** What are the advantages of using Pinterest for SMEs?

**2** What strategies should SMEs use when planning to begin using Pinterest?

**3** Why does Up Knörth include a range of PinBoards?

**4** How important is Pinterest for an SME's communication strategy?

**References:** Columbus Despatch (2015) Pinterest drawing wider audience $11 billion social-media hub hopes to corner market on brainstorming, www.dispatch.com (accessed 6 April 2015); WeMakeWebsites (2015) Blog: How to use Pinterest to grow your business, wemakewebsites.com/blog (accessed 6 April 2015); Up Knörth (2015) Pinterest Board, www.pinterest.com/upknorth/ (accessed 5 June 2018); Pinterest by the numbers: Stats, demographics&fun facts 1 January 2018 www.omnicoreagency.com/pinterest-statistics/ (accessed 5 June 2018).

## DISCUSSION QUESTIONS

**1** How can the smaller business compensate for its lack of resources and expertise in international marketing when trying to enter new markets?

**2** Why is international niche marketing likely to be a superior approach to export selling?

**3** As the leader of a rock group you have had moderate success in your home country but have noticed that you seem to be gaining fans in different countries. As you have not been signed up by a recognized music company, how might you exploit your popularity internationally?

**4** How does the mindset of a proactive international marketer differ from a reactive marketer?

**5** Small international marketing firms do not have the resources to carry out market research systematically. What advice would you give to a Danish renewable energy firm that wishes to enter the Southern African market?

## REFERENCES

1.  Ansoff, I. (1957) Strategies for diversification. *Harvard Business Review* 35(5): 113–124.

2.  Ayuso, S. and NavarreteBáez, F.E. (2018) How does entrepreneurial and international orientation influence SMEs' commitment to sustainable development? Empirical evidence from Spain and Mexico. *Corporate Social Responsibility and Environmental Management* 25(1), 80–94.

3.  Berrywhite (2018). www.berrywhite.com/our-story/ (accessed 5 June 2018).

4.  *Botswana Gazette* (2015) DHL realising increasing demand in retail sector. Available from www.thegazette. news/dhl-realising-increasing-demand-in-retail-sector/ (accessed 20 March 2018).

5.  Brown, L. and McDonald, M.H.B. (1994) *Competitive Marketing Strategy for Europe*. Macmillan.

6.  CBInsights (2018) www.cbinsights.com/research/startup-failure-reasons-top/ (accessed 5 June 2018).

7.  Columbus Despatch (2015) Pinterest drawing wider audience $11 billion social-media hub hopes to corner market on brainstorming. Available from www.dispatch.com (accessed 6 April 2015).

8.  Crick, D. and Crick, J. (2014) The internationalization strategies of rapidly internationalizing high-tech UK SMEs: Planned and unplanned activities. *European Business Review* 26(5), 421–448.

9.  Cui, A.P., Walsh, M.F. and Zou, S. (2014) The importance of strategic fit between host–home country similarity and exploration exploitation strategies on small- and medium-sized enterprises' performance: A contingency perspective. *Journal of International Marketing* 22(4), 67–85.

10. Cull, R. and Beck, T. (2014) Policy Research Working Paper 7018 'SME Finance in Africa'. World Bank Group.

11. Cusmano, L., Koreen, M. and Pissareva, L. (2018) 2018 OECD Ministerial Conference on SMEs: Key Issues Paper. OECD SME and Entrepreneurship Papers, No. 7, OECD Publishing. Paris. http://dx.doi. org/10.1787/90c8823c-en.

12. DHL (2014) LLP Newsletter August 2014 Nigeria Security Case Study. Available from: http://www.dhl.com/ en/logistics/customer_resource_area/logistics_news/ llp_newsletter_q6.html (accessed 7 June 2018).

13. DHL Botswana (2015) *Country Profile*. Available from www.dhl.co.bw/en/country_profile/key_facts.html (accessed 5 June 2018).

14. Doole, I., Grimes, A. and Demack, S. (2006) An exploration of the management practices and processes most closely associated with high levels of export capability in SMEs. *Marketing Intelligence and Planning* 24(6).

15. *Economic Times* (2017) Why SMEs on growth trajectory should consider outsourcing HR requirements.

Available from: https://economictimes.indiatimes.com/small-biz/hr-leadership/people/why-smes-on-growth-trajectory-should-consider-outsourcing-hr-requirements/articleshow/61078889.cms (accessed 23 March 2017).

16. Efrat, K., Gilboa, S. and Yonatany, M. (2017) When marketing and innovation interact: The case of born global firms. *International Business Review* 26(2), 380–390.

17. Fairtrade (2017) *Monitoring Report*. Available from: https://monitoringreport2016.fairtrade.net/en/ (accessed 5 June 2018).

18. Fairtrade Foundation (2018) *Farmers and Workers*. Available from: www.fairtrade.org.uk/Farmers-and-Workers (accessed 5 June 2018).

19. Fraudmann, A. (2017) SMEs and global growth: Meeting logistics challenges. *The Economist*. June 2017.

20. Global Entrepreneurship Monitor (2014) *Global Entrepreneurship Monitor 2014*. Available from: http://gemconsortium.org/report (accessed 7 June 2018).

21. Grimes, A., Doole, I. and Kitchen, P.J. (2007) Profiling the capabilities of SMEs to compete internationally. *Journal of Small Business and Enterprise Development* 14(1), 64–80.

22. Hagen, B., Zucchella, A., Cerchiello, P. and De Giovanni, N. (2012) International strategy and performance – Clustering strategic types of SMEs. *International Business Review* 21(3), 369–382.

23. IMF (2015) *Sub-Saharan Africa Navigating Headwinds*. April 2015. International Monetary Fund.

24. Johannson, J. and Vahlne, J.E. (1992) The mechanism of internationalization. *International Marketing Review*, Emerald Insight.

25. Kalinic, I. and Forza, C. (2012) Rapid internationalization of traditional SMEs: Between gradualist models and born globals. *International Business Review* 21(4), 694–707.

26. Katsikeas, C.S. and Leonidou, L.C. (1996) Export marketing expansion strategy: differences between market concentration and market spreading. *Journal of Marketing Management* 12.

27. Kim, W.C. and Mauborgne, R. (2005) *Blue Ocean Strategy: How to Create Uncontested Market Space and Make Competition Irrelevant*. Harvard Business Press.

28. Kulmeier, D.B. and Knight, G. (2010) The critical role of relationship quality in SME internationalization. *Journal of Global Marketing* 23(1).

29. Muller, P., Julius, J., Herr, D., Koch, L., Peycheva, V. and McKiernan, S. (2017) *Annual Report on European SMEs 2016/2017* © 2017 – European Union. All rights reserved.

30. Nueno, P. (2000) The dragon breathes enterprising fire. In S. Bailey and F. Muzyka (eds) *Mastering Entrepreneurship*. FT Prentice Hall.

31. OECD (2009) *Top Barriers and Drivers to SME Internationalization*. Report by the OECD Working party on SMEs and Entrepreneurship, OECD.

32. OECD (2014) *Economic Outlook Africa 2014*. Available from www.oecd-ilibrary.org (accessed 3 April 2014).

33. OECD (2017) www.oecd.org/cfe/smes/New-Approaches-SME-full-report.pdf (accessed 5 June 2018).

34. OECD (2017) Going digital: making the transformation work for growth and wellbeing. Available from www.oecd.org/going-digital/project/going-digital-information-note.pdf (accessed 5 June 2018).

35. Park, J. and Campbell, J.M. (2017) US SMEs' corporate citizenship: Collectivism, market orientation, and reciprocity. *Journal of Small Business & Entrepreneurship* 29(2), 120–139.

36. Peters, T.J. and Waterman, R.H. (1982) *In Search of Excellence*. Warner.

37. Pinterest by the numbers: Stats, demographics & fun facts 1 January 2018. Available from www.omnicoreagency.com/pinterest-statistics/ (accessed 5 June 2018).

38. Porter, M.E. (1990) *Competitive Advantage of Nations*. Free Press.

39. Sarathy, R., Terpstra, V. and Russow, L. (2006) *International Marketing*, 9th edition. Dryden Press.

40. Servais, P., Madsen, T.K. and Rasmussen, E.S. (2007) Small manufacturing firms involvement in international e-business activities. *Advances in International Marketing* 17, 297–317.

41. *SME Magazine Asia* (2014) Export data is showing e-commerce is heating up export trade, 2 April 2014. Available from www.smemagazine.asia (accessed 3 April 2014).

42. Solheim, E.M. (2012) The internationalization process of born global companies: A study of born globals without prior internationalization experience, Unpublished. NTNU School of Entrepreneurship.

43. Statista (2018) *Revenue of Fairtrade International Products Worldwide from 2004 to 2016 (in million euros)*. Available from www.statista.com/statistics/271354/revenue-of-fair-trade-products-worldwide-since-2004/ (accessed 5 June 2018).

44. UK Council for International Student Affairs (2018) *International Student Statistics: UK Higher Education*. Available from www.ukcisa.org.uk (accessed 20 March 2018).

45. Up Knörth (2015) Pinterest Board, www.pinterest.com/upknorth/ (accessed 5 June 2018).

46. WeMakeWebsites (2015) Blog: How to use Pinterest to grow your business, wemakewebsites.com/blog (accessed 6 April 2015).

47. WTO (2016) *World Trade Report: Levelling the Trading Field for SMEs*. Available from: www.wto.org/english/res_e/booksp_e/world_trade_report16_e.pdf (accessed 5 June 2018).

## CHAPTER 6

# GLOBAL STRATEGIES

## LEARNING OBJECTIVES

After reading this chapter you should be able to:

- Appreciate the various aspects of globalization and be able to compare and contrast the alternative global strategies

- Evaluate the factors that determine a firm's choice of global strategy

- Identify the challenges that firms, particularly from emerging markets, face in developing a global presence

- Appreciate the role of branding in globalization

- Understand the factors affecting global marketing management

## INTRODUCTION

Having discussed the nature of international development in smaller firms, we now consider the global marketing strategies of the largest firms that compete on a worldwide basis. The largest firms have the mindset of achieving **globalization** as the route to maximizing performance by introducing, where possible, standardized marketing programmes and processes to enhance efficiency and competitiveness. At the same time, they adapt certain operational activities to local needs in order to achieve effectiveness by maximizing short-term revenue generation. The problem that such firms face is exactly which aspects of their international activity to standardize and which to adapt. These decisions are often context specific and are affected by the particular factors which drive change within their particular industry. This leads to firms adopting a variety of global strategies, from those that are very similar from country to country, to those that are substantially different in each country in which the firm operates. These strategies substantially increase complexity. In the past, global marketing has been dominated by firms from developed countries, such as Coca-Cola, McDonald's and Microsoft. But an increasing number of firms such as LG and Samsung, from recently emerging markets, have become global players too. As the balance of economic power in global markets shifts further to the BRIC (Brazil, Russia, India and China) and MINT (Mexico, Indonesia, Nigeria and Turkey) countries, many more firms from those markets are poised to continue the trend.

In this chapter we start by reviewing the dimensions of the concept and drivers of globalization, before considering the alternative strategic approaches and the factors that drive strategic choice. This discussion is then followed by an examination of the strategy implementation issues that international and multinational enterprises (MNEs) might face in managing their global business and building their global presence. We place particular emphasis on global branding. We end the chapter with a discussion of the issues that must be addressed in order to manage global marketing effectively.

# The alternative views of globalization

Since the late 1980s, the term globalization seems to have led to a polarization of views. For some, globalization is associated with opportunity, the removal of barriers to prosperity for all countries of the world and greater exposure to, and understanding of, different cultures. Globalization encourages large and small businesses to be creative and innovative. Developing countries can quickly embrace new ideas and technology without going through the long and expensive research and development stages. Others see globalization, capitalism and MNE activity as the same thing. They believe global companies dominate international business, ruthlessly exploiting the countries' resources and adversely influencing the economy and culture of every country. They are seen as moving their operations from country to country according to whichever offers the lowest wage rates. Thus, they have no thought for those who lose their jobs or the well-being of those who are paid extremely low wages. In the last few years the actions of global companies have been blamed for a loss of cultural traditions.

In practice, globalization is about progress towards an, as yet, undefined goal. Few companies, even those with the most familiar brand names, are truly global. Table 6.1 lists the biggest firms in the world by revenues. It shows that half of the top ten companies are in the petroleum- and power-related industries. However, Walmart Inc. remains at number one and automobile organizations remain strong global businesses. This picture is similar to that presented in Table 6.2, which shows the top 20 transnational companies (TNC) ranked by foreign assets. UNCTAD (2017) provides a measure of the real transnationality of multinationals by identifying an index of transnationality (TNI), which is an average of the measures of transnationality (foreign to total assets, sales and employment).

The most dominant multinational companies still come from developed economies and are typically from the motor, petroleum and telecommunications sectors (see Tables 6.1 and 6.2). Multinational companies in countries such as Taiwan, Province of China and Republic of Korea (top 20 in Table 6.3) are gaining a significant presence. It is also clear that an increasing number of 'big businesses' are from BRIC and MINT countries and it is expected these companies and more will appear in the top 100 global companies as emerging countries grow.

There is no doubt that the world's largest firms seek a worldwide presence.

Table 6.1 Top ten companies in the world by revenues

| Rank | Company | Revenues (US$ billion) | Country | Industry |
|------|---------|------------------------|---------|----------|
| 1 | Walmart Inc. | 485.9 | United States | Mass merchants |
| 2 | State Grid | 315.2 | China | Electricity (utility company) |
| 3 | China Petroleum & Chemical Corporation (Sinopec Group) | 267.5 | China | Integrated oils |
| 4 | China National Petroleum | 262.6 | China | Oil and gas |
| 5 | Toyota Motor | 254.7 | Japan | Automobile OEM |
| 6 | Volkswagen | 240.3 | Germany | Automobile OEM |
| 7 | Royal Dutch Shell | 240.0 | Netherlands | Integrated oils |
| 8 | Berkshire Hathaway | 223.6 | United States | Multinational conglomerate |
| 9 | Apple | 215.6 | United States | Technology |
| 10 | Exxon Mobil | 205.0 | United States | Integrated oils |

Source: Adapted from Top 10 revenue worldwide companies, Bloomberg and Fortune 500 Global companies 2017.

Table 6.2   The top 20 non-financial multinational companies ranked by foreign assets 2016

| Ranking by foreign assets | Corporation | Home economy | Industry | Foreign assets (US$ million) | TNI* (per cent) |
|---|---|---|---|---|---|
| 1 | Royal Dutch Shell plc | United Kingdom | Petroleum refining and related industries | 349 720 | 74.3 |
| 2 | Toyota Motors Corporation | Japan | Motor vehicles | 303 678 | 60.2 |
| 3 | BP plc | United Kingdom | Petroleum refining and related industries | 235 124 | 74.9 |
| 4 | Total SA | France | Petroleum refining and related industries | 233 217 | 80.9 |
| 5 | Anheuser-Busch InBev SA/NV | Belgium | Food & beverages | 208 012 | 82.1 |
| 6 | Volkswagen Group | Germany | Motor vehicles | 197 254 | 60.3 |
| 7 | Chevron Corporation | United States | Petroleum refining and related industries | 189 116 | 57.9 |
| 8 | General Electric Co | United States | Industrial and commercial machinery | 178 525 | 56.8 |
| 9 | ExxonMobil | United States | Petroleum refining and related industries | 165 969 | 52.1 |
| 10 | SoftBank Group Corp | Japan | Telecommunications | 145 611 | 62.5 |
| 11 | Vodafone Group Plc | United Kingdom | Telecommunications | 143 574 | 81.4 |
| 12 | Daimler AG | Germany | Motor vehicles | 138 967 | 59.6 |
| 13 | Honda Motor Co. Ltd | Japan | Motor vehicles | 130 067 | 77.6 |
| 14 | Apple Inc. | United States | Computer equipment | 126 793 | 47.9 |
| 15 | BHP Billiton Group Limited | Australia | Mining, quarrying and petroleum | 118 953 | 79.1 |
| 16 | Nissan Motor Co., Ltd. | Japan | Motor vehicles | 116 612 | 70.1 |
| 17 | Siemens AG | Germany | Industrial and commercial machinery | 115 251 | 65.9 |
| 18 | Enel SpA | Italy | Electricity, gas and water | 111 240 | 55.3 |
| 19 | CK Hutchison Holdings Limited | Hong Kong, China | Retail trade | 110 515 | 84.5 |
| 20 | Mitsubishi Corporation | Japan | Wholesale trade | 107 860 | 62.5 |

*TNI: Transnationality Index, is calculated as the average of three ratios: foreign assets to total assets; foreign sales to total sales; and foreign employment to total employment.
Source: UNCTAD, Annex table 24. The world's top 100 non-financial MNEs, ranked by foreign assets, 2016a, based on data from companies' financial reporting corresponding to the financial year 1 April 2016 to 31 March 2017. Reprinted with the permission of the United Nations.

**Table 6.3**  The top 20 non-financial multinational companies from developing and transition economies, ranked by foreign assets 2015

| Ranking by foreign assets | Corporation | Home economy | Industry | Foreign assets (US$ million) | TNI* (per cent) |
|---|---|---|---|---|---|
| 1 | CK Hutchison Holdings Limited | Hong Kong, China | Retail trade | 118 250 | 85.8 |
| 2 | China National Offshore Oil Corp (CNOOC) | China | Mining, quarrying and petroleum | 66 673 | 23.8 |
| 3 | Hon Hai Precision Industry Co., Ltd. | Taiwan, Province of China | Electronic components | 64 040 | 84.3 |
| 4 | Samsung Electronics Co. Ltd. | Korea, Republic of | Communications equipment | 62 294 | 63.4 |
| 5 | PETRONAS | Malaysia | Mining, quarrying and petroleum | 47 912 | 42.5 |
| 6 | China COSCO Shipping Corp Ltd | China | Transport and storage | 43 076 | 49.8 |
| 7 | Vale S.A. | Brazil | Mining, quarrying and petroleum | 35 338 | 48.6 |
| 8 | China Minmetals Corporation Limited | China | Metals and metal products | 35 165 | 20.9 |
| 9 | América Móvil, S.A.B. de C.V. | Mexico | Telecommunications | 34 480 | 59.8 |
| 10 | Tata Motors Limited | India | Motor vehicles | 30 589 | 68.3 |
| 11 | Cemex S.A.B. de C.V. | Mexico | Stone, clay, glass and concrete products | 26 830 | 79.9 |
| 12 | Hanwha Corporation | Korea, Republic of | Wholesale trade | 26 326 | 20.4 |
| 13 | China State Construction Engineering Corp Ltd (CSCEC) | China | Construction | 25 472 | 12.6 |
| 14 | Singapore Telecommunications Ltd | Singapore | Telecommunications | 25 309 | 65.3 |
| 15 | New World Development Company Limited | Hong Kong, China | Construction | 24 990 | 47.6 |
| 16 | Formosa Plastics Group | Taiwan, Province of China | Chemicals and allied products | 24 490 | 24.9 |
| 17 | Tencent Holdings Limited | China | Computer and data processing | 24 086 | 36.1 |
| 18 | Oil and Natural Gas Corporation Ltd. | India | Mining, quarrying and petroleum | 23 921 | 32.8 |
| 19 | China National Chemical Corporation (ChemChina) | China | Chemicals and allied products | 23 795 | 46.3 |
| 20 | Hyundai Motor Company | Korea, Republic of | Motor vehicles | 23 450 | 32.2 |

Data based on companies' annual reports corresponding to financial year 1 April 2015 to 31 March 2016.

*TNI, Transnationality Index is calculated as the average of three ratios: foreign assets to total assets; foreign sales to total sales; and foreign employment to total employment.

Source: UNCTAD, Web table 20. The top 100 non-financial MNEs from developing and transition economies, ranked by foreign assets, 2016a. Reprinted with the permission of the United Nations.

## Globalization and standardization

In seeking to compete successfully in increasingly globalized markets, MNEs realize that a precondition of long-term growth is a worldwide presence. In previous chapters we have discussed the nature of global markets. A fundamental question is whether global markets require standardized products. Decades ago a number of writers such as Elinder (1961) and Levitt (1983) debated whether or not this would result in globally standardized products and services.

So far, there are few examples of product and service offers which have been completely standardized across the world. And these are probably limited to those sold over the Internet in the B2B sector. Some of the most widely available products which might be considered to be standardized are in fact substantially adapted. You can taste the Coca-Cola variants from around the world at the museum in Atlanta and try the different McDonald's menus as you travel. Computer companies use different language options in their service manuals. American baseball has the World Series competition in which only North American teams take part, in contrast to the football World Cup competition (in Qatar in 2022) where 32 countries will take part from the 210 countries that entered the qualifying rounds (islands within a general territory count as separate countries). The concept of globalization, therefore, is often characterized by contradictions. These include the need to standardize some elements of the marketing mix while, at the same time, accepting the requirement to respond to local desires and tastes by adapting the product or service. Some believe that the true nature of globalization is encapsulated in the phrase 'think global, act local', in which there is an acknowledgement of the need to balance standardization and adaptation according to the particular situation. Even this concept is challenged because it implies that the starting point for the strategy is based on a standardized marketing mix. For many international businesses and MNEs, 'think local, act global' may be more appropriate given that it implies focusing on local needs. But it also means taking the opportunity, whenever feasible and appropriate, to standardize elements of the marketing mix and globalize support services. Against this background the word globalization is associated in a very imprecise way with many different aspects of the international marketing strategy process. However, Illustration 6.1 shows how the Hard Rock Café has developed internationally and localized parts of its marketing mix.

## ILLUSTRATION 6.1

## Hard Rock Café localizing memorabilia and merchandising

Hard Rock Café was started by two Americans, Isaac Tigrett and Peter Morton, in London in 1971. They were travelling and just wanted an 'all American burger', and as they could not find one, they created a café to do just that. The first Hard Rock Café was based in a rented former Rolls Royce showroom. From there it has flourished into an international brand with cafés, hotels and casinos in hundreds of locations around the world. There are several pillars that support the iconic brand, three of which show how Hard Rock Café can standardize and localize effectively. The three pillars are:

1  Music

2  Memorabilia

3  Merchandising

Isaac Tigrett and Peter Morton not only liked burgers but they loved great music, namely rock 'n' roll music from the Beatles to the Rolling Stones and Stereophonics to Lucia Fontaine. At all times, day and night, music is played (loudly) at Hard Rock Café. Local rock bands also grace the stage playing covers of classic tunes intermingled with their own songs.

Memorabilia adorning the walls in Hard Rock Cafés are as famous as the cafés themselves. Each café has a range of memorabilia from rock stars, including guitars from Led Zeppelin, Elvis Presley's studded jumpsuits, John Lennon's glasses, Madonna's bra and posters of Miley Cyrus and the Black-Eyed Peas. There is also memorabilia, concert posters and album covers from local rock legends, all of which provide a global and local feel to each café.

Each Hard Rock Café also has a shop full of exciting merchandise such as standard pins, badges, clothing, drumsticks and toys. The iconic Hard Rock Café bear is often localized, not just with a hoodie with the Hard Rock Café city location emblazoned across the front, but with costumes symbolic to the local area. The bear sold in Warsaw has wings. The wings are symbolic of a Polish army troop, namely the Hussars. The Hussars were formed in 1503 and were known to be successful in battle. Legend has it that the Hussars were successful partly because they had long feathers attached to the infantryman's saddle. The long feathers made the infantryman look as if he had wings. When the Hussars charged into battle, the feathers vibrated and created such a noise that the sight and sound of the infantrymen frightened the enemy.

Warsaw is not unique. In Venice the Hard Rock Café bear is dressed as a gondolier (gondola driver) to signify a profession that is nearly 1000 years old.

## Questions

**1** Who benefits from the Hard Rock Café standardizing and localizing in its globalization strategy?

**2** New Hard Rock Café openings are Cairo in Egypt, Chengdu in China and Gramado in Brazil. What marketing mix elements would you localize?

## The drivers of globalization

Although globalization may be difficult to define satisfactorily, there are a number of drivers of globalization that can be used to explain its impact and discuss its implications (see Table 6.4).

*Globalization of market access* has increased as the number of inaccessible markets has reduced following the political changes that have opened up markets. For example, in central and eastern Europe and China there is now much greater MNE involvement. While these 'new' markets have become more accessible, firms entering them usually face difficult problems establishing their global products there. This can be because of differences in social and business culture and the lack of a reliable infrastructure. Also, the unfamiliar and unpredictable legal framework and the varying standards and values of business practice, which often lead to corruption, can also present problems. While these markets offer attractive growth prospects, many western global firms have shown themselves to be ill-equipped to exploit these opportunities. Initially, they were unwilling or unable to 'go it alone' in these markets. The markets were unsophisticated by developed country standards, and western global firms found it necessary to form partnerships with local firms, with mixed results.

In the short period since these markets have opened up many local companies have experienced phenomenal domestic growth, which has enabled them to build a platform from which they themselves can become global players.

**Market access** is also being improved by the increasing regionalization, resulting from the growth of trading blocs. Firms are reinforcing this effect by helping to reduce inter-country barriers. This improves market access by firms operating more standardized pan-regional marketing programmes and processes such as product development and advertising. Indeed, the market access challenges for global companies now relate not so much to externally imposed barriers but to internal management issues faced by competing in emerging markets against increasingly sophisticated competitors.

*Globalization of market opportunities* has increased with the continued deregulation of certain sectors. Financial services is one such sector, where the traditional barriers between the various parts of an industry,

Table 6.4 Drivers of globalization

| | |
|---|---|
| Market access | Customer requirements |
| Market opportunities | Competition |
| Industry standards | Cooperation |
| Sourcing | Distribution |
| Products and services | Communication and information |
| Technology | Company strategy, business programmes and processes |

such as banking, insurance, pensions, specialist savings, mortgage and loan suppliers, are being broken down. This has enabled supermarket groups to enter many market sectors, including financial services and pharmacy product retailing.

Removal of sector barriers has resulted in mergers or alliances of firms to form larger and more powerful groups which can offer a complete range of products or services to their customers in the sector. For such MNEs, the power base may be a large domestic or regional market, as has been the case with a number of mergers in financial services or automobiles.

The privatization of government-owned utilities such as electricity, gas and telephone is leading to industry restructuring where previously there were monopolies with tight operating restrictions. Vila and Peters (2016) highlighted many examples of privatization, including UK-privatized Royal Mail, Spain's AENA Airport, and Portugal's Energias de Portugal (EDP) and Redes Energéticas Nacionais (REN). This is allowing firms to compete in geographic areas and industry sectors from which they had previously been excluded.

An interesting example of this is shown in Management Challenge 6.1 in which two international airports are operated under private ownership.

## MANAGEMENT CHALLENGE 6.1

## International airports funded privately

There are a number of European airports that are no longer publicly owned; instead, some of them are now privately owned. That is to say, organizations can invest their money and become shareholders in airports in their own or other countries. The privately owned trend is moving upwards. There are 500 airports in Europe. In 2010 the number of fully privately owned airports was 9 per cent; by 2016 the percentage was 15.8 per cent. Airports are now considered to be businesses working within a competitive environment. Revenue streams from shareholders can be beneficial as it can help airports to innovate and improve. Heathrow Airport and London Gatwick are examples of two European airports funded by organizations overseas, details of which are shown below.

Privately owned airports such as Heathrow and London Gatwick need to satisfy shareholders. To do this, the airports need to be efficient, lean and still provide excellent service for customers and neighbouring communities.

### Question

1 What are the disadvantages of airports being owned by private shareholders?

| Airport | Airport code | Name of airport operator | Ownership of airport operator | % Shares | Shareholder name |
|---------|--------------|--------------------------|-------------------------------|----------|------------------|
| Heathrow Airport | **LHR** | Heathrow Airport Limited | Fully private | 25% | Ferrovial S.A. |
| | | | | 20% | Qatar Holdings |
| | | | | 13% | Caisse de dépôt et placement du Québec |
| | | | | 11% | Government of Singapore |
| | | | | 11% | Alinda Capital Partners |
| | | | | 10% | China Investment Corp. |
| | | | | 10% | Universities Superannuation Scheme (USS) |
| London Gatwick Airport | **LGW** | Gatwick Airport Limited | Fully private | 42% | Global Infrastructure Partners, LP |
| | | | | 17.2% | Future Fund Board of Guardians |
| | | | | 15.9% | The Abu Dhabi Investment Authority |
| | | | | 12.8% | The California Public Employees Retirement System |
| | | | | 12.1% | National Pensions Service of Korea |

Source: Airports Council International (2016) *The Ownership of Europe's Airports*. www.newairportinsider.com (accessed 5 June 2018).

*Globalization of industry standards* is increasing as technical operating standards, professional rules and guidelines are being adopted more widely. This is primarily due to the harmonization of regulations within trading blocs. More generally around the world, this is also as a result of the increased mobility of experts and advisers and the wider use of quality standards. Such standards include ISO 9001 for quality management and ISO 14000 for environmental management. It is a precondition of supplying major customers that firms operate to certain product and service standards that can be recognized regionally and globally.

The largest MNEs are expected to work to ethical standards that cover such diverse areas as employment, environmental protection and unfair competition. As a result, MNEs demand that their staff work to exacting company standards. Professional staff are usually also regulated by national bodies, so greater regional harmonization is affecting standards of behaviour and performance. Despite this, there is a long way to go, particularly where organizations outsource workforces and production centres.

*Globalization of sourcing* has increased as companies search the world for the best and cheapest materials, components and services rather than rely on local suppliers. Figure 6.1 identifies the benefits of global sourcing.

## FIGURE 6.1   The benefits of global sourcing

- *Cheaper labour rates*. Fashion and clothing marketers obtain supplies from low labour rate countries such as China, Indonesia, Costa Rica, Vietnam and Latin America. There can, however, be problems with product quality. There may also be criticism of unethical behaviour as these firms resort to 'island hopping' to the new lower labour rate areas that result from changes in local country economic development. Their contractors may also employ child labour.

- *Better or more uniform quality*. Certain countries and companies have competitive advantage over others as suppliers because of the local availability of materials and skills.

- *Access to the best technology, innovation and ideas*. Firms search the world to identify a particular research or design centre which might offer the specialist expertise they require. For example, Nissan set up design facilities in California. Microsoft has established research facilities close to Cambridge University in the UK.

- *Access to local markets*. Developing stronger links with a country through sourcing can help to generate new business in that country. For example, the aircraft maker Boeing has opened up the market in China following its decision to purchase components there.

- *Economies of scale advantages*. Where the location of a manufacturing or distribution operation is convenient to supply a whole region, it can lead to significant cost advantages.

- *Lower taxes and duties*. Certain countries may offer tax advantages to manufacturers and low rates of duty when shipping goods to the customer. The relocation of some higher added value activities can help by spreading currency risk.

- *Potentially lower logistics costs*. Global transport and warehousing companies use IT more effectively to control product movement and inventory.

- *More consistent supply*. Some foods would be restricted because of seasonality if steps had not been taken to arrange supplies from countries with different growing seasons.

Illustration 6.2 explains that new country destinations are being found for outsourcing.

The major risks in global sourcing are in dealing with countries where there might be political, economic and exchange rate risks. There are also specific risks associated with an individual supplier that might use the knowledge gained and power which results from a strong position in the supply chain to become a competitor. As increasing numbers of scientists and engineers are being trained in China, India and central and eastern Europe, so outsourcing of research and development to these countries will lead to increased competition from them in the future. Quality and service provided by the supplier can be critical and if not managed can begin to affect the reputation of the customer. What is crucial is that the MNE must retain its

## ILLUSTRATION 6.2

# J.P. Morgan: being the outsourcer and outsourcee

J.P. Morgan is a global leader when it comes to investment banking, financial transaction processing, private equity, commercial banking and asset management. It topped the Forbes' Worldwide Investment Banking Rankings. It is based in New York but is a multinational company and also researches market dynamics to inform other multinational organizations. J.P. Morgan is known to offer first-class B2B services. To do this, it employs the best people. In 2013 J.P. Morgan plunged into the uncharted waters of outsourcing. J.P. Morgan is now both an outsourcer and an outsourcee. An outsourcer is an organization that acquires some of its goods or services from other third-party organizations. When an organization is an outsourcee, the organization is the third party which offers goods or services to other organizations.

J.P. Morgan wanted to solidify its business service in Europe and Asia. To do this it scoured the globe for a country that would have highly skilled financial services employees. J.P. Morgan found these employees in Warsaw. As the outsourcer, J.P. Morgan will outsource a range of tasks including risk management and other central functions for clients in Europe and Asia through its newly formed global operations centre. The Polish Prime Minister, Mateusz Morawiecki, was delighted and said the opportunity to enable Polish workers to be outsourced to a high-profile, award-winning, top-ranking bank like J.P. Morgan is like a 'little Mercedes in the services sector'. Outsourcing in Poland created 2500 jobs in 2018.

J.P. Morgan is an outsourcee for Rebeco, an asset management company. This means it uses client money to invest or buy securities. Rebeco, based in Rotterdam, has been in business since the 1930s. It invests billions of dollars each year and has 15 offices worldwide and employs 877 people. Rebeco's strategy was to reorganize and meet demanding growth targets. Its 2017–2021 Strategic Plan included being an outsourcer and passing its operations and management activities to a skilled organization. It chose J.P. Morgan for this. The outsourcing activities began in 2018. Outsourcing at Rebeco meant that 70 Rotterdam-based employees lost their jobs.

## Question

**1** What are the main advantages and disadvantages of outsourcing?

**References:** Rebeco (2018) Rebeco outsources part of its operations activities to JP Morgan. Available from www.robeco.com/en/media/press-releases/2018/robeco-outsources-part-of-its-operations-activities-to-jp-morgan.html (accessed 5 June 2018); Shotter, J. (2017) JPMorgan plans to create 2,500 new jobs in Poland  www.ft.com/content/706c66f0-9f7a-11e7-9a86-4d5a475ba4c5 (accessed 5 June 2018); J.P. Morgan. www.jpmorgan.com (accessed 5 June 2018).

---

competitive advantage. It should not outsource its supplies to the point where it gives away all its technical and commercial secrets, power in the market or risks supply quality problems. This potential danger needs to be managed by purchasers improving their supplier–purchaser relationships or, perhaps, even forming longer-term strategic alliances. The additional benefit of better supplier–purchaser relationships can be improved communications and the avoidance of some unnecessary supply chain costs. These can result from inadequate specifications, misunderstandings about quality and generally poor management. As we will see later, the Internet has made the development of international supply chains easier but has also changed their nature.

*Globalization of core products and services.* More and more products are reaching the mature phase of their product life cycle and this is leading to greater commoditization of products and services. Consumers see very little difference between the offerings of many competing suppliers as they become less loyal to a single brand. The increased speed at which new innovations can be copied by other competitors means that core benefits can no longer be a point of differentiation between competitors. MNEs are responding to this and trying to gain competitive advantage over local competition. They do this by differentiating their products through developing their marketing and customer service capability in the form of the brand image and by providing higher levels of service or better technical support.

*Globalization of technology.* Technology is converging within and between industries, with similar processes and ideas being used, for example, in telecommunications, IT hardware and software, and entertainment and consumer electronics. This means that new multifunctional products and services cross the traditional boundaries between the industry sectors. New technologies are adopted around the world at ever greater speeds. In many industries this is being driven by a small number of global players. These global players have the market power to change the ways of working and generate sufficient demand from customers to make the wider application of the ideas more cost-effective. In this way the globalization of technology is contributing very significantly to the competitive advantage of the MNEs. This is because they are able to market products in a number of industry sectors because they have developed effective distribution channels and international promotion.

*Globalization of customer requirements* is resulting from the identification of worldwide customer segments, such as teenagers with similar worldwide tastes in music, fashion and fast food. The very rich, who live the celebrity lifestyle and buy the most expensive fashion brands, fly first class or hire their own plane, stay at the same luxury hotels and own super performance cars, are another customer segment. No matter where they originate, they consume the same products and services. With industries becoming more globalized, the demands placed on the business support services, such as advertising agencies, accountants, law firms and consultants, are converging too. Customers in both the consumer and B2B markets are demanding and getting what they perceive to be added value global products and services. These better meet their changing needs than those they have been used to receiving from national companies.

*Globalization of competition* between industry giants tends to result in the same fight being replicated in each corner of the world, with MNEs using largely similar competing product or service offers. Traditional national firms have been outmanoeuvred by aggressive fast-growing international competitors who are far better at exploiting technical changes and other globalization effects and winning customers with more sophisticated marketing. They are also able to cross-subsidize their activities between countries, so helping them to gain an unfair advantage over local competition.

Mature industries, as well as new technology sectors, are being affected by global competition. For example, while the majority of the top ten chemical companies are European, there is increasing competition, particularly from Asian companies. These companies have different cost structures and systems of industry regulation. Success in these component and raw material industries has traditionally been dependent upon the product portfolio, the relationship with customers and the levels of technical service and support provided. Increasingly, the fact that these are components in the supply chain of branded consumer products means that successful suppliers must carry out more effective marketing to members of the supply chain that are closer to the customer.

*Globalization of cooperation.* To compete in all the major world markets, it is necessary to make available huge financial resources, often outside the scope of individual firms. This is leading to the formation of alliances between major MNEs, members of a supply chain or between firms with complementary activities. The Japanese *keiretsu* go further in that they are formal organizations between banks, manufacturers and trading companies with cross-share ownership. They have the huge resources necessary to build businesses in the major world markets. This has enabled them to make investments over a number of years to establish a dominant long-term market position in a particular industry.

*Globalization of distribution* is occurring as the supply chain becomes increasingly concentrated on fewer, more powerful channel distributors, retailers and logistics companies. In addition, e-business technology dominates the exchange and transfer of data and the whole process of product and service transactions, including methods of product and service selling, ordering, customizing, progress chasing, payment arrangement and delivery confirmation. Finally, as logistics become a source of competitive advantage, for example in retailing, it contributes to the international success of Walmart, Ikea and Tesco. For many organizations it can be argued that a global approach to distribution means organizing according to factors such as proximity to the population and transport infrastructure, rather than country borders.

Globalization of distribution is particularly important for companies such as Amazon that use e-commerce. They must be able to make transaction and logistics arrangements to enable them to provide high levels of service and efficiency to customers, wherever they are located.

*Globalization of communication and information.* Major changes in telecommunications and IT have had three effects. First, global communications such as satellite and cable TV, and the World Wide Web have made it essential that MNEs develop a consistent worldwide corporate identity and brand image. As consumers travel physically or virtually by way of the media or World Wide Web, they are exposed to communications and advertising originating from MNEs from many parts of the world. Consistency of communication is vital for reinforcing brand familiarity, quality and values.

Second, digital technology is driving the localization and individuality of communications, for example through the proliferation of local TV channels, on-demand video and television and the continued development of the Internet. This allows greater exposure for individual communications. These developments go further than simply improving the accessibility of the traditional one-way communications with customers by adding a two-way, interactive dimension to the firms' relationships with their global customers. And clearly a three-way, interactive dimension is B2C, C2B and C2C.

Third, the explosion of social media through websites such as Facebook and Twitter, means that much more discussion of the MNE's activities takes place outside the influence and control of the company. Thus, while the globalization of communications leads to global access for customers, the need to integrate communications is becoming ever more difficult to manage.

*Globalization of the company's strategy, business programmes and processes.* The result of these globalization effects is to pose challenges to firms to achieve both improved global operational efficiency and greater global market effectiveness. The global firm's response to managing the complexity of international marketing must include developing an all-embracing global strategy supported by effective marketing programmes and processes that will integrate the various disparate activities of the firm's far-flung strategic business units.

In considering each of these areas of globalization in turn, it is possible to identify business sector examples in which the globalization trend is relatively advanced and others in which it is in its early stages. For example, accountancy and associated consultancy is dominated by four major players. Until the late 1990s retailing could be regarded as a largely national or, at most, subregional activity with few examples of retailers active in more than five or six countries. The challenge for global companies is to lead the development towards globalization in industry sectors where there is the greatest potential for growth. However, there is no guarantee that by simply being globally active in an industry sector a firm will benefit. Firms must be able to manage the environmental threats and exploit their market opportunities by building global competitive advantage. Illustration 6.3 shows how a firm from an emerging country has become a global player and is investing and expanding internationally, but keeping a global mission.

## Alternative strategic responses

It is against the background of the trend towards globalization and the need to build a worldwide presence that firms must develop strategic responses which are appropriate to their situation and are feasible to implement. For MNEs, the question may be how to rationalize their activities to gain greater focus and effectiveness. For firms that have progressed through the early stages of expansion into new country markets, the next stage is to decide whether or not to progress further. If yes, what strategy might they adopt to enable them to manage their involvement in many countries? Underpinning the growth strategy in either case must be some fundamental decisions about the product portfolio and expansion into new country markets.

ILLUSTRATION 6.3

# Tata Group reaching out around the world

In 2018 Tata Group turned 150 years old. It is now a global leader, a conglomerate from India that is successful in over 100 operating companies spread across 6 continents. Revenue was $100.4 billion (in 2016/17) and it employs 695 000 people within the Group.

Starting in 1868, Jamsetji Nusserwanji Tata began by establishing a trading business in Bombay. Being an entrepreneur at heart, he then provided seeding capital for businesses in steel, energy, textiles and hospitality and helped to build businesses. Jamsetji Tata also invested in the education of Indian children through JN Tata Endowment for the Higher Education of Indians, which began in 1892. Like all businesses, Jamsetji Tata's had a mission statement and goals. Mission statements and goals are often set to drive businesses towards gaining profit and/or collecting assets. However, the central tenet to Jamsetji Tata's mission statement was to be a righteous person; not just a righteous person who lives a good life but who makes life better for others. This mission statement showed the underlying values of Jamsetji Tata, which have remained the foundation of Tata Group's purpose and leadership style.

From the 1930s to the 1980s, the Tata business continued to thrive, expanding into insurance, soap and cooking oil. During this time Tata noticed many changes, notably that international businesses were expanding globally and entering the Indian market. While continuing to invest in businesses within India, Tata also began to look to other countries for expansion opportunities. Now Tata Group is a major player with multinational businesses including Tata Steel, Tata Motors, Tata Consultancy Services, Tata Power, Tata Chemicals, Tata Global Beverages, Tata Teleservices, Titan, Tata Communications and Indian Hotels.

To be part of such a complex international situation, Tata needs to have exceptional leadership and all-embracing values that drive the business forward collectively, with the values felt by each employee. Tata Group's mission statement today is: 'To improve the quality of life of the communities we serve globally, through long-term stakeholder value creation based on Leadership with Trust.' Clearly, this reflects the early philanthropic tenet of Jamsetji Tata. Tata Group shares profits with employees, shareholders and communities. It also invests in education and community causes to uplift the lives of those who are less fortunate.

## Question

**1** It is often expected that global businesses need to prove their success through profits and assets. How have Jamsetji Tata's values helped Tata be successful?

**Source:** Tata.com.

## The international competitive posture

The level of geographic development and product strength determine the strategic options available to a company. Gogel and Larreche (1989) identify four types of competitors along the two dimensions of product range and geographic coverage, as shown in Figure 6.2. The position of a company on the international competitive posture matrix will determine the strategic options that organizations can consider when deciding upon their international strategy.

**Kings** Because these firms have a wide geographic coverage and strong product portfolio, they are in a strong competitive position. They have been able to expand geographically and have not dispersed their resources into weak products. They are in the best position to have an effective global strategy and are the true global companies.

FIGURE 6.2   The international competitive posture matrix

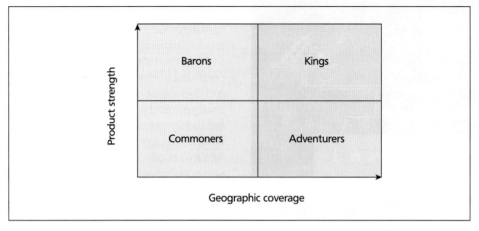

Source: Gogel and Larreche (1989). The battlefield for 1992: Product strength and geographic coverage, European Management Journal, Volume 7/2, 1989.

**Barons**   These companies have strong products in a limited number of countries. This makes geographic expansion attractive to them unless their domestic and close-by markets are large and untapped. In this case there is little need for international expansion. However, without domestic growth opportunities barons can be attractive to companies wishing to supplement their own product strength. Therefore, they may be takeover targets.

**Adventurers**   These have been driven to expand geographically, but they lack a strong portfolio. They are vulnerable to an increasing level of global competition. Their challenge is to consolidate their product position. They do this by focusing on internal product development, acquisition or by eliminating products to concentrate on a narrower portfolio in a classic global niche strategy.

**Commoners**   Commoners have a product portfolio with relatively weak international potential and narrow geographic coverage. They may have benefited from legal barriers protecting them from intense competition in their existing markets. They are likely acquisition targets. Before any geographical expansion they need to build their product portfolio. A likely international strategy could be one of supplying own-brand products to retailers.

Increasing geographic coverage and product strength means competition for resources and each quadrant of the matrix reflects the trade-offs that may become necessary. The position of a firm on the matrix reflects how it has been able to balance its resources between consolidation and expansion of geographic coverage and product strength. Technology companies such as Microsoft were initially adventurers, marketing their operating system widely before building up their product range to become the 'kings' they are today. Companies from Asian markets frequently are 'barons', developing a strong product range and building their home or close regional markets before developing internationally.

## Global strategy drivers

The fundamental driver of a global strategy is whether the market allows significant global standardization of the marketing activity or whether substantial adaptation is needed to address local differences and expectations. The challenge for global firm strategy development is to maximize the efficiency and effectiveness of their operations. Having a completely standardized marketing offer, products, services, communications, etc. would be very efficient. But, for most companies it would not maximize effectiveness in revenue generation, given the differing needs of customers from different countries and cultures. The second driver is what orientation the company adopts – in other words how it sees itself in the global market.

Before looking at the market factors it is useful to consider the company orientation, shown in Figure 6.3.

The standardization and adaptation drivers lead to the worldwide strategy options illustrated in Figure 6.4 with, at the one extreme, the concept of a multi-domestic approach in which the firm has a completely

**FIGURE 6.3**  Company orientation in global strategy development

| Global orientation | Focus |
| --- | --- |
| Ethnocentric | Because the domestic market is considered to be the most important, the company adopts home country standards and values. It assumes that the marketing offer in the home country will be acceptable in new country markets. Standardized products and services are typically designed for the domestic country and exported. The brand usually reflects the domestic country image. |
| Polycentric | Each country market is unique. The marketing offer is designed to meet the individual needs of the customers of each country. Typically, a country manager would ensure that the products and services are adapted locally. The brand is developed to incorporate cultural differences. This would typically result in a multi-domestic strategy. |
| Regiocentric | Developing a regional strategy as the geographic market focus, for example, a company might develop a product and service portfolio for Europe or for southern Africa. The organization gives the regional managers considerable autonomy. The regional focus, however, can leave missed opportunities to standardize. |
| Geocentric | This is the global or transnational company that sees the entire world as a potential market. The strategy adopted focuses on one global customer segment that requires a globally standardized product or service. Alternatively, a geocentric company develops a transnational strategy that uses a strategy based on a standardized identity and well communicated values. It would then integrate standardized and adapted elements of the marketing offer to efficiently meet the diverse needs of customers. |

different strategy for every single market. At the other extreme is a global approach in which everything in the marketing activity is standardized in all countries. In addition, an ethnocentric firm that is very focused on the domestic market might seek to export its home market model with few modifications. In practice, firms adopt a combination of standardization and adaptation of the various elements of the marketing management programmes and processes by globalizing some elements and localizing others. In broad terms it is possible to categorize a firm's strategic development as multi-domestic, global or regional. In regional development a firm implements separate, but largely standardized, marketing strategies across a region of the world.

**FIGURE 6.4**  Alternative worldwide strategies

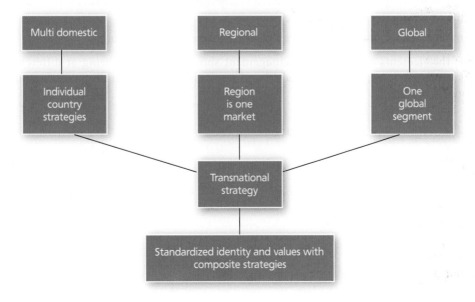

The largest, most complex companies in the world use a combination of all these strategies. A transnational approach is one in which the firm has a standardized identity and corporate values throughout the firm but delivers its strategic objectives through composite strategies. These contain elements of multidomestic, regional and global strategies. The global marketing strategy is influenced significantly by the supply chain decisions relating to location of operations and outsourcing arrangements.

Zou and Cavusgil (2002) identify three perspectives of global marketing strategy: the standardization perspective, the configuration perspective and the integration perspective. The global firm locates its supply chain activities in those countries where they can be carried out most efficiently. Components are then transferred to another country for assembly, before the highly standardized finished goods are exported to the countries in which they will be sold, supported by largely standardized marketing. Global firms then integrate their activities and competitive moves to enable them to become major players in all major markets. Increased outsourcing makes these tasks more challenging as success depends on customer requirements being met on time.

Standardizing the various elements of the marketing process has the aim of scale economies and experience curve effects in operations, research and development, and marketing. Concentrating value chain activity in a few country locations exploits comparative advantage and so improves efficiency. The experience curve effect or learning curve relates to the relationship between experience and efficiency.

## Standardization and adaptation

The challenge facing firms with aspirations to become truly effective global players appears to be turning widespread international presence into global competitive advantage. The critical success factor in achieving this is to offer added value for global customers. They do this by providing the customers with benefits that are significantly better than those provided by the competitors, particularly local competitors. The benefits can be tangible: for example, a global product such as Intel processors that are broadly the same worldwide. They may also be intangible: for example, a brand such as Rolex that is recognized worldwide. At the same time, they must aggressively seek cost efficiencies that will enable the firm to offer better value for money than their competitors.

In practice, firms manage these apparently incompatible requirements by using strategies that are appropriate to their own situation. They strike a balance between the different degrees of standardization or adaptation of the various elements of the international marketing process.

In general:

- Marketing objectives and strategies are more readily standardized than operational marketing decisions.
- Within the marketing mix, products are most easily standardized, promotion less so, and distribution and pricing only with difficulty.
- The more operational the decision the more likely it is to be differentiated.

Consequently, the elements of marketing management should be seen as being at different points of a continuum of standardization, where the product and service image are generally easier to standardize than individual country pricing.

| | |
|---|---|
| Pricing | Adaptation |
| Distribution | |
| Sales force | |
| Sales promotion | |
| Product image objective | |
| Strategy | Standardization |

Of course, as Akgün *et al.* (2014) state, some businesses will both standardize *and* adapt elements of their marketing mix. They might keep the product brand name standardized but adapt on-pack promotions or colour and distribution opportunities dependent upon which country they enter. See Management Challenge 6.2 for an example of a Turkish furniture business's marketing mix challenges.

## MANAGEMENT CHALLENGE 6.2

## Turkish B2B and their marketing mix

Domestic businesses often feel compelled to expand internationally because their domestic economy is weak and/or unemployment is high, both of which lead to low consumer spend. Alternatively, to take advantage of economies of scale, businesses consider it a wise move to make more of the same product and find new consumer marketing internationally. The latter is known as Ansoff's growth matrix (See Figure 5.4 in Chapter 5). A Turkish furniture business chose the market development growth strategy as it saw B2B opportunities outside their domestic market. During the research project they realized that they could standardize some of their marketing mix elements, but adapt others.

The product name, brand and style of furniture items were standardized across international markets. However, the colours of the products needed to be adapted as western European consumers preferred lighter or white furniture, whereas Romanian consumers preferred much darker colours. The price for the same product was adapted for each international country. The pricing policy was based on a competition-based policy. This meant that the Turkish furniture was costed at a price similar to other furniture of a similar standard available in each country. The marketing mix place was adapted too. In some countries, such as France and Greece, the Turkish furniture business could sell direct to independent franchisees. However, in Germany and Austria the Turkish furniture business could only sell to chain stores. Therefore, the distribution B2B network available in each country contributed to the level of standardization or adaptation required. The Turkish furniture business provided standardized advertising material for international stores that sold their furniture on an exclusive basis. However, they did allow the international stores to adapt the advertising material to suit local consumer needs.

### Question

**1** What are the advantages and disadvantages of the adaptation and standardization of marketing mix elements for the Turkish furniture?

**Reference:** Akgün, A.E., Keskin, H. and Ayar, H. (2014) Standardization and adaptation of international marketing mix activities: A case study. *Procedia – Social and Behavioral Sciences* 150, 609–618.

## Globally standardized strategy

A company adopting a global strategic orientation makes no distinction between domestic and foreign market opportunities. It seeks to serve an essentially identical customer segment appearing in many countries around the world. It develops global strategies to compete with other global firms. Global marketing can be defined as the focusing of an organization's resources on the selection and exploitation of global market opportunities consistent with and supportive of its short-term strategic objectives and goals.

Global marketing is the realization that a firm's foreign marketing activities, in whatever form they take, need to be supportive of some higher objective than just the immediate exploitation of a foreign market opportunity. Global marketing can, therefore, involve the selection of a country for its potential contribution to globalization benefits. A firm may even enter an unattractive market which has global strategic significance – for example, the home market of a competitor. Thus, an organization with such a global focus formulates a long-term strategy for the company as a whole and then coordinates the strategies of local subsidiaries to support this.

Many writers have offered views on this issue. For example, Levitt (1983) suggested that in order to be competitive in the world market, firms should shift their emphasis from local customized products to globally standardized products that are advanced, functional, reliable and low priced. Buzzell (1968) argued that product standardization has the benefits of (a) economies of scale, (b) faster accumulation of learning through experience that can aid efficiency and effectiveness, and (c) reduced costs of design modification.

In summarizing the forces at work in the standardization debate, Meffet and Bolz (1993) describe the globalization push and pull factors which are driving marketing standardization. But technology advances since the late 1990s have led to counter push and pull factors for customization to meet the needs and expectations of individual and small groups of customers. The globalization and customization drivers are shown in Figure 6.5. Many barriers to standardization across markets have been removed or reduced, enabling cost savings to be made. Also, the previously prohibitive additional costs of customization have been hugely reduced by technological advances.

The challenge for firms is to achieve efficiency and effectiveness in delivering marketing programmes and processes. The opportunity to standardize programmes and processes and reduce cost and improve efficiency through economies of scale and the experience effect (or learning curve) is driven by the globalization of customer demand and competition. There is also the possibility for global players to cross-subsidize markets to increase sales volume (offset losses in one market by profits from other markets). Moreover, globalization of technology means that new products have shorter lives. The rapidly increasing research and development costs require the high costs of innovation to be recovered more quickly due to the shorter payback cycles for new products. Rapid diffusion of new products into all possible global markets is necessary.

Driven by the customization push and pull factors, firms are also focusing on the effectiveness of their marketing by customizing their offer. It is still possible, however, to make cost savings by developing standardized processes, such as standardizing the product range, advertising campaigns and prices across all markets. While it may not be possible or desirable to completely standardize the marketing programmes, it is possible to globally standardize the processes. These processes include how the product portfolio is managed, new products are launched, marketing communications are delivered, and how online and offline advertising space is booked. It also includes how the marketing information system is populated with data and the marketing planning processes are integrated around the world. In this situation some of the globalization

## FIGURE 6.5  Globalization and customization push and pull factors

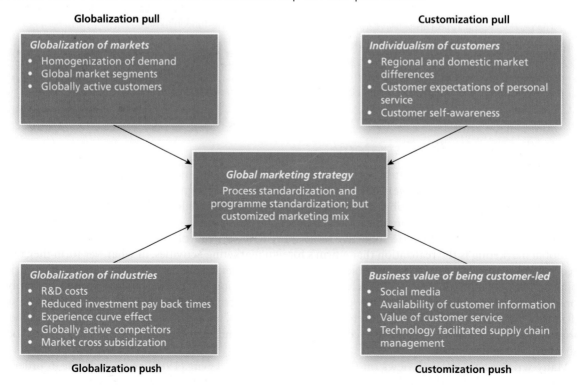

Source: Meffet and Bolz (1993) in Halliburton and Hunerberg (eds) *European Marketing Readings and Cases*, Addison-Wesley.

drivers such as economies of scale and the experience effect (or learning curve) can be achieved through process standardization.

Market fragmentation has increased. In practice, global firms have to strike an appropriate balance between the relative advantages of standardization, adaptation to local tastes and customization to individual customer needs. There is little point in standardizing programmes for marketing products and services if consumers reject them.

**Multi-domestic strategies** A company adopting a multi-domestic orientation assumes that foreign market opportunities are as important as home market opportunities. However, the company takes the view that the differences between its international markets are so acute that widespread adaptation is necessary to meet market needs and retain competitive leverage in local markets. Thus, the company essentially follows a differentiated marketing strategy with individual marketing mix strategies in many of their world markets.

For many major businesses there are few benefits to be obtained from widespread standardization of their activities. Consequently, a well-organized and managed multi-domestic strategy is an effective method for many companies for developing a global business.

An example of an organization which can be accurately characterized as having a multi-domestic strategy is ABB, discussed in Illustration 6.4.

ILLUSTRATION 6.4

# ABB: a new model of global entrepreneurialism – good while it lasted?

ABB was formed by a merger of Sweden's Asea and the Swiss company Brown Boveri. It had customers in the process industries, manufacturing and consumer industries and in utilities (oil, gas and petrochemicals). When chief executive Percy Barnevik was faced with merging two companies with different business cultures and operations, he decided to create a fundamentally different model of how a large MNE could be organized and managed. He created the new head office in Zurich to make the merger less like a takeover by the Swedes, and started dispersing the two head offices of 6000 staff among a number of frontline units.

He created a head office with 135 staff managing 1300 companies with 5000 profit centres. He cut 90 per cent of headquarters staff by moving 30 per cent into the small business units (SBUs), 30 per cent into free-standing service centres concerned with value-adding activities, and eliminated 30 per cent of the jobs. Similar huge cuts in management were made in the headquarters of the subsidiaries.

The management within the SBUs, which usually had fewer than 200 employees, were given a substantially enhanced role in managing their business. ABB was one of the most admired firms of the 1990s. Bartlett and Ghoshal (2015) said that Barnevik's achievement was combining the contradictions of big and small, local and global, economies of scale and intimate market knowledge to create a truly global organization.

ABB employed 160 000 staff in 100 countries. A large part of their manufacturing was moved away from the developed countries to the developing countries, including eastern Europe. By employing people in developing countries, ABB was in a position to sell further expertise and services as they helped build the countries' infrastructures.

Barnevik was succeeded by Jorgen Centremann in October 2000, but he lasted less than two years as the company's share price halved. ABB missed its profit targets, it nearly ran out of cash as its debts mounted, and in 2002 it made its first loss of US$787 million. The problems were compounded by the threat that a US unit would go bankrupt because of the potential liabilities (capped at US$1.3 billion by a US court) resulting from a number of massive lawsuits involving asbestos.

### Question

**1** Could the model be blamed for ABB's problems?

**Reference:** ABB, https://new.abb.com/

A key factor in the strategy is encouraging senior managers to be entrepreneurial in responding to local customer needs, industry standards and different stages of economic development.

Thus, while there are many forces driving companies towards achieving a global strategy through standardizing as many marketing activities as possible, there are also very important prevailing arguments persuading companies that they can also achieve an effective worldwide strategy through a multi-domestic approach. These forces are as follows.

**Industry standards remain diverse**   For many traditional industries such as those based upon engineering, and particularly those that involve large investment in plant and equipment, the cost of harmonization of standards is high and the progress to harmonization is slow. The markets for these industries often involve a country's infrastructure, transport and utilities. Consequently, they depend on often protracted government spending decisions. Usually in making decisions such as these, governments will give consideration not simply to market factors but also to the impact on the economy, environment and the electorate's expectations.

**Customers continue to demand locally differentiated products**   Cultural heritage and traditions still play a strong role in areas such as food, drink and shopping. While there are increasing moves to accept cross-border products, there is still resistance in many cultures.

**Being an insider remains critically important**   The perceived country of origin effect of goods still has a bearing on take-up of products. Local manufacturing of goods is frequently necessary to overcome this scepticism. In B2B marketing, there is a definite bias in favour of products sourced from particular areas, such as Silicon Valley in the USA, and so IT/electronic firms often decide to set up local manufacture there.

A further factor is that companies that make a significant commitment to a country by establishing manufacturing, research and development capability are likely to be consulted by the government as they prepare new legislation. This should result in providing greater opportunities for influencing than would be possible for a company that shows little commitment to the country, perhaps simply exporting to the country.

**Global organizations are difficult to manage**   In finding ways to coordinate far-flung operations, firms have to decentralize and replace home country loyalties with a system of corporate values and loyalties that is acceptable to the firm's staff around the world. For some companies this proves to be problematic. In some cases, the head office values and culture can be significantly different from those of the workforce. Their desire to impose standardized products with little or no consultation on their country's operations is very often seen as arrogant by local staff.

**Management myopia**   Many products and services that are suitable candidates for global marketing are ignored as managers fail to seize the opportunity to build their business in a wider range of markets. On the other hand, products that work well in the managers' home markets are often believed to be acceptable to customers worldwide without being given full consideration. Self-reference criteria often make it difficult for managers to take other than a narrow, national view of international marketing. Moreover, because there are no guarantees that a business can succeed, the firm must be willing to risk the heavy investment that the move from a multi-domestic to a global strategy requires. For some, the resources required and the risks involved are simply too great.

## Regional strategy

One of the most significant developments in global marketing strategy is how firms respond to the rise of the regional trading blocs. Even in globalized industries, company strategies are becoming more of a composite of regionally focused strategies and programmes. For many companies, regionalization represents a more manageable compromise between the extremes of global standardization and multi-domestic strategies. For example, there are some obvious differences in the challenges of marketing to North America, Africa and South East Asia. Different strategies are usually formulated for each region.

However, many firms create regional management for the convenience of creating manageable teams rather than to exploit regional similarities. For example, a number of MNEs create a regional division titled EMEA, which comprises Europe, Middle East and Africa – regions which might be characterized by their differences rather than their similarities.

## MANAGEMENT CHALLENGE 6.3

## Go global, stay local

Bernard Arnault is the owner of 60 LVMH luxury brands including the iconic Louis Vuitton hand-bags, Dom Perignon champagne, Bulgari jewellery and Dior fragrances. He and the family business are ranked 13th in Forbes' (2015) World's Billionaires list, based on their net worth of $38 billion. They have the largest share in the European luxury market with US$36.38 billion in sales. With their head office in Paris, Bernard Anault promotes the heritage and culture of French fashion through their luxury brands.

One of LVMH's competitors, Hermes, also has their head office in Paris. Hermes is also a family-run business gaining US$4.48 billion from the European luxury market. Hermes is known for its scarves, fragrances and of course the Birkin and Kelly handbags that have a celebrity A-list following.

Both companies are global 'big luxury' companies whose products are available online, through their own retail stores and concessions in airports and hotels around the world. Products and promotion are standardized; they feel no need for adaptations. Their prices remain high, appealing in the main to the middle and upper socioeconomic groups. Both brands are particularly popular in developing countries where such well-known brands clearly signify a person's wealth. Some, however, say that the Louis Vuitton logo is a 'look at me' status-driven brand. Others say that Hermes provides status as it often makes consumers wait six months for products to come to market. Nevertheless, both brands hold their value and resale value very well – with Hermes Birkin bags often selling for 50 per cent more than the original sale price.

### Questions

**1** Why can some brands go global, but stay local to their heritage?

**2** What are the benefits of this strategy for the businesses and the consumer?

**References:** Forbes (2015) *Billionaire List*. Available from www.forbes.com/profile/bernard-arnault/ (accessed 13 April 2015); *The Economist* (2014) Beauty and the beasts. Available from www.economist.com/news/special-report/21635758-think-global-act-artisan-beauty-and-beasts (accessed 13 April 2015).

Regional trading blocs tend to favour their own MNEs. For those companies located outside the region there can be significant tariff and non-tariff barriers. Public–private sector committees decide on standards, such as car emissions, safety standards and security. By shifting operations and decision making inside the region an MNE can gain advantage from being part of the consultation and decision-making process.

The key to developing effective regional strategies is deciding in what ways the marketing strategy for one region should be differentiated from the others and being able to respond quickly to threats or opportunities that emerge in the region.

However, while regional strategies are built around the common elements within a region and the distinctiveness of the region, in practice the differences within the region are still huge. Many organizations Think Global and Act Local and develop their product range accordingly. Therefore, the big differences in the country environments and markets require more responsive approaches rather than centralized multinational management. Companies are taking the opportunity from the formation of regional trading blocs to include regional objectives and plans as a significant part of their worldwide strategy. They build on existing, or form new, cooperative trading relationships. Starbucks has understood this concept, often known as glocalization, by offering to not only change the menus to suit consumer variations but it has also brought a different localization feel through the layout of their coffee shops. In New Orleans the store brings in the local spirit by enabling local artists to display their paintings; this has gone down very well with positive feedback on MyStarbucksideas.force.com.

The prime motivation in the formation of the regional trading blocs is to enable indigenous companies to build the critical mass of activity necessary within the home region to enable them to compete effectively in global markets. The European Union, for example, has strived to create collaborative working between participants in a common supply chain, or those offering complementary or competitive products. Where the companies come from different countries, political differences do still arise, particularly if national governments are concerned about the retention of jobs in sensitive industries, such as the defence and airline industries. Airbus is one such consortium in the manufacture of aeroplanes in Europe that has at different times benefited and suffered from political interference.

**Transnational strategies**   If a firm has sufficient power and resources to exploit all the available opportunities on a worldwide basis, with little need to adapt strategies or involve partners to any great extent, then a simple strategy can be developed. However, many multinationals have a wide range of products and services, some of which might be suited to global and others to multi-domestic development. The successful exploitation of these opportunities might require a much more flexible approach to strategic development. For example, it could involve a number of partners in licensing, joint ventures and strategic alliances as well as wholly owned operations.

Transnational companies integrate diverse assets, resources and people into operating units around the world. Through flexible management processes and networks, transnational companies aim to build three strategic capabilities:

- Global scale efficiency and competitiveness.
- National level responsiveness and flexibility.
- Cross-market capacity to leverage learning on a worldwide basis.

Nistor (2014) and Bartlett and Ghoshal (2015) state that transnational companies generally use standardized products that are sufficiently flexible to cope with local consumer needs. This leads to the firm's global scale efficiency and competitiveness in its totality. The firm needs the ability to recognize market opportunities and risks across national borders. The overall goal is to achieve global competitiveness through a fully integrated strategy and operations. Thus, a transnational approach is not a particular strategy, but a strategic perspective that evolves as firms and the markets in which they operate increase in complexity. Hewlett Packard is a transnational organization because some of its marketing operations and research and development are centralized and standardized, whereas other units operate with a substantial degree of independence. It has a strong corporate identity and some of its promotional themes, for example around e-business, are common throughout the firm. It has also formed strategic alliances with partners in order to carry out certain research and development activities where it is likely to benefit from the participation of partners. In such organizations the implications for strategic development are significant. A transnational strategy that is to achieve global competitive advantage needs to accommodate some, or all of the following:

- Simple and complex individual product and market policies which may be independent or interdependent.
- Customer segments that are specific and unique to a cross-national niche market so the resultant segments are transnational and valid across borders.
- Working closely with firms that are customers, suppliers, competitors and partners at the same time. In addition, they need to ensure that the values of the company are maintained and demonstrated to external stakeholders through establishing clear and unambiguous positioning in all markets.
- Maintaining and building meaningful and added value relationships in the supply chain.

## International marketing management for global firms

So far in this chapter we have identified the changing trends in the business environment that are leading to increasing globalization. We have also looked at the factors that affect the firms' response to this, particularly in the way they standardize or adapt their marketing programmes and processes. We have shown distinct differences in the way global strategies can be developed to meet individual firms' situations. Implementing these global strategies, however, poses considerable problems and it is to these that we now turn.

As in the previous chapter, it is useful for the discussion to be based loosely upon the McKinsey 7S framework, which includes the hardware elements of strategy, structure and systems and the software elements of management style, staff, skills and shared values. Again, we start with the hardware elements of strategy, systems and organization structure.

## Global strategy implementation

Global firms have the objective of developing effective business operations in all the major markets in the world in order to maximize their performance. In the past they may well have prioritized the developed economies in North America, Europe and Asia, principally Japan. More recently these firms have developed a significant presence in many more markets. Now the focus for investment is focusing on the BRIC countries. Research and investment will also soon turn to the MINT countries as growth prospects look healthy. Countries in the Middle East are seeking to grow and diversify their business activity away from a dependence on oil. They too are gaining a foothold in the other emerging markets of Asia, Africa and South America if they wish to benefit from the anticipated future development.

However, building a global presence is hugely expensive. Many firms see no value in expanding globally if their home country or region offers sufficient growth prospects without marketing their products and services in what they might perceive to be higher risk areas. US and Chinese companies have a large domestic market and, despite the rapid growth prospects of other regions of the world, their unfamiliarity often makes them unattractive. Despite this, with growth rates four times as high in Asia than in the rest of the world, almost all the Fortune 500 and leading European companies invest heavily in this area.

## Opportunities in emerging markets for global firms

Most MNEs, particularly from developed countries, focus on the customers that are wealthy enough now or will be in the future to purchase their premium goods and services. Companies such as McDonald's and Yum are opening new outlets at unprecedented rates.

However, for many multinationals, the very poorest parts of the world appear to be largely economically inactive and offer little opportunity for profitable growth. A small number of MNEs have traded with these countries for many years. They often buy and sell raw materials or sell processing machinery and develop a presence by selling basic products to the consumer and B2B market. Prahalad and Hart (2002) have suggested that there is a pyramid of wealth, shown in Table 6.5. They emphasize that those with the lowest incomes still have the potential to create a significant demand for goods and services if they meet the specific needs of poor consumers and ensure that products and services are marketed to them in a sensitive way. It might be expected that consumers from emerging markets simply want unsophisticated products. However, it may well prove a mistake to try to market to emerging markets those products that have reached the end of their life cycle and been replaced in developing countries. The particular situation in an emerging market may require a specific, innovative solution and this may miss out a particular technology development stage. For example, development of technology and changing economic environments is making MNEs consider new networks, as shown in Illustration 6.5.

Hart and London (2005) have identified examples of innovative solutions that include not only products and services that satisfy customer demand but also create new routes to market that are more efficient in these

Table 6.5   The global pyramid of wealth

|  | Global population (millions) | Purchasing power (US$) |
| --- | --- | --- |
| The wealthy | 800 | >15 000 |
| The emerging middle class | 1 500 | 1 500–15 000 |
| Low income markets | 4 000 | <1 500 |

Source: Adapted from Prahalad, C.K. and Hart, S.L. (2002) The fortune at the bottom of the pyramid. *Strategy and Business* 26, 54–67, Booz and Co.

## ILLUSTRATION 6.5

# Developing countries learning through the Internet of Things (IoT)

As stated earlier in this chapter, Indonesia is one of the MINT countries and its capital Jakarta is becoming a smarter city. To do this Jakarta is utilizing the Internet of Things (IoT) technology. IoT is a system of interrelated 'things', be they computers, smartphones, objects, machines, people or animals, being provided with a unique identifier which can transfer data to another 'thing'. This is done via a network rather than through human-to-human or human-to-computer interaction. A simple example of this is when a person downloads and connects the Alexa app and Smart Technology app on their smartphone. At home, the person can simply ask Alexa to 'turn on the fire' (or television, lights, seat-warming system in the car and so on). At work the person can tap their phone to engage the car seat-warming system or turn on the fire so the house is warm when they return home.

Jakarta wants to take IoT technology further by introducing the Jakarta One Card. The One Card is the size of a bank card. It can be used as a payment system for public transport, shopping and road tolls. It can also be used as an entry and exit card to museums and art galleries to monitor how many people visit these spaces and how long they stay. The One Card will eventually make Jakarta a 'no cash' city. The One Card also links to a person's bank and savings accounts, and contains details of their health and social security details. Alongside the One Card the government of Jakarta has introduced the Qlue mobile phone app, which gives Jakarta's 10 million citizens the opportunity to be the ears and eyes of Jakarta and provide feedback on the city's products and services. From 10 million citizens, 1400 messages are sent per day to the city's government. By analyzing this data from One Card, Jakarta's government ministers can make smarter and more effective policy decisions about town planning, public services, health and retail.

### Questions

**1** What are the advantages and disadvantages of the One Card for the citizens of Jakarta?

**2** In addition to shopping and museums/art galleries, what other leisure activities could be collected by One Card and what benefit would this be to Jakarta's government?

**Reference:** IBM. www.ibm.com/case-studies/jakartasmartcity (accessed 5 June 2018).

emerging markets. This often requires the MNE to work with partners through less formal channels and networks than they are used to. The resulting solutions, such as lower cost manufacturing techniques, design and distribution can then be marketed to other parts of the world.

The instability of emerging markets, crime and corruption are some of the main problems that MNEs have to deal with directly to ensure they protect their staff and reputation. However, their unfamiliarity with these markets makes this difficult, and here too local partners can prove invaluable.

## The emergence of MNEs from emerging markets

So far, we have focused on strategies of firms that already have a strong presence in developed countries and wish to extend that to emerging markets. A current feature of global marketing, however, is the emergence of future players. The high growth rates in the BRIC and MINT countries are providing the platforms for the new generation of global players. Bracken (2007) suggests that it will be multinationals from emerging markets that could achieve the greatest growth in the future, as shown by Tata in Illustration 6.3. Developing countries have traditionally depended upon foreign companies to supply job training and know-how. In exchange, multinationals, usually from western countries, could force concessions from national governments enabling them to build sales in new markets. Globalization and the requirements of a market economy, therefore, reduce the power of national governments. Now the governments of the strongest emerging countries are no longer willing to surrender their home market to foreign companies that exert undue influence in the industry sector. This might delay technology transfer into the developing country and so delay the economic development of the country. The size of the home markets in India and China provides domestic companies with a large base to build the potential multinational companies of the future. China, for example, has decided to develop its own car industry. India, following the removal of central planning and bureaucracy in the 1990s, has created some strong IT outsourcing businesses, such as Wipro, Tata and Infosys.

In emerging markets, volume and low cost have driven the hypergrowth and the ambitions of young managers. Entrepreneurs spot opportunities in other sectors than their own, so a property developer might move into computers (*The Economist*, 2010a).

Leggett (2013) suggests that while the BRIC countries have grabbed the attention of MNCs for a number of years, their deceleration is starting to move the major players to ASEAN (Association of Southeast Asian Nations), which includes Malaysia, the Philippines and Indonesia. However, success stories from these countries may take some time. Naturally, business success from the BRIC countries will be evaluated to support greater achievements in other developing nations. There is some evidence that this is changing, partly through organic development and partly through acquisition. Tata is meeting the needs of local, first time, middle class consumers through its Nano car development. But it has also taken over Citigroup's Global Services outsourcing division. China's BYD in batteries and Huawei, second largest supplier in the world to Ericsson in mobile telecom equipment, equally provide business customers with cost-effective solutions. These companies are building their global presence also through acquisition (*The Economist* 2010b).

Multinationals from developed markets will now have to work harder to access these fast-growing emerging markets. It will prove to be much harder to go it alone and more difficult to exert control over local partners who now see the possibility of developing their own global businesses.

Multinationals from the last generation of emerging markets have already become global players with dominant market shares in western markets. Toyota, from Japan, now close to becoming the leading US car maker, was virtually unknown in the west until 1965. Samsung from South Korea is vying with Apple for first place in the worldwide mobile/cell phone market.

For firms wishing to build a truly global presence, there are a number of challenges, including:

- Responding to the changing basis of competitive advantage.
- Increasing **global appeal** by building the **global brand**.
- Developing sustainable strategies.
- Creating a global presence by achieving **global reach**.
- Managing diverse and complex activities across a range of often similar but frequently disparate markets and cultures.

Regardless of which strategy is chosen, the Boston Consulting Group (2014) certainly recommends that to remain and emerge competitive in the global arena it is essential to understand the global challenges, develop and professionalize practices at all key stages and, most importantly, drive forward through innovation.

## Global appeal and the changing basis of competitive advantage

All major firms today are capable of offering good-quality products and services that offer value for customers. This is no longer a source of differentiation and competitive advantage as competitors quickly offer lower cost alternatives.

The rapid growth of the Japanese car industry was largely based on value for money criteria, with quality, reliability and performance at a reasonable cost being the basis of the appeal. Japanese manufacturers, such as Toyota, have continued to develop more sophisticated cars and establish local supply chains. But their competitors from the emerging economies, such as Kia and Hyundai, have replaced them in offering cheaper and even better value-for-money cars. At the same time a number of firms, such as Tata with its Nano, are competing for the very lowest price car segment. The car market is highly competitive and characterized by over-capacity. It is becoming ever harder for major global players to be consistently profitable. The question is how and where they should compete, particularly against the new players that are identifying new segments. A few of the car makers from the developed countries have substantially improved their quality and reliability and offer designs and brand imagery with better consumer appeal for the most affluent customers in developed and emerging markets.

It is possible to observe similar changes in the IT industry. Cost-conscious consumers increasingly expect computer suppliers to offer improved performance, functionality, quality, security and greater reliability as well as becoming more 'user-friendly' – all at considerably reduced prices. To attract affluent consumers, firms must now offer more intangible benefits. These include better styling, higher levels of service support and advice, more interesting and appealing software and online services, and a 'cool' brand. The spectacular performance of Apple was the appeal of the iMac, iPod, iPhone and iPad to a design-conscious segment. Consumers are becoming more confident with technology. They are willing to experiment by downloading software and multiple apps from a variety of online platforms.

Consumers are also prepared to mix and match basics with expensive items. The cost of basic clothing sold through supermarkets and stores such as Zara and Primark has fallen dramatically in recent years, making it difficult for retailers to operate in the middle ground between high fashion and low cost. But high fashion – and cost – items, shoes and handbags are also matched with basic items.

In B2B situations, the basis of competitive advantage is also changing. Specialty niches are becoming rarer especially when new technology such as 3D printing has a major impact on industry. 3D printing enables big growth opportunities in toys and footwear. The interesting part is not just the fact that technology can print an exact 3D copy of a 'must have' toy, but the fact that there would be no shipping or transportation costs (*Strategy and Business*, 2015).

## Increasing global appeal by building the global brand

Branding is usually considered within the marketing strategy as part of the product and service policy. Global brands, however, are inextricably tied up with achieving global appeal and building a global presence, so we have included a broader-based discussion of global branding at this point.

## Global brand management

Holt *et al.* (2004) noted that in the late 1980s, Levitt was arguing that organizations should offer standardized products globally. But now consumers find it difficult to relate to generic standardized products. So firms have adopted 'glocal' strategies in which they have customized product features, selling and marketing to local tastes. They build their efficiencies on a global scale around 'back office' activities of which customers are unaware.

Holt *et al.* found that most transnational firms are perceived differently from other firms because of their power. They have suffered because of this as they have been major targets for anti-globalization protests. However, most people choose one global brand over another based on three dimensions: quality, indicated by the firm's global stature; the cultural myths and stories created by the firm; and the firm's efforts in corporate social responsibility. In the past for some brands the country of origin of the brand was important as it was often part of the cultural myth. Holt *et al.*, however, believe that this is no longer important. Indeed, the trend for a number of global brands has been to dissociate themselves from their country of origin. For example, British Airways has renamed itself BA, British Petroleum has become BP and Kentucky Fried Chicken has become KFC.

For decades the power of the biggest global brands seemed to increase steadily. But their dominant position now seems to be more dependent on success in newer markets and responding to changes in their existing markets.

Khashani (1995) draws attention to changes in a number of factors which affect the performance of the brands:

- Customers are better educated, better informed, more sceptical, more willing to experiment, less brand loyal, much more media aware and have higher expectations of the total package.

- Competition is more aggressive, with more rapid launches of higher quality 'me-too' products.

- Retailers have installed better electronic point-of-sale technology and, as a result, have greater awareness of brand performance. In response to better consumer information, they have introduced better quality private labels.

These changes in the brand market environment have been compounded by weaknesses in brand management, including:

- low investment
- inadequate product development
- poor consumer communication
- an emphasis on quick paybacks rather than long-term brand building
- too little innovation,
- an emphasis upon small modifications.

For global brand success it is essential to listen to the market and get closer to global customers. It is necessary to be bold, think creatively, set new market and performance standards, and take risks. The aim must be to think globally, launch products and services sequentially and rapidly across markets and build world brands. There are many 'almost great' brands, but only a few are truly great.

While the progress of global brands seems to be unstoppable, they do not always succeed. Walmart withdrew from South Korea and Germany in 2006 because financial losses could no longer be tolerated. Despite promising for years that performance could be improved, it never managed a turnaround. In both countries Walmart failed to compete with dominant local companies that were better at catering for local tastes. Moreover, Barbaro (2006) notes that in Germany in the late 1990s Walmart changed the name of its stores from a well-known reliable local brand to Walmart, a name that was unfamiliar to local shoppers.

The global development of brands can lead to some dilemmas. Both Google in China and Apple's Face-Time ban in the United Arab Emirates have run into problems with government controls, which can result in the need to compromise on the brand values and functionality.

**B2B branding**   In business-to-business marketing, purchasers and users value the commitment of suppliers to the product and service and benefit from the added value from dealing with a firm. For example, buyers talk about suppliers such as Apple or Vodafone as brands, which lends a sense of authority to the purchasing decision. Users might also detail a specific product or service that must be purchased, e.g. an iPhone or the Apple Watch. In some situations, there may be benefits which can be gained from cobranding with globally recognized branded components (e.g. Intel microprocessors in computers). This trend is becoming increasingly important as consumers become more influential in the choice of components and services in the supply chain and demand products that contain branded components.

In international B2B branding firms use different naming strategies, with some firms concentrating less on corporate brand endorsement and more on the individual brand in the same way as Procter and Gamble and Unilever do in consumer markets. For example, the pharmaceutical product brands Zantac and Tagamet are promoted by GlaxoSmithKline without any obvious association with the manufacturer in the brand name.

Ultimately, the rationale for the existence of brands in B2B marketing is the same as in consumer goods marketing – to avoid the commoditization of products, which leads to decisions being based only on price.

Brands are also important in the not-for-profit areas. For example, although the charity sector is fragmented into many thousands of organizations, it is the global charities with well-marketed brands, such as Red Crescent/Red Cross, Oxfam and Save the Children, that are the most successful in terms of scale of activities. When major disasters occur, it is these organizations that have the resources to cope.

## Creating a global presence by achieving global reach

The aim of many MNEs is to dominate their market sector by building a presence in every worthwhile market. However, few firms have the resources to build a strong presence in all the countries in the world and so rely on third parties to enable them to reach into similar markets. Many firms cannot afford to wait until they have built the products, services, image and resources through organic growth within the firm.

Instead, they use a wide range of growth, market entry and marketing mix strategies to achieve global reach, and these are discussed in later chapters.

**Mergers and acquisitions**  The rationale for acquisitions and mergers has been that a well-managed company should take over a weaker rival marketer of competing or complementary products in order to achieve higher growth and savings in operating, management and marketing costs.

As market entry methods, acquisition or mergers are used to facilitate access to particular markets. In some business sectors, however, there appears to be a view that it is only by operating on a very large scale on a worldwide basis that customers can receive the level and quality of service that they need. This seems logical in the case of aircraft manufacture where industry consolidation has left only two main players, Boeing and Airbus. Scale economies in accountancy may not be so obvious and, of course, there are still many small accountancy practices. But the global sector is dominated by four companies: Deloitte, KPMG, EY and PwC, whereas there were eight major players in 1989.

Cross-border mergers and acquisitions are becoming increasingly common too, but often do not deliver the expected outcomes. For example, in telecommunications, Vodafone (UK) with Mannesmann (Germany), and in automobiles, Daimler-Benz (Germany) and Chrysler (US). One of the implications of mergers is the impact upon branding decisions and whether the merged firm will retain two separate brand identities or whether they will merge them. Illustration 6.6 provides an outline of why Uber merged with Grab in 2018. The decision often depends upon whether the senior management believes the brand is important for their

## ILLUSTRATION 6.6

## Uber decides to merge

Uber is a taxi-hailing service. It has provided us with a revolutionary way of getting a taxi, be it in your own city outside a concert venue or in a different city hailing a taxi from an international airport thousands of miles from home. One of the revolutionary elements of Uber is its app. The Uber app is simply downloaded to a smartphone and is an excellent way for consumers to 'hail a taxi and pay' in just a few taps. The Uber app is not just a benefit for consumers but for businesses as well, which can use the Uber app to book and pay for taxis to collect clients from train stations or as a means to transport clients to a hotel.

Uber operates in 60 nations and in more than 300 cities. Its growth and expansion has been phenomenal. However, there have been a number of setbacks along the way. For example, in 2016 Uber jumped into China. There was already a successful taxi-hailing and

car-sharing business in China named Didi. Didi had 450 million users in 400 cities and employed over 7000 people. Uber retreated when it struggled to compete and was losing billions of pounds. Uber continued to look east and during 2017 and 2018 went head to head with Grab. Grab is a popular taxi-hailing operator in South East Asia. Mr Tan, the Malaysian business tycoon who set up Grab, knows his customers. Being from the region, he knows the Ojek passengers of Indonesia are happy to hail motorbike taxis to get through the congested cities. Mr Tan also knows the nuances between the business commuter from Singapore and those of Kuala Lumpur. Grab has over 600 million users and, like Uber, users hail a taxi and pay through a smartphone app. However, the Grab app offers more than just a taxi-hailing service. It enables users to buy coffee, order food, have lunch delivered to their office or home and much more. Uber could not compete with the regional differences that Mr Tan knew about, the size of his marketplace and the extended services available through the app. Therefore, Uber needed to pull out of South East Asia and sell its assets. However, Uber still has its foot in South East Asia following its merger with Grab. Uber has a 27.5 per cent stake in Grab and a seat on the Grab board.

### Questions

1 Why did Uber fail in China and South East Asia?

2 What research should Uber have done that may have helped it be more successful in China and South East Asia?

particular company or industry sector. Smith (1998) reports research by McKinsey which suggests that there are three routes to brand consolidation:

- Phasing out brands over time, when the strategy is to retain loyal customers who will buy as long as the brand is available.
- Quickly changing some of the branding, which only works well if the firm has control over distribution, advertising and promotion.
- Cobranding to manage the transition, which is the most common approach, used, for example, when Whirlpool bought Philips domestic appliances.

**The pitfalls of mergers and acquisitions**    There are serious pitfalls associated with mergers and acquisitions, particularly where they involve cross-border ownership and cooperation. Finkelstein (1998) refers to a study of 89 US companies acquired by foreign buyers during the period 1977–90 and found the performance of most of them had not improved within one year.

There are obvious organizational challenges that follow from a merger, such as who will be in charge, whose products and services will be offered (or dropped) and where costs savings should be made. If the merger or acquisition was not entirely harmonious, there may be cross-cultural challenges, such as the different ways of doing business in Europe, the US and Asia. Other challenges are resolving different corporate governance, the status and power of different employee and management groups, job security guarantees, government regulations and customer expectations.

Finkelstein (1998) recommends that the integration process should focus on value creation by ensuring employees actually achieve the synergy that is promised before the deal is done. They should plan in detail how the various cross-border problems will be overcome and develop a clear communication plan to cope with the whole process.

## Managing diverse and complex activities across a range of similar but often disparate markets and cultures

The implications of pursuing a global strategy are that organizations must continually expand into what are likely to be less stable markets, perhaps tertiary opportunities from Figure 4.3 or incipient markets in Figure 4.1 (see Chapter 4). Typically, these will be in some way less attractive (at least at the present time) because of the associated political and economic risks of entering less developed markets, more difficult trading conditions and barriers to 'free' trade. By comparison with the firms' existing markets, these emerging markets may demand disproportionately high investment in management time and financial resources as well as involving the firm in considerable additional financial and reputation risk if things go wrong.

The risks associated with specific emerging country market involvement can be substantial, however, and include some or all of the following:

- Financial loss associated with inappropriate investment, such as buying unusable assets, being unable to achieve acceptable levels of performance from the purchased assets, losing the assets by misappropriation to the host country government or to partners.
- Damage to the firm's reputation through association with the country, its government and intermediaries, especially where they are seen to be corrupt, engage in unacceptable social or business practices, or have close relationships with other countries or organizations which are considered to be corrupt.
- Litigation arising from offering an unacceptable product and/or service to the country, or becoming involved in questionable business practices.
- Prompting an unexpected international competitor response by attacking a market which it considers to be its home territory.
- Initially making arrangements with joint venture partners, distributors, agents or government agencies to secure entry but which become inappropriate in the medium to long term.
- Damage to the firm's reputation through insensitivity in its operations in the country, when it might be accused of exploiting local labour, the country's resources or causing environmental damage to the country.

The problem for international strategic management in less developed countries is that the 'rule book' that managers rely on in developed countries does not always apply, because business infrastructure and processes are not well established.

## Organization structure for transnational firms

While the simple organization structures discussed in the previous chapter are appropriate for managing the international strategies of SMEs, the largest transnational companies, by their very nature, have complex structures that are specific to the firms' context. As a result, organization structures differ from firm to firm.

Most firms operate using a form of matrix structure. Majaro (1991) distinguished between:

- a macropyramid structure in which companies such as McDonald's exert usually highly centralized control
- an umbrella structure in which geographically based SBUs take responsibility for the global strategy of the MNE in specific activities, and
- the interglomerate, in which the SBUs of companies such as ABB, discussed in Illustration 6.4, and many Asian-owned comprises, such as Hutchison Whampoa, Tata and Guandong Investments, operate as quite independent international businesses.

## Systems, processes and control

Given the complexity of international strategic marketing in global firms, it is essential that the organization operates effective processes for the management of its complex operations, processes and systems to enable managers to be able to share information effectively.

## Control

Control is the cornerstone of management. Control provides the means to direct, regulate and manage business operations. A significant amount of interaction is required between the individual areas of marketing (such as market development, advertising and selling) and the other functional areas (such as human resources, finance, production, research and development).

However, for many firms, control means a separate activity through which senior managers are able to keep a check periodically (weekly, monthly or quarterly) on more junior levels of management, who often see this in terms of being called upon to justify their actions. Feedback and control systems should be regarded as an integrated part of the whole planning process. They are essential in ensuring that the marketing plans are not only being implemented worldwide but are still appropriate for the changing environment in each country.

There are a number of benefits of an effective strategic control system. It encourages higher standards of performance, forces greater clarity and realism and permits corporate management to intervene when necessary. Moreover, it ensures that the financial objectives do not overwhelm the strategic objectives, encourages clearer definition of responsibilities making decentralization work more effectively and so provides more motivation for managers.

There are three essential elements of the control process:

1 *Setting standards*: The standards that are set need to be relevant to the corporate goals such as:
   - growth and profits reported by financial measures, e.g. return on capital employed and on sales,
   - non-financial indicators, e.g. market share.

   Intermediate goals and individual targets can be set by breaking the plan down into measurable parts which, when successfully completed, will lead to the overall objectives being achieved. The standards must be understandable, achievable and relevant to each local country situation.

2 *Measuring performance against standards*: To obtain measurements and ensure rapid feedback of information, firms use a variety of techniques These include reports, meetings and special

measurements of specific parts of the marketing programme to obtain a thorough examination of every aspect of marketing in a particular country, such as:

- cost–benefit analysis of customers
- product lines,
- territories or marketing audits.

They also use benchmarking which allows comparisons of various aspects of the business, such as efficiency of distribution, customer response times, service levels and complaints, with other companies that are not necessarily from the same business sector.

3 *Correcting deviations from the plan*: Perhaps the most difficult decisions that must be made are to determine when performance has deviated sufficiently from the plan to require corrective action to be taken. This can be either by changing the plan or the management team charged with the responsibility of carrying out the plan. Evaluation of the performance of a particular management team is particularly difficult in international marketing as the performance of a particular SBU can only be compared with its own plan. This plan would have been determined by the headquarters or with the performance of a 'similar' SBU. There are obvious weaknesses in making any of these comparisons, resulting in considerable differences of opinion between the head office and its subsidiary.

A key element in the control process is the input from people, both the directly employed staff of the company but also the staff of the other members of the supply chain. Various quality management models, for example, Total Quality Management, Continuous Quality Improvement and Business Excellence, supported by international standards such as ISO 9001, are used by firms to underpin the control process. Consistency across the firm's global operations can be increased and general improvements made using a variety of techniques:

- Benchmarking against other SBUs within the firm, other firms within the business sector and the 'best in the class' in a particular activity, such as just-in-time operations control, service centre response rates or delivery performance.

- Identifying good practice wherever in the world it occurs and applying the lessons either in individual SBUs or across the firm.

- Encouraging performance improvement through self-assessment (individuals completing questionnaires and improvement plans alone), peer review (evaluation by staff at the same level) and appraisals completed by more senior managers.

Setting standards to achieve consistency and establishing continuous performance improvement projects throughout the global company can, however, be problematic. This is because of cultural barriers, differences in language and ethical standards causing different levels of motivation, communications problems and misinterpretation of instructions and advice. In addition, different measuring techniques, standards and imprecise reporting procedures and processes can create difficulties in achieving a meaningful control process.

## Return on marketing investment

One of the problems for marketing is the concern that marketing and promotion expenditure is simply seen as a cost to the business with no benefits linked to it. As a key control tool, therefore, measuring the return on marketing investment is essential for any B2B or consumer marketing manager looking to improve their ability to produce real results in revenue growth. In much of the traditional marketing activity it is difficult to define the specific benefits that can be attributed to one individual activity. With online marketing, as we shall see later, it is easier to link the marketing investment with its impact. In practice, firms need to measure the effect of an integrated marketing programme in order to learn good and bad practice.

## Planning systems and processes

The increasingly turbulent environment resulting from more rapid changes in technology, competition, consumer taste and fashion means that the traditional systems and processes for preparing the analysis, strategy development and action plans take too long. Balabanis *et al.* (2004) emphasize that global information systems are needed to enable headquarters and subsidiary managers to keep track of environmental changes (opportunities and threats), facilitate the coordination and control of operations in different locations and assist in sharing new ideas and knowledge.

Timescales must be reduced to make sure that the plan is still relevant when it is being implemented. Consequently, it is necessary to avoid planning that is too general and unfocused and to improve the quality of implementation and the relevance and responsiveness of the process.

As a result of this, increasing emphasis is being placed by MNEs on scenario and contingency planning to take account of things going wrong because of unexpected changes in the environment. Moreover, greater reliance is being placed on expert systems for understanding market changes, carrying out forecasting, resource planning and gap analysis. The plans prepared tend to be based on the understanding that they will be emergent and will evolve during the timescale of the plan rather than be decided before the time period of the plan begins. The plans may be designed to be incremental, with the start of each new phase being prompted by a change in the environment or by the successful completion of a previous implementation phase.

## Building skills in transnational organizations

While the structures outlined provide some general understanding of the alternative methods of organizing the management, they are for most companies an oversimplification. Cagni (2006) explains that old-fashioned, centralized, multinational management is no longer appropriate as it creates a single process overseen from head office. While this creates scale advantages, improved efficiency and the capability to share knowledge, local staff see a loss of autonomy. They see the creation of an ivory tower for the elite and the disempowerment of local managers, leaving them with less interesting jobs. The structure needs to be developed in a way that avoids rigidity as flexibility is needed to respond to the changes in environment and market.

This has implications for the roles of the international marketing manager, as Bartlett and Ghoshal (2015) have concluded. The management of transnational businesses must be highly specialized and understand that there is likely to be a great deal of resistance from consumers that receive highly sanitized, standardized, homogenized products. Global business or product division managers have the responsibility to further the company's global-scale efficiency and competitiveness, but not lose sight of the fact that the consumer may not like the 'one-size-fits-all' approach. They must combine the strategist skills of recognizing opportunities and risks across national and functional boundaries, be the architect for worldwide resource and asset utilization, and the coordinator of activities and capabilities.

The country manager must play a pivotal role by sensing local customer needs, but also satisfying the host government's requirements and defending the company's market position. The country manager is likely to have objectives that conflict with the business manager and so must be prepared to negotiate to overcome the differences. The functional manager's role is as the business environment scanner, cross-pollinator of ideas and champion of specific aspects of the business which are essential for success. The global manager may be required to play a number of roles, and no one person can fulfil the required tasks alone. This manager must provide leadership, while acting as the talent scout and the developer of the other levels of management.

As a result, patterns of activity in a transnational company will vary considerably in each new situation. Innovations, for example, should be generated at several locations and in several ways throughout the world, so that the company is not restricted to making centralized decisions. Since the late 1990s, firms such as Shell, Philips and Unilever have used an integrated network approach, with resources and capabilities concentrated in various locations and accessed through the free flow of knowledge, technology, components, products, resources and people. By developing matrix structures, firms can achieve efficiency, responsiveness and the ability to develop and exploit their knowledge and capability for competitive advantage.

As the international operations of firms increase in diversity and tangible ties between the activities become strained, so the nature of the formal systems and organizational structures must change too. Training programmes, career path planning, job rotation, company-wide accounting, evaluation and data-processing systems become more important as part of the shared value system of the firm.

## Staff and the problems of international management

Of the potential sources of problems of planning in international marketing, it is the relationship between headquarters and local subsidiary staff that is likely to be the largest single factor. Headquarters staff, as guardians of the overall company strategies, claim to have a far broader perspective of the company's activities. They might expect that subsidiary staff should simply be concerned with implementation of the details of the plan. Subsidiary staff claim that, by being closer to the individual markets, they are in a better position to identify opportunities and should, therefore, play a large part in developing objectives and strategies. This situation must be resolved if the planning process is to be effective. All staff need to have a clear idea of their own role in setting, developing and implementing policy, and understanding how their individual contributions might be integrated into the corporate objectives and strategies.

Govindarajan and Gupta (2001) comment on the need to create teams comprised of many nationalities to benefit from the synergies and collective wisdom superior to that of an individual. The failure rate of teams is high – in a survey one-third of teams rated their performance as largely unsuccessful. This can be due to a lack of trust or due to communication problems, even when members speak in the same language, including semantics, accents, tone, pitch and dialects. Mortensen and Beyene (2009) explain that to build trust it is necessary to spend time onsite observing the people, places and norms of the distant locale. This not only leads to direct knowledge of the other but also to knowledge of self as seen by the other (reflected knowledge), thus affecting trust through identification, adaptation and reduced misunderstanding.

Sebenius (2002) notes that decision-making and governance processes vary widely not only in terms of legal technicalities but also the behaviour and core beliefs that drive them. The solution is to map out the decision-making process and anticipate problems before they arise.

The difficulties of planning in international markets are further developed by Brandt *et al.* (1980), in a framework of international planning problems. Weichmann and Pringle (1979) identify the key problems experienced by large US and European multinationals.

Many companies recognize that for strategies to be successful they must be owned. So staff at all levels must be involved in the marketing planning process. This is becoming more difficult as MNEs have ever greater numbers of their workers employed outside the head office country. As the company grows, therefore, a company-wide planning culture should be developed, with the following objectives:

- Planning becomes part of the continuous process of management rather than an annual 'event'.
- Strategic thinking becomes the responsibility of every manager rather than being restricted to a separate strategic planning department.
- The planning process becomes standardized, with a format that allows contributions from all parts of the company.
- The plan becomes the working document, updated periodically for all aspects of the company, so allowing performance evaluations to be carried out regularly.
- The planning process is itself regularly reviewed and refined through the use of new tools and techniques in order to improve its relevance and effectiveness.

Brett *et al.* (2006) identify the advantages of multicultural teams in international firms, including deep knowledge of different product markets and culturally sensitive customer service. They also note the problems caused when cultural differences affect team effectiveness, direct versus indirect communication, trouble with accents and fluency, differing attitudes to hierarchy and authority, and conflicting norms for decision making. The authors emphasize the need to pinpoint the root cause of the problems, intervene early and see the challenges as stemming from culture rather than personalities.

## What makes a good international manager?

For many of the most powerful businesses, increasing globalization is the future scenario. The most successful will be managed by people who can best embrace and thrive on the ambiguity and complexity of transnational operations. Using Illustration 6.6, it is interesting to see that MNEs must clearly understand the culture of a country and the competitors operating in the country before they can class themselves as a good international manager; without that knowledge businesses fail.

A number of researchers have emphasized the need for managers to be able to handle national differences in business, including cultural divergence on hierarchy, humour, assertiveness and working hours. In France, Germany, Italy and a large part of Asia, for example, performance-related pay is seen negatively as revealing the shortcomings of some members of the work group. Feedback sessions are seen positively in the US, but German managers see them as 'enforced admissions of failure'.

The international manager, therefore, must be more culturally aware and show greater sensitivity. But it can be difficult to adapt to the culture and values of a foreign country while upholding the culture and values of a parent company. The only way is to give managers experience overseas. But the cost of sending people abroad is typically two-and-a-half times that for a local manager, so firms look for alternatives, such as short-term secondments, exchanges and participation in multicultural project teams.

Wills and Barham (1994) believe that international managers require four sets of attributes. They must:

1  Be able to cope with cognitive complexity and be able to understand issues from a variety of complicated perspectives.

2  Have cultural empathy, a sense of humility and the power of active listening. Due to their unfamiliarity with different cultural settings, international managers cannot be as competent or confident in a foreign environment.

3  Have emotional energy and be capable of adding depth and quality to interactions through their emotional self-awareness, emotional resilience and ability to accept risk. They must be able to rely on the support of the family.

4  Demonstrate psychological maturity by having the curiosity to learn, an awareness of time constraints and a fundamental personal morality that will enable them to cope with the diversity of demands made on them.

## Management culture

There has been considerable discussion about the difference between the Asian and western models of management and the reasons for the differences. Such differences include the elements of a deeply embedded culture and more recent history and the effects on management of working within a centrally planned economy. Deshpandé *et al.* (2004), however, also note the differences between Asian management cultures and suggest that Chinese and Vietnamese firms, emerging from centrally planned economies to some form of market socialism, tend to be bureaucratic. Indian firms tend to be entrepreneurial. Japanese culture is the most consensual and the least entrepreneurial. Hong Kong tends to be about average in that it reflects the mixed Chinese and western influences on its management culture.

They conclude that there are in fact four organizational culture types:

1  Competitive or market culture which is characterized by an emphasis on competitive advantage and market superiority.

2  Entrepreneurial or adhocracy culture which emphasizes innovation and risk-taking.

3  Bureaucratic or hierarchy culture in which regulations and formal structures are important.

4  Consensual or clan culture which emphasizes loyalty, tradition and internal maintenance.

They found that in each country more competitive and entrepreneurial firms perform better, and consensual and bureaucratic firms perform worse than their national peers. They also noted that market orientation has a greater effect on performance in Asia, and innovativeness has a greater effect in the more industrialized nations.

As the workplace becomes more globalized, having a multicultural team is becoming the norm (Agrawal and Rook 2013). In their research on Asian and western management cultures they found significant differences in key leadership behaviours. These relate to implementing company strategy, promoting responsiveness to customers and other stakeholders, fostering respect and understanding in the workforce and handling the pressures of the managerial lifestyle. However, rather than focusing on cultural differences, Carlos Ghosn, Chairman and CEO of Renault-Nissan Alliance (Kase *et al.* 2011), maintains strength comes from diversity and the richest solutions come when ideas are challenged by colleagues with different perspectives.

## Management style and shared values

The different contexts and stages in the global development of firms mean that there is no proven right or wrong management style and shared values for the firm. Indeed, the shared values, as we have seen earlier, may be the only common aspect of the company that binds the various parts together. It may be based upon a long tradition in the firm, built up over many years. This is particularly the case in companies dominated by extended family ownership, such as in many Asian businesses, or where the principles of the founding family of a business are maintained.

What is important to recognize is that although global businesses are complex and diverse, the chief executive can have a major effect on the business. The personality of entrepreneurs such as Ratan Tata, Steve Jobs, Michael Dell and Richard Branson has shaped the management style and shared values of the businesses they have created from their early days.

## SUMMARY

- The increase in global business activity has resulted from a number of drivers in the environment, particularly through technological developments. Clearly it is communications and IT that have had the greatest effect on creating a global marketplace. Firms have also accelerated the move towards greater globalization by developing a worldwide presence and strategy, and offering similar products and services.

- To exploit global markets firms have developed appropriate strategies for their particular situation. These range from multi-domestic strategies, in which each market is seen as separate and individual, through to globally standardized strategies in which the firm has identified one global segment with similar needs. In practice, the largest firms are too complex for one simple strategy to be appropriate. They therefore use a combination of different strategies to build global efficiency, local effectiveness and knowledge assets.

- In the past, global trade has been dominated by MNEs from developed countries. But now, companies from emerging markets that have built their capability and resources in the domestic market, are becoming global players investing in developed countries too. The competitive advantage that they have built in their home market must then be tested in the global marketplace.

- To succeed globally, firms must build global appeal through globally recognized brands. They must also innovate, as the basis of competitive advantage in many industries changes continually.

- An increasingly common feature of transnational strategies is the greater level of cooperation between firms that would otherwise be competitors, customers or suppliers.

- To enable managers to set and control the operations of the business, an appropriate organization structure is needed. International managers must also be able to recruit and develop the right staff that will have the skills necessary to deal with the complexity, diversity and conflicting challenges of global business development.

## KEYWORDS

| | | |
|---|---|---|
| globalization | World Wide Web | global brand |
| transnationality | standardization | global reach |
| market access | adaptation | business-to-business marketing |
| global sourcing | global presence | control |
| competitive advantage | global appeal | international manager |

## CASE STUDY 1

# Huawei: overcoming market obstacles

**B**etween 2016 and 2017, the fastest-growing major Chinese multinational company in China was Huawei, which grew 31 per cent. Huawei delivers ICT solutions, products and services to one-third of the world's population in 170 countries. Huawei's founder is Ren Zhengfei who was formerly deputy director of the People's Liberation Army engineering corporation before setting up the company in 1987. Its headquarters are in Shenzhen, China, and it employs 180 000.

In 2010, Huawei was included for the first time in the US magazine *Fortune*'s Global Fortune 500. In 2017 Interbrand ranked the Huawei brand 70th in its Best Global Brands.

### History

When Huawei was first started it primarily dealt in imported private branch exchange switches from Hong Kong. Within a few years, it made one of its first digital breakthroughs by launching the C&C08 digital telephone switch. This enabled Huawei to develop products to supply to multinationals in the sector. Hutchinson Whampoa, a Hong Kong based company, provided Huawei with its first overseas contract in 1997, supplying fixed-line network products. In the mid-2000s, the company built a third-generation network for a Danish company and signed supply agreements with Vodafone and British Telecom.

Huawei has continually focused on R&D, opening a centre in India to develop a range of telecom software. It has expanded into both the USA and Sweden, creating five R&D centres, one in Stockholm and the rest in the USA.

Huawei has worked with multiple companies including 3Com, Nokia, Siemens and Motorola, which have allowed it to advance its mobile technology and networking solutions. The company's partnership with Symantec also allowed it to branch out into storage and security solutions.

By 2018 Huawei had overtaken Ericsson in sales of telecoms equipment (with revenue of US$96 billion), was the third-largest handset supplier and a leader in the development of 5G technology, the next generation mobile standard essential for connected devices.

### The US market

Uniquely perhaps among technology businesses, Huawei has achieved its leading global industry position despite antagonism in the USA. There was suspicion in US government circles that its equipment could be used for 'snooping', that the company was too closely linked to the Chinese government and military, which could endanger security. However, many multinationals, including US firms, were happy to use Huawei equipment as they found it to be effective and cheaper than competitors.

Huawei's goal is to double the business every two years. To achieve this, the company aims to increase its focus on services, such as cloud computing. In addition, it aims to continue to build its telecoms equipment sales, which account for half its revenues, and its handset sales, which account for one-third of sales in the fast-growing enterprise sector. This sector is dominated by Amazon, Google, Microsoft from the USA, and Alibaba and Tencent from China. Key to achieving this potential growth, Huawei believes, is exploiting the Internet of Things and building greater industry and government collaboration.

### Questions

**1** What do you consider to be the reasons for Huawei's rapid global growth?

**2** What must Huawei do to maintain and build their global position?

**3** How important to Huawei's global ambition is success in the US market?

**4** What strategy should they adopt in the US market?

**References:** www.Huawei.com; *Financial Times* (2018) L. Lucas Huawei flourishes despite perennial hurdles in US, 4 April. Available from www.ft.com/content/2baaaaae-332c-11e8-b5bf-23cb17fd1498 (accessed 5 June 2018); Interbrand (2017). *Best Global Brand Rankings*. Available from http://interbrand.com/best-brands/best-global-brands/2017/ranking/ (accessed 4 April 2018).

## CASE STUDY 2

# Reshoring: rethinking global reach

The benefits for MNEs of offshoring and outsourcing have been outlined in this chapter. The most frequently cited are low wages paid to manufacturing workers and low land rents, for example in China and Mexico.

However, many MNEs are rethinking their strategies and bringing back product manufacturing and services, such as call centres, within their shores.

There are many reasons given, not least that cost benefits are reducing:

**Narrowing wages gap**: Recent times have seen increases in wages and land costs in China, Mexico, Turkey and Poland, making them less competitive for offshoring. Other countries such as Bangladesh and the Philippines still offer lower costs, but the calculation of low wages plus high transportation costs may make more businesses rethink the offshoring decision.

**Transportation, taxation and exchange rate costs**: The rising costs of shipping, fuel and associated taxes mean that profit margins on goods produced in northern China, Russia or eastern India and travelling long distances have been reduced. Changes in currency exchange rates have affected the competitiveness of low-cost supply countries.

**Social conscience**: Businesses such as Google, GE and the Ford Motor Company decided to invest in human capital and have brought production and service jobs back to the USA. This trend became more political in 2016, when in his election campaign slogan 'America First', the president promised to restore manufacturing jobs to the US 'rust belt' by applying tariffs on certain imports.

**'Made In . . .'**: Many consumers, usually encouraged by governments, want to buy products and services from suppliers in their own country. Rossignol built an ultra-modern factory in Sallanches (Haute-Savoie) to make 20 000 pairs of 'Made in France' skis, enabling consumers to feel patriotic and contribute more directly to their economy. Previously, they were made in a Taiwanese factory. Rossignol can fly the flag for French innovation while being able to respond more quickly to the demands of its mainly European and North American consumers.

**Speed to market and building an agile supply chain**: Consumers are increasingly impatient and do not want long delivery times. Zara, the fast-fashion brand, brought back manufacturing clothing and accessories to northern Spain. Fast for Zara means that over 60 per cent of fashion items go from 'the drawing board' to retailers in two weeks, difficult if outsourced from countries thousands of miles away.

Brooks Brothers, the US fashion brand, has re-shored manufacturing jobs to enable a quicker turnaround of smaller volumes of more exclusive designs. The smaller more frequent batches can be turned around in 5–14 days.

**Consumer demand**: Many banks, insurance and telecommunication businesses offshored their call centre services but have since re-shored them. Customers did not feel comfortable discussing personal financial matters with someone overseas.

**Quality**: B2B or B2C customers increasingly demand high-quality goods and services. A survey of 300 manufacturers in the UK found that one in six had re-shored some production in the last few years. The main reasons were quality concerns, reduced delivery times and to achieve more flexible lead times.

Mulberry makes 50 per cent of its bags in the UK to ensure quality.

**Mass customization**: Part of Burberry's decision to invest £50 million in a factory in northern England was to facilitate more customer participation in designs and flexibility in production. This is enabling the firm to run a monogramming service for customers.

**Product development**: In the USA the Makers Row database of 10 000 small furniture and fashion manufacturers facilitates greater collaboration and quick turnaround in design, prototyping and production of initial small quantities.

**The re-shoring challenge**: Decisions about re-shoring are complex and challenging. Many firms, such as Burberry, have re-shored only part of their production to keep their options open. Often, the workforce skills needed are no longer available in the developed countries. The investment in new factories and training can therefore be huge. Nike announced that it was going to relocate 10 000 manufacturing jobs back to the USA, but rather than investing itself, it has negotiated with Apollo Global Management, a New York private equity firm, to set up a US supply chain of existing and new players, headed by Tegra Global. Presumably Nike is supporting this venture with purchase quantity guarantees.

Experts question whether job creation through re-shoring, promised by politicians, will be fully realized. Justin Rose of Boston Consulting Group explains that a manufacturer of stainless steel kitchen rubbish bins moved production back from China to the USA. But his client replaced 70 Chinese workers with only 10 Americans by automating picking parts, putting parts on a production line, vehicle driving and unloading.

## Questions

**1** What are the advantages and disadvantages of off-shoring a supply chain?

**2** What are the marketing benefits of re-shoring?

**3** What are the likely supply chain challenges?

**4** What are the likely impacts for less developed supply countries?

**References:** Mellow, C. (2017) US Manufacturing The Reshoring Is Real, The Jobs Are Not. *Global Finance*. Available from www.gfmag.com/magazine/october-2017/us-manufacturing-reshoring-real-jobs-are-not (accessed 3 April 2018); Lloyds Bank (2016) Reshoring – how to assess location decisions for your business. Available from http://resources.lloydsbank.com/insight/gameplan/re-shoring-how-to-assess-location-decisions-for-your-business/ (accessed 3 April 2018); Abnett, K. (2016) Does reshoring fashion manufacturing make sense? *Business of Fashion*. Available from www.businessoffashion.com/articles/intelligence/can-fashion-manufacturing-come-home (accessed 3 April 2018); *Supply Chain Navigator* (2017) Nike takes the leap. Available from http://scnavigator.avnet.com/article/may-2017/nike-takes-the-leap/ (accessed 3 April 2018).

## REFERENCES

1. Abnett, K. (2016) Does reshoring fashion manufacturing make sense? *Business of Fashion*. Available from www.businessoffashion.com/articles/intelligence/can-fashion-manufacturing-come-home (accessed 3 April 2018).

2. Agrawal, A. and Rook, C. (2013) Global leaders in East and West: Do all global leaders lead in the same way? INSEAD Business School working paper. Available at www.insead.edu/facultyresearch/research/doc.cfm?did=52985 (accessed 5 June 2018).

3. Airports Council International (2016) *The Ownership of Europe's Airports*. www.newairportinsider.com (accessed 5 June 2018).

4. Akgün, A.E., Keskin, H. and Ayar, H. (2014) Standardization and adaptation of international marketing mix activities: A case study. *Procedia – Social and Behavioral Sciences* 150, 609–618.

5. Balabanis, G., Theodosiou, M. and Katsikea, E.S. (2004) Export marketing: developments and a research agenda. *International Marketing Review* 21 (4–5), 353–77.

6. Barbaro, M. (2006) Wal-Mart profits falls 26%, its first drop in 10 years. *New York Times*, 16 August.

7. Bartlett, C.A. and Ghoshal, S. (2015) Organizing for worldwide effectiveness. The transnational solution. Chapter 14 in Buckley, P.J. and Ghauri, P.N. (eds) *International Business Strategy: Theory and Practice*. Routledge.

8. Boston Consulting Group (2014) Redefining global competitive dynamics, September 2014. Part of the winning growth series. BCG.org.

9. Bracken, P. (2007) Revenge of the domestic tigers. Available from www.strategy-business.com/article/05316 (accessed 19 August 2015).

10. Brandt, W., Hulbert, J. and Richers, R. (1980) Pitfalls in planning for multinational operations. *Long Range Planning*, December.

11. Brett, J., Behfar, K. and Kern, M.C. (2006) Managing multicultural teams. *Harvard Business Review* 84(11), 84–91.

12. Buzzell, R.D. (1968) Can you standardize multinational marketing? *Harvard Business Review* 46(6), 101–114.

13. Cagni, P. (2006) Think global, act European. Available from www.strategy-business.com.

14. Deshpandé, R., Farley, J.U. and Bowman, D. (2004) Tigers, dragons and others: Profiling high performance in Asian firms. *Journal of International Marketing* 12(3), 5–29.

15. *The Economist* (2010a) The world turned upside down. *The Economist*, 15 April.

16. *The Economist* (2010b) Grow, grow, grow. What makes emerging-markets companies run. *The Economist*, 15 April.

17. *The Economist* (2014) Beauty and the beasts. Available from www.economist.com/news/special-report/21635758-think-global-act-artisan-beauty-and-beasts (accessed 13 April 2015).

18. Elinder, E. (1961) How international can European advertising be? *International Advertiser* December, 12–16.

19. *Financial Times* (2018) L. Lucas Huawei flourishes despite perennial hurdles in US, 4 April. Available from www.ft.com/content/2baaaaae-332c-11e8-b5bf-23cb17fd1498 (accessed 5 June 2018).

20. Finkelstein, S. (1998) Safe ways to cross the merger minefield, Mastering global business Part 4. *Financial Times*, 20 February.

21. Forbes (2015) *Billionaire List*. Available from www.forbes.com/profile/bernard-arnault/ (accessed 13 April 2015).

22. Gogel, R. and Larreche, J.C. (1989) The battlefield for 1992: product strength and geographical coverage. *European Journal of Management* 17, 289.

23. Govindarajan, V. and Gupta, A.K. (2001) Building an effective global business team. *MIT Sloan Management Review* 42(4), 63–71.

24. Hart, S.L. and London, T. (2005) Developing native capability: Why multinational corporations can learn from the base of the pyramid. *Stanford Social Innovation Review*, Summer. Available from www.ssireview.org/ (accessed 5 June 2018).

25. Holt, D.B., Quelch, J.A. and Taylor, E.L. (2004) How global brands compete. *Harvard Business Review* 82(9), 68–75.

26. Interbrand (2017) *Best Global Brand Rankings*. Available from http://interbrand.com/best-brands/best-global-brands/2017/ranking/ (accessed 4 April 2018).

27. Kase, K., Slocum, A. and Zhang, Y. (2011) *Asian versus Western Management Thinking, Its Culture-bound Nature*. Palgrave Macmillan.

28. Khashani, K. (1995) A new future for brands. *Financial Times*, 10 November.

29. Leggett, R. (2013) As emerging markets slow, firms search for 'new' BRICs. *Harvard Business Review* 28 November 2013 www.hbr.org/2013/11/as-emerging-markets-slow-firms-search-for-new-brics/ (accessed 14 April 2015).

30. Levitt, T. (1983) The globalization of markets. *Harvard Business Review* 61(3), 69–81.

31. Lloyds Bank (2016) Reshoring: How to assess location decisions for your business. Available from http://resources.lloydsbank.com/insight/gameplan/re-shoring-how-to-assess-location-decisions-for-your-business/ (accessed 3 April 2018).

32. Majaro, S. (1991) *International Marketing*. Routledge.

33. Meffet, H. and Bolz, J. (1993) Standardization of marketing in Europe needs effort. In C. Haliburton and R. Hunerberg (eds) *European Marketing Readings*. Addison-Wesley.

34. Mellow, C. (2017) US manufacturing the reshoring is real, the jobs are not. *Global Finance*. Available from www.gfmag.com/magazine/october-2017/us-manufacturing-reshoring-real-jobs-are-not (accessed 3 April 2018).

35. Mortensen, M. and Beyene, T. (2009) Firsthand experience and the subsequent role of reflected knowledge in cultivating trust in global collaboration. Working papers, Harvard Business School Division of Research, 1–65.

36. Nistor, C. (2014) Firms' transnationalization evolution of multinational groups operating in Romania. *SEA-Practical Application of Science* (5), 51–58.

37. Prahalad, C.K. and Hart, S.L. (2002) The fortune at the bottom of the pyramid. *Strategy and Business* 26(54), 67.

38. Rebeco (2018) Rebeco outsources part of its operations activities to JP Morgan. Available from www.robeco.com/en/media/press-releases/2018/robeco-outsources-part-of-its-operations-activities-to-jp-morgan.html (accessed 5 June 2018).

39. Sebenius, J.K. (2002) The hidden challenge of crossborder negotiations. *Harvard Business Review* 80(3), 76–85.

40. Shotter, J. (2017) JPMorgan plans to create 2,500 new jobs in Poland www.ft.com/content/706c66f0-9f7a-11e7-9a86-4d5a475ba4c5 (accessed 5 June 2018).

41. Smith, A. (1998) The conundrum of maintaining image. *Financial Times*, 8 May.

42. *Strategy and Business* (2015) s+b trend watch: 3D printing's impact on the transportation industry. Spring Issue 78, 19 January 2015.

43. *Supply Chain Navigator* (2017) Nike takes the leap. Available from http://scnavigator.avnet.com/article/may-2017/nike-takes-the-leap/ (accessed 3 April 2018).

44. Vila, S.T. and Peters, M. (2016) The Privatising Industry in Europe. *Amsterdam: Transnational Institute*.

45. Weichmann, U.E. and Pringle, L.G. (1979) Problems that plague multinational marketers. *Harvard Business Review*, July/August.

46. Wills, S. and Barham, K. (1994) Being an international manager. *European Management Journal* 12(1).

47. Zou, S. and Cavusgil, S.T. (2002) The GMS: A broad conceptualization of global marketing strategy and its effect on firm performance. *Journal of Marketing* 66, 40–56.

## CHAPTER 7

# MARKET ENTRY STRATEGIES

## LEARNING OBJECTIVES

After reading this chapter you should be able to:

- Identify the alternative market entry options available to firms seeking to develop new country markets

- Compare the different levels of involvement, risk and marketing control of these market entry methods

- Understand the criteria for selecting between the market entry options

- Appreciate the advantages and disadvantages of the different market entry methods

- Understand the motivations and challenges of market entry partnership strategies, such as alliances and joint ventures

## INTRODUCTION

For the majority of companies, the most significant international marketing decisions they are likely to take are how they should enter new markets, and how they will maintain and build their involvement in existing markets to increase their international competitiveness. We have already identified potential country, regional and world markets and discussed the development of international marketing strategies in both smaller and global firms. In this chapter we examine the different market entry options open to firms to enable them to select the most appropriate method for their given situation. For most SMEs this represents a critical first step. But for established companies, the problem is how to exploit opportunities more effectively within the context of their existing network of international operations and, particularly, how to enter new emerging markets.

There are advantages and disadvantages with each market entry method. Critical in the decision-making process are the firm's ambition and capability, assessment of the cost and risk associated with each method, and level of involvement the company is allowed by the government. These factors determine the degree of control it can exert over the total product and service offer and the method of distribution.

There is, however, no ideal market entry strategy. Different market entry methods might be adopted by different firms entering the same market and/or by the same firm in different markets. We particularly focus on the collaborative strategies adopted by the very largest firms.

# The alternative market entry methods

The various alternative market entry methods are shown in Figure 7.1. They cover a span of international involvement. At one end is almost zero domestic purchasing, where the firm merely makes the products available for others to export but effectively does nothing itself to market its products internationally. At the other is total involvement where the firm might operate wholly owned subsidiaries in all its key markets. These are approximate relative positions and vary according to the specific situation. E-commerce might be placed in a range of positions depending upon the particular business model adopted. For Facebook and Google, it is the complete offer, whereas for the manufacturer of capital equipment it might be simply an information source.

The market entry decision is taken within the firm. It is determined to a large extent by the firm's objectives and attitudes to international marketing and the confidence in the capability of its managers to operate in foreign countries. In order to select an appropriate and potentially successful market entry method, it is necessary to consider a number of criteria including:

- The company objectives and expectations relating to the size and value of anticipated business.
- The size and financial resources of the company.
- Its existing foreign market involvement.
- The skill, abilities and attitudes of the company management towards international marketing.
- The nature and power of the competition within the market.
- The nature of existing and anticipated tariff and non-tariff barriers, and other country-specific constraints, such as legal and infrastructure limitations.
- The nature of the product itself, particularly any areas of competitive advantage, such as trademark or patent protection.
- The timing of the move in relation to the market and competitive situation.

**FIGURE 7.1**   Market entry methods and the levels of involvement in international markets

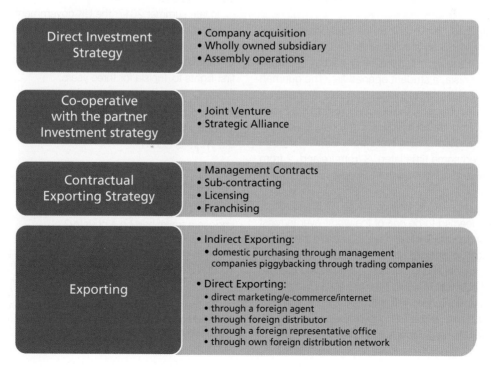

This list is not exhaustive, as the entry method might be influenced by other factors which are specific to the firm's particular situation. For example, the laws of a host country might prevent a firm from owning 100 per cent of an operation in that country. Trade embargos put in place by the United Nations may prevent a firm entering the country during times of war. Or terrorism in the country of origin of the product or service may make market entry inadvisable. It is not just the United Nations that prevents activity in countries because of terrorist action. More recently, governments banned all but essential travel to Tunisia following a terrorist attack in 2015, thus preventing existing travel companies from taking tourists to a country they had entered (see Illustration 7.1 for further discussion of this issue).

## ILLUSTRATION 7.1

# Thomas Cook's withdrawal and re-entry into Tunisia

Thomas Cook, like many other travel companies, was presented with a crisis when on 26 June 2015 in Port El Kataoui, near the busy holiday resort of Sousse, Tunisia, a student opened fire. The gunman fired his Kalashnikov indiscriminately at holiday-makers sunbathing on the beach in front of the 5-star Hotel Rui Imperia Marhaba. On the day 36 people were killed, 30 of whom were from Britain (another person died some time later), 3 from Ireland, 2 from Germany and 1 from each of Russia, Belgium and Portugal.

The random attack, later connected to Islamic State (IS), was deemed to be one of the worst-ever terrorist attacks on tourists. Incidents like this add to the level of geopolitical uncertainty that surrounds decisions made by governments and in this case travel-related companies and tourists. To avoid their citizens being at risk, a travel ban to Tunisia was imposed by governments including those of the UK, the Netherlands, Ireland, Denmark, Germany, France and Spain.

This incident, and the following travel ban, meant Thomas Cook had to react quickly. First, it had to get customers out of Tunisia. Second, it had to rearrange holidays for customers who had already booked Tunisia as their destination for the summer and winter season. And third, it had to remove Tunisia from its product offer; a country it had been trading in for many years.

During the travel ban imposed by the UK government, Thomas Cook was no longer able to trade in Tunisia. While this trading situation was outside its control, Thomas Cook accepted it, was keen to show it is a caring company with tourist security and safety at the top of its agenda.

The Tunisian Tourist Board stated that during 2014, the number of British travellers who visited Tunisia was 425 000. Following the terrorist attack and the UK government's travel ban, the number fell dramatically to just 18 000 in 2016.

In late summer 2017, the UK government's Foreign Office announced it had lifted the travel ban to Tunisia following developments in security and safety. Six months later, in February 2018, Thomas Cook began it first flights to Tunisia for three years.

## Questions

**1** What effect does terrorism have on tour operators like Thomas Cook?

**2** How would the terrorism attack have affected tourism-related businesses in Tunisia?

**3** What other situations may prompt governments to impose a travel ban on a country?

**References:** Morris, H. (2018) Thousands of holidaymakers are returning to Tunisia: But is it safe? Available from www.telegraph.co.uk/travel/destinations/africa/tunisia/articles/thomas-cook-tunisia-cheap-holidays-is-it-safe/ (accessed 3 April 2018); BBC (2017) Tunisia attack: What happened. Available from www.bbc.co.uk/news/world-africa-33304897 (accessed 4 April 2018).

Timing is another particularly important factor in considering entry. For example, emerging markets typically have bursts of optimism and growth which are often followed by setbacks caused by political or economic factors, or changing customer expectations. The Asian approach of allocating time and resources in the expectation of improved trading conditions in the future has paid off in many emerging markets. Chinese companies are investing heavily in the infrastructure in Africa in exchange for valuable resources and assets and in the expectation that the economies of African countries will improve in the near future. This approach contrasts with that of many western companies who seem to invest only when a particular country is about to 'take off'. But it may be too late if their Asian rivals are already well entrenched. International e-commerce brands such as Amazon and Alibaba lead the way in entering new markets (see Illustration 7.2). In doing so, they provide small businesses with the opportunity to export indirectly using Amazon or Alibaba's infrastructure.

# ILLUSTRATION 7.2

# Amazon and Alibaba: e-commerce giants moving to bricks and mortar retail

### Why e-commerce is a success

Amazon and Alibaba are major players in e-commerce, dominating different parts of the world. Amazon has entered many countries in North America and Europe. However, it has recently looked east and begun investing heavily in India, Australia and Singapore. Alibaba, on the other hand, dominates e-commerce sales in China, but it is also entering new markets, investing in India and Australia.

Clearly both e-commerce giants are embracing the general increase in global wealth and the increased availability of the Internet to more consumers around the world. Their growth is of great benefit to companies large and small who have the opportunity to use Amazon and Alibaba's infrastructure, international reach and brand, which in turn provides an unimaginable marketplace of products for millions of consumers.

Looking at Figure 7.1, Amazon and Alibaba use different market-entry modes to grow. Amazon generally tends to grow through company acquisitions, whereas Alibaba tends to invest in existing businesses. Despite the incredible e-commerce success, both Amazon and Alibaba have decided that they also need to include traditional bricks and mortar retail outlets as part of their portfolio.

### Why bricks and mortar?

Alibaba is the number one e-commerce business in China and 800 million Chinese can access the Internet. A high percentage enjoys online browsing and shopping. However, hundreds of millions of Chinese do not go online at all. Therefore, the traditional in-person bricks and mortar shoppers are a consumer market opportunity for Alibaba. To capture that market, Alibaba invested $2.9 billion into Sun Art Retail, one of China's largest hypermarket chains. The alliance with Sun Art Retail enables Alibaba to connect with the bricks and mortar shopper in the hope that, in time, these shoppers will be exposed to and use Alibaba's online retail store.

## Questions

**1** Why did Amazon and Alibaba invest money in existing companies when entering new markets?

**2** What are the benefits of e-commerce businesses opening bricks and mortar in-person retail stores?

**Reference:** CB Insights (2018) Amazon Vs. Alibaba: How the e-commerce giants stack up in the fight to go global. Available from: www.cbinsights.com/research/amazon-alibaba-international-expansion/ (accessed 3 April 2018); Bloomberg News (2018) What Drew Amazon and Alibaba to Bricks-and-Mortar: Q&A. Available from: www.bloomberg.com (accessed 3 April 2018).

## Risk and control in market entry

We referred earlier to the fact that one of the most important characteristics of the different market entry methods is the level of involvement of the firm in international operations. This has significant implications in terms of levels of risk and control and is shown in Figure 7.2. This figure also shows the four categories of market entry methods: indirect and direct market entry, cooperation and direct investment.

The cost of resourcing the alternative methods usually equates closely to levels of involvement and risk. The Figure 7.2 does suggest, however, that higher levels of involvement bring greater potential for control over its foreign country marketing activities and also higher potential risk, usually due to the high cost of investment. In practice, this is an oversimplification. Firms whose products are marketed internationally through domestic purchasing are at risk of losing all their income from international markets. They may not know why, because of their total reliance on their customer's strategy for success.

Partnerships, in the form of joint ventures and strategic alliances, have become increasingly common over the past few years. They are thought to offer the advantage of achieving higher levels of control in market entry at lower levels of risk and cost. This is on the basis that there is a high degree of cooperation between companies and that the individual objectives of the partner companies are compatible.

In making a decision on market entry, therefore, the most fundamental questions that the firm must answer are:

■ What level of control over our international business activities do we require?

■ What level of risk are we willing to take?

■ What cost can we afford to bear?

In answering these questions, it is important to consider not just the level of control, risk and cost. It is also important to review the relative importance that the firm might place upon the different elements of its marketing activity. For example, a lack of control over certain aspects of the marketing process, such as after-sales servicing, might become more important. After-sales servicing is often undertaken by third-party contractors. If this is of a poor standard, it may affect the reputation and image of a company or brand because consumers frequently blame the manufacturer rather than a distributor or retailer for the poor service they have received.

**FIGURE 7.2**  Risk and control in market entry

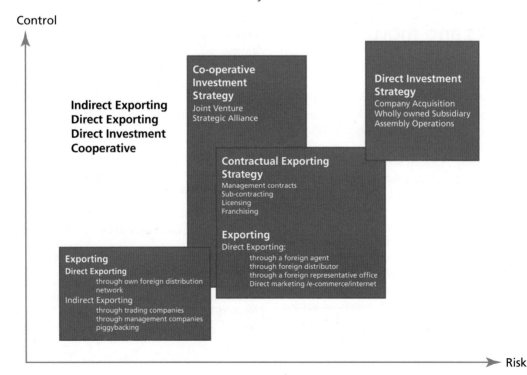

# Indirect exporting

For firms that have little inclination or few resources for international marketing, the simplest and lowest cost method of market entry is for them to have their products sold overseas by others. The objective of firms which use this method of entry may be to benefit from opportunities that arise without incurring any expense. Or they may simply want to sell off excess capacity into foreign markets with the least possible inconvenience. Firms such as these often withdraw from this activity as soon as their sales into the home market improve. While indirect exporting has the advantage of the least cost and risk of any entry method, it allows the firm little control over how, when, where and by whom the products are sold. In some cases, the domestic company may even be unaware that its products are being exported.

There are four main methods of indirect exporting, and these are by using:

- domestic purchasing
- an export management company (EMC) or export house (EH)
- piggyback operations,
- trading companies.

## Domestic purchasing

Some firms or individuals do not realize that their products or services have potential export value until they are approached by the buyer from a foreign organization. The buyer might make the initial contact, purchase the product at the factory gate and take on the task of exporting, marketing and distributing the product in one or more overseas markets. Examples of this include purchasing beads from the Maasai and cocoa beans from farmers in Africa. The Body Shop sourced naturally occurring ingredients for its ranges of toiletries and cosmetics and made domestic purchasing from deprived regions of the world a feature of its marketing activity. Taking a moral stance and demonstrating environmental concern, however, can make the firm a target for detractors. Ben and Jerry's took this route, in sourcing ingredients for their ice cream from community-based suppliers. When fashions changed, however, and certain ingredients were no longer popular, they were criticized for stopping supply arrangements with community-based social enterprises.

Local subcontractors to original equipment manufacturers (OEMs) fall into this category, as their international market potential is derived entirely from being a member of the OEM's supply chain. While for the manufacturer or supplier, domestic purchasing could hardly be called an entry strategy, it does provide the firm with access to and limited knowledge of international markets. However, the supplying organization is able to exert little control over the choice of markets and the strategies adopted in marketing its products. Small firms find that this is the easiest method of obtaining foreign sales. But, being totally dependent on the purchaser, they are unlikely to be aware of a change in consumer behaviour and competitor activity or of the purchasing firm's intention to terminate the arrangement.

If a company is intent on seeking longer-term viability for its export business, it must adopt a more proactive approach, which will inevitably involve obtaining a greater understanding of the markets in which their products are sold.

## Export management companies or export houses

Export houses or export management companies (EMCs) are specialist companies set up to act as the export department for a range of companies. They can help SMEs to initiate, develop and maintain their international sales. As well as taking orders from foreign buyers, they provide indirect access to international market information and contacts. By offering ranges of products from various companies, they provide a more attractive overall sales package to foreign buyers. By carrying a large range they can spread selling and administration costs over more products and companies, and reduce transport costs because of the economies of making larger shipments of goods from a number of companies.

EMCs deal with the necessary documentation. Their knowledge of local purchasing practices and government regulations is particularly useful in markets that might prove difficult to penetrate. The use of EMCs, therefore, allows individual companies to gain far wider exposure of their products in foreign markets at much lower overall costs than they could achieve on their own. There are a number of disadvantages, however. The export house may specialize by geographical area, product or customer type (retail, industrial or institutional). This may not coincide with the suppliers' objectives. As a result of this, the selection of markets may be made on the basis of what is best for the EMC rather than the manufacturer. EMCs are paid by commission. So they might be tempted to concentrate upon products with immediate sales potential rather than those that might require greater customer education and sustained marketing effort to achieve success in the longer term. EMCs may also be tempted to carry too many product ranges. As a result, the manufacturer's products may not be given the necessary attention from sales people. The EMC may also carry competitive products which they promote preferentially, again to the disadvantage of a particular firm.

Care is needed in selecting a suitable EMC. Resources should be allocated to managing the relationship, monitoring performance and learning more about the markets in which products are being sold in order to seize new opportunities. As sales increase, the firm may wish to manage its own exporting. The transition, however, may not be very easy. First, the firm is likely to have become very dependent on the export house. Unless steps have been taken to build contacts with foreign customers and increase market knowledge, moving from using EMCs could prove difficult. Second, the firm could find it difficult to withdraw from its contractual commitments to the export house. Many agreements are based only on the current and short-term situation. Third, the EMC may be able to substitute products from an alternative manufacturer and so use their customer contacts as a basis for introducing new competition against the original exporter.

E-business was expected to have a significant adverse effect on EMCs and even threaten their survival. However, in assessing the impact of e-business, Sharma (2013) found that EMCs are of great benefit to e-businesses as well as manufacturers as they play an efficient and effective role by engaging with B2B companies worldwide.

## Piggybacking

In piggybacking, an established international distribution network of one manufacturer might be used to carry the products of a second manufacturer. The second manufacturer is able to ride on the back of the existing reputation, contacts and administration of the carrier with little direct investment themselves.

The carrier is either paid by commission and so acts as an agent, or alternatively, buys the product outright and so acts as an independent distributor. There are also advantages in piggybacking for the carrier. They are able to carry a wider product range and so present a more attractive sales package to potential buyers. Furthermore, they can benefit from economies of scale by increasing their revenue without incurring additional costs of marketing, selling administration and distribution.

There can, however, be problems as the terms and conditions of the marketing arrangements are often poorly thought out. This is because piggybacking often starts on a 'try it and see' basis. Either company might become locked into an arrangement that proves unsatisfactory for them, particularly as a firm's strategic objectives change over a period of time. Decisions about such marketing mix issues as branding might not suit both companies. Arrangements for providing technical support and service for products often prove to be a source of disagreement and difficulty.

For smaller firms, piggybacking can work when two products are interdependent, or if the second product provides a service for the first. Larger companies, too, have found it successful. This might be if the rider has experienced some kind of barrier to entering particular markets, or the use of an existing distribution network can provide faster market development.

A form of piggybacking occurs when an MNE moves into an emerging market. This provides the opportunity for their key suppliers, such as advertising, market research and consultancy companies, to set up local offices there.

## Trading companies

Trading companies are part of the historical legacy from the colonial days. Although different in nature now, they are still important trading forces in Africa and Asia. There are many trading companies in Africa, such as Chimart Nexus Limited, which is a distributor of goods ranging from cosmetics to noodles, and Deflora Enterprises Limited, which is one of the largest importers of steel from around the world.

One of the major benefits of using trading houses is that their extensive operations and contacts allow them to operate in more difficult trading areas. One important aspect of their operations is to manage countertrade activities in which sales into one market are paid for by taking other products from that market in exchange. The essential role of the trading company is to quickly find a buyer for the products that have been taken in exchange.

Indirect exporting is often a small company's first experience of international marketing. It has the advantages of being a simple and low-cost method of gaining exposure of products in foreign markets without the company first having to gain the necessary expertise in the various aspects of international trading. However, the company has little control over its international marketing activities and is restricted to simply reacting to new situations and opportunities as they arise. It is extremely difficult to build up international marketing knowledge and expertise by marketing at arm's-length, or to develop any significant long-term product and promotional strategies. Moreover, because of the lack of direct contact between the firm and the market, indirect entry approaches are usually perceived as lacking long-term commitment. As a result, customers and other members of the distribution channels are likely to withhold their full commitment to the firm and its products until the firm becomes more involved in the market, by adopting a more direct approach.

## Direct exporting

If a company wishes to secure a more permanent long-term place in international markets, it must become more proactive through direct involvement in the process of exporting. Indeed, exporting is the most popular approach for firms as it requires fewer resources, has little effect on existing operations and involves low investment and financial risks. More importantly, by direct exporting, organizations learn more from their buyers on what to produce and how to produce their goods (Bai *et al.* 2017) In addition, Helm and Gritsch (2014) state that when marketers clearly understand the key components of the export marketing mix, they will significantly reduce uncertainty. However, this requires definite commitment from the company and takes the form of investment in the international operation through allocating time and resources to a number of supporting activities. The export marketing mix is summarized in Figure 7.3.

Figure 7.3  The components of the export marketing mix

| | |
|---|---|
| Product: | selection, development and sourcing |
| Pricing: | policy, strategies, discount structures and trading terms |
| Promotion: | corporate promotions and local selling, trade shows and literature |
| Distribution: | sales force management, agents, distributors and logistics |
| Services: | market research, training and sales servicing |
| Finance and administration: | budgets, order processing, insurance and credit control |
| Technical: | specifications, testing and product quality |

The benefits of direct over indirect exporting are that the proactive approach makes it easier to exert more influence over international activities. This results in a number of specific advantages for the exporter, such as greater control over the selection of markets, greater control over the elements of the marketing mix, improved feedback about the performance of individual products, changing situations in individual markets and competitor activity, and the opportunity to build up expertise in international marketing.

The disadvantages of direct exporting are that the direct investment necessary is considerable because the whole of the marketing, distribution and administration costs will now be borne by the company. In taking this decision, the company must be quite sure that the costs can be justified in the light of the market opportunities identified. Illustration 7.3 shows the benefits exporting can have on emerging countries which excel at exporting to other parts of the world.

## ILLUSTRATION 7.3

## Blooming success for Columbian flower farmers

The flower bouquet market depreciated from 2015 to 2016 by −4.6 per cent. The Netherlands is the world's number one exporter of flower bouquets. It now exports over 46 per cent of the world's flowers (it was 45 per cent in 2015), but its flower bouquet sales declined from US$3.8 billion in 2015 to US$3.5 billion in 2016. The second largest exporter of flowers is Columbia, accounting for 17 per cent of flower exports, with a like-for-like value of US$1.3 billion in both 2015 and 2016. The Columbian flower export business began in earnest in the 1960s when the US and Columbian governments set up an 'Alliance for Progress' programme focusing on export trade from Columbia to the USA in agricultural produce. Flowers are not the first thing that springs to mind when thinking of agricultural produce. However, Columbia has fine, temperate weather all year round. It has fertile, moist soil and plenty of water, making it a perfect place from which to grow and export flowers. While labour is cheap in Columbia, the country's government has strict labour legislation. Workers receive paid medical leave, and there is both maternity leave (18 weeks) and paternity leave. The 'minimum wage' is well established and all receive it. The USA is the main recipient of Columbian flower exports, as well as the UK, Japan and Russia. The fact that the Columbian government has introduced legislation to ensure its flower workers are not exploited is one reason importers and wholesalers like to do business with Columbia. Indeed importers 'are guilt-free' and feel they are acting responsibly through their suppliers. Additionally, consumers, as well as the World Health Organization and the Environmental Protection Agency, are calling for a ban on chemicals and pesticides on all agricultural items, from flowers to foodstuffs. The Columbian government does not allow Columbian flower farmers to use any pesticides, which adds to the reasons why flower importers choose and remain loyal to Columbia.

### Question

**1** What has the Columbian government done to help the flower industry flourish?

**Reference:**  Workman, D. (2017) Flower bouquet exports by country: world's top exports, www.worldstopexports.com/flower-bouquet-exports-country/ (accessed 4 April 2017); International Trade Centre (2018) Trade Map Colombia. www.trademap.org.

For those firms wishing to change from indirect to direct exporting, or to significantly increase their marketing efforts, timing can be critical. The extra costs involved can often place a huge financial burden on the company. The solution to this is, wherever possible, to make the transition gradually and in a well-planned way, starting with a beachhead or initial landing in one nearby foreign market.

## Factors for success in exporting

A considerable amount of research has been carried out into the barriers and motivations for new exporters and the stages of internationalization, and this was discussed in Chapter 5.

Katsikeas *et al.* (2000) conclude that the way exporting performance is assessed is important. The simplest measure is whether firms do or do not export. Measurement of the financial performance of the firm in terms of export sales volume, growth and profitability, and the ratio of export to total sales is useful to measure longitudinal firm performance. It is less useful for comparing firm performance between industry sectors, because the industry sectors may be structured quite differently. Subjective measurements of the performance of the management of the firm are often helpful but pose a problem, too, in their comparability between firms and sectors.

Katsikeas *et al.* do, however, conclude that a number of factors are important in contributing to successful exporting:

- Commitment of the firms' management.
- An exporting approach in the firm which emphasizes the importance of augmenting and maintaining skills.
- A good marketing information and communication system.
- Sufficient production capacity and capability, product superiority and competitive pricing.
- Effective market research to reduce the psychic distance between the home country and target country market. Given that it is knowledge that generates business opportunities and drives the international process.
- An effective national export policy which provides support at an individual firm level and emphasizes the need for knowledge-based programmes which prioritize market information about foreign market opportunities.

They find that the cost of export planning incurred by the firm does not correlate with export performance. They suggest that this might be explained by the fact that a major source of strength in exporting is flexibility and adaptability to export opportunities and the ability to make an immediate strategic response. Moreover, firm size and the managers' experience are not critical factors in export success. They do recognize that these factors may be the source of the export stimuli in the first place and could be major determinants of the firm's commitment to exporting and its ability to solve problems.

It is generally accepted, therefore, that in a small business, attitudes and commitment to international expansion are crucial for success. In larger companies other factors can have a bearing on performance. The size of a company can either hinder or encourage international development. This is because of the variations in the capability of the staff for planning, the lack of consistency of information and the degree to which adaptation of the mix is necessary. A number of other factors, such as the types of strategies that are pursued, segmentation, product and pricing can also affect export success.

International marketing of services is more fully explored in Chapter 8. Early stage exporting of services is different from exporting of products. Styles *et al.* (2005) find there is limited research into the unique success factors in the sector. They do, however, report some key success factors, emphasizing appropriate use of the tangible and intangible assets and personnel-related factors where there is high face-to-face contact.

## Selection of exporting method

The choice of the specific individual markets for exporting was discussed in Part I of this book. It is important to re-emphasize that the more subjective factors, such as a senior executive's existing formal or informal links, particular knowledge of culture or language and perceived attractiveness of markets, may well influence an individual firm's decision.

Once individual markets have been selected and the responsibilities for exporting have been allocated, the decision needs to be taken about precisely how the firm should be represented in the new market. Clearly, the nature, size and structure of the market will be significant in determining the method adopted. In a large market, particularly if a high level of market knowledge and customer contact is needed, it may be necessary to have a member of the firm's staff resident in or close to the market. This cannot be justified if the market is small or levels of customer contact need not be so high. Alternatively, a home-based sales force may be used to make periodic sales trips in conjunction with follow-up communications by telephone, fax and email.

Many other factors will affect the cost–benefit analysis of maintaining the company's own staff in foreign markets. These include whether the market is likely to be attractive in the long term as well as the short term and whether the high cost of installing a member of the firm's own staff will be offset by the improvements in the quality of contacts, market expertise and communications. The alternative, and usually the first stage in exporting, is to appoint an agent or distributor.

## Agents

Agents provide the most common form of low-cost direct involvement in foreign markets. They are independent individuals or firms who are contracted to act on behalf of exporters to obtain orders on a commission basis. They typically represent a number of manufacturers and will handle non-competitive ranges. As part of their contract they will be expected to agree sales targets and contribute substantially to the preparation of forecasts, development of strategies and tactics using their knowledge of the local market. Agents do not take ownership of the goods but work instead on commission, sometimes as low as 2–3 per cent on large value orders.

The selection of suitable agents or distributors can be a problematic process. The selection criteria might include:

- The financial strength of the agents.
- Their contacts with potential customers.
- The nature and extent of their responsibilities to other organizations.
- Their premises, equipment and resources, including sales representatives.

Clearly, the nature of the agreement between the firm and its agent is crucial in ensuring the success of the arrangement. The agreement should clarify what is expected of each party, set out the basis for the relationships that will be built up and ensure that adequate feedback on the market and product development is provided.

There are various sources for finding a suitable agent at low cost to the exporter:

- Asking potential customers to suggest a suitable agent.
- Obtaining recommendations from institutions such as trade associations, chambers of commerce and government trade departments.
- Using commercial agencies.
- Using agents for non-competing products.
- Poaching a competitor's agent.
- Advertising in suitable trade papers.

## Achieving a satisfactory manufacturer–agent relationship

To achieve success the exporter–agent relationship needs to be managed by:

- Allocating time and resources to finding a suitably qualified agent.
- Ensuring that both the manufacturer and agent understand what each expects of the other.
- Ensuring that the agent is motivated to improve performance.
- Providing adequate support on a continuing basis including training, joint promotion and developing contacts.
- Ensuring that there is sufficient advice and information transfer in both directions.

## Distributors

Distributors buy and stock the product from the manufacturer, organize selling and distribution and so take the market risk on unsold products as well as the profit. For this reason, they usually expect to take a higher percentage to cover their costs and risk.

Distributors usually seek exclusive rights for a specific sales territory and generally represent the manufacturer in all aspects of sales and servicing in that area. The exclusivity, therefore, is in return for the substantial capital investment that may be required in handling and selling the products. The capital investment can be particularly high if the product requires special handling equipment or transport and storage equipment in the case of perishable goods, chemicals, materials or components.

The issue of agreeing territories is becoming increasingly important. In many markets, distributors are becoming fewer in number, larger in size and sometimes more specialized in their activity. The trend to regionalization is leading distributors increasingly to extend their territories through organic growth, mergers and acquisitions. Also, within regional trading blocs competition laws are used to avoid exclusive distribution being set up for individual territories.

## Other direct exporting methods

There are three other modes of exporting which are considered to be direct: management contracts, franchising and direct marketing, typically online buying.

# Management contracts

Management contracts emphasize the growing importance of services, business skills and management expertise as saleable commodities in international trade. Normally the contracts undertaken are concerned with installing management operating and control systems, and training local staff to take over when the contract is completed. Many construction projects, such as the rebuilding of Afghanistan and Iraq, were undertaken in this way.

Other examples of management contracts may be as part of a deal to sell a processing plant as a turnkey operation. This is when the capital plant and a management team are provided by the firm to set up and run the plant for the first few months of operation, and then train the local team to take over. With increased privatization and outsourcing of facilities management by public and private sector organizations, there is a substantial growth in management contracts and in firms providing these services. Businesses are outsourcing many services, providing growth opportunities for businesses such as Flatworld Solutions (India), an international market research company, and ISS World, which provides cleaning, catering and security services in 77 countries.

# Franchising

Franchising is a means of marketing goods and services in which the franchisor grants the legal right to use branding, trademarks and products. The method of operation is transferred to a third party – the franchisee – in return for a franchise fee. The franchisor provides assistance, training and help with sourcing components, and exercises significant control over the franchisee's method of operation. It is considered to be a relatively less risky business start-up for the franchisee. However, it still harnesses the motivation, time and energy of the people who are investing their own capital in the business. For the franchisor it has a number of advantages, including the opportunity to build greater market coverage and obtain a steady, predictable stream of income without requiring excessive investment.

There are two main types of franchise. The first is known as a distribution franchise. For example, car dealerships such as Ford Motor Company and international drinks brands such as Coca-Cola. The franchisees are granted the right to distribute a manufacturer's (franchisor's) product in a specified territory. The other type of franchise is the business format franchise, which is a growing sector and includes many types of businesses such as restaurants (Café Rouge), convenience stores (Spar), fitness outlets (Fitness Space) and hotels (Intercontinental Hotels and Resorts). This type of franchise includes the licensing of a trademark, the system for operating the business and the appearance of the location.

Franchising can take the form of single-unit franchising in which the arrangement is made with a single franchisee, or multi-unit in which the franchisee operates more than one unit. The multi-unit franchisee may be given the responsibility for developing a territory and opening a specified number of units alone. Or, as is common in international markets, they may operate a master franchise, in which the master franchisee can sub-franchise to others. See Case Study 1 of Wagamama's international expansion.

Franchising, be it single or multi-unit business, is one of the major success stories in terms of international growth (King *et al.* 2013). Franchising is a basic contractual agreement between the franchisor, the owner of the brand and supporting marketing mix, and a franchisee who invests personal time and money into the franchisor's brand. Internationally, franchisors are able to draw upon the cultural knowledge of appointed franchisees. This is of great benefit when considering service delivery, tastes, local demands, expectations, competitors and, of course, accessing local suppliers. Local franchisees can make suggestions to fast food menus such as removing pepperoni from pizza toppings at Pizza Hut in India, providing more corn in Japanese restaurants, and suggesting that KFC include gravy, peas and pumpkin at Australian outlets. Local competitive knowledge is also helpful. By knowing the local market, McDonald's has added spaghetti to the menu to compete more effectively with Jollibee in the Philippines, especially as spaghetti is traditionally used to celebrate birthdays in the Philippines. For the franchisee the major benefit for investing in an international franchise business is to be supported by global brand awareness and advertising.

Currently, the top five international franchise companies are McDonald's, KFC, Burger King, Pizza Hut and 7-Eleven (Franchise Direct 2018). These are all US brands, but some other well-known franchise brands in the top 20 international franchise companies come from Europe. These include Intercontinental Hotel and Resorts from the UK, ranked 9th, and Carrefour and Europa, both from France, ranked 18th and 19th respectively.

The leading franchisor, McDonald's, has over 37 000 restaurants in the world, of which 85 per cent are owned by independent franchisees. McDonald's operates in over 100 countries and there are over 375 000 people employed by McDonald's worldwide.

Trading companies have frequently been appointed as master franchisees. While this has helped to accelerate the growth of franchising, it has also influenced the franchisor's internationalization process. Because of the global power of these trading companies, they are able to challenge the franchisor's decisions in the franchise process and have a considerable say in the strategic development of the business. There is an imbalance in power in franchising, which means that there is conflict between the goals of the franchisor and those of the franchisee. Similarly, the franchisee has fewer opportunities to use his or her entrepreneurial skills as he or she is burdened with standardization processes and procedures imposed by the franchisor (Terry *et al.* 2017).

Most US hotels are part of branded part-franchised/part-owned groups. There is considerable scope to franchise in China and India, where hotels remain independent.

## Direct marketing and online purchasing

**Direct marketing** is concerned with marketing and selling activities which do not depend for success on direct face-to-face contact. This includes mail order, telephone marketing, television marketing, media marketing, direct mail and e-commerce using the Internet. There is considerable growth in all these areas, largely encouraged by increased availability of information and the development of ICT to analyze it, and client management systems to manage customer contacts. The changing lifestyles and purchasing behaviour of consumers, and the increasing cost of more traditional methods of entering new markets, are further drivers of this trend. The critical success factors for direct marketing are in the standardization of the product coupled with the personalization of the communication. While technical data about the product might be available in one language, often English, the recipients of the direct marketing in international markets expect to receive accurate communications in their domestic language. International direct marketing, therefore, poses considerable challenges, such as the need to build and maintain up-to-date databases, use sophisticated multilingual data processing and personalization software programs, and develop reliable credit control and secure payment systems.

However, it can offer an advantage in entering new markets. Whereas US firms had trouble breaking into the Japanese market, catalogue firms were successful because they were positioned as good value for money for well-known clothing brands. Japanese catalogues were priced higher for similar quality items.

Direct marketing techniques can also be used to support traditional methods of marketing by providing sales leads, maintaining contact or simply providing improved customer service through international call centres. Where multiple direct channels are used for market entry, it is the integration of channels through effective customer relationship management systems that is essential to ensure customer satisfaction.

# Foreign manufacturing strategies without direct investment

Having so far considered market entry strategies that have been based upon the development, manufacture and supply of products and services from the firms' domestic operations, we now turn our attention to strategies which involve production and service supply from overseas plants. Before discussing the alternatives available for ownership and control of overseas operations, it is necessary to consider the factors which may lead a firm to start having its products and services produced in one or more of its international markets.

## Reasons for setting up overseas manufacture and service operations

The benefits of overseas manufacturing and service operations are:

- *Product.* Avoiding problems due to the nature of the product, such as perishability.
- *Services.* These are dependent for success on local intellectual property, knowledge and sensitivity to the local market.
- *Transporting and warehousing.* The cost of transporting heavy, bulky components and finished products over long distances is reduced.
- *Tariff barriers/quotas.* Barriers to trade, which make the market inaccessible, are reduced.
- *Government regulations.* Entry to some markets, such as central and eastern Europe, are difficult unless accompanied by investment in local operations.
- *Market.* Local manufacture and service operations may be viewed more favourably by customers.
- *Government contacts.* Firms are likely to be viewed more favourably if they contribute more to the local economy.
- *Information.* A strong local presence improves the quality of market feedback.
- *International culture.* Local presence encourages a more international outlook and ensures greater commitment by the firm to international markets.
- *Delivery.* Local manufacture and service operations can facilitate faster response and just-in-time delivery.
- *Labour costs.* Production, distribution and service centres can be moved to lower labour cost markets provided there are appropriate skills and adequate IT infrastructure to maintain satisfactory quality.

For most companies, the cost of setting up an overseas operation is initially much higher than expanding the domestic facility by an equivalent amount, as we indicated earlier in this chapter. The equipment costs are likely to be similar, and other costs such as labour, land purchase and building may even be cheaper. But it is the cost involved in transferring technology, skills and knowledge that normally proves to be expensive and is often underestimated.

Transferring operations from a domestic to an overseas plant reduces the demand on the home plant, which might have traditionally supplied all the firm's overseas markets. The firm must plan either to quickly reduce the cost of running the domestic plant or find new business to replace the production that has been transferred abroad, otherwise the viability of the domestic plant might be put at risk. Setting up new plants overseas involves large cash outflows and can put a significant strain on the firms' finances. Poor planning, underestimation of costs or unforeseen problems associated with setting up a plant overseas have frequently caused businesses to fail or be vulnerable to takeover.

The reason for locating the manufacturing plant close to the market may be due to the nature of the product. Increasingly, however, it is the costs of manufacture (including labour, raw materials and government support) as well as the costs of transport. For many firms, setting up foreign country operations for market entry reasons has prompted them to review their business. This has frequently resulted in them closing down their domestic operation and transferring labour-intensive activity to lower labour cost countries.

Regionalization is also having a significant effect on plant location. For example, in the car industry, location decisions are being based on a variety of factors, such as the participation of the country in monetary union, the different levels of productivity and the need to be closer to the most attractive potential markets. Mexico has expanded its car manufacturing business within NAFTA (North American Free Trade Agreement).

Hutton (2006) observes that eastern Europe has become the new Detroit: car manufacturers General Motors, Volkswagen, Audi, Suzuki, Toyota, BMS and Kia all have factories there. Interestingly, South Korean firms are looking to 'make where they sell' to avoid paying tariffs and high transport costs. Kia, however, noted that wage rates in Slovenia were one-fifth of those in South Korea. Reversing this trend, Hyundai invested around US$1.7 billion in an assembly plant in Alabama during 2004 to produce sports utility vehicles, and it was still going strong in 2018.

Having emphasized that a move into overseas manufacturing and service operations involves high cost and risk, firms can choose between different levels of financial commitment. They can, for example, embark upon foreign manufacturing strategies which do not involve direct investment. These include contract manufacture and licensing agreements, or strategies which do involve direct investment albeit at different levels of cost and risk. Such strategies include assembly operations, wholly owned subsidiary, company acquisition, joint venture and strategic alliances.

## Contract manufacture

A firm which markets and sells products into international markets might arrange for a local manufacturer to produce the product for them under contract. Examples include Nike and Gap, both of whom use contract clothing and shoe manufacturers in lower labour cost countries. The advantage of arranging contract manufacture is that it allows the firm to concentrate upon its sales and marketing activities. As investment is kept to a minimum, it makes withdrawal relatively easy and less costly if the product proves to be unsuccessful.

Contract manufacture might be necessary in order to overcome trade barriers. Sometimes it is the only way to gain entry to a country in which the government attempts to secure local employment by insisting on local production. If political instability makes foreign investment unwise, this may be the best way of achieving a marketing presence without having the risk of a large investment in manufacturing. The disadvantage of contract manufacture as an entry method is that it does not allow the buyer control over the manufacturer's activities.

Outsourcing from contract manufacturers allows firms such as Sara Lee Desserts to be very flexible by supplying differentiated food products for different regional markets and adjusting costs more quickly when necessary. It also has the financial benefit of lower capital employed. But the risks are that the local contractor may not achieve the desired quality levels or may not gain the necessary knowledge to market the product themselves and compete directly with the international marketer. The marketing firm has less control over the conditions in the factory (intentionally or unintentionally). Some years ago, Nike and Gap received bad publicity with the sweatshop conditions in plants they used in Asia. More recently, Primark was one of the retailers whose products were made in a sweatshop factory that collapsed, killing 1000 Bangladeshi workers. As a result, they had to sever contracts with plants which refused to comply with company standards for wage levels and working conditions. Primark stepped forward with compensation for the families of those that died.

Two Scottish companies, Young's and Dawnfresh, provide further examples of contract manufacture. They are processors and marketers of shellfish caught in Scottish waters. However, both companies announced that they were closing their processing plants in Scotland with the resulting loss of 190 jobs. Young's decided to ship 120 000 tonnes of scampi 12 000 miles to Thailand for peeling before they make the return journey. Dawnfresh shipped its scampi to China for peeling.

## Licensing

Licensing also requires relatively low levels of investment. Organizations involved in the film, television and sports industries have been particularly successful in licensing the use of brands, characters and themes, generating huge sales of licensed products. Such organizations include ones as diverse as Disney, the Olympic Games Committee and Manchester United Football Club. It is estimated that the global merchandising industry is worth US$191 billion. Instantly recognizable logos or characters are key, with cartoon characters making the most successful brands. *The Simpsons* is the most successful licensed TV show in history, with sales of more than US$8 billion. It is a form of management contract in which the licenser confers to the licensee the right to use one or more of the following: patent rights, trademark rights, copyrights and/or product or process know-how. In some situations, the licenser may continue to sell essential components or services to the licensee as part of the agreement. An example of the licensing activities surrounding Peppa Pig's launch into the Brazilian and Japanese market is shown in Management Challenge 7.1.

## MANAGEMENT CHALLENGE 7.1

## Peppa Pig: on the road in Brazil and Japan

Helped by brother George and Mummy and Daddy pig, Peppa with her characteristic laugh and love of muddy puddles is a popular British pre-school cartoon. Peppa Pig does everything a 3-year-old child does, and her adventures are adored by children in 180 countries. The cartoons are available in 40 different languages, often with a British accent. They have wonderful stories, some of which are country-specific, providing children with a fun glimpse of different cultures and traditions from around the world.

Recent entries into new countries include Brazil and Japan. In 2015 Peppa Pig was launched in Brazil and was a phenomenal success. Brazilians enjoy a carnival-style atmosphere so Peppa Pig went on the road showcasing new merchandise to adoring fans in 12 malls around Brazil, including Rio de Janeiro, São Paulo, Salvador and Londrina. Many licences to make Peppa Pig merchandise in Brazil were set up, giving toy makers, printing factories and even shoe manufacturers a boost. The master licensee in Brazil is Exim.

It did an amazing job finding manufacturers as Peppa Pig fans rushed out to buy 3 million pairs of Peppa Pig shoes, story books and magazines in anticipation of Peppa Pig's arrival.

In 2018 Entertainment One took Peppa Pig to the Japanese market in spring, fanfaring a new episode where Peppa Pig goes out into the sunshine with her friends to enjoy the cherry blossom. This new episode and launch coincided with Japan's traditional cherry blossom season. Just like the launch in Brazil, Entertainment One needed to award a master licensee to arrange the manufacture of Peppa Pig sticker books, toys and clothes. For the Japanese market, Saga Toys is the master licensee, who is tasked with finding the very best partners to manufacture Peppa Pig merchandise. At the spring launch of Peppa Pig, a pop-up shop called 'Peppa Pig Goes to London' sold over 100 merchandised products from 23 licensing partners.

### Question

**1** What are the benefits to Japanese manufacturers and retailers when an international icon like Peppa Pig enters their country?

**Reference:** Licensing Biz (2018) Entertainment One celebrates Peppa Pig in Japan with London-themed pop-up shop. Available from: www.licensing.biz/entertainment/entertainment-one-celebrates-peppa-pig-in-japan-with-london-themed-pop-up-shop (accessed 5 April 2018).

There are a number of reasons why licensing is a useful entry method for organizations. Financial and management commitments can be kept low, the high cost of setting up a manufacturing, retailing or marketing subsidiary can be reduced and tariff and non-tariff barriers can be avoided. Licensing is particularly useful, therefore, to deal with difficult markets where direct involvement would not be possible, and where the market segments to be targeted may not be sufficiently large for full involvement.

Licensing usually has a number of benefits for the licenser. The licensee pays for the licence normally as a percentage of sales. Thus, as sales grow, so does the revenue to the licenser. Considerable control exists as the licensee uses the rights or know-how in an agreed way for an agreed quantity of product. The licensee markets and purchases products for an agreed fee.

For the licensee, there are a number of advantages. For a relatively low outlay, it is possible to capitalize on established know-how with little risk and avoid the high research and development (R&D) cost associated with launching a new product in many markets. This is particularly important in the industrial market, for example, where licensing of proven technology enables companies to enter markets with products which would be prohibitively expensive to develop.

Problems can occur in licensing if the licenser does not respond to changes in the market or technology, or does not help to develop the market for the licensee. A very capable licensee may have learned so much about the market and product that the contribution from the licenser is no longer required. The licensee too may either be unwilling or unable to develop the market in the way that the licenser would wish. These sources of conflict often arise as a result of the environment, competitors and market demand changing over the licensing period.

Sarathy *et al.* (2006) identify a number of techniques that can be adopted to minimize the potential problems of licensing:

- Develop a clear policy and plan.
- Allocate licensing responsibility to a senior manager.
- Select licensees carefully.
- Draft the agreement carefully to include duration, royalties, trade secrets, quality control and performance measures.
- Supply the critical ingredients.
- Obtain equity in the licensee.
- Limit the product and territorial coverage.
- Retain patents, trademarks, copyrights.
- Be an important part of the licensee's business.

# Foreign manufacturing strategies with direct investment

At some point in its international development, a stage is reached when the pressure increases upon a firm to make a much more substantial commitment to an individual market or region. The reasons for investment in local operations are:

- *To gain new business.* Local production demonstrates strong commitment and is the best way to persuade customers to change suppliers, particularly in industrial markets where service and reliability are often the main factors when making purchasing decisions.
- *To defend existing business.* Car imports to a number of countries are subject to restrictions. As their sales increase, so they become more vulnerable to locally produced competitive products.
- *To move with an established customer.* Component suppliers or service providers often set up their own local subsidiaries to retain their existing business, compete with local component makers and benefit from increased sales.
- *To save costs.* By locating production facilities overseas, costs can be saved in a variety of areas such as labour, raw materials and transport.
- *To avoid government restrictions.* These might be in force to restrict imports of certain goods.

For most multinationals there is a strong requirement to demonstrate that they have a permanent presence in all their major markets. The actual form of their operations in each market is likely to vary considerably from country to country. But they must also reduce their own manufacturing and operating costs through making the supply chain more cost-effective. Some firms, for example in the shoe and footwear industries, obtain component or finished product supplies from the lowest labour cost areas. Ford locates its component suppliers on a manufacturing campus close to its assembly plants.

## Assembly

A foreign-owned operation might be set up simply to assemble components which have been manufactured in the domestic market. It has the advantage of reducing the effect of tariff barriers, which are normally lower on components than on finished goods. It is also advantageous if the product is large and transport costs are high, for example in the case of cars. There are other benefits for the firm too, as retaining component manufacture in the domestic plant allows development and production skills and investment to be concentrated, thus maintaining the benefit from economies of scale. By contrast, the assembly plant can be made a relatively simple activity requiring low levels of local management, engineering skills and development support.

There is an argument that assembly plants do not contribute significantly to the local economy in the long term. In initially attracting Nissan, Honda and Toyota assembly plants, the UK government claimed that many jobs would be created at relatively low cost. Critics, however, have claimed that the number of jobs created in the assembly plants was not very significant. In addition, unless the components were made locally, little transfer of technology would be achieved, and the assembly plants could relatively easily be moved to a new location. In practice, as other car manufacturers withdrew from the UK market, these Japanese manufacturers became the only major established firms. Both to counter threats such as this and also to generate further employment, countries can take steps to develop the component supply business. They can do this by interrupting the component supply chain through imposition of import or foreign exchange rate restrictions. Or, as in the case of CzechInvest, the inward investment arm of the Czech Republic, they can support local component manufacturers who can supply 'just-in-time'. Coca-Cola uses 50 per cent owned bottling and distribution companies in local countries, supplying them with concentrate to maintain control over the recipes.

## ILLUSTRATION 7.4

# Mexico: developing into a big player in manufacturing

The reasons for setting up overseas manufacturing businesses are outlined in this chapter and this illustration shows those principles.

Mexico's economic outlook is positive: GDP is growing, unemployment rates are reducing and inflation rates are falling. Export revenue is already valued at US$397.5 billion, with the vast majority of that relating to manufacture of cars, airplane parts, computers and mobile/cell phones. Therefore, the Mexican government is proud. They are not only promoting these facts but showcasing Mexico as a great place in which to do business. So much so they are changing regulations to incentivize manufacturing companies to build production factories in Mexico. In turn, this will help unemployment figures stay low and boost local economies.

Volkswagen and Nissan, both worldwide car manufacturing brands, are stepping up their investments in Mexico by building new and/or improved factories. And when big brands such as Volkswagen and Nissan show interest in a country, others will follow. Mazda is increasing its production capacity from 140 000 cars per year to 230 000 cars per year by 2016. South Korea is investing in Mexico for the first time with the production of their Kia.

In addition to the Mexican government's incentives, labour costs in Mexico are low. China, once heralded as the number one country for car manufacturing, is falling out of favour with big brands because of their ever-increasing labour costs. With the average wage in Mexico for an unskilled automobile worker being $900 per year less than an equivalent worker in China, it is no wonder car manufacturers are thinking of turning to Mexico.

Furthermore, there are many excellent skilled assembly workers in Mexico, something which foreign manufacturing investors find attractive as it saves money on intensive training from a zero to low-skilled workforce.

## Question

**1** What are the benefits and risks for foreign car manufacturers investing in Mexico?

**References:** Kynge, J. (2015) Mexico steals a march on China in car manufacturing. *The Financial Times*, 21 April. Available from www.ft.com/intl/cms/s/2/0bc33e06-e81e-11e4-894a-00144feab7de.html#axzz3YP0HhhQ3 (accessed 24 April 2015); The Offshore Group (2015) Foreign companies continue to invest in Mexico manufacturing. 2 February. Available from offshoregroup.com/2015/02/09/foreign-companies-continue-to-invest-in-mexico-manufacturing/ (accessed 24 April 2015).

## *Wholly owned subsidiary*

As we indicated in Figure 7.2, for any firm the most expensive method and high risk of market entry is likely to be the development of its own foreign subsidiary, as this requires the greatest commitment in terms of management time and resources. It can only be undertaken when demand for the market appears to be assured.

This market entry method indicates that the firm is taking a long-term view, especially if full manufacturing facilities are developed rather than simply setting up an assembly plant. Even greater commitment is shown when the R&D facilities are established in local countries too. If the company believes its products have long-term market potential in a relatively politically stable country, then only full ownership will provide the level of control necessary to fully meet the firm's strategic marketing objectives. There are considerable risks, too. Any subsequent withdrawal from the market can be extremely costly, not simply in terms of financial outlay, but also in terms of the firm's reputation in the international and domestic market, particularly with shareholders, customers and staff. Sometimes organizations enter other markets too quickly and are left in debt because they have expanded too soon and/or too fast, and/or because the external environment changes. Illustration 7.5 gives an example of how a solar panel organization was 'blinded by the light', invested too heavily and development was affected by an unanticipated fall in oil prices.

## ILLUSTRATION 7.5

# Overexpansion: blinded by the sun's energy

A total of 175 parties (174 countries and the European Union) signed the Paris Agreement on climate change. This drove a flurry of activity in the renewable energy market. Clearly, governments needed businesses to take up the challenge to innovate and supply renewable energy. Already there had been a significant increase in the number of orders for solar power installations in the USA and China. It seems that following the Paris Agreement, renewable energy suppliers could reap rewards. Abengoa, whose headquarters are in Spain, was already a major player in renewable solutions and was known to be one of the world's largest suppliers of sustainable energy. The company is passionate about reducing emissions and, together with its solar-power

insulations, it was clearly on a trajectory to be a driving force to reverse climate change.

However, it seemed Abengoa had been 'blinded by the sun's energy': it borrowed too much money and tried to expand too rapidly. Abengoa borrowed heavily to expand its business into North and South America, Africa, India and China. Unfortunately, the expansions caused problems and by 2015/16, Abengoa was 8.9 billion in debt and its debt to earnings ratio showed the company was in trouble. Clearly, Abengoa had borrowed too much money and could not sustain its operations. There were some factors out of Abengoa's control that affected the company, such as the slump in oil prices and the lack of government-led incentives for businesses to provide renewable energy. But, to put it simply. Abengoa had spent 'more than they had planned', particularly in developing its Brazilian projects. These factors meant that Abengoa had to keep borrowing to 'keep going'. And in 2017 it had to restructure its debts to stay afloat.

## Questions

**1** How could Abengoa have reduced its risks?

**2** In addition to oil prices and government-led incentives, what other external factors could have affected Abengoa?

**Reference:** Economist Intelligence Unit N.A. Incorporated (2016) Blinded by the light; Solar energy, *The Economist*. 419.8983, 2 April, p. 62 (US). Copyright 2016. http://store. eiu.com/

## Company acquisitions and mergers

In the previous chapters we discussed the role of acquisitions and mergers in achieving globalization. Illustration 7.6 demonstrates the justification for using acquisition as a means of strategic development to strengthen a long-term position and acquire new talent. It also shows that governments can play an important role in the process and can foil takeover attempts.

The considerable pressure to produce short-term profits means that speed of market entry is essential. This can be achieved by acquiring an existing company in the market. Among other advantages, acquisition gives immediate access to a trained labour force, existing customer and supplier contacts, recognized brands, an established distribution network and an immediate source of revenue. Companies from emerging markets have used acquisition as a fast route to acquire a globally recognized brand. Examples include: Lenovo's acquisition of IBM's PC division, Aspen Pharmacare's takeover of Australia's Sigma Pharmaceuticals to acquire market share, or India's Bharti Airtel's acquisition of the African assets of Kuwait's Zain to build its African telecoms business.

## ILLUSTRATION 7.6

## Facebook's Instagram acquisition photo-sharing businesses

Facebook has acquired over 40 different businesses since its launch including FriendFeed, Divvyshot and Chai Labs. Facebook did not purchase these businesses for their assets or market share. What they bought was talent inside the entrepreneurs who had set up the innovative and successful business, driven it forward and were future thinkers. Facebook bought talent to add to the existing pioneering culture that they are known for.

Two major photo-sharing businesses were acquired recently, Instagram and WhatsApp. Instagram was bought for US$1 billion; WhatsApp was bought for US$22 billion. The new photo-sharing businesses have been added to Facebook's portfolio of products, with the intention that they will help fulfil Mark Zuckerberg's (chief executive of Facebook) dream of connecting everyone to everybody else through virtual platforms.

At the time of purchase (2012) Instagram was one of the fastest growing photo-sharing networks but had only 30 million monthly active people and no income. Facebook bought the talent from Instagram and combined it with the advertising talent of Facebook employees. Advertising started to appear on a consumer's Instagram from 2013. Brands are still tentative about this space to advertise as promotions only appear to a highly targeted audience based on an Instagrammer's Facebook profile. So Ben and Jerry's, one of the earliest advertisers on Instagram, only promotes its brand to Facebookers that like ice cream.

Now there are 500 million daily active users on Instagram. More importantly for potential advertising revenue, there are 25 million businesses on Instagram. And to date, over 40 billion pictures have been shared. It is predicted that sales from Instagram adverts will grow from US$4.10 billion in 2017 to US$10.87 billion by 2019, which is a readjustment from 2015 when it was predicted that advertising revenue on Instagram would be $5.8 billion by 2020.

### Question

**1** What are the benefits and possible pitfalls of Facebook's acquisition of Instagram?

**References:** Aslam, S. (2018) Instagram by the numbers: Stats, demographics & fun facts. Available from www.omnicoreagency.com/instagram-statistics/ (accessed 1 April 2018); McCarthy, J. (2017) Instagram ad revenue to double to $10.87bn by 2019, says eMarketer. Available from: www.thedrum.com/news/2017/12/17/instagram-ad-revenue-double-1087bn-2019-says-emarketer (accessed 1 April 2018); Fiegerman, S. (2015) Instagram revenue projected to hit $5.8 billion in 2020, analyst says, 19 February. Available from mashable.com/2015/02/19/instagram-revenue-estimate-2020/ (accessed 8 June 2018); Facebook.com; Instagram.com.

In certain situations, acquisition is the only route into a market. This is the case with previously state-owned utilities. Many utilities and infrastructure companies in the UK are foreign owned. For example, water companies are owned by Australian investment fund Macquarie, Suez, Vivendi and Bouygues (France), Union Fenosa (Spain) and YTL (Malaysia); the British Airports Authority by Ferrovial of Spain; and electricity companies by EDF of France.

Expropriation is the opposite of privatization and occurs when a government, usually a nondemocratic regime, takes strategic assets from a company, such as an oil well or mine. Even the most powerful companies are unable to stop this and often receive little compensation.

Sometimes the reasons for international business acquisition are, perhaps, not driven by business logic. It seems questionable whether any of the takeovers of British premiership football clubs will make money, starting with Roman Abramovitch's purchase of Chelsea and the Glazer family ownership of Manchester United, even though the marketing opportunities are huge.

An acquisition strategy is based upon the assumption that companies for potential acquisition will be available. If the choice of companies is limited, however, the decision may be taken on the basis of expediency rather than suitability. The belief that acquisitions will be a time-saving alternative to waiting for organic growth to take effect may not prove to be true in practice. It can take a considerable amount of time to search and evaluate possible acquisition targets, engage in protracted negotiations and then integrate the acquired company into the existing organization structure.

Another disadvantage of acquisition is that the acquiring company might take over a demotivated labour force, a poor image and reputation, and out-of-date products and processes. All of these problems can prove costly and time-consuming to overcome.

While takeover of its companies is often accepted by government as a way of increasing investment, takeover of companies which are regarded as part of a country's heritage or key to security can raise considerable national resentment if it seems that they are being taken over by foreign firms. A country looking to develop its own technology and manufacturing is likely to believe that acquisition of a domestic company by an MNE is not as desirable as the MNE setting up a local subsidiary. See Management Challenge 7.2 where governments are setting up joint ventures.

Moreover, acquisition by a large international firm is often associated with job losses and transfer of production facilities overseas. In the past few years there has been considerable debate about acquisition and mergers as a method of achieving rapid expansion. The rationale that is used for acquisition is that an ineffective company can be purchased by a more effective company. This company will be able, first, to reduce costs; second, improve performance through applying better management skills and techniques; and third, build upon the synergy between the two companies and so achieve better results. Many takeovers in the UK and the USA were financed by huge bank loans justified on the basis that an improvement in future profits would be used to pay the high interest charges. In practice, few companies are able to realize the true benefits of synergy. If the other parts of the acquirer's business underperform, for example during a recession, then the acquired company is used to service an increasing debt and is starved of investment.

Some firms use acquisition to focus on their core business and sell off peripheral activities to raise the necessary investment funds for new projects or to plug holes in their finances. As part of its commitment to raise US$30 billion by the end of 2011 to meet the obligations of the Gulf of Mexico oil spill, BP sold assets in many countries around the world.

## Cooperative strategies

There are a number of situations in which two or more firms might work together to exploit a new opportunity. The methods that are adopted are joint ventures, strategic alliances and reciprocal ownership, in which two firms hold a stake in each other's business.

### Joint ventures

Joint ventures occur when a company decides that shared ownership of a specially set up new company for marketing and/or manufacturing is the most appropriate method of exploiting a business opportunity. It is usually based on the premise that two or more companies can contribute complementary expertise

Table 7.1 Who provides what in partnerships between firms from developed and developing countries?

| Developed | Developing |
|---|---|
| Marketing systems | Customer insights |
| Brands and communication | Land |
| Financial management | Buildings and equipment |
| Forecasting | Distribution networks |
| Planning | Skills |
| Technology | Low costs |
| Information systems | Beneficial wage rates |
| Capital | Tax relief |
| Supply chain management | Political connections |
| Know-how | Neighbouring markets |
| Human resources | |
| Financial incentives | |

Source: Schiffman, L.G. and Kanuk, L.L. (2000) *Consumer Behaviour*, Prentice Hall.

or resources to the joint company, which, as a result, will have a unique competitive advantage to exploit. Table 7.1 shows the contributions of partners from developed and developing countries.

While two companies contributing complementary expertise might be a significant feature of other entry methods, such as licensing, the difference with joint ventures is that each company takes an equity stake in the newly formed firm. The stake taken by one company might be as low as 10 per cent, but this still gives them a voice in the management of the joint venture.

There are a number of advantages to setting up joint ventures. These include:

- Countries, such as the Philippines, try to restrict foreign ownership.
- Many firms find that partners in the host country can increase the speed of market entry when good business and government contacts are essential for success.
- Complementary technology or management skills provided by the partners can lead to new opportunities in existing sectors, for example, in mobile communications.
- Global operations in R&D and production are prohibitively expensive, but necessary to achieve competitive advantage.
- The two companies can share investment costs and risk.
- The firms can learn from each other, particularly how to participate in local markets.

There are, however, some significant disadvantages to joint ventures as a market entry method. As joint venture companies involve joint ownership, there are often differences in the aims and objectives of the participating companies. These can cause disagreements over the strategies adopted by the particular companies. If ownership is evenly divided between the participant firms, these disagreements can often lead to delays and failure to develop clear policies. In some joint ventures the greater motivation of one partner rather than another, particularly if they have a greater equity stake, can lead to them becoming dominant and the other partner becoming resentful. Some firms more effectively learn their partners' skills. In a General Motors–Toyota joint venture, Toyota learned about supply logistics and managing US staff, whereas General Motors failed to learn Toyota's manufacturing methods.

The other disadvantages of this form of market entry compared to, for example, licensing or the use of agents, is that a substantial commitment of investment of capital and management resources must be made in order to ensure success. Start-up costs for management and control and developing cultural understanding can be high. Many companies would argue that the demands on management time might be even greater for a joint venture than for a directly owned subsidiary. This is because of the need to educate, negotiate and agree many of the operational details of the joint venture with the partner.

Some experts recommend that a joint venture should be used by companies to extend their capabilities rather than merely exploit existing advantages. It is not recommended if there are potential conflicts of interest between partners. The role of the government in joint ventures can be particularly influential, as it may control access to the domestic market. Moreover, a government may be persuaded to adapt its policy if a firm is bringing in advanced technology or is willing to make a major investment. Most of the major multinationals have increased their involvement in joint ventures. The implications of this, however, are that it leads to increasingly decentralized management and operations, more closely aligned to transnational operation than to global standardization, in which more centralized control is necessary.

Where joint ventures are used for emerging market entry there is also the possibility of a conflict of objectives. This can occur between the international company, which wishes to develop a new market, and the local company, which wishes to develop its own foreign markets or withdraw profits from the joint venture to finance other projects.

In analyzing the results of joint ventures in China, Vankonacker (1997) observes that joint ventures are hard to sustain in unstable environments. He concludes that more direct investment in China will be wholly owned, offering Johnson & Johnson's oral care, baby and feminine hygiene products business as a success story. Management Challenge 7.2 shows that joint ventures do not have to take place between two businesses; governments are also engaging with the benefits of joint ventures.

## Strategic alliances

While all market entry methods essentially involve alliances of some kind, during the 1980s the term strategic alliance started to be used, without being precisely defined. It was used to cover a variety of contractual arrangements that are intended to be strategically beneficial to both parties but cannot be defined as clearly as licensing or joint ventures. The Star Alliance of airlines that includes Lufthansa, BMI, Scandinavian Airlines, Singapore Airlines and South African Airways is one example. Bronder and Pritzl (1992) have defined strategic alliances in terms of at least two companies combining value chain activities for the purpose of competitive advantage.

Some examples of the bases of alliances are:

- technology swaps
- R&D exchanges
- distribution relationships
- marketing relationships
- manufacturer–supplier relationships
- cross-licensing.

Perhaps one of the most significant aspects of strategic alliances has been that many involve cooperation between partners that might also be competitors. This can pose problems for the participants, who must be careful about sharing information with their alliance partner but avoid information leakage where the organization may be competing.

There are a number of driving forces for the formation and operation of strategic alliances.

*Insufficient resources*: the central argument is that no organization alone has sufficient resources to realize the full global potential of its existing, and particularly its new, products. Equally, if it fails to satisfy all the markets which demand these products, competitors will exploit the opportunities which arise and become stronger. In order to remain competitive, powerful and independent, companies need to cooperate.

*Pace of innovation and market diffusion*: the rate of change of technology and consequent shorter product life cycles mean that new products must be exploited quickly by effective diffusion out into the market. This requires not only effective promotion and efficient physical distribution but also needs good channel

## MANAGEMENT CHALLENGE 7.2

## Joined-up thinking: Africa and the Gulf

The United Nations (UN) advise that agricultural production including fruit, vegetables, wheat, corn and rice needs to increase by 100 per cent in developing countries. They also advise that in the more developed countries, food production needs to increase by around 70 per cent. These increases need to take place by 2050 to feed the world's rising population. Many countries will not be able to achieve the increases that the UN recommends. The main reason for this is because many countries have only small areas of agricultural land, limited farming expertise and, more importantly, their land is arid. The UAE recognizes it cannot increase its agricultural production to that recommended by the UN. While UAE land is rich in energy reserves, such as oil, they have very limited fresh water supplies and limited land for agricultural growth. Indeed, for many years, the UAE has purchased food from outside its borders.

Parts of North Africa have a history of famine, disease, poverty and hunger. Over 80 per cent of African people live and work on farms. They should, therefore, have abundant crops of fruits, vegetables, cotton, rice and wheat. However, due to low productivity, no investment in technological advances, poor irrigation systems and a chaotic infrastructure, production is very low.

A joint venture has been formed between the Middle East and Africa. The Middle East will provide a multi-million dollar investment in African agriculture. Africa, in exchange for the investment, will feed the Middle East.

Two examples of how this joint venture is working are Qatar and Saudi Arabia. Hassad Food from Qatar has invested US$1 billion in Sudan's agriculture. Sudanese farmers will grow wheat, corn and soya, which will then be exported to Qatar. Saudi Arabia has invested US$2.5 billion in Ethiopia's agriculture. In exchange for the investment Ethiopian farmers will produce rice for Saudi Arabia. The joint venture will be of mutual benefit to both parties.

### Questions

**1** What are the benefits of joint ventures?

**2** Why has the joint venture between the Middle East and Africa been formed?

**3** What are the benefits of this joint venture?

**Reference:** Rafaty, M. (2014) View from Middle East and Africa: Can Africa feed the Middle East? 14 August. Available at www.fdiintelligence.com/Locations/Middle-East-Africa/View-from-Middle-East-and-Africa-can-Africa-feed-the-Middle-East (accessed 26 April 2015).

management, especially when other members of the channel are powerful. So, for example, the strength of alliances within the recorded music industry including artists, recording labels and retailers, has a powerful effect on the success of individual hardware products such as the MP3 player.

*High R&D costs*: as technology becomes more complex and genuinely new products become rarer, so the costs of R&D become higher.

*Concentration of firms in mature industries*: many industries have used alliances to manage the problem of excess production capacity in mature markets. Sometimes this leads to takeovers as has occurred in the 'oneworld alliance' between BA and Iberia.

*Government cooperation*: as the trend towards regionalization continues, so governments are more prepared to cooperate on high-cost projects rather than try to go it alone. There have been a number of alliances in Europe – for example, the European Airbus has been developed to challenge Boeing, and the Eurofighter aircraft project is a collaborative venture by the UK, Germany, Italy and Spain.

*Self-protection*: a number of alliances have been formed in the belief that they might afford protection against competition in the form of individual companies or newly formed alliances. This is particularly the case in the emerging global high technology sectors such as IT, telecommunications, media and entertainment.

*Market access*: strategic alliances have been used by companies to gain access to difficult markets. For instance, Caterpillar used an alliance with Mitsubishi to enter the Japanese market.

Further benefits to a strategic alliance are shown in Management Challenge 7.3 where businesses need each other's expertise to take their own products to market.

## MANAGEMENT CHALLENGE 7.3

# Plastic and food: the perfect strategic alliance

KOR Food Innovation was founded by Chef John Csukor and he has an insatiable passion for food. Csukor has been a food innovator and developer for many years. He has many marketing, food production and purchasing talents. Through Csukor's employment in mass catering at Motorola Hospitality Group, Compass Group and Starbucks Coffee Company, he has fed thousands of hungry workers. More recently, John Csukor has set up his own business called KOR Food Innovation. KOR Food Innovation helps other businesses design and implement a menu strategy for their workforce. They run focus groups to establish the latest trends in food and/or home-based cooking and even design food product labels. Csukor and his research team made up of dieticians, food designers and fine-dining chefs, develop a range of amazing food that is commercially ready for hotels, restaurants and supermarkets.

Dupont, original makers of gunpowder, now has many business segments including industrial bioscience, agriculture and performance materials. They found their fame through researching and manufacturing plastic, polymer and lycra for sportswear and women's hosiery. One area of their business is to provide plastic covers to protect ready-made food, meats and cheese from bacteria and, of course, to help keep food fresh for longer periods.

KOR Food Innovation and Dupont have formed a strategic alliance. KOR Food Innovation has designed new meat-based products that need a plastic packaging. The plastic packaging designed by Dupont enables KOR Food Innovation's meat-based products to be cooked in the oven to over 400°F, without the packaging shrivelling and shrinking. The plastic can be used on fresh or frozen meat produce and can go straight to the oven. There are even air-vents in the plastic to release steam and baste the meat-based products.

### Question

1 What are the benefits of the strategic alliance between KOR International and Dupont?

**Reference:** Dupont (2013) Data Book; KOR Food Innovation. www.korfoodinnovation.com/ (accessed 6 June 2018).

As with all entry strategies, success with strategic alliances depends on effective management, good planning, adequate research, accountability and monitoring. It is also important to recognize the limitations of this as an entry method. Companies need to be aware of the dangers of becoming drawn into activities for which they are not designed.

Voss *et al.* (2006) emphasize the importance of cultural sensitivity in cross-border alliances and the implications for trust and quality information exchange.

## Minority stake share holdings

In this chapter we have considered many different methods of cooperation between partners. Over the years many firms have taken an equity stake in another firm for a variety of reasons. Russia, for example, restricts foreign ownership to 49 per cent. The main reason is that it is regarded as less risky to build an ownership stake over time to reduce uncertainty in the workforce. Volkswagen took a 31 per cent stake in koda, the remainder being owned by the Czech government. Now, because of the trust, honesty and huge investment from Volkswagen in koda in the Czech Republic, the government has enabled Volkswagen to move from being a minor shareholder to being the main shareholder. It might provide the opportunity to influence the strategy of that firm, create a basis upon which to share expertise between the firms or establish a platform that might lead to a more formal business relationship, such as a merger, as well as generating an immediate return on the investment. Renault took a stake in Nissan to save the company from bankruptcy and succeeded in turning the company around by helping it to launch a more attractive and competitive range of cars. Renault then became the recipients of Nissan's expertise in improving quality and production efficiency.

What is quite clear is that global firms are adopting a range of market entry partnership arrangements to maximize their global performance and presence. The businesses are becoming increasingly complex as they embark on joint ventures. The associated formal responsibilities, strategic alliances, short-term contractual obligations and shareholdings might be the basis for closer future cooperation.

Inevitably, the challenge for management is to manage the various stakeholder expectations and maximize the opportunities that come from synergy and the complementary activity of the partners. To do this it is necessary to select partners that are willing and able to contribute at least some of:

- complementary products and services
- knowledge and expertise in building customer relationships
- capability in technology and research
- capacity in manufacturing and logistics
- power in distribution channels,
- money and management time.

The management must also deal with the added complexity and potential for conflicts between two quite different partners that arise because of differences in:

- objectives and strategies
- approach to repatriation of profits and investment in the business
- social, business and organization cultures,
- commitment to partnership and understanding of management responsibilities.

While cooperative strategies promise synergy, the potential for cost saving and faster market entry, it requires considerable management effort to overcome the inherent difficulties and dedication to see the partnerships through to success.

## SUMMARY

- For a firm at the start of internationalization, market entry can be regarded as a critical first step. It is vital not only for financial reasons but also because it will set a pattern of future international involvement. It determines not just the opportunities for sales but also a valuable source of market information.

- Market entry methods can be seen as a series of alternatives available to international firms. A global strategy might utilize a number of different approaches. A firm can make individual decisions based on the factors affecting one specific country or the whole region and choose the most appropriate method for the particular set of circumstances.

- The choice of market entry method should be based on an assessment of the firm's desired involvement in the market and the level of control of its marketing mix in the country, set against the financial and marketing risks.

- For large established companies that already have extensive involvement in international markets, the market entry decision is taken against the background of the competitive nature of the market, the environment, its global strategy and an existing and substantial network of operations.

- The company's competitive strategy is likely to require simultaneous decisions affecting its arrangements in a number of markets in order to improve its competitive position by entering untapped or emerging markets, or expanding its activities in existing markets.

- In order to achieve these objectives within a very short timescale, rather than relying on organic growth the companies use a variety of market entry strategies, including joint ventures and alliances, often with competitors. This is leading to increasingly complex operations being created in which companies strive to balance the opposing forces of competitiveness and cooperation. Quite frequently such arrangements fail to deliver the expected benefits.

# KEYWORDS

| | | |
|---|---|---|
| market entry | trading companies | wholly owned subsidiary |
| market involvement | indirect exporting | contract manufacture |
| risk and control | exporting | licensing |
| indirect exporting | distributors | acquisition |
| domestic purchasing | management contracts | joint venture |
| export houses | franchising | strategic alliance |
| piggybacking | direct marketing | |

## CASE STUDY 1

## Wagamama's international expansion

Created by Alan Yau in 1992, Wagamama is a restaurant chain with its headquarters in the UK. The restaurant is designed around the concept of a Japanese ramen bar, serving a variety of noodles, rice, vegetarian and vegan dishes with pan-Asian flavours. By 2018, the chain had grown to 185 restaurants, 129 of which are in the UK (see Table 7.2). Other restaurants are located in Europe, the Middle East and New Zealand. A total of 51 Wagamama restaurants are franchised and it operates in 23 countries.

One of the reasons that Wagamama has had the opportunity to grow is because the trend for consumers eating out has shifted towards casual dining. However, Wagamama is not alone in the casual dining market. Its main competitors include Gondola Group, Casual Dining Group, Gordon Ramsey Holdings and YO! Sushi Group. The brand has been a key player when it comes to healthy eating, something that is becoming prevalent within the casual dining market. And to respond to the growing number of vegans in the UK, a 360 per cent increase since the late 2000s (Mintel 2017), Wagamama introduced vegan dishes to its menu. This introduction was popular with consumers and received great press coverage particularly after winning an award at PETA's 2017 Vegan Food Awards for 'Best Curry', namely their Yasai Samla Curry (PETA 2017).

Wagamama has many strengths, the brand itself being one of them. Its Chief Executive has made a conscious effort to develop Wagamama as an 'urban brand' with restaurants in prime locations in large, vibrant cities. Recognition does not just come from the internal team, as it has received many awards ahead of its competitors such as the Gordon Ramsey Group and Nobu London (Dodkin 2016). Its strong brand image has encouraged an extensive social media following from over 500 000 followers on Wagamama GB Facebook; 55 000 followers on @wagamama_uk twitter and 63 000 on @wagamamas_uk Instagram, used as leverage to maintain loyal customers. Loyal fans are invited through social media to book and be VIPs at pre-launch events. The brand also introduced a mobile app which aims to improve customer engagement, while understanding customer behaviour, to aid new business development and marketing strategies. But more importantly the wagamamaGO app provides a bill-less pay system which saves diners around 12 minutes at each meal because they do not have to wait for the bill to arrive and go through the process of paying with the waiter or at the till.

Financially, Wagamama is strong, with group turnover increasing 12.5 per cent like for like to £72.1 million in Q3 2017–18. In the UK it has traded ahead of the

## Table 7.2  Wagamama restaurant chain composition

| | For the 12 weeks ended | | For the 40 weeks ended | |
|---|---|---|---|---|
| | January 28, 2018 | January 29, 2017 | January 28, 2018 | January 29, 2017 |
| **Company-operated restaurants** [1] _____ | **134** | **127** | **134** | **127** |
| *United Kingdom restaurants* _____ | 129 | 123 | 129 | 123 |
| *United States restaurants* _____ | 5 | 4 | 5 | 4 |
| *Company-operated restaurant openings during the period* _____ | 1 | 2 | 8 | 8 |
| *Company-operated restaurants closures during the period* _____ | 0 | 0 | (2) | (5) |
| Franchised [2] _____ | 51 | 40 | 51 | 40 |
| **Total** _____ | **185** | **167** | **185** | **167** |

(1) Company-operated restaurants include all of our restaurants in the United Kingdom and the United States.
(2) Franchised restaurants as at the dates listed were located in Belgium, Greece, Ireland, Malta, The Netherlands, Northern Ireland, Denmark, Sweden, Cyprus, Slovakia, Turkey, Qatar, United Arab Emirates, Bahrain, New Zealand, Gibraltar, Saudi Arabia, Bulgaria, Spain, Italy and Oman.

Source: Wagamama (2018) *Q3: 2017–18 Report Interim Financial Statement www.wagamama.com/ p. 7.*

competition consistently for over three years. However, over 90 per cent of its revenue is generated from the UK market. Clearly, as shown in Table 7.2, Wagamama is moving beyond the UK borders and has announced plans to provide franchising opportunities in Croatia, Finland, Germany, Hungary, Kuwait, Luxemburg, Norway, Poland, Romania and Switzerland. By expanding the business further, it will allow the brand to strengthen operational capabilities, effectively and efficiently delivering products and services which are customer driven (Coleman 2016). Finally, expanding globally will enhance the geographic footprint, capturing market share and new target markets everywhere.

Though there is limited information on specific costs and training details provided by Wagamama, Point Franchise states the minimum investment for a Wagamama franchise is approximately £40 000. This does not include further information on additional advertising fees, operating fees or royalties. However, evidence can be seen of Wagamama's care for its brand and franchisees in what it calls the 'whole life' system – an on-going process and training structure to ensure each franchise reaches its full potential in leadership and management (Wagamama 2018).

The restaurant's innovation, connectivity and dedicated expansion through their Company Operated and Franchised businesses has not gone unnoticed,

earning them the prize of Multiple Casual Dining Restaurant of the Year at the Casual Dining Restaurant & Pub Awards 2017.

## Questions

**1** Why is Wagamama successful?

**2** What research did Wagamama complete before it chose Croatia, Finland, Germany, Hungary, Kuwait, Luxemburg, Norway, Poland, Romania and Switzerland as countries in which to offer franchise opportunities?

**3** What research needs to be done by a franchisee before applying for a franchise with Wagamama?

**Author:** Victoria Jasmine Robertson Leeds Beckett University

**Sources:** Coleman, A. (2016) Going for growth ... how to expand without destroying your business. *The Guardian*, 26 September; Dobkin, K. (2016) Now open: British import Wagamama arrives in NYC. Available from www.zagat.com/b/now-open-british-noodle-shop-wagamama-arrives-in-nyc (accessed 8 June 2018); Mintel (2017) Attitudes towards casual dining – UK – June 2017, s.l.: Mintel Oxygen Reports; PETA (2017) Wagamama and Starbucks among winners of PETA's 2017 Vegan Food Awards. Available from www.peta.org.uk/media/news-releases/wagamama-starbucks-among-winners-petas-2017-vegan-food-awards/ (accessed 5 June 2018); Wagamama (2018). Q3: 2017–18 Report Interim Financial Statement www.wagamama.com/ (accessed 5 June 2018).

## CASE STUDY 2

# IKEA in China: market entry flat packed?

A rapidly growing middle class in China seeking a more comfortable home and lifestyle offers an attractive market to those companies whose success has been secured in more mature markets by helping customers to realize their dreams. IKEA of Sweden and Home Depot of the USA both saw China as their next big opportunity. The difference, however, is that IKEA is succeeding in China whereas Home Depot has failed, closing its final big box stores in 2012, with the loss of 850 jobs and taking a US$160 million hit in the process.

The reason for this appears to be that Home Depot expected middle-class Chinese to behave as American middle-class consumers would. However, due to low labour costs, there is no do-it-yourself (DIY) culture in China. The Chinese prefer to pay a handyman or contractor to complete a project, whereas US homeowners would often undertake the task themselves. Home Depot's products were mainly about providing the tools and materials to complete tasks that often required DIY skills.

By contrast, IKEA's huge stores use room settings to show consumers how to furnish and decorate and give them experience of western culture. All the products to do this can be taken away from the store.

IKEA has not been an overnight success in China. It took a decade to open 11 stores. But growth is expected to accelerate. IKEA recognizes that it must adapt to each market and visits thousands of homes close to its stores, sitting in the kitchen to listen to householders' frustrations, ambitions, resources and alternative purchases. It recognizes that it must adapt its range in each of its 28 country markets. In the USA, for example, it needs to make beds bigger; in China it needs to provide firmer mattresses. Chinese apartments are smaller and so its room layouts and products reflect this.

IKEA has faced a number of further challenges. Chinese consumers tend to buy low-priced products. IKEA had to cut its prices substantially to compete with local suppliers. Its Beijing store can now attract over 25 000 visitors on a Saturday, equivalent to the number of visitors in a week at its European stores. This means that stores in China need to be larger and located nearer the population as few Chinese consumers have their own transport. Chinese consumers are less used to taking away flat-packed furniture – the key to IKEA's success – so the firm is expanding its delivery, assembly and installation services, as well as offering IKEA staff to get goods off the shelves – almost unheard of in European markets.

The company has perhaps been slow to realize the need for e-commerce. Young Chinese born in the late 1980s are becoming a key segment of the market, used to buying on the Internet and having their purchases delivered to their home. IKEA's 22 stores in China can physically only reach a small percentage of the population. In 2017 IKEA started testing e-commerce using third parties to reach more consumers. Another reason to do this was that Alibaba opened Home Times, an IKEA lookalike competitive home furnishing store, in Hangzhou that was supported by Alibaba's e-commerce expertise.

Another problem for IKEA has been that many of the visitors are not really shoppers at all. They are likely to be taking advantage of IKEA's air-conditioning to escape the heat and smog of the city, or perhaps picnickers with their tea flasks and plastic bags of snacks strewn around the showroom, young lovers posing for 'selfies' in apartment room sets, toddlers left to play on model furniture and people asleep on the beds and chairs around the store. Gradually IKEA's patience with them is paying off as growth accelerates.

## Questions

**1** What are the main reasons for IKEA's success and Home Depot's failure in China?

**2** What are the key learning points from IKEA's market entry into China?

**3** What would have been the advantages and disadvantages for IKEA of a more collaborative market-entry strategy?

**4** What effect is the emergence of a major local competitor likely to have on IKEA's market-entry strategy?

**References:** *People's Daily* (2017) IKEA to team up with third party e-commerce site in China. 24 July; npr (2017) IKEA in Shanghai tries to kick out freeloading senior citizens. 26 October. Available from www.npr.org/sections/goatsands oda/2016/10/20/498719746/ikea-in-shanghai-tries-to-kick-out-freeloading-senior-citizens (accessed 9 June 2018); *China Money Network* (2017) Alibaba's IKEA-like super store marks next step in offline retail expansion. 25 September; Reuters (2013) One size doesn't fit all: IKEA goes local for India, China. 7 March. Available from https://in.reuters.com/article/ikea-expansion-india-china/one-size-doesnt-fit-all-ikea-goes-local-for-india-china-idINDEE92603L20130307 (accessed 8 June 2018).

# REFERENCES

1. Aslam, S. (2018) Instagram by the numbers: Stats, demographics & fun facts. Available from www.omnicoreagency.com/instagram-statistics/ (accessed 1 April 2018).

2. Bai, X., Krishna, K. and Ma, H. (2017) How you export matters: Export mode, learning and productivity in China. *Journal Of International Economics* 104, 122–137.

3. BBC (2017) Tunisia attack: What happened. Available from www.bbc.co.uk/news/world-africa-33304897 (accessed 4 April 2018).

4. Bloomberg News (2018) What drew Amazon and Alibaba to bricks-and-mortar: Q&A. Available from www.bloomberg.com (accessed 3 April 2018).

5. Bronder, C. and Pritzl, R. (1992) Developing strategic alliances: a conceptual framework for successful co-operation. *European Management Journal* 10(4), 412–421.

6. CB Insights (2018) Amazon vs. Alibaba: How the e-commerce giants stack up in the fight to go global. Available from: www.cbinsights.com/research/amazon-alibaba-international-expansion/ (accessed 3 April 2018).

7. *China Money Network* (2017) Alibaba's IKEA-like super store marks next step in offline retail expansion. 25 September. Available from www.chinamoneynetwork.com/2017/09/25/alibaba-opens-ikea-like-store-targeting-furniture-sector-offline-expansion (accessed 9 June 2018).

8. Coleman, A. (2016) Going for growth . . . how to expand without destroying your business. *The Guardian*, 26 September.

9. Dobkin, K. (2016) Now open: British import Wagamama arrives in NYC. Available from www.zagat.com/b/now-open-british-noodle-shop-wagamama-arrives-in-nyc (accessed 8 June 2018).

10. Dupont (2013) Data Book; KOR Food Innovation. Available from www.korfoodinnovation.com/ (accessed 6 June 2018).

11. Economist Intelligence Unit N.A. Incorporated (2016) Blinded by the light; Solar energy, *The Economist*. 419.8983, 2 April, p. 62 (US). Copyright 2016. http://store.eiu.com/.

12. Fiegerman, S. (2015) Instagram revenue projected to hit $5.8 billion in 2020, analyst says, 19 February. Available from mashable.com/2015/02/19/instagram-revenue-estimate-2020/ (accessed 8 June 2018).

13. Franchise Direct (2018) Top 100 global franchises – rankings. Available from www.franchisedirect.com/top100globalfranchises/rankings/ (accessed 13 March 2018).

14. Helm, R. and Gritsch, S. (2014) Examining the influence of uncertainty on marketing mix strategy elements in emerging business to business export-markets. *International Business Review* 23(2), 418–428.

15. Hutton, R. (2006) Eastern Europe the new Detroit. *Sunday Times*, 15 October.

16. International Trade Centre (2018) Trade Map Colombia. www.trademap.org.

17. Katsikeas, C.S., Leonidou, L.C. and Morgan, N.A. (2000) Firm-level performance assessment: review, evaluation and development. *Journal of Academy of Marketing Science* 28(4), 493–511.

18. King, C., Grace, D. and Weaven, S. (2013) Developing brand champions: A franchisee perspective. *Journal of Marketing Management* 29(11–12), 1308–1336.

19. Kynge, J. (2015) Mexico steals a march on China in car manufacturing. *The Financial Times*, 21 April. Available from www.ft.com/intl/cms/s/2/0bc33e06-e81e-11e4-894a-00144feab7de.html#axzz3YP0HhhQ3 (accessed 24 April 2015).

20. Licensing Biz (2018) Entertainment One celebrates Peppa Pig in Japan with London-themed pop-up shop. Available from: www.licensing.biz/entertainment/entertainment-one-celebrates-peppa-pig-in-japan-with-london-themed-pop-up-shop (accessed 5 April 2018).

21. McCarthy, J. (2017) Instagram ad revenue to double to $10.87bn by 2019, says eMarketer. Available from www.thedrum.com/news/2017/12/17/instagram-ad-revenue-double-1087bn-2019-says-emarketer (accessed 1 April 2018).

22. Mintel (2017) Attitudes towards casual dining – UK – June 2017, s.l.: Mintel Oxygen Reports.

23. Morris, H. (2018) Thousands of holidaymakers are returning to Tunisia: But is it safe? Available from: www.telegraph.co.uk/travel/destinations/africa/tunisia/articles/thomas-cook-tunisia-cheap-holidays-is-it-safe/ (accessed 3 April 2018).

24. npr (2017) IKEA in Shanghai tries to kick out freeloading senior citizens. 26 October. Available at www.npr.org/sections/goatsandsoda/2016/10/20/498719746/ikea-in-shanghai-tries-to-kick-out-freeloading-senior-citizens (accessed 9 June 2018).

25. The Offshore Group (2015) Foreign companies continue to invest in Mexico manufacturing. 2 February. Available from offshoregroup.com/2015/02/09/foreign-companies-continue-to-invest-in-mexico-manufacturing/ (accessed 24 April 2015).

26. *People's Daily* (2017) IKEA to team up with third party e-commerce site in China. 24 July.

27. PETA (2017) Wagamama and Starbucks among winners of PETA's 2017 Vegan Food Awards. Available from www.peta.org.uk/media/news-releases/wagamama-starbucks-among-winners-petas-2017-vegan-food-awards/ (accessed 5 June 2018).

28. Rafaty, M. (2014) View from Middle East and Africa: Can Africa feed the Middle East? 14 August. Available from www.fdiintelligence.com/Locations/Middle-East-Africa/View-from-Middle-East-and-Africa-can-Africa-feed-the-Middle-East (accessed 26 April 2015).

29. Reuters (2013) One size doesn't fit all: IKEA goes local for India, China. 7 March. Available from https://in.reuters.com/article/ikea-expansion-india-china/one-size-doesnt-fit-all-ikea-goes-local-for-india-china-idINDEE92603L20130307 (accessed 8 June 2018).

30. Sarathy, R., Terpstra, V. and Russow, L. (2006) *International Marketing*, 9th edition. Dryden Press.

31. Schiffman, L.G. and Kanuk, L.L. (2000) *Consumer Behaviour*, Prentice Hall.

32. Sharma, V.M. (2013) Enhancement of trust in the export management company-supplier relationship through e-business. *International Journal of Commerce and Management* 23, 1, 24–37.

33. Styles, C., Patterson, P.G. and La, V.Q. (2005) Executive insights: Exporting services to South East Asia – Lessons from Australian knowledge-based service exporters. *Journal of International Marketing* 13(4), 104–128.

34. Terry, A., Di Lernia, C. and Perrigot, R. (2017) The obligation of good faith and its role in franchise regulation. In F. Hoy *et al.* (eds) *Handbook of Research on Franchising*. Edward Elgar p. 169.

35. Vankonacker, W. (1997) Entering China: An unconventional approach. *Harvard Business Review*, March-April.

36. Voss, K.E., Johnson, J.L., Cullen, J.B., Sakano, T. and Takenouchi, H. (2006) Relational exchange in US–Japanese marketing strategic alliances. *International Marketing Review* 23(6), 610–635.

37. Wagamama (2018) *Q3: 2017–18 Report Interim Financial Statement*. Available from www.wagamama.com/ (accessed 9 June 2018), p. 7.

38. Workman, D. (2017) Flower bouquet exports by country: World's top exports. Available from www.worldstopexports.com/flower-bouquet-exports-country/ (accessed 4 April 2017).

## CHAPTER 8

# INTERNATIONAL PRODUCT AND SERVICE MANAGEMENT

## LEARNING OBJECTIVES

After reading this chapter you should be able to:

- Understand the nature of international product and service marketing and appreciate the elements that make up the product and service offer

- Evaluate the factors affecting international product and service strategy development both external and internal to the firm

- Explain the issues that affect international product and service management across borders

- Identify the implications of the image, branding and positioning of products and services in international markets

- Understand how innovation contributes to the international product and service strategy

## INTRODUCTION

Success in international marketing depends to a large extent upon the value proposition, satisfying the demands of the market and ultimately, on whether the product or service offered is suitable and acceptable for its purpose. More markets are reaching maturity and fewer products can be differentiated by their core benefits and so are becoming commodities. In defining the term 'product', therefore, we include additional elements such as packaging, warranties, aftersales service and branding that make up the total product and a complete package of tangible and intangible benefits for the customer. Services are taking an increasing share of international trade, but managing services internationally poses particular challenges. This is because the delivery of services is so dependent on the context, which is usually influenced by the varying cultural perceptions of what is acceptable service. In both product and service markets increasing customer expectations and competition mean that it is essential for firms to continually add better value through innovation and new product development (NPD). Much of this innovation is related to technological developments.

In this chapter we focus upon some of the key aspects and recent trends of international product policy. We consider the changes in the nature of the products and services offered individually and within the portfolio, their relationship with the market and how innovation can create new products and services. Particularly important is the need to provide customers around the world with a satisfactory experience when using the product or service. To achieve this requires a clear understanding of when to meet the similar needs and wants of transnational customer segments and when to adapt to local tastes and requirements.

# The nature of products and services

The reason that the majority of companies initially develop international markets is to generate new market opportunities, increase sales of an existing product or service or to offload excess capacity. However, the product must be seen as a bundle of satisfactions, providing people not just with products but with satisfying experiences in terms of the benefits they provide rather than the functions the products perform. These concepts are particularly important in international marketing, because, for example, the growth of such global consumer products as McDonald's 'I'm lovin' it' and Coca-Cola's 'Taste the feeling' cannot be attributable solely to a distinctive taste. Much of their success might be attributed to the aspirations of their international customers to be part of the 'Coca-Cola Culture'. This comes from deriving satisfaction from a close association with the product and the brand and also being reminded of the experiences associated with the product, such as enjoying music, being with friends or watching sport.

In understanding how products can provide satisfying experiences and benefits for people, it is necessary to clearly identify and understand the motivations of the target consumer and not make assumptions about them.

## International product and service marketing

The term 'product' is used in marketing to refer both to physical goods, such as a can of baked beans or a refrigerator, and services, such as insurance or a holiday. In fact, few products can be described as pure product with no service element – salt is often suggested as approaching a pure product. Education is probably the closest to a pure service. All offers are a combination of product and service components, as shown in Figure 8.1. Before considering the total product 'offer' in more detail, it is important to consider the specific characteristics of services and the challenges they pose in international marketing.

Service characteristics are:

- **Intangibility:** Services include both tangible and intangible elements. Intangible elements cannot be touched, smelt or seen. An intangible element of a service could be 'magical'. A magical experience is what parents want for their children when they visit a Disney resort. A 'magical' experience cannot be touched, smelt or seen. However, 'magical' can be experienced when children see the Disney characters on parade, receive a big hug from Goofy or when Elsa from the film *Frozen* sings 'Let it go'. Tangible elements of this magical service offer from Disney include the magic castle, costumes of heroes and heroines, and music. Air transportation has intangible elements such as 'feeling safe' or 'enjoyment'; the tangible elements include safety belt, the life jackets stowed under the passenger seat, food, drink and the in-flight safety video. For car insurance the intangible element is 'peace of mind'; the tangible elements are a written policy received by mail or email and possibly a free gift. And for education, the tangible elements include a certificate, wearing a cap and gown, having

**FIGURE 8.1**   The product-service continuum

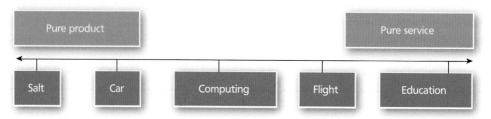

a graduation photograph, all to demonstrate success in education. From a marketing point of view, there are elements that can be standardized. Intangible examples include the anticipation of throwing caps in the air following the graduation ceremony or life-long memories. These cannot be standardized. Therefore, tangible elements are used as reminders and reinforcements of the service to confirm the benefits and suggest experiences which, in turn, will enhance the perceived value of the service. However, the physical evidence of the service that is offered may be valued very differently by people from different countries and cultures.

■ Perishability: Services cannot be stored. For example, the revenues from unfilled airline seats cannot be sold once the aircraft has taken off. This characteristic causes considerable problems in planning and promotion when attempting to match supply and demand during peak holiday season, or knowing how many baristas to have on duty during the busy and quiet times of the day. Perishability is also a problem for event organizers. An event that has only sold 900 of the 1000 tickets for a rock band's gig in Manchester cannot be sold after the gig has taken place, especially as the rock band has moved to Edinburgh for a gig that was a 'sell-out'. Therefore, for service organizations it can be problematic predicting unfamiliar patterns of demand and managing capacity, especially in distant and varied international locations.

■ Heterogeneity: Services are rarely the same because they often involve interactions between different people with different expectations. For international fast food companies this can cause problems in maintaining the consistent quality expected of employees representing the brand. This is particularly challenging when service organizations operate in international markets where there are quite different attitudes towards customer service. Consumers presume that employees of international brands will provide the same quality of service throughout the world. And because consumers expect this, if they receive poor service in Frankfurt, the international brand's reputation, in their mind, will diminish and poor service will be expected in all outlets.

■ Inseparability: The service is produced and the experience consumed simultaneously. For example, actors perform on stage at the theatre in front of an audience, barbers provide a Turkish shave while their customer is 'in the chair' and surgeons complete laser-eye treatment to improve their patients' vision in real time. This means that economies of scale and the experience curve benefits can be difficult to achieve. Supplying the service in scattered markets can be expensive. Where the service involves some special expertise, such as pop music or sporting events, the number of consumers is limited by the size and number of venues that can be visited by the performer. If the fans are in a market which is remote, they are unlikely to see the artist or their football team. Therefore they need to engage in other forms of communication such as videos, website and books, in order not to feel too separated from the performer. Instagram is a platform used by celebrities to maintain continual contact with their devoted followers. And with Selena Gomez and Cristiano Ronaldo having 133 million and 121 million followers respectively, it is clear there is a fan base that is inseparable from these entertainers.

## The three additional marketing mix elements

These differences between product and service offers have certain implications for the international marketing mix and, in addition to the usual four Ps for products – product, price, place and promotion – another three Ps for services are added. Because of the importance and nature of service delivery, special emphasis must be placed upon:

■ *People.* Consumers must be educated in order for their expectations of the service to be managed. Employees must be motivated and well trained in order to ensure that high standards of service are maintained. However, because of cultural differences, staff and customers in various countries often respond differently, not only to training and education but also in their attitudes to the speed of service, punctuality, willingness to queue and so on. To an MNE customer firms such as consultancies, advertising agencies or IT management supplying services around the world will be expected to maintain the same standards in every country. But local staff and customers may have different attitudes to service in each. *People* also includes call centre staff, online 'chat help' contacts and, of course, all the people who reply, like or share Facebook, Twitter and Instagram posts. Even though these employees are often physically remote from the consumer they must also be well trained and communicate the brand's values at all times.

- *Process*. As the success of the service is dependent on the total customer experience, a well-designed delivery process is essential. Customer expectations of process standards vary with different cultures. Standardization is difficult in many varied contexts. Frequently, the service process is affected by elements for which the service deliverer may be blamed by frustrated customers but over whom they have little control. Sports fans might travel at great expense to major events such as the Olympics, the football World Cup or golf's Ryder Cup, only to experience delays at an airport, excessive policing or bad weather. Although their team may perform well, the fans may be reluctant to travel to future matches because of their unsatisfactory overall experience. Process is a key element for restaurants. Some restaurateurs meet and greet their consumers, guide them to the table, provide a menu, discuss the meal options and offer advice on dishes and wines that complement each other. Other restaurateurs expect their consumers to find their own table, review the menu, pay up front for drinks and food, and collect their own food from the buffet table. Clearly, the process of moving the consumer through their meal experience is not the same and demonstrates the difference between high and low service restaurants. At its most basic, the process of customer management should be to make it easy for the customer to interact with the firm no matter where they are in the world.

- *Physical aspects*. Many physical reminders, including the appearance of the retail outlets, provide an atmosphere through the choice of product displays, layout of the store, logos, background music and even the branded bag in which consumers take home their purchases. The physical aspects make the service more tangible and can enhance the overall customer experience. Apart from using appropriate artefacts to generate the right atmosphere, constant reminders of the firm's corporate identity help to build customer awareness and loyalty. For example, the familiar logos of Louis Vuitton, Google, BBC and Etihad Airways may give the reassurance necessary for a consumer to buy the brand or use the service in a foreign market.

As suggested earlier, there are some specific problems in marketing services internationally. Achieving uniformity of standards of the three additional Ps in remote locations can be particularly difficult to control. Pricing, too, can be extremely problematic, because fixed costs such as taxes, rent for buildings and wages paid to employees can be a very significant part of the total service costs and vary in different locations. As a result, the consumer's ability to buy and their perceptions of the *promised experience*, *added value* and *received service* may vary considerably between markets. This has led to international service organizations providing largely standardized services. This clearly poses considerable challenges to international service providers. For example, an MNE might employ an international law firm to protect its interests. But the scope for offering a standardized service is limited by the fact that every country has its own legal system.

There are a number of generalizations that can be made about international marketing of services. Foreign markets present greater opportunities for gaining market share and long-term profits for MNEs if local firms are less experienced in customer management and communication and quality of service delivery. If cultural sensitivity and local knowledge are key, then local service companies are likely to succeed. Companies such as Google, eBay and Facebook have lost out to local imitators in China and India. IT and the development of expert knowledge networks are the sources of competitive advantage for international service marketers. Due to the high initial cost of financing overseas operations, joint ventures and franchising are rapidly growing entry methods. Frequently, the market entry strategy is based on forming alliances or piggybacking as existing clients move into new markets. Government regulations and attitudes to the protection of local suppliers vary considerably from country to country. As new markets open up, organizations have to learn what is acceptable.

While it might seem appropriate to categorize physical goods as tangible and services as intangible, marketing increasingly appears to be concerned with blurring this distinction. For example, a product such as perfume is not promoted as a complex chemical solution, but instead, marketers develop a fantasy. For example, Azzaro fragrance house created Chrome X Under The Pole. It discussed men's fragrance with North Pole explorers who talked about the fresh air they breathe at the North Pole, how the salt water splashes their faces and the extreme depths they go to underwater. From many meetings and discussions, this unique fragrance emerged, with an intangible fantasy created in the advertising message, namely extremes of freshness.

Azzaro competes with other fragrance houses by creating intangible fantasies. On the other hand, many services appear to compete over tangible 'add-ons'. Examples of competing over tangible 'add-ons' can be seen by reviewing the offers provided by low-cost airlines such as Ryanair (Ireland), Mango (South Africa), Flynas (Saudi Arabia) and Lion Air (Indonesia). Low-cost airlines develop elements of the marketing mix, using their websites to introduce yield management software that not only maximizes revenue opportunities but enables the airline to compete with other low-cost airlines based on the 'extras'. Extras include pre-ordering in-flight meals, seats with extra leg-room, priority boarding or pre-booking seats.

## The international marketing of service

One of the achievements of the Uruguay Round of negotiations on the General Agreement on Trade in Services (GATS) was to identify four modes of delivery or ways in which services may be exported. This is useful in detailing the nature of international services:

1 *Cross-border trade*, where the trade takes place from one country to another, without the movement of persons. Only the service itself, for example market research or training, crosses the border electronically (direct online/through service clouds or email), by telecommunications (telephone, radio) or by infrastructure (air, rail).

2 *Consumption abroad*, where the customer travels to the country where the service is supplied (tourism, education or training, legal services).

3 *Commercial presence*, where the supplier establishes a commercial presence abroad (banks, construction project offices, or warehousing and logistics).

4 *Movement of natural persons*, where the provider of the services crosses the border (arts and culture, recreation and sports).

Any of the four modes constitutes trade so long as the local firm is being paid by the foreign firm, no matter where the service is provided.

Illustration 8.1 shows how a dining experience in a monastery provides both tangible and intangible elements.

## ILLUSTRATION 8.1

## Gastronomy in sacred places

The Hostel San Marcos Monastery in Leon, Spain is just one of the sacred places that is a tourist attraction in itself and has been transformed into a wonderful 5-star hotel. The 16th-century building was once a hospital for pilgrims who were on the road to Santiago de Compostela where it is pronounced the Biblical apostle, St James, is buried.

Now the 5-star hotel filled with Jacobean motifs, magnificent carvings in wood and stone, and tranquil gardens also provides hospitality for exhibitors and delegates in its conference rooms and diners in its beautiful restaurants.

Many monasteries were self-sufficient, growing fruit and vegetables and some brewed their own beer. Monasteries were a place of refuge for the sick and homeless who were given food. Similarly, all travellers who knocked on the door of a monastery were welcomed and also given food, drink and a bed for the night. The transformation of the Hostel San Marcos, like many monasteries, into a hospitality venue seems to be a natural development. In particular, the income from hotel guests, conference exhibitors and delegates and diners enables monasteries to stay in good repair so that travellers and tourists can enjoy their splendour and history for many years to come.

Monasteries are holy places. Within the walls are hundreds of years of history of worship and contemplation. Visitors can feel a transcendental connection with history and the world outside themselves. Dining guests for example enjoy gastronomic delights in the restaurants in the Hostel San Marcos Monastery. They have a unique experience through the tangible and intangible attributes provided by the hotel.

The tangible attributes are the sacred heritage of the monastery, shown through art, architecture, the impressive dining tables, chairs, plates, the uniforms of the waiting staff and, of course, the beautifully presented food. The intangible attributes come from the cultural references, the history of the building, the notion that silence, prayer, rituals, worship and devotion happened within the building in which the diner is present. The combination of the tangible and intangible provides a wonderful experience for guests.

## Questions

**1** Monasteries are just one way a business and marketing manager can create an experience through tangible and intangible attributes, inside a building. What other buildings could be used to provide an experience for diners?

**2** What would be the tangible and intangible attributes?

'Invisible' services contribute to all aspects of economic activity. For example, infrastructure services (transport, communications and financial services) provide support to any type of business. Education, health and recreational services influence the quality of labour available, and professional services provide the specialized expertise to increase firms' competitiveness. Services make up an increasing proportion of GDP and are also used to add value to the product offer as outlined in the following section.

# The components of the international product offer

In creating a suitable and acceptable product offer for international markets, it is necessary to examine what contributes to the 'total' product. Second, it is necessary to decide what might make the product acceptable to the international market. Kotler and Armstrong (2014) suggest three essential aspects of the international product offer, which should be considered by marketers in order to meet consumer needs and wants:

1 *Core customer benefits*. These are the elements that consumers perceive as meeting their needs and providing satisfaction through performance and image. When consumers go to their bank, they do so to get honest and reliable investment advice and the security of knowing their savings are in a safe place.

2 *Actual products*. These are the elements most closely associated with the core product, such as features, specifications, styling, branding and packaging. To make the core customer benefits tangible, an international bank, Santander (head office Spain), provides actual products such as basic savings, mortgage and current accounts, plus recognizable logos, staff uniforms (the same the world over) and easy to understand product information to educate and enlighten consumers as to what is available. And as Santander promotes itself as being driven by innovation and technology, consumers would expect it to pioneer online banking features and 'on the go' smartphone banking apps for instant transactions.

3 *Augmented products*. These are the additional elements to the core product which contribute to providing satisfaction and include delivery, after-sales service and guarantees. For Santander, augmented products include customer service staff, via phone, email and Twitter. It also includes certificated mortgages, investments, a comprehensive website, regular engagement with social media, loyalty programmes, pension planning advisers, and terms and condition documents providing guarantees for the services and products of Santander.

**FIGURE 8.2** The three elements of the product or service

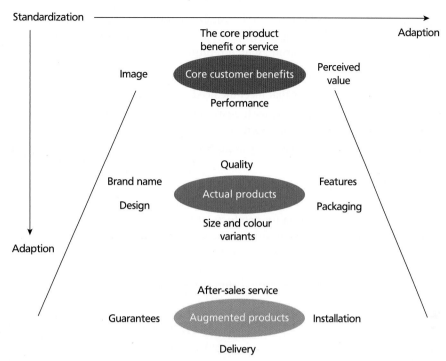

These elements form the augmented product, an extended version of which is shown in Figure 8.2. Moving down and to the right of the figure shows the elements that are relatively more difficult to standardize in different country markets.

Having introduced the concept of the total product offer, it is essential to evaluate each aspect of the product in terms of what benefits the consumer might expect to gain and how the offer will be perceived by consumers. This can be done by answering the following six questions for each market:

1 For what purpose has the product been developed, and how would the product be used in that country?

2 What distinctive properties does the product have?

3 What benefits is the consumer expected to gain?

4 How is the product positioned, and what image do consumers perceive it to have?

5 Which consumer segments of the total market are expected to buy it, on what occasions and for what purposes?

6 How does the product fit into the total market?

The main issue for a company about to commence marketing internationally is to assess the suitability of the existing products for international markets. As a minimum, a purchaser in an overseas market expects to have a clear explanation of how a product should be used. So the instructions on the domestic packaging usually have to be translated for international markets. Interestingly, one cosmetics marketer found that in some countries customers objected if their language was not printed first on multilingual packs.

The question is, however, to what extent the components of the total product offer can and should be adapted for international markets. In the case of a product where only the packaging needs to be changed, the effect on the overall cost is likely to be minimal. If more fundamental changes to the product itself are required, because of differences in use or safety regulations, the higher cost might prove prohibitive for a small company. Such problems can be circumvented by taking an alternative market entry approach such as licensing or franchising.

## Products, services and value propositions

The distinction between products and services is becoming increasingly blurred. In practice there are few 'pure' products and services. Most offerings from firms are a combination of the two. But to succeed it is essential they focus on value-based marketing, which requires:

- ■ A deep understanding of customer needs and decision-making processes.
- ■ The formulation of value propositions that meet the needs of customers and create a differential advantage.
- ■ The building of long-term relationships with customers, so that loyalty and trust are built on the satisfaction with and confidence in the supplier.
- ■ The necessary superior knowledge, skills, systems and marketing assets (including brand) to deliver superior value.

At this point it is worth noting that customer expectations are increasing. A value proposition that simply claims to offer a good quality product or reliable service no longer satisfies customers. Customers will be dissatisfied if they do not receive good quality products and service. They will only be satisfied if they are delighted with the product or service because of some extra benefits that exceed their expectations. Of course, what will delight customers around the world varies considerably. With this in mind, it is important to understand and interpret added value. Sometimes added value can be emotional. Illustration 8.2 presents details of a funeral service that provides emotional support and care when needed.

## ILLUSTRATION 8.2

## Ecoffins help you to care for the planet during emotional times

As shown in Chapter 1, sustainability and caring for the environment are high on many businesses' agenda. Consumers are also choosing to buy products and enjoy services from organizations that show their Fair Trade, eco-friendly and sustainable credentials. At a difficult time, such as when a person loses a loved one, the values of that person do not disappear. Therefore, despite feeling emotional, people who care for the planet are seeking environmentally aware organizations when choosing a coffin or urn.

Ecoffins is a supplier of coffins and urns made from bamboo, banana, recycled cardboard and willow. It supplies to funeral homes and individuals. Furthermore, it is the main eco-friendly supplier of coffins and urns

in the UK, although it does supply eco coffins and urns to other countries. Its products are 100 per cent natural (not nails or screws) and are biodegradable. Ecoffins has many accreditations such as the Association of Green Funeral Directors and the World Fair Trade Organization (WFTO), which demonstrates its credentials. People going through the bereavement process can identify quickly that Ecoffins can satisfy their own environmental values.

Being a member of WFTO certainly shows that Ecoffins is passionate about the environment, the rights of workers and fair payment of goods and services. Not only does Ecoffins say it is passionate, it has to prove it by engaging in the Ten Principles of Fair Trade. For example, one of the ten principles is No Child Labour/ No forced Labour and another is Respect the Environment. To demonstrate these, Ecoffins was inspected by two independent bodies at its factory in China to prove it adhered to the 'No Child/No Forced Labour' principle. To show it respects the environment, Ecoffins states that when products are shipped from China, it does this by stacking coffins inside one another like 'Russian Dolls'. Doing this saves space. Also, because the coffins are relatively light the fuel used during the transportation is calculated to be around the same as driving a car for about five miles.

Ecoffins has recently won the 'Coffin Supplier of the Year Award' from Good Funeral Awards.

### Question

1 How does Ecoffins help socially and environmentally aware people during their bereavement?

# Factors affecting international product and service management

There are a number of factors that affect the international management of products and services including:

- the balance between standardization and adaptation owing to:
  - cultural factors
  - usage factors
  - legal factors
- product acceptability
- shortening product life cycles
- the effect of different market entry methods
- changes in marketing management
- ethical and green environmental issues.

The discussion in Chapter 6 on globalization leads to the conclusion that for the largest companies in the world the benefits of marketing standardized products are very significant indeed. But while firms may be prepared to invest heavily to achieve **standardization**, in practice, virtually all products must be adapted to some degree. The issue then becomes to what degree their industrial or consumer product or service should be standardized or adapted to the needs of the local market. Even the most obviously global companies achieve only partial standardization of products. For example, while Coca-Cola adopts a global standardized branding strategy, it modifies the product for particular customer segments by offering Diet, Light and Caffeine-Free Coca-Cola. Coca-Cola Life also offers a lower calorie drink using leaves of the stevia plant to provide an intense, natural sweetness. McDonald's, too, alters its menu in different countries to cater for local tastes and accommodates their health and food safety needs.

All firms must identify the benefit or satisfaction that the consumer recognizes and will purchase. This benefit must provide the basis upon which the company differentiates its products from those of its competitors. For a product such as the smartphone, when it was first introduced the competitive advantage was a technical breakthrough, the first portable long-distance mobile voice communication. So this was a standardization of the core benefit. Now the core benefit is just the same: communication. But the types of communication used differ from one consumer to another. As products were copied and developed, so new sources of competitive advantage were sought for smartphone developers. This led to the standardization of actual products as all smartphones now have a long battery life, fingerprint recognition, and front and rear cameras with around 12 MPs and 64/128 MB options. Therefore, smartphone developers are turning to innovative accessories marketed as 'must haves' (augmented products) to populate the augmented product. iPhone's augmented 'must haves' include silicone anti-skid wireless chargers, the 'Tile' Bluetooth tracker that can be attached to car/house keys to instantly be found by the iPhone, or a foldaway tripod to use while video conferencing.

The decision for most companies to standardize or adapt is based on a cost–benefit analysis of what they believe the implications of adaptation and standardization might be for revenue, profitability and market share. In normal circumstances, the cost of adaptation would be expected to be greater than the cost of successful standardization. Only if the needs and tastes identified in the target market segment are significantly different and substantial additional business will be generated, can the extra cost involved in making and delivering adapted products be justified. Illustration 8.3 shows how Red Bull sponsors extreme sports in different countries.

Some companies are tempted to adopt a policy of adaptation in order to satisfy immediate demand. Others believe that continual exposure to the standardized products will redefine customer needs and ultimately change their tastes, leading to greater market share in the longer term. In summary, the advantages of product standardization are that the company benefits from more rapid recovery of its investment and easier organization and control of its product management. In addition, it can reduce costs through economies of scale and gain the experience effect throughout most of its operations, such as production, advertising and distribution.

## ILLUSTRATION 8.3

# Red Bull adapts as it flies round the world

Red Bull is in the energy drink business and has its headquarters in Austria. In fact, it is the leading energy drink over Monster Beverages in value terms, although in volume terms Monster Beverages is ahead. Red Bull reaches its target market in many ways including Red Bull TV, Red Bull Magazine, through music, social media and apps. Additionally, Red Bull sponsors athletes from different countries. It does not standardize by sponsoring one athlete that represents the brand worldwide. What it prefers to do is adapt and localize. For example, it chooses to sponsor extreme athletes from different countries; Hiroto Arai, from Japan, claims he was born to surf. He is famous in his country for his expertise and also in the surfing world. Red Bull, therefore, can appeal to the young Japanese market and also surfing fans through its sponsorship of a high-profile surfer such as Hiroto. Hiroto is also of benefit for Red Bull through his more than 8000 Instagram followers who will see the Red Bull logo. Hiroto's followers are an audience that Red Bull may not have been able to reach. Thus, sponsorship provides a happy bonus in terms of the number of potential consumers that see the Red Bull brand.

On the other side of the world in Canada, Red Bull sponsors Kaya Turski who is a freestyle skier with 38 500 followers on Instagram. Kaya is from Canada which means the Red Bull brand is represented through its sponsorship of a world champion freestyle skier and to the Canadian audience . . . and of course, through Kaya's large Instagram following.

In terms of product, positioning and pricing Red Bull generally standardizes when entering new markets. As stated earlier, Red Bull is a premium energy drink. Whichever market it enters it does so as a premium energy drink. Red Bull has entered Brazil with that proposition. There are other lower priced, non-premium energy drink brands in Brazil. Being a developing country where citizens are on lower incomes, it may be that Red Bull cannot compete because of its high price/premium drink strategy; time will tell.

Red Bull does need to adapt when rules, laws and regulations are imposed by governments of countries it is already in or those it wishes to enter. For example, Red Bull had good sales in Latvia. However, the Latvian government recently brought in a regulation which stated that no outlets can sell any energy drink (not just Red Bull) to anyone under the age of 18. In the UK, energy drinks cannot be sold to under 16s. Also, Saudi Arabia's government banned energy drink advertising and sponsorship at events.

## Questions

**1** Choose two countries from different continents and recommend a cultural celebrity who could embody the Red Bull brand in the chosen countries.

**2** Provide reasons why you have chosen that celebrity and why they embody the Red Bull brand.

**3** Why has Saudi Arabia banned energy drink advertising and sponsorship at events?

**References:** Redbull (2018). www.redbull.com; *Gulf News* (2018) UK Shops ban sale of energy drinks to under-16s. Available from https://gulfnews.com/news/europe/uk/uk-supermarkets-ban-sale-of-energy-drinks-to-under-16s-1.2183027 (accessed 9 June 2018).

Product standardization is both encouraging and being encouraged by the globalization trends in markets, including:

1 Markets are becoming more homogeneous.
2 There are more identifiable transnational consumer segments.
3 There is an increase in the number of firms moving towards globalization, so forcing greater standardization throughout industry sectors.

There are some disadvantages to product standardization too. Market opportunities might be lost when it is impossible to match very specific local requirements. Some managers of local subsidiaries who are only expected to implement global or regional product policies can become demotivated and miss market opportunities if they are not given the opportunity to be entrepreneurial.

Greater standardization of products makes it easier for competitors to copy at ever lower prices. Inevitably, this leads to standardization within a product category so that consumers are unable to differentiate between competing products. The result is the creation of a 'commodity market'. To counter this, competition is focused increasingly upon the augmented product elements. In the family car market, for example, there is very little to choose between the performance, reliability and economy of the main competitors, including Ford, General Motors, Renault, Toyota, Peugeot and Nissan. Against this background, the promotion of individual cars focuses upon design, image, warranties and financing arrangements and rather less on individual performance comparisons. The industry is also continually developing products for subsegments, examples being the Renault Twizy or Toyota's Prius hybrid energy source car and sports utility vehicles.

## Reasons for adaptation of the product

In some instances, product standardization may not be possible due to environmental constraints through mandatory legislation because of such reasons as differences in electrical systems, legal standards, safety requirements or product liability. It may also be because the firm believes that the product appeal can be increased in a particular market by addressing cultural and usage factors.

**Cultural factors**   Certain products and services, such as computers and airline flights, are not culturally sensitive as the benefits they offer are valued internationally. Here the adaptation is peripheral to the main benefit, for example the translation of instructions into different languages. Other products and services are more culturally sensitive and might need to be adapted more substantially. Food is a particularly difficult area for standardization, as the preparation and eating of food are often embedded in the history, religion and/or culture of the country. This presents specific problems for fast food firms, for example, where the main ingredients of McDonald's and Burger King, beef and pork, prove unacceptable to many potential customers. Also, the necessary ingredients for fast food, such as the specific type of wheat for pizza bases, suitable chicken and mozzarella cheese are unavailable, or are of variable quality in certain countries.

One example of service development is Islamic banking, which for many years was regarded as a small niche activity. However, the growing sense of religious identity in the Muslim world, together with the significant increase in construction in the Middle East, has led to rapid growth in the sector.

Changes are taking place in product acceptance, however. For example, fashion is becoming increasingly globalized. The traditional domination of the fashion industry by western designers is gradually being broken down. Denim jeans infiltrated countries like India which had hitherto only accepted traditional dress. Some people believe that the erosion of the country's traditional heritage and culture, particularly by the media and MNE advertising, is unethical and should be resisted. Others suggest that larger countries such as India and China simply take those international products which serve a particular need and ignore other global products.

**Usage factors**   The same product might be used in quite different ways in different markets, partly due to the culture of the country, but also due to the geographical factors of climate and terrain. Unilever and Procter & Gamble have a large variety of products adapted and branded for different markets because of the different ways products are used. For example, French people wash clothes in scalding hot water, while the Australians tend to use cold water. Most Europeans use front-loading washing machines, whereas the French and Americans often use top-loaders. Equipment supplied to armies fighting in unfamiliar and inhospitable climates has often proved ineffective.

Honda found that when they first introduced motorcycles into the USA, they were unreliable and frequently broke down. Japanese riders were only able to travel short distances, whereas some US riders were used to riding the bikes over longer distances and much rougher terrain. Honda also realized that other US riders and Indonesian riders that lived near cities were fascinated by their 50cc to 125cc bikes and promoted them instead. Honda quickly became established and was soon able to introduce better-performing larger bikes to a smaller but active market.

**Legal standards**   The standardization of products and services can be significantly affected by legislation. Legal standards are often very country-specific, sometimes because obscure laws have been left unchanged for decades. There have been considerable problems for European exporters of simple products such as confectionery, jams and sausages as they need to consider the legal standards that different countries have.

Lack of precise, reliable, understandable and universally accepted scientific information, for example in food safety (beef, lamb and chicken), serves only to make it more difficult to achieve a satisfactory industry standard. Pharmaceutical companies experience problems in introducing products into different markets because individual governments have differing standards of public health and approaches to healthcare. Many countries insist that they carry out their own supervised clinical testing on all drugs prior to the products being available on the market. Furthermore, the instructions and contraindications might need to be changed and agreed with health authorities locally.

**Product liability**   In the USA over the past few years there has been a considerable increase in litigation, with lawyers seeking clients on a no win–no fee basis. For marketers, particularly those selling potentially life-threatening products such as pharmaceuticals and cars, this demands much greater caution when introducing standard products based on the home country specification. In extreme circumstances litigation can lead to huge financial settlements, for example in cases related to the oil, tobacco and asbestos industries.

## Product acceptability

Consumers generally are becoming much more discerning and have greater expectations of all the elements of the augmented product. The manufacturer must take responsibility for controlling the pre- and post-purchase servicing and warranties provided by independent distributors and retailers. The packaging, branding and trademark decisions are becoming increasingly important because global social media no longer allows mistakes and failures to go unpublicized.

Consumers, too, have different perceptions of the value and satisfaction of products. Their view of what is acceptable will vary considerably from country to country. The product usage, production process or service offered may not fit with the culture and environment of the country. The product or service may not be acceptable for its intended use. Certain healthcare services, such as abortion, plus gambling, banking products and alcohol are unacceptable to some cultures.

## Shortening product life cycles

The merging of markets through increasing globalization is leading to greater concentration of powerful suppliers. They have the resources to rapidly copy a competitor's product or develop their own products to exploit a new market opportunity. The increasing pace of technology means that a technical lead in a product is not likely to be held for very long, as competitors catch up quickly. This means that product life cycles are becoming shorter, by a third in some cases. Improvements are introduced more frequently, often annually. These must be added to the much higher cost of research, development and commercialization of new products. This places much greater pressures on the firm to distribute the new product throughout world markets as quickly and widely as possible in order to achieve a high return on R&D investment before new products are introduced.

## Franchising, joint ventures and alliances

The pressure to exploit new technology and products as quickly and widely as possible has encouraged the rapid expansion of more creative and cost-effective ways of achieving cooperation in research, development and distribution. These include franchising, joint ventures and strategic alliances. As discussed in Chapter 7, while these market entry methods allow less control than total ownership, they do enable firms to develop a wider sphere of activity than they could do alone. Of course, the challenge is to find partners with truly complementary expertise, knowledge and capability.

## Marketing management

These trends have led to significant changes in the way that marketing management operates, allowing a more creative approach to be adopted in developing product policy. First, there is a wider range of options available in international marketing management, particularly through innovation and integration of the marketing mix elements, which will be discussed later in this book. Second, there have been significant improvements in the tools available for performance measurement, real-time data analysis and planning. Third, there are more insightful and widely available sources of information through online marketing research, involving customers, suppliers and the web community in product and service evaluation and innovations. These allow greater power for global brand management. It must be pointed out that success in using these tools requires managers to be more flexible in redefining niche segments and creative in innovating in all areas of the marketing mix. Fourth, with improved internal and external networking, NPD can become much more integrated within the firm's strategies and be capable of more satisfactorily meeting customer needs through the management of supply chain relationships.

## Environmental and social responsibility issues

By way of contrast, unscrupulous companies have exploited the different legal controls and lower risks of litigation by sending hazardous products, such as chemical waste, to less developed countries with lower standards for disposal. However, this practice is being increasingly challenged by international pressure groups. It is also backed by the United Nations which encourages all countries and companies to consider environmental issues (United Nations 2014).

Concern for environmental issues is becoming greater in many countries and has considerable implications for product policies. But the nature, patterns and strength of interest vary considerably from country to country.

The United Nations states that businesses should engage in environmental issues, take the initiative to support environmental responsibilities and choose environmentally friendly technologies. Additional social responsibility issues that businesses should engage in and be transparent about, through annual reports, press releases and newsletters, include:

- *Governance*: Environmental and social responsibilities should be at the heart of businesses in their mission and vision statements and of course how they 'do business'.

- *Workforce*: all employees, particularly in the service and manufacturing industries, must be given fair and equal rights, be paid a fair wage and receive training and career opportunities.

- *Advertising and communication*: must be honest and truthful.

- *Supply chain*: Businesses should only engage with other organizations that also care for the environment and conduct their business in a responsible manner.

Against this background, MNEs and SMEs must respond in an appropriate way to global and local concerns. They should take a more comprehensive approach to dealing with environmental and socially responsible issues by anticipating and, where appropriate, initiating changes. They must also evaluate and manage proactively all the effects on the environment of their operations. See Management Challenge 8.1 to see how global fashion brands must take more care when choosing clothing manufacturers in their supply chain. Contracts should only be given to factories from the ready-made garment industry (RMG) in Bangladesh that allow inspections to check their health and safety conditions (Accord 2018).

Malagasy is a gourmet food company that sells high quality products to supermarkets. It has partners in Madagascar that produce and package the chocolate, nuts, spices and honey it uses. It is a social enterprise that balances its commercial aims with social and economic objectives. The company realized that with many firms, 95 per cent of the final value of a chocolate bar is created outside the country from which the chocolate ingredients originate. However, more value can be retained in the country where the ingredients originated if the finished product is made and packaged in that country – and that is what Malagasy does (Stone 2006).

## MANAGEMENT CHALLENGE 8.1

## Global brands: do they care what happens down the supply chain?

In 2013, shocking news spread around the world that an eight-storey factory in Bangladesh had collapsed. Immediate thoughts were that an earthquake had shaken the ground or that the factory had been a target for a terrorist attack. But this was not the case. A total of 1134 garment workers in the factory were killed and over 2000 injured due to a negligent construction company. The company that had constructed the Rana Plaza in Dhaka, Bangladesh, had not taken the care and attention needed to provide a safe working environment for the garment workers. The construction of the building was poor, weak and was cheaply and quickly constructed. The main reason for the hurried construction of the factory was to satisfy the pressing needs of western consumers that wanted low-cost fashionable items. To satisfy the insatiable desire for fashionable clothes, retailers such as Zara and Benetton subcontracted clothing orders to agents in Bangladesh. Their brand labels were found in the rubble after the building had collapsed.

The global brands insisted they had asked the subcontractors to provide fair wages and working conditions. Clearly the global brands did not check the Bangladeshi employees received those basic rights. Retailers from many countries became signatories to an organization called 'Accord on Fire and Building Safety in Bangladesh', to help factories in the ready-made garment industry (RMG) and improve safety issues and fairness for employees. The key components of the Accord agreement are as follows:

1 The agreement between retail brands and trade unions is a legally binding treaty that lasts for five years. Its purpose is to ensure there is a safe working environment in the ready-made garment industry in Bangladesh.

2 There would be an independent inspection program supported by brands in which workers and trade unions were involved.

3 Public disclosure of all factories, inspection reports and corrective action plans (CAP) would be shared publicly.

4 Retail brand signatories stated they were committed to provide sufficient funds to help Bangladeshi RMGs complete necessary improvements and to maintain sourcing relationships.

5 Democratically elected health and safety committees in all factories were deployed to identify and act on health and safety risks.

6 Workers received extensive training which gave them the knowledge and confidence to refuse unsafe work.

Clearly, factories not willing to be inspected would no longer receive contracts from the signatories. Following the inspection, factories with health and safety issues received notice of the issues, plus guidance on what to improve. Factories that did not rectify the issues received a formal notification advising them that the signatories from the Accord on Fire and Building Safety in Bangladesh would terminate all relations with that organization. Samsons Winterwear Ltd was inspected and was given a range of improvements to make; however, the improvements were not made. The Accord on Fire and Building Safety in Bangladesh contacted all signatories to advise that they needed to terminate their contracts with Samsons Winterwear Ltd. In March 2018 the signatories including Kmart Australia, Dansk Supermarket Group Denmark, Hugo Boss Germany, Mango Spain, M&S UK, terminated all contracts with the company.

### Question

1 What benefits can the ready-made garment (RMG) industry gain following the introduction of the Accord on Fire and Building Safety in Bangladesh?

**Source:** Accord on Fire and Building Safety in Bangladesh (2018). Available from: http://bangladeshaccord.org/about/.

A number of companies have set corporate strategies which address these issues. Sony, for example, incorporates environmental considerations into the planning of every product, and Ford has adopted the environmental standard, ISO4001, worldwide.

The goal is to achieve environmental excellence, with firms such as The Body Shop, 3M, British Telecom, Johnson Matthey, Merck, Norsk Hydro and Rank Xerox taking a strategic approach rather than making ad hoc decisions. There are many problems in building environmental considerations into corporate strategy, including the uncertainties of the science. These include different views on global warming, and the difficulty in deciding on appropriate action because replacement processes or chemicals often give rise to new problems.

# Product policy

Having considered the factors which underpin the development of an international product portfolio, the next steps are to look first at the suitability of the existing products before embarking on the development of new or modified products. The decision about which products should be included in the range to be marketed internationally is determined by several factors:

- The company's overall objectives in terms of growth and profits.
- The experience, philosophies and attitude of the company to international development, and which of the company's financial and managerial resources will be allocated to international marketing.
- The characteristics of the markets such as economic development and the barriers to trade of the firm's domestic and host countries.
- The requirements, expectations and attitudes of the consumers in the market.
- The products and services themselves, their attributes, appeal and perceived values (their positioning), the stage that they are at in the life cycle and economies of scale.
- The ease of distributing and selling them.
- The support the products require from other elements of the marketing mix and after-sales services.
- Environmental constraints (such as legal or political factors) which must be overcome.
- The level of risk that the company is prepared to take.

Illustration 8.4 shows how disposal of products should be a matter of concern for businesses.

## Product strategies

Against the background of so many variables, it is inevitable that companies adopt a very wide range of product strategies in international markets. In formulating product policies, Mesdag (1985) postulated that a company has three basic choices:

| | |
|---|---|
| SWYG | Sell What You have Got. |
| SWAB | Sell What people Actually Buy. |
| GLOB | Sell the same thing GLOBally disregarding national frontiers. |

All three strategies have been used for a long time. Heinz, Mars, Heineken and Johnnie Walker have been international brands for decades using global product and brand strategies to enable them to clearly position their products as global brands. The Danes have long dominated the UK bacon market by following a SWAB strategy. The disadvantage of the SWAB strategy is that it is only possible to penetrate one market at a time. It may also be difficult to compete with local firms on their own terms. Furthermore, it is sometimes difficult for a foreign company to establish credibility as a supplier of products which have a strong domestic demand. For example, Suntory of Japan make good whisky but could not market it in the UK. So it acquired Morrison Bowmore Distillers, which produces distinctively Scottish single malt whisky brands.

**ILLUSTRATION 8.4**

# Recycling services: dealing with the world's waste

Many organizations send old and out-of-date computers, mobile/cell phones and electrical equipment to India. The organizations pay India to dispose of the waste on their behalf. The majority of the waste ends up on waste dumps, which are where thousands of homeless people live. The people that live there and their children, known as collectors, try to find items among the waste that they can sell to make money. One of the prized finds on dump sites is e-waste. E-waste includes computer circuit boards. The collectors dismantle e-waste computers to get to the prized circuit board, which contains precious metals such as gold or copper. However, the next step in the process is to extract the gold and copper from the circuit board. This process is extremely hazardous. The process involves collectors using cyanide to break down the circuit board connectors, thus extracting the gold and copper. The fumes from the cyanide sometimes kill collectors. Additionally, cyanide waste contaminates the surrounding soil and local water systems.

Nitin Gupta and his brother Rohan love e-waste. They have built, thanks to international financial aid, a state-of-the-art factory that recycles old and broken computers. They actively encourage organizations around the world to use their factory to recycle old and broken computers, instead of sending the e-waste to dumps. Over two-thirds of Nitin's business comes from organizations that want to use their recycling services. One-third of their business comes from the 'unregulated' collectors. Nitin pays the collectors more money than they would get for circuit boards 'on the street'. He also takes the complete circuit board, so the collectors do not have to use cyanide to extract the precious metals.

There are many service organizations like Nitin's that recycle waste. Indeed, e-recycling computer and mobile/cell phone e-waste is big business. And the disposal of e-waste is on the political agenda in many countries, which means many organizations will have to pay more attention to the disposal of their products and electronic goods.

## Questions

**1** Who should be responsible for disposing of or recycling e-waste?

**2** What should organizations do to promote their recycling policies?

**Reference:** Ives, M. (2014) In developing world, a push to bring e-waste out of the shadows. 6 February. Via Environment360, www.e360.yale.edu (accessed 6 May 2015).

---

The SWAB approach is the classic differentiated approach. While it is responsive to market needs, it does make considerable demands on the firm's development, manufacturing, logistics and financial resources. It is often impractical for these very reasons.

SWYG are the most common form of export strategies, but they are also the most common reason for failure. The key objective for most firms following such strategies is to fill production lines at home rather than meet a market need. By concentrating only on a few markets, however, many companies do successfully implement this kind of strategy. Mesdag argues also that some of the most successful global products started off as domestic products with a SWYG strategy, for example pizza, hamburgers and yoghurt. Success has been the result of the company's ability to meet new international emerging demand for the convenience of fast foods. The products may not necessarily be formulated identically across markets, but they appeal to a pan-regional or global need and can therefore be positioned as cross-frontier brands. The success of the strategy has been based on identifying and meeting the needs of transnational customer segments. Heineken, the Dutch brewing firm, took over Egypt's only brewery, Al Harham Beverages Company, in 2002 and in so doing acquired Fayrouz, a fruit flavoured non-alcoholic malt drink popular in Egypt and certified Halal by Al Azhar, a leading Sunni Islam religious institution. Heineken then had the opportunity to market Fayrouz in the Indian subcontinent and to Muslims in the UK, Germany, the Netherlands and France. In 2011 they strengthened the authenticity of the Fayrouz brand when they changed the flavours of their drinks and updated the packaging to something much more fun and trendy for their target audiences.

Keegan and Green (2014) have highlighted the key aspects of international marketing strategy as a combination of standardization or adaptation of product and promotion elements of the mix. They offer five alternative and more specific approaches to product policy:

**One product, one message worldwide**  These are the truly global brands. Since the 1920s, Coca-Cola has adopted a global approach which has allowed it to make enormous cost savings and benefit from continual reinforcement of the same message. While a number of writers have argued that this will be the strategy adopted for many products in the future, in practice only a handful of products might claim to have achieved this already. A number of firms have tried and failed.

**Product extension, promotion adaptation**  While the product stays the same, this strategy allows for the adaptation of the promotional effort to target either new customer segments or appeal to the particular tastes of individual countries. For example, Yoplait yoghurt (US) attempts to capture the mood of the country in its various television adverts.

**Product adaptation, promotion extension**  This strategy is used if a promotional campaign has achieved international appeal, but the product needs to be adapted because of local needs. Many suppliers of capital goods, IT management and consultancy, promote the idea of providing technical solutions rather than selling industrial plants or computer hardware. IBM has used 'solutions for a small planet'.

**Dual adaptation**  By adapting both products and promotion for each market, the firm is adopting a totally differentiated approach. This strategy is often undertaken by firms when one of the previous three strategies has failed. In particular, the strategy may be used if the firm is not in a leadership position and, instead, must react to the market or follow the competitors. This is closest to a multidomestic strategy.

**Product invention**  Product invention is adopted by firms, usually from advanced nations, who are supplying products to less well-developed countries. Products are specifically developed to meet the needs of the individual markets. European innovators and IBM worked together to create a drone that delivers medicine or food to remote areas. The 'flying donkeys' as they have been named are a simple engineering answer to a big logistical problem.

# Managing products across borders

## The product life cycle

In the domestic market, models such as the product life cycle and Boston Consulting Group's (BCG) portfolio matrix are used to manage a portfolio of products. The concepts can be applied in international markets to the management of a product, brand or product range across a portfolio of countries.

The life cycle concept is used as a model for considering the implications for marketing management of a product passing through the stages of introduction, growth, maturity and decline. It can also be applied to international marketing.

The international product life cycle suggests that products in international markets can have consecutive 'lives' in different countries. Soon after the product was launched in its domestic market, it was introduced into another developed country, A. Later it was introduced to other developed and newly industrialized countries, B and C, and only recently to a less developed country, D. In the domestic market and country A, a replacement product is required, while considerable growth is still possible in the other countries. This illustrates the dilemma that firms often face. They must decide how to allocate scarce resources between product and market development (Figure 8.3).

In some hi-tech markets it is now possible to accurately predict when new technology will force a new product's introduction. As a result, it is now necessary for the product to be project managed for a limited

**FIGURE 8.3**   The international product cycle

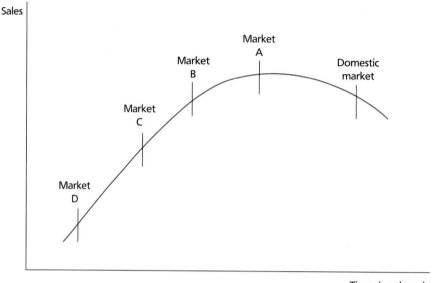

and specific lifetime. This ensures that by the end of its life the product has been profitable, recouped the initial investment and a replacement new innovation is ready for launch. Illustration 8.5 shows how Gillette is addressing this situation.

The most significant change for life cycle models is that global communications lead to global companies having to launch new products into many markets simultaneously to meet customer expectations. So the sequential approach to marketing and manufacturing that is encapsulated in the original model applies less frequently. However, as we established earlier, not all companies operating internationally are global corporations. Neither are they based on leading-edge technology. It is therefore important not to ignore the model altogether. The concept of phases in the life cycle is still useful for a company that is not in a fast-changing market. This could simply be exporting specialist engineering components and tools from an advanced economy or rolling out a service into new country markets as the opportunity arises.

On balance, therefore, although the validity of the product life cycle has at various times been attacked by a variety of writers, it does have a role to play for certain types of company insofar as it is a model that provides a framework for thinking in detail about product policy, NPD, product introduction and product elimination.

## Product portfolio analysis

The use of portfolio approaches in international product management centres around the BCG growth–share matrix, the General Electric/McKinsey screen and the Arthur D. Little business profile matrix. They are designed primarily to clarify the current strategic position of a company, its products and those of its competitors, and to help identify any future strategic options.

The complexity of the analysis increases as the competitive positions occupied by a product and the intensity of competition differ significantly from one market to another. Comparing the strength of a portfolio across a variety of markets becomes difficult as the analytical base constantly changes. For these reasons, the BCG matrix, for example, might be based on one product range or on one brand with the circles in the matrices representing country sales instead of different product sales, as shown in Figure 8.4. This then provides a basis for analyzing the current international product portfolio, assessing competitors' product/market strengths and forecasting the likely development of future portfolios both for itself and its competitors. The key decisions will be whether to use cash generated in 'cash cow' countries to maintain the position by introducing new products or to build positions in emerging markets (stars and question marks) where growth will be higher.

## ILLUSTRATION 8.5

# Gillette planning a close shave

In the late 1970s and 1980s the change to disposable razors by many consumers in the USA and Europe meant that shaving products appeared to be turning into a commodity market. For Gillette, which had a 65 per cent share of the market, this was extremely serious. Gillette in the USA cut advertising by a quarter and appeared to have almost given up on razors.

In Europe, however, Gillette started to spend on a pan-European campaign featuring the slogan 'Gillette – the best a man can get' to promote the top-of-the-range Contour Plus brand. This led to a gain in market share and an increase in margins.

Gillette's mission statement since the late 1980s has been 'There is a better way to shave and we will find it'. Sensor, launched in 1989, spearheaded Gillette's fightback. Sensor was shown to be significantly better than anything else on the market. User tests showed that 80 per cent of men who tried it kept on using it. Gillette decided to centralize its marketing by combining the European and US sections into one group, headed by the previous European head, to ensure an effective launch of Sensor. Previously, marketing had been carried out by brand managers in each local country.

Sensor helped Gillette to a 70 per cent share of the world razor market. By 1997, however, the sales growth was flattening, signifying the need for a new product. The successor, Mach 3, cost well over US$1 billion to develop but sold at a premium of 25–35 per cent over the price of Sensor, which Gillette retained as it does not withdraw older products.

The competition started to fight back. Schick, recently taken over by Energiser, used the Wilkinson Sword brand in some markets with its four-blade Quattro, followed by Schick Hydro. A South Korean company, Dorco, developed a Mach 3 competitor with prices 30 per cent cheaper than Gillette. Men and women do not shave more often, so the only way to increase sales and profits is to increase prices in developed countries, persuade customers to buy more products and win new customers in emerging markets. The Fusion range was the last new product to be introduced before Procter & Gamble bought Gillette in 2005. Five years passed before the Fusion ProGlide Series became the first introduction under Procter & Gamble. With its five-blade razor and range of skincare products, Gillette's aim was to 'address every aspect of interaction with hair and skin' claiming in tests involving 30 000 men that there was a 2:1 preference for ProGlide over Fusion. Gillette sells in over 75 countries.

## Questions

**1** How should Gillette keep its technological lead?

**2** Will technology be the only factor in its future success in the global shaving market?

## Introduction and elimination activities

While the major focus of product policy is upon new product and service development, the increased pace of the activity has a number of consequences for product management at both ends of the product life cycle. The factors that need to be taken into account in managing the product portfolio are:

- The firm's objectives.
- The profitability of the company's existing range of products and services.
- The stage in the life cycle that the products and services have reached.
- The manufacturing and service delivery capacity available.
- The likely receptiveness of the market to the new product or service.
- The competitive structure of the market.

**FIGURE 8.4**   The portfolio approach to strategic analysis (BCG matrix)

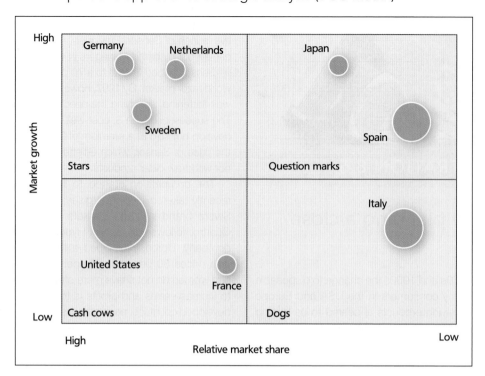

These factors have a number of implications for the product policy. Too many product and service introductions can risk overburdening the firm's marketing system. There is a constant need for a regular review of the range and for elimination decisions to be made where a product or service is either in its decline stage or simply failing to generate sufficient profit. The international perspective, however, means that decision making is more difficult. A product may be manufactured principally in a plant in one country but exported to many countries, be a 'cash cow' in one market and a 'dog' in another. Careful analysis is therefore needed before the product elimination decision is taken. The identification of overlaps in the product range or poor performance of specific products may necessitate elimination of products. This can arise if they are in the declining stage of the product life cycle, have been duplicated or have been replaced by a newer product.

The complexity of managing a wide portfolio of products is discussed in Illustration 8.6. It raises some fundamental issues about the product strategy alternatives.

# Image, branding and positioning

Of all the elements of the product or service offer, it is the image of the brand which is the most visible. It is the perceived value which consumers attach to this that is the central factor in positioning the products in the various markets.

The image and reputation of products, companies and countries can confer different values to consumers in different countries. Research by a number of writers has shown that products from particular countries have a stereotyped national image for such attributes as quality, price and reliability. Individual corporate brands either benefit from positive country of origin perceptions or must overcome negative perceptions to succeed in international markets.

## Country of origin effects

Buyers evaluate the products that they may wish to purchase based on their assessment of intrinsic (taste, design, performance and quality) and extrinsic cues (brand names, packaging and country of origin).

Where the buyers' knowledge about the product is limited, for example because they do not understand the technology, country of origin perceptions influence their buying decisions. The consumers' perceptions of companies are usually based on national stereotypes. For example, Japanese products tend to be regarded as high quality, reliable and 'miniaturized'. US products are seen as big and 'brash'. German products are perceived as well engineered and of high specification. Products from developing countries are often seen by western consumers as low quality, unreliable, inexpensive and usually copies of products from developed countries. This was the perception of Japanese products some decades ago, and shows that it is possible to change consumer attitudes.

There are significant differences between countries in the willingness of consumers to buy locally produced products. Usually this appears to be related to the feeling of nationalism that exists in the country at the particular time the assessment is made. As countries develop there is often a greater satisfaction with home-produced products and services.

The country of origin effect does extend further. For example, the stereotyping relates just as much to developed countries. There are strong associations between countries and the products that they are known for: Italy and pizza, Germany and machine tools. Overcoming these stereotypes is often the first challenge for international marketers who must prove that their product does not reinforce negative stereotypes. This is particularly important as customers become more knowledgeable. For example, many new car buyers know where their car has been designed and manufactured as well as the country of origin of the brand. Increasingly, of course, the MNE's headquarters, the brand's perceived 'home', the location of product design and places of manufacture may all be in different countries. Many MNEs such as Nike are marketing, not manufacturing, companies and source products from many countries. Their brand becomes the 'badge of quality' that overlays the country of origin effect.

*Product image*: As we have already emphasized, product image is one of the most powerful points of differentiation for consumers. The aspirational and achiever groups of purchasers wish to belong to particular worldwide customer segments and are keen to purchase products associated with that group. This is a major buying factor that has driven the sales of Apple's iPhones, iPods and iPads. An interesting example of this is that the sales of luxury goods remained buoyant during recent recessions due to increased sales to emerging countries as the 'new' rich sought to buy similar products and services from the 'old' rich.

*Company image* is becoming increasingly important in creating a central theme running through diverse product ranges. It reinforces the vision and values of the company, which can be recognized by employees and customers alike. For this reason, many companies have spent considerable effort and resources on controlling and enhancing the corporate identity through consistent style and communications, discussed in more detail in Chapter 9.

Image can be equally important at the other end of the product spectrum to luxury goods. Aldi (Germany), Netto (Denmark) and Lidl (Germany) use a no-frills approach to retailing by reinforcing their message of low prices with simple decor, warehouse-type displays and single colour understated packaging.

The image of a company also plays a vital role in B2B marketing, for example when quoting for international capital projects. Decisions are likely to be made on the grounds of the perceived reputation of the company. Without a strong international presence, it can be quite difficult to break into a small elite circle of international companies, even if very low prices are quoted.

Connections too can be important. Reconstruction projects following tsunamis, hurricanes and wars are extremely lucrative and are usually awarded to global companies. For example, Samoa was devastated after the tsunami in 2012. The Post-Tsunami Reconstruction Project was established so that global companies could help in rebuilding damaged roads and seawalls. In 2014 Hurricane Sandy hit New York City and there are still hundreds of reconstruction contracts available under the Build it Back Reconstruction Project.

## International branding

The image and reputation of an organization and its products and services are increasingly important differentiators from competitors' offers in international markets. The management of international branding is vital in adding value. The role of branding, important as it is in domestic markets, takes on an additional dimension in international markets. It is the most visible of the firm's activities, particularly for global companies, as we discussed in Chapter 6. Brands allow customers to identify products or services which will 'guarantee' satisfaction by providing specific benefits, such as performance, price, quality or status. Brands have the potential to add value to the organization by providing the following benefits:

- *Price premium*. They should allow higher prices to be charged than for products that have an equivalent specification but no brand.
- *Higher volumes*. Alternatively branded products can generate higher volumes than non-branded products if they are priced at market rates, rather than at a premium.
- *Lower costs*. Higher volumes should lead to cost reductions from the economies of scale and the experience effect, so improving competitiveness.
- *Better utilization of assets*. The predictably high level of sales should lead brand managers to make effective use of assets such as equipment, the supply chain and distribution channels.

The constituents of the brand include tangible benefits, such as quality and reliability. They also include intangible benefits which may bring out a whole range of feelings, such as status, being fashionable or possessing good judgement by purchasing a particular brand. Very young children are now fully aware of which fashion label is 'cool' at the moment. Advertisers are equally alert to the effects of 'pester power' on all the family purchasing decisions.

## Brand categories

Three brand categories are identified (Doyle 2000):

1 *Attribute brands* are created around the functional product or service attributes. These include quality, specification and performance, to build confidence among customers in situations where it is difficult for them to evaluate the difference between competitive products. The brand provides a 'guarantee'. Examples include Volvo for safety, Walmart for everyday low prices and Intel for computer processing.

2 *Aspirational brands* create images in the minds of customers about the type of people who purchase the brand. They convey the standards and values that the brand is associated with. Such brands do not simply deliver the customer's functional requirements of the products and services, such as high specification and quality. They also recognize the customer's status, and the recognition and esteem that can be associated with the brand. Examples include Ferrari and Louis Vuitton, or choosing to take a holiday at a high-end hotel, such as The Royal Penthouse Suite at Hotel President Wilson in Switzerland, which is currently $65 000 per night.

3 *Experience brands* focus on a shared philosophy between the customer and brand and on shared associations and emotions. They do not necessarily focus on claims of superiority. Examples include Nike, Virgin and Mini Cooper. Coca-Cola won the Best Brand Experience Event following the launch of its 'Share a Coke' campaign where Coca-Cola bottles were personalized with names from Alex to Oleg to Zak, all names appropriate for customers in 34 countries.

The appeal of these different types of brand varies according to the context of the purchasing decision. In luxury product markets aspirational brands are likely to be most successful. In consumer markets, where there is little to distinguish between the attributes and performance of products, experience branding is more appropriate. Attribute branding would be more appropriate in B2B markets where the purchasing process should be more rational, objective and based on specifications.

In global markets, too, because of different cultures, customer expectations and market sophistication, the appeal of a particular branding approach might be more relevant for a similar product. For example, in some cultures, such as in Germany, the attributes, functionality and specification may be more important. In others, such as in emerging markets, aspirational branding might be more appealing.

The brand value equation (Figure 8.5) draws attention to the offer to consumers of the intangible benefits that the brand adds over and above the tangible, functional benefits of a commoditized product or service. The challenge for international branding, of course, is to what extent the intangible benefits from branded products and services vary between countries, cultures and individuals.

FIGURE 8.5   The brand value equation

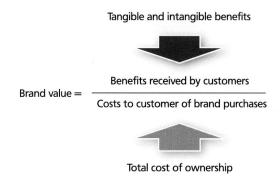

Apple products are the 'must haves' for the teenage and young adult generation. This is not just because of their functionality and design but also because of peer pressure for some and 'being part of the Apple club' for others.

Rappa and Hirsh (2007) find that superb service was the indispensable ingredient of successful high-end brands and identify four principles to deliver customer satisfaction:

- Create a customer-centred culture.
- Use a rigorous staff selection process.
- Constantly retrain employees.
- Systematically measure and reward customer-centric behaviour.

Tangible and intangible benefits must also be valued against the background of the total cost of ownership of the branded product by the customer. The total cost of ownership and the tangible and intangible benefits are accrued over the lifetime of the product. For example, car ownership offers different benefits and costs in different markets. This is especially so when considering the longer-term implications of, for example, warranty and servicing costs, car resale value and changing car fashions. Brand strength for cars is, to some extent, determined by the second-hand car values, with car marques such as BMW and Mercedes holding their value exceptionally well and some cars, such as Ferrari, even increasing in value.

## Brand value

It has been suggested that the strongest brands convey a core value to all their customers by the associations that are made with their name. Great brands (Table 8.1) have achieved their global status through high levels of investment and consistent management across their country markets of the dimensions used to value the brand over a long period of time. They are highly innovative and excellent communicators across a variety of platforms. These include traditional media as well as on social media as commentators and active participants. Furthermore, international brands promote their values and products through a significant commitment to advertising. They also engage in consumer research to understand their customers' needs and wants and to be committed to consistent quality, reliability and continuous innovation. These factors are just as important for achieving widespread customer loyalty and recommendations through user-generated content on social media channels. To gain brand strength, the brands shown in Table 8.1 engage with their consumers, are relevant and authentic, have excellent governance and are committed to their workforce. Apple and Google remain the number 1 and 2 Best Global Brands, having been top in 2014 and again in 2017 (Interbrand 2018). Table 8.1 provides details of the Best Global Brands for 2014 and 2017. As shown, Microsoft was Best Brand number 5 in 2014 but it was number 3 in 2017; IBM was number 4 in 2014 but moved down to number 10 in 2017.

Table 8.1 also provides details of the top growing brands of 2017 (change in brand value %). Interbrand (2018) reports that Facebook took the number 1 position in terms of growth percentage at 48 per cent, and Amazon ranked second with growth of 29 per cent.

Table 8.1    The 30 best global brands 2014 and 2017

| Rank 2017 | Rank 2014 | Brand | Sector | Change in brand value (%) | Brand value (US$ million) |
|---|---|---|---|---|---|
| 1 | 1 | Apple | Technology | +3 | 184 154 |
| 2 | 2 | Google | Technology | +6 | 141 703 |
| 3 | 5 | Microsoft | Technology | +10 | 79 999 |
| 4 | 3 | Coca-Cola | Beverages | −5 | 69 733 |
| 5 | 15 | Amazon | Retail | +29 | 64 796 |
| 6 | 7 | Samsung | Technology | +9 | 56 249 |
| 7 | 8 | Toyota | Automotive | −6 | 50 291 |
| 8 | 29 | Facebook | Technology | +48 | 48 188 |
| 9 | 10 | Mercedes-Benz | Automotive | +10 | 47 829 |
| 10 | 4 | IBM | Business services | −11 | 46 829 |
| 11 | 6 | GE | Diversified | +3 | 44 208 |
| 12 | 9 | McDonald's | Restaurants | +5 | 41 533 |
| 13 | 11 | BMW | Automotive | 0 | 41 521 |
| 14 | 13 | Disney | Media | +5 | 40 772 |
| 15 | 12 | Intel | Technology | +7 | 39 459 |
| 16 | 14 | Cisco | Technology | +3 | 31 930 |
| 17 | 16 | Oracle | Technology | +3 | 27 466 |
| 18 | 22 | Nike | Sporting goods | +8 | 27 021 |
| 19 | 19 | Louis Vuitton | Luxury | −4 | 22 919 |
| 20 | 20 | Honda | Automotive | +3 | 22 696 |
| 21 | 25 | SAP | Technology | +6 | 22 635 |
| 22 | 24 | Pepsi | Beverages | +1 | 20 491 |
| 23 | 21 | H&M | Apparel | −10 | 20 488 |
| 24 | 36 | Zara | Apparel | +11 | 18 573 |
| 25 | 26 | Ikea | Retail | +4 | 18 472 |
| 26 | 18 | Gillette | FMCG | −9 | 18 200 |
| 27 | 23 | American Express | Financial services | −3 | 17 787 |
| 28 | 30 | Pampers | FMCG | +2 | 16 416 |
| 29 | 27 | UPS | Logistics | +7 | 16 387 |
| 30 | 35 | J.P. Morgan | Financial services | +11 | 15 749 |

Source: Interbrand (2018). *Best Global Brands 2017 and 2014*. Available from www.interbrand.com (accessed 9 June 2018).

FIGURE 8.6   Brand valuation

The most basic criteria for brand evaluation include:

- Title to the brand has to be clear and separately disposable from the rest of the business.
- The value has to be substantial and long term, based on separately identifiable earnings that have to be in excess of those achieved by unbranded products.

Brand valuation is inevitably subjective to some degree. The dimensions indicated in Figure 8.6 suggest that building the brand requires dedicated management of the complete marketing mix across the various markets. There is evidence of this in all the successful brands. Brands can, of course, also decline in value from time to time. This may be due, for example, to failure to understand changing customer expectations (some fast food brands), inappropriate brand stretching (a number of the top fashion brands), failure to respond to market problems (banks and financial institutions) product and service problems (Toyota) or failure to respond to new competition (formerly state-owned airlines and telecoms businesses and many of the developed world car manufacturers at some point in their recent history).

## Branding strategies

**Branding strategies and the brand portfolio**   The first decision is to choose between the alternative branding strategies that can be applied to the brand portfolio. The alternatives are:

- *Umbrella brands*: occurs when one brand supports several products, as is the case with Google (see Management Challenge 8.2).
- *Product brands*: occur when, for example, Unilever, Procter & Gamble and pharmaceutical firms give each product a unique and distinctive brand.
- *Line brands*: occur where a company has a number of complementary products sharing the same brand concept, for example, L'Oréal sells haircare products under the Studio Line name.
- *Range brands*: are similar to line brands but include a broader range of products, for example Heinz uses Weightwatchers, and Nestlé uses Findus for frozen foods.
- *Endorsing brands*: is a weaker association of a corporate name with a product brand name and is often used after acquisition. Over time, Nestlé has gradually increased the size of 'Nestlé' on the packaging of its acquired brands, such as Kit Kat. This may be one step towards umbrella branding.
- *Source brands*: occur where products are double branded with a corporate or range name and a product name, for example, Ford Mondeo.

Essentially the decision about which strategy to use is determined by whether the benefits of a shared identity outweigh the importance of differentiation between the individual product brands.

A further branding strategy, private branding, is the practice of supplying products to a third party for sale under their brand name. The two South Korean companies, Samsung and LG, achieved success initially by being original equipment manufacturers (OEM). But they have rapidly developed internationally to the point where they now have high shares of certain product categories by building their own brands.

Private branding is used widely in retailing. As the major retailers become more powerful, so the private brand share of the market has increased significantly, especially during times of recession. This is because the consumers perceive private brands as providing value for money. This has been supported as retailers have promoted their own label products and continually improved the quality too.

## Brand piracy

One of the most difficult challenges for brand management is dealing with brand piracy. Research suggests that the problem of forgery of famous brand names is increasing. Many but by no means all fake products

## MANAGEMENT CHALLENGE 8.2

# Google: the number 2 umbrella technology brand

Google's Googlers (their employees) create and design a range of products and services under the worldwide second-highest ranking brand.

There are over 40 000 Googlers who ask the question 'what can Google develop for you?' By asking this question every day Google stays in touch with the consumers and gives them solutions to their problems and, of course, products that consumers didn't know they needed.

The main products, familiar to Google and non-Google consumers, are:

1  Web-based products: These include the very simple and easy to use Google search engine. The fun thing about the search engine is the Google doodle logo, which has hundreds of different images showing Mother's Day, An Earth Day quiz, doodles of dancing Shamrocks for St. Patrick's Day and a special Google logo for Martin Luther King Jr Day.

2  Google Chrome – a superfast web-browser for consumers and businesses.

3  Google Bookmarks – a filing system to help consumers organize and keep their favourite topics, videos or fashion pages at their fingertips.

For businesses there are also Google products:

1  Google Adsense, which is a free service for businesses that publish a webpage. If a business has a webpage, they can earn money by simply allowing other web-based publishers to post an advertisement on their site.

2  Google Hangouts – rivalling Skype for businesses that want to connect face-to-face with employees that are remote or have meetings with colleagues overseas.

3  Google Adwords – for businesses that want to attract more customers to their website or telephone number. A coffee shop in Leeds using Adwords can pay a small fee to have an advertisement viewed on Google. A consumer search for 'coffee shop in Leeds' will increase business by attracting more customers either globally or locally.

And for leisure there are:

1  Google Books – which enables consumers to download books from the classics to children's books to academic text books. Some books are free and some have a small fee.

2  Google Play – is another fun platform for consumers on the go. Games, music and TV can be accessed and downloaded. There are also hundreds of magazines and newspaper articles available straight to PCs and Android phones.

Other Google products and services under the umbrella brand include Google Maps, Google Translate, Google Drive, Google Scholar and YouTube. Google has something for everyone. Their Google products and services are provided under a range of subcategories, which are:

Web, mobile, business, media, geo, specialized search, home and office, social and innovation.

### Questions

1  Which target markets are Google appealing to?

2  Why did Google choose the umbrella brand strategy?

3  What are the weaknesses of using an umbrella brand strategy?

**Reference:** www.google.co.uk.

---

have been found to originate in developing countries and in Asia. It is important to recognize the differences between the ways in which forgery takes place. Kaitiki (1981) identifies:

- *Outright piracy*: in which a product is in the same form and uses the same trademark as the original but is false.
- *Reverse engineering*: in which the original product is stripped down, copied and then undersold to the original manufacturer, particularly in the electronics industry.
- *Counterfeiting*: in which the product quality has been altered but the same trademark appears on the label. Burberry, Levi Strauss and Lacoste have all been victims.
- *Passing off*: involves modifying the product but retaining a trademark which is similar in appearance, phonetic quality or meaning, for example Coalgate for Colgate and Del Mundo for Del Monte.

■ *Wholesale infringement*: is the questionable registration of the names of famous brands overseas rather than the introduction of fake products. This might be considered brand piracy, but it is entirely within the law. This has been very prevalent in e-business with the registration of dotcom sites by individuals hoping to sell the site later, at substantial profit, to the famous name.

There is a vast trade in pirated brands and copied products. It has been estimated that 90 per cent of the software used in India and China is counterfeit. However, some cultures do not accept that individuals should gain from ideas which ought to benefit everyone, so there are substantial differences in the perception of the importance of counterfeiting. Others believe that the development of many underdeveloped economies would have been set back considerably if they had paid market rates for software. This raises the ethical question of whether oligopolistic companies such as Microsoft should be allowed to make fortunes for certain individuals by charging very high prices while effectively excluding customers in underdeveloped countries who cannot afford to pay.

The issue of brand piracy clearly is costing MNEs vast revenues. The USA has led the way in insisting that governments crack down on the companies undertaking the counterfeiting. However, such firms have sophisticated networking operations, with much of their revenue coming from sales to consumers in developed countries. Trying to reduce or eliminate their activities is costly and time-consuming and unlikely to be a priority for governments in less developed countries. Moreover, pursuing legal action in foreign markets can be expensive, particularly for small companies, and can result in adverse publicity for larger firms.

The music industry has particularly suffered from illegal practices. The myth of music piracy was of a victimless crime, but the International Federation of the Phonographic Industry (IFPI) claims that billions of dollars go to support criminal gangs as well as sucking money out of the legitimate music industry (IFPI 2003).

## Positioning

Closely related to brand strategy and at the heart of its implementation is positioning. Positioning is largely concerned with how a product or service might be differentiated from the competition. However, it is important to stress that it is the customers' perceptions of the product or service offer that will indirectly confirm the positioning and so determine its success. Firms can only seek to establish and confirm the positioning in the consumers' minds through their management of the marketing mix. In countries at different stages of economic development the customer segments that are likely to be able to purchase the product, and the occasions on which it is bought, may be significantly different. For example, KFC and McDonald's restaurants aim at everyday eating for the mass market in developed countries. In less developed countries, however, they are perceived as places for special occasion eating and out of the reach of the poorest segments of the population. A Mercedes car may be perceived as a luxury car in many countries but as an everyday taxi in Germany.

Unilever has a different approach. It introduced a new logo for its ice cream so that while the familiar names stay the same, for example, Wall's in the UK and Ola in the Netherlands, the background design and font are being standardized around the world.

There appears to be an increasing demand for standardized products among market segments that are mobile and susceptible to influence by the media and through travel. There is also a strongly emerging demand for the same products among consumers in less developed countries, too. Achieving unique positioning for a product or service must come from the creative dimensions of positioning rather than resorting to simple price positioning.

In confirming the positioning of a product or service in a specific market or region, it is necessary, therefore, to establish in the consumers' perception exactly what is the value proposition and how it differs from existing and potential competition.

# Innovation and new product development

A recurring theme of discussions of international marketing issues is the increasing need for companies to have a dynamic and proactive policy of innovation for developing new products and services. This is to satisfy the apparently insatiable demand of consumers for new experiences and to reinforce and, where necessary, renew, their source of competitive advantage. Some companies have new product development (NPD) as a corporate objective. Today, Johnson & Johnson generates 35 per cent of its sales from products that are less than five years old, compared to 30 per cent in 1980. Lim *et al.* (2006) argue that faster NPD capability is essential for firms striving for a higher degree of export involvement. At the outset, however, it is important to stress that the most competitive firms encourage innovation in every aspect of their marketing activity. The space in which innovation takes place includes new products and services; new processes; position innovation which includes creativity in brand identity and communication; and paradigm innovation which changes the underlying mental models that frame what the organization does. For example, IBM has reinvented itself from being a hardware company (International Business Machines), to a software and solutions provider, to a business process outsourcing company. Nestlé's new medical nutrition division aims to create a new industry between food and pharmaceuticals, in which foods are developed for people suffering, for example, from metabolic disorders. An increasing trend among online businesses is architectural innovation (Tuschman and Anderson 2004) and the adoption of innovative business models. For example, Google does not charge for search but generates income from advertisers. Mobile/cell phone companies give away expensive phones for free and generate income from monthly rental contracts and connection.

While product or technological innovation is quite obvious – for example the average person knows that Edison invented the light bulb – getting the bulbs into houses and schools and selling electricity is service innovation. However, due to the increase in personal economic circumstances in both the developed and developing countries, and of course increased global knowledge, consumers expect and demand more, particularly for services such as healthcare, education, leisure and entertainment. One of the key aspects that is helping services innovate and grow is technology. Barrett *et al.* (2015) state that technological innovation is particularly useful in advancing consumer self-service opportunities, such as telephoning a doctor for a diagnosis, which is popular in developed countries and rural areas in Peru. Additionally, mobile payments and delivery services enhance the consumer's opportunity to shop online from any device. IBM, Oracle and other tech companies have formed a non-profit consortium www.thesri.org to advance the concept using an open web social networking community and public archive. It maintains that innovation is about culture and values rather than processes and notes that the best ideas are, at first, laughable. If an innovation is truly and substantially new, it must by definition carry with it uncertainty and ambiguity.

## The most innovative companies

Deciding which are the world's most innovative companies rather depends on which measure you use. Jaruzel *et al.* (2014), from Strategy& (formally Booz and Company), show that in the annual study of the world's biggest R&D spenders cars, computing and electronics, and healthcare were the biggest industries for R&D spending. The top five companies were Volkswagen, Samsung, Intel, Microsoft and Roche. By contrast, a survey of innovation executives to explore the relationship between innovation capabilities, corporate strategy and financial performance resulted in overwhelming votes for Apple, Google, Amazon and Samsung as the world's most innovative companies.

Patent filing is used by some as another measure of the innovativeness of firms. Huawei Technologies, China's largest telecoms equipment maker, is the world's top international patent seeker followed by Panasonic and Philips Electronics which had dominated for a decade. Next come Japan's Toyota and Fujitsu, Germany's Robert Bosch and Siemens, Finland's Nokia, South Korea's LG Electronics and Sweden's Ericsson. China was the sixth largest patent filer by country, behind the USA, Japan, Germany, South Korea and France.

## The nature of new product development

Few new products and services are actually revolutionary. Figure 8.7 shows the various categories of new products in terms of their newness to the market and company. Innovative firms encourage their staff to undertake incremental innovation in every aspect of business activity. This is to ensure a continual improvement process intended to refresh and reinforce the product range by complementing the existing company and brand image, rather than causing a change of direction.

Periodically, step change innovation occurs as a result of a technological breakthrough, such as the mobile/cell phone, or ground breaking creative ideas often related to marketing that achieve a change of industry direction. Renewable energy innovations require technological and business innovations, step change and are incremental. Patagonia decided to extend its environmental innovations beyond recycling to sustainable beer.

**FIGURE 8.7**  New product categories

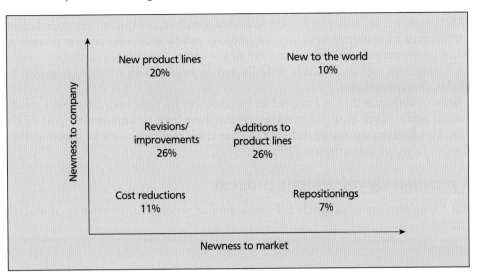

ILLUSTRATION 8.6

# Patagonia innovators with plastic, goose and duck down, and beer

Patagonia began as a small organization that made tools and clothes for climbers. It expanded to make clothing for other 'silent sports' including skiing, snowboarding, surfing, fly fishing, paddling and trail running. 'Silent sports' are those that do not need a motor. This fitted perfectly with Patagonia's ideals that it needed to work hard to stop the planet's environmental health declining further.

Patagonia's mission is to 'build the best product, cause no unnecessary harm, use business to inspire and implement solutions to the environmental crisis'. One product it is known for is its fleece-wear which is made of plastic bottles, thus saving the bottles from going to landfill or joining the many cubic metres of plastic floating in the world's seas. Patagonia also recycles goose and duck down from cushions and duvet bedding that can't be resold. The recycled goose and duck down is then stuffed into parkas, vests and jackets.

Patagonia does not just stop at being innovative with recycled materials. It is branching out and making agriculture sustainable. There are conversations the world over that due to the intensification of agricultural farming, for both food and bio-fuels, the land is exhausted. And something has to happen as it is likely that by 2050, when there will be around 9 billion people, natural resources will not be able to cope. Patagonia Provisions (an off shoot of Patagonia the company that provides clothing) has found a solution: to make beer from a grain that is grown from regenerative agricultural practices. The grain is called Kernza© and is beneficial for many reasons. The following four are key. First, the roots of the grain are long and because of this they do not need as much water from a watering system. Second, Kernza© sucks in more carbon from the atmosphere than wheat does. Third, Kernza© is a perennial plant which means it can continue to grow for two or three years, maybe longer. And fourth, as the plant is hardy and resilient, no chemical fertilizers or pesticides are needed. These key reasons make the plant itself an ecological dream. Patagonia teamed up with Hopworks Urban Brewery to create the first beer from Kernza©. The beer, aptly named Long Root Ale, is particularly popular worldwide, due to the resurgence of real ale and craft beers.

## Questions

**1** In what ways are Patagonia's innovations helping to improve the health of the planet?

**2** How can a company such as Patagonia be a business to inspire others to become involved in improving the health of the planet?

Usually, developing new technologies is hugely expensive. For example, it is estimated that the cost of developing a new drug is between US$800 million and US$2 billion and takes over 15 years. In order to recover the R&D costs it is necessary to market new ideas simultaneously in all developed countries. This is because the time taken by competitors to copy or improve products and circumvent patents is shortening. Moreover, when pharmaceutical products come out of the patent period, they can legitimately be copied as generic drugs. Companies such as Ranbaxy in India and Aspen in South Africa have grown fast and built a strong global business doing this.

Even the largest companies do not have sufficient resources on their own to achieve rapid diffusion of a new product or service into all world markets. So this is at least as important a part of the process as the initial idea. This leads to the use of different market entry methods, such as licensing, franchising and strategic alliances, to secure cost-effective diffusion.

## The new product development process

In its simplest form, developing products follows a similar process for international markets to that in domestic situations:

- idea generation
- initial screening
- business analysis
- development
- market testing
- commercialization and launch.

Particular emphasis must be placed upon the quality of the information system, as it is essential that the product or service meets the needs of the customers and is positioned accurately in each market from the outset. With this in mind, the international development process should incorporate the following elements.

*Idea generation* must ensure that ideas worldwide are accessed so that duplication is avoided. Synergy is then optimized by effectively using all available internal and external resources to generate new ideas. These include employees, R&D departments, competitors, sales people, customers, distributors and external experts.

*Initial screening* involves establishing rigorous international criteria, including both production and marketing factors, to test the ideas for suitability in all world regions so that opportunities and limitations are not overlooked. Ideas that may, for example, be inappropriate for western Europe might be appropriate for South America. In doing this an assessment should be made of the degree of adaptation that will be necessary for individual markets.

*Business analysis* must involve establishing criteria for potential success or failure of the product and linking the criteria with regions and/or markets. It must make provision for contingencies such as environmental and competitive situations and unexpected events which might adversely affect the business case.

*Product development* must include ensuring that all relevant functions such as production, design and packaging become involved in the process. The most appropriate R&D centres for the development process should be selected, with particular attention being paid to such factors as access to technological expertise and location near prime target and lead markets.

*Market testing* must involve ensuring the test area is representative of the prime target markets. Ensuring an adequate infrastructure in terms of the necessary services, such as advertising and market research agencies, and an appropriate distribution network is in place, are also essential. It should also take account of potential competitor response both in the test market and globally.

*The launch* must be planned either to be sequential, with an initial concentration upon prime markets or lead markets, or to be a simultaneous launch. Allowance must be made for aggressive competitive responses, as few competitors will give up market share without a fight.

*To protect the firm's competitive advantage* the company needs to pay particular attention to defending its intellectual property and anticipate the ability of competitors to copy a new product and launch it in a separate market. There are a number of actions that companies might take to protect their intellectual property, such as taking strong patent protection, or entering into licensing arrangements to ensure fast, widespread penetration of the world or regional markets.

*Timing* is perhaps the most critical element of the process, not only in terms of exploiting an opportunity or competitive weakness at the right moment but also minimizing the time to market. This includes how long it takes from when the idea was first generated to making it available commercially and the time it takes to achieve the desired level of diffusion.

## Approaches to technology transfer and the benefits for marketing

This traditional, sequential and largely internal approach to NPD has considerable disadvantages because of a number of factors, including:

- The shortening of product life cycles.
- The cost and risk of funding development internally.
- The time needed to get the new product to market.
- 'Non-core' activities such as product and packaging design and process development, as part of the in-house development process.

In an attempt to resolve these problems, many firms are adopting a more interactive approach in which new product and service developments are carried out jointly between the manufacturer, component maker, designer and technology supplier. Bogers *et al.* (2018) explain that open innovation is an approach in which a variety of specialist organizations, including businesses, policy makers and academia, pool their knowledge of key trends and potential solutions. The main benefits of an interactive approach to NPD for the company are the concentration of skills and expertise on core activities, the ability to condense timescales and access to the best knowledge available on a particular topic.

It can be difficult to obtain contributions to the innovation process from staff around the world. Eppinger and Chitkara (2006) note that companies in many industries have engineering teams located in different parts of the world, but that without frameworks to support collaboration, managers find it difficult to achieve the necessary cohesion in the operation to drive efficient growth and innovation. The authors highlight Hyundai, Hewlett Packard and Alcatel as firms that have achieved this.

To further speed up the NPD process, the stages can be regarded as simultaneous rather than linear. For example, testing the concept on customers around the world, carrying out the detailed analysis for the business case and designing the product packaging, could go ahead at the same time.

## R&D strategies

No matter which approach is adopted, major international companies must still decide upon the aims of their own R&D, the exact nature of the activities undertaken and where they should be located. They must take decisions on:

- The location of their own internal R&D facilities.
- The extent to which they embrace open innovation and contract out certain parts of their research and development programme, as large pharmaceutical companies do.
- Whether they might acquire a company which can provide either the required new technology or a new product.
- Licensing the technology and process from another company.
- Funding joint ventures or strategic alliances with companies that have complementary technology.

In general, the R&D activities of international companies tend to follow an evolutionary path. But for many the major question is whether or not they should move away from the dominance of their domestic country R&D location and, if so, where should their R&D facilities be located.

Many companies still concentrate a large proportion of R&D activity in their country of origin. But as they move increasingly towards transnational operations, so the concept of the home country becomes increasingly meaningless. It is, however, useful to consider the arguments for and against the centralization of R&D activities, and these are shown in Figure 8.8.

FIGURE 8.8   The arguments for and against centralization of R&D

| Arguments for centralization | Arguments against centralization |
|---|---|
| • economies of scale<br>• easier and faster communication<br>• better coordination<br>• greater control over outflow of information with implications for secrecy<br>• greater synergy<br>• avoiding duplication<br>• overcoming problems of ownership | • pressure from subsidiaries<br>• pressure from governments<br>• benefits of public relations<br>• use of wider range of skills and abilities<br>• benefits from comparative advantage<br>• greater sensitivity to local tastes<br>• better monitoring of local competitive activity<br>• closeness to possible acquisitions<br>• access new technology wherever it is located |

## Success and failure in new product development

One of the most difficult aspects of NPD is to reduce the high levels of risk (and therefore the cost) of new product failure. The classic studies of success and failure of new products in developed countries, particularly in the USA and UK, emphasize that for success it is necessary to place greater emphasis upon marketing rather than technical factors. The key to success is an effective NPD strategy. This includes the development of the central and supporting processes to generate a flow of new products that might vary in market impact, but will include some high revenue or high-margin generators. In emerging markets, the key is to develop products and services that meet the needs of customers for more basic items. So the concept of 'frugal engineering' has been introduced, see Management Challenge 8.3. The aim of the innovation is to completely re-engineer products and services rather than simply try to reduce the costs of the established processes. These new products created are not of inferior quality and will find new markets in developed countries too.

Griffin (2003) suggests three fundamental requirements of the innovation process:

1 Uncover unmet needs and problems.
2 Develop a product with competitive advantage.
3 Shepherd the products through the firm.

Tzokas et al. (2003) suggest that market information is central to achieving success in NPD. They summarize the research studies that have highlighted its role within the strategic success factors:

■ Ensuring product performance improvements over what is already available.
■ Achieving synergy with existing firm technologies and manufacturing capability and learning new capabilities quickly.
■ Achieving marketing synergies, such as channels and promotion, often because of the need to target a new segment.
■ Integrating the contributions of marketing and R&D.

MANAGEMENT CHALLENGE 8.3

# Meeting emerging market needs with frugal engineering

Over many years, innovation has (and still is) mainly concerned with improvements that embrace new technology. They typically add value for those customers that can afford to pay for increasingly sophisticated products and services. In Chapter 6 we introduced the concept of customers at the bottom of the pyramid, highlighting the huge number of people, particularly in markets such as China, India and Brazil, that are moving out of poverty, enjoying prosperity for the first time and shopping for basics, rather than 'nice to have' features.

The term 'frugal engineering' has been coined not to describe stripped down engineering – removing features to enable products to be sold at lower prices – but to take a 'clean sheet' approach. Cost discipline is an intrinsic part of the process and avoids needless costs in the first place. In developed nations expansion of features has contributed most to the profitability of firms. So, for example, many car manufacturers make profit on the top-of-the-range models and little or no profit on the low specification models. But this means that production lines are not geared to producing basic items. For example, manual car windows are virtually extinct in the USA. Firms in emerging markets, such as Tata with its Nano, are showing how 'frugal engineering', a term coined by Renault CEO, Carlos Ghosn, can create products with costs that are unimaginable in the developed nations.

It is not just cars that are fit for purpose in emerging markets but also 'Little Cool' refrigerators with a fan rather than a compressor. Also, basic function laptop computers, unsophisticated X-ray machines and mobile/cell phones that just make calls. Western firms are beginning to wake up to the opportunities. After watching customers using mobile/cell phones in India, Nokia developed its best-selling phone costing between \$15–\$20. It sends and receives calls and texts, has a monochrome display, lacks complex software so extending battery life, and is designed to cope with high humidity and dust.

Its one added feature is an energy efficient flashlight, popular where blackouts are common.

Some customers in developed countries also see the value in frugally engineered products. Deere from the USA started selling small, lower-powered tractors in India but did not sell them into the US market until an Indian company, Mahindra and Mahindra, beat them to it. Now Mahindra and Mahindra is competing for Deere's large tractor market. By contrast, GE is selling its low-cost electrocardiogram machine in the USA, which was developed for India.

Another innovation for Kenyan people was provided by MPESA, a company that enables people in remote villages to save, spend and transfer money using their mobile/cell phones without needing to have a bank account. Additionally, Kenyan SteamaCo, a supplier of renewable energy, provides kit for Kenyan people to fully charge their mobile/cell phones from the sun.

## Questions

**1** How can firms such as Tata, Nokia and GE manage their portfolio to include 'frugal engineering' but also include top-of-the-range models for more demanding customers?

**2** SteamaCo and MPESA use frugal engineering. However, these companies are not global companies. What can local and global companies learn from each other?

**References:** Radjou, N. and Prabhu, J. (2013) Frugal innovation. A new business paradigm, INSEAD Knowledge, published 10 January 2013; Sehgal, V., Dehoff, K. and Panneer, G. (2010) The importance of frugal engineering. *Strategy and Business* 59. Available from www.strategy-business.com (accessed 25 May 2010); Maina Waruru (2015) Microgrids and mobile tech bring solar power to rural Kenya. *Reuters* 16 April. Available from www.reuters.com/article/2015/04/16/us-kenya-energy-solar-idUSKBN0N70TK20150416 (accessed 11 May 2015).

- Identifying attractive markets with growth potential.
- Effectively carrying out the NPD process, including pre-development activities, such as idea generation, screening, concept and business case investigation.
- Obtaining support from top management.
- Speed in development.

Key to success in technology sectors is generating a continual flow of new product introductions, but success is by no means guaranteed. Even for technologically leading edge companies, not every idea will make it to the market and be a commercial success. So risk-taking and tolerating failure must be accepted by the firm's management. The main focus, however, should be to add value to meet the needs of customers wherever they are in the world.

## SUMMARY

- In many business sectors product and service strategies are being affected by the increased globalization of consumer tastes, communications, technological advances and the concentration of business activity. At the same time, however, given the level of competition and choice available, there is an increasing expectation among customers that their individual needs will be met.

- Product managers are balancing the efficiency benefits of standardization in terms of economies of scale and the experience effect, with the need and cost of adapting products and services to meet the needs of local customers, regulations and usage conditions.

- The growth of international services is a feature of international marketing and is being driven by low labour costs and increasing demand in developing countries. It also provides increased possibilities for transferring information through IT and communications.

- As more products are reaching the mature phase of the life cycle they are becoming commodities. There is a need to use additional services to differentiate them from competitor offerings. However, services are often difficult to standardize globally because they are affected significantly by the different expectations of service delivery that exist in different cultures.

- The product or service strategy is usually at the centre of international marketing operations. Branding is a key part of product and service management, particularly in international markets. But it is difficult to establish global brands that are truly distinctive and have images that appeal to cross-cultural customer segments.

- New product and service development and innovation throughout the marketing process are essential for growth and the renewal of the international portfolio. In particular, for culturally sensitive products and services, it is vital to obtain input from the different stakeholders around the world in order to ensure that they will be successful.

## KEYWORDS

| | | |
|---|---|---|
| intangibility | adaptation | international branding |
| perishability | international product portfolio | branding strategies |
| heterogeneity | product strategies | brand piracy |
| inseparability | international product life cycle | new product development |
| international product offer | country of origin effect | |
| standardization | services | |

## CASE STUDY 1

# Autonomous cars: looking for a driver!

For existing multinational enterprises, the emergence of a new technology that has the power to transform the market in which they operate can offer the opportunity to become a global powerhouse. However, if they fail to embrace such a disruptive technology quickly enough, they may find that they are left behind by existing competitors or much more agile newcomers.

To create a successful business start-up based on new technology in a global market dominated by MNEs requires an entrepreneur with vision and the development of products and services that excite customers, meet their needs, are safe to use and fit into the business and physical environment for which they are intended.

It could be claimed that all the technologies required to create autonomous or driverless vehicles have been invented for quite some time. Putting the components together in the form of safe and economical products and services, however, is fiendishly difficult and expensive. Many of the global firms that will be affected by such technology have introduced their prototypes or initial products and explained their vision for autonomous cars, self-driving taxis/hire cars (the two services would merge), drone delivery of packages and so on. Many more firms – MNEs, SMEs and start-ups – are working on solving the myriad technology implementation challenges. These firms will also be key players in the future supply chains of autonomous car suppliers.

However, while it is important to communicate an exciting vision of the future to engage and enthuse potential customers who will become the early adopters and buyers of the product and service, it is also essential to convince the rather more sceptical global mass market. This might mean introducing a more basic product to generate income while the ultimate visionary product is being developed.

Global investors in exciting new business opportunities are risk-takers – some perhaps gamblers – and back firms that appear to promise them a fortune in the future. However, they will sell their share of a business if they no longer see the prospect of a satisfactory return on their investment. Investors expect firms to deliver on their promises and within their budget.

Billionaire and serial entrepreneur Elon Musk founded Tesla in 2003 to make innovative electric cars with driver-assisted technology, leading ultimately to the production of fully autonomous (driverless) cars. In March 2018 Tesla lost a fifth of its market value after a series of negative stories, but still had a higher value than Ford. Tesla admitted that its Model X autopilot system was operating when the car crashed into a barrier in California killing the driver. It was forced to recall 120 000 of its Model 3 series due to a faulty bolt.

Due to high R&D costs, the company had huge debts. To generate the necessary income to service the debt and avoid the firm running out of cash, Tesla was more dependent on sales of its Model 3 'electric car for the masses', launched in 2016 with a starting price of $35 000, than the much more expensive Tesla S luxury saloon or the Tesla X 7 seater SUV. The initial promise to make 5000 Model 3 cars per week had been cut to a target of 2500 per week, and less than 800 per week were produced in the last weeks of 2017. In the last week of March 2018, the factory in Fremont, California made just over 2000 cars.

More than 500 000 orders (as of 2017) had been placed for the Model 3 car from around the world. The firm was promising to reach its target production by the third quarter, when the high volume, good gross margin and strong positive cash flow would stem the losses.

## Questions

**1** How can Tesla's key market segments be characterized?

**2** What are the drivers for Tesla's product strategies for each segment?

**3** How can Tesla manage its competing demands for resources?

**4** How might Tesla maximize the global opportunities for its products, and should they?

**References:** www.tesla.com; Jones, C. (2018) Tesla 'out-accelerating the Model T'. *The Times*, 4 April. Available from www.thetimes.co.uk/edition/business/tesla-out-accelerating-the-model-t-x9cptpg5g (accessed 9 June 2018).

## CASE STUDY 2

## Accor inseparable services: online and face-to-face

Accor, the hotel brand that has many sub-brands, is known for its excellent service and hospitality around the world. In 2018 Accor was present in 100 countries, had 4300 hotels, and 260 000 employees. Its business model has two arms, AccorInvest, a subsidiary hotel investor, and AccorHotels, a hotel operator. This means that its hotel portfolio includes franchised, managed and owned/leased hotels and other related hospitality activities. Through continual acquisitions under Accor's sub-brands, the company satisfies different hospitality experiences.

Accor's fastest-growing regions are in Asia Pacific (particularly China and India) and sub-Saharan Africa and Latin America. But it is also investing heavily in the renovation and redevelopment of hotels in its more traditional markets. Accor's Le Club AccorHotels is the largest hospitality loyalty club with 32 million members.

The Accor brand and its sub-brands are one of the tangible elements that employees need to know the values and working practices of. The brand names are also useful for consumers to recognize and associate with different levels of service, quality and price.

The customer experience is of paramount importance to Accor. And because of its worldwide portfolio, Accor is keen to offer a heterogeneous but superior customer experience. Accor knows that inseparable moments occur both on and face-to-face along the customer's journey. It works hard on two particular contact points along the customer journey.

### 1. Online
Over 300 million inseparable moments occur each year when consumers visit Accor's websites. Accor ensures the inseparable moments include tangible elements

| International Brands | |
| Brand category | Sub-brands |
| --- | --- |
| Luxury and upscale | Raffles<br>Orient Express<br>Banyan Tree<br>Rixos<br>Angsana<br>Fairmont<br>Sofitel<br>Sofitel Legend<br>So Sofitel<br>Swissôtel<br>Pullman Hotel and Resorts<br>M Gallery<br>Grand Mercure<br>The Sebel<br>25 Hours Hotels |
| Lifestyle, mid-scale boutique and economy | Novotel<br>Mercure Hotels<br>Adagio<br>Mama Shelter<br>Jo&Joe<br>Ibis<br>Ibis Styles<br>Ibis budget<br>HotelF1 |
| Private rental | onefinestay |
| Coworking | Nextdoor<br>Mamaworks |
| Concierge | John Paul<br>Accor Local |
| Dining &Events | Potel & Chabot<br>Noctis |
| Digital solutions | Availpro<br>Fastbooking<br>Gekko<br>Verychic |

that consumers find both useful and enjoyable. Geolocation software identifies where customers are situated. Therefore, if someone visits Accor's website in France, the website text will be in French; or if located in Brazil the website text will be in Portuguese. Currently, Accor accommodates 16 languages through geolocation technology, making this inseparable moment easy for consumers to navigate around the website and book accommodation. With people booking rooms directly through Accor websites every five seconds, this inseparable moment is certainly helpful in driving consumers to purchase. Social media also shows intangible elements of Accor Hotels. Sofitel's website exudes luxury and identifies with upscale consumers, especially the artistic photographs of concierge services. For the busy, budget-conscious customer, Accor provides dedicated mobile applications for Hotel F1 so consumers can geo-search for a hotel, SMS a booking query, book and send payment within seconds. Accor's online connections, web or mobile, are excellent ways to ensure inseparable moments are useful and engaging.

**2. Face-to-face**

'Welcomers' are a new innovation of face-to-face service at Accor Pullman Hotels and Resorts. Welcomers move fluidly around the hotel's floor areas speaking to guests, answering questions, inspiring ideas and making special, individual relationships with each guest. These inseparable moments make Accor guests feel special. In other Accor hotels the barrier of the reception desk has been banished. Reception desks have been replaced with 'Host pods'. Hosts, carrying mobile tablets, check guests in, check train timetables, show local street maps and book guests into a local ice-hockey game. This innovative service also provides a more informal, personal, inseparable moment that Accor guests enjoy. Consumers can also use digital smartphone technology to check in and out of Accor hotels.

### Questions

**1** How has Accor used technology to improve inseparability moments?

**2** What tangible changes has Accor made online and in its hotels to improve intangible guest experiences?

**3** What are the advantages and disadvantages of having so many sub-brands?

**4** How can Accor ensure that good practice in service is shared across brands and across country borders?

**Source:** Accor (2017) 2016 Business Review. 5 May. Available from www.accorhotels.group/en/business-review (accessed 6 April 2018).

## DISCUSSION QUESTIONS

**1** Identify the major macro-environmental trends in world trade. Using examples from one product and one service sector, explain how these trends have affected product and service portfolio management across international markets.

**2** In an ideal world, companies would like to manufacture a standardized product. What are the factors that support the case for a standardized product, and what are the circumstances that are likely to prevent its implementation?

**3** Examine the ways in which a major company operating in many countries around the world can use new product development and commercialization to enhance its ambitions to become a global company.

**4** What challenges would you expect to face in marketing products and/or services from:

**(a)** A developing country to a developed country?

**(b)** A developed to a less developed country?

**5** How might these challenges be overcome? Illustrate your answer by focusing on a product or service of your choice.

**6** International services marketing is a major growth area. Using one service sector as an example, explain what the main barriers are to success and what strategies might be used to overcome them.

## REFERENCES

1. Accor (2017) *2016 Business Review*. 5 May. Available from www.accorhotels.group/en/business-review (accessed 6 April 2018).
2. Accord on Fire and Building Safety in Bangladesh (2018). Available from http://bangladeshaccord.org/about/ (accessed 9 June 2018).
3. Aguiar, M., Bradtke, T., Erica Carlisle, D. Khanna, D. Lee, Michael, D.C., Nettesheim, C., Pai-Panandiker, R. and Ullrich, P. (2014) *Meet the 2014 BCG Global Challengers*. 10 September. Available from www.bcgperspectives.com/content/articles/globalization_growth_meet_2014_global_challengers/ (accessed 22 September 2015).

4. Barrett, M., Davidson, E., Prabhu, J. and Vargo, S.L. (2015) Service innovation in the digital age: Key contributions and future directions. *MIS Quarterly* 39(1), 135–154.

5. Bogers, M., Chesbrough, H. and Moedas, C. (2018) Open innovation: Research, practices, and policies. *California Management Review* 60(2), 5–16.

6. Doyle, P. (2000) *Value Based Marketing Strategies for Corporate Growth and Shareholder Value*. Wiley.

7. Eppinger, S.D. and Chitkara, A.R. (2006) The new practice of global product development. *MIT Sloan Management Review* 47(4), 22–30.

8. Griffin, A. (2003) Marketing's role in new product development and product decisions. In Douglas Hoffman, K. (ed.) *Marketing Best Practice*. Thomson South-Western.

9. IFPI (2003) *Commercial Piracy Report*, July, London. Available from www.ifpi.org.

10. Interbrand (2018). *Best Global Brands 2017 and 2014*. Available from www.interbrand.com (accessed 9 June 2018).

11. Ives, M. (2014) In developing world, a push to bring e-waste out of the shadows. 6 February. Via Environment 360, www.e360.yale.edu (accessed 6 May 2015).

12. Jaruzel, B., Staack, V. and Goehle, B. (2014) The top innovators and spenders. Available from www.strategyand. pwc.com/global/home/what-we-think/innovation1000/top-innovators-spenders (accessed 11 May 2015).

13. Jones, C. (2018) Tesla 'out-accelerating the Model T'. *The Times*, 4 April. Available from www.thetimes.co.uk/edition/business/tesla-out-accelerating-the-model-t-x9cptpg5g (accessed 9 June 2018).

14. Kaitiki, S. (1981) How multinationals cope with the international trade mark forgery. *Journal of International Marketing* 1(2), 69–80.

15. Keegan, W.J. and Green, C. (2014) *Global Marketing*, 8th edition. Pearson Education.

16. Kotler, P. and Armstrong, G. (2014) *Principles of Marketing*, 15th edition. Pearson. Electronic Copy.

17. Lim, J., Sharkey, T.W. and Heinrichs, J.H. (2006) Strategic impact of new product development on export involvement. *European Journal of Marketing* 40, 44–60.

18. Maina Waruru (2015) Microgrids and mobile tech bring solar power to rural Kenya. *Reuters* 16 April. Available from www.reuters.com/article/2015/04/16/us-kenya-energy-solar-idUSKBN0N70TK20150416 (accessed 11 May 2015).

19. Mesdag, M. van (1985) The frontiers of choice. *Marketing*, 10 October.

20. Radjou, N. and Prabhu, J. (2013) Frugal innovation. A new business paradigm, INSEAD Knowledge, published 10 January 2013.

21. Rappa, R. and Hirsh, E. (2007) The luxury touch. Available from www-strategy-business.com (accessed 3 April).

22. Sehgal, V., Dehoff, K. and Panneer, G. (2010) The importance of frugal engineering. *Strategy and Business* 59. Available from www.strategy-business.com (accessed 25 May 2010).

23. Stone, A. (2006) Profits save the world. *Sunday Times*, 10 December.

24. Tuschman, M.L. and Anderson, P. (2004) *Managing Strategic Innovation and Change*, 2nd edition. Free Press.

25. Tzokas, N., Hart, S. and Saren, M. (2003) New product development, a marketing agenda for change. In S. Hart (ed.) *Marketing Changes*. Thomson.

26. United Nations (2014) Environment. Available from www.unglobalcompact.org/Issues/Environment/index.html updated 22 January 2014 (accessed May 2015).

# INTERNATIONAL MARKETING PLANNING: STRATEGY DEVELOPMENT

## Introduction

In Directed Study Activity 1, against the background of information on the market structure and customer needs, a segmentation approach was developed. In this activity we focus on possible strategic alternatives and the development of a global marketing strategy by companies from emerging markets who are becoming global players in the industries within which they operate.

Arguably the most significant change in international marketing over recent years has been the changing competitive landscape globally, as major players who were previously national champions in their own countries in emerging economies, ranging from China and Taiwan to Korea and Brazil, have developed as potential global players.

These companies have not really developed their global strategies through the traditional multinational route. But they are becoming global by developing global brands, either organically or by buying western companies to aid their global growth. However, as they develop, considering the possible alternative approaches to transnational development is valuable, given the very different contexts in which they operate. In this activity we consider a number of companies from emerging markets who are highly competitive and who are aiming to become truly global. You are able to choose one to investigate. Essentially the activity is about analyzing the basis of the competitive capability of the firms involved and thinking through how this has to develop and shift if they are to build and sustain a global competitive advantage. This gives you the opportunity to consider how a changing global competitive landscape modifies the competitive behaviour of companies in their struggle for a global competitive advantage. It is these issues and how the company you choose should resolve them that are explored in this activity.

## Learning objectives

On completing this activity you should be able to:

- Critically appraise the global marketing strategy that a company is following and evaluate the potential for their success or failure

- Understand the role and value of global marketing planning and its implications for the organization structure

- Understand the concept of globalization and how it affects the strategies of organizations

## The scenario: the future global players from emerging markets

Boston Consulting Group (BCG) has identified 100 newcomers (called the RDE 100) from developing economies, such as China, India, Brazil, Mexico and Russia – firms who are cash rich and hungry for global growth. BCG has also identified 40 fast growing and globalizing companies from Africa.

Previously, newcomers from emerging markets have focused on building their competitive advantage through marketing low-value manufacturing and service activities. These firms, however, are building the capability to compete with established firms by the use of much more sophisticated marketing approaches. They do this by, for example, using their success in meeting customer needs in their huge and rapidly growing domestic markets as a platform for global expansion. The question for all of these companies is whether they can compete on a more sustainable basis in the global marketing environment.

Not too many years ago, companies such as Toyota, LG and Samsung would have been regarded as 'newcomers' from emerging markets. More recently, companies that have been discussed in earlier editions of this book have rapidly become quite established global operators in their particular sectors in a period of 20 years. These companies include Mittal, a previously unknown steel producer in Indonesia – now as ArcelorMittal it is the world's largest steel producer. Lenovo, which bought IBM's personal computer division, is the fourth largest PC maker. South African Breweries, a local brewer in South Africa, is now one of the three largest beer companies. Which companies will be the stars of tomorrow?

## The following ten firms are typical of the firms identified by BCG

1 Concha y Toro: www.conchaytoro.com
   Concha y Toro from Chile is the largest Latin American wine producer and the seventh largest in the world, with vineyards in Argentina, Chile and the USA. Exports account for over 70 per cent of revenue and are growing rapidly. The company has demonstrated its desire to become a global brand through its sponsorship of Manchester United Football Club.

2 Marcopolo: www.marcopolo.com
   Founded in 1949 in Brazil, Marcopolo is one of the biggest manufacturers of bus bodies in the world. It recently initiated activities in the Light Commercial Vehicles sector, parts and components and also in the plastic products sector. It has factories in Brazil, Colombia, Argentina, Mexico, India, Egypt and South Africa.

3 Etisalat: www.etisalat.ae
   Etisalat is one of the largest telecommunications companies in the world and the leading service provider in the Middle East. The company operates in 19 countries across Asia, the Middle East and Africa and has 170 million customers.

4 Jollibee: www.jollibee.com.ph
   Jollibee started in 1975 as an ice cream stand in the Philippines, but its move into burgers and Filipino fast food accelerated its growth. Through internal growth and acquisitions it now has over 2000 outlets in Brunei, China, Indonesia, Taiwan and the USA. A quarter of its revenues come from its overseas restaurants.

5 Aspen Pharmacare: www.aspenpharma.com
   Aspen Pharmacare of South Africa is Africa's largest pharmaceutical manufacturer and a major supplier of branded pharmaceutical, health care and nutritional products to 47 countries. The group has 26 manufacturing plants at 18 sites on 6 continents.

6 Embraer: www.embraer.com
   A Brazilian company, Embraer (the Empresa Brasileira de Aeronáutica S.A.) is a Brazilian aircraft manufacturer. It produces commercial jets up to 120 seats, military and corporate aircraft. It is the fifth largest manufacturer of executive jets in the world and is one of the top three Brazilian exporters. It has a workforce of 19 000 and competes with Bombardier to be the third largest aircraft manufacturer behind Boeing and Airbus.

7 Tencent: www.tencent.com
   Tencent is a wholly online-based company. Its base is in China but already 100 of the 600 million users of its WeChat social messaging service are located outside China. Through heavy investment overseas, more than half its revenues are generated from gaming and this appears to be where growth will be generated. It owns Riot Games that created the popular League of Legends video game.

8 Infosys: www.infosys.com
   Infosys Technologies was started in 1981 by seven people with $250. Today, the company is a global leader in 'next generation' IT and consulting with revenues of US$8.7 billion in 2015. Infosys defines, designs and delivers technology-enabled business solutions for major companies offering business and technology consulting, application services, systems integration, product engineering, software development, IT infrastructure services and business process outsourcing.

9 EuroChem: www.eurochemgroup.com
   EuroChem Mineral and Chemical from Russia is in the top ten producers of fertilizer and is growing rapidly through having a vertically integrated business model from extracting raw materials through to distributing the final product. It has built a production plant in the USA and has a joint venture in China. Some 80 per cent of its revenues are generated from exports.

10 Yildiz: https://english.yildizholding.com.tr
   Yildiz from Turkey has long been successful in selling packaged food in Africa, central and eastern Europe and the Middle East. In 2007 it acquired Godiva, a premium chocolate company with outlets in Asia, Canada, Europe and the USA. The company is the largest in its sector in Turkey and it is expected to grow its international revenues, currently 20 per cent, rapidly over the next few years.

# Developing a strategy for a global challenger from an emerging market

You are required to select one of the companies listed, all of whom come from emerging markets and are embarking on global expansion. Your brief is to develop an outline global marketing strategy to enable it to challenge the existing competitors in the market.

You should prepare a report of approximately 3500 words.

## The task

1 Critically and briefly evaluate the trends in the international market sector in which the company operates.

2 Against the background of your answer to Question 1, comment on how well your chosen firm is placed to develop globally.

3 Advise the company on how to develop a sustainable long-term global marketing strategy.

The report should include the following sections:

### Section 1

■ Trends in the environment and market for the sector.

■ The market structure for the sector, including the geographic spread of products, customer segmentation and competitive positioning of key global players.

### Section 2

■ Summary of product and market focus, including reasons for the company's domestic, regional and international success to date.

■ Basis of current competitive advantage.

■ The strategic marketing challenges it is likely to face as it aims to improve its international competitive position.

### Section 3

■ Recommendations on how to build sustainable competitive advantage in the future.

■ Implementation actions that will be critical in building competitive advantage.

## Useful websites

Concha y Toro: www.conchaytoro.com

Marcopolo www.marcopolo.com

Etisalat www.etisalat.ae

Jollibee: www.jollibee.com.ph

Aspen Pharmacare www.aspenpharma.com

Embraer www.embraer.com

Tencent: www.tencent.com

Infosys www.infosys.com

EuroChem: www.eurochemgroup.com

Yildiz: https://english.yildizholding.com.tr

www.businessweek.com

www.telegraph.co.uk

www.oecd.org/statistics

www.ft.com/markets/emerging

www.businessmonitor.com/risk

## Getting started

In this section the Directed Study focuses on the companies from emerging markets that are developing global competitive positions. You should use the information outlined above to obtain an understanding of who the companies are, where they come from and why they may be interesting to examine, as well as for general background information. It is important of course to use the information to decide which company you are going to use as a basis for this learning activity. To complete the learning activity, however, you will need to access a range of research material from libraries and web-based sources as well as perhaps external sources of information.

In Task 1 we build on the skills developed in DSA 1. However, in this task, it is important to pay particular attention to the key trends affecting the development of the company you have chosen, their competitive positioning and how the trends in the market are impacting on the way the global market is structured.

In considering Task 2, you will need to carry out some research to understand the company's background, its activities and progress to date. You will also need to gain an understanding of the competition and the market environment.

Given that your company may be relatively unknown, you should not expect to obtain very detailed information on the company. You should not try to carry out a critical evaluation of its strategy.

You are, however, required to demonstrate your understanding of the global challenges (threats and opportunities) that a firm from an emerging market faces, and you are encouraged to be creative in your response to the questions asked.

The starting point for Task 3 is articulating an overall vision and setting appropriate corporate objectives for the firm in terms of developing globally. The global marketing strategy that is developed should be based on a relevant response to the analysis you have developed in answering questions 1 and 2. Against the background of the firm's capabilities, existing and potential future competition, the firm should consider the strategic options it has and develop a positioning statement. This will ensure the firm can build a global competitive position in which its products and services are clearly differentiated from the competition.

Key decisions in the strategy development will relate to the degree to which the firm wishes, and is able, to standardize its product and service offerings or needs to adapt them to the requirements of the local markets. Market entry methods need to be selected if it is to enter new markets. The products and services that will be in the portfolio need to be chosen. You also need to consider how the recommendations made contribute to the development of a long-term global competitive advantage across the region and the implications your recommendations have for resource allocation and portfolio management for the specified company. In summary, in completing the task, you need to ensure you consider the key factors listed in the key pointers below.

# Key pointers for Directed Study Activity 2

## Task 1

- The key international trends impacting on the development of the market.
- An evaluation of how the global market is structured/segmented.
- The competitive positioning of the key global players.
- The ability to analyze and synthesize material from a variety of sources.
- Relevance and coherence of analysis.

## Task 2

- Assessment of the current competitiveness of the specified company.
- Identification of the key strategic marketing issues the company needs to address to compete effectively in the global market.

## Task 3

- Clearly stated recommendations.
- Ability to contextualize.
- Clear and logical link between analysis and response.
- Innovation and creativity in your response.
- Coherence and justification of your recommendations.
- Appreciation of the contribution to a long-term global competitive advantage.

# The way forward

The task in this activity shows how the diversity encountered in developing a global marketing strategy makes it a difficult activity to carry out satisfactorily. After studying Part III of the text, you may wish to revisit the solutions you have recommended in this activity and consider how your recommendations could be successfully implemented.

In doing so you may wish to consider such aspects as:

- What is an appropriate organization management structure for delivering your strategy?
- How can you ensure a systematic planning system throughout the globe that will enable the company to satisfactorily implement the strategy, organize the diverse operations and ensure the managers around the globe respond to the challenges you have identified?

All of this is hard to achieve in a global marketing strategy. For senior managers, the problem is how to maintain cohesion between all staff in order to ensure uniform standards, a coherent worldwide strategy, retain a unique vision and purpose and yet at the same time create an operation which has empathy with consumers in each host country.

For most firms the international planning process is concerned with managing a number of tensions and ambiguities. It is how you would resolve such tensions that you may wish to consider on completion of Part III. There is a need to adopt a regular, thorough and systematic sequence, but at the same time provide the flexibility which allows more junior managers to realize opportunities and address problems when and where they occur. While detailed analysis is necessary to fully appreciate the complexities of a situation at the host country level, there is also a need for a clear uncluttered vision, shared by all staff, of where the company intends to go.

# References

Aguiar, M., Bradtke, T., Erica Carlisle, D. Khanna, D. Lee, Michael, D.C., Nettesheim, C., Pai-Panandiker, R. and Ullrich, P. (2014) *Meet the 2014 BCG Global Challengers*. 10 September. Available from www.bcgperspectives.com/content/articles/globalization_growth_meet_2014_global_challengers/ (accessed 22 September 2015).

## AIMS AND OBJECTIVES

Having defined the international marketing strategy and determined the market entry method and product policy in Part II, we now turn to implementation. The aim of Part III of *International Marketing Strategy* is to examine the implementation issues and determine the activities that will ensure the strategies are competitive and sustainable, and the products and services are effective in meeting the needs of the customers. While we address the elements of the marketing mix in turn, throughout the section we emphasize the need to integrate the various elements of marketing activity, as they are mutually reinforcing. Where possible, many firms seek to standardize their marketing activities but recognize too that they need to be adapted to the needs of the specific markets in which they are operating. In this respect, market entry and product and service management are also considerations in both strategic development and implementation.

The first chapter in Part III, Chapter 9, is a broad examination of the importance of integrating communications. International communications is not only concerned with the promotion of products and services and differentiating them from those of competitors. It is also about achieving effective communications internally, establishing a corporate identity that is understood worldwide and building long-term relationships with customers.

In Chapter 10, we turn to the more operational aspects of the marketing mix, involving the distribution of goods and services that make up a significant proportion of costs and contribute to customer satisfaction. This includes the different retailing infrastructures around the globe and the challenges of physically distributing products.

For most firms pricing is a complex area, especially so when pricing across international markets. Firms face currency risks, transaction risks and the risks of not being paid at all. In Chapter 11 we examine the problems companies face when pricing across foreign markets. We also look at some of the tools and techniques used by companies to combat these problems.

Finally, in Chapter 12, we explore the increasing role technology plays in providing a source of growth and enabling managers to implement their international marketing strategy efficiently and effectively. Technology is expected to provide the solution for many global sustainability problems. We discuss corporate social responsibility in this chapter too.

# CHAPTER 9

# INTERNATIONAL COMMUNICATIONS

## LEARNING OBJECTIVES

After reading this chapter you should be able to:

- Appreciate the nature and role of communications in implementing international marketing strategies

- Understand the challenges faced in the successful management and effective integration of international marketing communications

- Be able to explain the use of the elements of an international communications strategy, including corporate identity, products and services promotion, and the development of relationships with customers

- Identify the use and the limitations of the communications tools in international marketing

- Recognize the value of integrating the communications to meet the requirements of different audiences offline and online

## INTRODUCTION

The geographical and cultural separation of a company from its marketplaces causes great difficulty in communicating effectively with its stakeholders. In this chapter we take a broad view of communications and include the traditional promotional mix of personal selling, advertising, sponsorship, sales and public relations. We also look at other methods of communications which have the objective of developing better and more personalized relationships with global customers, often using online media. In our discussions we acknowledge the fact that the target audience extends beyond existing and potential customers and includes other stakeholder groups that have a potential impact on the global development of firms and their international reputation.

In doing this, the development of internal relationships between staff from different strategic business units within the global organization and with close business partners is vital in influencing overall performance. Some remote strategic business units often appear to have a closer relationship with their customers and competition than they have with the parent organization. Ensuring good communications seems to be particularly important as firms embark on joint ventures and strategic alliances.

Building a convincing value proposition for stakeholders and achieving cost-effectiveness requires the integration of marketing communications and the distribution channel. Success in this depends upon building good relationships with all of these interested parties.

# The role of marketing communications

Marketing communications are concerned with presenting and exchanging information with various stakeholders, both individuals and organizations, to achieve specific results. This means not only that the information must be understood accurately but that, often, elements of persuasion are also required. In a domestic environment this process is difficult enough. But the management of both offline and online international marketing communications is made particularly challenging by a number of factors. These include the complexity of different market conditions, differences in media availability, languages, cultural sensitivities, regulations controlling advertising and sales promotions, and the challenge of providing adequate resourcing levels.

A variety of approaches have been taken to define and describe the marketing mix area, which is concerned with persuasive communications. Some writers refer to the communications mix, others to the promotional mix and others, for example Kotler and Armstrong (2014), use the two terms interchangeably to mean the same thing. Communications, embracing as it does the ideas of conveying information, is the most helpful term and implies the need for a two-way process in international marketing and is at the core of digital media. It also includes internal communications between the organization's staff, especially as organizations become larger, more diverse and complex. In addition, 'internal staff' might include collaborative partners that add value to the organization's offer and are part of the supply chain. Some online organizations encourage greater involvement of customers in the business, and these situations redraw the boundaries between internal and external staff.

Figure 9.1 shows the external and internal marketing communication flows and emphasizes the need to consider three dimensions: external, internal and interactive or relationship marketing.

## Internal marketing

For a large diverse multinational firm, it is a key task to ensure that all staff employed in its business units around the world are aware of the strategies, tactics, priorities and procedures to achieve the firm's mission and objectives. Increasingly, organizations form closer collaborations with supply chain and distribution channel members, franchisees, joint venture and strategic alliance partners, all of whom participate

**FIGURE 9.1** External, internal and interactive or relationship marketing

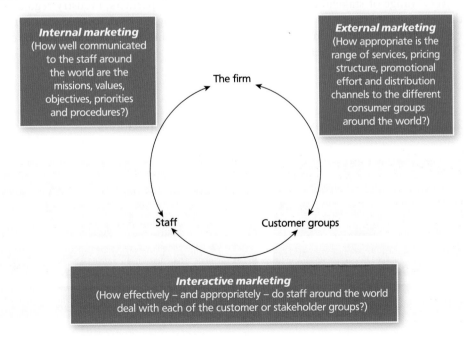

collectively in marketing networks. Organizations are dependent on staff in the extended organization working to a common set of objectives. They need to be informed about the appropriate marketing strategies.

Staff in remote locations are often overlooked in communications. They may receive messages that become unclear as they cross cultural and language boundaries, in the same way that external audiences may misunderstand the firm's external communications. Therefore, internal communication is vital with employees in locations overseas or in remote locations. This is so that they understand the brand, regularly receive helpful information about their brand's strategy, as well as be reminded of the organization's standards and values.

## Interactive marketing

As many customers of MNEs are MNEs themselves, it is essential for staff around the world to deliver consistent service. This includes service delivery staff, call centre operators, service engineers and salespeople in each location. Staff are trained in how to communicate with stakeholders in a consistent way, take appropriate decisions that fit with the strategy and deliver a standardized service. This ensures that the reputation of the organization is enhanced.

Consistent and effective two-way interactive communication is at the heart of online marketing businesses, where the Internet provides the underpinning link between the staff undertaking the various business functions and their customers. As we discuss later, it is this process that creates the nature of the relationship that online businesses strive to build and maintain.

## External marketing

The traditional role of international marketing communications is largely concerned with providing a mechanism by which the features and benefits of the product or service can be promoted as cost-effectively as possible to existing and potential customers in different countries. Details of the features and benefits are communicated through the promotion mix. This includes online and offline communications, personal selling, advertising, sales promotion and public relations, with the ultimate purpose of persuading customers to buy specific products and services. International marketing communications, however, have now become much more important within the marketing mix. The purposes for which marketing communications might be used externally in international markets are now more diverse. They include the need to communicate with a more diverse range of stakeholders, including supply chain partners, industry regulators, pressure groups and the community in general. They also need to build higher levels of customer service through interactive or relationship marketing. International marketing communications could now be considered to include the four distinct strategic elements shown in Figure 9.2.

**FIGURE 9.2**   The dimensions of external marketing communications

## Communicating product and service differentiation

As we discussed in Chapters 6 and 8, increased competition and the maturation of markets have led to many firms offering largely similar core product and service specifications. This means that in addition to its traditional role of promoting products and services, international marketing communications is increasingly used to provide the firm with an important source of differentiation. This can be by providing customers with an easily recognizable and distinctive brand image, or by explaining the unique positioning of the product.

Online and mobile communications have contributed to the vast increase in the range and volume of communications to which consumers are exposed as they go about their day-to-day lives. And, with the communication messages being delivered across multiple platforms 24/7, making one product or service distinctive becomes an ever-increasing challenge. There are a wide variety of promotional tools that might be used to persuade customers to buy the firm's products and services. Newer information and communications technologies are increasing this choice all the time. The challenge for the firm is to use these tools as cost-effectively as possible to reach out to consumers – wherever they are in the world.

## Communicating the corporate identity to international stakeholders

As stakeholders in general have become more aware of how they are affected by international organizations – both good and bad – companies have found it necessary to justify their international activities by constantly and more widely communicating their core values and standards to their internal and external audience. This is essential to demonstrate their responsibility to shareholders, trustworthiness to customers and care and concern for the local community, environment and local employees. The corporate image or logo is the most visible part of the identity and, in some firms, is the only standardized element of the marketing mix, because it constantly reminds stakeholders of the organization's reputation. The corporate identity of the firm should be deeper and more pervasive and reflected in a clear and distinctive message supported by appropriate and proactive public relations activity. Illustration 9.1 shows how a brand can improve its brand image and sales by understanding consumer behaviour.

More intense global competition has provided consumers with greater choice of products and services which they perceive to be capable of satisfying their needs and providing new experiences. Customers also feel that there is less risk of dissatisfaction in switching to alternative products and services, and so are becoming less likely to stay loyal to one supplier or brand.

With the increasing cost of marketing communications and the need to reach an ever wider international audience, organizations are becoming much more aware of the high costs of winning new customers and the relatively lower costs of retaining existing customers. Attention has been drawn to how much a single customer of one product might purchase over his or her lifetime. Readers might like to calculate how much they buy from a food retailer, car manufacturer or a travel company if they stay loyal to that supplier for 5, 10 or 20 years. Food retailers offer incentives for customer loyalty, such as bonus cards and money-off vouchers for other products and services they offer, such as petrol and insurance services. They routinely communicate with consumers using direct mail, email, tweets and online banner advertisements to inform them of new product offers.

The concept of **relationship marketing** has taken on greater significance with e-commerce where communications, promotion and delivery of services have been integrated with **customer relationship management** (CRM) systems. More recently, CRM has also been integrated with **social customer relationship management (SCRM)** to enable firms to communicate in a much more intelligent, efficient and effective way. They base their messages on a better knowledge of the characteristics and responses of their existing and potential customers, and a better understanding of what they might wish to hear. In this way firms are able to be sensitive to different cultures and environmental contexts and develop better relationships with their customers and other influential stakeholders, irrespective of their location in the world. It is useful to reflect on the key characteristics of the Internet communication, see Table 9.1. The key drivers for communicating via the Internet are similar to the general communication strategies shown in more detail later in this chapter. Social media marketing communications actively encourage stakeholders (including consumers and employees) to respond, comment upon and engage directly with the communication message.

Table 9.1   Drivers for online communications

| To increase brand equity |
| To increase brand awareness |
| To improve brand perception |
| To engage with key influencers |
| To reach all stakeholders |
| To create a buzz online |
| To encourage word-of-mouth recommendations |
| To increase customer satisfaction |
| To drive traffic to sales platforms, e.g. website |
| To generate leads |
| To increase sales |
| To create brand loyalty |
| To co-create new product ideas |

# The fundamental challenges for international marketing communications

All forms of international marketing communication have a fundamental purpose, which is to ensure that the intended messages (those which are part of the firm's international marketing strategy) are conveyed accurately between the sender and the receiver. Also, that the impact of unintentional messages (those which are likely to have an adverse effect on the firm's market performance and reputation) are kept to a minimum. The communications process should be two-way. The sender should always make provision for feedback to ensure that the receiver has understood the message as it was intended and has responded positively to it, as Figure 9.3 shows.

FIGURE 9.3   Model of communication

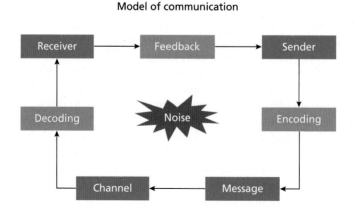

Model of communication

## ILLUSTRATION 9.1

# Weetabix: have you found yours?

Weetabix and its slogan 'Have you had your Weetabix?' were struggling in the cereal market. Hypermarkets, supermarkets and local stores have an eye-watering number of cereals on display. And Weetabix did not know what 'it' was that made consumers choose Weetabix instead of all the other cereals. So, Weetabix commissioned research to find out what 'it' was.

Consumers visit retail outlets and shop for their favourite food and drinks. However, consumers' habits change on a regular basis. Without exploring consumer behaviour, some food and drink brands find their sales go down and competitors' brands increase. This was happening to Weetabix and it took charge to try to reverse this trend. It asked a research company to help it understand the following four challenges:

1 Understand the cereal category consumer.

2 Establish what influences cereal consumers to choose one cereal brand over another.

3 Improve the cereal category consumer experience.

4 Present ways in which Weetabix brands could improve sales.

To do this, qualitative and quantitative research was completed. State-of-the-art cameras were installed in supermarkets, with the cameras directed at the shelves selling cereal. They recorded data of how the consumers behaved, which cereal boxes they picked up, promotions read and how long they spent in the cereal aisles. The research company filmed consumers for 72 hours. In addition to the filmed data, fieldworkers were inside the supermarkets and observed shoppers in the cereal aisles, recording even more detailed behaviour patterns in addition to the behaviours being filmed by the cameras.

In the main, the cameras and fieldworkers wanted to establish dwell time (how long consumers took to make their decision on which cereal to buy) and reoccurring behaviours, such as consumers knowing where their favourite box of cereal was located and thus did not look at any other brands. They also looked at consumers who moved around trying to find different brands, different pack sizes or special offers and those who only shopped for premium brands.

Some consumers were also asked to wear eye-tracking glasses. The eye-tracking glasses recorded everything the consumer saw and how they moved around the cereal aisles. Again, this was measuring dwell time and which brands of cereal were viewed more often than others. In addition, consumers who wore eye-tracking glasses were interviewed to ascertain why they behaved in the way that they did. To add to the data, surveys were completed.

Findings from the data revealed that:

1 Weetabix had too many different types of on-pack promotions. This made it difficult and confusing for busy consumers to know which offer was best for them. The solution was to keep promotional offers to a minimum and help consumers further by keeping similar offers in the same place and associate the offer with a specific coloured self-edge label. For example, keep all '3 for £3' offers together with a yellow shelf-edge label and all '4 for the price of 3' offers together with a blue shelf-edge label.

2 Weetabix had too many on-pack designs. The solution was to provide all packaging and point-of-sale labels with the same logo. For example, its general Weetabix range now has a big corner-to-corner Weetabix logo. And its Alpen logo became bigger, brighter and had a clearer, bolder picture of the Swiss mountains.

## Questions

1 How did the research company fulfil the four challenges?

2 How do you think the consumer will benefit from the solutions?

In practice this apparently simple process poses considerable challenges for firms trying to manage their international marketing communications. This is often discussed in the business press, which contains many serious but frequently amusing anecdotes about the failed attempts of major firms to communicate in international markets. Mistakes in the use of language, particularly using messages which do not translate or are mistranslated, are a particular problem. More serious is a lack of sensitivity to different cultures among international communicators. Management Challenge 9.1 also shows how product advertising can meet customer needs but can be seen as unethical and controversial, including being seen as racist.

Many of the failures of communications are unintentional, of course. Following negotiations with the Council on America–Islamic Relations, Nike had to scrap almost 40 000 pairs of sports shoes because the flame design which was used bore a resemblance to the Arabic for Allah. Two years earlier Nike was forced to withdraw a billboard showing a basketball player above the caption 'They Called Him Allah' when it caused an outcry among Muslims.

## MANAGEMENT CHALLENGE 9.1

## Dove apologizes for an advertisement considered to be racist

Unilever has a range of sub-brands within its skin care and cosmetic range. Ponds is one of its international brands. On Asian Facebook it recently promoted a soap called White Beauty. The strap line for White Beauty is 'Dark Out, White In'. The special feature of Ponds' face wash soap is that it whitens skin. Facebook viewers were asked to click LIKE for fairer skin (there is a need for products like this as skin whiteners account for 46 per cent of total facial care retail sales, according to Mintel). Despite this, care must be taken when advertising such products. A make-up artist named Naomi Blake responded to a Dove soap Facebook advertisement saying it was racist. The images in the advertisement presented a black woman who took off her T-shirt to reveal an Asian woman, who took off her T-shirt to reveal a white woman. A Dove body wash bottle was shown throughout the advertisement. Many consumers on social media agreed it was racist, some saying it depicted the idea that black women were dirty and using the Dove body wash would make a black woman clean and white. Others said they would boycott Dove products. Within hours Dove advised via Facebook that it deeply regretted the advertising campaign for Dove body wash, stating that it was sincerely sorry it had caused offence and did not condone any activity that shows insulting imagery. Dove also promised to assess its processes to ensure it did not make the same mistake again. On Facebook over 12 000 were 'talking about this'. Dove removed the advertisement.

### Question

1 What damage can advertisements like this have on a brand such as Unilever?

**Reference:** The Conversation (2017) http://theconversation.com/dove-real-beauty-and-the-racist-history-of-skin-whitening-85446 (accessed 5 June 2018); Mintel (2015) cited in Cosmetics Design-Asia (2016) Skin whitening in India gathers pace. Available from www.cosmeticsdesign-asia.com/Article/2016/10/11/Skin-whitening-in-India-grows (accessed 5 June 2018).

Besides the often highly visible failures which make firms appear to be incompetent and insensitive, there are many examples of wasted effort and resources which are not so widely publicized. There are a number of reasons for international marketing communications' failure, including:

- Inconsistency in the messages conveyed to customers by staff at different levels and from different countries and cultures.
- Different styles of presentation of corporate identity, brand and product image from different departments and country business units which can leave customers confused.
- A lack of coordination of messages, such as press releases, advertising campaigns and changes in product specification or pricing across the various country markets.

- Failure to appreciate the differences in the fields of perception (the way the message is understood) of the sender and receiver. The field of perception tends to be affected significantly by the self-reference criteria of both parties. This is, perhaps, where the greatest problems arise because, as we have already discussed, avoiding this requires knowledge of different market environments, cultural empathy and the willingness to adapt the communications programmes and processes to local requirements.

This last area is influenced by knowledge, attitudes and empathy. The other three areas of potential communications failure are concerned with the effectiveness of the firm's strategy and planning and the degree to which the staff within the organization understand and are involved in the communications planning process. It is almost inevitable that some communication failures occur from time to time. But it is vital that firms learn from their mistakes.

While it can be argued that the majority of these failures are ultimately within the control of the company, a number of situations arise where the firm's communications can be affected by factors which are outside its control or are extremely difficult to control. Examples of these are situations where:

- *Counterfeiting or other infringements* of patents or copyright take place (see discussion in Chapter 8). Not only does the firm lose revenue but it may also suffer damage to its image if consumers believe the low-quality goods supplied by the counterfeiter are genuine. Even if the customer knows the product is counterfeit, the brand name might still be subconsciously associated with a poorly performing product.

- *Parallel importing* communicates contradictory messages that do not reflect the image of the brand and thus confuse consumers (discussed in greater detail in Chapter 11). This can be particularly problematic if the parallel importer seriously undercuts the prices charged by the official channel, leading customers to feel they have been 'ripped off'.

- *Competitors, governments or pressure groups* attack the standards and values of the MNE by alleging, fairly or unfairly, bad business practice. Despite their huge resources, some of the largest firms are not very effective in responding to allegations from relatively less powerful stakeholders. Companies such as Shell, Coca-Cola, KFC and McDonald's have suffered following criticism of their lack of concern for the environment or animal rights. Stakeholders are also powerful enough in some cases to change government policy. China is known for a history of animal issues, particularly testing drugs and cosmetics on animals. Until recently all cosmetics had to be tested on animals – testing on animals is the law in China to avoid products being launched that irritate and/or cause damage to human beings. The *Be Cruelty-Free China* campaign, launched by Humane Society International, has held many events, conferences and demonstrations with the sole purpose of changing the law. Now cosmetics can be tested for skin and eye-irritation using non-animal testing mechanisms. Consumers, as stakeholders, were successful in their battle.

Customers increasingly believe reviews posted on websites rather than more rigorous and independent assessments, perhaps not realizing how much these informal reviews can be manipulated. The most significant challenge is that anyone can now comment on a firm's product and service through social media. This is increasingly at the expense of formal communications. The firm has less control or even influence over the identity, image and reputation created in the media.

## *International marketing communications, standardization and adaptation*

The most obvious tactic for reducing instances of international communications failure might appear to be to adopt a strict policy of standardization in the implementation of communications plans. Firms adopt this principle, for example, in their use of corporate identity and global advertising campaigns. However, International communications should be adapted to local market needs. This demonstrates cultural sensitivity and empathy with a wide range of international customers *and* avoids the type of mistakes referred to earlier.

## Towards standardization

The drivers for standardization of international marketing communications come first from the organization's desire to improve efficiency. Cost-saving activities in marketing communications include benefits from economies of scale. Examples include in advertising creative work, media buying, making better use of staff time and from the experience effect. Efficiencies are achieved through replicating successful marketing communications programmes and processes in different countries.

Customers believe that they gain additional benefit and value from a consistent and widely recognized brand image that reflects their own self-image. For example, teenagers (as well as rather more elderly sports enthusiasts too) gain peer recognition, credibility and prestige from wearing branded sportswear which has strong associations with international sports stars. A company may use a top international business consultancy or advertising agency with a prestigious image just as much. This is because the association is perceived positively by the company's suppliers and customers rather than for the cost-effectiveness of the work that is carried out.

Consistency in the corporate identity and branding reinforces awareness in stakeholders' minds. It also provides the familiarity with the company which leads to a feeling of confidence, trust and loyalty. For example, it may be reassuring for a visitor to see the familiar logo and appearance of a fast food outlet, hotel chain or bank in a foreign country that they are visiting.

Over the years changes have led to greater prosperity. Greater buying power – at least for some people – has resulted in greater acceptance of imported products. Consumers and B2B customers often prefer internationally available products with which they have become familiar through increased travel, Internet, radio and television communications and the written media. Satellite and cable television have created worldwide customer segments for many more globally standardized products and services.

The Internet allows customers to access products from organizations from very distant locations. It allows specialist suppliers to make their standard products and services globally available to customers. It enables smaller companies to compete essentially on equal terms with their much larger competitors, so 'punching above their weight'. Of course, companies that only communicate using the Internet are limiting their customer base to those customer segments that can access the Internet or buy online.

At an operational level, advertising standardization is possible when:

- Visual messages form the main content of the advertisement.
- Well-known international film stars, popular celebrities and sports personalities are featured.
- Music is an important part of the communication.
- Well-known symbols and trademarks are featured. For example, in China, symbols used in advertisements include dragons and ancient manuscripts, and traditional or female-related images such as flowers to symbolize fertility and harmony with nature. The Grand Canyon in the USA can be used to symbolize certain types of outdoor US values.

Advertisements do not travel well to other countries:

- When the use of spoken and written language forms an important part of the communication.
- If humour is used – humour is often *very* specific to certain cultures.
- If personalities are used who are well known in one country but are not known internationally.
- If campaigns are used that rely on specific knowledge of previous advertising.

## Towards adaptation

The principal drivers of international marketing, communications adaptation, are the cultural differences that must be managed when communicating with customers in different countries. As we have already seen in this text, there are some fundamental differences in the ways that consumers from different cultures respond to different communication approaches. More specifically, however, in a comparison between the US and Chinese responses to advertising, Zhang and Neelankavil (1997) observe that, overall, US subjects preferred the individualistic appeal (self-orientation, self-sufficiency and control, the pursuit of individual gains) whereas Chinese subjects favoured the collective appeal (subordination of personal interests to the goals of the group, with emphasis on sharing, cooperation and harmony, and a concern for the group's welfare).

Koptseva and Reznikova (2017) investigated Chinese advertisements to see how the country was represented through their reflection of Chinese society. They concluded that Chinese advertisements show not only local and traditional culture but also global culture. The advertisements often feature children and youth to demonstrate their future is essential. They also include depictions of 'the Dream', including a rich culture, healthy environment, collectivists' foundations and equal standards in both rural or urban areas. Nonetheless, international organizations need to recognize that despite globalization, advertisements still depict traditional values and culture. However, as shown in Chapter 7, within countries there is a convergence across cultures and moves towards standardization.

Advertisers believe that advertising is most effective when it is relevant to the target audience. One area where there are significant differences is in the portrayal of women in advertising. An article in *Campaign* magazine (Kemp 2017) referred to the following instances of gender stereotyping:

- Depicting family members creating a mess while a woman has sole responsibility for cleaning it up.
- Suggesting a specific activity is inappropriate for boys because it is stereotypically associated with girls, or vice-versa.
- Featuring a man trying and failing to undertake simple parental or household tasks.

More research is being done on gender stereotyping in advertising. In the meantime, UK-based brands and advertisers working in other countries are pulling away from using stereotypical characters. Social media posts from frustrated and annoyed consumers soon advise companies when they get it wrong. For example, a Billabong outdoor clothing advertisement that drove consumers to their website's shopping portal created a frenzy. There were two images on the landing page of the US website. The first showed a male surfer spectacularly riding a wave. The second showed the lower torso and legs of a woman, dressed in a bikini, sunbathing. In the Czech Republic, Aurosa, a beer company, showed an image of a beer bottle in a bed of white roses. The beer bottle was pink and the strapline was 'The first beer for women. A representation of a woman's strength and a girl's tenderness'. After the social media outcry at these advertisements, Billabong changed the advert, although some still criticized it as it again displayed a bikini-clad woman, but this time on a surf board. Aurosa did not change its advertisement.

In research carried out by Siu and Au (1997) in China and Singapore, they found that sex-role stereotyping was more apparent in China. Women were depicted as product users and men as having product authority. In Singapore women generally appeared as the spokesperson for the product, to have product authority and be the providers of help and advice. Positive stereotypes of women are also being shown in Indian newspapers and magazines.

Kataria's (2014) study shows that the historical portrayal of women in Asia as weak and powerless is changing. Advertisements show women to be assertive and financially independent, which in turn shows the different roles that Asian women now engage in.

There are many local reasons why firms may need to adapt their communications strategy. Many companies have to change their brand names because of different meanings when they move to new markets. The New Zealand Dairy Board, a large exporter of dairy foods, uses the brand name Fern for its butter in Malaysia, although Anchor is the flagship brand well known in western Europe. In Malaysia, Anchor is a widely advertised local beer. Malaysian housewives are unlikely to buy dairy products for their children which they would subconsciously associate with alcohol.

When Johnson & Johnson entered the Hong Kong market they used the name *zhuang-cheng* which means 'an official or lord during feudal times'. This upper-class association was seen as inappropriate for China. The more upbeat modern tone of *qiang-sheng*, meaning 'active life', was used instead, to better reflect the drive for modernization.

Illustration 9.2 shows the importance of regulations regarding advertising to ensure government and advertising guidelines are adhered to.

Firms use a variety of ways of becoming more sensitive to cultural differences. Unilever has set up innovation centres in Asia in order to bring together research, production and marketing staff to speed up development of international brands which have a local appeal. In Bangkok there are innovation centres responsible

## ILLUSTRATION 9.2

# Advertising regulations around the world

Many government and advertising regulators/associations provide regulations for brands to adhere to when advertising in new countries. The regulations are put in place so that advertisements will not offend or insult their citizens. Italy has introduced Article 10 of the Code of Marketing Communication Self-Regulation. The regulations advise that advertisements should avoid discrimination of all forms, including gender. Sweden has the Redlamonbudsmannen, which has criteria to ensure advertisements avoid discrimination based on gender, such as portraying men or women in a degrading way.

The USA has a Children's Advertiser Review Unit (CARU) to regulate advertising aimed at or for children. India also has rules that state advertisers should not ridicule anyone, specifically around gender issues. Clearly many regulators are involved, and they have powers to ban advertisements should offences occur.

In Finland, complaints came flooding into the advertising regulatory body regarding an online toy store, which recommended to potential consumers that the dolls were appropriate for girls and the tracks for cars were appropriate for boys. This was considered to be discriminatory and the complaints were upheld: the advertisement was withdrawn. A poster advertisement in Germany received complaints. The strapline was 'Real Men Score'. The product was aftershave. The woman in the advertisement was objectified and sexualized in that the man's eyes were fixated on the sexual region of the woman. It was also deemed to be harmful to men, the advertisement suggesting that only 'real men' would be successful with women. The poster advertisement was withdrawn.

South Africa's advertising regulatory body, the Advertising Standards Authority of South Africa (ASASA), champions guidelines for brands to ensure advertisements consider human dignity and equality. A recent TV car insurance advertisement was withdrawn as it depicted sexist and unfounded claims that men were irresponsible drivers.

## Questions

**1** When entering a new country, what research should brand and creative directors do to ensure adherence to online, social media and traditional advertising regulations?

**2** Could there be a worldwide set of regulations that all countries adhere to? If yes, explain why this could be so. If no, explain why.

for ice cream, laundry detergents and hair care. Asian Delight is a regional brand of ice cream – between the Magnum brand and local brands – and uses English and Thai on its packaging in Thailand. But it uses only English in Malaysia, Singapore and Indonesia. It is sold from Wall's mobile units and cabinets in convenience stores and supermarkets. The flavours have a local appeal and include coconut milk-based ice cream mixed with fruits and vegetables traditionally used in desserts or chewy strings of green flour, black beans and sago.

## International marketing communications strategy

So far in this chapter we have highlighted the need to consider the nature and role of international marketing communications more broadly than was the case in the past. We focused on both internal and external communications and a wider range of communications tools. In thinking about developing strategy there are two significant issues to address. First, there is a need to state clear and precise objectives for the international marketing communications strategy. Second, how might the various communications activities be coordinated to maximize their cost-effectiveness?

The promotional objectives can be categorized as sales-related and brand/product communications-related. Sales can be increased by:

■ Increasing market share at the expense of local and/or international competitors.

■ Identifying new potential customers.

■ Obtaining a specific number of responses to a promotional campaign.

■ Reducing the impact of competitors in the market.

Brand/product communications can be maximized by:

■ Increasing the value of the corporate brand and product image.

■ Helping to establish the position or to reposition the product or brand.

■ Increasing awareness levels especially in new country markets.

■ Changing consumers' perceptions of products, brands or the firm.

These objectives must be set for each country or region in order to fit with the firm's international development ambition.

The options that are available for a generic marketing communications strategy centre on the extent to which a **push** or **pull strategy** could and should be adopted (Figure 9.4). A push strategy means promoting the product or service to retailers and wholesalers in order to force the product or service down the distribution channel. This is done by using promotional methods, such as personal selling, discounts and special deals. A pull strategy means communicating with the final consumer to attract them to the retailer or distributor to purchase the product. In this case mass advertising, sales promotions and point of sales promotions are the most obvious promotional methods. In domestic markets, firms realize the need to have a combination of push and pull strategies, including both encouraging the intermediaries and retailers to stock the products and attracting end users to buy.

In international markets the nature of the market structure that already exists may well affect the degree to which push and pull strategies are used. This includes how well the distribution channel is established, how powerful the retailers or distributors are, how well established the competitors are and whether the firm marketing its products or services wishes or has the power to challenge the existing 'route to market' by setting up a new channel.

Frequently, the international marketing communications strategy of a firm has to be adapted because of the variation in the market structures and distribution channels from country to country (for example, some are highly fragmented, while others are very concentrated). More often than not, however, it is the

**FIGURE 9.4** Push and pull strategies

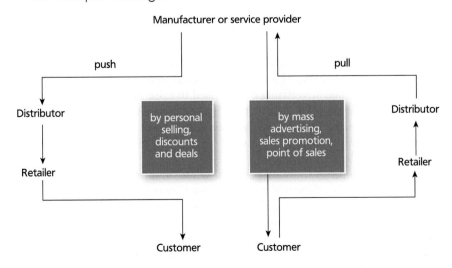

lack of resources, expertise and local knowledge of the firm in the target country markets that limits its communications strategy options. It may well not be able to transfer its successful domestic strategy to the new market. The firm may be forced into making use of and relying heavily upon established intermediaries to do the promotion for them through existing channels. For this reason, it is possible to find organizations that have a pull strategy in their domestic or other established markets and a push strategy in their newer markets.

Having determined the objectives and decided upon the degree to which a push and pull strategy might be used, the dimensions of the international marketing communications implementation strategy can be defined. These are:

- The message to be communicated.
- The target audience to which the message will be directed.
- The media that will be used to carry the message.
- The ways in which the impact of the communications will be measured.

As we said at the start of this chapter, continually evaluating the impact of the communications is vital, not only in improving the effectiveness of the communication but also in assessing the degree to which each of these dimensions can be standardized across international markets.

## Communicating with existing and potential customers

The primary objective of international marketing communications is to persuade customers to buy products and services which will meet their requirements. It is therefore appropriate to consider how international marketing communications are used strategically to influence each of the stages of the buying process and to help customers to complete their purchase.

A number of writers have developed models of buying behaviour which tend to vary according to the context of the study. However, all acknowledge that there are a number of stages in the buying process. A simplified version of these stages (AIDA) includes:

- Awareness of the firm, its products and services and their reputation.
- Interest in the products and services, because they may be suited to the consumers' needs and worthy of consideration for potential purchase.
- Desire to buy the product or service, in preference to that of the competitor, after consumers have become better informed about its performance.
- Action by the customer in overcoming any remaining reservations or barriers and purchasing the product or service.

Illustration 9.3 provides an example of raising awareness for parents whose children play hard and come home in dirty clothes.

Different messages must be prepared. The most appropriate promotional tool must be selected for each part of the buying process in order to persuade customers to move to the next stage. There are significant differences between consumer markets, B2B and institutional market purchasing. For example, in fast-moving consumer goods marketing, advertising can be used to raise awareness, create interest and encourage consumers to purchase. But this can only happen if the messages are sensitive and appealing and the customers have access to the media used for advertising. Other tools such as point of sale promotion can be used to support the strategy, provided it is possible for the firm to maintain some level of control over the displays used by local retailers.

Capital equipment usually depends more on personal selling and providing technical service to a buying committee. This would typically be supported by awareness-raising in the trade press, using PR and corporate advertising. Here the need for monitoring the consistency of approach, and ensuring good communications with the manufacturing operation, must be balanced against the need for sensitivity to the way that business is done in that particular country. Institutional purchasing is often undertaken through competitive tenders which often, directly or indirectly, favour local suppliers.

## ILLUSTRATION 9.3

## Targeting parents and schools: dirt is good – free the kids

Persil is a global brand that parents and guardians use to get rid of dirt from children's clothes. It has been using the 'Dirt is good' strapline for a number of years. Advertisements show children enjoying themselves outside: playing and getting dirty. They might be collecting specimens of soil, putting worms in pockets, getting grass stains from football games and general exercise, and have mud ingrained in their socks, shorts, tops and even hair from their 'adventures' in puddles and streams. Persil suggests that getting dirty is part of playtime. Cynically, it could be thought that Persil is just trying to sell more washing pods, tablets or power. However, its motive for the 'Dirt is good' campaign is genuine. Persil does not want to be known as the biggest and best brand for washing clothes – no. Its goal is to 'help restore childhood across the world. We can drive change by encouraging everyone to prize REAL PLAY as essential for children, to ensure that every child under 13 has the chance to experience the benefits of play, every day'.

Persil's marketing team completed market research with 12 000 parents/guardians around the world to establish how much outdoor play time children have each day. They also investigated how much outdoor time prisoners get each day. It was revealed that on average children have less outdoor time than prisoners. (Prisoners get two hours outdoor time per day.)

As part of its social responsibilities, Persil goes outside its core business to improve the lives of citizens, in this case children. So its advertising message is motivated to get children playing outside, enjoying the outdoors and realizing it really is fun to get dirty.

Additional communication channels also extol the virtues of play. For example, its website provides great ideas about taking children out of the classroom and prioritizing play. The 'Outside Classroom Day' tab (www.outdoorclassroomday.com) provides teachers with excellent resources for encouraging play, learning and discovery. These include 'A nature passport', which is a science lesson outdoors. The children get down on their hands and knees and observe bugs and worms, estimate their size, body shape, where they travel and what they eat. An outdoor music lesson is all about listening to a 'nature orchestra' and composing their own tunes based on the sounds they hear outside.

### Questions

**1** Why was Persil's survey with 12 000 parents/guardians useful?

**2** Why does Persil have a mission statement about play?

**Reference:** Persil (2018) Dirt is good. Available from www.persil.com/uk/dirt-is-good/real-play/why-do-we-think-dirt-is-good.html (accessed 5 June 2018).

## The integration of communications

Stakeholders receive messages, both intended and unintended, from every part of the organization's activities. Davidson (2002) explains that an organization communicates in eight ways:

1  Actions: what it does.

2  Behaviour: how things are done, for example, how the telephone is answered.

3  Face-to-face by management: through talks, visits and meetings it shows what the management thinks is important.

4  Signals, from the organizations' actions, facilities and objects, including executive bonuses, dress, buildings.

5  Product and services, and particularly their quality.

6  Intended communications, such as advertising, which is not always received as the organization expects.

7  Word of mouth, e-word of mouth (all online communications).

8  Comment by other organizations, such as pressure groups, competitors and the media.

The number of communications has increased dramatically, and customers have become more critical and sceptical. So the importance of integrated marketing communications has been emphasized in order to avoid conflicting messages and instead communicate consistent and mutually supporting messages. Fill (2006) points out that traditional mass-communication strategies have given way to more personalized, customer-oriented and technology-driven approaches. This has continued particularly as data can enable firms to communicate through a variety of different approaches, focusing on the individual customer. Kotler *et al.* (2014) say that companies must integrate many communication channels, be they personal selling, social media, TV/press advertising, PR, sales promotion and direct marketing (via mail and/or online websites and social media). They go on to say that the communications need to be interesting and compelling messages that are clear and focused for their target market and remain consistent regarding the organization's brand and values (*ibid.*).

Andrews and Shimp (2018) provide a definition of integrated marketing communications which puts the customer at the centre:

1  Start with the customer or prospect.

2  Use any form of relevant contact and/or touch points, personal and online.

3  Communicate using a single voice, a single message.

4  Build relationships.

5  Affect behaviour.

The emphasis of Andrews and Shimp's approach is on marketing promotion whereas digital media encourages a two-way communications process. Interactivity between the organization and its customer is a key component of integration. Social media touch points are growing in importance. Reputation Institute (2018) states that the key touch points on social media are:

■  Company advertisements on social media

■  Social media postings

■  Expert/CEO/senior management – discussion on websites and blogs

■  User-generated postings about the company

In terms of user-generated postings, organizations need to listen to online conversations to ensure that comments from consumers are positive. If they are not, organizations need to step in quickly and recover the situation so that their brand reputation stays intact.

### The benefits of integration

Individual messages on their own have little overall impact on customers. So it follows that the effect of communications will be significantly greater if the many messages are consistent, uniform and mutually supporting. In this way they build the image of the brand, product and service and reinforce the reputation, standards and values of the organization around the world.

It is easier to justify the cost and control communications activities if they are integrated so that the cumulative effect, rather than individual effect, is assessed. Measurement of individual actions is difficult, given the 'noise' in the environment, and so it is more sensible to measure the effects of the combined actions.

### Integration with the global strategy

Although usually considered to be a part of the marketing mix, in many organizations communications takes on a much more important role. It is essential in explaining the organization's corporate business unit and marketing mix strategies to stakeholders, including shareholders. Global integration is needed so that the consistency of internal and external communications across borders is maintained.

**Business unit integration** At business unit level, managers in charge of communications must work closely with colleagues responsible for development, operations, key account management, sales and customer service centre management. This develops a highly integrated global approach that offers a seamless service to customers.

**Marketing mix integration** Customers continually receive communications from the organization that are the result of marketing mix actions. Every element of the marketing mix communicates with customers.

It is important to remember that non-verbal communications in many markets has a greater impact than verbal communications or written words, especially given the amount of time (milliseconds!) that a customer concentrates on one communication. For example, the colours and styles used in creative packaging or signage work communicate non-verbally with the customers, reinforcing the images and customer perceptions. This differs between cultures, however. Customers can pick up small errors in colour matching and design, so discipline in the use of the corporate identity is essential. In different cultures the significance of colours, symbols and numbers is so great that they alone could deter customers from buying a product.

## Coordination and planning of the international marketing communications strategy

To achieve its objectives, the communications strategy will almost certainly include a variety of promotional tools. The key to success is integrating the various promotion elements in a cost-efficient way and adding value through choosing the communications methods that will have the most impact on the customers. The actual mix chosen will depend upon a number of issues surrounding the context of the purchasing situation, including:

- The market area and industry sector.
- Whether it is consumer, institutional or B2B marketing.
- The customer segment to be targeted.
- The participants in the purchasing process, their requirements and expectations and the best methods to reach and influence them.
- The country or region, the culture, the communications infrastructure and the preferred methods of communicating.
- The resources made available by the organization and the implications for the level of involvement and control it wishes to exert over the communications process.

The value of different promotional methods varies according to the context in which the marketing communications are being used and the degree to which they are integrated within a marketing communications strategy, as shown in Figure 9.5.

The critical issue is the extent to which they must be adapted so that they can be effective in international markets. Management Challenge 9.2 shows how difficult it is for managers to make decisions that require them to go against their instincts and self-reference criteria.

## The marketing communications tools

There are a number of offline and online marketing **communications tools** for the external market and it is to these that we now turn. For convenience we have grouped these tools within broad categories. In practice there is some flexibility in the way the tools are used within a coordinated strategy, but the tools are listed as follows:

- Communicating **product and service differentiation**. This group includes personal selling and word-of-mouth communications, exhibitions and trade fairs, trade missions, advertising and the use of agencies, sales promotion and direct marketing.
- Communicating with a wider range of stakeholders. This includes corporate identity, sponsorship and public relations.

**FIGURE 9.5**   Internal and external international communications programmes

| Marketing programmes influencing communications | International communication aims |
|---|---|
| **Internally focused programmes** | |
| Corporate identity | Consistency in all aspects of company logo, signs and image |
| Internal marketing communications | Reinforce motivation through telling staff what is happening |
| Sales force, dealer and distributor training and development | Training through conferences, manuals and brochures |
| Retailing merchandising | Point of sale persuasion through displays and shelf facings |
| First contact customer service | Welcoming first contact through telephonist and receptionist training |
| After-sales service | Customer retention and satisfaction through staff training and brochures |
| Quality management | Assuring a continuous quality approach in all programmes |
| Brand management | Achieving common brand standards and values |
| **Externally focused programmes (marketing mix)** | |
| Product attributes | Offering innovative, high-quality products |
| Distribution channel | Ensuring easy access to products and frequent customer encounters with the products |
| Price | Messages about quality and status |
| Product/service promotion | Managing customer expectations through the integration of the marketing mix communications |
| People | Using staff–customer interactions to reinforce the aims, standards and values of the firm |
| Customer service process | Providing a satisfactory total experience through the service offer |
| Physical evidence for the service delivery | All contacts with the facilities reinforce the firm's messages |

Online communications are used in all areas of communications, both complementing and replacing offline communications.

## Word-of-mouth and personal selling

**Word-of-mouth**   The role of the consumer must be considered within internal and external communication programmes. Brand and marketing managers are no longer the custodians of the brand and the messages it communicates. Consumers, through user-generated content, can comment freely about the brand, its products and services, and the advertisements or the celebrities chosen to endorse the brand. Consumer-generated content is the online word-of-mouth that organizations need to listen to. They can do this through a variety of social media analytics software. The software tracks and analyzes positive and negative word-of-mouth comments posted through social media platforms. The examination of the positive and negative comments is called *sentiment analysis*, which provides further guidance to organizations on whether they are satisfying their consumer's needs.

**Personal selling**   For many companies the first proactive communication tool to promote exports is personal selling. Selling is often used to gain the first few orders in a new market. It is also the main component of a push strategy to persuade distribution channel members, such as agents, distributors or retailers, to stock the product. It is expensive, however.

The use of personal selling tends to be limited to situations in which benefits can be derived from two-way information flows, negotiation is required and when the revenue from the sale is sufficiently high to justify the costs. This is typically the case with B2B marketing and in consumer markets where the purchase price and complexity of negotiations justifies the high cost of personal selling. Examples include cars, holidays, homes and consumer durable products. Even here the need for personal selling is being challenged as direct marketing, particularly using the Internet, is now being used routinely to purchase these products.

In countries where labour costs are very low, personal selling is used to a greater extent than in high cost countries. This ranges from street and market trading to quite sophisticated multilevel distribution chains for B2B products. In high labour-cost countries personal selling of low unit cost products is used rarely, except for illegal trading, for example of drugs.

## MANAGEMENT CHALLENGE 9.2

## Self-reference criteria in advertising decisions

Advertising managers who are involved in cross-border campaigns face the problem of self-reference criteria. A European brand manager for Heinz, based in the UK, was responsible for approving advertising campaigns that had been developed by local agencies for the local country subsidiary as part of a pan-European campaign. In Germany the local agency produced a television advertising campaign. The European brand manager, his boss and his boss's boss, all English, turned down the agency's creative work.

The advertisement was meant to be humorous, but they did not find it at all funny. They were concerned that it would devalue the brand and the campaign. The agency insisted that they had tested the ad on consumers and the humour would work in Germany. After various delays the manager had to make the decision whether or not the ad should go ahead on the following Monday. However, it was the weekend and he could not reach his bosses for help with the decision.

The campaign would cost £1 million, which would be lost if it did not go ahead. If the campaign adversely affected the product it would be a greater disaster – his job could be on the line! Against his better judgement, and overcoming his self-reference criteria, he decided the advert should be broadcast. The campaign was a great success!

Western firms also realize that it is important to appreciate the levels of intelligence and sophistication of emerging markets. When Heinz first launched tomato ketchup in Russia they used an existing TV ad from the UK with minor modifications. Now it would be unacceptable as the Russian audience is more sophisticated. Russian actors would be needed on the advertisement. Heinz is particularly sensitive to the need to adapt to local markets and this is part of their strategy.

Consumers are very knowledgeable and well aware when some big brands are behaving in an arrogant manner and telling them what to buy. They can become annoyed when firms insult their intelligence. A number of firms have seen their reputation and share price suffer because of insensitive promotion and PR.

### Question

**1** Should a firm insist on standardization and consistency of its communications approach, and when should they trust partners with local knowledge?

Effective selling in international B2B and consumer markets involves a wide range of tasks and skills, including product and market knowledge, listening and questioning skills. However, it is in the core selling activities of negotiation and persuasion, discussed in Chapter 3, that higher-order expertise is required. It is likely that local people will be more effective than home-based representatives in understanding the subtleties of the negotiation process as they apply within the local business culture. They will have fluent language skills and an intimate knowledge of the culture of the country.

However, negotiation of high-value contracts may well require specialist technical knowledge, an understanding of the processes and systems and strict adherence to the firm's standards and values. For these reasons the company may well prefer to use staff from its head office to ensure that the sales people are well informed about the firm's capabilities and that their activities can be controlled.

This is particularly the case if the opportunities to make a sale are very infrequent (e.g. with capital goods) when high levels of technical skill and an understanding of the company's systems are needed but not easily learnt by new people. For example, Rolls-Royce uses a complete team of UK-based engineers, accountants and sales people to sell aero engines to customers in foreign markets. Some of the team will make frequent visits, others will be based in close online and offline contact with the customer for a period of many months. The sheer complexity of the contracts means that only Rolls-Royce employees could understand the detail sufficiently to handle the negotiations. The high contract price provides sufficient revenue to pay for the costs of the UK-based sales team.

An alternative to employing local or head office sales staff (both have their advantages and disadvantages) is to employ expatriates, staff from the domestic country to work for extended periods in the host country in order to bridge the culture and company standards gap.

In practice the expatriate is likely to experience a culture shock caused by living in a foreign culture where the familiar symbols, cues and everyday reassurances are missing. This can often cause feelings of frustration, stress and anxiety. The expatriate can respond to the situation in one of three ways. At one extreme, adjustment is made to the expatriate culture only. In effect the expatriate adjusts to the way of life of a ready-made cultural island within the host country and makes little attempt to adjust to the host culture. At the other extreme the expatriate completely embraces the host culture and minimizes contact with the expatriate community – and the firm too. Ideally, the expatriate adjusts to both the local culture and the expatriate culture. In this way the expatriate retains the home country and firm's system of values and beliefs, but is considerate and respectful towards the people of his or her host country and to their culture. It is this last option that is usually most beneficial for the firm's sales effort.

Whichever approach to selling is adopted, it is through relevant training that firms aim to manage their sales staff's involvement with the firm and the market, and maintain their enthusiasm for selling. Multinational companies are excellent at ensuring that sales staff are trained in product knowledge, 'soft skills' and cross-cultural understanding (Subramanian 2015). However, Attia *et al.* (2014) state that training sales staff is not universal. They researched Egyptian domestic firms and found that in comparison with international firms, Egyptian companies gave little attention to even basic training on customer relationship management (CRM), supply chain management and 'soft skills'. This may put Egyptian firms at a disadvantage as 'soft skills' such as quality customer service, leadership, decision making and listening are high on the agenda for MNC companies. They see skills such as these, together with positive personality traits, to be essential in the global market.

## Exhibitions, trade fairs and experiential marketing

Exhibitions and trade fairs are an effective way of meeting many existing and potential customers from different countries. The cost of exhibiting at international trade fairs is very high when the cost of the stand, space rental, sales staff time and travelling expenses are taken into account. It is for this reason that the selection of the most appropriate fairs for the industry is critical. Also important are the creative work for the stand, preparation of sales literature and selection of suitable personnel for the stand, bearing in mind the need for cultural and language empathy.

Conferences and conventions are attended by people hoping to network and listen to professionals speaking about their new products, services and research findings, advance their career and in some cases enhance their reputation with their peers (Mair *et al.* 2018; Rogers 2008).

Exhibitors benefit from being at conferences, trade fairs or exhibitions as they can generate high-quality leads, increasing awareness and perception of the corporate brand. Of course, they also benefit by gaining contact with existing and potential customers (Verma 2014). Both exhibitors and delegates also want information regarding the security and safety at the venue, ease of access via efficient and effective transport, good accommodation, dining facilities, shopping and sightseeing opportunities. These attributes encourage more exhibitors and delegates and must also be communicated clearly to further encourage participation at trade fairs and conferences (Whitfield *et al.* 2014). An additional benefit of exhibitions is that they can provide experiential marketing, a rapidly growing communications approach also called customer experience marketing. In this, customers obtain an engaging, entertaining and interactive brand experience. There are of course other ways of providing experiential marketing. For example, Apple operates stores in which customers can try out their products. Harley Davidson provides opportunities for visitors to ride its bikes.

Tommy Hilfiger turned this experience on its head when he installed a booth in his retail stores that enabled customers to don a virtual reality headset to watch his fashion show, as though they were sitting in the front row of the New York Fashion Show! Therefore, experiential marketing is gaining in importance, not just at events and conferences but for all service organizations that want to enhance the consumer's enjoyment and engagement with their product offer.

## Trade missions

Trade missions are organized visits to a country or region by a group of senior business managers from a number of firms, perhaps from the same geographic region or the same industry. They are often subsidized by national or local government. Discussions with potential customers are arranged in advance in the host country.

Trade missions are usually associated with exporting. They may be used to carry out introductory talks with prospective clients or to negotiate a contract. As with trade fairs, good preparation work before the visit is essential to ensure that meetings are arranged with appropriate customers where there is a genuine possibility of business being generated. Usually the home country's local embassy staff will provide support for trade missions. Often, too, depending on the importance of the mission, there will be discussions with the host government, civil servants and politicians about how trade between the two countries can be developed.

## Advertising

Online and offline advertising are usually the most visible forms of communication. They are often considered the most important part of the whole strategy for consumer products in countries with a well-developed media industry. Traditionally, offline advertising has disadvantages because it is essentially a one-way method of communication. In international marketing, for example, it can be difficult to control the reach of TV (the geographic area in which consumers are exposed to the messages and specific customer segments). The objective is to obtain the maximum exposure of the product or brand to the largest possible target audience.

In most B2B markets, advertising tends to be used as a supporting activity, for example, to increase awareness or interest in the company as a whole or in a new concept. In B2B markets the number of important customers is often comparatively small. So it is essential that advertising is precisely targeted, using appropriate specialist trade media.

Together with the increased harmonization of consumer demands for some products and the benefits of standardized products and services to firms, there is a strong move to pan-regional advertising campaigns. Consumers increasingly share common values and characteristics, but there are differences. For example, consumers in developing markets are still developing their habits as consumers.

There are considerable differences in the availability and usefulness of other advertising media such as radio, cinema and posters. These differences make it essential to obtain data about media effectiveness in order to make informed decisions about international media schedules. For instance, in remote regions, exposure to certain media is prevented. This is because of the poor transmission output quality from radio stations, lack of electricity to power TVs or computers, the target audience having insufficient disposable income to afford television or radio, and low adult literacy levels preventing significant numbers of adults from reading printed advertising.

Mass communications are becoming less effective for reaching target segments, particularly in developed countries, because of the increasingly fragmented nature of the national press and television. Many households have access to multiple TV channels, films and TV on-demand, and alternative leisure activities such as gaming and social media. The traditional channels have lost audiences, particularly in the 16–24 age group. This group hardly watches mainstream commercial television stations. Indeed, major changes are taking place online and offline, with many organizations replicating or creating new advertisements to stream on YouTube (see Management Challenge 9.3).

In these situations, it may be necessary to develop a campaign based upon a multitude of individual media activities. But this does mean that the measurement of the cost-effectiveness of the campaign is extremely difficult, given that individual components of the campaign may produce different effects.

Mass marketing is still valuable in emerging markets and to help organizations create a global brand. Increased spending has led to Coca-Cola becoming the best-selling soft drink in China and overtaking Pepsi in a number of central and eastern European republics. Pepsi's response to this has been to embark on diversification by buying a stake in Russia's largest food group, Wimm-Bill-Dann. Conglomerates from emerging countries, such as Hyundai, HTC and Huawei, recognize the value of moving from product orientation to marketing orientation and have built substantial brands through global advertising. However, there is a change in where organizations are choosing to spend their advertising budget. Table 9.2 shows the global advertising spend by medium. In 1996 the total global advertising spend was US$251 995.9 million. This rose to US$535 894.9 in 2016. However, the spend by medium has changed dramatically. The number of newspaper and magazine print advertisements fell by over 50 per cent between 2006 and 2016. The money seems to have shifted to Internet sales, which have grown dramatically, and also mobile advertising, which only started in 2006. Mobile advertising is already showing signs of being a medium that organizations are choosing to place their advertising budget.

Table 9.2 shows the global advertising expenditure from 2007 to 2021.

Table 9.2   Global advertising expenditure 2007–2021 (US$ billion)

| Year | Expenditure |
| --- | --- |
| 2007 | 388 |
| 2008 | 383 |
| 2009 | 345 |
| 2010 | 376 |
| 2011 | 393 |
| 2012 | 412 |
| 2013 | 429 |
| 2014 | 499 |
| 2015 | 466 |
| 2016* | 493 |
| 2017* | 511 |
| 2018* | 533 |
| 2019* | 552 |
| 2020* | 579 |
| 2021* | 600 |

Source: Statista (2018). www.statista.com/statistics/272850/global-advertising-forecast/ (accessed 13 June 2018).

*Forecast

## Television advertising

The main influence on television advertising expenditure is the size of the economy in GDP per capita. But the regulatory environment also affects spending, particularly television which tends to be more closely regulated than other media.

Cable and satellite television have contributed to a proliferation of television channels so that viewers can receive a rapidly increasing number of programmes. This means that there is a greater capacity for television advertising. But, of course, there is greater competition for prime television advertising spots (and much higher costs) if there is likely to be a large audience. Both satellite and cable television have the potential to cross country borders and attract large audiences for programmes of common international interest, for example, major sporting events.

It is not only overt television advertising in large amounts that sells. The prominent placing of products on television shows, or sponsorship of programmes that are likely to be transmitted in other countries, can also become an important part of the advertising campaign. This is particularly so because placements and sponsorship cannot be removed by viewers 'zapping' between channels. More often than not consumers will have at least two 'screens up' at one time while they are watching TV or streaming channels. 'Screens up' devices are mobile smartphones, laptops and tablets where consumers catch up on Facebook, YouTube and Instagram plus emails from work and, of course, downloading films which are then cast directly onto the television screen. At the same time friends and family may be Skyping, Facetiming or WhatsApp videoing. This behaviour shows just how important an integrated marketing communications message is across many social media platforms, in addition to traditional media. An interesting development is shown in Illustration 9.4 which shows how offline and online communications can embed a local message on national television through integrated communication. With a more sceptical and knowledgeable audience, advertisers are adopting different, more inclusive approaches that will certainly win over customers.

## Press advertising

Media availability and effectiveness are particularly important in deciding the nature of campaigns, because they can vary from country to country. The lack of mass-circulation national titles might cause distribution difficulties too, as it is easier to distribute quickly in small compact countries than in much larger ones such as France or Spain. Vast countries like the USA have a regional press. Newer publishing and printing technology has allowed many more local and free newspapers and specialist magazines to be introduced to both consumer and B2B markets. By their very nature they tend to be highly targeted at specific market segments and can be useful to niche marketers. Advertising spend in the printed newspapers in many countries is declining as advertising spend in the printed press has gone down, but is prolific in and around online subscription magazine sites. Sales of mass audience newspapers in many countries are declining as readers turn to the Internet for general and specialist news coverage. For mass marketers the resulting fragmentation of readership means that national campaigns are more difficult to coordinate.

## The use of agencies and consultancies

Most companies in which marketing communications are an important part of the marketing mix use agencies and consultancies. The reasons why this is so can be explained by financial considerations, specialist knowledge, creative input and external perspective.

- *Financial*. Advertising agents that are recognized by the media are eligible for a commission based on booked advertising space. The agency can, therefore, perform the advertising services of creation, media planning and booking more economically than the client.
- Agencies and consultancies can use specialist people and resources, such as a database for media planning, with a number of clients. This helps spread costs for both the agency and client.
- *Specialist knowledge*. By concentrating on one particular area, agencies and consultancies can become experts in specialized techniques, for example international database marketing or training sales people. Client companies might have an infrequent need for these services and so find it more cost-effective to subcontract the work.
- *Creative input*. Creativity is very important in marketing communications. The organization culture of client companies is unlikely to encourage true creativity in external communications. The challenge of new and different projects for different clients contributes to the creativity of agencies.
- *External perspective*. The external view of agencies reduces some of the myopia of the client company. This might be particularly valuable at times of major transition, for example in moving from international marketing towards global marketing.

## ILLUSTRATION 9.4

# Budweiser's integrated marketing communication: thanks to cold and wet football fans

Television viewing figures on the last day of the UK's football leagues (Premiership, Champion's League, Division One and Division Two) are extremely high as football results signify teams that have won their division, been promoted to a higher division or been relegated to a lower division. In 2015, the winner of the Dream Goal was announced on 22 May.

Roll back now to March 2015 when Budweiser launched the Dream Goal #ToTheDream campaign. The integrated marketing campaign started with Budweiser realizing there is a great deal of football talent in the UK. A lot of it happens on a cold and wet Sunday morning in front of between 10 and 50 equally cold and wet but avid fans. Welcome to amateur league football. Budweiser and ABInBev UK Limited set a competition to find the best amateur league football goal. The competition required fans to video their local amateur team's

football game and upload it to Budweiser.co.uk. Calls to football fans came through different media channels. First, the Budweiser.co.uk website, a dedicated Facebook page, Twitter, Google+ and youtube.com/BudweiserDreamGoal. Second, calls to fans were made through press releases where newspapers like the *Daily Mirror* championed the competition.

Talksport (radio) also supported the Budweiser competition both live on air and through their website www.talksport.com/budweiser.

Budweiser then joined forces with two well-known Sky Sports commentators and sports writers – Jamie Rednapp (retired English footballer and Premiership player for Liverpool FC, Tottenham Hotspurs, Southampton and Bournemouth) and Gary Neville (retired England footballer and Premiership player for Manchester United).

The videos from the amateur teams were shown to Jamie Rednapp and Gary Neville and critiqued in front of a studio audience. This event was made into an advertisement and shown regularly on UK television. The advertisements lasted between 60 seconds to 1 minute 30 seconds, making it an expensive advertisement campaign. Neville commented on the organization of the team and how the players knew exactly which positions to be in. Jamie Rednapp discussed the amateur team's performance and how 'big Dad's' attention to the old-fashioned techniques was amazing. The commentators had a lot of fun analyzing the game just as they do on national television for Sky Sports Saturday Night Football and Monday Night Football.

From March to May advertisements for the Dream Goal #ToTheDream campaign took place. All other communication channels were also active in promoting the Dream Goal, recruiting fans to video amateur football goals and of course promoting Budweiser. The Facebook page has 12 million followers, Twitter has 12 000 followers and the YouTube videos have over 300 000 views.

## Questions

**1** How has Budweiser used integrated marketing communications for the Dream Goal campaign?

**2** What benefits have links to celebrities brought to the advertisement?

**3** How could Budweiser engage with consumers?

**4** How could Budweiser use this integrated marketing communications format in different countries?

**Reference:** Budweiser (2015) www.budweiser.co.uk.

The selection of agencies and consultants is an important business decision. If the agency is going to be involved over a long period and be trusted with large expenditures of time and money, the decision process will be significant. A dilemma for global marketers is whether they should select one central agency or many local agencies in their target countries, both of which approaches have advantages and disadvantages.

## Sales promotions

Sales promotions are used as an extra incentive for the purchaser at the point of sale. In some markets there may be no meaningful differences between a number of companies or brands, except for the degree of attractiveness of the sales promotion offer. The customers' perception of the relative value of the alternative promotions depends to a great extent on their cultural values and differences, which lead to certain types of sales promotion being very successful in one country but failing in another.

Legal restrictions also affect the opportunity for firms to standardize sales promotions across country borders. There are limitations on the amount of cash discounts and special sales promotions in some countries in Europe. Different legal definitions of the rules for lotteries, too, prevent some competition-based promotions being operated across borders.

## Direct marketing

In the past, direct marketing has usually taken the form of direct mail or telephone selling. But in markets with high computer ownership the Internet has taken the lead. The key elements of direct marketing are an accurate up-to-date database, the ability to purge the database of incorrect data and to merge the database with a firm's promotional message. Usually firms subcontract direct marketing to specialist agencies which provide the various services, such as list brokering, purging and merging.

## Communicating with the wider range of stakeholders

At the outset we said that the principal objective of the international marketing communications strategy was to sell products and services. However, customers in a host country are unlikely to even contemplate buying from a foreign firm that is unknown. Worse still, the firm might be perceived to be exploiting its local workers, bribing government officials, showing little regard for environmental protection issues, offering poor or variable product quality or likely to pull out of the country at any moment and thus be unable to fulfil its guarantees and obligations. A foreign firm can build increased loyalty among its customers at the expense of local firms if it is perceived to offer better quality and value for money, to be a more reliable supplier, more caring about the local community and, in some cases, through association, to be respected by world personalities.

Firms need to build their reputation with all their influential stakeholders, pressure groups and the community in general as well as customers. They do this in a number of ways:

- Corporate identity
- Sponsorship
- Public relations and lobbying.

## Corporate identity

Corporate identity is concerned with consistently communicating not just what business the firm is in and what image it wishes to project in the market, but also how it does its business. It must reflect the standards and values it aims to uphold in its dealings with all its stakeholders. Corporate philanthropy is a key factor as Illustration 9.5 shows. But the aims of the organization and recipients of corporate giving may not always coincide. For this reason, there are two distinct elements. For many MNEs the focus is upon the image it wishes to create. This is reinforced by consistency in the way the company name and logo is presented and applied to the vast range of physical outputs and assets of the company. These include signs, staff uniforms, letterheads, visiting cards, gifts, annual reports, packaging specification and promotional literature.

ILLUSTRATION 9.5

# Reputation Institute: which company has the best reputation in the world?

A company's corporate identity is everything. Its reputation enables all stakeholders to understand the values and trustworthiness of that company.

Companies are facing different challenges from those of the late 2000s. Trust in businesses, governments and social media, particularly with the run of fake news stories, is declining. Moreover, employees do not stay loyal to their company and neither do consumers. Loyalty to brands is also declining. This means organizations must try harder to win the hearts and minds of employees, consumers and all other stakeholders. What is more important is that they need to try harder in different ways. Employees, consumers and stakeholders judge companies on their citizenship, morality, ethics and transparency. Now it is expected that companies are first to market with innovative products and services that have a positive effect on society, care about the well-being of their workforce, have an environmental conscience and engage with good causes.

For the third year in a row, Rolex has been judged as the most reputable company in the world by the Global RepTrak 100 produced by the Reputation Institute. Rolex's corporate identity is exceptional. Virginie Chevailler, Head of Public Relations at Rolex, states, 'Continuous innovation, perpetual exploration and lasting excellence are the foundations of our company. We are pleased to be ranked first on the Global RepTrak 100 for the third year in a row. This is hard-earned recognition of our sustainable contribution to society and our commitment to inspire future generations through our products as well as our philanthropic, environmental and sports partnerships'.

Rolex cannot be complacent about its success. In order to remain at the top, it must continue to get its voice heard and champion the excellent things it does. This will ensure its messages rise above the constant barrage of news, advertising and social media rantings. Through social media it is essential that Rolex posts information about its citizenship, showing how it has embraced a modern culture, provides sustainable, high-quality products, shows that it is committed to providing excellent customer service and engages within the community for the greater good of all citizens

## Questions

**1** What could companies such as Rolex do to ensure they are the number one most reputable company for the fourth year?

**2** Suggest three topics that Rolex should post messages about on social media that would enhance its reputation.

**Source:** Reputation Institute (2018) Global RepTrak® www.reputationinstitute.com/ (accessed 5 June 2018).

In principle, while these can all be controlled by the firm, there are many challenges in applying them consistently in all the countries where the firm operates. This is especially so where it develops alliances with partners who might also wish to maintain their corporate identity in joint communications.

Arguably of more importance is the underlying identity of the firm and its beliefs, standards and values, which will show through in everything it does. These may pose more difficulties in the firm's attempts to achieve consistency and a favourable impact throughout the world because of the different cultural values of its staff and stakeholders in different countries.

## Sponsorship and celebrity endorsement

Sponsorship involves a firm (the sponsor) providing finance, resources or other support for an event, activity, firm, person, product or service. In return the sponsor would expect to gain some advantage, such as the exposure of its brand, logo or advertising message. Sponsorship of music, performing arts and sporting events provides opportunities for:

- Brand exposure and publicity.
- Entertaining and rewarding customers and employees.
- Association between brands and events, with the events often reinforcing the brand positioning.
- Improving community relations by supporting community-based projects.
- Creating the opportunity to promote the brands at the event, either through providing free products or gifts such as T-shirts carrying the brand logo.

Expenditure on global sponsorship has expanded rapidly since the late 1990s. It is being used much more for the following reasons:

- Restrictive government policies on tobacco and alcohol advertising make sponsorship the most effective way of communicating the brand imagery to a mass market, for example in Formula 1 car racing.
- The escalating costs of media advertising.
- Increased leisure activities and sporting events.
- The cost-effectiveness of sponsorship of successful events.
- Endorsement of the product or service through association with the event.
- Greater (free) media coverage of sponsored events.
- The reduced efficiencies of traditional media advertising because of clutter and zapping between television programmes, especially during advertising breaks.

Masterson (2005) explains the need to achieve a fit between the sponsor and the activity being sponsored. She also introduces the concept of integrated product relevance and explains the ways in which this can be used to affect the consumers' responses to the sponsor's products, by focusing on function and image similarity.

There has been an increase in the amount of broadcast sponsorship in film, television and radio programmes. This can result in the benefit of the event sponsorship being reduced. For example, Heinz sponsored a Rugby World Cup only to find that Sony sponsored the national commercial television coverage in the UK, resulting in most viewers thinking that Sony had sponsored the whole event.

## Product placement and celebrity endorsement

As many television viewers record programmes and are able to fast-forward through advertising, product placement within the programmes is becoming more attractive. Those films that will gain a global TV audience, such as James Bond, offer the most potential from product placement for global firms.

Sponsorship of individuals such as sports stars and the use of celebrities to endorse brands are very beneficial because of the perceived shared values and image association between the celebrity and the brand. The problem is that individuals can be unpredictable. This can lead to unfortunate and undesirable associations. Celebrities are increasingly advertising their own merchandise on TV shopping channels.

Global brand ambassadors need to be leaders in their field and recognizable by global consumers. As David Beckham came towards the end of his footballing career, he was replaced as the face of Gillette by Tiger Woods, Thierry Henry and Roger Federer, then Denny Hamlin, Ryan Lochte and Kyle Busch. Woods attracted unfavourable media comment because of his behaviour in his private life, which adversely affected his sporting performance. However, as Management Challenge 9.3 shows, Tiger Woods still receives money from big brand names and up and coming brands.

## Public relations

Public relations (PR) is concerned with communicating news stories about the firm, its people, standards and values – particularly its attitude to social responsibility – products and services through the media. It is also concerned with developing relationships, goodwill and mutual understanding between the firm and its stakeholders. The press is always hungry for stories to fill their ever expanding programmes and newspapers, and are grateful for interesting and newsworthy stories that are inexpensive to obtain.

The purposes of PR are as follows:

- Helping to foster the prestige and reputation of the firm through its public image.
- Raising awareness and creating interest in the firm's products.
- Dealing with social and environmental issues and opportunities.
- Improving goodwill with customers through presenting useful information and dealing effectively with complaints.
- Promoting the sense of identification of employees with the firm through newsletters, social activities and recognition.
- Discovering and eliminating rumours and other sources of misunderstanding and misconceptions.
- Building a reputation as a good customer and reliable supplier.
- Influencing the opinions of public officials and politicians, especially in explaining the responsible operation of the business and the importance of its activities to the community.
- Dealing promptly, accurately and effectively with unfavourable negative publicity, especially where it is perceived to be a crisis which might damage the firm's reputation.
- Attracting and keeping good employees.

## MANAGEMENT CHALLENGE 9.3

## Tiger Woods returns with new sponsors

Tiger Woods became Steve Stricker's vice-captain for the 2018 Ryder Cup Team. This was the year that Tiger made his comeback as a player in prestigious golf tournaments. The first half of the year was a little up and down. At the Arnold Palmer Invitations, Tiger tied in fifth place. In the US Masters at Augusta National Golf Course, he tied in 32nd place; at the Valspar Championship he tied in second place; and at the Honda Classic he was 12th. Despite his up and down comeback, fans shouted 'Tiger, Tiger, Tiger' just as loudly as they ever had.

One of Tiger Woods' most prominent sponsors was Nike Golf. Nike signed Tiger Woods in 1999 when he was just 20 years old. This was during the days when Tiger was a formidable player. In 1997 he was ranked number one in the world. In 1999 Nike included Tiger as its golf ball sponsor and he used its balls in some of his most spectacular championships.

Nike Golf only started producing golf clubs in 2002 and provided Tiger with a full set of golf clubs as his official sponsor. In 2011, Tiger fell down the rankings amid bad publicity around extra-marital affairs, but returned to being ranked number one again in 2013. In 2014 Tiger suffered back pain and needed surgery so only played 23 rounds of competition golf between 2014 and 2017. At the end of 2017 Tiger had slipped to being the 656th player in the world. During Tiger's periods of absence, Nike Golf stopped providing and selling golf clubs and balls. Therefore in 2018 Tiger needed to get a new sponsor for his comeback. In 2018 Tiger was back playing at major golf tournaments. He was still sponsored by Nike for his clothing, but TaylorMade sponsored his golf clubs and Bridgestone Golf sponsored his golf balls. Tiger was the celebrity endorsing Full Swing, an indoor golf simulator, and he was the face on TV advertisements in Japan for Kowa, a pharmaceutical company, for pain relief products.

### Question

1 How does Tiger's performance and behaviour affect the brands that sponsor him?

An important aspect of PR is explaining the corporate social responsibility policy of organizations and dealing with the cynicism of pressure groups and individuals communicating online and using traditional media.

PR is concerned with a wide variety of activities to deliver these objectives, including:

- Dealing with press relations.
- Arranging facility visits.
- Publishing house journals and newsletters.
- Preparing videos, audiovisual presentations, printed reports and publications describing the firm's activities.
- Training courses.
- Arranging community projects.
- Lobbying governments.

From a communications perspective the effect of PR-generated stories in the media is different from advertising. The viewer, listener or reader will perceive the information differently. Editorial material in the media is perceived by consumers to be factual and comparatively neutral. Advertising material, on the other hand, is expected to be persuasive and present a positive statement for the advertiser's products. Whereas the firm controls every aspect of advertising, a press release covering a firm's news story will be interpreted by the journalist who writes the story for the press or edits the videotape for television.

## Crisis management

In international marketing one of the most important responsibilities of public relations is to manage unexpected crises which occur from time to time. Over the past few years there have been a number of examples of good and bad practice in managing information when dealing with a crisis. Examples include environmental pollution, unethical promotion, exploitation of labour and health scares caused by food contamination. The golden rule is that the firm should be seen to act, before the media or government forces it to do so, in order to show that it is sorry that an incident has occurred. However, it should neither accept responsibility nor apportion blame until the evidence is investigated and the real cause of the problem identified.

Many MNEs consider government lobbying an essential part of international communications, with the aim of influencing foreign governments both directly and indirectly through asking the home country government to help. Recent examples of lobbying have been US firms seeking to reduce Chinese piracy of products and services, and allowing greater access to Japanese markets.

As government lobbying becomes increasingly important, it raises issues for the company about how high profile it should be in pressing its case, particularly where it is seen to be exerting undue pressure on politicians or civil servants to behave unethically or reverse policy.

Some firms go one stage further by making donations to political parties. This, of course, can have the effect of alienating other stakeholders. There is little doubt that firms are increasingly making lobbying a major responsibility of senior management, given the pivotal role of governments in making decisions which might affect MNEs.

## Online communications

In Chapter 12 we will discuss the use of technology in shaping the international marketing strategy of firms at greater length and, clearly, facilitating communications is at the heart. Here, however, we discuss the tactical use of online integrated marketing communications.

### The nature of online communications

A number of online tools are used by marketers to create brand awareness, product and service associations and drive users to their websites, where customers might obtain further information, purchase an item from an online store or direct the customer to a traditional store. One significant advantage of online communications is that it is easier to measure the actions of customers and their responses, and so marketing metrics are more accurate.

*Advertising* is placed on partner sites that charge a 'click-through' fee in return for providing the sales lead and link. Search engines and comparative pricing sites provide sales leads by listing websites based on brand searches or brand associations with key words. Being listed on the first page of a key word search is essential. Firms pay heavily and also manage their web content carefully to ensure that this happens in all their international markets.

*Websites* Some websites are clearly defined as marketplaces either owned by one specific organization or where links to commercial sites should be expected, for example, financial services supermarkets, online travel agents or insurance brokers.

*Email* Organizations use email to convey their marketing messages directly to their customers. However, many customers have been irritated by the large volume of spam they receive. Around 269 billion emails are sent and received each day, which equates to around 3.1 million emails per second (Internet live stats 2018). In terms of other social media interactions 8000 tweets are sent per second, 840 Instagram photos are uploaded per second and 73 464 YouTube videos are viewed per second. This means that the effect of individual messages is diluted among this volume of what is referred to as interruption marketing (spam). The term 'permission marketing' suggests that the communications will be more effective if customers agree to receive more communications from the firm. This opt-in approach is preferable to an opt-out, in which the customer would have to take the initiative in asking a firm not to send messages.

*Viral marketing* has extended the effectiveness of online communications by encouraging recipients of email messages to pass them onto others to create a 'buzz' in the marketplace.

*Mobile communications* For some time it has been predicted that mobile communications would be valuable and, as we saw in earlier chapters, multifunctional mobile devices, such as smartphones and tablets, now provide more comprehensive services and interactive communications, see Illustration 9.6.

## ILLUSTRATION 9.6

# We are social: latest details of consumer social spaces

It is essential that international brands understand the behaviour of their target audiences. This is particularly true where social media is concerned as online behaviour varies in different countries. What international brands definitely know is social media activity is growing day by day. Therefore, advertisers need to ensure their communication messages are shown to target markets via the most appropriate social media channel.

By 2018 there were 7.6 billion people in the world. Over 4 billion of these people are active Internet users. The most important statistic that advertisers need to know is how many active users there are. The answer is that there are 3.2 billion active *social media* users. There are 5.2 billion unique mobile users and 3 billion active *mobile social* users. These data enable advertisers to know that their communication messages must reach the online social consumers, grab their attention and raise brand awareness and/or increase sales potential.

The dynamics of online and social media activity vary around the world. For instance, worldwide, the number of hours spent per day on the Internet is six hours (via desktop/laptop/tablet/phone – in fact any device). This has increased from 4.4 hours per day in 2015. Table 9.3 shows the number of hours spent on the Internet by consumers from different countries (36 countries in all were investigated).

The amount of Internet activity – both work and leisure time – is growing. Advertisers realize the potential for communicating with consumers via Internet channels. And as familiarity and usage of the Internet grows, Internet brand presence online is essential.

E-commerce over the Internet is big business, but greater in some countries than others. In the UK, 78 per cent (up from 64 per cent in 2015) of consumers stated they had 'bought something' online in one particular month during 2017. The UK has the highest penetration of the population 'buying something' online.

**Table 9.3** Number of hours spent on the Internet by consumers from different countries via any device

| Country | H = hours M = minutes |
|---|---|
| Thailand | 9H 36M |
| South Africa | 8H 32M |
| Taiwan | 7H 49M |
| Portugal | 6H 31M |
| UK | 5H 51M |
| France | 4H 48M |
| Japan | 4H 12M |
| Morocco | 2H 53M |

Sources: We are Social and Hootsuite (2018).

E-commerce activity is also high in Germany (74 per cent) and South Korea (74 per cent). However, e-commerce activity is low in other countries. As shown in Table 9.4, the lowest e-commerce penetration is Egypt at 22 per cent and the second lowest is India at 26 per cent. Thus, brands advertising online will have different strategies and targets for different countries. Brands advertising to UK, German and South Korean consumers will heavily promote a 'call to action' to improve sales, while in the Philippines, Indonesia and India, online advertisements will have strategies for brand awareness and loyalty building, and brand switching.

The opportunity to use social media is not the same worldwide. The percentage total of active accounts on social media in the USA is 70 per cent, in Northern Europe 66 per cent, South-East Asia 55 per cent and

**Table 9.4** E-commerce penetration: % of population by country that bought something online (via any device) in one particular month during 2017

| | |
|---|---|
| UK | 78% |
| USA | 69% |
| France | 61% |
| Malaysia | 59% |
| Poland | 57% |
| Saudi Arabia | 47% |
| India | 26% |
| Egypt | 22% |

Source: We are Social and Hootsuite (2018).

just 6 per cent in Africa. Therefore, advertisers of international brands will direct their efforts through traditional and social media marketing channels that are available to the consumer.

## Questions

**1** Why is social media marketing essential for international brands?

**2** Why is it important for advertisers to know about the online behaviours of consumers from different countries?

**3** Highlight some of the different behaviours of e-commerce consumers and what this means to an international brand.

**Sources:** Kemp, S. (2018) Digital in 2018. We are Social and Hootsuite. Available from www.wearesocial.com.

*Privacy* There is a conflict between the interests of the firm and customer in developing databases. In order to offer more individually targeted, personalized and relevant communications, the firm requires ever more detailed and potentially sensitive information from the customer. However, the customer is reluctant to give firms personal information. They appreciate that certain firms such as insurance companies might need the information in order to process a transaction, can be trusted and will respect local country privacy laws, such as the 1998 Data Protection Act in the UK. They have more concern over the possibility of the firms passing on the sensitive information – deliberately or accidentally – to other firms that will not be so scrupulous in its use. It is very easy to pass information electronically to other companies or countries.

# Developing profitable, long-term marketing relationships

So far in this chapter we have focused upon the communications strategies that might be used to ensure that the firm's broad base of stakeholders around the world is aware of the company's standards and values, the distinctiveness and quality of its brands, products and services and that customers are exposed to the messages that will encourage them to buy the firm's products and services rather than the competitor's. Once customers have been won over, usually at a considerable cost, firms increasingly realize that it is less costly if they can persuade them to stay loyal to the firm rather than lose them to a competitor. Otherwise they face the cost of winning them over again.

Customer retention is particularly important for B2B marketing, where the number of opportunities to win over new customers may be very limited and the loss of a major customer could have a disastrous effect on the firm. The lifetime value of the customer is considerable, but the cost to the customer of changing to a new supplier can be considerable too. Both supplier and customer have something to gain from the relationship marketing concept. This is concerned with developing and maintaining mutually advantageous relationships between two or more firms in a supply chain and using their combined capability and resources to deliver the maximum added value for the ultimate customer. It involves a more holistic approach to understanding the market dynamics and developing implementation strategies to respond to the changes in the market needs that have been identified.

## The concept of relationship marketing

There are significant differences between adopting a traditional marketing approach based on individual transactions, in which the emphasis is placed on the 4Ps of the product marketing mix (particularly the product P), and an approach based on building relationships by emphasizing the three extra Ps of the service mix (particularly the people P). At the core of relationship marketing is the idea that rather than simply trying to add customer service onto a predetermined product offer, based on a rigid marketing mix, the firm should provide customer satisfaction by using the marketing mix flexibly to meet the customer's evolving needs.

Horovitz (2000) suggests that in relationship marketing the 4Ps of the traditional marketing mix are changed altogether and replaced by the 4Cs of relationship marketing: customer needs and wants; costs; convenience; and communication. Clearly, given the need to meet diverse cultural requirements, relationship marketing makes sense for high-involvement B2B purchases where value can be added and sales generated by relationship marketing. It is less so for low-involvement purchases of consumer packaged goods. It is important to recognize that consumers do not want a relationship as such but do want interactivity, one-to-one marketing and more personalized communications. This can be done by replacing conventional offline with online communications.

Throughout the firm the objectives of relationship marketing are to:

- Maintain and build existing customers by offering more tailored and cost-effective business solutions.
- Use existing relationships to obtain referral to business units and other supply chain members that are perhaps in different parts of the world and not currently customers.
- Increase the revenue from customers by offering solutions that are a combination of products and services.
- Reduce the operational and communications cost of servicing the customers, including the work prior to a trading relationship.

Relationships must be built with those that might influence the final purchase decision. These include internal staff as individuals and groups, experts, celebrities and other influential individuals that have the power to connect the organization with the market.

The power and influence of the organization's stakeholders in these markets will vary considerably around the world. Their relative importance depends upon the specific context of the firm's activity. In the technology sector, for example, key influencers and high profile lead customers may be located in a particular country market. But their decisions might influence purchasing decisions across the world.

## Database development

Managing and influencing potentially millions of interactions between staff, customers and partners requires a systematic approach. Chaffey *et al.* (2003) explain that the key objectives are: customer retention, customer extension (increasing the depth and range of customers) and customer selection (segmenting and targeting).

The starting point is to build an information technology system that will integrate the relationship marketing activity. Central to the system is a database that will identify those customers with which it is worthwhile developing a relationship. The database can best be built from the company records of its interactions with customers and then supplemented with purchased lists of possible customers. Chaffey *et al.* explain that the details about the customer should include:

- Personal and profile data, including contact details.
- Transaction data, including purchase quantities, channels, timing and locations.
- Communications data, including response to campaigns.

Wasserman *et al.* (2000) explain that data mining is used to 'discover hidden facts contained in databases'. Identifying trends in behaviour and attitudes from data provides a basis for targeting prospective customers cost-effectively, developing cooperative relationships with other companies and better understanding the patterns of customer purchasing behaviour.

## Customer relationship management

International consumer markets are characterized by their sheer size and the relative anonymity of their customers. Even small retailers cannot possibly know their customers' individual behaviour, attitudes, intention to purchase and experiences (good or bad) in dealing with the firm. An industrial marketer, on the other hand, with only a few customers possibly can. As we have discussed in the section on databases, technology has been developed to try to integrate relationship marketing activity and manage the vast amounts of supporting information. Customer relationship management (CRM) is effectively computer software coupled with defined management processes and procedures to enable staff throughout organizations to capture and use information about their customers to maintain and build relationships. Companies such as Siebel (US) have built their businesses around such concepts.

Although CRM should play a decisive role in integrating communications and developing relationships with the customer as the focus, Kotler (2003) points out that, in practice, many firms have embraced the concept and spent between US$5 million and US$10 million on CRM systems, but been less than satisfied with the results. He quotes the CRM Forum research that suggests fewer than 30 per cent of companies are satisfied with their systems. The problems that companies identify in establishing the systems tend not to be associated with software failure (2 per cent), but rather organizational change (29 per cent), company politics/inertia (22 per cent), lack of CRM understanding (20 per cent), poor planning (12 per cent), lack of CRM skills (6 per cent), budget problems (4 per cent), bad advice (1 per cent) and 'other' (4 per cent).

The problems arise when firms see CRM systems as a quick fix to try to manage vast amounts of data. They make broad generalizations about customer segments and are often too insensitive to different consumer cultures and concerns. Too often CRM is not adopted on an organization-wide basis and instead is adopted by individual departments for very specific reasons. It also gets modified because of the need to interface it with existing legacy systems and so becomes fragmented and, rather than reducing cost, actually increases it. The introduction of CRM leads to raised expectations of service levels among customers and staff. If this is not delivered, CRM can have a detrimental effect on the business.

The opportunities for relationship marketing to offer benefits are increasing because of improvements in communications, IT and increased cross-border purchasing. However, it is important to understand that the consumer is not necessarily a willing participant in the relationship mission and, unless this is recognized, relationship marketing will prove to be of limited value. Indeed, the question must be asked whether the majority of consumers will derive any benefit from a relationship with an MNE – the benefits will be mainly for the firm.

For relatively low purchase price items there is a danger that the costs to the firm of building customer loyalty might outweigh the costs of a more traditional approach to marketing products and services. It is difficult to measure the relative merits of short-term costs against longer-term revenues. Few companies are willing to take a long-term view based upon their assumptions of what might happen in the future.

In practice the methods of relationship marketing in the consumer markets are diverging from relationship marketing in the business sector. In consumer markets relationship marketing will become more concerned with making one-to-one connections with customers through interactivity and promoting and placing products and services in the appropriate media at just the right moment.

## SUMMARY

- To be effective in global markets external international marketing communications are driven by the need to have a uniform corporate identity, clearly differentiated product and service offers supported by consistent promotion and strategies in place to build long-term customer relationships.

- Firms also need to focus on internal and interactive communications and ensure that their staff and partners' staff in remote locations deliver consistent and integrated international marketing communications.

- There are benefits to the firm of standardizing the promotion processes and programmes to benefit from economies of scale and the learning effect, wherever possible. But communications are extremely sensitive to local culture and conditions and, without attention to detail, they can be the source of problems worldwide for firms.

- The communication tools must be used appropriately to suit the context of the markets being served, different customer needs and the firm's objectives. Media availability, cultural and legislation differences and the nature of the products and services being marketed will influence the communications strategy decisions and choice of tools.

- Customer perceptions can be damaged by poor communications management within the firm and by external factors over which the organization may have no control. The international firm must concentrate on communicating consistency in its image, standards and values to a diverse range of stakeholders, as well as making its direct appeal to existing and potential customers. It must also integrate the traditional communications with online communications to further develop interactive, one-to-one customer relationships.

- Due to the high cost of winning and losing customers, firms, particularly in the B2B market, must build relationships to retain their most valuable customers in the long term. They must also measure the impact of their marketing communication investment as far as possible to ensure value for money.

## KEYWORDS

communications mix

promotional mix

corporate identity

relationship marketing

customer relationship management (CRM)

social customer relationship management (SCRM)

failures of communications

standardization of international marketing communications

communications adaptation

push strategy

pull strategy

communications tools

product and service differentiation

transactions

## CASE STUDY 1

# UNiDAYS: a good deal for students worldwide

UNiDAYS was set up by Josh Rathour and three co-founders in 2011 to help companies reach the global Generation Z cohort, born since the mid-1990s, who are digitally savvy and have grown up with social media.

Global organizations want to reach this marketing segment of customers as they first achieve financial independence and while their opinions, preferences and loyalties, particularly towards brands, are still being formed. This is a global segment with huge potential but expensive to reach by any mass communication approach.

Rathour's solution and business proposition was to develop the technology that could verify whether or not these people were students. If they could ensure that only students were being targeted, then brands could be persuaded to use their technology to offer student specific discounts as a first step in building customer loyalty. The discounts could be offered online, through social media as well as in shops. The potential customer brands of UNiDAYS would come from many markets, including food and drink, fashion and beauty, fitness and technological equipment.

A year after start up, UNiDAYS had secured its first major customer – fashion retailer Asos. Major international players including Apple, Nike and Samsung followed. By 2016 the company had signed up 600 global brands. One particularly attractive, exclusive deal was a 50 per cent discount off the Apple Music streaming service.

In 2018 UNiDAYS claimed to have an online community of more than 10 million students worldwide and a social media following of 800 000. Key to its success is engaging with its global audience to ensure that it stays relevant to its customers, that appropriate new brands are added to its network and that its platform is continually improved. Together with its social media following, it has set up a number of initiatives, including student councils in the UK, the USA and Australia with 20 000 members.

UNiDAYS started operations in Nottingham, UK, and has offices in London, New York and Sydney. In 2017 it helped generate £1.9 billion in revenues for its partners. Of its overall turnover of £15.7 million, its overseas sales were £3.3 million, up from £209 000 two years earlier, gaining it first place in the 2018 *Sunday Times* league table of SMEs with the fastest-growing international sales.

The company already operates in 114 countries and plans to grow rapidly, expecting to recruit an additional 30 software developers in Nottingham and increase its worldwide staff count from 144 to 400. The company is looking to open new offices in France, Germany and Canada.

## Questions

**1** Achieving a win–win is key to a successful business partnership. Why is this business successful?

**2** What are the communications priorities for UNiDAYS to succeed in its new markets?

**3** Identify the challenges that UNiDAYS faces in entering newer markets and supporting its brand partners.

**4** What are the longer-term risks that the business faces and how should it address them?

**References:** www.myunidays.com/; *The Sunday Times* (2018) Britain's SMEs with the fastest-growing international sales. The Sunday Times SME Export Track 100. February 2018. Available from www.fasttrack.co.uk/league-tables/sme-export-track-100/league-table/ (accessed 9 June 2018).

## CASE STUDY 2

# Greenpeace: global campaigner

Greenpeace campaigns to change attitudes and behaviour in order to protect and conserve the environment and promote peace in a number of areas, such as: energy conservation, reducing waste of resources and use of hazardous chemicals, promoting sustainable agriculture, protecting the world's great forests, the animals, plants, and people that live in them, and its oceans, working for disarmament, elimination of nuclear weapons and tackling the causes of conflict.

### Fund-raising

Greenpeace must influence governments and large commercial organizations, the politicians and policy makers if it is to achieve its objectives. Given these primary targets and the need to take an independent stance, Greenpeace only raises funds from individual donors and does not accept donations from any commercial or politically based organizations.

Although it is a global operation with branches in 40 countries, 3 million donors and more than $350 million in annual contributions, Greenpeace's international strategy is based on a franchise system in which each country-based Greenpeace operation contributes 17.5 per cent of its income to Greenpeace International to fund global campaigns, but is also responsible for local management, campaigns and fund-raising. This reflects the fact that different cultures and geographically based audiences may place a different emphasis on the relative importance of Greenpeace's campaigns.

### Getting heard

Greenpeace adopts professional marketing and management strategies but most of its activities are controversial. Greenpeace's main marketing weapons are high-profile actions that make dramatic news items in the worldwide broadcast and social media. To support these public relations campaigns, Greenpeace uses targeted marketing communications to get its message across. Greenpeace has realized that trying to persuade governments to take action on promoting ethical behaviour has been largely ineffective. There is also little point in using its limited funds to highlight unethical practices in companies that consumers have not heard of, as this is unlikely to result in a change of behaviour. Instead, Greenpeace focuses on the global brands supplied by companies that are using illegal or unethical practices. For example, Greenpeace forced Lego to end its long partnership with Shell, worth a reported £68 million. It used Lego figures, including polar bears, in an advert to show the damage caused by Shell drilling oil in the Arctic: 700 000 petition signatures and eight million YouTube views of the advert persuaded Lego to end the partnership. Lego was committed to using 100 per cent renewable energy and phasing out oil-based components anyway. Lego protested that Greenpeace should have complained to Shell, but this would not have gained the same publicity.

Asia Pulp and Paper (APP) was persuaded to cease its deforestation activity when Greenpeace publicized the fact that toymakers Mattel – makers of the Barbie doll – was buying cardboard traced back to the destruction of precious rainforests. As an Asian company, APP initially found the harsh criticism of Greenpeace difficult to take but has since adopted a zero-deforestation policy.

It took UK food retailer Waitrose 3 hours and 20 minutes to respond to an attack on it by Greenpeace for selling the John West brand of tuna. Waitrose said they would stop selling the the brand if it did not change its methods. Having committed to source 100 per cent sustainable tuna by the end of 2015, John West was still catching 98 per cent of its tuna using 'destructive' methods that also killed other species. In this way the global brands force their suppliers to behave ethically.

The BBC programme *Blue Planet 2* explained how 12.7 million tonnes of plastic end up in the oceans every year – a truckload every minute – resulting in 90 per cent of seabirds and 1 in 3 turtles having ingested plastic. Greenpeace demanded that companies such as Coca-Cola (which produces an estimated 110 billion single-use plastic bottles a year worldwide) should lead the way in addressing the problem. Greenpeace accuses some global brands, such as Volkswagen regarding vehicle emissions, of lying to its customers and encourages consumers to challenge the marketing communications of global brands.

Greenpeace recognizes that different segmentation and communication strategies are required for each donor segment, campaign and stakeholder. Individuals, for example, cannot just be divided into 'donors' and 'members'. As people go through life, their charity-giving, their contributions to the causes and their political and economic influence also go through different stages, so Greenpeace must build their communications strategies to respond to this. Customer relationship management and social media strategies to develop viral marketing campaigns are most effective. In doing this, however, the charity also needs to behave ethically and manage its activities effectively to retain the loyalty of its donors.

## Questions

**1** Advise Greenpeace on the strategic marketing decisions it needs to consider if it is to maintain and grow its level of donations and increase membership over the longer term.

**2** In light of your answer to Question 1, recommend to Greenpeace how it can develop an integrated communications strategy that would help it to achieve its long-term objectives.

**3** Which communications methods do you consider to be the most effective for Greenpeace as it implements its integrated communications strategy?

**4** What should big global brands learn from Greenpeace's campaigns?

**References:** www.greenpeace.org; Hobbs, T. (2016) Greenpeace on 'policing' the world's biggest brands and what marketers can learn from its unconventional advertising. 16 May, *Marketing Week*. Available from www.marketingweek.com/2016/05/16/greenpeace-on-handing-out-vigilante-justice-to-the-worlds-biggest-brands/ (accessed 9 June 2018).

## DISCUSSION QUESTIONS

**1** Communications are becoming increasingly fragmented. Why is this so and what are the critical success factors in planning, executing and controlling an integrated international communications strategy?

**2** Critically examine the case for and against using one advertising agency to create and implement an international advertising campaign.

**3** How might a small firm with few resources use online communications to build its international business? Using examples, show how this might be done (1) in the business-to-consumer market and (2) in the business-to-business market.

**4** Select an economic region. Identify the advantages and disadvantages of pan-regional advertising. How would you manage a pan-regional campaign for a product or service of your choice?

**5** A key element of communications for a global company of your choice is maintaining relationships with all its international stakeholders. Identify the various stakeholders and prepare an outline international communications plan to promote the company's values, its reputation and increase its profile.

## REFERENCES

1. Andrews, J.C. and Shimp, T.A. (2018) *Advertising, Promotion, and Other Aspects of Integrated Marketing Communications*, 10th edition. Cengage.
2. Attia, A.M., Asri Jantan, M., Atteya, N. and Fakhr, R. (2014) Sales training: Comparing multinational and domestic companies. *Marketing Intelligence & Planning* 32(1), 124–138.
3. Chaffey, D., Meyer, R., Johnston, K. and Ellis-Chadwick, F. (2003) *Internet Marketing: Strategy, Implementation and Practice*. FT/Prentice Hall.
4. The Conversation (2017) http://theconversation.com/dove-real-beauty-and-the-racist-history-of-skin-whitening-85446 (accessed 5 June 2018).
5. Davidson, H. (2002) *Committed Enterprise: How to Make Values and Visions Work*. Butterworth-Heinemann.
6. Fill, C. (2006) *Marketing Communications: Engagement, Strategies and Practice*. FT/Prentice Hall.
7. Hobbs, T. (2016) Greenpeace on 'policing' the world's biggest brands and what marketers can learn from its unconventional advertising. 16 May, *Marketing Week*.

Available from www.marketingweek.com/2016/05/16/greenpeace-on-handing-out-vigilante-justice-to-the-worlds-biggest-brands/ (accessed 9 June 2018).

8.  Horovitz, J. (2000) Using information to bond customers. In D. Marchand (ed.) *Competing with Information*. Wiley.

9.  Internet Live Stats (2018) One second. Available from www.internetlivestats.com/one-second/ (accessed 8 June 2018).

10. Kataria, M. (2014) Presentation of women ads in print advertisements. *Asian Journal of Multidisciplinary Studies* 2(10). Available from http://ajms.co.in/sites/ajms2015/index.php/ajms/article/view/630/532 (accessed 9 June 2018).

11. Kemp, N. (2017) ASA to introduce new guidelines on gender stereotyping in ads. Available from www.campaignlive.co.uk/article/asa-introduce-new-guidelines-gender-stereotyping-ads/1439657#DEsqhHVI5C5zUrmz.99 (accessed 9 June 2018).

12. Koptseva, N.P. and Reznikova, K.V. (2017) The cultural aspects of advertising communications in modern China. *East Asia* 34(4), 249–269.

13. Kotler, P. (2003) *Marketing Insights from A To Z: 80 Concepts Every Manager Needs to Know*. John Wiley.

14. Kotler, P. and Armstrong, G. (2014) *Principles of Marketing*, 15th edition. Pearson. Electronic Copy.

15. Kotler, P., Bowen J.T. and Makens, M. (2014) *Marketing for Hospitality and Tourism*, 6th edition. Pearson Education Limited.

16. Mair, J., Lockstone-Binney, L. and Whitelaw, P.A. (2018) The motives and barriers of association conference attendance: Evidence from an Australasian tourism and hospitality academic conference. *Journal of Hospitality and Tourism Management* 34, 58–65.

17. Masterson, R. (2005) The importance of creative match in television sponsorship. *International Journal of Advertising* 25(4), 471–488.

18. Mintel (2015) cited in Cosmetics Design-Asia (2016) Skin whitening in India gathers pace. Available from www.cosmeticsdesign-asia.com/Article/2016/10/11/Skin-whitening-in-India-grows (accessed 5 June 2018).

19. Persil (2018) Dirt is good. Available from www.persil.com/uk/dirt-is-good/real-play/why-do-we-think-dirt-is-good.html (accessed 5 June 2018).

20. Reputation Institute (2018) Global RepTrak® www.reputationinstitute.com/ (accessed 5 June 2018).

21. Rogers, T. (2008) Foreword. In Rogers, T (ed.) *Conferences and Conventions: A Global Industry*. Butterworth Heinemann, pp. xiii–xvii.

22. Siu, W. and Au, A.K. (1997) Women in advertising: A comparison of television advertisements in China and Singapore. *Marketing Intelligence and Planning* 15(5), 235–243.

23. Statista (2018) www.statista.com/statistics/272850/global-advertising-forecast/ (accessed 13 June 2018).

24. Subramanian, R. (2015) Soft-skills training and cultural sensitization of Indian BPO workers: A qualitative study. *Communications of the IIMA* 5(2), 2.

25. *The Sunday Times* (2018) Britain's SMEs with the fastest-growing international sales. The Sunday Times SME Export Track 100. February 2018. Available from www.fasttrack.co.uk/league-tables/sme-export-track-100/league-table/ (accessed 9 June 2018).

26. Verma, R. (2014) Why attend tradeshows? A comparison of exhibitor and attendee's preferences. *Cornell Hospitality Quarterly* 55(3), 239–251.

27. Wasserman, T., Khermouch, G. and Green, J. (2000) Mining everyone's business. *Brandweek*, February.

28. We are Social and Hootsuite (2018) *Global Digital Report 2018*. Available at: https://digitalreport.wearesocial.com/ (accessed 8 June 2018).

29. Whitfield, J., Dioko, L.D.A., Webber, D. and Zhang, L. (2014) Attracting convention and exhibition attendance to complex MICE venues: Emerging data from Macao. *International Journal of Tourism Research* 16(2), 169–179.

30. Zhang, Y. and Neelankavil, J.P. (1997) The influence of culture on advertising effectiveness in China and the USA: A crosscultural study. *European Journal of Management* 31(2), 134–149.

## CHAPTER 10

# THE MANAGEMENT OF INTERNATIONAL DISTRIBUTION AND LOGISTICS

## LEARNING OBJECTIVES

After reading this chapter you should be able to:

- Strategically evaluate potential foreign distribution options for a given situation
- Discuss the complexities of efficiently managing intermediaries in an international marketing context
- Appreciate the difference in retailing infrastructures across the globe
- Advise and recommend potential solutions to developing a logistics strategy in foreign markets
- Understand the export documentation process

## INTRODUCTION

In Chapter 7 we examined strategies for international expansion and the options available for firms entering foreign markets. In this chapter we will build on the issues discussed in Chapter 7, but focus on managing the distribution and logistics within foreign markets.

The management of foreign channels of distribution is a key area in a firm's efforts to gain competitive advantage. As products become more standardized across the world, the ability to compete on customer service becomes more vital. In order to be effective in this area, a firm must have a well-managed integrated supply chain within foreign markets and across international boundaries.

International marketing involves companies operating in countries other than their own. The trend to a more globalized world implies an interconnected and interdependent world where capital, goods and services are freely transferred across national frontiers. As companies continue to pursue global strategies and operate in more and more countries, customers in every corner of the world expect to be served better, faster and by whatever channel suits them. To meet those expectations, organizations need to give a global, holistic view of their customers and really understand how to develop a globally integrated distribution system.

The ultimate goal may be to have a single system that offers all global customers a streamlined efficient service. In order for many companies in many markets to achieve that, they first have to develop a real understanding of the mechanics of the operations of the distribution systems of the countries in which they operate.

> In this chapter, we will examine the strategic issues in managing distribution channels and discuss the issues of selecting intermediaries and how to build long-term effective relationships in international markets. We will also examine the developments in retailing and the differences in retailing across markets at different levels of economic development.
>
> Finally, we will examine the logistics of physically moving goods across national boundaries and the importance of efficient distribution management to minimize costs in international markets.

# The challenges in managing an international distribution strategy

Recent events that have affected international marketing include the global recession and its recovery, austerity measures and emerging economies, all of which have changed the distribution channels for products and services. This chapter is dedicated to the challenges and opportunities around international distribution strategies.

Distribution channels are the means by which goods are distributed from the manufacturer to the end user. Some companies have their own means of distribution, some only deal directly with the most important customers. But many companies rely on other companies to perform distribution functions for them. These functions include:

- the purchase of goods or services
- the assembly of an attractive assortment of goods
- holding stocks or inventory
- promoting the sale of goods or services to the end customer
- the physical movement of goods.

Technology has enabled other distribution functions to take place, such as the movement of products and services, online. An example of the movement of services online is when hotels use online travel agents (OTAs) to distribute details of their rooms or conference facilities; see Illustration 10.2. Physical goods can also be 'distributed' through a 3D printing process. This starts with a 3D Computer Aided Design (CAD) model, which is then exported via the Internet to be printed anywhere in the world. Management Case 10.1 shows Siemens revolutionizing distribution by investing in 3D printing.

In international marketing, companies usually take advantage of a wide number of different organizations to facilitate the distribution of their products. The large number is explained by considerable differences between countries, both in their distribution systems and in the expected level of product sales. The physical movement of goods usually includes several modes of transport – for example, by road to a port, by boat to the country of destination and by road to the customer's premises. The movement of services can be delivered to the consumer in many forms. For example, data storage can be uploaded to a cloud storage facility, or language learning apps for consumers can be distributed via mobile apps. The selection of the appropriate distribution strategy is a significant decision. While the marketing mix decisions of product and marketing communications are often more glamorous, they are usually dependent upon the chosen distribution channel. The actual distribution channel decision is fundamental as it affects all aspects of the international marketing strategy. Therefore, the whole channel (also referred to as the supply chain) relies on each part of the distribution channel performing its task perfectly and on time.

The key objective in building an effective distribution strategy is to build a supply chain to your markets. In fact, as Kotler and Armstrong (2014) state, the distribution channel 'performs better if it includes a firm, agency or mechanism that provides leadership and has the power to assign roles and manage conflict' (p. 367).

To achieve this across international markets is a daunting task. It will mean the international marketing managers have to meet a number of important challenges in order to ensure they develop a distribution strategy which delivers the effective distribution of products and services. The major areas they will need to consider are as follows:

- *Selection of foreign country intermediaries.* Should the firm use indirect or direct channels? What type of intermediaries will best serve their needs in the marketplace?

- *How to build a relationship with intermediaries.* The management and motivation of intermediaries in foreign country markets is especially important to firms trying to build a long-term presence, competing on offering quality services.

- *How to deal with the varying types of retailing infrastructure across international markets.* Achieving a coordinated strategy across markets where retailing is at varying stages of development, and the impact of the growth of retailers themselves globalizing, are important considerations in the distribution strategies of firms competing in consumer goods markets.

- *How to maximize new and innovative forms of distribution.* Can be achieved particularly through opportunities arising through the Internet and electronic forms of distribution.

- *How to manage the logistics of physically distributing products across foreign markets.* Firms need to evaluate the options available and develop a well-managed logistics system.

In the following sections of the chapter, we will examine the issues in each of these areas of international distribution and logistics.

## Selecting foreign country market intermediaries

A distribution decision is a long-term decision, as once established it can be difficult to extract a company from existing agreements. This means that channels chosen have to be appropriate for today and flexible enough to adapt to long-term market developments.

In some instances, difficulties may arise because of legal contracts, as in the case of the termination of an agency. In other situations, they result from relationships that need to be initiated and then nurtured. For example, the development of sales through wholesalers and distributors might be substantially influenced by the past trading pattern and the expectation of future profitable sales. Therefore, a long-term relationship needs to be developed before a firm is willing to invest significantly in an intermediary.

The long-term nature of distribution decisions forces a careful analysis of future developments. If new forms of distribution emerge, including TV or mobile shopping, interactive media, e-retailing or 3D printing, these channels will certainly have an impact on manufacturing distribution channels. See Management Challenge 10.1.

Another important challenge is the comparative inexperience of managers in the channel selection process in international markets. In domestic marketing, most marketing managers develop marketing plans which will usually be implemented within the existing arrangement of the company's distribution channels. This is quite a different proposition to the pioneering process of establishing a distribution channel in the first place and then achieving a well-supported availability through channel members in different country markets.

Furthermore, if foreign market channels are being managed from the home market, there may be preconceived notions and preferences that home market systems can operate elsewhere. As they are unfamiliar with the market, managers may underestimate the barriers to entry erected by local competitors and even government regulations. For instance, in France and Japan there are restrictive laws which inhibit the growth of large retailers. In Japan there is limited floor space, so convenience stores are about 100 m$^2$ on average, and typically stock about 3000 products. They are highly competitive, very busy and have a high turnover of stock.

## MANAGEMENT CHALLENGE 10.1

Increasing the number
of 3D printers from now
until 2035

In 2018 Siemens, a German company, invested £27 million in a 3D printing manufacturer in the UK. The manufacturing plant in Worcester belongs to Materials Solutions Ltd, an established 3D printing solutions business. The investment will bring jobs to the area as it includes the purchase of new 3D printers, increasing the number from 15 to 50 by 2035.

Back in 2015, Siemens noticed the advances Materials Solutions was making with its 3D printing and decided to make a strategic investment. This meant Materials Solutions could advance its technology and operations in manufacturing turbines. Its expertise flourished. So it was no surprise when Siemens wanted 'the best in the business' to print metal parts: it chose Materials Solutions.

3D printing, often called additive manufacturing, builds objects layer upon layer, from the bottom up, to form paper plates, plastic heart valves and now metal objects. When Siemens wants Materials Solutions to make a product such as a gas turbine, it simply draws a model of the product using CAD (Computer-Aided Design) software, clicks 'SEND' on a computer and within moments the designed product is on a computer screen in Worcester. The Materials Solutions 3D printer then sets to work building the turbine by fusing together metal powder with laser technology.

### Question

**1** What are the many benefits of using 3D printing technology with regards to distribution?

**Reference:** Siemens www.siemens.com.

## Indirect and direct channels

One of the first decisions to make in selecting intermediaries for international markets is, should the product be distributed indirectly? In other words, using outside sales agents and distributors in the country. Or should the product be distributed directly, using the company's sales force, via a company-owned distribution channel or via other intermediaries in a foreign country? The former option is an independent channel which is non-integrated and provides very little or no control over its international distribution. It affords virtually no links with the end users. On the other hand, direct distribution, which is an integrated channel, generally affords the supplier more control and, at the same time, brings responsibility, commitment and attendant risks. As we have discussed, distribution decisions are difficult to change. It is therefore important for firms to consider the alternatives available and the differing degrees of commitment and risk, evaluate the alternatives and select the most appropriate type of distribution.

Integrated (direct) channels of distribution are seen to be beneficial when a firm's marketing strategy requires a high level of service before or after the sale. Integrated channels will be more helpful than independent channels in ensuring that high levels of customer service will be achieved.

Indirect channels on the other hand require less investment in terms of both money and management time. Indirect channels also are seen to be beneficial in overcoming freight rate, negotiating disadvantages, lowering the cost of exporting and allowing higher margins and profits for the manufacturer. An independent channel, therefore, allows the international firm to tap the benefits of a distribution specialist within a foreign market, such as economies of scale and pooling the demand for the distribution services of several manufacturers.

The advantages and disadvantages of indirect exporting were discussed in Chapter 7. In this section we will focus on issues facing firms who have made the decision to involve themselves with intermediaries in foreign country markets, either through the use of agents or distributors or using their own company-owned sales force. These intermediaries offer a wide range of services:

- *Export distributors*: usually perform a variety of functions including stock inventories, handling promotion, extending customer credit, processing orders, arranging shipping, product maintenance and repair.

- *Export agents*: responsibilities often include buyer/seller introductions, host market information, trade fair exhibitions and general promotional activities.

- *Cooperative organizations*: carry on exporting activities on behalf of several producers and are partly under their administrative control (often used by producers of primary products, e.g. bananas, coffee, sugar).

A company-owned sales force may be one of three types:

1 *Travelling export sales representatives*. The company can begin by sending home-based sales people abroad to gather important information, to make the necessary customer contacts and to conduct the negotiating and selling process.

2 *Domestic-based export department or division*. An export sales manager carries on the actual selling and draws on market assistance as needed. It might evolve into a self-contained export department performing all the activities in export and operating as a profit centre.

3 *Foreign-based sales branch or subsidiary*. A foreign-based sales branch allows the company to achieve greater presence and programme control in the foreign market. The sales branch handles sales and distribution and may also handle warehousing and promotion. It often serves as a display centre and customer service centre as well.

The choices available to a firm may well be determined by whether they are operating in the B2B or B2C sector and if they are using online facilities, as the movement of B2B and B2C physical goods is a major activity. Figures 10.1 and 10.2 illustrate the choices for organizations. Figure 10.1 suggests the main organizations along the distribution chain, from supplier to business buyer in international B2B transactions.

The main channels in the B2B market tend to be agents, distributors and companies' wholly owned sales forces. The main distribution channels in the B2C market are shown in Figure 10.2.

Service organizations such as hotels are embracing online opportunities. They can offer rooms and conference facilities directly through their own online sales platforms such as their website, Facebook or through

**FIGURE 10.1**   Distribution channels for business goods

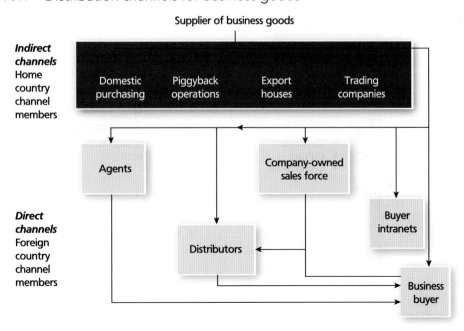

FIGURE 10.2   Distribution channels for consumer goods

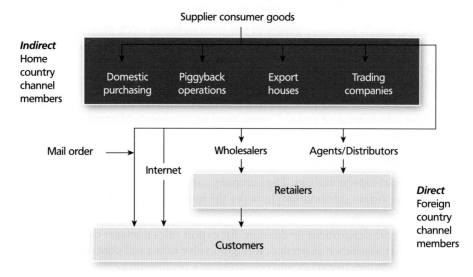

mobile apps. Additionally, there are land-based agents that are available for consumers who wish to discuss their holiday requirements in person.

Over the past few years, there have been considerable developments in retailing across national boundaries. In a later section in this chapter, we will examine these trends and other new forms of retailing. First, however, we will look at the factors to consider in selecting channels of distribution and then building effective relationships with intermediaries.

## Channel selection

In selecting appropriate channel intermediaries, a firm has to consider many factors. Czinkota and Ronkainen (2012) suggest the 11C model to explain the factors a firm should consider in their selection process. Figure 10.3 shows the 11C elements split into elements that are external to the organization and internal to the organization.

FIGURE 10.3   The 11 Cs

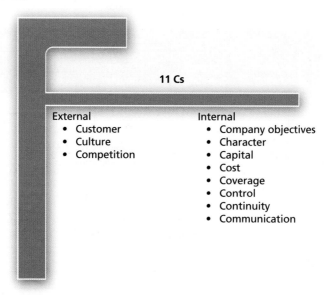

Source: Czinkota, M. and Ronkainen, I. (2013) *International Marketing*. Cengage Learning.

## Customer characteristics and culture

Channels of distribution have usually developed through the cultural traditions of the country. Therefore, there are great disparities across nations, making the development of any standardized approach difficult.

The distribution system of a country can vary enormously. In Finland the main sectors of the Finnish economy are dominated by oligopolies. Consumables for everyday use are marketed by an integrated system of distribution dominated by two big groups. These are S Group, which includes sub-brands of Prisma, S-Market and Alepa, with around 47 per cent of the market in Finland, and K Group with sub-brands K-citymarket, K-market and K-Supermarket with around 36 per cent of sales. In total 83 per cent of the grocery market is with just two organizations (Société Générale 2018).

In Japan, the entire distribution system is based on networks with lots of wholesalers selling to other wholesalers. There are over 300 000 wholesalers and over 1.2 million retailers. Due to the price of land being so high in Japan, many wholesalers cannot carry stock in the traditional sense, so may order on a daily basis. This means that there are many layers between the foreign company entering the market and the final consumer.

The Japanese system centres on distributor linkages to *dainyo* manufacturers, where the distributor accepts a subservient social status in return for economic security. From this interaction emerges vertical distribution networks called *Ryūtsū keiretsu*, in which units are arrayed in hierarchical layers and power resides at the 'commanding heights' of large *keiretsu*.

*Keiretsu* refers to a uniquely Japanese form of corporate organization. A *keiretsu* is a grouping or family that forms a tight-knit alliance to work towards each other's mutual success through long-term relationships. It can best be understood as the intricate web of relationships that links banks, manufacturers, suppliers and distributors with the Japanese government. Now the *keiretsu* are more corporate. Family groups no longer form the basis of the *keiretsu*. Shareholders are the ones that bring together Japanese firms, often from different types of businesses. One *keiretsu* is called Mitsubishi. The Bank of Tokyo-Mitsubishi is the lead member working with Mitsubishi Motors, Mitsubishi Trust and Banking, and Meiji Mutual Life Insurance Company. This *keiretsu* has a collective goal, which is to distribute goods around the world and together seek new global markets (Twomey 2018).

Distributors at 'lower' layers in the structure are tied to the *Ryūtsū keiretsu*, (distribution *keiretsu*) system by bonds of loyalty, mutual obligation, trust and power that extend throughout existing distribution structures. While this arrangement guarantees members some degree of security, it also deprives them of economic freedom. Distributors that choose to deal with firms outside of the established group risk severing their ties with the group.

While distributors lack the freedom to transact with whomever they wish, they are also relieved of many costs associated with being independent. These include smaller distributors in the system that need not shoulder the risk of carrying inventories of products that will not sell and can depend on reliable delivery and financial help where necessary.

Since the late 2000s the power of the *keiretsu* has started to diminish. Many faced debts through bad loan portfolios and were forced to merge or go out of business. The changes in automotive distribution have also had a major impact on the power of the *keiretsu*, as can be seen in Illustration 10.1.

Sometimes non-Japanese businesses are described as *keiretsu*. The Virgin Group (UK) and Tata Group (India), and airline alliances such as Oneworld and the Star Alliance (USA), are seen to have similar characteristics to those of the Japanese *keiretsu*.

Thus, the characteristics of the customer and the cultural traditions of the country have a major impact on the choices available to a firm. A Belgian shopper may buy groceries from huge hypermarkets, concentrating on purchases which have long shelf lives and are easy to store in their spacious apartments and houses. The Japanese customers on the other hand can be characterized by their logistical imperatives, as confined living space makes storage of goods very difficult. Therefore, customers make frequent visits to shops and rely on stores to keep their inventories. Moreover, Japan's narrow roads and lack of parking spaces (except for suburbs) predispose most of its population to do its shopping on foot.

## ILLUSTRATION 10.1

# Japanese *keiretsu* and the automotive industry

Toyota, the global automotive brand, has used many distribution channels to move their cars from the manufacturer to the consumer. Toyota have traditionally moved their cars by ship, rail and other large road transport vehicles. Cars have moved from Toyota's manufacturing plants in Japan to London, Washington, Jakarta, Paris, in fact anywhere where there is a consumer market. Traditionally, Toyota has also used Japanese suppliers to provide parts for their cars, from steering wheels to seats, engines to headlight bulbs.

However, Toyota and their suppliers are facing a crisis. First, both are facing problems due to the recent economic changes brought on by the global recession, recession recovery and emerging markets. Second, the huge migration of Japanese citizens means their home market for cars and parts is diminishing year on year. And third, the *keiretsu* system has broken down.

The *keiretsu* system in Japan embodies a 'trust system' which brings with it a *favoured and guaranteed* distribution and purchasing system. Therefore, organizations in Japan, such as Toyota and their suppliers, have a further partnership system. An example of the partnership system comes in the format that Toyota invests money in their 'favourite suppliers' and the suppliers provide their best, most innovative products for Toyota. The age-old tradition of the bonded relationship between a car manufacturer, such as Toyota (the *father*) and their 'favourite *son*' (the supplier of

automotive parts) is at a turning point. Neither *father* nor *son* can continue solely within their *keiretsu* system. In fact, both partners **must** find new partners to succeed.

### Why the son needs to go beyond the *keiretsu* system

Automotive parts suppliers need to grow their businesses internationally because they too see their market shrinking due to the migration of Japanese citizens. Therefore, suppliers must seek new markets overseas, form new relationships (that do not have and/or know the *keiretsu* system) to survive. The markets that suppliers seek are other car manufacturers coming to set up business in Japan. Or they must go outside their country's borders to surrounding areas such as Indonesia and Thailand. This means the 'favourite *son*' is going outside the *keiretsu* system in order to grow its business.

### Why the father needs to go outside the *keiretsu* system

Major Japanese car manufacturers including Toyota, Nissan Motor Corporation and Honda Motor Company, are no longer making all their cars in Japan. All three are choosing to change their distribution model from manufacturing cars in Japan and distributing them around the world, to investing in new manufacturing plants nearer new consumer markets. Indeed Mexico is one such country that large manufacturers see as a place to do business. Manufacturing plants in Mexico will need suppliers to provide steering wheels, seats, engines and headlight bulbs. However, to save distribution costs, the Japanese car brands manufacturing cars in Mexico are no longer asking their 'favourite *son*' in Japan to supply the parts. Thus the *keiretsu* system from the *father*'s side is also breaking down.

## Question

1 What are the strengths and weaknesses of the *keiretsu* system?

**Reference:** Griemal, H. (2014) Japan's keiretsu suppliers: At risk in a new reality, published 29 November 2014 in *Automotive News* 89 (6640), 3–49. Available from www.autonews. com/article/20140929/OEM10/309299984/japans-keiretsu-suppliers-at-risk-in-a-new-reality (accessed 13 June 2015).

## Company objectives and competitive activity

The channel choice will also be determined by the company's objectives and what the firm's competitors are doing in a particular market. The distribution policy is part of a firm's international direction. Therefore, the distribution system developed will depend on the company's objective, i.e. whether their strategic objective is long term or short term and how quickly they need to realize their investment.

Most firms operating in international markets will endeavour to maintain a cost-effective balance between direct and indirect channels of distribution. Firms will use direct channels, perhaps their own sales force, in foreign country markets where their company's objective is to deliver high-value solutions to buying problems in order to maximize customer satisfaction. Thus, the firm is practising 'interaction' marketing as opposed to 'transaction' marketing. A firm whose objective is to build long-term, stable relationships with its foreign customers will have quite different objectives in the building of relationships throughout the supply chain than a firm with relatively short-term objectives in foreign country markets who purely wishes to complete the transaction before moving onto the next customer. Illustration 10.2 shows how a service can be distributed using online direct and indirect channels.

## Character of the market

The characteristics of the market will also determine the choice available. Products often are introduced later into international markets than to the home domestic market. The company's image and awareness are normally lower, in many cases much lower, than in the domestic market. The market share attainable in the market is lower, at least initially. This makes it a much less profitable business proposition for distribution channel intermediaries. Furthermore, distribution channels are already being used by other companies who will have built up relationships with the intermediaries. This provides less space and opportunity for firms newly entering the market.

Developing countries are characterized by distribution systems consisting of a myriad of intermediaries and retail outlets. Such fragmentation results in cost inefficiencies, as large volumes of product cannot be centralized and moved quickly from manufacturers to wholesalers to retailers.

Fragmented and circuitous channels also diminish possible competitive advantage by reducing the abilities of firms to get their products and services quickly and efficiently to masses of buyers. This is particularly the case for time-sensitive products. For example, overnight package couriers in a number of markets have failed in some cases to live up to delivery promises due to flight cancellations, poor road conditions and insufficient phone lines.

Often in emerging markets, the problems of fragmented distribution are compounded by legal restrictions as to which channels of distribution can be used by foreign importers.

The World Trade Organization is working towards the opening up of participation in distribution systems by foreign firms in a number of countries. India and Indonesia have eased restrictions, making it much easier for international companies to develop their own distribution systems. Previously, foreign companies had not been allowed to set up their own distribution networks. Thailand has welcomed foreign investment, but then Tesco (UK) faced severe restrictions in Thailand when the ruling military council restricted their expansion plans in the country. However, many regions are actively encouraging the development of a global retailing industry.

## Capital required and costings

In evaluating the financial implications of channel selection, a firm needs to assess the relative cost of each channel, the consequences on cash flow and the capital required.

**The relative costs of each channel**   It is generally considered that it may be cheaper to use agents than set up a firm's own sales force in international markets. However, the firm has little control and may have little commitment from the agent. Also, if the company has long-term objectives in the market, then as sales develop, the use of agents may be more expensive than employing the company's own sales force. A break-even analysis is necessary to evaluate the relative cost of each channel alternative over time.

## ILLUSTRATION 10.2

# Distribution networks full of accommodation for leisure travellers

Hotels are using online distribution channels to sell their rooms direct to leisure travellers. They showcase rooms via a direct booking platform on their website, which can be accessed via a consumer's PC, phone or hotel app. Leisure travellers receive many benefits by choosing to book via the hotel website. A hotel's website is the most cost-effective way of providing marketing messages, prices for rooms, visibility of company values, social responsibilities, environmental credentials and, of course, facilitating bookings. And more importantly for the busy leisure traveller, the online booking can even be made at the last minute while waiting for holiday/business luggage to arrive from the aeroplane. The reason this is possible is because hotel websites are open 24/7 and working in real time.

Hotels also have other ways to indirectly receive bookings, for example, by selling rooms to consumers via a travel company. Worldwide travel companies include Kuoni, TUI, First Choice and Explore: Adventure Travel Holidays. Hotels sell rooms directly to travel companies (B2B) which then sell directly to the leisure traveller (B2C).

Another way hotels indirectly sell rooms to consumers is through OTAs, which for hotels is a B2B transaction. Well-known OTAs include Experian.com, Priceline.com, Orbitz.com, Trivago.com and Hotels.com. The hotel pays a commission to OTAs for bookings made. The commission is around 15 to 25 per cent of the price of the room sold. The OTAs sell directly to the leisure consumer.

However, many leisure consumers still book their holiday by walking down the high street and speaking face-to-face with a travel agent. The travel agent still gets commission for selling rooms for a hotel. High-street travel agents are seeing an upturn in the number of visits to their stores because leisure consumers are becoming frustrated and stressed with arranging their own travel. The reasons for their frustration are:

1  There are so many online hotel booking sites to choose from.

2  There are so many 'deals'; it is not clear which is best for them.

3  Searching for the right hotel takes too much time.

4  Once the hotel room is booked, consumers then need to organize the 'add-ons' such as travel insurance and transport to and from the airport from the hotel.

## Questions

**1** How are online distribution networks beneficial to hoteliers?

**2** What impact do OTAs and the sharing economy have on the hotel industry?

**3** Name five other B2B and B2C relationships that are similar to hotels selling a room to a travel company who then sells the same room to a leisure traveller.

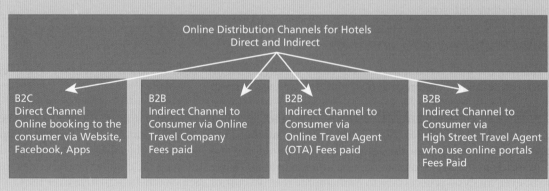

Online Distribution Channels for Hotels
Direct and Indirect

**B2C**
Direct Channel
Online booking to the consumer via Website, Facebook, Apps

**B2B**
Indirect Channel to Consumer via Online Travel Company
Fees paid

**B2B**
Indirect Channel to Consumer via Online Travel Agent (OTA) Fees paid

**B2B**
Indirect Channel to Consumer via High Street Travel Agent who use online portals Fees Paid

**Consequences on cash flow**   If a firm uses wholesalers or distributors then traditionally they take ownership of the goods and the risks. This has a positive impact on cash flow. If the firm wishes to circumvent such channels and deal direct with the retailer or even the consumer, it means they have to be prepared to take on some of the traditional wholesaler services. These include the offering of credit, breaking bulk and small orders. This means the firm will have capital and resources tied up in managing the distribution chain rather than developing the market.

**Capital required**   Direct distribution systems need capital injected to establish them. Non-recurring capital costs, as well as the recurring running costs when evaluating expected return in the long term, have to be taken into account.

A company also needs to evaluate whether it can raise the finance locally or whether borrowing restrictions are placed on foreign companies, what grants are available and what the regulations on earnings capital repatriation will be.

## The coverage needed

Required coverage will also be a determining factor. In some markets, to get 100 per cent coverage of a market, the costs of using the company's own sales force may be too high. This would make indirect channels more appropriate, especially in countries which are characterized by large rural populations. However, firms who rely on sparse retail outlets can maximize the opportunities that fragmented distribution channels afford. Avon has recruited and groomed armies of sales representatives to sell its cosmetics directly to millions in all reaches of Brazil, Mexico, Poland, China and Argentina. Altogether Avon has successful sales operations in 56 countries and is distributing to 18 others in a diverse set of countries that includes emerging economies as well as developed countries (Avon Company 2018). There are now over 6 million Avon representatives achieving a revenue of $5 715.6 million (2017), which was $5 717.7 million.

## Control, continuity and communication

If a firm is building an international competitive advantage in providing a quality service throughout the world, then channels that enable the firm to achieve rapid response in foreign markets will be important. Also of importance will be the development of a distribution system which gives them total control in the marketplace and effective direct communication to their customer.

It is the drive to achieve high levels of quality of service that, to some extent, has led to the breakdown of conventional barriers between manufacturers, agents, distributors and retailers. This is when firms strive to develop effective vertical marketing systems. Such firms will be selecting intermediaries which will enable them to be solution-oriented service providers operating on high margins across a multitude of international markets.

To achieve this, some manufacturers have bought themselves into retailing and other parts of the supply chain. Others, such as Benetton, have pursued similar results by franchising. From small beginnings, Benetton launched its business in 1965 and now operates in 120 countries with over 5000 retail stores in the Benetton network (Benetton Group 2018).

## The selection and contracting process

Having evaluated the criteria, a firm must select intermediaries capable of helping the firm achieve its goals and objectives. The intermediaries chosen must provide the geographic coverage needed and the services required in the particular international market(s). It is often desirable to select intermediaries that are native to the country where they will be doing business, as this will enhance their ability to build and maintain customer relationships.

The selection process for channel members will be based upon an assessment of their:

- sales volume potential
- geographic and customer coverage
- financial strength (which will be checked through credit rating services and references)
- managerial capabilities

- the size and quality of the sales force
- any marketing communications services
- the nature and reputation of the business.

In some countries, religious or ethnic differences might make an agent suitable for one part of the market coverage but unsuitable in another. This can result in more channel members being required to give adequate market coverage.

Before final contractual arrangements are made, it is thought wise to make personal visits to the prospective channel member. The long-term commitment involved in distribution channels can become particularly difficult if the contract between the company and the channel member is not carefully drafted. It is normal to prescribe a time limit and a minimum sales level to be achieved, in addition to the particular responsibilities for each party. If this is not carried out satisfactorily, the company may be stuck with a weak performer that either cannot be removed or is very costly to buy out from their contract.

# Building relationships in foreign market channels

Management of sales activities and business relationships across international boundaries is a particularly complex and often overwhelming task. The combination of diverse languages, dissimilar cultural heritages and remote geographic locations can create strong barriers to building and maintaining effective buyer–seller relationships. Further, in international settings, communications are often complicated by a lack of trust – a critical dimension in any business relationship. Non-verbal cues, product origin biases, sales force nationality issues and differences in intercultural negotiation styles add even more complexity to the international business environment. Added to the traditional responsibilities of a sales manager, these factors make managing international relationships in distribution channels a unique and challenging task. Thus, it is crucial for firms and their sales managers both to understand and be able to work within various international markets throughout the world.

## Motivating international marketing intermediaries

International marketing intermediaries can pick and choose the products they will promote to their customers. Therefore, they need to be motivated to emphasize the firm's products. As difficult as it is for manufacturers to motivate their domestic distributors or dealers, it is even more difficult in the international arena. The environment, culture and customs affecting seller–intermediary relationships can be complicating factors for the uninitiated. Organizations need to understand this too.

Motivation, whether in the context of domestic or international channels, is the process through which the manufacturer seeks to gain the support of the marketing intermediary in carrying out the manufacturer's marketing objectives. Three basic elements are involved in this process (Rosenbloom 2012):

1 Finding out the needs and problems of marketing intermediaries.
2 Offering support that is consistent with their needs and problems.
3 Building continuing relationships.

First, the needs and problems of international marketing intermediaries can be dramatically different from those at home. One of the most common differences is in the size of the intermediary. In emerging economies in Asia, Africa and Latin America, dealers may be family businesses with little desire to grow larger. This may also be true for more developed economies in eastern Europe, Japan and Italy. Thus, they may not aggressively promote a foreign manufacturer's product.

Second, the specific support programme provided by the manufacturer to its international intermediaries should be based on a careful analysis of their needs and problems. Factors to be included are:

- the adequacy of the profit margins available
- the guarantee of exclusive territories
- the adequacy and availability of advertising assistance
- the offer of needed financial assistance.

In light of the cost structures faced by many foreign market distributors and dealers, the need to provide them with good margin potentials on the imported products they handle is even more important. Doing so, however, may force manufacturers to change their ideas of what constitutes a 'fair' or 'reasonable' margin for foreign market distributors.

Territorial protection or even the guarantee of exclusive territories sought by many distributors in the domestic market can be even more desirable in foreign markets. On some international markets, distributors, many of whom may have quite limited financial resources, will not want to assume the risk of handling and promoting a foreign manufacturer's product line if other distributors will be competing in the same territory for the same customers.

Advertising assistance for distributors and dealers is another vital form of support. A foreign manufacturer, especially a large one, can have an advantage over indigenous firms in providing advertising support because of its often greater financial resources and experience in the use of advertising. The top two distributors (Source Today 2018) of electronic goods are:

1  Avenet, Inc., which has built its organization because business customers wanted a trusted organization that would handle their supply chain. Its sales amount to $25.17 billion and it has 17 700 employees.

2  Arrow Electronics also deals with distributions for its business customers in over 80 countries. Its sales amount to $83.8 billion and it has 18 700 employees.

Distribution is big business; therefore, businesses that manufacture and supply electronic equipment to customers around the world need to trust a third party to ensure that it arrives on time and undamaged.

Financial assistance in countries where intermediaries are small and fragmented is essential. Levi-Strauss found in Russia that they needed to give a six-month credit period to persuade intermediaries to stock their products. Their usual credit period was 30 to 60 days. Such constraints do not mean that manufacturers selling through foreign market intermediaries cannot build strong relationships with them – it is certainly possible to do so. However, the approach used may have to be quite different from that taken with intermediaries in their home market. Companies from the USA predominantly motivate distributors through financial incentives. However, in many other cultures motivating factors such as status, personal recognition and, in some cases management support, are much more important.

It is vital to keep in regular contact with intermediaries. A consistent flow of all relevant types of communications will stimulate interest and sales performance. The cultural interface between the company and the channel member is the essence of corporate rapport. Business people from low context cultures may be thought to be insensitive and disrespectful by agents in high context culture countries. The problem can be compounded if sales performance is discussed too personally. According to Usunier and Lee (2009), precise measurement of sales people's performance, for example of the agent or the distributors, may be considered as almost evil in some countries. In South East Asia the ethic of non-confrontation clearly clashes with an objective to review performance. Various types of motivation need to be considered. In some cultures, intrinsic and group-related rewards work best. In the USA, a country in which individualism and rationalism are the foundations of its society, individual and extrinsic rewards work best. In the UAE relationships and feedback are important. Businesses need to understand that UAE intermediaries are not motivated by negative feedback, but are motivated by positive feedback. So, delivery of on-site training, on-site visits and joint agreement on objectives and task are beneficial.

## Controlling intermediaries in international markets

The process of control is difficult. Control problems are substantially reduced if channel members are selected carefully, have appropriately drafted contracts which have been mutually understood and agreed, and are motivated in a culturally empathetic way.

Control attempts are often exercised through other companies and sometimes through several layers of distribution intermediaries. Control should be sought through the development of written plans with clearly expressed performance objectives. These performance objectives would include some of the following:

- sales turnover per year
- number of accounts
- market share

- growth rate
- introduction of new products
- price charged
- marketing communications support.

Control should be exercised through a regular report programme and periodic personal meetings. Evaluation of performance and control against agreed plans has to be interpreted against the changing environment. In some situations, economic recession or fierce competition activity prevent objectives from being met. However, if poor performance is established, the contract between the company and the channel member will have to be reconsidered and, perhaps, terminated. In an age in which relationship marketing is becoming more important in the western world, the long-term building of suitable distribution relationships provides something of the eastern flavour of obligation and working together.

## Channel updating

In managing distribution channels, firms need to ensure that, as they increase their involvement in global markets, they are able to adapt and update their channel strategy accordingly. Thus, the management monitoring and control mechanisms a firm puts in place should give them the ability to develop their presence in the marketplace. In China, Kodak ensured this capability was in place in their early negotiations when setting up their local manufacturing and distribution operations by taking over three lossmaking Chinese companies. They also extended a package to all their distributors offering help including marketing assistance to corner shops in exchange for becoming a Kodak Express and evicting competing film brands from the stores. Kodak's presence in China has been strong over the years, so when the Chinese government called for 'green printing' to take place in China, Kodak was there. In 2017 it launched the opening of a new technology centre. The output will be distributed across the Asia Pacific region (Kodak 2017). Dell built a global brand by focusing on a direct sales model. However, they too have adapted their strategy in response to customer needs and have introduced a retail presence.

## Developing a company-owned international sales force

Firms with expansion plans and an interest in becoming more involved in global markets will eventually take control of implementing their own marketing strategies. They will establish and manage their own international sales force. Generally, the firms begin to gradually move from indirect exporting to direct exporting via marketing intermediaries to a company-owned sales force (Kotler and Armstrong 2014). The company can do this in several ways, including travelling export sales reps, a domestic-based export department or division and a foreign-based sales branch or subsidiary.

The advantages of using a company-owned sales force include:

- It provides far greater control over the sales and marketing effort because the sales force is now directly employed by the company.
- It facilitates formation of closer manufacturer–customer relationships.
- Once established, the company-owned sales force can be helpful in identifying and exploiting new international marketing opportunities.

The disadvantages of developing a company-owned sales force include:

- A relatively larger resource commitment.
- Somewhat higher exit costs should the firm decide to no longer serve a particular market.
- Increased exposure to unexpected changes in the political/social environment of the host country.

One common strategy is to begin export operations by establishing a domestic-based export department and/or using home-based travelling salespeople. Then, as sales reach a certain volume in the new market, the decision is made to set up a foreign-based sales branch or subsidiary in the country.

The new unit may be strictly a marketing/sales arm or may also involve a production or warehouse facility. In either event, the firm must make a commitment of resources to develop its own direct sales force to sell the firm's offerings and build relationships with the firm's customers in that market.

It may well be that a firm uses its own sales force for key accounts and agents and distributors for small accounts. Equally, its own sales force may work in conjunction with international intermediaries, building links directly with customers but always with and through the intermediaries. This has the advantage of enabling the firm to build relationships with the customer and the intermediaries, while not having to make the capital investment required to run a wholly owned subsidiary.

However, for many multinationals, managing international operations is an issue of 'does the company control operations centrally or allow sales subsidiaries around the world a high degree of autonomy?' In some countries they may have little choice, due to the strength of local competition and the loyalty of local distributors to locally made brands.

# Trends in retailing in international markets

Retailing structures differ across countries, reflecting their different histories, geography and politics. Retailing varies across the different levels of economic development and is influenced by cultural variations. The cultural importance attached to food in France provides the opportunity for small specialist food retailers to survive and prosper. In other developed countries, for example the USA, the trend is towards very large superstores which incorporate a wide range of speciality foods. The French approach relies on small-scale production by the retail proprietor. The US approach encourages mass production, branding and sophisticated distribution systems to handle inventory and freshness issues.

In this section, our discussion will be concerned with three important issues for international marketers. First, the differences in the patterns of retailing around the world with particular reference to emerging markets and developing countries. Second, the internationalization of retailers and its impact on distribution channel structures. Third, the emergence of new forms of retailing which are particularly relevant to firms competing on international markets.

## The differing patterns of retailing around the world

The concentration of the retailing industry varies significantly between markets. Low concentration ratios of retailer ownership give more power to the manufacturer. A 'no' decision from any one retailer does not make a big impact on total sales. While the low concentration ratios to be found in Japan and Italy and in many lesser developed countries increase the relative power of the manufacturer, there are problems. First, low concentration ratios in retailers might be counterbalanced by powerful wholesalers. Second, the costs of the sales force in calling on a multiplicity of very small retailers and the logistics of delivering products to them can reduce the manufacturer's profitability. If economies are sought by using wholesalers, the power balance might tilt away from the manufacturer to the wholesaler.

The main differences between traditional retailing structures found in lesser developed countries and the advanced retailing structures in more developed economies are illustrated in Table 10.1.

Retailing in developing countries is characterized by low levels of capital investment. The large size, purpose-built retail outlet, full of specialist display shelving and electronic point of sale equipment, is rarely found in less developed countries. The more likely picture is of a very small space with goods sold by the counter service method and technology limited to a cash register or a pocket calculator. That does not mean to say that there are not innovations or exciting things happening in these markets. As you can see in Illustration 10.3, Nina Interiors, an East African retailer, is changing the way retailing business is done in that region.

Retail stores are often managed by the owner/proprietor and staffed by the extended family. The lack of capital input is partially offset by large quantities of low-cost labour, and the management style is usually based on limiting risks. The retailer will seek to stock goods with a proven demand pattern. In addition, the retailer will try to obtain interest-free credit from the interface channel partners: the wholesaler and the manufacturer.

Distribution channels in developing countries depend on manufacturers and wholesalers for their sales promotion ideas and materials. In developed countries retailers often take the initiative regarding sales promotions and will develop their own schemes. The opportunities for the manufacturer to influence the retailer in advanced countries are becoming fewer and fewer.

## ILLUSTRATION 10.3

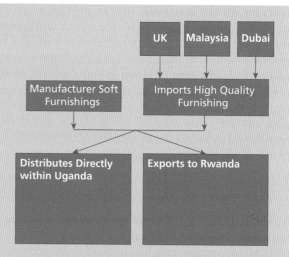

UK | Malaysia | Dubai

Manufacturer Soft Furnishings

Imports High Quality Furnishing

Distributes Directly within Uganda

Exports to Rwanda

# Nina Interiors: from a soft furnishing store to an importing and exporting superbrand

One of the superbrands of East Africa is Nina Interiors. Before moving into the world of soft furnishings, Mrs Alice Karugaba worked as a secretary for the East African Development Bank in Uganda during the early 1980s. She also had a creative side and in 1981 had started to bake her favourite (and her customers' favourite) cakes and buns. Baking cakes and buns supplemented her income from the bank but also helped Mrs Karugaba to become an international entrepreneur. In 1989, she wound up her cake and bun business and partnered with McCrae's who made high quality interior furniture such as beds, sofas, cupboards, wardrobes, tables and chairs. However, McCrae's did not make soft furnishings, such as cushions, curtains and bed spreads. To provide their consumers with a full package of goods, they employed Mrs Karugaba. The McCrae and Karugaba partnership was successful, but in 1991 they parted company. So Mrs Karugaba gathered her savings and created her own business called Nina Interiors.

Mrs Karugaba also wanted to offer her customers a full package of goods, but she and her part-time seamstress could only make soft furnishings and repair covers for chairs and sofas. She decided to research high-quality interior furniture and found that Malaysia, the UK and Dubai provided the best. She then imported them into her home country of Uganda.

Currently, Nina Interiors distributes products to a store based in Kampala and exports to another store in Kigali, Rwanda. Products are also displayed and shown on its retail store's website where orders can be placed online. Currently, Mrs Karugaba only exports to Rwanda. However, products now include home and office interior furniture and accompanying soft furnishings. Her office interior furniture is purchased by international brands that have stores or offices in Uganda. The international brands include Barclays and Toyota. Clients of Mrs Karugaba's interior furniture, the office of the President, the National Water and Sewerage Corporation and the offices of the Ministry of Education.

Nina Interiors has been recognized by the International Trade Centre as a successful company that is exporting from Uganda, especially when it comes to the gender dimension of trade from Uganda. The staff working for Nina Interiors are mainly women making soft furnishings. The store in Uganda was also the first furniture store in Uganda that had a large store format (2000 m$^2$). This has paved the way for other Ugandan retailers to showcase their products in an open, design-led format.

## Questions

**1** What do you think the main distribution challenges were for Nina Interiors?

**2** Why do international brands choose Nina Interiors for their offices?

**Reference:** Nina Interiors (2018) http://ninainteriors.co.ug/.

Table 10.1   Retailers: typical differences between developing and developed countries

| Retailing issues | Traditional retailers in developing countries | Advanced retailing structures in mature economies |
|---|---|---|
| Concentration of retail power | Low | Often high |
| Site selection and retail location | Limited to the immediate locality | Very important, often sophisticated techniques to pinpoint the most valuable sites |
| Size of outlet | Limited | Large and tending to get larger |
| Retailer initiation of product assortment | Limited to the buy/no buy decision | Wide range of stock possible. Use of own-label and store-specific sales promotions |
| Retail concepts, images and corporate identity | Rarely used | Very important |
| Retailer-initiated sales promotion | Rarely used. Reliance on manufacturer and wholesaler-developed sales promotion and point of sale material | Very important |
| Use of retail technology | Limited | Vital, e.g. EDI, EPOS |
| Service | Mainly counter service | Mass customization, sophisticated CRM systems |

Small-scale retailing limits the opportunities to follow own-label strategies. The minimum economies of scale cannot be reached by the small urban and rural retailer in developing countries. The balance of power lies with the manufacturer to innovate and adapt products.

The proliferation of very many small-scale retailers means that the retail market is widely dispersed. The levels of concentration of ownership are much lower than are found in mature economies with relatively structured levels of retailing.

These differences give rise to principally four stages of retailing around the world: traditional, intermediary, structured and advanced.

## Traditional retailing

'Traditional retailers' are typically found in Africa, Asia, Latin America and Japan. The concentration of operators is weak, segmentation is non-existent and the level of integration of new technology is very low. These are often small-scale family retailing businesses employing few people and with a low turnover. Traditionally, the retail market in India fell into this group and was largely unorganized. But with changing consumer preferences, organized retail is gradually becoming popular. Unorganized retailing in India consists of small and medium grocery stores, medicine stores, Subzi Mandi, Kirana Stores, Paan shops. Many countries have unorganized and organized types of retail activities. However, considering the market size of India is expected to increase to around US$1.1 trillion in the next ten years or so, it is worth looking at the breakdown of the unorganized and organized retail sectors:

Unorganized retail sector: 91% of the total retail sector

Organized retail sector: 9% of the total retail sector

Source: India Brand Equity Foundation (2018) Retail Industry in India www.Ibef.org.

This divergence in the sector brings particular challenges to global operators (see Illustration 10.4).

## ILLUSTRATION 10.4

# Comparative retailing traditions

In the UK, consumers are used to shops being open 7 days a week and in the USA 24/7. In Germany, however, it is only recently that shops have been allowed to open on Saturday afternoons. A new federal law allows city centre shops to open until 8 p.m. However, outside the city most still close at 4 p.m. for the weekend and Sunday opening is still highly restricted. This is much the same as New Zealand where stores close at 5.30 p.m. except for one night each week when they are open until 9.00 p.m. Stores are also closed on Sundays and many are closed on Saturday afternoons.

In India, opening hours are unrestricted, but most retail stores are family owned and are much smaller in size. With the exception of a few (small) super bazaars, consumers are not allowed to walk freely inside the stores, examine and compare labels of different brands before making the selection. The salesperson collects the items which the customer wishes to purchase, having made a list beforehand.

Retailing in Greece has until recently been small-scale and highly traditional. The majority of stores are family owned and small in size. Shopping for pleasure is less popular. However, the entry into the country of some of the big global retailers is starting to change the face of retailing there.

## Question

1 How can a company achieve a global distribution strategy when retailing infrastructures vary so much?

## *Intermediary retailing*

Retailing in Italy, Spain and eastern Europe is in the process of transformation, being both modern and traditional, and so examples of intermediary retailing. Most businesses are independent with a turnover lower than the European average. However, there is a marked tendency towards concentration, particularly in the food sector, where the number of food retailing outlets per 1000 people is dropping. The importance of wholesalers and voluntary chains is still very strong, particularly in Italy, where there are 192 000 wholesale businesses. See Management Challenge 10.2 for an example of a distribution channel used by farmers.

In the major cities of China there have been huge developments in the retail structure of the country, taking retailing in the major cities to a very advanced status. China is encouraging mergers and partnerships between indigenous retailers to reduce costs and improve competitiveness. China also wants to ensure they have the capacity to compete against such global operators as Walmart and Carrefour, who are fighting for a share of the US$1.8 trillion retail market. Shanghai Bailian Group Co., Ltd, China's largest retailer, is a vertical integrated organization that manages the entire operation process from product design, to production, to sales. At present, products under the brand name of 'Bailian' are sold in more than 300 direct outlets throughout China. However, like India, outside the major cities of Shanghai and Beijing, China's retail sector is still dominated by small neighbourhood stores and local markets.

Countries with intermediary retailing structures are obviously attractive locations for retailers expanding internationally as they are seen as latent markets ripe for expansion. The level of economic development and the intermediary structure of retailing has historically meant that these countries are not host to large domestic retailers, making entry into the market relatively easy.

Since the late 2000s, the entry of foreign operators into regions such as Latin America have altered the retailing landscape. There are now hypermarkets, variety stores and non-food specialists which have stimulated competition and greatly modernized retailing across the continent.

## MANAGEMENT CHALLENGE 10.2

# Government and e-Choupal: farming in the Wardha District

Agriculture in India is big business and accounts for 66 per cent of the workforce. This group of workers produces 23 per cent of the GDP for India. However, the distribution channel for farmers of small-holdings may be unfair. The vertical distribution channel is shown in Figure 10.4.

The distribution channel is flawed as the farmers are often unaware of global agricultural pricing trends. In addition, the farmers may be exploited as the price given at auction may be fixed between the purchasing agent and the national and international traders. Finally, farmers often have to wait for hours, if not days, to sell all their produce.

ITC Ltd are an exceptionally successful business in India. One of their core values is to generate economic value for the nation. They do not mean just their business should bring value to India. So when they saw the plight of rural farmers in India they decided to help. ITC Ltd developed an agricultural Internet platform called e-Choupal for rural farming communities in India.

Choupal is Hindi for village meeting place. The e-Choupal provided a kiosk through which there is a virtual meeting place for rural farmers and a process for selling produce.

Farmers pay a very small fee to have ITC Ltd, which includes hardware, such as a PC and Internet wireless hub, and software, such as the agro farming package. The e-Choupal provides rural farmers with the opportunity to discover crop prices, soil-testing services, scientifically proven farming practices and weather reports, as well as have informal chats with other farmers throughout the world.

There are two special services available via the e-Choupal kiosk:

1  Spot quote system: A farmer brings a small bag of produce, it is weighed and an on-the-spot price is given.

2  Produce handling system: The farmers arrange for all the produce they want to sell, following the spot price of course, to be collected. The collected produce is delivered to an ITC Ltd collection centre. Upon arrival of the produce at the collection centre the farmer is paid within two hours.

An unexpected benefit of e-Choupal is that school children have used the PC and wireless Internet system to help them with their homework.

**FIGURE 10.4**  Vertical distribution channel

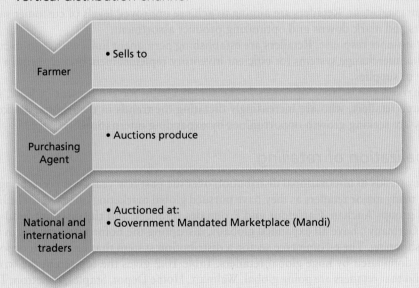

**Farmer**
• Sells to

**Purchasing Agent**
• Auctions produce

**National and international traders**
• Auctioned at:
• Government Mandated Marketplace (Mandi)

**Reference:** Admane, R.A. (2014) ITC's e-Choupal: A market-ing strategy for rural transformation – A case study of Wardha District. *Maharashtra International Journal of Management Research and Business Strategy* 3(1), 249–257.

## Questions

**1** For an emerging market discuss the disadvantages of the vertical distribution system shown in Figure 10.4.

**2** What benefits has the Internet brought to rural farm-ers in India?

## Structured retailing

Retailing in the north of Europe tends to be fairly structured, reflecting the level of economic development. Denmark, Luxembourg, the Netherlands and France have enterprises that are larger in size, have a higher level of concentration and a greater level of productivity per employee than southern European retailers.

In these markets, retail competition is fairly well developed, and there is a mature relationship between suppliers and retailers.

Retailers also have introduced fairly sophisticated technologies facilitating more elaborate competitive strategies. They are also finding growth through opportunities overseas and new retailing formats.

## Advanced retailing

The US, Germany and the UK are all examples of countries in which retailing is the most advanced in terms of concentration, segmentation, capitalization and integration. Retailer strategies are advanced, very market focused and generally incorporate five important dimensions.

Interactive customer marketing. Targeting of customers as individuals, developing strategies to improve retention and increase sales per shop visit.

Mass customization. Retailers are looking for improved margins through higher volumes, reduced costs and achieving low levels of returns.

Data mining. Retailers are using technology and electronic point of sale information to improve knowl-edge of customers, ensuring the ability to make targeted offers which are timely and clearly differentiated. Data mining is beginning to be used by retailers in emerging and developing markets where previously there has been little reliable data on which to base decisions, as can be seen in Illustration 10.3 in the case of Nina Interiors.

Category management. Retailers are aiming to achieve improved levels of customer satisfaction through reducing costs and mark downs and optimizing product assortment.

Effective consumer response. Retailers are establishing permanent links with manufacturers, establishing electronic data interchange systems for efficient inventory replenishment and ensuring a continuous just in time delivery of supplies.

In these markets the balance of power in the supply chain, for the present at least, seems to lie firmly with these large retailers, who are increasingly dictating the trends in their home markets. As these reach maturity they are seeking growth opportunities by expanding internationally.

## The globalization of retailing

One of the key trends in international distribution over the past few years has been the aggressive strategies employed by many major retailers as they have pursued global marketing objectives. The likes of Tesco (UK); hypermarket groups Auchan, Carrefour and Promodes (France); and the discount food retailers Aldi, Lidl and Swartz (Germany), have all expanded globally, disrupting the home retail sectors in terms of price and out of town shopping. The e-commerce sector, a distribution system that has grown exponentially in recent years, is now dominated by huge global retailers. Table 10.2 gives the top ten in the world. However, it is not just in food that retailers are going global. Walmart, Home Depot, Staples, Benetton, The Body Shop and Hertz are all now global retailers. Hong Kong retailers A S Watson and Dairy Farm have entered neighbour-ing countries with supermarkets and pharmaceutical chains. Japanese department stores Takashimaya and

Table 10.2   Top ten global powers of retailing

| Top retailer rank FY$_{16}$ | Name of company | Country of origin | FY$_{16}$ retail revenue (US\$ million) | FY$_{16}$ retail revenue growth % |
|---|---|---|---|---|
| 1 | Walmart Stores Inc. | US | 485 873 | 0.8 |
| 2 | Costco Wholesale Corporation | US | 118 719 | 2.2 |
| 3 | The Kroger Co. | US | 115 337 | 5.0 |
| 4 | Schwarz Group | Germany | 99 256 | 5.3 |
| 5 | Walgreens Boots Alliance Inc. | US | 97 058 | 8.3 |
| 6 | Amazon.com, Inc | US | 94 665 | 19.4 |
| 7 | The Home Depot, Inc | US | 94 595 | 6.9 |
| 8 | Aldi Group | Germany | 84 923* | 4.8 |
| 9 | Carrefour S.A. | France | 84 131 | −0.4 |
| 10 | CVS Health Corporation | US | 81 100 | 12.6 |

\* estimate

Source: Deloitte (2018) *Global Powers of Retailing 2018*. Available from www2.deloitte.com/uk/en/pages/consumer-business/articles/global-powers-of-retailing.html (accessed 5 June 2018).

Isetan have established outlets across Asia. More recently this trend has accelerated, with German retailers Metro, Rewe and Tengelmann expanding into the Czech Republic, Hungary and Poland, often using joint ventures with former socialist cooperatives. Three western European retailers, Tengelmann (Germany), Ahold (Netherlands) and Delhaizae Le Lion (Belgium), now generate more sales and profit from their foreign activities, which include the US, central Europe and Asia, than they do in their home markets. The smaller high-growth economies such as Ireland have also been attracting the particular interest of the expanding globals. The e-commerce markets with top e-commerce companies, like Amazon, Alibaba, Walmart, Otto and JD, have also expanded their distribution networks far and wide.

The expansion of international activity of retailers around the world has given rise to five different types of international retailers:

1  the hypermarket
2  the power retailers
3  the niche retailer
4  the designer flagship stores who target particular global cities for their stores
5  the online international retailer which tends to have warehouses in out of town sites or uses the distribution networks already available in that country.

Examples of high-end international brands that adorn fashionable city high streets with speciality stores include Alberta Ferretti, Joseph, Alexander McQueen, Manolo Blahnik, Agent Provocateur, Galliano, Tom Ford and Lanvin.

As well as the growing sophistication of the industry and the opening up of new markets around the world, the globalization of retailers can be attributed to a number of 'pull' and 'push' factors.

The 'push' factors are:

■  Saturation of the home market or over-competition.

■  Economic recession or limited growth in spending.

■  A declining or ageing population.

- Strict planning policies on store development.
- High operating costs – labour, rents, taxation.
- Shareholder pressure to maintain profit growth.
- The 'me too' syndrome in retailing.

The 'pull' factors are:

- The underdevelopment of some markets or weak competition
- Strong economic growth or rising standards of living.
- High population growth or a high concentration of young adults.
- A relaxed regulatory framework.
- Favourable operating costs – labour, rents, taxation.
- The geographical spread of trading risks.
- The opportunity to innovate under new market conditions.

## Marketing implications for development of international distribution strategies

The internationalization of retailing has meant a new era of distribution is developing. This new competitive landscape in distribution has a number of implications for the development of the distribution strategies of international firms. The most important of these are:

- Power shifts in supply chains towards retailers.
- Intense concentrated competition with significant buyer power across country markets.
- Rapidly advancing technology facilitating global sourcing and global electronic transactions.
- Unrelenting performance measures being demanded of suppliers by international retailers.
- Smart, demanding consumers expecting high levels of customer service.

Thus, power in many international markets is moving from the supplier down the supply chain to the consumer. This means effective management is critical to suppliers competing in international markets. It again highlights the importance of ensuring the distribution strategy across international markets is driven by an understanding of the target market segments, both within each foreign country market and across national market boundaries.

This intensive growth in the size and power of retailers in countries with advanced retailing structures and retailers internationalizing means there is now tremendous pressure on suppliers to improve the quality of service to them. Retailers are demanding:

- Streamlined and flexible supply chains.
- Suppliers who can guarantee quality and reliability across global markets.
- The ability to supply high volumes and close relationships with intermediaries in the supply chain.
- Suppliers who can meet the global sourcing requirements of large-scale retailers who wish to buy centrally across the globe.

It could mean, therefore, that the firms who are successful are the firms who develop the capability to compete effectively in the supply chain activities compared to their international competitors. It is for this reason that the distribution strategy of the international company has taken on such an important dimension in recent times.

## Internet retailing

Multimedia technology has provided a number of opportunities for interactive shopping which offer particular opportunities in international markets. Tele-shopping and the Internet offer suppliers the retailing opportunities for direct contact with consumers throughout the globe. What is more, they can achieve this without the problems and expense of having to establish infrastructures in foreign country markets. For example, Amazon.com, like other bookshops, which sell purely over the Internet, carries no books as they are directly shipped from the publishers' or distributors' warehouses; or read online via a Kindle. This means Amazon has few inventory or real estate costs. Amazon proactively traps individual information on consumer purchases and then flash messages back telling consumers of other products bought by consumers making similar purchases. The diffusion of the Internet is increasingly challenging the traditional channels of distribution. It has the capacity to bring together buyers and sellers around the world through the creation of an online marketplace. The number of digital buyers worldwide in 2014 was 1.32 billion. This is estimated to increase to 2.05 billion by 2019 and 2.14 billion by 2021 (Statista 2018). This means e-commerce will continue to change distribution and logistics services. Management Challenge 10.3 below shows the challenges with distribution.

---

## MANAGEMENT CHALLENGE 10.3

## The Philippines: growth potential but distribution headaches

If a country is to be successful in the current business environment it must have a good infrastructure. There are four elements that when combined together make a good infrastructure. The elements are (1) power supply, (2) transport network, (3) telecommunications, and, of course, (4) water and sanitation. If any of the elements is poor or inadequate, the quality of life for the country's citizens, and also the potential for growth, is severely affected.

The Philippines has the potential to grow. It is also a country which many global franchise brands are eager to do business with. However, there are some infrastructure issues in the Philippines. For example, around only 50 per cent of the population (20 per cent in rural areas) have piped water supplied to their homes. Open sewers and solid waste is commonplace in cities due to the deterioration of pipes and sanitation systems. Adequate sanitation and power supplies of electricity cannot keep up with the growth in urbanization and city living. Clearly, investment in power and sanitation is needed.

Investment in roads has also been limited in the Philippines. Distribution of products or building materials for hotels, restaurants, office blocks and housing is problematic. Of the 11 000 kilometres of paved roads, around 50 per cent is considered to be of poor quality. This means distribution of products is slow and the pot-holes can seriously damage the vehicles that transport products.

The Philippines has many seaports, with Manila being one of the busiest seaports in the world. However, cargos and containers full of produce, cars or building materials are often delayed or hampered by inadequate logistics from many of the seaports.

The market entry rules and regulations for telecommunications companies are slow, bureaucratic and very expensive. All telecommunication service providers have to have a franchise agreement and a certificate from the National Telecommunications Commission (NTC). Further, some telecommunication service providers are reluctant to complete the franchise agreement and get the certificate from the NTC as both are seen to be politically driven and corrupt processes.

### Question

**1** What should the Philippines do to be successful in the global business environment?

---

In international marketing the major impact, as we will discuss in Chapter 12, has been the ability of the Internet to enable SMEs to access niche markets around the globe that were previously too logistically difficult for them to access. By simply setting up their own sites, a company in effect becomes global and can sell goods and services throughout the world. However, there has also been the development of market sites which have impacted on the way business transactions take place internationally, such as:

- *Auctions*. Online marketplaces where negotiations of price between independent buyers and sellers are implemented through a standard auction open to all participants, including eBay and Dabsexchange. Even Sotheby's of London (established 1744) enables participants to bid for rare bottles of wine with estimated selling prices of £2600.

- *Single buyer markets.* Where a large buyer establishes an online intranet market for its own suppliers (e.g. GE TradeWeb). Usually for suppliers to gain access to the site they will have achieved the status of approved supplier.
- *Pure exchanges.* Where individual buyers and sellers are matched according to product offers and needs.

The most promising products are often those where existing intermediaries do not perform many of the traditional 'wholesaler' functions for a broad market owing to the high cost of servicing small diverse and geographically or functionally dispersed players. There are several market characteristics in international markets which favour the development of Internet-based distribution:

- *Inefficiencies in traditional distribution channels*, as in Japan where it is difficult for international operators to penetrate the market, so sellers cannot gain access to customers.
- *Market fragmentation.* Niche market players where customers are geographically dispersed across the globe and are not concentrated in any one country.
- *Minimum scale barriers.* Smaller exporters have traditionally been restricted from operating globally because of the costs and difficulties of exporting. They therefore lose out to larger players who reap economies of scale and exploit distribution relationships.
- *Commodity-type products.* Products with well-known technical specifications, or manufacturer brands that can easily be price-compared across countries and do not require substantial after-sales service.
- *Short life cycle products.* Product-markets with short life cycles create large quantities of obsolete and discontinued items. Customers may experience difficulty finding spare parts or compatible accessories for earlier generations of product.

# The management of the physical distribution of goods

Physical distribution management is concerned with the planning, implementing and control of physical flows of materials and final goods from points of origin to points of use to meet customer needs at a profit (Kotler and Armstrong 2014).

In international physical distribution of goods, the total distribution costs will be higher than domestic distribution. The extra activities, increased time taken and the need to adapt to special country requirements will all increase costs. The extra costs centre around three areas:

1 *Increased distance.* This means, in terms of costs, increased transport time, inventory, cash flow and insurance.
2 *New variables to consider.* New modes of transport (air, sea, rail, road), new types of documentation, packaging for long transit times.
3 *Greater market complexity.* Language differences require the translation of documents, the extra costs of bureaucracy and longer lines of communication.

It is important for the firm to take full account of all these extra costs when evaluating alternative distribution strategies. In taking the total distribution cost approach, firms will include the costs of transport, warehousing, inventory, order processing, documentation, packaging and the total cost of lost sales if delays occur. Companies find that changes to one element of distribution influence the performance and the costs of other elements. Management Challenge 10.3 shows that infrastructure problems can also make the physical distribution of products difficult.

## The logistics approach to physical distribution

Many writers on physical distribution use logistics and physical distribution as terms meaning the same thing. Kotler and Armstrong (2014) make the distinction between physical distribution as a more traditional activity and logistics as being more market-oriented. In this way, physical distribution thinking starts with the finished product at the end of the production line and then attempts to find low-cost solutions to get the product to the customer. Logistics thinking, on the other hand, considers the customer and then works back to the factory. In this section we will use the market-oriented view. We will use the term logistics to mean an integrated view of physical distribution management in which customer demand influences are at least as important as cost-cutting forces. More and more companies are integrating their physical distribution strategies and linking their operations in different countries with more common processes. In this way, they are rationalizing their manufacturing and distribution infrastructure to make more effective use of business resources and so taking a logistical view of their distribution operations.

In Europe, 75 per cent of businesses operating across European markets have a pan-European logistics or distribution strategy in place. McKinsey Consultants estimate the European logistics market to be worth about US$400 billion. The logistics function is having an increasing influence in many parts of the business, especially in inventory planning, IT, purchasing and manufacturing.

There are a number of factors influencing this change:

- Customers demanding improved levels of customer service.
- Electronic data interchange (EDI) becoming the all-pervading technology for firms to build links with customers, suppliers and distribution providers.
- Companies restructuring their physical distribution operations in response to the formation of regional trading blocs.

In the following sections, we will briefly examine the developments in each of the above areas.

## Customer service

The main elements of customer service will revolve around:

- order to delivery time
- consistency and reliability of delivery
- inventory availability
- order size constraints
- ordering convenience
- delivery time and flexibility
- invoicing procedures, documentation and accuracy
- claims procedure
- condition of goods
- salesperson's visits
- order status information
- after-sales support.

In developing customer service levels, it is essential to use the elements of service that the customer regards as important. Delivery reliability might be more important than a quick order to delivery time that is unreliable in meeting delivery schedules. Understanding the way in which the international customer perceives service is important. There will be considerable differences. Customers who are distant might be more concerned about the guarantees of reliable rapid availability than customers much closer to the production source. The corporate capability to meet widely differing customer requirements in different countries needs to be managed.

In all countries, customers are becoming increasingly demanding. Partnership arrangements are becoming significant in many sectors as supply chains become more integrated. These developments are usually driven by customer-led demands for improved service. Consumers are demanding ever quicker delivery and ever more added value from their products that increasingly require just in time distribution. Companies increasingly allow customers to track the progress of products through the distribution system via the Internet. The websites which allow customers to track the progress of their packages are attracting 1 million hits a day. The other major area of IT involvement is in stock control and buying. Despite having 1575 stores in

22 countries, the last ones opening in Serbia, C&A is still using 12 different own labels. In some locations it is delivering nine times a day to its stores due to its efficient centralized buying operation for men's, women's and children's wear.

## The restructuring of physical distribution operations

In mature trading regions such as the USA and Europe, a large number of firms have restructured their distribution networks in response to changes in the trading structures in the region. Cross-border deliveries have increased, and the number of factories and warehouses has decreased. The number of distribution centres serving more than one country has increased, whereas there has been a decrease in the number of warehouses dedicated to within-country movements.

Lucent Technology dispatches all its products from its factory in Spain to a test and assembly centre in Singapore before final delivery. It might go back to a customer sitting 10 kilometres away from the factory in Spain, but it will still go to Singapore first. The company gives a 48-hour delivery guarantee to customers anywhere in the world, posing demanding logistical challenges.

The physical movement of goods is a high-cost activity. Companies often incur 10 to 35 per cent of their expenditure on physical distribution. As distribution is so expensive, it is now receiving close attention from general management and from marketing management.

The logistics approach is to analyze customer requirements and to review what competitors are providing. Customers are interested in a number of things. These include deliveries to meet agreed time schedules, zero defect delivery, supplier willingness to meet emergency needs, supplier willingness to replace damaged goods quickly, and supplier willingness to engage in just in time delivery and inventory holding.

If a company is to achieve a logistically effective system of distribution, it will become involved in a highly complex and sophisticated system. It will, therefore, need to:

- clearly define areas of responsibility across foreign country markets
- have a highly developed planning system
- have an up-to-date and comprehensive information support system
- develop expertise in distribution management
- have a centralized planning body to coordinate activities and exercise overall control.

Thus, a logistical system helps the company to pay attention to inventory levels and think through market relationships. In this way it can minimize costs of stock out and maximize distribution efficiency across a large number of markets.

In developing an efficient logistical system of physical distribution across international markets there are a number of important considerations:

- how intermediaries such as freight forwarders can enhance the service
- what modes of transportation should be used
- how the firm can make effective use of export processing zones
- what documentation is required
- what are the packaging requirements for transit and the market
- how the export sales contract should be organized.

In the following sections, we will briefly discuss some of the important issues in each of these areas.

## The use of intermediaries

Traditionally, intermediaries such as forwarders and freight companies, simply offered transportation by land, sea and air. There are now many types of intermediaries which offer global logistical services. FedEx, UPS and DPWN (Deutsche Post World Net, which absorbed DHL) have global networks to offer express-delivery services which they also use to offer customized logistics solutions. Brokering houses such as Kuehne + Nagel offer their skills in tying together different modes of transport. Other companies offer specialized services, for instance transport and warehouse-management firms which organize the physical movement and storage of goods. Still others are dedicated contract carriers and freight forwarders who buy capacity on ships and cargo planes and put together loads from different companies to fill them. Most freight forwarders will offer services such as preparation and processing of international transport documents, coordination of transport services and the provision of warehousing. (See Illustration 10.5).

However, as we have seen, recent trends such as just in time delivery, outsourcing of non-core activities, cutting inventories and the trend to build to order (BTO) have meant international firms have had to build a comprehensive but flexible logistics operation. This is to ensure goods reach their customers around the world in the right place at the right time. It is such a challenging task that companies are no longer able to do it all themselves, so more of them are using intermediaries and outsourcing the logistical functions.

## ILLUSTRATION 10.5

# Freight forward 900 million tins of baked beans

A freight forwarder is a company that dispatches shipments via carriers, and books or otherwise arranges space for shipments. Carriers could include vessels, aeroplanes, trucks or railroads.

Freight forwarders 'arrange cargo to an international destination and have the expertise that allows them to prepare and process the documentation *and* perform activities that are needed for international shipments'.

During 2014 European freight business saw a positive growth in business. Overall 46.9 million 'twenty-foot equivalent units' (TEUs) passed through European seaports alone. This is an increase of 5.4 per cent on the previous year. While it is difficult to imagine something of this scale, a container is 20 ft (length) × 8 ft (width) × 9 ft (height). There are around 6000 'very large' container ships that carry around 16 000 TEUs. Therefore, an enormous number of products are imported and exported via the sea. Some container ships will commence their voyage and take a week to deliver their cargo, often calling at a number of seaports along their journey. The world's biggest container ship, called the *CSCL Globe*, made its maiden voyage

and docked at Felixstowe in Suffolk, UK on 7 January 2015. The owner of the port of Felixstowe, Paul Davey of Hutchison Ports (UK) Limited, was extremely proud to see the *CSCL Globe* docked. He stated that 30 000 local people are employed in the transport industry, so getting mega container ships to dock in Felixstowe is positive news economically. He and the hundreds of spectators who saw the *CSCL Globe* dock were amazed at the size of the ship. She carries 19 100 containers.

Four thousand of the containers held food, drink, clothing, electrical goods and furniture, which equates to 57 000 tonnes of cargo. The actual ship measures 400 m (1312 ft) from bow to stern, which is slightly longer than four football pitches placed end to end. Instead of carrying 900 million tins of baked beans, it is estimated the *CSCL Globe* could carry 156 million pairs of shoes or 300 million tablet computers.

Not all seaports could dock the *CSCL Globe* because (a) it is too large, or (b) the cranes or lifting-gear to load and unload the ship are inadequate. The port of Felixstowe invested £300 million in their port to accommodate the mega cargo ships. So much so that in March 2015 the *MSC Oscar* docked in Felixstowe. The *MSC Oscar* is slightly smaller than the *CSCL Globe*, but can carry 124 more containers than the *Globe*.

## Question

**1** What are the benefits of using container ships as a distribution channel?

**References:** BBC News (2015) *CSCL Globe*: Felixstowe arrival for world's largest container ship, published 7 January. Available from www.bbc.co.uk/news/uk-england-suffolk-30700269 (accessed 18 May 2015); BBC News (2015) World's largest container ship *MSC Oscar* in Felixstowe, published 9 March. Available from www.bbc.co.uk/news/uk-england-suffolk-31798664 (accessed 18 May 2015); http://www.rammargroup.com/index.html.

This has meant the global freight-transport industry itself has had to reshape, as manufacturers seek service suppliers with global reach. Manufacturers want custom-designed delivery systems, using all types of transport – land, sea and air. Many of the larger firms now offer a whole range of options beyond their original specific function. This has meant that distinctions between the various intermediaries, such as freight forwarders, transport companies, express couriers and logistics services are blurring.

All intermediaries deal with three parallel flows: physical goods, information and finance (leasing, lending and brokerage). What is happening now is that while previously intermediaries specialized in one of the flows, they are now offering the full range of services. Even global manufacturers are entering the logistics business. Caterpillar, which makes construction equipment, uses the global distribution network it has already developed as a channel for the products of other manufacturers.

There have been two driving forces for this. First, global competition has meant a downward pressure on costs. This has spawned the phenomenon that began in the logistics sector with outsourcing, but has extended to the whole range of other services now regarded as legitimate logistics tasks. Indeed, many of the multinational logistics companies such as DPWN, FedEx, UPS and TNT, the so-called integrators, themselves outsource the functions they take on to small specialist suppliers. See Management Challenge 10.4 for a recent addition to distribution channels.

## MANAGEMENT CHALLENGE 10.4

## Amazon Prime Air

Some products take weeks to arrive if the manufacturer chooses to use freight as their distribution channel. Music can be purchased and downloaded within minutes. The 21st-century young consumer is more inclined to want their products and services quickly. Amazon understands this and offers an exciting 'be first to have it' opportunity by enabling consumers to pre-order an item such as the latest PS4 game, new Batman toy, etc. By clicking on the release delivery date, the consumer can get the product delivered to their home on release day. Additionally, the speedy delivery postal option for products is on the increase, and the delivery of products within five days is on the decline. Amazon has devised a way to deliver products, usually delivered by post, to customers within 30 minutes. Amazon promotes the fact that their Prime Air will deliver products anywhere within 30 minutes. The Amazon Prime Air is a drone which takes to the skies from an Amazon Depot. It will deliver products to consumers at home, their office, on a boat on a lake, or even to a person hiking across the Yorkshire Pennines. Consumers are at the heart of this logistical operation. And it is through the consumer's GPS signal on their Smartphone that the Amazon Prime Air will locate the consumer and deliver the parcel. The drone has been fitted with flight sensors, sonar, cameras and radar to ensure the drone avoids any obstacles that may damage the product it is delivering.

The non-manned machine-2-machine air delivery service is also being used by DHL who uses drones, called parcelcopters, to deliver health parcels to a remote island off the German coast. Google is also using drone-based delivery services to deliver cattle vaccines to farmers in Australia.

### Question

1 What are the benefits of the non-manned machine-2-machine air distribution channel used by Amazon, DHL and Google?

**Reference:** BBC (2015) Amazon details drone delivery plans, published 8 May. Available from www.bbc.co.uk/news/technology-32653269 (accessed 13 May 2015).

Second, the technological advances discussed earlier mean that logistics specialists are able to offer increasingly sophisticated services to exporters that firms cannot provide in-house. For example, a firm's products might once have passed from factory to national warehouse and then on to a foreign regional warehouse, then to a local depot, before delivery to the end consumer. This was a wasteful process in terms of time and cost. Today, using state-of-the-art systems, a logistics specialist taking responsibility for the warehouse function will deliver to the customer direct from the main warehouse, cutting out three of four links in the chain.

At the more advanced end of the logistics services spectrum, companies are handing control of more and more roles to their logistics partners. This is partly driven by the sheer geographical complexity of many exporters' operations where, for example, head office, factory and customer may be separated by thousands of miles.

As more companies attempt to develop the newly opened emerging markets where they have little knowledge or understanding of the distribution system, the use of third-party intermediaries to organize logistics is becoming an essential part of a global marketing strategy.

## Transportation

The physical handling and movement of goods over long distances will practically always have to be performed by third parties.

Transportation is the most visible part of the physical distribution strategy. The main options are:

- *Ocean transport*: capacity for large loads of differentiated products, raw materials, semi-finished goods, finished goods. Handling of goods in bulk, in packaged or unitized form, pallets, containers.
- *Inland waterway transport*: heavy and bulk products. Growing container transport. Restrictions because of need for suitable loading/unloading terminals.
- *Air transport*: urgent shipments, perishables, low-density light/high value, relatively small shipments.
- *Road transport*: most flexible door-to-door transport for all kinds of products but mostly finished goods. Container transport.
- *Rail transport*: long distance heavy and bulk products. Container transport.

**Ocean and inland waterways**  Sea and inland waterways provide a very low-cost way to transport bulky, low value or non-perishable products such as coal and oil. Water transport is slow and is subject to difficulties caused by the weather; for example, some ports are iced over for part of the winter. Water transport usually needs to be used with other modes of transport to achieve door-to-door delivery.

One of the policies used to encourage growth in South Korea, a newly industrialized country, has been the stimulation of its shipping and shipbuilding industry.

Ocean shipping can be open market, i.e. free ocean where there are very few restrictions, or it can be organized in conferences which are essentially cartels that regulate rates and capacities available on routes.

As in other areas of distribution, the containerization of ports and the impact of IT have meant sea transport has become a capital-intensive industry where there is high pressure to achieve full capacity utilization.

The costs of ocean freight, as a result, have decreased since the late 2000s. So it is still the most cost-effective method of transporting goods to distant markets.

The average cost for a 6 m dry cargo container to be shipped from the UK to Shanghai in China will be £1000–£1550 and the approximate transit time would be 20–25 days.

However, a number of hidden costs can arise in overseas shipping:

- overseas warehousing costs due to having to send large inventories in container loads
- inventory losses from handling spoilage, theft, obsolescence and exchange rate charges
- cost of time in transit
- lost sales from late arrival.

Inland waterways are very important in countries with poor infrastructures. In Vietnam the most popular mode of transportation is by water. A dense network of waterways exists, although even this system will suffer the vagaries of both flood and drought conditions.

**Air freight**  This is considerably more expensive per tonne/kilometre than the other modes of transport. Air freight is particularly appropriate for the movement of high-value low-bulk and perishable items. For example, diamonds, computer software, specialist component parts and cut flowers use air freight. Air freight is extending its market through promoting its advantages. The higher freight charges can often be offset. Packing costs and insurance rates are significantly less by air. Storage en route, overseas warehousing and inventory losses may all be less by air as will the actual cost of the time in transit. In addition, the development of larger and more flexible aeroplanes for air freight has helped reduce costs.

**Road**   Very flexible in route and time. Schedules can deliver direct to customers' premises. Very efficient for short hauls of high-value goods. Restrictions at border controls can be time-consuming, however. Long distances and the need for sea crossings reduce the attractiveness of freight transport by road. In some parts of the world, particularly in less developed countries, road surfaces are poor and the distribution infrastructure inadequate. In Vietnam, an attractive emerging market for many international firms, the majority of the road network is beaten track which, during the wet season (six months of the year), makes transporting anything by road very difficult. There are often problems of transporting goods across African countries due to poor road infrastructure.

**Rail**   Rail services provide a very good method of transporting bulky goods over long land distances. The increasing use of containers provides a flexible means to use rail and road modes with minimal load transfer times and costs.

In Europe, we are seeing the development of the use of 'Bloc Trains' as a highly efficient means of rail transport. In the USA they use 'Double Bloc' trains to transport goods across the vast plains. In a number of markets, rail transport is fraught with difficulties. In China, a shipment from Shanghai to Guangzhou, a distance of approximately 2000 kilometres, can take 25 days. Across the interior it is even slower. Shanghai to Xian, 1500 kilometres, can take 45 days. Much of the rail capacity is antiquated and many of the rail lines are old, leading to frequent derailments. See Illustration 10.6 for further details about train transportation issues along the '21st Century Silk Road'.

## ILLUSTRATION 10.6

# A slow train to China?

Distribution channels come in many forms: road, rail, air, ship and of course clouds for internet-based products and services. Choosing which channel to use is often based on two variants:

1 Time,

2 Cost.

The longest rail track now spans between China and Spain. The train track, the longest in the world, is called the 21st Century Silk Road. The first major trading journey carried a 30-carriage train from Yiwu, a manufacturing distribution centre in China, to Madrid in Spain. The journey broke all speed records for a trading journey; however, it still took 21 days to travel the 8000 miles between China and Spain. The first delivery from China brought thousands of toys and goods for Christmas 2014. The return cargo from Spain to China was full of traditional Spanish produce, including olive oil, wine and ham. To make the 16 000 mile round trip the train goes through Kazakhstan, Russia, Belarus, Poland, Germany and France. However, in some areas of Kazakhstan, temperatures often drop to around −7 degrees Celsius (20 degrees Fahrenheit). Products like the Spanish ham and wine can freeze, which will ruin the produce. There are trains that have containers which keep temperatures inside warmer than −7 degrees Celsius. These are used for more sensitive hardware such as laptops, smartphones and computer equipment. The temperature controlled train containers cost more money than *general* containers.

Another long train container journey is between China and Poland, which takes around 14 days and costs $10 000 for a 10 ton 40 foot load. A similar load going by air takes around four days (including passage through customs and delivery time at each end of the journey) and would cost $40 000. If a manufacturer chooses to send a similar cargo of products by boat, the cost would be $5000. The cargo of products sent by sea would take around six weeks.

## Questions

**1** Which is the cheapest distribution channel and which distribution channel takes the longest?

**2** What are the strengths and weaknesses of train transportation?

**Reference:** Mount, I. (2014) Spain to China by rail: A 21st Century Silk Road riddled with obstacles. *Fortune*, published 24 December.

**The final decision on transport**   The decision concerning which transport mode to use is discussed by Branch (2005). He identifies four factors as decisive in choosing transport: the terms of the export contract, the commodity specification, freight and overall transit time.

In the terms of the export contract, the customer can specify the mode(s) of transport and can insist on the country's national shipping line or airline being used. In considering different modes of transport, the specification of the commodity will have a strong influence on modal choice. For example, transport of fresh food will have requirements to prevent spoilage and contamination. The cost of transport is of major importance. It creates extra costs above the normal domestic cost. It is important, therefore, that transport options are researched thoroughly so that the best value arrangements can be made for both the buyer and the supplier.

## Export processing zones

The principle of the **export processing zone** (EPZ) started with the opening of the world's first EPZ at Shannon in the Republic of Ireland. Since then there has been a proliferation in the establishment of EPZs worldwide, with notable examples being Jebel Ali at Dubai in the UAE and Subic Bay in the Philippines. The principle of the EPZ has been embraced as a worldwide instrument for national economic development by the United Nations.

The concept of the EPZ concerns the duty-free and tax-free manufacture or processing of products for export purposes within a customs-controlled ('offshore') environment. Components may be imported into the zone duty free and tax free to be processed or manufactured into the finished product, or stored for onward distribution and then re-exported without any liability of import duties or other taxes. The purpose of the EPZ is to ensure that at least 70 per cent of the zone-produced articles are re-exported. The remaining percentage of items produced within the zone may be imported into domestic territory upon payment of the appropriate import duty and tax for the finished article.

Companies trading from within the EPZ can be wholly owned by foreign-based enterprises and, in most cases, all profits may be repatriated to the home country. Foreign direct investment by overseas-based companies is encouraged in zone operations, since normal national rules regarding profits or ownership do not apply. It is also possible for locally based companies to engage in zone operations as long as they are involved in import and export operations.

It is also likely that the workforce used will cost the zone company less than for home-based operations, since the majority of the EPZs are located in developing countries, especially East and South East Asia and Central America.

The benefits for companies in taking advantage of EPZs are:

- All goods entering the EPZ are exempted from customs duties and import permits.
- Firms can use foreign currency to settle transactions.
- EPZs can be used for assembly of products and so help reduce transportation costs.
- EPZs give a company much more flexibility and help avoid the unwanted bureaucracy of customs and excise.

China has developed 124 EPZs in the coastal regions and special economic zones (SEZs) in the interior of China to help develop export sea trade. Examples of EPZs in China are Hong Kong, Shenzhen, Shanghai and Tianjin.

## Administrative problems resulting from the cross-border transfer of goods

For many companies, particularly those that are infrequent exporters or that have insufficient resources for effective **export administration**, the process of ensuring that goods reach their ultimate destination is beset with difficulties. These include goods held in customs warehouses without apparent reason, confusing paperwork, high and apparently arbitrary duties, levies and surcharges, and the need to make exorbitant payments to expedite the release of goods. The UN Conference on Trade and Development (UNCTAD) believes these additional costs to world trade could be as much as 10 per cent of the US$12.5 trillion total world trade. UNCTAD also believes that those costs could be cut by US$250 billion by improved efficiency. It is unlikely, however, that such changes as these will happen quickly. So companies face a series of decisions about how to manage their own risks and costs, while still providing an effective service to their customers.

## Documentation

A number of different documents are required in cross-border marketing. These include invoices, consignment notes and customs documents. SITRO, the Simpler Trade Procedures Board, has been involved in developing simpler documentation and export procedures with the aim of encouraging international trade. Electronic data interchange is expanding and now provides a fast integrated system which is reducing documentation preparation time and errors.

The process of documentation has more importance than its rather mechanistic and bureaucratic nature would suggest. Errors made in documents can result in laws being broken, customs regulations being violated or, in financial institutions, refusing to honour demands for payment. Country variations are considerable with regard to export documentation procedures. Different documents are required in different formats. Figure 10.5 shows a typical export order process.

Documentation problems have five main causes: complexity, culture, change, cost and error. Complexity arises from the number of different parties requiring precise documents delivered at the correct time. In addition to the customer, banks, chambers of commerce, consulates, international carriers, domestic carriers, customs, port/terminal/customs clearance areas, insurance companies and the exporting company or freight forwarding company are being used by the exporter.

Different countries require different numbers of copies of documents, sometimes in their own language and sometimes open to official scrutiny that is strongly influenced by the culture of that country. Document clearance can, therefore, be slow and subject to bureaucratic delays.

Errors in documentation can have serious consequences. The definition of an 'error' is open to interpretation. Errors can result in goods being held in customs or in a port. Clearance delays cause failure to meet customer service objectives. In extreme cases, errors result in goods being confiscated or not being paid for.

The development of regional trading blocs is reducing some of the complexity of documentation. Businesses outside free market arrangements need to complete import and export documents and pay the necessary taxes as agreed between the different countries. Some companies seek to minimize their exposure to documentation problems by using freight forwarders to handle freight and documentation. Other companies develop their own expertise and handle documentation in-house.

**FIGURE 10.5**  The export order and physical process

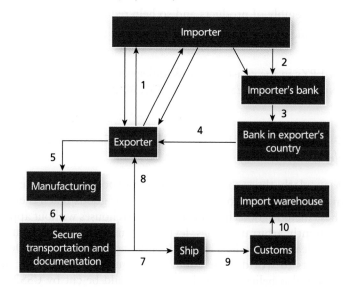

## Packaging

Packaging for international markets needs to reflect climatic, geographical, economic, cultural and distribution channel considerations. In this section we will concentrate on the specific requirements that particularly relate to transport and warehousing.

The main packaging issues of interest for the exporter are: loss, damage and the provision of handling points. These all need to be considered within the range of transport modes and the levels of handling sophistication and types of equipment used throughout the entire transit.

■ *Loss.* The main concerns of loss of goods relate to misdirection and to theft (pilferage). The use of containers has reduced some of the opportunities for theft. Misdirection can be minimized by the appropriate use of shipping marks and labelling. High-value consignments need to be marked in such a way as to avoid drawing them to the attention of potential thieves. Marking needs to be simple, security-conscious and readily understandable by different people in different countries.

■ *Damage.* The length of transit and variations in climate and physical movement give rise to many opportunities for damage to occur. Goods stowed in large ships might be contaminated by chemical odours or corroding machinery. Goods might be left out in the open air in equatorial or severe winter conditions. Walmart found that local Brazilian suppliers could not meet their standards for packaging and quality control.

A good balance needs to be achieved between the high costs of the substantial export packing required to eliminate all or almost all damage and the price and profit implications that this has for the customer and the exporter. See Case Study 2 at the end of this chapter for more details about packaging.

Over the years, export packaging has been modified from wooden crates and straw, etc., towards fibreboard and cardboard cartons. Different countries have different regulations about what materials are acceptable. In addition, export packaging influences customer satisfaction through its appearance and in its appropriateness to minimize handling costs for the customer.

## The export sales contract

The export sales contract covers important terms for the delivery of products in international trade. There are three main areas of uncertainty in international trade contracts, which Branch (2005) identifies as:

■ uncertainty about which legal system will be used to adjudicate the contract

■ difficulties resulting from inadequate and unreliable information

■ differences in the interpretation of different trade terms.

The International Chamber of Commerce (ICC) has formulated a set of internationally recognized trade terms called Incoterms. The use of Incoterms will reduce these uncertainties. However, because there are many different ways in which the customer and the supplier could contract for the international delivery of products, the possibility of ambiguity can exist unless care is taken.

At one extreme, the customer could buy the product at the factory gate, taking all the responsibility for permits, arrangements and costs of transport and insurance. At the other extreme, the supplier can arrange and pay for all costs to the point where the product is delivered to the customer's premises. There are a variety of different steps between manufacture and delivery to the customer. Keegan and Green (2010) identify nine steps:

1   Obtaining an export permit, if required. An example would be for the sale of armaments.

2   Obtaining a currency permit, if required.

3   Packing the goods for export.

4   Transporting the goods to the place of departure. This is usually road transport to a seaport or to an airport. For some countries, for example within continental Europe, transport could be entirely by road.

5   Preparing a bill of lading.

6   Completing necessary customs export papers.

7 Preparing customs or consular invoices as required in the country of destination.

8 Arranging for ocean freight and preparation.

9 Obtaining marine insurance and certificate of the policy.

There are a number of Incoterms specifying many variations of responsibility for the required steps in the delivery process. The main terms are defined below:

- *Ex-works (EXW).* In this contract the exporter makes goods available at a specified time at the exporter's factory or warehouse. The advantage to the buyer in this arrangement is that of obtaining the goods at the lowest possible price.

- *Free on board (FOB).* In this contract the exporter is responsible for the costs and risks of moving the goods up to the point of passing them over the ship's rail. The FOB contract will specify the name of the ship and the name of the port. The benefit to the buyer in this arrangement is that the goods can be transported in the national shipping line of the buyer and can be insured using a national insurance company. In this way the amount of foreign currency needed to finance the contract is reduced.

- *Cost, insurance, freight (CIF).* This contract specifies that the exporter is responsible for all costs and risks to a specified destination port indicated by the buyer. The buyer benefits from receiving the goods in the home country and is, therefore, spared the costs, risks and management of the goods in transit. The exporter can benefit from a higher price for the contract. Whether the contract is more profitable will depend on the extra total distribution costs associated with the CIF contract. From a national point of view, the use of CIF contracts by a country's exporters is preferred as invisible earnings through extra freight and insurance services are increased when CIF contracts are used rather than FOB contracts.

Governments of all types of political and economic persuasion sometimes develop policies to favour their own national companies. They can also try to influence the availability of transport modes. In addition, the extra incentive to increase foreign currency earnings can change the export sales contract and with it the specification of the Incoterms.

## SUMMARY

- The management of international distribution channels and logistics is challenging because it is frequently determined more by the available infrastructure and host country channel structure than by what the firm would like to do.

- The lack of experience in distribution decision making is exposed further by explicit and implicit cultural differences. It is important to understand and manage cultural differences among different members of the variety of distribution channel arrangements in different country markets.

- Cultural differences add to control difficulties. Typically, companies have less control over international channels than they have in their domestic market. The usual pattern is to have a smaller market share and to use longer distribution channels, that is, using more layers of distribution intermediaries. Both of these factors reduce the power of the manufacturer. Less channel power usually results in less control over other channel members.

- The changing nature of retailing patterns influences distribution planning. The long-term commitments that form the basis of successful distribution need to be nurtured. However, change also implies some adapting of distribution channel arrangements. It is a considerable challenge to add new types of distribution intermediaries while holding onto long-established accounts.

- Successful management of international distribution channels and logistics represents a significant challenge to the international marketer. The proximity of the company, the distribution intermediaries and the customer make cultural interactions an important influence on success.

- Success in international distribution channel and logistics management has to be based on high-quality strategic decisions and consistent and efficient tactical implementation.

## KEYWORDS

| | | |
|---|---|---|
| logistics | distribution channel structures | total distribution cost |
| integrated supply chain | interactive customer marketing | logistics or distribution strategy |
| physical movement | mass customization | electronic data interchange |
| movement of services | data mining | build to order |
| foreign market channels | category management | open market |
| indirect channels | effective consumer response | export processing zone |
| direct channels | multimedia technology | export administration |
| buyer–seller relationships | interactive shopping | |

## CASE STUDY 1

## Bulk wine shifts the global wine market

The bulk wine sector is growing at a rate of 6 per cent pa with up to 30 per cent of wine produced in the world being sold under this label. A combination of the popularity for bulk wine among retailers able to sell directly to consumers and a high number of wine producers adding to the market has led to the growth in the bulk wine sector.

The advantages of bulk wine shipments tend to favour suppliers in countries with large-scale production of wine and distant export markets. South African, Argentinian and Chilean producers use bulk shipping to provide low shipping costs to their export markets.

Bulk buying has also become available to wine producers in Turkey, Romania, Poland and the Ukraine. This has happened due to increasing access to contract suppliers and an online trading exchange in London.

The growth of the sector has led to major changes in the way wine is distributed internationally. Bulk wine, which was once seen as the commodity low end of the market, has now become a major player in the distribution of wine globally.

Due to the changes in competitive market structure caused by this new phenomenon, some commentators have referred to it as being disruptive to the global wine industry. It has allowed a decrease in price and an increase in varieties of wine across Asia and China as distributors can buy large amounts of wine at reasonably cheap prices.

Chile has used bulk wine to become an appealing supplier to the market in China, which now makes up more than $200 million of its exports. Historically, the two have never had any established trading routes making the situation a major market shift.

Chile's palatable wine is appealing to China's importers, distributors and retailers due to the fact it can easily be shipped, bottled and distributed across China.

However, the international supply chain of bulk wine is a complex one involving on the supply side producers, brokers and contract suppliers, and on the demand side, retailers and on-premise operators. Together with a toughening legislative environment this makes the wine market in China a tough market to navigate.

### Questions

**1** Discuss the pros and cons of the growing bulk wine sector to the global wine market.

**2** Evaluate the advantages and disadvantages to Chilean wine producers using this route to build a global competitive advantage.

**References:** Deborah Parker Wong (2017) Incredible bulk: The changing nature of the international bulk wine market is creating opportunities for brokers, retailers, and distributors. Available from www.spiritedbiz.com/author/deborahparkerwong/ (accessed 8 June 2018); *The Buyer* (2017) Why bulk wine is the industry's most disruptive sector. Available from http://www.the-buyer.net/opinion/ richard-siddle-on-how-bulk-wine-is-the-most-disruptive-sector-in-the-wine-industry/ (accessed 9 June 2018); Barnes, A. (2017) China becomes the biggest overseas market for Chilean wines. *Decanter China*. Available from https://www.decanterchina.com/en/news/china-becomes-the-biggest-overseas-market-for-chilean-wines (accessed 9 June 2018).

### CASE STUDY 2

# Poor packaging = lost profits

Correct transportation packaging is a priority for every business, be it a rural Bangladeshi farmer or a global soft drinks giant such as Coca-Cola, particularly during transportation. If a rural farmer does choose poor quality or inappropriate cloth bags in which to transport his rice, flour or wheat, there is a good chance the cloth bags will split. Split bags spill produce which means less produce can be sold. Similarly, if Coca-Cola chooses incorrect packaging, its bottles could be punctured or broken when being lifted on or off ships or trains, which again means stock losses during transportation.

Philip Luijckx, the marketing manager of industrial and consumer packaging for Dow Performance Packaging, states that it is important for businesses to choose packaging that is sustainable and 'fit for purpose'. In fact, many businesses underestimate the stresses that products go through during the transportation process. Products can be vibrated constantly when packaged and transported on trains. Equally, products receive regular 'shocks' when the transportation lorry goes over a pot-hole or when train containers are connected/disconnected from the engine.

The consequences of choosing packaging which is not 'fit for purpose' and does not protect the valuable products can result in a loss of sales for the manufacturer and a loss of profit for the supply chain. Consumers are now much more aware of the packaging they choose when shopping and its impact on the environment. Therefore they may choose a product container which is not going to increase food and product waste.

Many international brands were prompted to redesign their packaging after the amount of plastic found in oceans around the world came to light in the media. The increased numbers of consumers who choose to shop online has also meant packaging has become more of an issue for consumers. They want their products to reach them intact, a desire shared by the companies themselves.

According to Mintel the five key trends in packaging in 2018 are:

- **Packaged Planet**: a focus on package innovations that protect and ensure safe delivery.
- **rEpackage**: the use of e-commerce packaging that reflects consumer expectations from e-shopping with that of the brand in-store.
- **Clean Label 2.0**: the next generation of clean labels to packaging designed to provide clarity for shoppers
- **Sea Change**: a renewed effort towards the circular economy is to keep packaging material in use.
- **rEnavigate**: The use of transparent materials, contemporary design, recyclability or unique shapes.

Forward thinking companies now aim for packaging designs that enlighten and inform consumers' purchase decisions and are now rejecting approaches that offer too much non-recyclable material.

At the World Economic Forum in Davos, Switzerland (2017), Proctor & Gamble unveiled its plan to collect plastic on beaches around Europe and turn it into shampoo bottles.

The new Head and Shoulders is being produced with recycled plastic from beaches.

However, these trends are not only in the B2C market. International B2B customers such as Lockheed Martin Corporation, a global security and aerospace company, now insist that their suppliers deliver product to it with environmentally friendly packaging. Lockheed Martin Corporation goes so far as to provide details of the types of packing it wants their products wrapped and boxed in. Suggestions include:

- Biodegradable bags that are air cushioned to 'absorb shock' and protect hard-edged products during transportation.

- Bubble wrap, also biodegradable, which like air-cushioned bags absorbs shock and vibration, which is especially useful for fragile products.

- Recycled moulded cardboard boxes and sheets particularly useful for absorbing constant vibrations experienced during long train transportation.

## Questions

**1** What are the major priorities with regards to packaging for companies marketing goods internationally?

**2** How should companies respond to the global packaging trends identified by Mintel?

**3** Identify examples of recent innovations in packaging of companies marketing goods internationally.

**References:** www.headandshoulders.co.uk/; www.ift.org; Mintel (2017) Mintel announces five global packaging trends from 2018. Available from www.mintel.com/press-centre/retail-press-centre/mintel-announces-five-global-packaging-trends-for-2018 (accessed 9 June 2018).

# DISCUSSION QUESTIONS

**1** How might companies use the Internet to increase the competitiveness of their international distribution strategy?

**2** How might the analysis of the retailer infrastructure and retailer marketing practices in advanced economies influence the development of marketing plans for retailers based in less-developed countries?

**3** Discuss what factors contribute to the increasing complexity of global logistics operations. Explain why cooperative relationships are so important in this aspect of international marketing operations.

**4** The arrival of the global village has had a major impact on companies' distribution methods. Identify four factors involved and explain how each has influenced distribution.

**5** Fully evaluate the statement: 'Distribution and logistics are increasingly becoming the battleground in international markets as companies seek to gain global competitive advantage.'

# REFERENCES

1. Admane, R.A. (2014) ITC's e-Choupal: A marketing strategy for rural transformation – A case study of Wardha District. *Maharashtra International Journal of Management Research and Business Strategy* 3(1), 249–257.
2. Avon Company (2018) *Report and Accounts*. Available from www.investor.avoncompany.com (accessed 9 June 2018).
3. Barnes, A. (2017) China becomes the biggest overseas market for Chilean wines. *Decanter China*. Available from www.decanterchina.com/en/news/china-becomes-the-biggest-overseas-market-for-chilean-wines (accessed 9 June 2018).
4. BBC (2015) Amazon details drone delivery plans, published 8 May. Available from www.bbc.co.uk/news/technology-32653269 (accessed 13 May 2015).
5. BBC News (2015) *CSCL Globe*: Felixstowe arrival for world's largest container ship, published 7 January. Available from www.bbc.co.uk/news/uk-england-suffolk-30700269 (accessed 18 May 2015).
6. BBC News (2015) World's largest container ship *MSC Oscar* in Felixstowe, published 9 March. Available from www.bbc.co.uk/news/uk-england-suffolk-31798664 (accessed 18 May 2015).
7. The Benetton Group (2018) http://www.benettongroup.com (accessed 10th May 2018).
8. Branch, A.E. (2005) *Export Practice and Management*, 5th edition. Thomson Learning.
9. *The Buyer* (2017) Why bulk wine is the industry's most disruptive sector. Available from www.the-buyer.net/opinion/

richard-siddle-on-how-bulk-wine-is-the-most-disruptive-sector-in-the-wine-industry/ (accessed 9 June 2018).

10. Czinkota, M. and Ronkainen, I. (2012) *International Marketing*. Cengage Learning.

11. Deloitte (2018) *Global Powers of Retailing 2018*. Available from www2.deloitte.com/uk/en/pages/consumer-business/articles/global-powers-of-retailing.html (accessed 5 June 2018).

12. Griemal, H. (2014) Japan's keiretsu suppliers: At risk in a new reality, published 29 November 2014 in *Automotive News* 89(6640), 3–49. Available from www.autonews.com/article/20140929/OEM10/309299984/japans-keiretsu-suppliers-at-risk-in-a-new-reality (accessed 13 June 2015).

13. Keegan, W.J. and Green, M.J. (2010) *Global Marketing Management*, 6th edition. Pearson.

14. Kodak (2017) Kodak opens new technology center in China to support Flexo growth. Available from www.kodak.com/us/en/print/blog/blog_post/?contentid=4295001487 (accessed 9 June 2018).

15. Kotler, P. and Armstrong, G. (2014) *Principles of Marketing*. Pearson Prentice Hall, p. 367.

16. Mintel (2017) Mintel announces five global packaging trends from 2018. Available from http://www.mintel.com/press-centre/retail-press-centre/mintel-announces-five-global-packaging-trends-for-2018 (accessed 9 June 2018).

17. Mount, I. (2014) Spain to China by rail: A 21st Century Silk Road riddled with obstacles. *Fortune*, published 24 December.

18. Rosenbloom, B. (2012) *Marketing Channels*. Cengage.

19. Société Générale (2018) *Finnish Market Distribution*. Available from http://import-export.societegenerale.fr/en/country/finland/market-distribution (accessed 9 June 2018).

20. Source Today (2018) *Top 50 Electronics Distributors 2017*. Available from: www.sourcetoday.com (accessed 9 June 2018).

21. Statista (2018) Number of digital buyers worldwide from 2014 to 2021. www.statista.com/statistics (accessed 9 June 2018).

22. Twomey, B. (2018) Understanding Japanese keiretsu. Available from www.Investopedia.com.

23. Usunier, J.C. and Lee, J.A. (2009) *Marketing Across Cultures*, 5th edition. Prentice Hall.

24. Deborah Parker Wong (2017) Incredible bulk: The changing nature of the international bulk wine market is creating opportunities for brokers, retailers, and distributors. Available from www.spiritedbiz.com/author/deborahparkerwong/ (accessed 8 June 2018).

## CHAPTER 11

# PRICING FOR INTERNATIONAL MARKETS

## LEARNING OBJECTIVES

After reading this chapter you should be able to:

- Discuss the issues that affect international pricing decisions

- Evaluate different strategic options for pricing across international markets

- Differentiate between the problems facing companies engaged in foreign market pricing and those faced by companies trying to coordinate strategies across a range of global markets

- Find solutions to the problems of pricing in high-risk markets

## INTRODUCTION

Many organizations believe that pricing is the most flexible, independent and controllable element of the marketing mix and that it plays a major role in international marketing management. This is largely based on the fact that pricing changes appear to prompt an immediate response in the market. However, despite the apparent simplicity of using pricing as a major marketing tool, many managers find pricing decisions difficult to make. This is in part due to the fact that most firms recognize the importance of pricing at a tactical level in stimulating short-term demand. Far fewer, however, recognize the importance of the strategic role of pricing in international marketing.

In this chapter, we focus upon both the internal and external factors that affect international pricing decisions, the role that pricing plays in developing strategies to meet corporate objectives, and the relationship between pricing and other aspects of the firm's activities. In addition to considering the stages involved in developing a comprehensive international pricing policy, we discuss the specific problems associated with pricing in international marketing which do not affect the domestic business. We then go on to explore the financial issues in managing risk in pricing and of non-payment of debts.

# Domestic vs international pricing

For many companies operating in domestic markets, pricing decisions are based on a relatively straightforward process. This involves allocating the total estimated cost of producing, managing and marketing a product or service between the forecast total volume of sales and adding an appropriate profit margin. Problems for these firms arise when costs increase, sales do not materialize or competitors undercut the prices. In international markets, however, pricing decisions are much more complex. This is because they are affected by a number of additional external factors, such as fluctuations in exchange rates, accelerating inflation in certain countries and the use of alternative payment methods such as leasing, barter and countertrade. The global financial crisis of 2008 still affects the complexities of pricing in a global market. Additionally, where there is economic and political uncertainty, pricing decisions become even more difficult for many companies. They are often now trading in countries with high levels of inflation, high levels of debt, high unemployment and political tensions.

In recent years, too, it has become more apparent that customer tastes have become much more sophisticated. Purchase decisions are made less frequently on the basis of price consideration, but are increasingly influenced by wider expectations of product performance and perceptions of value. This has particular implications for international products, which are often perceived to be of significantly different value – higher or lower – than locally produced products. Pricing strategies are also strongly influenced by the nature and intensity of the competition which exists in the various local markets.

For these reasons, it is important to recognize at the outset that the development and implementation of pricing strategies in international markets should go through the following stages:

1 Analyzing the factors which influence international pricing, such as the cost structures, the value of the product, the market structure, competitor pricing levels and a variety of environmental constraints.

2 Confirming what impact the corporate strategies should have on pricing policy.

3 Evaluating the various strategic pricing options and selecting the most appropriate approach.

4 Implementing the strategy through the use of a variety of tactics and procedures to set prices at strategic business unit (SBU) level.

5 Managing prices and financing international transactions.

# The factors affecting international pricing decisions

A firm exporting speculatively for the first time, with little knowledge of the market environment that it is entering, is likely to set a price based largely on company and product factors. Due to its restricted resources, the firm places particular emphasis on ensuring that sales revenue generated at least covers the costs incurred. It is important that firms recognize that the cost structures for production, marketing and distribution of products and services are of vital importance. But they should not be regarded as the sole determinants when setting prices. Sarathy *et al.* (2006) identify many other factors that firms should take into consideration – environment, market, company and specific product factors – and these are summarized in Table 11.1. It is by giving full recognition to the effect of these factors on pricing decisions that the company can develop a strategic rather than a purely tactical approach to pricing.

Companies operating internationally must consider all the above factors detailed for each specific country market. However, as with all the other marketing mix factors, the individual country pricing policies need to be integrated and coordinated within a wider regional or global strategy in order to enable corporate objectives to be met.

While it is important that companies consider all the factors listed, some of them, such as corporate objectives, market and product factors, consumer perceptions, competitor responses and cost structures, are of particular significance.

## Table 11.1   Factors influencing the pricing strategy

### Company and product factors

- corporate and marketing objectives
- firm and product positioning
- product range, life cycle, substitutes, product differentiation and unique selling propositions
- cost structures, manufacturing, experience effect and economies of scale, taxes, and production costs
- marketing, product development
- available resources
- inventory
- channel costs such as shipping, rail, air, data in and out of Cloud services.

### Market factors

- consumers' perceptions, expectations and ability to pay
- need for product and promotional adaptation, market servicing, extra packaging requirements
- market structure, distribution channels, discounting pressures
- market growth, demand elasticities
- need for credit
- competition objectives, strategies and strength.

### Environmental factors

- government influences and constraints including price controls, taxes and duties
- currency fluctuations and exchange rates
- business cycle stage, level of inflation
- use of non-money payment and leasing.

## Company and product factors

**Corporate objectives**   The short-term tactical use of pricing such as discounts, product offers and seasonal reductions is often emphasized by managers, at the expense of its strategic role. Sometimes firms will use export markets if they have excess production capacity to dump those excess products. This means they use marginal pricing strategies, pricing at really low prices, so they cover only the variable costs. Yet pricing over the past few years has played a very significant part in the restructuring of many industries, resulting in the growth of some businesses and the decline of others. New global brands from emerging markets such as LG (Korea) and Haier (China) have approached a new international market for a specific product with the intention of building market share over a period of years. They do this by maintaining or even reducing pricing levels, establishing the product and the brand name, and setting up effective distribution and servicing networks. As a result of this strategy they are now beginning to dominate a whole range of market sectors, especially in markets such as consumer electronics. This has usually been accomplished at the expense of short-term profits, as the company will have a long-term perspective on profits.

By contrast, US firms have relied in the past more on international corporate strategies with greater emphasis on factors such as advertising and selling, believing that these reduce the need to compete on price. The reason for this is that the cost base of US manufacturing is usually much higher than that of its foreign competitors. However, the rapid growth of brands from China, Korea and the Asian economies has led to a change in the priorities of US firms. In a recent survey US firms ranked pricing as more important than any other element of the marketing mix. Asian firms, which have been aggressively reducing their cost base for years, now place greater emphasis upon other factors as they seek to build global brands. The move of many Asian manufacturers from being contract manufacturers to marketing their own brands globally has seen them placing much more emphasis on innovation and marketing. They are upgrading and developing their products and differentiating themselves by building their own distinctive brands.

The international nature of competition leads to the question of whether firms should aim for a broadly standardized price structure, or whether prices should be adapted in each country.

## Product and service factors

While in theory standardization in pricing might appear easier to manage and therefore be preferable, in practice the different local economic, legal and competitive factors in each market make it rarely achievable. The occasions when price standardization is achievable are more usually related to the nature of the product and its stage in the life cycle. For example, standardized pricing can be adopted for certain hi-tech products where limited competition exists. Cavusgil *et al.* (2014) in their examination of export pricing, state that exporting goods can be problematic as changes in tariffs, exchange rate fluctuations and differing trade barriers can affect business dramatically and quickly. They go on to say that SMEs are affected more than MNCs as they are less likely to make plans years in advance (*ibid.*). Aircraft makers, for example, because of the relative uniqueness and complexity of the technology, tend to charge the same price regardless of where the customer is based. However, in contrast, shipbuilders, with products in the mature phase of the product life cycle, adapt prices to meet each particular purchase situation.

In developing pricing strategies, a company needs to be aware of the price dynamics of specific products in the various markets. Five characteristics of the product are important in pricing:

1 *Frequency of purchase.* Frequently purchased products, for example, baby food, petrol, tea and bread, tend to be very price-sensitive in all international markets, whereas occasional purchases are not.

2 *Degree of necessity.* If a product is essential for its users, price changes are unlikely to affect the market size, except in countries where extreme poverty exists and people cannot afford even the most basic necessities.

3 *Unit price.* High-priced products such as holidays and cars are evaluated in greater detail in terms of the consumer's perceptions of value for money. Therefore, besides price, issues such as, for example, reliability, style and features of cars, are extremely important to consumers.

4 *Degree of comparability.* Consumers are less price-conscious about insurance policies than grocery products, because the alternatives are more difficult to compare. Price-setting is particularly difficult in certain services, such as advertising, consultancy and accountancy, which have a different perceived value from country to country.

5 *Degree of fashion or status.* The high prices of luxury goods are seen as establishing their quality. It is usually the goods that have prestige.

Developing pricing strategies for services across international markets is difficult for several reasons. Services are highly perishable. Human resource constraints often restrict the capacity to grow a service business in foreign country markets. Therefore, companies are restricted by the high costs of expansion and managing short-term capacity issues. Likewise, the intangibility of services compared with goods may lead to higher marketing costs. This is because the company has to build the market reputation on the actual service experience of consumers, rather than building a brand image in anticipation of the consumer experience. This means positioning optimum prices in foreign country markets can be difficult to judge. In B2B marketing, the growth of international services predominates. Managers are often tasked with developing effective global pricing strategies for B2B customers that are characterized by different cultures and differing perceptions as to the value of the different service attributes they are buying. The intensive customer contact, extensive customization requirements and the costs of building a service quality reputation in the market, make the challenge of formulating international pricing strategies for services across international markets particularly problematic.

The characteristics of the product or service, particularly the high unit price items, lead international marketers to adopt local pricing strategies which are broadly similar for individual markets. Therefore, the positioning of specific products can remain consistent from country to country. M&S sells basic foods at higher prices than other food retailers in the UK by guaranteeing extremely high consistency of quality.

This difference is not perceived to be so great in other countries, however, where consumers feel that the general quality is not significantly different to justify a substantially higher price. Illustration 11.1 suggests other factors that influence prices.

## ILLUSTRATION 11.1

## Milk: global pricing and politics shake the UK dairy farmers' profits

Since the late 1990s, dairy farms in the UK have reduced in number. Of those that are left, 50 per cent of milk is sold directly, mainly to wholesalers or retailers, while the other 50 per cent is sent to manufacturers to make into cheese, yoghurt and butter. However, a high percentage of these products are also made from milk imported from overseas.

UK farmers are affected by international pricing, which sometimes can make their profits go down. Huge farms in the USA and New Zealand (with average herds three to four times bigger than the average herd owned by a UK dairy farmer) have recently benefited from fantastic weather. The yields from their cows has grown to such a high level that the price at which milk is sold has reduced. This is bad news for the UK dairy farmer as milk prices are dictated globally. Therefore, a reduction in milk prices in one country affects dairy farmers worldwide.

Recently, politics has impacted on UK (and European) dairy farms. The milk supplied to manufacturers to make cheese, yoghurt and butter was left standing in factories and ports. Russia's recent (2015) import ban on products from Europe meant cheese from the UK could not be sold in Russia. Russia had previously imported a lot of cheese from Europe. This created a 'cheese mountain' which in turn reduced cheese prices. UK and European dairy farmers saw their profits reduce again for issues outside their control. Most businesses are in control of the key elements of the marketing mix. However, this is not the case for the UK dairy farmer.

### Questions

**1** What are the main factors that affect the price of milk?

**2** What factors can farmers control and which can they not control?

**Reference:** *The Guardian* (2015) Editorial. The Guardian view on milk prices: dairy farmers are being driven out of business. The groceries regulator should find out why. 12 January.

Price plays an important role in product differentiation by enhancing the perceived value of the product and helping consumers to distinguish between offers from different competitors in order that their needs can be met. Watch prices, for example, range from very little for a child's watch, to a high premium price for a Rolex. Within this range, individual manufacturers normally confine specific brands within particular pricing bands. These are linked to the positioning of the brand and the profile of the watches within the range, and to the characteristics of the target segment.

The key role of price in differentiating products within a category and within a particular market can be used as an offensive strategy. This is demonstrated by the South Korean car manufacturer, Kia. It entered the US car market knowing that its brand name had little credibility there and that the market was already saturated with broadly equivalent products. It targeted its Japanese equivalents, the Honda Civic and Toyota Corolla, by offering a similar car at a 25 per cent lower price.

## The influence of cost structures on pricing

There is a close relationship between prices, costs and sales volume of a product, because the price charged affects sales volume by increasing or decreasing the overall demand. As a result of producing or marketing larger volumes the unit cost of an individual product reduces. Therefore, of all the factors, this often becomes the initial stimulus for firms taking the decision to export.

**The relationship between demand and sales volume**   The way price affects demand is influenced by many factors. Some products are characterized by having elastic demand and being extremely price-sensitive. So sales volumes increase significantly as prices are reduced. In underdeveloped markets, where there is low penetration but considerable desire for western products such as soft drinks or fast food, sales will increase rapidly if the price is reduced relative to consumers' ability to pay.

By contrast, other products are characterized by inelastic demand. For example, suppliers of power generation equipment cannot significantly stimulate demand in individual markets by reducing the price. For such firms, an increase in business revenue is largely determined by changes in external factors, such as an improvement in the economy. The potential market for the European power generation equipment suppliers National Power and ABB was increased by the political decision in Malaysia to partially privatize state utilities.

**The relationship between cost and sales volume**   A second situation of inelastic demand occurs if a firm finds that it has reached saturation in its home market. In other words, even if prices were reduced, there would not be significant extra sales to offset the loss of profit. The firm might conclude that exporting would provide an alternative method of increasing sales and thereby generate additional profit.

This is especially so when firms can increase sales by entering an export market, make use of existing spare production capacity and so price purely to cover their variable costs. Consider the situation shown in Table 11.2 where all the fixed costs are absorbed by the sales in the domestic market, but in addition, 10 per cent extra sales are obtained in export markets at the same prices. Provided there are no increases in fixed costs, there would be over recovery of the fixed costs because of the additional 10 per cent export business. This recovery of fixed costs by the export business would be shown as an additional contribution to the general overheads of the business. The contribution from the export business would all be additional profit.

The fixed production cost of the product includes depreciation of equipment, building rental and business rates. General overheads include advertising, selling, distribution and administration.

The example shows that, in practice, the additional £100 000 sales have generated an additional £40 000 profit (6.3 per cent on total sales) – far greater than the £30 000 profit generated on the £1 million domestic sales (3 per cent profit on total sales). The firm could, therefore, afford to reduce its export price considerably and still make a profit. This is as long as no extra general overhead costs are incurred, there is spare production capacity and no extra investment has to be made.

Table 11.2   The effect of additional export sales on contribution

| | Domestic sales (100 000 units) £000 | + 10% Export sales | Domestic + 10% export sales (110 000 units) £000 |
|---|---|---|---|
| Sales | 1000 | 100 | 1100 |
| Fixed production costs | 300 | | 300 |
| Variable production costs | 500 | 50 | 550 |
| Total costs | 800 | 50 | 850 |
| Contribution to general overheads | 200 | 50 | 250 |
| General overheads | 170 | 10 | 180* |
| Profit | 30 | 40 | 70 |

* General overheads are higher due to additional exporting costs.

In export markets, the firm might choose one of the following four alternatives, setting the selling price at:

- Production cost plus general overhead plus added profit (this would normally be the list price).
- Production cost, but without general overhead or profit added.
- Below production cost.
- Production cost with specific export costs added.

The choice of alternatives will depend on the firm's objectives in entering international markets. The first leads to the safest, albeit least competitive, price and is frequently the approach adopted by new exporters who are unwilling to take any significant risk. The firm might even take the list price, including the domestic gross margin, and add to it all the costs of exporting such as marketing, distribution and administration, resulting in the export price being far greater than the domestic price. In most international markets, however, a list price calculated in this way is unlikely to gain significant market share, and so a lower selling price is required.

The arguments for using the second option, to set a lower export selling price, are based on the belief that export costs should not include domestic sales costs such as advertising, marketing research, domestic and administration costs. While this option has some merit, it might well fail to take account of high specific export costs.

The third option is clearly quite risky as it is designed to substantially increase volume. The danger, of course, is that if the increased volume generated does not absorb the fixed and general overhead costs, the product will be unprofitable and losses will result. This approach is often used in overseas markets and is based on marginal costing, whereby unused production capacity or extended production runs can provide extra goods for sale with little or no change in fixed costs, so that the extra production can effectively be produced at a lower cost than the original production schedule. Another risk with this strategy is that the firm could be accused of dumping excess capacity in foreign markets. This sometimes is exacerbated as a result of government policy, particularly in declining industries. This can arise if governments continue to subsidize their own inefficient industries by providing various incentives such as subsidies.

The fourth option begs the question of whether export pricing should reflect the entire costs specific to export sales, and if so, which costs can be directly attributable to exports. It could be argued that it is vital to know exactly what the realistic costs for foreign markets are. This is important particularly if a firm intends ultimately to commence manufacturing in foreign markets. Allocating costs such as R&D accurately and appropriately, however, can be difficult. See Illustration 11.2 for details of hidden costs.

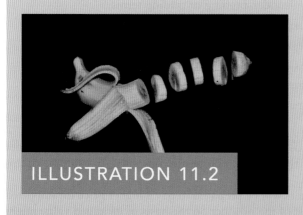

ILLUSTRATION 11.2

## Fruit Ninja: extra costs for online gaming success

The Australian government encourages businesses to export goods and services by providing loans, grants, education packages, regular road shows and guidance on free trade agreements. In conjunction with the Australian Trade Commission and Australian Chamber of Commerce and Industry, the Australian government hosts an award ceremony entitled the Australian Export Awards. Winning such an award not only puts Australia on the map for innovation, creativity and business excellence but it is an excellent PR opportunity for the winners. Halfbrick Studios is a B2B and B2C company that develops software for online games.

Their most famous gaming character is the Fruit Ninja. Fruit Ninja software was exported B2B to Apple via their iOS platform for iPhone devices. The game became Halfbrick's first export. It was an instant success with 500 million copies downloaded onto Apple platforms. When the game became available on non-Apple platforms its popularity increased further as it was downloaded 1 billion times! The game also became a B2C export so gamers can download the software onto Windows platforms, or purchase it for X-Box and Gameboy Advance. During the R&D stage of Fruit Ninja, Halfbrick completed a competitor analysis of games to explore gaps in the market that their chosen target market would want. The target market for Fruit Ninja is game-loving children. To reach their target market, Halfbrick had to set up a range of social media platforms which included a lot of time and effort in staffing. But the ongoing (daily) posts on social media keep the target market interested in their brand. Fruit Ninja's Twitter followers are now 37 800 (2018), up from 24 900 (as of 2015). Fruit Ninja's Twitter fans are regularly encouraged to eat fruit with 'Watermelon Wednesdays', watermelon lollypops and amazing watermelon carvings linked to Chinese New Year and The Last Jedi.

New games from Halfbrick have also been launched and exported including Shadows Remain and Siege Breakers. These were Halfbrick's first engagement with augmented reality games and were popular due to the launch of the iPhone X. To do that employees of Halfbrick visited certain countries and set up networks around the world. In some countries Halfbrick pays agents, distributers or provides office space for employees (Los Angeles, San Francisco, Madrid and Bulgaria) as they understand the local market better than Halfbrick employees based in Australia. To localize even further, they set up a partnership with iDreamSky, a Chinese games publisher.

Future exports are planned for India and Brazil, where new research activities are required to understand the needs of this new market of gamers (and their parents).

### Question

**1** What are the other hidden and extra costs that Halfbrick has had to pay?

**Reference:** Halfbrick (2018) www.halfbrick.com.

## Specific export costs

While export volumes are small in comparison to the domestic market, some experimentation in export pricing is possible. As exporting becomes a more significant part of the activities of the company, however, perhaps requiring the allocation of dedicated equipment or staff, it is necessary to reflect all costs that are specific to export sales. These costs include tariffs, special packaging, insurance, tax liabilities, extra transport, warehousing costs and export selling as well as money transmission, hedging and foreign exchange costs.

However, often when operating across international markets, cost elements can frequently be overlooked or underestimated by companies. These include:

- Additional freight and handling costs due to a misunderstanding of trading terms.
- Last-minute product modifications to meet an export standard.
- Packaging and labelling requirements (language, ingredients, use-by dates).
- Documentation requirements such as certificates of origin and invoices.
- Insurance (including credit insurance), finance and banking charges.
- Delays in customs clearance if documentation, packaging and labelling are not in order.
- Vaguely worded contracts or agreements.

The most immediate and obvious result of all these costs being passed on is that the price to the consumer in an export market is likely to be much greater than the price to a domestic consumer. An example of this is shown in Table 11.3.

This raises the question of whether foreign consumers will be prepared to pay a higher price for imported rather than locally produced goods. Justifying the cost of the product on the basis of its added value might be possible in the short term. However, it is unlikely to provide the international marketer with a basis for long-term viability in each local market. A strategy must be developed to deal with this situation in which the cost to the ultimate consumer is reduced. The main options available to the exporter include:

- aggressively reducing production costs, modifying the product if necessary and sourcing overseas
- shortening the distribution channel, for example, by selling direct to retailers
- selecting a different market entry strategy, such as foreign manufacture, assembly or licensing to avoid the additional costs of exporting.

Table 11.3   Escalation of costs through exporting using the 'cost plus' export pricing model

| FOB | Free On Board | |
|---|---|---|
| | EXW (ex-works) price plus | 100 |
| + | Transport to carrier (e.g. wharf, airport) | 17 |
| + | Customs clearance | 8 |
| + | Additional packaging/labour for transport | 5 |
| + | Agent's commission | 13 |
| | **FOB** | 143 |
| CFR | Cost And Freight | |
| | or | |
| CPT | Carriage Paid To | |
| | FOB price plus | 143 |
| + | Sea/air freight charges to wharf/airport | 32 |
| + | Sea/air document fees (e.g. airway bill, B/L) | 11 |
| + | BAF (bunker adjustment factor) | 2 |
| + | Transport contingency | 2 |
| | **CFR or CPT** | 190 |
| CIF | Cost, Insurance, Freight | |
| | CFR or CPT price plus | 190 |
| + | Marine insurance premium | 2 |
| | **CIF** | 192 |
| DDP | Delivery Duty Paid | |
| | CIF price plus | 192 |
| + | Import duty/tax (calculated as 20% of CIF price) | 39 |
| + | Customs clearance fees | 8 |
| + | Delivery charge from airport to customer | 10 |
| | **DDP** | 249 |

Source: Adapted from *Austrade Guide to Export Pricing,* www.austrade.gov.au.

The implications of changing the market entry and distribution strategy have been dealt with in earlier chapters of this book; here we discuss strategies for reducing cost.

Top down pricing is another way for businesses to decide how much they will charge for goods and services when they export them to countries. During the research and development stage, an important stage that businesses go through when deciding to export goods and services overseas, it is highly recommended that businesses complete a competitor price analysis. By completing a competitor price analysis, businesses will:

- understand what the consumer is prepared to pay for goods and services, and
- gain an indication of the price at which they should sell goods and services to an agent or distributor.

This process is called the 'top down' export pricing model.

Table 11.4 provides an example of how the 'top down' export pricing model works. The example provided is for a case of wine being sold from an Australian vineyard to a retailer in Hong Kong. A case of wine contains 12 bottles. The marketer from the Australian vineyard will need to complete a number of calculations to decipher the price they will sell the wine for in Hong Kong retail outlets. See Table 11.4 for details of the calculation and Management Challenge 11.1 for top down pricing of sugar.

**Table 11.4**  'Top down' export pricing model: wine sold from an Australian vineyard to retail outlets in Hong Kong

|  | Per Bottle | Quick Tips |
|---|---|---|
| **Similar wine per bottle at retail store** | **HK $305** | |
| Deduct VAT | HK $0 | |
| **Consumer's price per bottle excluding VAT[1]** | **HK $305** | |
| Deduct retail margin of 150% | HK $183 | 305 × 0.60 |
| **Retailer's buying price per bottle** | **HK $122** | 305 − 183 = 305/2.5 |
| **Importer's buy price per bottle HK$ –** Deduct: Importer's margin of 30%[2] + clearance & warehouse allowance of 3% + advertising & promotion allowance of 5% = 38% | HK $88 | 122/1.38 |
| **Importer's buy price per case with duty HK$** | HK $1056 | 88 × 12 |
| **Importer's price per case before duty – deduct duty (80%) of CIF** | HK $587 | 1056/1.8 |
| **Convert to AUD$[3]** | AUD $146 | 587/4 |
| **CIF per case** | **AUD $146** | |
| Deduct freight[4] | AUD $1 | |
| Deduct marine insurance | AUD $1 | |
| **FOB per case** | **AUD $144** | |

Source: Adapted from *Austrade Guide to Export Pricing*. www.austrade.gov.au.

Notes:
[1] VAT and sales taxes are applied in many overseas markets. In this example there are no VAT or Sales Taxes in Hong Kong.
[2] Retailers take a full margin on the selling price not the buying price.
[3] Assumes an exchange rate of AUD$1 to HK$4.
[4] Assumes a freight rate of AUD$1200 for 20 foot FCL sea freight container that packs 1200 cases.

## MANAGEMENT CHALLENGE 11.1

## Top down pricing model for sugar exports

Australia's largest export market is China (27 per cent of total exports). China is also the largest country that Australia imports from. China consumes about 4 million tonnes of sugar per year. Australia supplies 250 000 tonnes of sugar to China. Therefore, any new sugar business that wants to export their products to China will need to calculate the price they are willing to sell their sugar for.

### Question

Using the 'top down' export pricing model shown in Table 11.4, what is the FOB of a bale of sugar that

Australian sugar growers should price up for retailers in China?

Use the following information within your calculations:

**1** VAT and sales taxes are applied in many overseas markets. For this example, there are no VAT or sales taxes in China.

**2** Retailers take a full margin on the selling price not the buying price.

**3** Assumes an exchange rate of AUD$1 = CNY4.76036.

**4** Assumes a freight rate of AUD$1200 for 20 foot FCL sea freight container that packs 1200 bales.

**5** Bales contain 25 bags of sugar.

Use the following table to complete your calculation:

| Top down pricing model for sugar exports | Bag of sugar | Quick tips |
|---|---|---|
| Similar bag of sugar at a retail store in China, assumed price = AUD$1 = CNY4.76036 | CNY | 4.76 |
| Deduct VAT | CNY | |
| Consumer price per bag of sugar excluding VAT **(1)** | CNY | |
| Deduct retail margin of 150% | | |
| Retailers buying price per bag of sugar | CNY | |
| Importers buying price per bag of sugar CNY − deduct importers margin of 30% **(2)** + clearance & warehouse allowance of 3% + advertising & promotion allowance of 5% = total 38% | CNY | |
| Importer buy price per bale with duty CNY | CNY | |
| Importer price per bale before duty – deduct duty (80%) of CIF | CNY | |
| Convert to AUD$ **(3)** | AUD | |
| CIF per bale | AUD | |
| Deduct Freight **(4)** | AUD | |
| Deduct marine insurance | AUD | |
| FOB per bale of sugar **(5)** | AUD | |

## Cost reduction

The rationale behind any firm's decision to enter international markets is usually to increase profitability. This is based on a recognition of the fact that the size of the firm's actual market share is a primary determinant of profitability. Thus, the argument goes that firms with a larger market share normally have lower unit costs. They are perceived by customers to market higher-quality products, leading to relatively higher market prices. Both of these factors result in higher profits for the firm.

Most companies in international markets have the potential to benefit from driving down costs through achieving economies of scale, exploiting the benefits of the **learning curve** and making strategic decisions on the location or relocation of manufacturing plants within the context of worldwide operations.

## Economies of scale

Economies of scale are obtained as a result of manufacturing additional products with the same or only slightly higher fixed costs, so that, in practice, for every additional product produced, the unit cost reduces. This is a slight over-simplification of the situation as, for example, installation of new plant might in the short term increase unit costs during the period when the plant is running at below its economic capacity. In domestic markets the benefits from economies of scale follow directly. In international markets, however, these economies must more than offset savings achieved by having local plants, which result in reduced transport costs and the avoidance of import tariffs.

## Learning curve

Some authors have suggested that, although it is less well known than economies of scale, the learning curve has potentially greater benefit for cost reduction. Its origins lie in the production of aircraft in the Second World War. The observation was made that the time needed to perform a specific task reduced as the operatives become more familiar with it. Since then a series of studies by the Boston Consulting Group has found evidence that the effect was much more widespread than this. It discovered it in all aspects of business, including high and low technology, products and services, and consumer and industrial products. They point out that there is a direct relationship between the cumulative volume of production and the costs incurred in producing the same product benefits. The major sources of savings from the experience gained through the learning curve are:

- greater labour efficiency
- task specialization and method improvement
- new production processes
- better performance of existing equipment
- changes to the mix of resources
- greater product standardization
- improved product designs.

Thus, the learning curve provides an opportunity for cost reductions, although if managers do not make a concerted effort, costs will rise.

The combined effects of economies of scale and the learning curve are seen in the electronics market, where aggressive firms slash prices to gain market share, knowing that cost reductions will follow. On the other hand, with experience, prices can be raised to exploit opportunities. At the Ramon Sanchez Pizjuan stadium in Spain, Manchester United fans were charged around £89 (allowing for exchange rates) for a ticket to watch the Champions League game against Sevilla. At a previous Champions League game at the Ramon Sanchez Pizjuan stadium, Liverpool fans were charged around £54. Manchester United threatened to increase the price for Sevilla fans for their away game at Old Trafford in the UK.

## Location of production facility

Driven by the continual need to reduce costs, companies have increasingly considered selective location or relocation of production facilities. As firms increasingly market their products globally, so their choice of manufacturing locations is determined by many considerations other than simply being close to particular markets. They might choose to locate a factory in a less developed country in order to take advantage of lower labour costs. They may also develop specific skills and areas of specialization in those locations. For example, a large proportion of televisions, radios, calculators and jeans are manufactured in China and South East Asia. Bangladesh is another country which is becoming a location for the production of televisions, mobile/cell phones and refrigerators. Due to the skills of its employees, location and price advantage, Walton's, the manufacturing arm of WALTON Group headquartered in Dhaka, Bangladesh, has a stated mission to lead the field in technology advancement and innovation. So much so that Walton's 2020 vision is to show to the world that 'Made in Bangladesh' is a sign that means aspiration and quality in the minds of consumers. And with its product portfolio ranging from freezers to LED/LCD televisions, headphones to laptops, motorbikes to screws, they offer something for everyone. Walton's mantra is to compete on quality and price. It sees its expansion through other economically developing countries.

India is another country with an excellent location which attracts organizations eager to do business. India has over 1.2 billion inhabitants, 125 million of whom are considered to represent a financially aware middle class. This not only presents a highly skilled but cheap workforce for multinationals but also a growing consumer market for the goods India produces. The Indian government has a range of incentives that encourage Foreign Direct Investment, such as stamp duty exemption for land acquisition and exemption from value added tax. These incentives will certainly attract global brands who can adapt their prices accordingly. India's government is so confident in its ability to provide products and services that they have set up their own website entitled www.makeinindia.com, together with a guidance team to encourage more brands to invest.

Thomson-CSF (France), Coca-Cola, Motorola, IBM and Hewlett Packard have invested heavily in the Indian region. Brands such as ThyssenKrupp Aerospace the German-based conglomerate, chose India to produce aerospace materials. Twitter, a San Francisco-based company, investing outside the USA for the first time, chose India to be their new R&D centre. In 2018, when India relaxed its foreign direct investment, fashion brands such as Uniqlo (Japan) and H&M (Sweden) as well as electronics and software company Xiaomi Inc., were the first to invest in India.

Problems associated with manufacturing in western countries have helped to accelerate this transfer of manufacturing to South Asia. Lagging productivity, reluctance to source materials and parts globally, strong unions and high standards of living were the causes of the decline in the US manufacturing base. Nevertheless, with the improvements in technology, together with greater efficiency and productivity, the number of employees in manufacturing has fallen but output has increased. Therefore, many regions and countries, like India, are responding to this opportunity for inward investment by marketing a variety of incentives and attractions to companies wishing to relocate.

It is not only in manufacturing that relocation of activities can benefit from lower labour costs. For instance, the introduction of fibre optic cables allows considerably more information to be transferred quickly and accurately by telecommunications. This can lead to high labour-content jobs such as data input, order processing and invoicing being carried out in other countries. It is on this foundation that India has built a global advantage in offering hi-tech services such as data processing, call centres and software application.

## Market factors

**Consumers' response**  Perhaps the most critical factor to be considered when developing a pricing strategy in international markets, however, is how the customers and competitors will respond.

There are nine factors which influence the sensitivity of customers to prices. All have implications for the international marketer. Price sensitivity reduces:

- the more distinctive the product is
- the greater the perceived quality

- the less aware consumers are of substitutes in the market
- if it is difficult to make comparisons, for example, in the quality of services such as consultancy or accountancy
- if the price of a product represents a small proportion of total expenditure of the customer
- as the perceived benefit increases
- if the product is used in association with a product bought previously so that, for example, components and replacements are usually extremely highly priced
- if costs are shared with other parties
- if the product or service cannot be stored.

The issue with all these factors is that it is customer perceptions and purchasing behaviour which are most important in setting prices. In France, Disneyland Paris suffered considerably from weaknesses in its financial structure. The fundamental problems were that customer perceptions and demand for Disneyland Paris were out of step with forecasts. The explanation for the weaknesses in their offer was found to be in the factors affecting price sensitivity. High interest rates and high labour costs in France were underestimated. The availability of disposable income of potential consumers was overestimated, particularly during and following the recent global financial crises. This means that Disneyland Paris still runs at a loss, with external forces not helping the situation. In 2014 Walt Disney provided a US$1 billion bailout for its French resort (Possebon 2014). It was hoped that, following the launch of the Star Wars attraction in 2017, Disneyland Paris would make a profit; unfortunately, it has not. There are three external factors that may reduce the number of visitors to Disneyland Paris in future. The factors include: first, the terror attacks in Paris during 2017; second, that many European countries are not growing economically leading to a lack of salary increases; and third, Paris has just been declared one of the top ten most expensive cities, which may deter travellers. Nevertheless, Disney supported its European sister with a further recapitalization of 1.5 billion. Customers' perception of credit can also influence purchasing behaviour. In central Europe and Asia consumers have been reluctant to borrow money to buy goods.

**Competitors' response**   As competition increases in virtually every product and market, the likely response of the competitors to a firm's pricing strategy becomes increasingly important. An attempt should be made to forecast how competitors might react to a change in pricing strategy by analyzing the market and product factors which affect them, consumer perceptions of their product offers and their internal cost structures. Competitors' pricing strategies will be affected by such issues as their commitment to particular products and markets, and the stance that they might have adopted in the past during periods of fierce competition.

Before implementing pricing strategies and tactics, therefore, it is essential to estimate the likely consumer and competitor response by evaluating similar situations which have arisen in other international markets or countries. The responses of competitors who adopt a global strategic approach are likely to be more easily predicted than a competitor adopting a multi-domestic strategy.

## Developing pricing strategies

Having discussed the factors which firms should consider in the pricing process, we now turn to the development of international pricing strategies. The first question to be addressed is to what extent prices should be standardized across the markets. There are three approaches to international pricing strategies.

*Standardization*, or ethnocentric pricing, based on setting a price for the product as it leaves the factory, irrespective of its final destination. While each customer pays the same price for the product at the factory gate, they are expected to pay transport and import duties themselves, either directly or indirectly. This can lead to considerable differences in the price to the final consumer.

For the firm, this is a low-risk strategy as a fixed return is guaranteed and the international buyer takes all the exchange rate risk. However, no attempt is made to respond to local conditions in each national market, and so no effort is made to maximize either profits or sales volume. This type of pricing strategy is often used when selling highly specialized manufacturing plant.

*Adaptation*, or polycentric pricing, allows each local subsidiary or partner to set a price which is considered to be the most appropriate for local conditions. No attempt is made to coordinate prices from country to country. The only constraints that are applied when using this strategy relate to transfer pricing within the corporate structure.

The weakness with this policy is the lack of control that the headquarters has over the prices set by the subsidiary operations. Significantly different prices might be set in adjacent markets, and this can reflect badly on the image of multinational firms. It also encourages the creation of grey markets (which are dealt with in greater detail later in this chapter), whereby products can be purchased in one market and sold in another, undercutting the established market prices in the process. Firms marketing on the Internet find it very difficult to pursue such strategies because of the free flow of information across markets. Gap customers soon discovered they could save up to 40 per cent of the price of a garment by buying online rather than in their local store, leading to a speedy change in their pricing strategy.

*Invention*, or geocentric pricing, involves neither fixing a single price, nor allowing local subsidiaries total freedom for setting prices either. It attempts to take the best of both approaches. While the need to take account of local factors is recognized, particularly in the short term, the firm still expects local pricing strategies to be integrated into a company-wide long-term strategy. The benefits of this approach are shown in the following example. A firm which intends to establish a manufacturing base within a particular region may need to rapidly increase market share in order to generate the additional sales necessary for a viable production plant. In the short term, the local subsidiary may be required to sell at what for them is an uneconomic price, so that by the time the new plant comes on stream, sufficient sales have built up to make the plant and the individual subsidiaries profitable.

## The objectives of pricing

The objectives of the firm's pricing strategy are directly related to the various factors which have been discussed. But it should be emphasized that they will be affected as much by the prevailing company culture and attitudes to international marketing as by market and environmental conditions. The most common pricing objectives for companies are listed here, but it must be recognized that firms also adapt or add other specific objectives according to their own specific and changing circumstances. The alternative approaches are:

- *Rate of return.* Cost-oriented companies set prices to achieve a specific level of return on investment and may quote the same ex-works (EXW) price for both domestic and international markets.

- *Market stabilization.* A firm may choose not to provoke retaliation from the market leader, so that market shares are not significantly changed.

- *Demand-led pricing.* Prices are adjusted according to an assessment of demand, so that high prices are charged when demand is buoyant and low prices are charged when demand is weak.

- *Competition-led pricing.* In commodity markets such as coffee and wheat, world market prices are established through continual interaction between buyers and sellers. Selling outside the narrow band of prices that have been mutually agreed will either reduce sales or unnecessarily reduce profits.

- *Pricing to reflect product differentiation.* Individual products are used to emphasize differences between products targeted at various market segments. Carmakers, for example, charge prices for the top-of-the-range models which are far higher than is justified by the cost of the additional features which distinguish them from the basic models. But problems arise in different international markets, as consumers' perceptions vary as to what is considered to be a basic model.

- *Market skimming.* The objective of market skimming is for the firm to enter the market at a high price and lower the price only gradually, or even abandon the market as competition increases. It is often used by companies to recover high R&D costs.

■ *Market penetration*. Low prices can be used by a firm to rapidly increase sales by stimulating growth and increasing market share. At the same time this discourages competition. Japanese companies have used this strategy extensively to gain leadership in a number of markets, such as cars, home entertainment products and electronic components.

■ *Early cash recovery*. A firm may aim for early cash recovery to increase sales and generate cash rapidly. It might need to do this if faced with liquidity problems, products in the mature or declining phase of the product life cycle, or products with an uncertain future in the market because of changes in government policy. A variety of mechanisms are used, including special offers, discounts for prompt payment and rigorous credit control. These are all types of marginal cost pricing.

■ *Prevent new entry*. Competitors can be discouraged from entering a market by establishing low prices which will indicate to potential competitors the prospect of low returns and price wars. Domestic firms have used this strategy to attempt to prevent entry by international competitors. However, the danger is that the other firm might successfully enter the market with a quite different positioning, such as higher specification or quality, or with improved service levels. The defending firm, due to its low-price strategy, may not have the income to make the necessary investment to compete with the new entrant.

## Setting a price

Having determined suitable strategies for pricing in international markets, a company must then consider the options available in setting individual prices. Companies can decide on the basis of their knowledge, objectives and situation to take either a cost, market or competition-oriented approach.

Cost-oriented approaches are intended to either:

■ achieve a specific return on investment, or

■ ensure an early recovery of either cash or investments made to enter the market.

Market-oriented pricing approaches give the company the opportunity to:

■ stabilize competitive positions within the market

■ skim the most profitable business, or

■ penetrate the market by adopting an aggressive strategy to increase market share.

Competition-oriented approaches are designed to:

■ maintain and improve market position

■ meet and follow competition

■ reflect differences in the perceived value and performance of competitive products, or

■ prevent or discourage new entrants in the market.

No matter which of these broad strategies is adopted, the process for determining export pricing is essentially the same:

■ determine export market potential

■ estimate the price range and target price

■ calculate sales potential at the target price

■ evaluate tariff and non-tariff barriers

■ select suitable pricing strategy in line with company objectives

■ consider likely competitor response

■ select pricing tactics, set distributor and end-user prices

■ monitor performance and take necessary corrective action.

# Problems of pricing and financing international transactions

There are a number of specific problems which arise in setting and managing prices in international markets. Problems arise in four main areas:

1 *Problems in multinational pricing.* Companies find difficulty in coordinating and controlling prices across their activities sufficiently to enable them to achieve effective financial performance and their desired price positioning:

   ■ How can prices be coordinated by the company across the various markets?
   ■ How can a company retain uniform price positioning in different market situations?
   ■ At what price should a company transfer products or services from a subsidiary in one country to a subsidiary in another?
   ■ How can a firm deal with importation and sale of its products by an unauthorized dealer?

2 *Problems in managing foreign currency and fluctuating exchange rates.* Considerable problems arise in foreign transactions because of the need to buy and sell products in different currencies:

   ■ In what currency should a company price its products in international markets?
   ■ How should the company deal with fluctuating exchange rates?
   ■ How can a company minimize exchange rate risk over the longer-term transactions?

3 *Problems of obtaining suitable payment in high-risk markets.* Obtaining payment promptly and in a suitable currency from the less developed countries can cause expense and additional difficulties:

   ■ How might/should a company deal with selling to countries where there is a risk of non-payment?
   ■ How should a company approach selling to countries which have a shortage of hard currency or high inflation?
   ■ How can a company obtain payment upfront on long-term transactions?

4 *Administrative problems of cross-border transfer of goods.* Problems of bureaucracy and delays arise as a result of simply moving goods physically across borders:

   ■ At what point should an exporter release control and responsibility for goods?
   ■ What steps can be taken in the export order process to minimize delays?

These four major problem areas will now be dealt with in the following sections.

# Problems in multinational pricing

## Coordination of prices across markets

The pressure on companies to market truly global products backed by globally standardized advertising campaigns is caused by three major trends. These are the homogenization of customer demand, the lowering of trade barriers and the emergence of international competitors. At the same time, these largely undifferentiated global products can be sold at very different prices in different countries, based on factors such as purchasing power, exchange rate changes, and competition and consumer preferences.

Until recently, this has been a perfectly acceptable practice. However, since the late 2000s, it has become increasingly difficult for companies to maintain a differentiated pricing strategy across international markets when they are marketing similar if not standardized products. Readily available information on worldwide prices through modern data transfer and the Internet have greatly increased price transparency. Advances in telecommunications systems have also greatly reduced international transaction costs. Global companies, who obviously follow differentiated pricing policies, are often under pressure on two fronts. First, they may suffer an erosion of consumer confidence as customers learn of the more attractive pricing policies in other markets. Second, a grey market may emerge where products are distributed through different channels to those authorized and controlled by the manufacturer. See Management Challenge 11.2.

## MANAGEMENT CHALLENGE 11.2

## Fighting back: unauthorized watch dealers – watch out!

Unauthorized sellers of watches compete against the legitimate authorized dealers. This is frustrating for watch marketing managers. Choosing the 'right' bricks and mortar retailer to sell a luxury watch, such as the Audemars Piguet Royal Oak automatic timepiece in rose gold, is an important decision for a brand. A brand's carefully crafted timepiece needs to be sold by retailers that extol the values of the organization that designed and made the watch. Retailers need to exude quality in their service and, more importantly, sell the watch at an appropriate price for a watch that is prestigious to own and be admired by others.

A popular Audemars Piguet Royal Oak sells for around £42 600. However, via parallel markets (grey markets), they can sell for around £27 000. Clearly the difference is apparent. Indeed, when visiting the Audemars Piguet website to view the exclusive Royal Oak Tourbillon Chronograph, there are beautiful pictures, details of the wonderful features of the watch and details of the warranty, but no prices are shown. Audemars Piguet point the viewer to a notice which states 'Please contact your preferred boutique for pricing information'. This model of the Audemars Piguet Royal Oak Tourbillon Chronograph is currently for sale via Chrono 24 at £338 069.

Grey market stores include Chrono 24, authentic-watches.com and jamashop.com.

Brian Lee of L2, a business intelligence service, suggests consumers are driving up the increase in demand for sales of watches via the grey market. Currently many luxury retailers do not quote prices on their websites. Quotations are via appointment or through one-to-one correspondence by email or phone call. However, grey market retailers and online stores provide prices for as many as 10 000 watches. With 10 million visitors to Chrono 24's website and 2.7 million app downloads, it is clear there is a market that wants to view watches online – perhaps it is the prices.

Grey market stores obtain their watches directly from brands and authorized dealers of watches because they have unsold stock they want to unload when watches become obsolete, unpopular or are simply gathering dust. The total watch market is worth around $62.5 billion dollars. The luxury watch market is just a part of that but around 20 per cent of sales in the luxury market range are now through the grey market.

### Question

1 What can luxury watch brands do to ensure their brands do not diminish by being sold through parallel markets?

**References:** *Financial Times* (2018) The billion-dollar grey market in watches upsets big brands. Available from www.ft.com/content/4a4fc942-582d-11e7-80b6-9bfa4c1f83d2. ©The Financial Times Limited 2018. All rights reserved; Audemars Piguet www.audemarspiguet.com; Chrono 24 www.chrono24.com.

**European Monetary Union**   The issue of achieving price coordination across markets has become particularly pertinent in the European Union since the establishment of the European Monetary Union (EMU). The EMU, sometimes called the Eurozone or Euro area, is the name given to the union of countries using the euro as a domestic currency.

National price levels across the EU are far from uniform. Among the Eurozone countries, Austria and Finland are viewed as high-priced markets; France, Belgium and Germany are seen as average; and Portugal and Spain are seen as having much lower prices. Price levels in Scandinavia can be 40 per cent higher than in southern parts of the Eurozone.

Differences in taxation and excise duties as well as disparities in production costs and wage levels lead to price differentials and difficulties in managing problems in the economy. Firms in product markets have tended to adapt their prices to the buying power, income levels and consumer preferences of national markets. However, in the service sector and particularly the tourism industry, it is not very easy to differentiate prices to reflect the differences in buying power and consumer preferences of the variety of national and international consumers that a company may be targeting.

Prior to the formation of the EMU, these differences were largely concealed from the European consumer, despite the formation of the Single European Market. The formation of the EMU and the introduction of the euro has changed all that. Now prices are no longer distorted by fluctuating exchange rates. This means companies competing on the European market need to consider the implications of price transparency in the Eurozone. The onset of price transparency impacts firms in different ways. Highly specialized products with few direct rivals are largely immune to the risk of price transparency generating more intense competition. However, companies marketing goods that are supplied direct to the consumer have come under increasing pressure from retailers to reduce margins if retailers themselves have had to cut prices to meet new price points set in euros. Furthermore, more retailers and businesses have moved to a policy of European-wide sourcing and using the Internet to search for the lowest prices for products. It has, therefore, become virtually impossible for companies to operate on the European market without a sophisticated strategy to effectively coordinate prices across the EU. It is this that has led to so many companies revamping their approach to managing their European marketing strategies.

Firms who have failed to meet this challenge have left themselves open to the threat of grey market goods cannibalizing their sales in high-priced national markets.

## What is grey marketing?

Grey marketing has become a particular problem for companies operating across Europe where there are huge price differentials and no trade barriers, so goods are able to flow freely across borders. Grey marketing is a business phenomenon that has seen unprecedented growth in the past few years. Information on prices flows across countries, and consumers have discovered how varied prices can be when companies try to pursue highly differentiated pricing strategies across markets that can no longer be kept separate.

Grey marketing occurs when trademarked goods are sold through channels of distribution that have not been given authority to sell the goods by the trademark holder. This could occur within a country, but more and more it is becoming common across countries. This becomes problematic, especially for global marketers trying to manage a coordinated marketing strategy across different markets. Coca-Cola had to bring forward the European launch of Vanilla Coke after it found the product was already being sold in the UK by a distributor who had imported it directly from Canada, where it had been launched several months previously. Typically, however, grey market goods are international brands with high price differentials and low costs of arbitrage. The costs connected with the arbitrage are transportation, tariffs, taxes and the costs of modifying the product, that is, changing the language of instructions.

Economic and monetary union and the euro were introduced to help achieve the goal of a single European market. One particular objective was to create a single market where currency could move as freely and cheaply in the Eurozone as it could within national markets. However, to achieve a truly single market, integration of payment facilities across borders was needed to create a single financial services market across the Eurozone. This is known as the Single European Payments Area (SEPA).

The key problem SEPA resolves for companies marketing across the Eurozone is the differences they face between the way domestic and cross-border payments operate and are priced. With SEPA in place, companies can execute any payment within the Euro area as easily and at the same cost as they could in their existing domestic markets.

The objective of SEPA, introduced in 2008, is to create a single payment area. Consumers and businesses can make cross-border payments as easily, safely and efficiently as they can within their own countries and, perhaps most importantly, as cheaply. Cross-border euro payments are treated exactly like domestic payments, whatever their amount. It can still take three business days from order to receipt for cross-border payments, as opposed to a single day within a country. It also still means companies face cross-border pricing difficulties with customers outside of SEPA. In SEPA there has been a consolidation of the cross-border payment infrastructure, which means there are now common rules for clearing and settlement. So costs are minimized and processes quicker. The harmonized European payments infrastructure also makes it possible to implement efficient e-solutions. According to GTnews.com, e-payments will soon account for 95–99 per cent of the total volume of payments.

It is perhaps important to point out that there is nothing illegal about grey market goods. It is purely the practice of buying a product in one market and selling it in other markets in order to benefit from the prevailing price differential. Grey markets tend to develop in markets where information on prices for basically the same product in different countries is cheap and easy to obtain (e.g. cars, designer goods, consumer durables). Sadly, despite the wonders that the Internet brings to marketers in terms of global consumers, extensive 24/7 promotional opportunities and innovative distribution/place channels, the Internet is a breeding ground for grey market activity. Just like all the positive things that the Internet brings, the downside of the Internet grey market is that often products are sold at as much as 25 per cent less than the authorized price. This can have the biggest influence on pricing, product availability and movement of products across borders. KPMG estimates the revenue generated by international grey marketing activities to be about US$25 billion a year. While grey marketing is seen by its critics as a free-riding strategy, it is being increasingly seen as a viable international strategy by smaller firms who, with limited resources, can use it to compete against larger firms in international markets.

There are three types of grey markets (see Figure 11.1):

1   *Parallel importing.* When the product is priced lower in the home market where it is produced than the export market. The grey marketer in the export market will parallel import directly from the home market rather than source from within their own country. An example is Levi's® jeans where there is a strong parallel import trade between the USA and Europe. Levi Strauss & Co. took out a lawsuit against the retail chain Tesco for selling Levi's® jeans they sourced directly from outside the EU. Levi Strauss & Co. insisted that jeans in Europe should only be sourced from authorized dealers within the EU. The judgment by the court, which shocked consumer rights groups everywhere, was that Tesco should not be allowed to import jeans made by Levi Strauss & Co. from outside the EU and sell them at reduced prices without first getting permission from the jeans maker. The high-end market in particular suffers from grey marketing, which is why Louis Vuitton is worried about their increased sales figures. See Illustration 11.3.

2   *Re-importing.* When the product is priced cheaper in an export market than in the home market where it was produced, re-importation in this case can be profitable to the grey marketer.

3   *Lateral importing.* When there is a price difference between export markets, products are sold from one country to another through unauthorized channels.

**FIGURE 11.1**   Three types of grey market

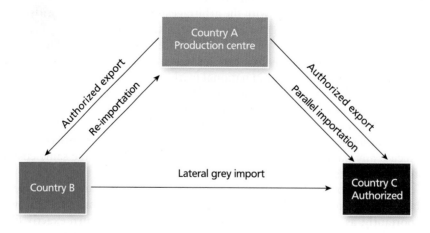

Note: Price in Country B < price in Country C

Source: Assnus, G. and Wiesse, C. (1995) How to address the gray market threat using price coordination. In Doole, I. and Lowe, R. (eds) *International Marketing Strategy: Contemporary Readings*. International Thomson Business Press.

## ILLUSTRATION 11.3

# Louis Vuitton sells to 'retailer tourists'

LVMH Moët Hennessy states that it is product innovation and fashion shows that keep its clothes and handbags *alive* and *desired*, particularly by the fashionable elite in Japan, the USA and Europe. It is for this reason its sales have increased. However, LVMH is worried that it is *competing with itself* as grey markets are creeping in.

Its main fear is the Chinese grey market. The average wealth of Chinese citizens has grown in recent years. The number of Chinese millionaires has grown to 3 per cent of the world's total number of millionaires. With this increase in wealth, Chinese consumers are a major force behind the increased sales of many luxury items. The desire for global, luxurious but discerning brands

is unabated. What is interesting, but worrying to LVMH, is that 50 per cent of luxury items that are bought by Chinese consumers are bought outside China.

LVMH's products, such as handbags, are sold for higher prices in China than they are sold in Europe. The reason for this is that import duties on luxury goods to be sold in China can be as high as 25 per cent, VAT 17 per cent and Consumption Tax can be as much as 45 per cent. Consumption Tax is especially high for luxury items. Chinese consumers are aware of this and flock to Europe or the USA to 'snap up a bargain' LVMH handbag. Chinese 'holiday retailers', who do not declare themselves as retail buyers, buy LVMH handbags in bulk at lower prices in Europe or the USA. Upon return to China, 'holiday retailers' resell LVMH handbags at inflated prices or worse still below the price of LVMH handbags sold through official distribution channels.

LVMH could of course reduce the price of handbags in China to stop the 'holiday retailer'. Or it could increase the price of handbags in Europe and the USA to reduce the price gap between China and Europe/USA.

## Question

**1** What can international companies do to try stop consumers buying from countries where their products are cheaper?

**References:** Atsmon, Y., Ducarme, D., Magni, M. and Wu, C. (2012) Luxury without borders: China's new class of shoppers take on the world. McKinsey and Company. Available from www.mckinseychina.com (accessed 9 June 2018); Brinnded, L. (2015) LVMH is cannibalising itself in China, published 14 April. Available from http://uk.businessinsider.com/lvmh-q1-revenue-analyst-call-on-pricing-policy-luxury-goods-arbitrage-and-the-grey-market-2015-4 (accessed 13 June 2018); Credit Suisse (2018) *Global Wealth Report 2017*. Credit Suisse AG: Switzerland. www.credit-suisse.com/corporate/en/research/research-institute/global-wealth-report.html (accessed 13 June 2018).

A disturbing example of this can be found in the pharmaceutical industry, where it is estimated that US$18 million of reduced-price HIV drugs intended for African markets were diverted back to Europe to be sold at much higher prices on the grey market. Consumers are now challenging the prices that brands place on their products. This is because consumers, not just businesses, are purchasing big brand products via the Internet that are sold more cheaply in other countries.

## Price coordination strategies

Typically, firms try to defend themselves against grey market activities by calling for government intervention or legal protection. As seen in the previous section, companies may resort to imposing restrictions or even threats on retailers. In the USA, Walmart sourced products through grey markets and suffered the resultant threats from firms such as Adidas and Levi Strauss & Co. Other reactive measures have included the refusal to issue warranties in certain markets, or even buying out the grey marketer.

Companies competing in international markets who wish to develop more effective strategies to deal with the problem of price coordination across increasingly interdependent markets and the threat of grey market goods have four options open to them:

1 *Economic measures.* The company can influence the country manager's pricing decision by controlling the input into those decisions. A multinational can do this through transfer pricing (see the later section in this chapter). By raising the price by which it transfers products to the low-priced country, the headquarters essentially imposes a tax on that market. Closely related to transfer pricing is rationing the product quantities allocated to each country or region and so limiting the number of units sold in the diverting country.

2 *Centralization.* The company can move towards more centralization in the setting of prices. Traditionally many multinational companies have given country managers a high degree of decision-making autonomy. Usually they are in the best position to assess consumer response to any given pricing decisions, and they are able to react swiftly to competitor activity. A centralized approach, however, could overcome difficulties with grey market goods, although it does usually result in dissatisfaction among country managers. A compromise approach is to shift the decision-making authority in pricing from a country to a regional level; however, increasingly, grey market goods are becoming a global issue.

3 *Formalization.* The company can standardize the process of planning and implementing pricing decisions. Thus, the company influences prices at the local level by prescribing a process that is followed by country managers when establishing pricing policy.

4 *Informal coordination.* A number of companies have moved towards a more informal system of coordination without either a high degree of centralization or formalization. This thinking is usual in the transnational company where international subsidiaries make differentiated and innovative contributions to an integrated worldwide operation. While this approach may incorporate a variety of techniques, the essential asset is that there are common shared business values across the subsidiaries that are backed by compatible incentive systems.

In a proactive approach to coordinating its pricing decision across international markets, a company has to select the appropriate strategy which will in effect be determined, first, by the level of local resources available and, second, by the level of environmental complexity, as illustrated in Figure 11.2.

**FIGURE 11.2**    A framework for selecting a coordination method

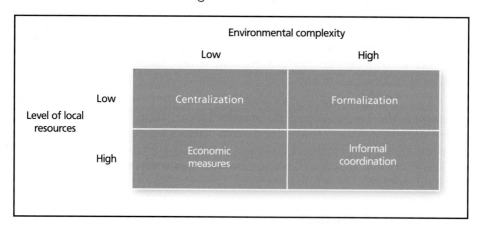

Source: Assnus, G. and Wiesse, C. (1995) How to address the gray market threat using price coordination. In Doole, I. and Lowe, R. (eds) *International Marketing Strategy: Contemporary Readings*. International Thomson Business Press.

## Transfer pricing in international markets

Transfer pricing is an area that has created complications for many international marketing firms. It is concerned with the pricing of goods sold within a corporate family, when the transactions involved are from division to division, to a foreign subsidiary or to a partner in a joint-venture agreement. While these transfer prices are internal to the company, they are important externally because goods being transferred from country to country must have a value for cross-border taxation purposes.

The objective of the corporation in this situation is to ensure that the transfer price paid optimizes corporate rather than divisional objectives. This can prove difficult when a company internationally is organized into profit centres. For profit centres to work effectively, a price must be set for everything that is transferred, be it working materials, components, finished goods or services. A high transfer price, for example, from the domestic division to a foreign subsidiary, is reflected in an apparently poor performance by the foreign subsidiary, whereas a low price would not be acceptable to the domestic division providing the goods. This issue alone can be the cause of much mistrust between subsidiaries – at best leading to fierce arguments and at worst leading to loss of business through overpricing.

There tend to be three bases for transfer pricing:

1 *Transfer at cost.* In which the transfer price is set at the level of the production cost, and the international division is credited with the entire profit that the firm makes. This means that the production centre is evaluated on efficiency parameters rather than profitability.

2 *Transfer at arm's length.* When the international division is charged the same as any buyer outside the firm. Problems occur if the overseas division is allowed to buy elsewhere when the price is uncompetitive, or the product quality is inferior. Further difficulties arise if there are no external buyers, making it difficult to establish a relevant price. This is the strategy most preferred by national governments and the agreed general principle of the OECD. The OECD say this principle should govern transfer pricing transactions and has published detailed guidelines to guide companies.

3 *Transfer at cost plus.* This is a compromise, where profits are split between the production and international divisions. The actual formula used for assessing the transfer price can vary. Usually it is this method which has the greatest chance of minimizing executive time spent on transfer price disagreements, optimizing corporate profits and motivating the home and international divisions. Often a senior executive is appointed to rule on disputes.

However, the real interest of transfer pricing is how it is used strategically by companies either to act as a barrier to entry or to marshal resources around the world.

## To create barriers to entry

Most oil companies are vertically integrated, from oil exploration right through to selling petrol at the pumps. They use transfer pricing as part of their strategy to maintain barriers to entry. The major cost for oil companies is at the exploration and refining stage. So, by charging high transfer prices for crude oil, profits are generated at the refining stage of the process, rather than in distribution where it is relatively easy to enter the market. Oil companies, therefore, attempt, by the use of transfer pricing, to make petrol distribution unattractive to potential competitors. Supermarkets and hypermarkets, with their huge purchasing power, have managed to challenge the dominance of the oil companies by using low-priced petrol as a loss-leader to entice customers to stores.

## To avoid domestic tax liabilities

When countries have different levels of taxation on corporate profits, firms try to ensure that profits are accumulated at the most advantageous point. Companies operating in countries with high corporation tax may be tempted to sell at low transfer prices to their subsidiaries in countries with lower corporate taxation.

## To avoid foreign tax

Foreign tax authorities wish to maximize the taxable income within their jurisdiction. There are a number of strategies a company might use to avoid tax, for example, by charging lower transfer prices if there is high customs duty on goods. The impact of such avoidance strategies is diminishing, as customs authorities become more aware of this practice. Recently, the US government demanded huge taxes from Sony when it discovered that it generated 60 per cent of its global sales in the USA but very little profit due to Sony's management of transfer pricing. Japan then retaliated by doing the same to Coca-Cola. However, it can be argued that as the general level of import duties is reducing as international trade agreements come into effect, so the need to take avoiding action is declining.

## To manage the level of involvement in markets

If a firm has both a wholly owned subsidiary and a joint venture in a particular country, it will wish to sell at a higher price to a company with which it has a joint venture than one that is a wholly owned subsidiary. Selling at a low price to foreign partnerships or licensees has the effect of sharing more of the profit with the partner.

Transfer pricing is an area where profit objectives, managerial motivations and government regulation interact. The expertise of many people – accountants, legal counsel, tax advisers and division managers – is needed to achieve an agreement. The international marketing manager's contribution is primarily concerned with two aspects of the problem:

■ achieving an effective distribution of goods to world markets, and

■ ensuring that the impact of the transfer price does not affect foreign market opportunities.

# Problems in managing foreign currency transactions

Perhaps the most critical issue for managers is how to deal with the various problems involved in managing transactions which involve currency exchange. Another difficulty is what action to take when selling to countries where there is high inflation. See Mangement Challenge 11.3 for the challenges when there is a volatile exchange rate and fluctuating market condistions.

## What currency should the price be quoted in?

In any international marketing transaction, the exporter has the option of quoting in either the domestic or the local currency. If the exporter quotes in its own domestic currency, then not only is it administratively much easier but also the risks associated with changes in the exchange rate are borne by the customer. Quoting prices in the foreign currency means the exporter bears the exchange rate risk. However, there are benefits to the exporter in quoting in foreign currency:

■ It could provide access to finance abroad at lower interest rates.

■ Good currency management may be a means of gaining additional profits.

■ Quoting in foreign currency could be a condition of the contract.

■ Customers normally prefer to be quoted in their own currency in order to be able to make competitive comparisons and to know exactly what the eventual price will be.

Furthermore, customers in export markets often prefer quotations in their own currency to enable them to more easily compare the tenders of competitors from a range of countries.

Often the choice of currency for the price quotation depends partly on the trade practices in the export market and the industry concerned. Suppliers competing for business in the oil industry, wherever in the world they may be supplying, may well find they are asked to quote in US dollars. In the airline industry things are more complicated. EADS, the European group manufacturing the Airbus plane, has all its costs in euros. But on the global market, planes are priced in US dollars. This gives the US company Boeing an

## MANAGEMENT CHALLENGE 11.3

# Commodity price challenges

African leaders have, after years of talks and numerous meetings, signed the largest free trade agreement for decades. The agreement is known as the African Continental Free Trade Area (CFTA) agreement. Out of the 55 member states of the African Union, 44 signed. The agreement affects 1.2 billion people and is a major triumph for them economically. African nations are rich in resources, but there are many barriers that have held them back. Within the CFTA, trading will take place tariff-free, which will be of benefit in terms of time and will reduce costs when importing and exporting.

Exporting inside Africa and out to the rest of the world is important for African countries, especially those that trade oil. Interestingly, of the largest oil producers in the world, five out of the top ten are in Africa. Moreover, when the dollar price per barrel fell from $100 to $30, it had a major impact on Africa's economy. Generally, African countries export raw commodities. In addition to oil, these include gas, precious metals (e.g. gold), diamonds and maize. Africa has experienced the volatility of prices in these raw materials.

### Questions

**1** Now that the CFTA has been signed, what are the advantages and challenges that come when removing tariffs in free-trade areas?

**2** Commodity prices rise and fall regularly, particularly for raw commodities on which Africa relies quite heavily. What can African countries do so they do not solely rely on oil, gas, precious metals, diamonds and maize?

**Reference:** Associated Press (2018) African nations sign largest free trade agreement since WTO. Available from https://wtop.com/africa/2018/03/african-nations-sign-largest-free-trade-agreement-since-wto (accessed 9 June 2018).

advantage competing on international markets, because they do not have the same exchange risk as EADS and can forecast their costs and prices with much more certainty than their arch rival Airbus.

When exporters experience a period of strong home currency it reduces their competitiveness on international markets and makes them vulnerable to price-cutting pressures from international customers. Thus, as well as the decision as to what currency to quote in, the main worry for both suppliers and customers on international markets is fluctuating exchange rates and how to deal with them.

The introduction of the euro has effectively eliminated exchange rate risk in the Eurozone countries. Even countries who have decided not to enter the EMU for the present time, increasingly find that companies selling goods into Europe are pressurized to quote prices in euros.

## Should prices be raised/lowered as exchange rates fluctuate?

One of the most difficult problems that exporters face is caused by fluctuating exchange rates.

Sarathy *et al*. (2006) identified three types of risk affecting firms, arising from exchange rate fluctuations:

**1** *Transaction risk*. This occurs when the exporter quotes in a foreign currency, which then appreciates, diminishing the financial return to the firm. US hoteliers in Hawaii experienced a noticeable decline in Japanese tourism when the dollar rose in value from ¥90 to ¥120 in just over a year.

**2** *Competitive risk*. Arises because the geographic pattern of a firm's manufacturing and sales puts them at a disadvantage compared to their competition. If, for instance, the firm is manufacturing in a country with an appreciating currency but trying to compete in a marketplace where currencies are depreciating, it could lose out to a local manufacturer. Firms may then try to maximize their expenditure in the marketplace. This is why Mercedes and BMW are now manufacturing in the USA.

**3** *Market portfolio risk*. This risk occurs because a company with a narrow market portfolio will be influenced to a much greater extent by changes in exchange rates than a diversified firm that is better able to balance changes in exchange rates through operating in many countries.

Various tactics can be adopted to deal with currency fluctuations. When the domestic currency is weak, the firm should:

- compete on price
- introduce new products with additional features
- source and manufacture in the domestic country
- fully exploit export opportunities
- obtain payment in cash
- use a full-cost approach for existing markets, but use marginal costs for new more competitive markets
- repatriate foreign-earned income quickly
- reduce expenditure and buy services (advertising, transport, etc.) locally
- minimize overseas borrowing
- invoice in the domestic currency.

When the domestic currency is strong, the firm should:

- compete on non-price factors (quality, delivery, service)
- improve productivity and reduce costs
- prioritize strong currency countries for exports
- use countertrade for weak currency countries
- reduce profit margins and use marginal costs for pricing
- keep the foreign-earned income in the local country
- maximize expenditures in local country currency
- buy services abroad in local currencies
- borrow money for expansion in local markets
- invoice foreign customers in their own currency.

## Problems in minimizing the risk of non-payment in high-risk countries

The international marketing manager increasingly needs to be knowledgeable about the various complexities of financing international marketing transactions and sources of finance to support international marketing strategies. This is especially so when trading with markets seen to be high risk due to adverse economic and political conditions, high inflation or perhaps lack of hard currency. For a company exporting goods to such markets there is a considerable risk of non-payment for a variety of reasons, such as:

- the buyer failing or refusing to pay for the goods
- insolvency of the buyer
- a general moratorium on external debt by the host
- government political and legal decisions
- war
- failure to fulfil the conditions of the contract
- lack of hard currency
- high inflation.

Traditionally, managers will seek financial support to help reduce the risk of non-payment due to these factors through home governments, commercial banks or some kind of cooperation agreement.

**Government-sponsored finance**   Governments are often willing to financially support companies in financing international trade transactions in the hope that increased exports will generate economic growth at home and boost employment. National governments approach such support in a variety of ways. But in most countries, there is an export–import bank or perhaps export bank or, as in the UK, a government department (Trade Partners UK) who fund a variety of support packages to help companies finance export strategies. Governments will also provide low-cost export guarantee insurance to protect their exporters against non-payment by foreign buyers. However, such protection may not be available in particularly high-risk markets.

**Commercial banks**   Commercial banks compete intensively to offer international trade services to companies operating in international markets. However, they tend only to be willing to support low-risk activities, which sometimes makes it difficult for companies expanding into emerging markets. Commercial banks may also be more interested in short-term financing. So this is potentially not such a good source for companies making a long-term investment decision in incipient markets where it may be several years before a full return on investment can be achieved. Many banks who made long-term loans to developing markets have suffered losses when countries not experiencing the growth rates expected have been unable to meet debt repayments. This has led to a number of banks being less willing to have exposure to long-term high-risk markets.

One of the ways banks can help against the risk of non-payment is by forfaiting.

**Forfaiting**   This is a way of financing without recourse. It means that companies selling products essentially transfer the transaction risk to a forfaiting house. A bill of exchange, usually requiring a bank guarantee or, as in the USA, a back up letter of credit, is drawn up to the value of the contract. The seller then transfers the claim resulting from the transaction to the forfaiting house. The seller immediately receives the full amount of the contract minus the discount agreed for the period of the contract. This discount will vary depending on the length of the contract, the level of country risk and whether the invoice is guaranteed by a commercial bank. For the company it provides a source of finance to support medium-term contracts in a market and a means of reducing the risk of non-payment.

**Cooperation agreements**   These agreements are special kinds of countertrade deals that extend over long periods of time and may have government involvement. They may be called product purchase transactions, buyback deals or pay as you earn deals. For instance, a company may obtain finance to help set up a factory in a particular country if they then agree to buy back the output of the plant.

## Countertrade and leasing

So far in this chapter we have focused upon largely conventional approaches to international pricing. However, since the late 1990s, there has been a dramatic increase in the use of leasing and countertrade deals. These are used as a response to the lack of hard currency, particularly among less developed countries.

Countertrade deals are more prevalent when companies are trying to enter emerging or less developed markets. The reasons for this are threefold:

1 It is sometimes difficult to obtain finance commercially to enter such markets.
2 The markets themselves may have limited access to hard currency, which means the finance of joint ventures or strategic alliances has to be sought through less traditional means.
3 Emerging markets may see such deals as a way of encouraging job creation in their own countries and so actively encourage such financing deals.

**What is countertrade?**   Countertrade covers various forms of trading arrangements where part or all of the payment for goods is in the form of other goods or services. Price-setting and financing are then dealt with together in one transaction. The original and simple barter system has been developed in order to accommodate modern trading situations. Estimates of countertrade activity range from 20 to 30 per cent of world trade. It is predicted to grow further due to its ability, first, to overcome market imperfections and, second, to provide opportunities for extraordinary profits to be made. See Illustration 11.4 for an outline of the bartering system used in Ecuador.

## ILLUSTRATION 11.4

# Ecuador's bartering system: everyone wins

In northern Ecuador bartering is a way of life. It is a way of exchanging goods and services. This way of trading is based on an Andean principle around the idea of someone engaging in a need exchange. A person has bananas; they need blankets and so the person seeks someone with whom he can exchange his bananas for blankets. The value attached to each item is to satisfy a need and not to have any monetary value attached. The practice of bartering promotes seven characteristics.

Bartering in northern Ecuador has been going on for generations. The whole family is involved in preparing 'for the bartering' by discussing what they have to exchange, what they need and what will be brought home following the bartering. There are other specifics to bartering in northern Ecuador. Some bartering takes place every week when the northern Ecuadorian families do their 'weekly shop'. Families in surrounding areas visit their local hub to exchange goods amounting to around $8. At other times some families from an area will go on an itinerant journey representing the whole village. They exchange oranges for vegetables or wooden containers for sleeping mats. At specific times of the year, whole villages attend bartering events that can take over a week. These bartering events are held after a harvest, during Holy Week and in the spring.

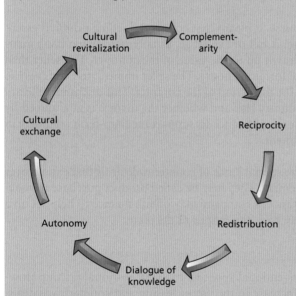

## Questions

**1** What are the advantages of engaging in bartering that promote the seven characteristics shown in the figure?

**2** What examples of bartering have you seen? What need do you have and what would you give in exchange?

**Reference:** Infotrac Newsstand (2017) Washington: The culture of nonmonetary bartering. US Official News, 4 December. Available from http://link.galegroup.com/apps/doc/A517355250/STND?u=lmu_web&sid=STND&xid=9da66980 (accessed 21 April 2018).

There are many variants of countertrade, resulting from the need to adapt arrangements to meet the needs of individual transactions. The following are the basic forms:

*Barter.* This is a single exchange of goods with no direct use of money and does not require intermediaries. It is the simplest form, but has become unpopular because, first, if the goods are not exchanged simultaneously then one participant is effectively financing the other. Second, one of the parties may well receive unwanted goods as part of the deal. Coca-Cola has entered several barter deals in eastern Europe. Russia paid Coca-Cola in vodka, Poland did the same with Coca-Cola but paid in beer. See Illustration 11.4 for a traditional way of bartering for needs in Ecuador.

*Compensation trading.* This involves an agreement in which payment for goods is accepted in a combination of goods and cash.

*Counter-purchase.* This involves the negotiation of two contracts. In the first, the international marketer agrees to sell the product at an established price in local currency. In the second, simultaneous contract, the international firm buys goods or services for an equivalent or proportionate cash payment from another local supplier.

*Offset*. This is similar to counter-purchase, but in this case national governments cooperate to support the deal. Sometimes called a product purchase transaction, it is a way in which the international firm is able to obtain more saleable goods from the country in exchange. For example, Boeing sold AWACS aircraft to the UK Ministry of Defence on the basis that the purchase price would be spent on UK goods.

*Switch deals* involve a third party (usually a merchant house) which specializes in barter trading, disposing of the goods. For example, if an eastern European company importing western products can only provide in return heavily discounted relatively low-quality products, these may not be saleable in the west. Therefore, a third country will need to be found so that a switch deal can be set up in which these lower-quality goods can be exchanged for other products that are more suitable for the original western markets.

*Cooperation agreements*. These can cover buyback deals, pay as you earn deals or a range of other beneficial arrangements made between two parties. It is an arrangement whereby part or all of the cost of

## ILLUSTRATION 11.5

## B2B cooperation between Diageo and pension trustees

Diageo is the owner of global brands including Smirnoff, Baileys and Johnny Walker. Despite continued success in expanding their business internationally, recently they had a big problem. The big problem was the fact Diageo had a pension deficit. The pension

deficit meant that Diageo did not have enough money in the pension pot to pay employees when they retired. Diageo was very innovative and organized a cooperation agreement between themselves and the Trustees of Diageo's pension plan. Diageo transferred ownership of £430 million worth of Johnny Walker whisky to the Trust. The 2.5 million barrels of whisky did not physically move to the Trustees. This was because the barrels of whisky had not actually matured. However, the barrels of whisky were a physical asset that Diageo had that would be turned into cash at a future date. The future date would be when the whisky had matured and sold on the open market. The B2B cooperation agreement was accepted between Diageo and the pension trustees, which in turn meant Diageo could pay retiring employees their pensions.

Diageo is not the only company in the UK that has a pension deficit. M&S and Sainsbury's also have pension deficits and, like Diageo, they have engaged in a cashless cooperation exchange. M&S and Sainsbury's did not use stock (such as whisky barrels), they used their high-street retail stores as an asset for collateral. British Airways also was in a similar situation and it used aeroplanes in its cooperation exchange. Cooperation exchanges like these are often known as an asset-backed funding (ABF) arrangement.

### Question

1 What are the advantages and disadvantages of the cooperation arrangements?

**References:** Kaikati, A.M. and Kaikati, J.G. (2013) Doing business without exchanging money: The scale and creativity of modern barter. *California Management Review* 55, 46–71; Mistry, B. (2013) Plugging the pension blackhole, published November 2013, *The Treasurer*. Available from www.treasurers.org/ACTmedia/Nov13TTtowerswatson38-39.pdf (accessed 31 May 2015).

purchase of capital equipment might be paid for in the form of production from the equipment supplied, either over time or in the form of some other benefit. See Illustration 11.5.

In Japan and South East Asia, compensation and offset are the most frequently used forms of countertrade. Barter and counter-purchase tend to be more common in lesser developed countries.

So far, the examples of countertrade have involved deals of products, but many other less tangible elements such as know-how, software and information can be included in agreements. Many of the deals set up are complicated. In some cases they have stretched over many years.

## Advantages and limitations of countertrade

The advantages of countertrade are as follows:

- New markets can be developed for a country's products, as marketing and quality control skills are often 'imported' with the deal. It can lead to gaining experience in western markets.
- Surplus and poorer quality products can be sold through countertrade whereas they could not be sold for cash. Moreover, dumping and heavy discounting can be disguised.
- Countertrade through bilateral and multilateral trade agreement can strengthen political ties.
- Countertrade and contract manufacture can be used to enter high-risk areas.
- Countertrade can provide extraordinary profits as it allows companies to circumvent government restrictions.

However, there are disadvantages and limitations to using countertrade:

- There is a lack of flexibility, as the transactions are often dependent on product availability. Countertraded products are often of poor quality, overpriced or are available due to a surplus.
- Products taken in exchange may not fit with the firm's trading objectives or may be difficult to sell.
- Dealing with companies and government organizations may be difficult, particularly in locating and organizing countertrade products.
- Negotiations may be difficult, as there are no guide market prices.
- Countertrade deals are difficult to evaluate in terms of profitability and companies can, through countertrade, create new competition.

It is likely that in the future, countertrading will develop further in the form of longer-term rather than shorter-term partnerships as multinationals seek permanent foreign sources for incorporation in their global sourcing strategy. Less developed countries offer the benefits of low-cost labour and materials, as well as relatively untapped markets for goods. This has resulted in multinationals reversing the traditional countertrade process by first seeking opportunities and then identifying potential countertrade partners with which to exploit the opportunities. For an example of countertrade, see Illustration 11.6.

## Leasing

Leasing is used as an alternative to outright purchase in countries where there is a shortage of capital available to purchase high-priced capital and industrial goods. Usually the rental fee will cover servicing and the costs of spares too. Therefore, the problem of poor levels of maintenance, which is often associated with hi-tech and capital equipment in less developed countries, can be overcome. Leasing arrangements can be attractive, too, in countries where investment grants and tax incentives are offered for new plant and machinery. In this case, the lessor can take advantage of the tax provisions in a way that the lessee cannot, and share some of the savings. It is estimated that leased aircraft account for about 20 per cent of the world's aircraft fleet.

## ILLUSTRATION 11.6

# Leasing a cloud

Cloud computing consists of a series of networks that have 'a cloud' or set of computer servers housed on the Internet. These store, manage and process data on behalf of a business or consumer that would do the same thing but on a local server or a PC, tablet or phone.

From cloud computing the leasing of cloud data storage and processing data is on the rise. Many consumers and businesses from born global companies to small businesses and MNEs lease assistance from cloud service providers to store data, provide a back-up service and run transactions.

The benefits of using the cloud are as follows:

- It lowers capital expenditure as leasing enables businesses to lease cloud space. Prior to this, businesses often purchased basic computer memory drives through to gigantic computer data storage units.

- It reduces operating expenditure. There is no longer a need to use electricity to run or cool down computer data storage units.

- It enables organizations to be mobile. The cloud is 'anywhere' and is not a physical entity for the organizations leasing cloud space. Therefore, businesses can move cities or even countries and their data does not need to move.

- It reduces the need to rent or buy physical space as data storage units can take up large amounts of space.

- It reduces the need to keep up-to-date with the latest data storage and data transacting technology as the cloud service providers do that.

Banking organizations hold vast amounts of data and need technology to deal with millions of transactions, particularly around busy times such as Christmas or Black Friday. Therefore, they are taking advantage of cloud service providers to run transactions that consumers generate from shopping on the high street or via their mobile/cell phones.

Microsoft is the number one cloud service provider. Many consumers use Google Drive as their cloud service provider, storing university assignments, photos and videos. Google Drive allows everyone 5GB for free. After that the price is £1.59 per month for 100GB, £7.99 for 1TB and £79.99 for 10TB of data. Over 10TB will be discussed between the consumer and Google.

Cloud leasing is a global phenomenon that amounts to $30.7 billion dollars and is expected to rise to $88.9 billion by 2022.

## Questions

**1** Discuss the advantages of cloud data storage and cloud service providers running consumer transactions for banks.

**2** What are the risks of using cloud service providers for (a) banks and (b) consumers?

# Deciding at what stage of the export sales process the price should be quoted

Export price quotations are important, because they spell out the legal and cost responsibilities of the buyer and seller. Sellers, as previously mentioned, favour a quote that gives them the least liability and responsibility, such as FOB or EXW, which means the exporter's liability finishes when the goods are loaded onto the buyer's carrier. Buyers, on the other hand, would prefer either free domicile, where responsibility is borne by the supplier all the way to the customer's warehouse, or CIF port of discharge, which means the buyer's responsibility begins only when the goods are in their own country.

Generally, the more market-oriented pricing policies are based on CIF, which indicates a strong commitment to the market. By pricing EXW, an exporter is not taking any steps to build relations with the market and so may be indicating only short-term commitment. The major stages at which export prices might be quoted are articulated through internationally agreed terms called Incoterms. The main ones are as follows:

- EXW: ex-works or ex point of origin
- FAS: free alongside ship
- FOB: free on board
- C and F: cost and freight
- CIF: cost, insurance freight
- DAF: delivered at frontier
- DDP: delivered duty paid to destination point.

In deciding at what stage of the export sales process to price, a company has to be clear about the responsibilities and the costs it is including in its price and what responsibility they wish to pass onto the buyer. Tables 11.5a and b illustrate these costs for each of the main stages in the export sales process.

## The export order process

To further emphasize the complexity of managing international pricing, a major task of the marketer is to choose payment terms that will satisfy importers and at the same time safeguard the interests of the exporter. The transactions process for handling export is illustrated in Figure 11.3.

In the process, the customer agrees to payment. The customer begins the process (1) by sending an enquiry for the goods. The price and terms are confirmed by a pro forma invoice (2) by the supplier, so that the customer knows what amount (3) to instruct its bank to pay and the method of payment (4). The method of payment is confirmed and arranged. If this is by letter of credit this will be opened by the issuing bank (5) in the supplier's country.

When the goods are shipped (6), the shipping documents are returned to the supplier (7) so that shipment is confirmed by their presentation (8) together with all stipulated documents and certificates for payment (9). The monies are automatically transmitted from the customer's account via the issuing bank. The customer may only collect the goods (10) when all the documents have been returned to them.

While letters of credit and drafts are the most common payment method, there are also several other methods of payment:

- A *draft* is drawn by the exporter on the importer, who makes it into a trade acceptance by writing on it the word 'accepted'. A *sight draft* is an unconditional order to pay a sum of money on demand or to the order of a specified person. Drafts which are payable at a future date are called *term drafts*.

- A *letter of credit* is similar to a draft, except it is drawn on the bank and becomes a bank acceptance rather than a trade acceptance. There is greater assurance of payment, as an unconditional undertaking is given by the bank that the debts of the buyer will be paid to the seller.

- A *bill of exchange* is an unconditional order in writing which is signed by one person and requires the person to whom it is addressed to pay a certain sum of money on instruction at a specified time.

- A *documentary collection* is when a bill of exchange is presented to the importer via the banking system. Alternatively, the exporter can present the bill direct. If the importer pays the bill of exchange on presentation, usually by authorizing the bank to transfer funds to the exporter's bank account, then no further action is required.

Table 11.5a   Incoterms stages and services at each stage of the export sales process – rules for any mode of transport

| Services | EXW Ex-works Who pays | FCA Free Carrier Who pays | CPT Carriage Paid To Who pays | CIP Carriage & Insurance Paid To Who pays | DAT Delivered at Terminal Who pays | DAP Delivered at Place Who pays | DDP Delivered Duty Paid Who pays |
|---|---|---|---|---|---|---|---|
| Export Packing | Seller | Seller | Seller | Seller | Seller | Seller | Seller |
| Marking & Labelling | Seller | Seller | Seller | Seller | Seller | Seller | Seller |
| Block and Brace | 1 | 1 | 1 | 1 | 1 | 1 | 1 |
| Export Formalities | Buyer | Seller | Seller | Seller | Seller | Seller | Seller |
| Freight Forwarding Fees | Buyer | Buyer | Seller | Seller | Seller | Seller | Seller |
| Inland Freight to Main Carrier | Buyer | 2 | Seller | Seller | Seller | Seller | Seller |
| Origin Port/Terminal Fees | Buyer | Buyer | Seller | Seller | Seller | Seller | Seller |
| Vessel Loading Fees | Buyer | Buyer | Seller | Seller | Seller | Seller | Seller |
| Ocean or Airfreight | Buyer | Buyer | Seller | Seller | Seller | Seller | Seller |
| Nomination of US Freight Forwarder | Buyer | Buyer | Seller | Seller | Seller | Seller | Seller |
| Marine Insurance | 3 | 3 | 3 | Seller | 3 | 3 | 3 |
| Unload Main Carrier Charges | Buyer | Buyer | 4 | 4 | Seller | Seller | Seller |
| Destination Terminal/Port Fees | Buyer | Buyer | 4 | 4 | 4 | Seller | Seller |
| Nomination of On-Carriage | Buyer | Buyer | Seller | Seller | Seller | Seller | Seller |
| Security Information Requirements | Buyer | Buyer | Buyer | Buyer | Buyer | Buyer | Buyer |
| Customs Entry Service Fees | Buyer | Buyer | Buyer | Buyer | Buyer | Buyer | Seller |
| Duties, Taxes, Customs Fees | Buyer | Buyer | Buyer | Buyer | Buyer | Buyer | Seller |
| Deliver to Buyer | Buyer | Buyer | 5 | 5 | 5 | 5 | Seller |
| Delivering Carrier Unloading | Buyer | Buyer | Buyer | Buyer | Buyer | Buyer | Buyer |

Source: Adapted from *Austrade Guide to Export Pricing*. www.austrade.gov.au.

**Table 11.5b**   Incoterms stages and services at each stage of the export sales process – **rules for sea and inland waterway transport**

| Services | FAS Free Alongside Ship Who pays | FOB Free on Board Who pays | CFR Cost & Freight Who pays | CIF Cost, Insurance & Freight Who pays |
|---|---|---|---|---|
| Export Packing | Seller | Seller | Seller | Seller |
| Marking & Labelling | Seller | Seller | Seller | Seller |
| Block and Brace | 1 | 1 | 1 | 1 |
| Export Formalities | Seller | Seller | Seller | Seller |
| Freight Forwarding Fees | Seller | Seller | Seller | Seller |
| Inland Freight to Main Carrier | Seller | Seller | Seller | Seller |
| Origin Port/Terminal Fees | Seller | Seller | Seller | Seller |
| Vessel Loading Fees | Buyer | Seller | Seller | Seller |
| Ocean or Airfreight | Buyer | Buyer | Seller | Seller |
| Nomination of US Freight Forwarder | Buyer | Buyer | Seller | Seller |
| Marine Insurance | 3 | 3 | 3 | Seller |
| Unload Main Carrier Charges | Buyer | Buyer | 4 | 4 |
| Destination Terminal/Port Fees | Buyer | Buyer | 4 | 4 |
| Nomination of On-Carriage | Buyer | Buyer | Buyer | Buyer |
| Security Information Requirements | Buyer | Buyer | Buyer | Buyer |
| Customs Entry Service Fees | Buyer | Buyer | Buyer | Buyer |
| Duties, Taxes, Customs Fees | Buyer | Buyer | Buyer | Buyer |
| Deliver to Buyer | Buyer | Buyer | Buyer | Buyer |
| Delivering Carrier Unloading | Buyer | Buyer | Buyer | Buyer |

Source: Adapted from *Austrade Guide to Export Pricing*. www.austrade.gov.au.

Notes:

[1] Incoterms® 2010 do not deal with the parties' obligations for stowage within a container and therefore, where relevant, the parties should deal with this in the sales contract.

[2] FCA seller's facility – buyer pays inland freight; FCA qualifiers. Seller arranges and loads pre-carriage carrier and pays inland freight to the 'F' delivery place.

[3] Incoterms® 2010 does not obligate the buyer nor must the seller to insure the goods, therefore this issue be addressed elsewhere in the sales contract.

[4] Charges paid by buyer or seller depending on contract of carriage.

[5] Charges paid by seller if through Bill of Lading or door-to-door rate to buyer's destination.

FIGURE 11.3 The export order process

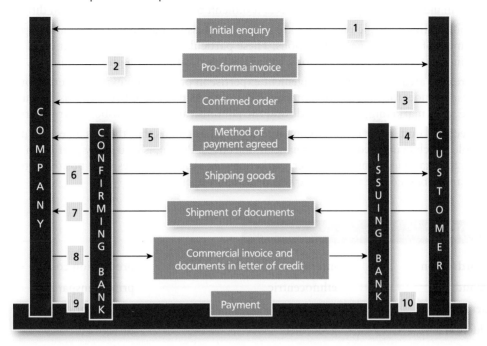

- *Open account* is when the sales terms are agreed between buyer and seller, but without documents specifying clearly the importer's payment obligations. There is less paperwork but greater risk of non-payment, so it is only used when a trusting relationship has been developed between the trading parties. In countries where foreign exchange is difficult to obtain, drafts and letters of credit will be given priority in any currency allocation.

- *A consignment note* is when the exporter retains title of the goods until the importer sells them. Exporters own the goods longer in this method than any other, and so the financial burden and risks are at their greatest. In addition, the recovery of either goods or debt could be very difficult. It is for this reason that consignments tend to be limited to companies trading with their subsidiaries.

The credit terms given are also important in determining the final price to the buyer. When products from international competitors are perceived to be similar, the purchaser may choose the supplier that offers the best credit terms, in order to effect a greater discount. In effect the supplier is offering a source of finance to the buyer. In some countries, for example, Brazil, government support is given to firms to help them gain a competitive advantage through this method. There have been a variety of international agreements to try to stop such practices, but it is still quite prevalent in some countries.

## SUMMARY

- In international markets pricing decisions are much more complex because they are affected by a number of additional external factors. These include fluctuations in exchange rates, accelerating inflation in certain countries and the use of alternative payment methods such as leasing, barter and countertrade.

- Many factors and problems contribute to making effective pricing management one of the most difficult aspects of international marketing to achieve. As well as the market factors associated with pricing decisions in each country, it is necessary to deal with the complexities of financing deals based in different currencies and trying to maintain cross-border consistency of pricing.

- While there are cost benefits in standardizing products, services and processes, local factors affect the cost base in individual countries. This makes it difficult to maintain similar prices in different markets.

- In addition to this strategic role, there are a number of issues relating to the detailed operational management of international transactions. These particularly relate to the reduction of risk in carrying out international trade transactions, especially when trading in high-risk countries.

- There are also areas of specific management expertise in pricing that exist in international marketing. These include, for example, the management of transfer pricing between business units within an MNE, grey marketing, countertrade and the administration of cross-border transfers of goods.

- What becomes quite clear in developing international pricing is that there is a need to use pricing in a key role in achieving a company's financial objectives. Pricing is also a key part of an integrated strategy, for example, along with other marketing mix elements, to respond positively to the opportunities and threats of the various markets in which it operates.

## KEYWORDS

| | | |
|---|---|---|
| price standardization | internal cost structures | production costs |
| elastic demand | ethnocentric | price transparency |
| inelastic demand | polycentric | transfer pricing |
| fixed production cost | geocentric | foreign currency |
| marginal costing | marginal cost pricing | exchange rate risk |
| dumping | exchange rate | Eurozone |
| economies of scale | grey marketing | countertrade |
| learning curve | price coordination | market-oriented pricing |

## CASE STUDY 1

## The impact of cryptocurrencies

The payment world has been revolutionized because of **cryptocurrency**; 'a digital asset that works as a medium of exchange using cryptography to secure transactions. Cryptocurrencies are unlike other currencies as they do not feature centralized economic money or a centrally controlled banking system. Instead control of them is decentralized through a blockchain. Blockchains are public transport databases which can act as a distributed ledger for cryptocurrencies.

Bitcoin was the first decentralized digital cryptocurrency, but in this emerging technology numerous other ones are now being developed. While not the most popular, Ripple, for example, is seen to be better for cross-border trade and business as it is able to better communicate with other currencies than Bitcoin. Ripple is a self-contained blockchain system. Whereas Bitcoin is fundamentally a currency, Ripple is a decentralized method of exchanging currencies.

The advantages to companies trading internationally using such cryptocurrencies are a lack of exchange rate, fast money movement, lower taxes and fees and detailed records kept of all transactions.

However, many companies are fearful of using cryptocurrencies. This is because they are difficult to understand, the technology is complex, they are not accepted widely and if the coins are lost, they are difficult to retrieve. There is also no way to reverse the payment. The main fear, however, is that since cryptocurrencies are so new, they are also very volatile. Many companies do not want to deal with a form of money that is going to go through huge swings in volatility.

All of these reasons make the acceptance of cryptocurrency seem riskier. However, despite the risks, cryptocurrencies are gaining ground. In particular, developing countries are starting to legalize and regulate the use of cryptocurrencies. Even countries with high political restrictions such as Russia and China are trying to ensure people can use them freely. Singapore and Switzerland are currently the most advanced in the use of cryptocurrency.

A number of companies are also now engaging with cryptocurrencies. Examples of companies accepting a cryptocurrency are Expedia, Microsoft, Subway, PayPal, Kodak and Shopify.

## Questions

**1** Discuss the pros and cons of using cryptocurrencies for companies competing on international markets.

**2** What impact do you think these currencies will have on the way companies trade internationally in the future?

**3** Do you think cryptocurrencies will replace traditional forms of payment for export transactions?

**References:** https://en.wikipedia.org/wiki/Bitcoin; www.tradeready.ca; www.globaltrademag.com; https://cointelegraph.com; www.nasdaq.com; https://coinpupil.com; www.bubblestranslation.

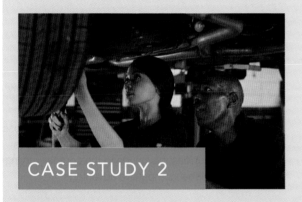

## CASE STUDY 2

# Torque Developments International plc

Torque Developments International plc develops and manufactures pneumatic anti-lock braking systems, electronic braking systems, automated manual transmission systems and an array of conventional products, such as actuators, air compressors and air control valves. In addition, it provides replacement parts, diagnostic tools, training and other services to vehicle distributors, repair shops and fleet operators. Its customers also include a commercial vehicle distributor network that provides replacement parts.

The company markets its products primarily in the USA, Asia and Europe through its global sales force.

## Global challenges

To maintain its global market presence, Torque faces a number of challenges. With its focus on bespoke design, new products are generally developed in response to the performance specification of the customer. Although Torque drives a best cost strategy, the ability to exploit economies of scale and design efficiencies is limited. The sustainability of providing such a high level of solution service also makes it difficult to compete in a market where customers are looking for cost-effective solutions. This means efficient and effective solutions are needed for the company to be sustainable.

Another challenge they face is calculating a sales price across global markets. Traditionally, Torque used a full absorption costing approach to their pricing. The fixed costs, material costs, labour and process and full export costs, and a defined margin, would be included in a bottom up approach to building the price for all quotation requests across global markets. However, this gave the global sales force little flexibility when negotiating in different country markets and meant they were often unable to respond to local market conditions. It also meant they found it problematic when pitching themselves against competitors with a much lower cost base.

The company responded to this challenge by initiating a value-based pricing approach to its global markets. The aim was to focus the engineering resources on those developments which clearly built value for the customers and for which the customer was therefore willing to pay. This enabled the company to achieve higher value margins in targeted areas and focus resources on those areas which delivered a high margin. The aim was to avoid setting prices that were either uncompetitive for customers or lower than they were willing to pay.

An example of the value-based approach to pricing is the method used to price a new brake disc. This brake consists of a turning disc which is mounted to the axle and on top of a brake calliper, carrying the brake pads and the adjuster unit. Torque developed a monobloc brake calliper which reduced the weight. The better distribution of the forces within the single bloc used less material than in the previous version of two halves screwed together.

By using the value-based pricing approach, it was possible to justify a higher added value price for the monobloc solution than the previous cost-plus approach. By communicating and explaining these commercial advantages, the customer was willing to pay for the clear added value, and the delivery contract was extended over a five-year period. This generated additional sales with a higher margin and improved customer satisfaction.

## Questions

**1** Critically evaluate the global pricing strategies pursued by Torque plc.

**2** Discuss how far the value-based approach to pricing meets the global challenges outlined.

**3** What other market-based approaches to pricing could it take?

## DISCUSSION QUESTIONS

1 What are the arguments for and against using price and non-price factors when competing in international markets?

2 What pricing problems might a multinational company face in marketing to less developed countries, and how might they be overcome?

3 Increasingly, competing on global markets requires substantial investment, often undertaken by two or more firms in a joint venture or strategic alliance. Consider the implications of such ventures in developing a strategic approach to coordinating pricing strategies across international markets.

4 Why should a domestic supplier invoice export goods in a foreign currency? What are the advantages and disadvantages of foreign currency invoicing?

5 The Internet is increasing price transparency across international markets. Fully evaluate the problems and opportunities this brings to the company trying to build a global competitive advantage.

## REFERENCES

1. Assnus, G. and Wiesse, C. (1995) How to address the gray market threat using price coordination. In Doole, I. and Lowe, R. (eds) *International Marketing Strategy: Contemporary Readings*. International Thomson Business Press.

2. Associated Press (2018) African nations sign largest free trade agreement since WTO. Available from https://wtop.com/africa/2018/03/african-nations-sign-largest-free-trade-agreement-since-wto (accessed 9 June 2018).

3. Atsmon, Y., Ducarme, D., Magni, M. and Wu, C. (2012) Luxury without borders: China's new class of shoppers take on the world. McKinsey and Company. Available from www.mckinseychina.com (accessed 9 June 2018).

4. Austrade (n.d.) *Austrade Guide to Export Pricing*. Available from www.austrade.gov.au (accessed 9 June 2018).

5. Brinnded, L. (2015) LVMH is cannibalising itself in China, published 14 April. Available from http://uk.businessinsider.com/lvmh-q1-revenue-analyst-call-on-pricing-policy-luxury-goods-arbitrage-and-the-grey-market-2015-4 (accessed 13 June 2018).

6. Cavusgil, S.T., Ghauri, P., Knight, G. and Riesenberge, J. (2014) *International Business*, Global Edition, 3rd edition. Pearson.

7. Credit Suisse (2018) *Global Wealth Report 2017*. Credit Suisse AG: Switzerland. www.credit-suisse.com/corporate/en/research/research-institute/global-wealth-report.html (accessed 13 June 2018).

8. *Financial Times* (2018) The billion-dollar grey market in watches upsets big brands. Available from www.ft.com/content/4a4fc942-582d-11e7-80b6-9bfa4c1f83d2. ©The Financial Times Limited 2018. All rights reserved.

9.  *The Guardian* (2015) Editorial. The Guardian view on milk prices: Dairy farmers are being driven out of business. The groceries regulator should find out why. 12 January.

10. Infotrac Newsstand (2017) Washington: The culture of nonmonetary bartering. US Official News, 4 December. Available from http://link.galegroup.com/apps/doc/A517355250/STND?u=lmu_web&sid=STND&xid=9da66980 (accessed 21 April 2018).

11. Kaikati, A.M. and Kaikati, J.G. (2013) Doing business without exchanging money: The scale and creativity of modern barter. *California Management Review* 55, 46–71.

12. Mistry, B. (2013) Plugging the pension blackhole, published November 2013, *The Treasurer*. Available from www.treasurers.org/ACTmedia/Nov13TTtowerswatson38-39.pdf (accessed 31 May 2015).

13. Possebon, M. (2014) Why Euro Disney is a 22-year money-losing failure. Business Insider (UK), published 7 October. Available from www.uk.businessinsider.com/euro-disney-announces-1-billion-crisis-plan-2014-10 (accessed 28 May 2015).

14. Sarathy, R., Terpstra, V. and Russow, L. (2006) *International Marketing*, 9th edition. Dryden Press.

## CHAPTER 12

# STRATEGIC PLANNING IN TECHNOLOGY-DRIVEN INTERNATIONAL MARKETS

## LEARNING OBJECTIVES

After reading this chapter you should be able to:

- understand how technology creates disruption, presents opportunities and poses challenges for international marketing strategy development

- appreciate the role of the enabling technologies in the international marketing environment and how businesses operate

- understand how technology can be used to integrate international marketing activities

- review the international marketing strategic planning process and understand the role of technology in creating change in business sectors.

## INTRODUCTION

Strategic planning is necessary because organizations need to respond to change. If an organization does not intend to change, then there is no need to plan! Technology brings about change and is at the forefront of economic development. It drives business growth in most business sectors and connects the increasingly global marketplace. Technology has accelerated the major changes taking place in global marketing, such as global sourcing, social networking and mobile access to the media. New technology has also generated new products, services and processes that have contributed in no small part to the unsustainability of the world today. Technology is expected by many to solve global problems. These include the generation of renewable energy, making better use of resources, eliminating waste and overcoming environmental pollution. International marketing is at the heart of many of these new initiatives. At the same time, technologies in the hands of malevolent governments and individuals can harm countries, organizations and consumers by reducing their security, spreading fake stories that might influence outcomes and enabling criminal activity. Moreover, the introduction of disruptive technologies eliminates thousands of jobs, but through history has created many more that were not predicted.

As we saw in the first part of the book, technology is a major driver of both the pace and magnitude of change in international marketing. It provides more immediate methods of gathering marketing information from around the world, quicker and more effective methods of analysis and prediction of future customer needs and wants. It is revolutionizing individual and organizational communications. It provides the enabling mechanism by which effective and integrated responses can be made to changing marketplaces. It is, therefore, an essential element in the development of the international marketing strategy. Technology underpins the choice of implementation strategies of the marketing mix. It also facilitates the process of learning and sharing best practice and enables more effective control of a firm's diverse international activities.

In this chapter, therefore, we focus on the challenges and opportunities faced in international markets in the future and consider the role technologies play in the development of appropriate and responsive international marketing strategies. We look at the ways in which technological, business and marketing innovation facilitate further development of international marketing strategy in providing solutions to international marketing problems and the mechanisms to exploit opportunities. The technology tools that are available to develop appropriate strategic responses are identified. As we shall see, this involves integrating separate elements of international marketing into a cohesive approach. We then discuss how firms can pull together the various aspects of corporate social responsibility discussed throughout this book into a cohesive sustainable strategy.

# The challenge

At its most basic, developing a strategic plan for the future involves effectively managing an organization's current business and exploiting new growth opportunities. In developed markets there are still opportunities to provide consumers with new exciting products and services but also many challenges to retaining existing business. Technology enables new competitors to move into a market with a new business model disrupting the traditional businesses. For example, consumers preferring to buy from online retailers are putting at risk shops with a physical presence. Innovations in robotics and artificial intelligence are threatening the production, service jobs and income of those same consumers.

The greatest growth opportunities will be in the emerging markets because of population increases added to an emerging middle class. In planning, it is important to take a critical look at data to understand its implications. In the media there are constant stories about the widening gap between rich and poor, and the plight of those living in poverty. Rosling (2018) explains, however, that *every day* for 25 years the number of poor has fallen by 137 000 through economic growth. Using a measure of the number of people living on less than $2 a day (in 2017 money), 85 per cent of people lived in extreme poverty in 1800, 50 per cent in 1966, 29 per cent in 1997 and 9 per cent in 2017. By 2100, more than 80 per cent of the world's population will live in Africa and Asia. They will be healthier, wealthier and better educated, largely the result of technological advances. Marketing managers will be aware of this; they innovate and organizations will acknowledge this in their strategic plans.

It is also important to fully understand risk and appreciate the background of why, through history, certain regions of the world are more advanced than others, have been more prone to conflict and whether their prospects are likely to change. Marshall (2016) discusses geopolitics and explains why some countries are strong and stable because of their geography – enclosed by mountains, oceans and rivers – whereas others have been and are still vulnerable because they are open to potential aggressors. Colonial rulers often left countries with artificial borders that would continue to be the source of continuing conflict and instability. Marshall also explains that in contrast with Europe, for example, the lack of navigable rivers and harbours in much of Africa and South America constrained trade and harmed development for centuries. Major investment in physical and technological infrastructure by major world powers seeking greater influence should overcome many of the historical barriers and help accelerate growth. However, the use of robotics in production and artificial intelligence could threaten many of the low-paid jobs in underdeveloped countries that have helped people escape extreme poverty.

The challenge for international marketing planning is managing uncertainty (as we saw in Chapter 2), especially in emerging markets too often disrupted by wars. The uncertainty is the need to be present in a market where no one knows 'when it will take off'.

# The enabling technologies

Down the centuries, advances in technology, business and marketing innovations have provided solutions for business problems. These include design, manufacturing, operations, internal and external communications, inventory control, managing finances and so on. Technological advances have enabled innovative firms to make product and service developments that provide distinctive benefits to customers. The technology is either industry sector specific or generic in nature. Of course, a specific industry technology may sometimes start off being used in one sector and over time be transferred to others. For example, the Internet was initially developed for use in the defence industry. Facebook was initially built for college students.

Marketing and business innovations have often built on and enhanced technological inventions. For example, the mobile/cell phone was initially designed to take phone calls when away from the home or office! It is now a platform for mobile computing using hundreds of thousands of apps.

The Internet has had the effect of 'shrinking the world' and has facilitated the worldwide integration of the different technologies, systems and processes in supply chains that are used locally by different parts of the organization and its partners. It enables experts around the world to be accessed virtually and instantly.

We refer here to enabling technologies, because there is no single technology that supports international marketing. The major steps forward in recent years have been associated with the integration of many technologies. These include those that support e-commerce, data collection, management and search, mobile communications and social media, customer relations management, computer-aided design, process, inventory and logistics management. So, enabling technologies in international marketing provide the solutions to old problems, such as:

- How can customers in remote locations around the world contribute to the design of a new global product as much as the customer next door?
- How can an organization use the advocates for its products to share their good experiences with potential customers around the world?
- How can a ten-person business market its products or services to its potential customers in 40 or 50 countries when managing market entry in so many countries through agents and distributors would probably be beyond the resources of most small businesses?

Technology does not remove the elements, challenges and dilemmas associated with the international marketing process. These include the need for cultural sensitivity, the need to make products and services available to customers worldwide with minimum investment, or the need to be both efficient and effective by achieving an appropriate balance between the standardization and adaptation of the international marketing process and programmes. It does have a major impact on the nature of the international marketing strategy that is used. In addition, it enables creative solutions to be found which will increase the organizations' competitive capability.

## *Technological innovation*

In considering the application of technology it is useful to focus specifically upon how technological advancement both creates new marketing opportunities and poses new challenges for firms, for example, in energy generation, conservation and waste recycling discussed in previous chapters. For international marketers, timing of the introduction of innovations is critical. The Energy Saving Trust states it is imperative that not only should governments and businesses engage in the conversations and actions about climate change and fuel poverty, but so should consumers in their choices. It goes on to explain that because innovative technology and environmental initiatives are available now for businesses premises, roads/highways, cruise ships, tourist attractions, to name but a few, steps towards reducing carbon emissions are already taking place. Its push is to encourage businesses and consumers to engage in renewable energy. This comes in all shapes, sizes and budgets, from advanced biofuels, ground source heat pumps, concentrated solar power, wind turbines, hydro technology from small streams, to rivers. Technological innovations that help reduce $CO_2$ emissions are highly saleable as multinational companies and individual business entrepreneurs want to reduce their carbon footprint and demonstrate they care for our planet's future. Decision making by governments is around building the necessary support infrastructure to reduce carbon ($CO_2$) emissions in the hope that this will slow

## ILLUSTRATION 12.1

# China quietly becoming greener through technology

China has a lot of fossil fuel and oil which it uses and imports and exports around the world. With that comes the label that China is pumping $CO_2$ into the atmosphere. Quietly, China is investing in green technology to the tune of US$132 billion. By 2020 China plans to spend US$360 billion on renewable energy and, more importantly, begin to decommission coal-fired plants. This builds on the Chinese government's aggressive green buildings and ecocities campaign.

Investing in innovative technology for the supply of energy through renewables is already having an impact. China's economy grew by 7 per cent from 2016 to 2017. When an economy grows there is always a huge surge in the amount of emissions sent into the atmosphere. However, China only saw a 1.7 per cent increase in emissions, which was seen as a reflection of their investment in the latest renewable technology.

So what has China been doing to become green? It is investing in renewables such as wind, solar PV and bioenergy. To put this into context, China's solar PV is equivalent in capacity to that of France and Germany combined, countries known for embracing environmental issues. China has also overtaken the USA in terms of being the world leader for non-hydro renewable-based electricity generation. And to help the consumer be green, China has invested in plant and technology to be the world leader when it comes to global sales of electric cars.

China has a long way to go. But it clearly wants to invest in green technology, support itself energy-wise and reduce carbon emissions released into the atmosphere. This of course is of benefit to the world as we all share the same air. However, if China can become self-sufficient in energy, it may become protectionist, which may damage shared knowledge and the exchange of ideas in how to improve green technology. In addition, China may not buy renewable energy technology from the rest of the world's suppliers.

### Questions

**1** How is China leading the way in green technology?

**2** What should organizations that design and manufacture green technology be including in their long-term strategy?

**References:** *The Conversation* (2017) China's green planning for the world starts with infrastructure. Available from www.theconversation.com (accessed 9 June 2018); *The Economist* (2018) China is rapidly developing its clean-energy technology. Available from: www.economist.com/news/special-report/21738578-there-plenty-room-international-co-operation-environment-china-rapidly (accessed 9 June 2018).

down climate change. Details of government commitment is shown in the Kyoto Protocol. Such initiatives are increasingly demanded by customers. See Illustration 12.1 to see how China is becoming greener.

It is important to emphasize that technology is of no value until it has a practical application, as illustrated in Figure 12.1. Those firms that are first to embrace a new technology and find a practical application will gain a new source of competitive advantage. Examples include creating a new product or service, a new route to market or a lower energy consuming process.

This sets new standards for the industry sector that means competitors also have to achieve those standards if they wish to compete in the future. Global communications make customers worldwide aware of the latest products and create new stakeholder expectations. In this way, all competitors in the sector, wherever they are in the world, have to catch up by embracing the new product and service offers and industry standards if they wish to survive.

## Disruptive technologies

From time to time technological advances make existing products and services redundant. They also sometimes challenge the very existence of businesses if they fail to react quickly enough. For example, the conventional worldwide photography sector was virtually destroyed when digital camera technology was introduced to

## FIGURE 12.1 The vicious circle of technology and competitive advantage

New technology → Practical applications identified → Firm embraces new technology → Firm develops new competitive advantage → Change of industry standards or new customer expectations set → Competitors must follow with 'me-too' → New technology

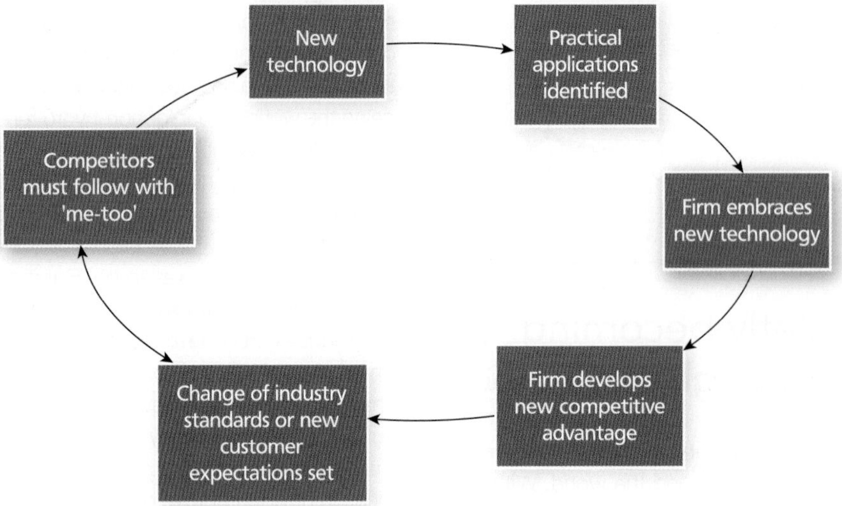

mobile/cell phones. Traditional fixed line telephony was the cornerstone of the former state-owned telecommunications firms for over a century. The introduction of mobile and Internet systems, such as Snapchat, Skype, WeChat and Google Hangouts, however, has completely changed the economics of the sector. Often it is entrepreneurial born global firms that exploit the disruptive technology if a new competence is required that the organization that previously led the sector does not have. Artificial intelligence and robotics are likely to be the source of disruption in many business sectors. It may also be the source of opportunity for both existing and start-up businesses. The winners will be the firms that can successfully integrate these operations into their activities. Illustration 12.2 highlights the need for humans and robots to work effectively together.

## ILLUSTRATION 12.2

# Humans and robots working together

It is estimated that the number of robots 'at work' in 2019 is 2.5 million. With a statistic like this comes many geopolitical fears that automation and the continued use of robots will have a negative impact on jobs. However, there are others who look at this positively and claim that robots 'at work' will create jobs.

Only around 10 per cent of jobs can be fully automated. Of the other 90 per cent, some have elements that can be automated within them. This means humans and robots should and will work side by side. Humans can sense when another person is near them, they can see them and without any conversation can tell how that person is feeling. Humans will see and be aware of the robot.

Robots often cannot see or be aware of humans. As Maurice Clark of Autodesk explains: 'Robots are blind. They have no perception of the space they are in. They can easily do serious harm to a human'. Autodesk developed software that gives robots sight and touch so the robot is aware of its human colleague.

Once the robot could see and had sensors so that it knew it was touching something, it was developed further. For example, the Autodesk team has now provided a computer program to tell the robot to build a metal object. Computer instructions are issued to the robot to make it weld metal segments together using a blow torch. What is revolutionary in the process is programming the robot to 'see' if it has welded the objects together perfectly. If it has not, the robot reprogrammes itself using the camera as eyes, paying attention to what it has done wrong. Over time, the robot has been able to build and weld the objects together perfectly.

It took a team of skilled people from programmers to software developers, CAD designers and engineers to achieve this innovation. Robots are here to stay; therefore, it is important that for those 10 per cent of jobs that could be fully automated, new jobs are created. For the jobs where humans and robots can be at work

togeth
that are p
leagues throug

**Reference:** Lindberg, R.
except in the productivity
bloomberg.com/news/articles/2
everywhere-except-in-the-productivi
June 2018).

A more recent trend, frugal engineering, was discussed earlier and has challenged the assumption that innovation should focus on adding additional features for wealthy customers. Technological innovation is being applied to address the needs of cost-conscious customers in emerging markets. Potentially this could be disruptive for many established companies.

When expanding internationally, companies often choose cities that are ranked high on the City Competitive Scale. These are places that attract talent and are spaces that thrive on innovation and often have creative industry clusters. Currently the top five cities are New York, London, Singapore, Paris and Hong Kong (Economist Intelligence Unit 2012).

## Convergent technology

An important trend is the integration of technologies and technology gadgets for business and consumer markets. So, for example, the mobile/cell phone has become a mobile communications and computing device that embraces voice, text and games, music, video, television and Internet access, particularly to social media. It is used to remotely control home or office heating and lighting. In the same way, traditional home television and recording devices are being wirelessly connected with personal computers and notebooks/tablets. With the ability to cast videos from phones to TV to tablet, this puts users in control, building flexibility and completely changing the way personal entertainment is consumed. Firms can generate revenues by products such as the hardware, including mobile devices and tablets, services (e.g. streaming downloads) and content (e.g. music, podcasts, films, games, and social media) enabling media organizations such as Netflix to grow quickly.

As the functionality increases so mobile computing is replacing 'fixed position' computing. Increasingly, objects will communicate with each other in the Internet of Things (IoT). Major players such as Apple, Amazon and Google are establishing themselves as dominant, branded players at the centre of this convergence. Other less powerful firms are seeking to connect a more open and inclusive network. Management Challenge 12.1 shows just how convergent smartphones can be.

# The Internet and international business communications

The Internet is the central pillar of the economies of developed countries. The growth of emerging economies is increasingly dependent on the Internet too. A report by Boston Consulting Group (2015) ranked Sweden, Denmark, South Korea, Netherlands, Norway and the UK as the six highest countries on its 'e-intensity index', a measure of the reach and depth of the Internet. The report noted that the UK was a net exporter of e-commerce goods and services, exporting £2.80 for every £1 imported, whereas in the 'off-line' economy, only 90p was exported for every £1 imported.

In the B2B market, the development of the Internet, external networks and extranet internal organizational networks have revolutionized demand and customer information management, supply and value chain management, and distribution channel management and control. It has sped up the process so that real-time decisions can be made in virtual, global marketplaces or 'hubs' that manage supply and demand. Mobile technology is essential to support high speed decision making.

y
t',
Su... kia
Lumia or ... as
'phablets' because ... size
(measured diagonally) and the... things
that can be done on a mobile phone and ... et.

Through cloud storage and apps, consumers can upload and download photographs, read books, convert currencies, pay for online purchases from Amazon, or Skype loved ones. But the more recent technologies enable consumers to use their phones on a Machine 2 Machine (M2M) basis.

M2M and the IoT give consumers the opportunity to join the *technology connected* revolution by interacting with their phablet. This in turn interacts with other technology/machines that consumers have at home. M2M has happened because many consumers do not have 9 to 5 jobs. So, through apps on their phablets,

...ners can use smart technology to, for example, ... on their central heating in their home from any... in the world or even just 30 minutes from home! ...elkin WeMo is a cooking pot that can also be linked ... consumer's home Wifi system. The cooking pot can ... switched on via an App on a phablet to ensure the ...onsumer's evening meal is ready upon their arrival at ...home. To ensure the consumer's journey home is stress-free, M2M technology, developed by Cisco, will change traffic lights and redirect traffic through cities more effectively. So, when the consumer arrives home they can kick off their shoes and Bluetooth their favourite music from their phablet to their beautiful, sleek speakers.

Technology converging with other technology via the mobile/cell phone is predicted to ensure brands stay connected with their consumers on a regular basis during their day-to-day lives.

## Questions

1 What are the arguments for and against businesses including M2M technology in their products as part of their marketing strategy?

2 What are the benefits for the consumer of engaging with M2M technology on their phablets?

**References:** Belkin (2015) Setting up the WeMo Slow Cooker (Crock-Pot®) Available from www.belkin.com/uk/support-article?articleNum=101177 (accessed 10 June 2015); Cisco (2014) AGT and Cisco Traffic Incident Management Solution: Improving Traffic Safety and Efficiency. Available from www.cisco.com/web/strategy/docs/agt-s-cc-city-tim-aag.pdf (accessed 10 June 2015).

In consumer markets, communications technology is regarded as a utility, similar to power and water. It has helped people around the world to become more aware of changes in the market environment and exciting new products and services that are introduced anywhere in the world. Customers have changing lifestyles, are more easily bored with their existing products and services, and are always looking for innovative new products and services that will regain their interest. They have less brand loyalty, so if one firm does not meet the needs of the customer, then a competitor will.

Customers find out about new products and services online. They have new ways of assessing their suitability and likely performance, believing online peer reviews more than company advertising. They have become deeply sceptical of the communications of multinational organizations and suspicious of the motives of the most powerful. Online reviews can be biased and unreliable, however, as they are often the highly subjective opinions of bloggers and celebrities who are frequently covertly paid to promote particular brands or products. Opinions expressed by individuals on Twitter can be retweeted so that a single bad experience can end up being blown up out of all proportion to the original problem it caused.

Information must be available in two or three clicks and products must be accessible to purchase quickly and more cost-effectively. Delivery is now often expected on the same day. Customers live on their phones and seem to prefer to lose their wallet or purse than their mobile/cell phone!

The key function of the Internet is provided by search engines (such as Google, Bing, Yahoo! and Ask), enabling users to find the information and services they need. This is critical for international marketers who want potential customers to be able to find them. Customers are impatient, so it is vital for organizations that they appear high on the list of search results. Firms can guarantee a place high on the list if they pay the search firm to manipulate the results. Many would argue that the current search functions can be highly frustrating, and little progress has been made since the late 2000s by the dominant providers to satisfy the needs of average users. However, there is evidence to suggest that the search providers are at last aiming to improve the situation. Google suggests that there are three layers of search: content, social and local. It is aiming to capture the market for location-based searches using its automatic Location Search function to enable consumers to reach a satisfactory answer. It should also provide new sources of revenue by attracting local advertisers. Given the number of mobile/cell phone connections and size of the e-commerce market, geo-advertising will continue to grow. Therefore, Google, Bing, Facebook and Twitter see huge potential for advertising income as more businesses promote their products and services across a range of social media platforms.

All businesses need to respond to these opportunities and threats. They must embrace new methods of communicating in order to gain more customer insights, retain their customers and connect with them in a better way. Many people in emerging economies do not have access to older technologies, such as

## ILLUSTRATION 12.3

# mHealth and text-baby

Health care in Africa is still at breaking point. This is particularly acute in rural areas where there is often only one health care worker per 1000 people. Many diseases, such as malaria, kill one African child every 30 seconds. Diseases such as Lassa fever, polio and leprosy, virtually eradicated elsewhere in the world, are still debilitating and/or fatal in Africa.

Simon Spurr, the Chief Executive of FOLUP, saw this problem and is one of many technology-driven organizations that has provided a helpful solution. FOLUP web and mobile platforms can help South African patients get a real-time diagnosis from expert doctors. Using smartphones/phablets or PSs, patients in remote parts of Africa can upload their symptoms, provide readings of their blood pressure or feedback on their reaction to medicines provided. Patients take an active part in their health care with a medical expert through wireless interaction. Together, the patient and the doctor come to a collaborative decision. Mobile technology is high in Africa. Two-thirds of people in Africa own a mobile/cell phone. Ownership, due to its low cost, is predicted to grow very quickly in the next few years. FOLUP technology not only provides connections to expert doctors but there are also mHealth apps for communities. The apps are forums for people with similar diseases to share information, motivate one other and not feel isolated. Therefore, FOLUP's connection to health care experts and a supportive community is a fantastic enabler for African citizens.

A further development of mHealth, called mBaby, is available in Tanzania for women who are pregnant or caring for babies and young children. The *Healthy Pregnancy, Healthy Baby Text Messaging Service* provides a free text messaging advisory service. The text messages include advice about morning sickness, breast feeding and dietary care. For mothers giving birth at home, there are text details of how to cut and clean the umbilical cord.

## Question

**1** What advice regarding investment in information and communications technology would you give to an African company seeking to develop and improve current mHealth and mBaby businesses?

**References:** Mulligan, G. (2015) Good prognosis: The rise of e-health in Africa. 17 March. *New African*. Available from http://newafricanmagazine.com/good-prognosis-rise-e-health-africa/ (accessed 11 June 2015); Our Africa (2015) Health. Available from www.our-africa.org/health (accessed 11 June 2015).

reliable electricity, fixed line telecommunications, radio and television, let alone the latest information and telecommunications technology. Increasingly, however, these markets are being recognized for their potential. It is possible to leapfrog existing technology with innovations that are appropriate to a specific situation. Recent innovations in remote areas of Africa include the wind-up radio, solar energy systems to power communications equipment and recharge mobile/cell phone batteries, and mobile/cell phones as a tool for making online payments. The cost of a fixed line telecommunications structure would be prohibitively expensive in most of the largely rural countries of Africa. But with more than 500 million mobile subscriptions there is a high level of demand. Despite having 14 per cent of the world's population, Africa accounts for only 2 per cent of Internet users. Of the 20 countries with the most expensive broadband subscription fees (over $1000 per month in some countries), 14 are in sub-Saharan Africa. The technological leap will be interesting. Cable systems are being laid around coasts, so bandwidth increase will become huge and costs will fall sharply. The challenge will be to connect rural broadband users with wireless technologies through 3G/4G networks to the communications providers. For international marketers to and from Africa this will bring about another industrial revolution, which is discussed in Illustration 12.3.

Email and text messaging can be frustrating for users, particularly in some of the emerging countries such as Nigeria and Indonesia. In these countries there are millions of Internet devices but connectivity is not countrywide, not secure and often not available. Other communications mechanisms, such as Twitter which limits message size to 280 characters, work differently but are preferred by many users for social and increasingly business networking. And when consumers sign up to Pinterest and Instagram, the suggested number of pins and photographs becomes overwhelming. However, technology platforms enable customers around the world to continually develop more efficient and effective integrated communication of word, stationary and video imagery, sound and complex data.

## Online strategies

The advances in communications technology enable internationally trading firms to develop new international marketing strategies. No longer is international marketing limited by the physical boundaries of the media footprint or the salesperson's or distribution company's territory. At a local level new developments in hand-held devices allow connection between users that is almost unlimited, offering opportunities for promotions close to location and point of sale (for example, restaurants, entertainment and shops). Few of these opportunities, however, have yet been exploited.

The Internet provides a global marketplace that is open to everyone. It is also:

- a method of collecting, searching for and exchanging marketing and business information
- an alternative route to market to traditional distribution channels
- a means of building customer relationships
- a device for the digital delivery of certain information services
- a networked system for managing the supply chain
- a virtual marketplace, trading floor and auction house.

The Internet also provides a mechanism for social networking through dedicated websites. The relevance of social networking for international marketing, which will be discussed in more detail later, is that it provides the opportunity for individuals and groups to discuss new products and services, problems encountered in dealing with organizations and dissatisfaction with the behaviour of organizations.

## The purpose of websites

Websites are created by individuals and organizations as a shop window or for facilitating activities. While they are used for many purposes, their relevance for international marketing falls into the following main categories:

- organization sites
- service online

- information online
- business transactions online (e-commerce websites are also used for m-commerce transactions).

Where much of the online communication about its products, services and organizational behaviour cannot be controlled by an organization, its website can, enabling it to communicate a clear and consistent message.

## Organization sites

Many organizations use their website to provide information to their stakeholders about the organization. This includes information on its origins; business mission and areas of activity; its standards and values; its brands; its financial performance; any job opportunities; and contact points. In addition the website should include quite specific information about the firm's products and their applications. Firms appealing to global customers must consider the degree to which their website should build much closer relationships with customers by providing a site in the local language (Motamedi and Choe 2015).

There are, of course, dangers too in just translating web content without addressing the need for it to be sensitive to cultural needs.

As well as providing information about products, some sites take customers through the purchasing process. For example, BMW helps customers to design their new car from a range of options, such as whether to have cruise control, petrol or diesel, metallic paint and alloy wheels. When the customer has designed the car, they are then referred to their local dealer to complete the purchase.

## Service online

Online banking puts customers more in control of their accounts, enabling them to obtain information from anywhere in the world and make transactions any time of the day or night. The saving to the bank through increased automation includes being able to reduce the resourcing of bank branches and service centres and cutting the cost of individual banking transactions.

Delivery firms, such as Federal Express, have been able to make huge savings by providing an online tracking service instead of employing staff to answer queries from customers. The system involves applying a barcode to the package, which is then scanned each time it progresses past a key point on its journey. This information is then transferred to the website and accessed by customers worldwide. Another example is real-time in-flight information that can be accessed online informing those meeting a flight whether the plane is delayed.

## Information online

Organizations in the business of providing information, such as Wikipedia or the *Financial Times*, provide websites that enable customers to access current and archived past files of news, data and images. Often, such sites provide one level of access free, but may charge a subscription for heavier users or may require payment for more valuable information. As this information is in digital form, it can be accessed and delivered online anywhere in the world.

Sites of media organizations, such as the BBC or CNN, are used to maintain and build the relationship with their consumers considerably beyond the scheduled content.

## Business transactions online

These websites typically include elements of the previous categories but, in addition, enable customers to complete a transaction and purchase products or services online. These websites comprise two parts. The first provides the shop window, which must be eye catching for any potential customer. The second is an easy-to-use checkout process that also reassures the buyer of its security, which is particularly important when the purchase is cross-border. Analysis of the purchaser's previous orders, browsing behaviour, beliefs and interests are collected using big data management to enable recommendations for additional purchases to be made.

## Social networking

The disadvantage of websites is that consumers have to visit them to receive the information they want. It has been suggested that platforms and networks will soon become more important as media for sharing information. One example is Digg, which aggregates social media news and provides links to interesting stories that can be voted on by users.

Social networking has always been a feature of the Internet. People recorded web logs well before the term 'blogs' was coined. As early as 1995, Amazon allowed users to write reviews and consumer guides. The phrase Web 2.0 was coined to indicate a second generation of Web services including social networking websites and online communications tools. It emphasizes collaboration. The Web is used as a platform, with users owning and exercising control over the data rather than hierarchical control being exercised. Web 3.0 is all about expressing human values into products and services so that online audiences can relate to them more. Web 4.0 is engaging with online consumers across every media channel with interactions along every part of their purchase journey.

Weblogs, chat rooms and community websites, such as Taobao, MySpace and Ibibo, provide a platform for millions of consumers to air their views. Blogs are updated thousands of times an hour. Many of the comments relate to products, services and opinions about companies, and it is essential for organizations to know what is being said about them. This requires intelligent search engines, such as Attentio, that can dig deeper than general searches and aggregate the data to provide a fuller picture of the trends and conversations that are taking place.

Businesses increasingly see the benefit of some involvement in other types of websites, even if the purpose is only to hear what is being said about the company, its competitors and their products. Blog and forum websites, such as Google's Blogger, enable people to meet others with common views and thus enable firms to quickly hear about any dissatisfaction. They can also be used by companies to inform and keep their staff around the world up to date. Social websites, such as Facebook, are effectively member groups or communities with common interests. File-sharing websites, such as Flickr and YouTube, have on numerous occasions been used to share both photo and video files that have either enhanced the reputation of a company and its staff or proved embarrassing. Perhaps the most significant developments are likely to come from mobile device websites that support smartphones.

# International e-markets and e-marketing

There are a number of e-marketing business models and e-marketplaces that originally started as digital extensions of physical marketing models. These business models focus on business-to-business marketing (B2B), discussed next, and business-to-consumer marketing (B2C) and other models, discussed later.

## Business-to-business (B2B)

The interactions involved in B2B marketing are much more complex because they involve the exchange of significant amounts of information between the seller and the customer before, during and after any transaction. The information includes such things as specifications, designs and drawings, purchase contracts, supply chain management, manufacturing and delivery schedules, inventory control, negotiation of price, distribution channel management and delivery. The information comes from different departments within the firms and is exchanged between the firms involved in the value chain.

For many years firms have been using information technology to improve the efficiency and effectiveness of the internal firm processes, for example, demand forecasting, inventory control, computer-aided design and manufacturing. The Internet enables this to be linked with external organizations and customers. The Internet has enabled a far wider range of data to be exchanged without restriction on the number of participant organizations. The mechanisms by which the exchanges take place and business can be transacted are called Web portals. These are 'hubs' where all the interested participants congregate. Typically, there are two types of hubs:

1  Industry-specific hubs, such as automobile or aerospace manufacturing.
2  Function-specific hubs, such as advertising or human resource management.

Using e-hubs, firms improve the efficiency of the processes of transactions and thereby lower costs. The hubs can reduce the transaction cost by bringing together all the purchasing requirements of many hundreds of customers worldwide (Kaplan and Sawhney 2000). E-hubs attract many buyers who are able to negotiate bulk discounts on behalf of a range of smaller, individual buyers.

If the products are commodities with no need to negotiate specifications, then dynamic pricing enables buyers and sellers to negotiate prices and volumes in real time. In sectors such as energy purchasing, the peaks and troughs of supply and demand can be smoothed.

The USA originally dominated B2B. Much of the innovation in B2B came from the USA. But firms around the world recognize that the potential savings can be quite significant with the increasing internationalization of sourcing and supply chain management. A culture change in the attitude of firms is needed as companies that may normally be competing should cooperate for the mutual benefit of reducing costs. Illustration 12.4 shows how Jack Ma has helped millions of Chinese entrepreneurs to access global business markets.

ILLUSTRATION 12.4

## Jack Ma supporting global entrepreneurs

To thousands of Chinese, Jack Ma has achieved rock star status to the point where he needs bodyguards to hold back the adoring fans. He is one of the wealthiest men in the world. He is listed in *Time* magazine's top 100 most influential people in the world and has achieved this status by enabling many Chinese to become their own boss – a dream ingrained in the Chinese culture. Ma set up Alibaba in 1999. It is now the world's largest and most valuable retailer, with sales and profits exceeding those of Walmart, Amazon and eBay combined. The company provides C2C (through Taobao), B2C and B2B (through Alibaba), sales services through its websites as well as operating many other businesses related to online services. Its growth in cloud computing has exceeded that of Amazon, Microsoft and Google.

Alibaba was set up as a marketplace for firms across the world to trade with one another and to build markets for the many Chinese SMEs that make a vast array of manufactured goods to trade with western traders. Ma led the Chinese development of online communities and social networking with a consumer auction site, Taobao, which has an innovation that reflects a cultural difference.

Whereas eBay transactions are largely between anonymous buyers and sellers, Taobao facilitates instant messaging, voicemail and allows personal photographs and details to be posted, creating a community of 'friends' in a country where there is a lack of trust.

The interesting aspect of Ma is that he is a business entrepreneur rather than a computer geek like the founders of Yahoo! and Google. He believes that 'someone as dumb as me should be able to use technology'. He will not accept a new feature unless he can understand it and use it.

Ma is encouraging entrepreneurship in many of the 200 countries in which Alibaba operates and has five top tips for entrepreneurs:

1 Always be optimistic and get negative thoughts out of your head.

2 Surround yourself with like-minded people who will chase the dream.

3 Expect to make sacrifices – it might take three or ten years to win.

4 Don't focus on things that are hot – most people thought e-commerce would not take off when he started.

5 Move early, move fast and don't wait for everything to be ready for you.

### Questions

1 What are the critical success factors in creating successful B2B and C2C electronic marketplaces?

2 What do you consider to be the best advice for would-be international entrepreneurs?

**Sources:** *South China Morning Post* Alibaba founder Jack Ma's 5 top tips for entrepreneurs, 22 November. Available from www.scmp.com/tech/leaders-founders/article/2121081/alibaba-founder-jack-mas-5-top-tips-entrepreneurs (accessed 22 April 2018); www.alibaba.com/.

The benefits of e-procurement, such as convenience and cost saving through group purchasing, appeal to governments for public sector and private–public sector purchasing. However, often progress is much slower than in private business.

## Disintermediation and re-intermediation

The Internet offers the possibility for an organization to efficiently handle many more transactions than was possible previously. With the benefit of the enabling Internet technology, many organizations have reassessed the value contribution of the intermediaries (distributors and agents) with the intention of managing the distribution themselves and cutting out the intermediary. The benefits to the organization are the removal of channel infrastructure costs and intermediary margins and the opportunity to develop a direct relationship with the final customer. 'Cutting out the middleman' is described as disintermediation. Chaffey *et al.* (2006) observe that at the start of the e-business boom, it was expected that there would be widespread disintermediation. While it has happened in some sectors, in others there has been little change. The results of disintermediation in some sectors have been disappointing, with the marketing organization incurring substantial additional IT, order management and logistics costs, offsetting the forecast savings. And this idea of 'cutting out the middleman' has grown into 'Bring-Your-Own-Device' (BYOD), 'Bring-Your-Own-Apps' (BYOA) and 'Bring-Your-Own-Network' (BYON). Many businesses enable their employees to BYOA by synching their work email via a mobile platform so they can read emails on the go without having to go through their organization's website. In addition, travellers with Etihad, for example, can store their flight booking form via an Etihad app for faster boarding. Additionally, many consumers 'Bring-Their-Own-Cloud' and have many gigabytes of data from Word documents to photographs available to them through their Google Drive or Dropbox app.

The counter to disintermediation is re-intermediation and the creation of new firms that add value in the purchasing situation, such as travel and household goods. While many financial services products and offers from utilities lend themselves to online selling, it is a laborious task to compare the many offerings from competing companies. Consequently, many brokers have set up websites such as uSwitch and Moneyextra to allow customers to compare many different financial product offerings. Of course, this means that the Internet marketer must ensure they are represented on key sites where there are high volumes of potential customers and ensure that they are offering competitive prices.

The alternatively strategy is for the marketer to set up his or her own intermediary to compete with the existing intermediaries: this is referred to as counter-mediation. A group of airlines set up www.Opodo.com as an alternative to www.expedia.com to offer airline tickets.

## Business-to-consumer (B2C)

In the B2C sector, well-designed websites, whether from small or large companies, provide a satisfying experience for the online shopper. This means customers are able to browse through the information that is available about the products and services they are seeking to buy, and do so at their leisure. The best websites offer potential customers the choice of which language they wish to communicate in and are sensitive to the local culture and legal frameworks. Having selected the product, they enable customers to easily purchase and pay for the product online, using credit cards to make payment. In practice, many more customers are prepared to use the Internet to carry out their information search on companies, products and services, but are still unwilling to pay online because of fears about the security of online payment and the potential for fraud. In emerging markets, problems are exacerbated because of the lack of a suitable payment method, such as a credit card. Firms that have both virtual and physical stores allow customers to find out information and then choose whether to buy online or go to the store.

Some services can be supplied as digital services online over the Internet. For example, information, software, financial advice, ticketless travel and music can be downloaded direct to the customer's computer, laptop, tablet or phone. For physical products, however, the supplier still needs a suitable distribution method to deliver the goods to the consumer. Fulfilment of the order depends on more traditional distribution, with its associated limitations of the country's existing infrastructure and the availability of appropriate logistics in each customer's country. Small items, such as cosmetics or books, can be posted. But delivering valuable bulky goods such as furniture, or goods that require special storage conditions such as food, directly to the door also requires arrangements to be made for the customer to receive them. However, to accommodate for the fact that some people work, Amazon has drop-off zones which hold much bulkier items that cannot be left at a PO Box or posted through a letter box. The drop-off zones are often placed at petrol stations or supermarkets.

Using the Internet simply to transact business underutilizes its potential, however, and does little to build competitive advantage, or improve the overall effectiveness of the operation in winning global customers and developing their loyalty. Moreover, without building competitive advantage and unique selling propositions, firms using the Internet to sell their products are vulnerable to lower priced offers from other global competitors, because sophisticated search engines identify the cheapest offers of comparable products or services. Many companies believe they can survive and grow by offering the lowest priced products direct to customers. Inevitably, however, new entrants will always offer lower prices, even if they are not sustainable in the longer term.

E-business operations are expensive to establish and maintain, given the large outlay for IT, systems, management and website development. Moreover, e-commerce firms require sophisticated systems to fulfil orders promptly and accurately and need to innovate constantly to retain customer interest and loyalty. The challenge for a business is therefore to maximize income. Chaffey *et al.* (2006) identify a number of opportunities for generating income from a website These include charging for sponsorship, advertising, and for 'click-through' fees for sales generated by a second firm that has a direct link to its own site. Income such as this is a primary revenue generator for many websites such as Google and Facebook.

## Consumer-to-consumer (C2C)

Timmers (1999) identifies other Internet business models involving exchange between supplier and customer. These include C2C in which consumers sell to each other through an online auction. One of the most successful sites for trading between individuals by online bidding is eBay. This type of buying and selling tends to become almost a hobby in itself for customers. They take a fee to insert the advertisement and a fee based on the final value. It has been successful internationally but has had problems competing in certain markets. As stated in the previous section, eBay pulled out of Japan and failed to compete with Alibaba, partly because it did not really understand the Chinese culture.

New models of international business are being developed that incorporate a number of aspects of business, consumer and social networking websites.

# International marketing solution integration

The most significant international marketing strategy development facilitated by technology is business solution integration. As competition increases, so firms must seek new sources of competitive advantage, secure ever-lower costs, increase their speed of action and responsiveness, and demonstrate their adaptability to new situations and flexibility in offering new innovative products and services perceived by customers to be valuable. They must also develop better relationships with their customers and business partners in order to retain their business. The strategy to achieve these outcomes is based on the effective integration of the elements of the marketing and business processes.

## Knowledge management

The move to an increasingly global market served by e-business has prompted firms to redefine their sources of competitive advantage. In a global market the traditional sources of competitive advantage can be easily challenged. A company that operates in a small number of countries or within a restricted business sector may believe that its competitive advantage comes from low-cost manufacturing, design capability, sales expertise and distribution efficiency. However, when exposed to global competition, it may find that its own competitive advantage cannot be transported to new countries. It can discover, instead, that regional or global competitors have even greater competitive advantage in their own domestic market as well as in the target country market.

By contrast, knowledge, expertise and experience have the potential to be transferable if they can be effectively collected, stored, accessed and communicated around the world (hence the term knowledge management). Later we discuss the processes for managing knowledge to support the customer–client interface. **Knowledge management** is essential to maximize added value throughout the supply chain. There is a danger in building competitive advantage through knowledge management, of course, because the knowledge assets of a firm are locked into their staff and their records, typically contained in their computers. Staff are becoming increasingly mobile, computer systems are still notoriously insecure and the potential loss of knowledge to a competitor is an ever greater problem for firms. Business espionage is growing in many countries and increasingly appears to be government-sponsored.

## Supply chain management

Technology-enabled supply chain management has helped firms to grow through exploiting market development opportunities, reducing investment by buying rather than manufacturing components and enabling small firms to have similar costs to large firms through e-procurement. It is vital that each part of the supply chain of the product maximizes the added value. This is made possible by integrating the activities. A supply chain for a complex product might typically involve such distinctly different activities as design, manufacture of raw materials, component assembly, advertising, logistics and local servicing. It is highly unlikely that one company could be the leader in each of these areas of activity, particularly when the most efficient members of the supply chain will increasingly be located around the world.

The implications, of course, are that through using e-commerce for procurement, partnerships can be set up and dissolved instantly. Of course, suppliers need to have huge flexibility and excellent systems to manage the rapid changes that are necessary to survive in this type of market. Suppliers are in completely open competition with other firms around the world.

Cost savings can be made in all areas of the supply chain, such as inventory reduction and just in time sourcing. Amazon is able to offer millions of books and music titles and other items by quickly obtaining stocks held anywhere in the world, whereas an average traditional bookstore might physically hold only 170 000 titles. Savings can be made in evaluating suppliers, specifications and delivery times and arranging scheduling. Marketing costs can be reduced because it is easier, quicker and cheaper to make alterations to Web content than incur the design and printing costs of a new brochure.

Advantest America, Inc. supplies measuring instruments, semiconductor test systems and related equipment. It outsourced the delivery of its replacement parts, e-commerce and supply chain management services to FedEx Corporation, which provides transport. Using FedEx's sophisticated integrated systems it was able to reduce its delivery times by more than 50 per cent, to 48 hours in Asia and 24 hours for customers in the USA and Europe. Previously, starting from the time the order was taken, it could take between 25 and 42 hours even to get through customs and onto a commercial aeroplane. Extending the system to the firm's customized printed circuit boards would avoid the need for the customer to hold stock on site, thus considerably reducing their inventory.

Every element in the logistics process must be tackled in order to improve performance. In service call centres the cost of employing a person capable of dealing with service calls in India is about one-tenth of the cost of employing a person in the UK for an equivalent level of performance. Very often service centre calls are routine, and technology can be used to make further savings by replacing people-based transactions with 'intelligent' computer-based responses.

## Value chain integration

The key question is how effectively the individual supply chain members around the world can work in partnership to maximize the effectiveness of their contributions towards improving efficiency and adding value across the entire value chain, so-called value chain integration. Success is then likely to be dependent on the effectiveness of the working relationship between the members of the supply chain, the speed and openness of information sharing and the degree of collaboration between each party. These include the company, its suppliers and customers and has the objective of adding value and removing transaction costs.

So, for example, a supermarket chain will allow its hundreds of suppliers to have access to its data warehouse. Each supplier then knows how their particular product is selling in each individual store, and access to the inventory system ensures that the supermarket never runs out of that supplier's stock. This system makes it easier for additional suppliers to be included and managed at low additional cost, allowing consumers more choice and more competitive prices. Hagiu (2013), however, explains that although multi-sided platforms (MSPs), such as PayPal, Microsoft, Google, Facebook and Apple, can lower costs, there are dangers with online collaboration as firms cede too much power to the MSPs. A recent MSP success is Airbnb, a platform where consumers can rent out space in their house or apartment usually to holiday makers. If Airbnb were not populated by people who rent out their properties and reviews from happy holidaymakers who have rented them, then the MSP would not be successful.

## Virtual enterprise networks

The possibility for Internet technology-supported collaboration between supply chain members is being extended and applied to SMEs and individuals with complementary expertise. These parties form themselves into a virtual enterprise network to bid for and carry out projects and routine business. Snyder (2005) explains that the Internet has reduced transaction costs and outsourcing risks, enabling individuals and organizations to form a more efficient form of organization, based on virtually integrated collaborative networks rather than hierarchical bureaucracies. Virtual enterprise networks are expected to become more common, international in nature and focused on international marketing opportunities.

## Customer relationship management

Customer relationship management (CRM) is the process of identifying, attracting, differentiating and retaining customers (Hoffman 2003). It allows a firm to focus its efforts on its most lucrative customers, no matter where they are from, and is based on the 'Pareto Law' that 80 per cent of a firm's profits come from 20 per cent of its customers. It is also designed to achieve efficient and effective customer management. As pressures on costs and prices increase, firms must manage customers as inexpensively as they can without losing customer loyalty. To answer a customer query with an automatic Web- or text-based service can be less than one-tenth of the cost of a person handling it by telephone through a service call centre. But the question is whether it can be as responsive to customer queries.

CRM allows customers to be categorized on the basis of their past profitability. The most profitable customers will be recognized and routed to the area that will handle calls fastest. For example, this can be done automatically by transferring telephone calls with a particular number. The profitable customers can then be targeted with attractive deals. The information is shared throughout the company to ensure integration of the firm's activities, so that profitable customers get priority service throughout the firm and also from partner firms. Sometimes this can lead to unethical behaviour by firms. Online gambling firms have been accused of offering incentives to their best (most losing), 'addicted' customers to continue betting even when they already cannot meet their debts.

To deliver a CRM strategy the key component is the database of customer information. Techniques and systems are used to manage and extract data (data mining) to identify trends and analyze customer characteristics that enable the targeting to be carried out. Building and sustaining a competitive advantage using a consumer-centric approach, coupled with CRM technology, often on a global scale, should be at the heart of every business (Richardson *et al.* 2015). Richardson *et al.* also argue that businesses no longer provide goods and services for consumers. There is a partnership where the consumer and the business co-create products and services, both seeking value from a transaction.

The system involves the retention of large amounts of detailed information about individual customers in a firm database. Customers often resent firms holding information about them. In some countries, this would infringe privacy laws. Companies analyze the data that they have, but only past behaviour has been recorded. This data, therefore, may not be an accurate predictor of future behaviour. Finally, there is an assumption that customers want a 'relationship' with suppliers and that in some way they will benefit from it. If the benefit is not clear, then customers will not remain loyal.

## Customization

As we have suggested on a number of occasions, customers increasingly want to be treated as individuals and not simply be the unwilling targets of mass market advertising. The Internet allows companies to mass customize their offering, and a variety of firms are exploiting the flexibility of online mobile communication. A number of firms are providing software applications that are designed to personalize or more individually target the firm's interactions. For example, Lindgren (2003) explains how Poindexter (USA) uses statistical analysis to identify the shared characteristics of online advertising viewers and be able to cluster those customers who respond to websites and online advertisements in a similar way. The clusters can then be offered a customized marketing mix and customized promotions and product offers. For example, an online shopper who puts products in an online basket but does not go through with the purchase immediately might be offered a discount by the online retailer as an incentive to go through with the purchase. As more viewers are analyzed, the system learns the best response and so delivers better performance.

Customers can be targeted and made aware of special deals being offered in their own neighbourhood, perhaps on travel, at a restaurant or at the wine shop. Global positioning systems coupled with mobile telephony enable firms to text consumers about deals available in the shop that they are just passing.

## Strategic planning

Against the background of how technology and innovation both disrupt and enable all aspects of international marketing, we now explore how a much more dynamic approach to international strategic planning is needed. To emphasize this, Management Challenge 12.2 illustrates the kind of problems WPP faces, as one of the largest organizations in its sector.

---

### MANAGEMENT CHALLENGE 12.2

## Finding a place for the ad man

In 2008 WPP overtook Omnicom to become the largest and most profitable marketing group in the world. It owned four of the world's largest advertising agencies – JWT, Ogilvy & Mather, Young & Rubicam and Grey – as well as other subsidiaries providing the full range of marketing services, including market research, design, digital branding, corporate identity, public relations and relationship marketing. WPP owned marketing agencies that served most country markets around the world.

Sir Martin Sorrell left his job as finance director at Saatchi & Saatchi and became WPP's first chief executive in 1987. Through acquisitions Sorrell built the company to its leading position but retired after 33 years in charge in April 2018, following allegations of personal misconduct and misuse of company assets. There had also been criticism of his excessive pay deals, amounting to about £200 million in options, bonuses and share awards in his last five years.

Storm clouds were already gathering for WPP, however. Sorrell announced that 2017 was the company's worst year since the 2009 recession. In 2009 WPP fired 14 000 of its workforce, but job cuts were less severe in 2017 when 1400 jobs were cut, around

1 per cent of its 134 000 workforce. In 2017 it reported a 0.9 per cent fall in revenues, prompting an immediate 14 per cent drop in its share price. A rapidly increasing share of WPP's business, and up to 90 per cent of new business, was being spent with tech companies such as Facebook and Google. Increasingly, firms placing ads with these companies were working directly with the tech companies, cutting the 'middleman', WPP, out of the deals. As well as the likes of Facebook and Google becoming new non-traditional competition, the firms providing specific marketing services and local agencies with specialist country and regional knowledge also compete with WPP for business. In a further blow, Ford Motor Company revealed that after working together for 75 years, it was putting its creative account up for review, putting at risk US$4 billion of advertising business for WPP in 40 countries.

### Questions

**1** How should WPP respond to the disintermediation in the market?

**2** In replacing Martin Sorrell, what management skills should the recruiters be looking for?

**References:** www.wpp.com; Sweeney, M. (2018) Martin Sorrell's WPP reports worst year for growth since 2009, *The Guardian* 1 March. Available from www.theguardian.com/media/2018/mar/01/martin-sorrell-wpp-reports-worst-year-growth-since-2009 (accessed 23 April 2018); Tay, V. (2018) Trouble brews on for WPP as Ford puts global creative account up for review, *Marketing*. Available at www.marketing-interactive.com/ford-global-creative-account-up-for-review-wpp-on-alert/ (accessed 23 April 2018).

## Technology-driven analysis

Demand patterns are now changing more quickly because of changes in the environment, customer needs, wants and expectations, and existing and new competition. It is therefore vital for firms to track changes through an effective marketing information system. Much of the data that must be gathered from around the world can be more effectively collected, managed and communicated through integrated big data systems. Firms can track political, economic and legal changes and competitor activity by using search engines and sites that provide up-to-date expert analysis. Point of sale information is collected and analyzed by retailers on a daily basis. This provides information about what products are selling and not selling, so that appropriate action can be taken to avoid unnecessary inventory and build a supply chain that is flexible and responsive. For example, for clothing products to sell in the USA, the fabric production, garment making and logistics must be fast, flexible and quickly adaptable to changing fashion needs to avoid stock write-offs or write-downs. For some brands it may not be possible to source these from Asia.

In the past, fashion magazines and newspaper articles provided information about the latest trend and images of celebrities wearing the next 'cool' brand or 'must have' product. Now social networking websites, chat rooms and bloggers provide the response and opinions from customers that are likely to affect their purchasing habits. Because of the informal, non-regulated nature of the websites, firms can influence their perceptions of the products.

The Internet provides not only general information about the firm's products but also makes it easier and faster to apply questionnaires to existing and potential customers around the world. These gauge not only opinions but also help to build up a psychological profile, enabling organizations to anticipate, reinforce and influence behaviour. Customer behaviour can be monitored on websites by tracking navigation through the site to provide new insights, thought processes and predict likely purchasing intentions. Egol *et al.* (2010) explain how online shopping behaviour can lead to six consumer segments:

1  *Shoppers* 2.0, the most technologically advanced group, price sensitive with little brand loyalty.

2  *Deal hunters*, price sensitive but gather information online and then get the best deal in-store.

3  *Online window shoppers*, gather information online and in-store, but are less price sensitive and less likely to switch brands.

4  *Channel surfers*, hunt out the brands they love and try to source the brands at reasonable prices.

5  *Loyalists*, least likely to switch brands or retail formats.

6  *Laggards*, least likely to change behaviour and carry out little online research.

The Internet carries negative information as well. This comes from blogs and social networking sites that spread negative and sometimes fake stories and extreme views, usually without any counter arguments or corrections. Firms can suffer considerable damage at the hands of such sites and comments.

As we discussed in Part 1, organizations are collecting this type of information in a much more systematic way. For example, Procter & Gamble and Unilever have a database of observed behaviour accessible to staff worldwide through an intranet.

Radian6 is an organization which uses algorithms to understand what consumers feel about products and services. They do this by analyzing comments shared on Facebook, Twitter, websites, blogs and so on. All happy consumers that say they enjoyed their visit to a theme park, or compliment a receptionist or shout out about a chef's fabulous food, are analyzed as providing a positive sentiment to the brand. However, consumers that share bad experiences and comment that a product was terrible or service staff were not courteous are analyzed as providing a negative sentiment to the brand. There are hundreds of companies like Radian6 that help businesses analyze and review internet 'chatter', so they can understand and customize their products and services to different customer needs identified through social media. Social media comments can be highly customized. A consumer who complains, via Twitter, that they are waiting in a queue to check in at a hotel can be identified immediately. The team tracking social media comments will advise the hotel that a person in the queue is complaining. Extra staff can be brought to reception to help alleviate the situation and give refreshments to all people who are waiting as an apology.

It seems therefore that a huge amount of micro and big data can be generated and analyzed. However, Ofek and Wathieu (2010) observe that while managers recognize major social, economic and technological trends, their focus is often on short-term goals. Also, they often fail to realize the significance of these trends in reshaping the business.

## Internal data

Technological advances have enabled internal organizational systems to collect and analyze data from across global operations. Using artificial intelligence means not only repetitive activities but also decision making can be undertaken without humans. However, key elements of organizational behaviour in international markets are increasingly under the spotlight of global communication and require even higher levels of internal monitoring and control. Such elements include cultural sensitivity; corporate social responsibility; moral, ethical and legal behaviour; political alignment; avoidance of criminality; support for staff; and knowledge leadership.

## The impact of technology on international strategy development

For some firms their international marketing strategy is inextricably linked to technology either because of the nature of the business, in the case of firms such as Huawei, Microsoft and Acer, or because it is the route to market in the case of Expedia, Uber or Airbnb.

For firms in most industry sectors, technology, business and marketing innovations are a major source of international competitive advantage. As we discussed earlier, organizations in developed countries cannot compete against the low-labour and other associated costs, operational scale benefits and lower R&D costs of firms from developing countries, such as India and China. As educational attainment levels increase in these firms, they are able to compete in the most technologically challenging markets, traditionally dominated by firms from developed countries. Moreover, the danger for established firms is that using these newly emerging firms in the supply chain can lead to the creation of a future competitor. As these firms from developing countries succeed, however, so their costs rise, too, as employees become more aware of their worth. So their competitive advantage of low cost will cease to be sustainable.

Their source of competitive advantage in the future, whether the firm is from a developed or less developed country, is likely to come from several areas. These include technological, business process and marketing innovations; knowledge management of the organization's intellectual property and assets; its ability to manage effectively; and the contributions of the supply chain to maximize customer value. For these reasons technological competence and capability, understanding the competitive market position and gaining in-depth customer insights will become key success criteria in the future.

## Internet-based market entry

The Web provides a less expensive market entry method than building a presence. It is particularly suitable for smaller, widespread niche markets. However, while the website might be accessible worldwide, the firm may need to select markets to focus on, possibly excluding those where there may be particular barriers, such as language, legal, payment and fulfilment problems. The cost of organizing the distribution to serve certain markets might still outweigh the possible benefits. For firms that already have a strong presence in many markets, the Web cost effectively supports all aspects of their activity.

Web-based services are successful if firms develop a global strategy based upon the integrated value chain. As this is a pervasive method of entry, based on global communications, it can facilitate lower-risk access to difficult markets. By building online delivery capability it is possible to serve markets profitably where there might be limited demand. Of course, an e-commerce strategy is limited in scope simply because it appeals to a very specific transnational segment – those that are able to gain access to the firm's website. But as Internet access, particularly high-speed access, continues to grow, this is a diminishing problem.

## The impact of technology on strategy implementation and control

**Product and service management**   Technological advances are key to innovation and facilitate worldwide contributions to the development, production, delivery and communication to customers of new products and services. Technology supports the delivery and control of all the elements of the augmented product and service offer (see Chapter 8, Figure 8.2) and integrates the worldwide members of the supply chain.

## ILLUSTRATION 12.5

# Health insurance where it is needed

Seeing the husband of her maid lose his life because they didn't have $25 to get medical help was a wake-up call for Lilian Makoi, founder of Jamii Africa. She found that 50 million Tanzanians had no health insurance. Jamii was set up in 2015 by Lilian, and Chris Rabi was her first angel investor. This micro-health insurance company was built around a mobile policy management platform that performs all the administrative activities of an insurer, including mobile premium collection and cashless services from over 400 hospitals, with very cheap insurance starting at $1 per month.

A key step was the formation of strategic partnerships with the largest insurer – Jubilee Insurance – and the largest telecom firm – Vodacom Tanzania – in the country. The next big break was being accepted onto the Barclays Techstars accelerator programme, which helped in the business design, provided connections and ultimately helped raise $750 000 seedcorn funding. By 2017 Lilian was planning to launch in five other East and Central African countries.

## Question

**1** Jamii Africa was named number 5 in the Disrupt 100, 2017 (at www.disrupt100.com), celebrating companies with the potential to influence, change or create global markets. Why could this company prove to be disruptive?

**Reference:** Hasson, Y. (2017) Meet Jamii Africa: Microhealth insurance startup, Techstars, January 24. Available from www.techstars.com/content/accelerators/meet-jamii-africa-microhealth-insurance-startup/ (accessed 22 April 2018).

In so doing, technology is increasingly supporting the standardization of the components of the product and creating worldwide product 'platforms' on the one hand. For example, car firms such as VW, and household appliance manufacturers such as Whirlpool, use a common platform and make minor adaptations for different models and markets. On the other hand, however, it is enabling firms to offer increased customization of products and services and one-to-one marketing. Illustration 12.5 shows how customers can be encouraged to spend money on essential services, in this case health insurance, if the price is within reach and the provider's costs can be controlled through the innovative use of technology.

**Pricing**   As we discussed earlier in the chapter, technology is driving down costs and prices through supply chain efficiencies, economies of scale, the experience curve effect and greater price transparency. Price transparency for customers and other stakeholders is created because of the ease with which it is possible to compare prices offered by competing potential suppliers across borders by searching through the information on their websites. Some sites such as Expedia in travel, Kelkoo on a range of products in B2C markets, and the sector and function e-hubs in B2B, provide the opportunity for customers to compare prices on one site.

The Internet makes grey marketing easier and also makes it much more difficult for firms to operate specific geographic territories and price differentials across country borders. Grey marketing may therefore become less of an issue in international markets as firms give up any hope of trying to control it. Price transparency has the effect of driving mature products towards commoditization in which products become less differentiated and competition is based largely on price. When there are many competitors, price transparency forces down prices as suppliers have to respond by cutting the costs of their products and services. This usually forces them to find ever lower cost sources. The alternative is to innovate and develop new products and services or add additional services, many of which, such as loyalty reward schemes, are operated online. However, these strategies will only work if customers around the world perceive the additional services to be valuable and of additional benefit over the commodity product alternative.

Customization is clearly the opposite of commoditization and, therefore, can be used partially to counter price transparency. Product and service elements can be bundled together with other aspects of the marketing mix. For example, international pricing embraces both pricing and financing the transaction; technology allows pricing to be customized. It can enable complex calculations to be made to facilitate the negotiation of mutually beneficial deals between supplier and customer with flexible pricing and financing. It can also control non-standard repayment schedules that ensure the transaction is ultimately profitable. Airlines have long had the ability to change prices over time to manage demand. Increasingly, online sellers can charge different prices every minute, in different locations and to different customers, to manage cash flow, inventory and customer relationships.

It is important to understand the business model operating and who is ultimately paying for the service. Services such as Google Search and Facebook are free to 'customers' because consumers are prepared to give away their personal data in return. Advertisers are only too willing to pay Google and Facebook for the data and direct access they get in return.

**Channel management**   Electronic marketing has encouraged disintermediation, or the removal of intermediaries from the supply chain, as suppliers market directly to customers. Technology now enables firms to efficiently manage thousands of small transactions that previously would have been left for a local intermediary to undertake. This is possible because e-marketing has typically lower transaction costs and is capable of managing large inventories, logistics, ordering and payments. It also allows the virtual bundling of products that might be sourced from different partner suppliers. Disintermediation provides the manufacturer with stronger control of its activities in the market and avoids being so reliant on third parties. It also enables the distribution channels to be customized to the specific needs of the customers.

For those firms that are maintaining intermediaries within their distribution channel, technology allows much closer cooperation through sharing of market information. It also allows greater control of intermediaries by making it easier to check on a daily basis whether they are fulfilling their commitments to the supplier.

Channel management also covers physical distribution. It can be argued that the 'want it now' demands of consumers create extra delivery costs, pollution and congestion on the roads. Illustration 12.6 shows the opportunities and potential challenges of drone delivery.

**Communications**   The main advantage of e-marketing communications is that they are targeted and often based on one-to-one communications using accumulated big data. They are also interactive. Customers are required to do something rather than being passive recipients of untargeted advertising, such as billboards and TV. As customers become more involved, so they are more likely to buy.

Marketing through websites, even interactive ones, is reactive. This is because potential customers must take the initiative and locate the site first, typically by using a search engine. It is therefore essential that the firm features high on the list of search results. Word of mouth referral or viral marketing is important in building traffic to the website, but to gain a large market in unexciting business sectors it is not enough just to have a website. It is also necessary to proactively market and promote the brand and the site in the traditional media. The fundamental questions of marketing need to be asked, such as who are we targeting, where will we find the target customers on the Internet and how will we get them directed to our site? How best can we then communicate our message to them globally and at low cost? The key is to deliver the right message to the right people at the right time in the right place using the right e-based communication channels.

**Control, evaluation and learning**   Technology enables firms to collect, transfer and analyze vast amounts of data from anywhere in the world. Using Enterprise Resource Planning (ERP) software they are able to control the use of resources and improve the efficiency of their operations. Financial management and control can be more immediate and more detailed. Firms use other processes and systems to control the supporting operations. These ensure quality and efficiency of the manufacturing and distribution operations and measure the effectiveness of the marketing processes and programmes.

These techniques can be applied in worldwide operations because they can be supported by IT and systems. Underpinning all these techniques is the need to develop a learning organization that follows good practice, shares new ideas and creates greater confidence in the abilities of its staff. They then become empowered to take decisions in their own area of expertise and knowledge.

## ILLUSTRATION 12.6

# A sky full of drones

In May 2018 the Federal Aviation Administration (FAA) gave approval for selected US cities and states to start commercial drone operations. This followed applications from 149 bidding consortiums comprising local governments and firms, and ranging from package delivery to property damage assessment for insurance. The use of drones in the USA had been delayed for some time by unclear regulations.

One of the bidders, Zipline, a Silicon Valley start-up, was already using drones to deliver blood for hospitals and clinics in Rwanda. North Carolina, in partnership with a number of companies, including Zipline, proposed delivering blood and medicines to rural areas, where life expectancy was eight years shorter than in the cities. Zipline founder, Keller Rinaudo, said that drone delivery was certain to replace large swathes of the existing supply chain, explaining that instant delivery by Prime and Deliveroo already existed, but using a 3000 lb (1361 kg) vehicle with a combustion engine to deliver a 1 lb (0.5 kg) hamburger didn't make sense, so drones could be used for more than just delivery of medical products.

The development of rules covering drones is moving more slowly in Europe. The European regulator has banned hobbyists from flying drones out of sight. In France a law has been proposed that drones over 800 g must be fitted with electronic tracking and with flashing beacons visible from 150 metres away. Risks associated with drones, such as the potential for accidents, invasion of privacy, use by drug dealers and terrorists, are expected to slow down law making. Legislators are also seeking assurances on the reliability of operating the equipment out of sight, at night and over populated areas.

### Questions

**1** In what way and how quickly are drone deliveries likely to affect the supply chain in different business sectors?

**2** How do you expect drone delivery to be used in different countries and regions of the world?

**Reference:** Fortson, D. (2018) Drone armada takes off. *The Sunday Times* 22 April 2018.

## Some limitations of e-commerce for international marketing strategy

There are some disadvantages in operating e-business globally. These include the high cost of providing a global website with 24-hour service for customers who expect interactive capability, wherever possible, in their own language and culture and adapted to their own environment. There are also some significant perceived and real dangers associated with e-commerce. Customers are concerned with data security and the risks, for example, of credit card fraud. Customers are also concerned with identity theft, data protection and the use, storage and passing on to third parties of personal information to firms anywhere in the world. Of course, technology is being continually developed and improved to try to overcome these difficulties. However, the next generation of supercomputers has extraordinary computing power which has the potential not only to solve some of the world's most difficult problems but could mean that personal data may no longer be secure.

Firms basing their business on e-commerce must recognize that there are typically low entry barriers, and competitors have greater and easier access to information that can be used to challenge the existing supplier. For example, Yell, the business directory company, blamed a decline in profits on a rival business set up by ex-sales staff made redundant in the USA by the company. Computer systems are still prone to system failure and corruption, and it is still alarmingly easy for computer hackers and computer viruses to cause severe damage to MNEs. Often MNEs, particularly banks, do not publicize such difficulties as it may well deter customers. There is also a proliferation of anti-MNE websites that through social networking can publicize damaging stories – true or not – virtually without challenge. This is possible, of course, simply because of the relatively uncontrolled nature of the Internet.

International e-business marketing businesses face several challenges:

■ The decisions of customers in e-commerce are strongly affected by cultural issues. Customers from some countries, typically low context countries, embrace the Internet in different ways to those in high-context cultures because of the lower emphasis placed on implicit interactions when building relationships and purchasing products.

■ Brand values often depend on the different communication methods that people use, both explicit and implicit, such as image, reputation, word of mouth and continual exposure online and offline. This emphasizes the need for an integrated communications approach involving virtual and physical media.

■ By being global, e-commerce still favours global players. Consumers expect high quality of performance and image, but these can be severely tarnished by a poor online presence and slow or inaccurate order fulfilment.

■ The effectiveness of websites is influenced by such factors as the ease of navigation, company and products information, shipping details and sensitivity to language and culture.

■ The barriers to entry must be significant if the defenders of domestic or limited country niches wish to retain their market share. It must be recognized by marketers that the marketing skills to ensure success in e-business are different from traditional skills. Success depends on attracting consumers to sites, and this is typically more difficult because of the increased media 'noise'.

■ The development of intelligent agents that search for specific pieces of information on markets and potential suppliers means that marketers cannot base their appeal to customers on traditional marketing-mix factors. They must find a new sustainable competitive advantage.

# Legislation

The aspect of the Internet that seems to raise most concern is the fact that there is very little control exerted. Consequently, the Internet is used for unethical and illegal purposes and to circumvent the law. The Internet has grown extremely rapidly and the application of existing law and introduction of legislation to control activities has lagged behind. Governments do not want to stifle development, so legislation is being developed not in anticipation but only as problems arise. However, as stories of ever more serious hacking, loss of personal privacy, theft of business secrets and political interference increase, so legislators increasingly act, for example, in the USA, China and the EU.

## Problems of application of existing law to the Internet

The Internet removes traditional geographic boundaries, so that virtually anyone anywhere in the world can access communications. Websites are subject to the laws of individual countries, both home and host country, where customers are based. Websites are also subject to regional trade agreements (e.g. EU and NAFTA) and regulations of organizations such as the WTO, the World International Property Organization (WIPO) and the Berne Convention on copyright law. Many countries either do not conform or interpret many conventions differently.

The result is a chaotic situation in which multiple and contradictory laws apply to the same transaction, leaving a marketer open to the possibility of unintentionally violating the laws of a foreign country. A whole series of issues arise in e-marketing, including what constitutes a contract in cyberspace, how international tax can be harmonized and how tax should be collected for online transactions.

There are many issues of intellectual property protection, including copyright infringement, inappropriate linking to information from another website and trademark infringement, such as the registering of existing trademarks as domain names for the website. Countries, including the UK, Mexico and Russia, have taken a 'first come, first served' approach to this. Companies such as Nike, Chrysler and Sony initially failed to register as widely as they should have and have suffered as a consequence.

Consumer protection for international consumer clients must be provided to avoid unfair and deceptive trading practices, such as unsubstantiated advertising claims and false endorsements. Relationship marketing, especially for small firms, is based on building substantial data on customers in order to retain their loyalty. But in a number of countries, gathering such information is still illegal as laws exist to protect consumer privacy. Marketers must also know the difference between what is considered free speech and what is defamation and disparagement. Furthermore, many firms ask customers to tick a box to indicate that they agree with their terms and conditions on the basis that few customers will read or understand them. They then use this agreement to allow them to use customer data in a way that customers would not normally accept.

## Other Internet problems

The problems discussed so far have related to the application of largely existing legislation to the new medium and the fact that the Internet crosses country borders indiscriminately. Other issues are the ease of access and lack of control of illegal activity, such as sales of drugs and weapons. It has been estimated that a large percentage of international consumer e-commerce is devoted to pornography, A worrying part of this traffic is illegal and supporting paedophilia and people trafficking. It requires close cooperation between country law enforcement agencies to catch the culprits.

The ease of communicating with many recipients makes it easy to send out 'junk mail' (spam). Millions of messages can be sent out worldwide in the hope of getting just a few responses. Many firms sell to potential customers through emails and text messages. However, if this is overused it degenerates into spam. Spam is the intrusive, offensive and often pornographic junk email that fills up the inboxes of email systems. It threatens to create gridlock on the Internet if it is not controlled. The USA has proposed opt-out legislation so that spam would be legal unless the receiver has opted out of receiving it. The EU legislation is opt-in – spam could not be sent unless the receiver had given consent to receive it – and would be more effective in controlling spam.

# Moving to a customer-led strategy

The Internet and developments in the media have revolutionized business communications and transactions. It has changed marketing for ever by allowing anyone anywhere in the world to buy online from anyone else. The range of communication methods has increased significantly as a result of technological advances and entrepreneurialism. The growth in social networking has transformed communications. Sometimes blogging is well informed and sometimes it is completely incorrect and often malicious. But it strongly influences consumer purchasing and usage decisions. The technology advances were expected to level the playing field between small and large firms so that the most innovative firms, small or large, would become the winners. It was thought that the technologists rather than the marketers would be in control. In reality, consumers have become more sophisticated in their use of technology and media, and used it to their advantage. As a result, consumers are increasingly in control of events. So even greater customer insights are needed and marketing expertise has never been more vital.

At the start of the chapter we proposed the idea that technology is an enabler. Hamill and Stevenson (2003) suggest that technology facilitates cost-effective relationship building but does not automatically achieve a customer-focused approach. Ritter and Walter (2006) examine the impact of IT on customer relationships in the B2B context. They conclude that while IT competence can replace parts of relationship management, it cannot do so totally.

Technology has shifted the balance of power from suppliers to customers. Consequently, customer dominance must be accepted. Those arrogant firms that take customers for granted will suffer. Organizations must adopt a customer-led approach in order to achieve sustainability. This means that they must develop innovative approaches to sales, marketing and overall corporate strategy that are driven by what customers need and want.

The objective of being customer-led is to identify, acquire, retain and grow 'quality' customers. Nykamp (2001) suggests that organizations must achieve competitive differentiation by building impermeable customer relationships. The challenge is to use the interactive power of the Internet to facilitate this by helping the organization to build close one-to-one relationships with their most valuable and growable customers.

Many firms have recognized the need to be customer-led and have responded by implementing sophisticated and expensive CRM systems. Hamill and Stevenson (2003) suggest that many of these systems have failed to produce the expected return because they have been technology-driven rather than customer-led. The term CRM has been hijacked by software vendors promising 'out-of-the-box' solutions to complex strategic, organizational and human resources problems. They claim that technology has a part to play. But customer-led is not about software, database marketing, loyalty programmes, customer bribes or hard selling. It is about building strong one-to-one relationships with quality customers, achieving customer loyalty, maximizing customer lifetime earnings and re-engineering the firm towards satisfying the needs of 'quality' customers on a customized and personalized basis. The most convincing reason for a customer to buy from any company in the world is that they are totally satisfied, have no reason to complain about the service they receive, and are surprised and delighted by some of the firm's innovative actions.

To deliver this requires a more fundamental reinvention of the firm if it wishes to really succeed in the future. A new mindset is needed, together with an innovative approach to the strategy. In practice, firms will need to:

■ Focus not on markets but on quality customers from anywhere in the world. By quality customers it is the strategically significant, most valuable and 'growable' customers that should be given the highest priority. The suggestion is that, over time, firms have moved from supplying markets to serving market segments and are now focusing on serving individual customers one at a time.

■ Focus on one-to-one relationships. To do this firms must learn about customers and deliver personalized and customized products, services and support in order to maximize the up- and cross-selling opportunities. The implications of this are that at one level, firms must be sensitive to the customer's business and social culture and the customer's business dynamics. At another level, the firm must be able to form supply and value chain alliances that enable the up- and cross-selling to be developed for the customer's benefit.

■ Increase, both lifetime and short-term revenue from customers. Firms must focus on the delivery of exceptional value by developing an effective worldwide supply chain, building ever-closer relationships both with customers and partners, and finding ways to erect barriers to entry by competitor firms.

■ Create a win–win situation. The long-term business relationships must be valuable for both supplier and provider, and so long-term value for the customer and firm must be maximized. This could require some compromises by both parties to achieve this.

■ Develop an integrated and coordinated approach. The success of a customer-led relationship building approach is that it requires commitment at all levels, creating, communicating and delivering value. For all businesses, but particularly global businesses, this is clearly a major challenge.

Most firms would claim to be customer-led, but the real test for them is whether they would be willing to change their strategy radically because of the trends that are being perceived in the marketplace. Lindstrom and Seybold (2003) report on research that suggests that marketing strategies in the future may need to be changed radically in order to be customer-led. Very young, computer literate child consumers have a large influence on family purchasing decisions. They are extremely well-informed through online networking sites that influence their behaviour. It is necessary to ask just how far firms should change their international marketing strategy to respond to these changes.

## Sustainability and corporate social responsibility

Sustainability is the topic of ever more intense public attention and debate. We have discussed various aspects of sustainability and corporate social responsibility (CSR) in this book. Much of the public debate has centred on the green environment, reduction in the consumption of the world's non-renewable energy and other resources, the dumping of waste, pollution of the landscape and sea, and so on. It is becoming increasingly important for global firms to address these issues responsibly as they will affect the reputation of the company and its brand value. However, for some firms, the failure to secure viable energy and resources, minimize waste, particularly finding alternatives to 'one-trip' plastics, and develop a sustainable, competitive cost base will put at risk the future of the business. Technological solutions from renewable sources of energy, plus recycling and using recycled components and improved processes, are essential.

Corporate social responsibility covers many more areas from treating staff well and paying them a living wage, not using child labour, paying suppliers a fair price and treating customers fairly. It also covers adopting fair competition practices and not resorting to bribery, fraud or other illegal practices. Berns *et al.* (2009) found from a survey of 50 global thought leaders the barriers that impede decisive corporate action include:

- a lack of understanding of what sustainability is and means to the enterprise
- difficulty modelling the business case,
- flaws in execution after a plan has been developed.

The growing awareness of consumers of the issues and their ability to access information about company practices worldwide means that more firms will come under pressure to provide answers. Along with technological advances, marketing will need to provide the answers. However, taking an eco-friendly stance is also fraught with problems, as Management Challenge 12.3 shows.

## MANAGEMENT CHALLENGE 12.3

## Palm oil and social responsibility

In January 2018 Richard Walker, managing director of UK supermarket group Iceland, pledged to become the first big retailer to eliminate plastic packaging. In a further initiative to reinforce the group's eco-friendly stance, he announced that palm oil would be removed from all its own brand foods. Both announcements were praised by environmentalists. Palm oil production has been cited as the cause of huge deforestation in South East Asia. Tropical rainforests have been cut down to create space for plantations for oil palms from which the product is produced.

However, this decision enraged those with palm oil interests in the region. A lobbying group, funded partly by the Malaysian government, bought Twitter ads to show a video that attacked Walker personally. He was portrayed as the Bentley-driving son who inherited the supermarket from his 'Daddy' and took a polluting jet to Malaysia to attack poor palm oil small farmers, who were using palm oil to create wealth for their families and a bright future for their communities. Environmental activists claimed that the website, Human Faces of Palm Oil, was created anonymously and the slick video was probably produced by a western PR company with the intention of damaging the supermarket's reputation.

### Questions

**1** How can a firm manage the competing corporate social responsibilities of sustainability of the environment and avoiding damage to the affected communities?

**2** What are the advantages and disadvantages of the palm oil interests using social media in this way?

**Reference:** Moore, M. (2018) Palm oil lobby smears Iceland boss Richard Walker. *The Times*, 20 April.

## The elements of the strategic plan

Having considered in the previous chapters of this book the factors that influence and shape international marketing strategy and, in this chapter, how technology specifically is both enabling and disrupting strategy analysis, development and implementation, we finish with Table 12.1. This is a checklist of the key elements that make up the plan.

**Table 12.1**   Checklist for international strategic planning

| Elements of the plan | Issues to be addressed |
| --- | --- |
| Analysis | • What assumptions have been made about the world economy using environmental (SLEPTS) scanning with particular focus on potentially disruptive new technology?<br>• Have the global trends, regional and local forecasts for growth in the sector been identified?<br>• Using data sets, how are customer needs, wants, beliefs and behaviour changing?<br>• What strategies are competitors in the sector using?<br>• Are new competitors using disruptive business models likely to emerge?<br>• Has a detailed evaluation of the firm's strategy and historical performance (sales, costs and profitability) by market been made?<br>• Have forecasts been made using extrapolation of the past and alternative scenarios?<br>• What are the firm's strengths, weaknesses and future capabilities in comparison to local and international competition?<br>• Has a summary of the critical factors for success been made? |
| Strategy development and planning | • What is the firm's vision?<br>• What are the corporate, subsidiary and country long-term aims and objectives, and is there a suitable strategy to achieve them?<br>• How might technology assist in further refining the firm's segmentation, targeting and positioning strategy?<br>• Are changes needed to the company's structure and business model?<br>• What new innovations, sectors and countries will be targeted?<br>• Is the firm's knowledge accumulation and data management effective, appropriate and valued? |
| Country and business division strategies | • Have one-year marketing objectives and individual strategies (for example, budgets, brand objectives and development of personnel) been set?<br>• Are there country-by-country forecasts and targets?<br>• Are there country-by-country plans for all marketing activities and coordination with other functions (for example, supply chain management)?<br>• Is there an explanation of how country plans will be integrated regionally or globally if appropriate?<br>• Has an assessment been made of the likely competitor response? |
| Implementation | • Are the corporate and brand identities clear and distinctive, and what plans have been made to further reinforce them?<br>• What steps are being taken to further differentiate products and service elements from competitor offers?<br>• Are intended and unintended communications to customers and other stakeholders being managed as effectively as possible?<br>• How might the supply chain be changed to achieve maximum effectiveness and customer satisfaction?<br>• Are costs managed efficiently, and does the business model and the pricing strategy maximize income for the firm?<br>• Are potential high-value customers being identified and targeted?<br>• Is the best use being made of technology to integrate systems and support customer relationship management? |

(*Continued*)

## Table 12.1   Continued

| Elements of the plan | Issues to be addressed |
| --- | --- |
| Control and management | • Are the financial and marketing measures and controls, the performance management and improvement processes effective?<br>• Do internal communications with global staff and partners contribute to performance?<br>• Is there a timely control process for feedback, evaluation and taking corrective action in place?<br>• Is there a contingency plan for when the unexpected happens (as it inevitably will!)? |

## SUMMARY

- Technology is creating new market opportunities and continually changing the way business is done in international markets. New technology provides solutions to solve old problems but also sets new challenges for international marketing management. Firms will under-perform or even fail if they are not able to exploit the global opportunities offered by the new technology or if they take the wrong decisions about how new technology might affect their industry sector.

- Consumer e-marketing, and especially innovative business models, attracts the interests of global consumers and facilitates new routes to market. Consumers are enthusiastically embracing new ways of communicating, through mobile devices and social media, collecting information about products and services, sharing opinions and making purchase and usage decisions.

- Although the Internet and advances in telecommunications have had the most dramatic effect on international marketing, other technologies and software to support integrated marketing solutions, such as robotics and drone delivery, are part of this change.

- Greater cooperation because of improvements in communication and the ease of information sharing make supply chains more effective. However, excess capacity and increased competition mean that the power in the supply chain is increasingly favouring the customer.

- Technology will provide some of the solutions to achieve sustainability of resources and strategies, and companies will have to take a more responsible attitude to the green environment. But they will also have to adopt greater corporate social responsibility as communications increasingly enable the community to scrutinize their actions.

- Because of this, firms will need to work ever harder to find new customers, gain deeper insights about the behaviour and opinions of different global segments and retain the loyalty of existing customers. Their international marketing strategies will have to be customer-led to develop compelling added value offers.

## KEYWORDS

| | | |
| --- | --- | --- |
| Internet | information technology | knowledge management |
| enabling technologies | industry-specific hubs | customer relationship management |
| e-commerce | function-specific hubs | mass customize |
| websites | supply chain management | legislation |
| business-to-business marketing | e-procurement | customer-led |
| business-to-consumer marketing | online auction | |

## CASE STUDY 1

## Heart problems? Wearable tech could save your life

The Internet of Things (IoT) was introduced in Challenge 12.1 showing the benefits for consumers who are *technology connected*. Technology can also help consumers improve their health and save their lives. The technology referred to in this case study is a Wireless Body Area Network (WBAN). Converging WBANs and the Internet can make significant improvements to a patient's health and wellbeing. Patients who have a heart condition are finding the WBAN particularly beneficial. Figure 12.2 shows the different layers of technology needed to keep a heart patient healthy.

The person in Figure 12.2 suffers from heart problems. They have a WBAN microchip implanted in their body. The data monitors and collects the person's temperature, blood pressure and heartbeat. The data is transferred from the WBAN microchip onto the person's smartphone app, which is then sent immediately to a cloud database. The person's data can then be downloaded by a medical doctor or clinician. The positive benefits for both the person who suffers from heart problems and their doctor is that data is transmitted in real time and is transmitted constantly. If the person's heart begins to beat irregularly or the person has a heart attack, the cloud data will provide alerts. Should the person call for an ambulance or go to hospital, their heart data before, during and after the irregular heartbeat or heart attack will be transmitted to the ambulance or hospital. This enables medical staff to attend to their patient's needs and save lives.

The technology that enables life-saving opportunities has two layers: the product layer and the service layer.

Technology for the product layer includes the WBAN microchip, IoT, medical cloud computing data storage facility and, of course, the laptops/desktops etc. that medical doctors and clinicians use.

The service layer of technology includes software to read and store data in the implanted microchip and the software that stores and/or analyzes the data.

The benefit of WBAN technology is immeasurable for patients, doctors and clinicians.

However, there are many people who argue that medical data should remain as private as possible between the patient and their doctor. Therefore, it is necessary for any business that develops WBANs or medical cloud computing data storage facilities to ensure the patient's name, medical details, their address and details of past diagnoses and medical treatment are secure. As shown in the chapter, privacy

**FIGURE 12.2**   Layers of technology

laws are not consistent or robust in some countries. This means it is important for WBAN businesses to choose carefully which cloud computing data storage facility they will use. WBAN businesses may not choose a cloud computing data storage facility in their own country because they feel that better, safer facilities are available in different countries.

## Questions

**1** Referring back to the strategic planning checklist, what issues are likely to be the most significant for wearable health devices?

   **a** What assumptions can be made regarding global and country trends in the market, for example,

people with health problems, and the contributory factors, such as lifestyle, obesity and fitness?

   **b** How might customer needs, wants, beliefs and behaviours affect demand? For example, how strong is the need for privacy, and are patients willing to accept diagnosis by computer as well as by a human (doctor)?

**2** Given similar assumptions and understanding of consumer attitudes, what other uses could there be for wearable devices?

**Reference:** Sawand, A., Djahel, S., Zhang, Z. and Nait-Abdesselam, F. (2015) Toward energy-efficient and trustworthy eHealth monitoring system. *Communications, China* 12(1), 46–65.

## CASE STUDY 2

# Yum! Brands: eating into new markets

Yum! Restaurants International is the world's largest restaurant group with 45 000 restaurants in 135 countries. It was spun off from PepsiCo in 1997 and owns and franchises KFC, Pizza Hut and Taco Bell brands worldwide. The brands employ 1.5 million people worldwide and it is the fourth-largest employer in the USA with 420 000 employees. Some 60 per cent of its restaurants are located outside the USA, up from 30 per cent in the late 1990s.

Chief executive Greg Creed notes that the company is the worldwide leader in emerging markets with 17 000 restaurants, almost twice as many as the nearest competitor. The opportunity for growth is huge in emerging markets, provided that consumers in emerging markets want similar fast food offers. In the top 10 emerging markets, there are 3 restaurants

per 1 million people compared to 57 restaurants per 1 million people in the USA.

A number of problems led Yum! to restructure in 2016 and focus on its core brands. Sales had declined in the USA as consumers sought what they considered to be healthier, fresher and less standardized food. Pizza Hut suffered declining sales. Although outside the USA the demand for global fast food brands had grown rapidly, problems such as food safety issues, changing consumer tastes and underperforming franchisees had been encountered in different countries. The involvement of an activist investor led to Yum! China being spun off and becoming a licensee of the parent company. The remaining markets reported directly to Yum! in the USA as the company pursued its strategy of 98 per cent of restaurants being franchised by 2018.

KFC was the first quick service restaurant chain to enter China in 1987. It has over 5000 units in 1000 cities. The development of the Chinese market was much faster than the company originally anticipated. As it owned the outlets, Yum! Brands was able to exert tight control over operations and learn quickly about the Chinese market. Typically, the initial investment was repaid out of profits over two to three years. Success was attributed to the establishment of an effective and efficient local supply chain and distribution infrastructure, based on what seemed to be a strong network of partners. However, customer confidence was adversely affected by a report that highlighted excessive levels of antibiotics in some chicken supplied to KFC. Also, a government investigation found that a KFC supplier was altering expiry dates on the chicken it was supplying.

The market is still expected to expand fast as the middle class grows from 300 million to 800 million by 2040. Yum! China has exploited Pizza Hut and Taco Bell, as well as developing its Little Sheep Hotpot and East Dawning brands and in total has 7300 restaurants.

Yum! China faces some challenges, however. Consumer preferences change quickly. The next generation of consumers already has different wants and expectations. Local knowledge, insights and clever adaptation of the KFC menu so far has maintained consumer loyalty. But the question is how much more can the menu be changed? The competition from existing Chinese restaurants is fierce. Despite its success, KFC has only a small market share. The brand is no longer aspirational. One KFC innovation in China has been home delivery because it was a cheaper and more practical alternative to 'drive thru'. If Yum! China can use technology to provide excellent service, deliver to the next generation of smartphone-owning consumers, avoid negative media and food safety problems, it should continue to grow.

### Yum! Restaurants International

Yum! divided its markets outside the USA and China into three types of region, where different strategies were needed: developing; developed – underpenetrated (for example, France, Italy and Germany); and developed – established. Sales were split: Europe 30 per cent, Asia 27 per cent, Americas 19 per cent, Middle East/South Africa 13 per cent and Australia/New Zealand 11 per cent.

Gone are the days when firms such as Yum! believed they could roll out the same formula in all global markets. India was hailed as the stand-out business opportunity by Creed in 2017. But the Yum! Brands might well perform differently in each country market. For example, the leading growth markets for Taco Bell were India, Brazil, China and Canada.

Future growth in outlets and profitability will come from the developing and underpenetrated developed markets. The franchising model has the benefit of leveraging additional investment and local management expertise to assist in adapting to local tastes and lifestyles. Each new territory presents local challenges that are often best understood by a local partner. The third restaurant planned in Mongolia was designed to be a drive thru, but deciding which side to place the delivery window was a problem as half the cars had left-hand drives and the other half right-hand drives!

However, lead franchisees are usually keen to build their own business and not simply rely on the brand licensee. A key partner for Yum! throughout the Middle East is Americana Group, established as a trading company in Kuwait in 1964. Americana manufactures food products for the Middle East and North Africa as well as operating many international franchises and its home-grown brands. Franchising can inadvertently help to create new competition.

Yum! Brands has been successful through its willingness to work with partners, adapt its menu and customer experience to fit with local needs and culture. But there is always the problem of controlling different business models to ensure quality and profitability. Yum! must build its appeal and adapt its business model to suit the next generation of tech-savvy consumers as well as take corporate social responsibility seriously, given how quickly negative stories spread about such issues as obesity, ill treatment of staff, overuse of packaging, questionable sourcing of food products and cultural insensitivity.

## Questions

1 Using the earlier checklist, what issues must Yum! pay particular attention to when developing its international marketing strategic plans?

2 How should the company respond to the changing nature of expectations of customers and consumer-purchasing behaviour in markets around the world?

3 What are the key marketing mix implementation challenges for Yum! Brands, including market entry, brand development, product selection, service delivery and communications issues?

4 Franchising adds additional flexibility in managing marketing strategies. What are the challenges in control, management and continuous improvement of the Yum! Brand operations when using the franchising model?

**Reference:** www.yum.com.

# DISCUSSION QUESTIONS

**1** The fundamental concerns of international marketing strategy analysis, development and implementation are to add stakeholder value and remove unnecessary costs. How can innovation in information and communications technology assist in this process of global consumer marketing?

**2** For a company providing international consultancy in the use of robotics and artificial intelligence to a

major multinational of your choice, identify the key areas for decision making in the marketing process.

**3** How might mobile computing continue to change international marketing strategies?

**4** What are the opportunities and potential pitfalls of using social media as a primary marketing approach? How can some of the problems be mitigated?

# REFERENCES

1. Belkin (2015) Setting up the WeMo Slow Cooker (Crock-Pot®). Available from www.belkin.com/uk/support-article?articleNum=101177 (accessed 10 June 2015).

2. Berns, M., Townend, A., Khayat, Z., Balagopal, B., Reeves, M., Hopkins, M.S. and Krushwitz, N. (2009) The business of sustainability, what it means to managers now. *MIT Sloan Management Review* 51(1), 20–26.

3. Boston Consulting Group (2015) The 2015 BCG e-Intensity Index. 18 November. Available from www.bcg.com/en-gb/publications/interactives/bcg-e-intensity-index.aspx (accessed 10 June 2018).

4. Chaffey, D., Mayer, R., Johnston, K. and Ellis-Chadwick, F. (2006) *Internet Marketing*. FT Prentice Hall.

5. Cisco (2014) AGT and Cisco Traffic Incident Management Solution: Improving Traffic Safety and Efficiency. Available from www.cisco.com/web/strategy/docs/agt-s-cc-city-tim-aag.pdf (accessed 10 June 2015).

6. *The Conversation* (2017) China's green planning for the world starts with infrastructure. Available from www.theconversation.com (accessed 9 June 2018).

7. *The Economist* (2018) China is rapidly developing its clean-energy technology. Available from: www.economist.com/news/special-report/21738578-there-plenty-room-international-co-operation-environment-china-rapidly (accessed 9 June 2018).

8. Economist Intelligence Unit (2012) *Hot Spots: Benchmarking Global City Competitiveness*. Commissioned by Citi Economist Intelligence Unit.

9. Egol, M., Clyde, A. and Rangan, K. (2010) The new consumer frugality. www.strategy+business.com, 15 March.

10. Fortson, D. (2018) Drone armada takes off. *The Sunday Times*, 22 April.

11. Hagiu, A. (2013) *Strategic Decisions for Multisided Platforms Magazine: Winter 2014*. Research Feature Published 19 December. MIT Slone Management Review. Available from http://sloanreview.mit.edu/article/strategic-decisions-for-multisided-platforms/ (accessed on 11 June 2015).

12. Hamill, J. and Stevenson, A. (2003) Customer-led strategic Internet marketing. In S. Hart (ed.) *Marketing Changes*. Thomson Learning.

13. Hasson, Y. (2017) Meet Jamii Africa: Microhealth insurance startup, Techstars, January 24. Available from www.techstars.com/content/accelerators/meet-jamii-africa-microhealth-insurance-startup/ (accessed 22 April 2018).

14. Hoffman, K.D. (2003) *Services Marketing in Marketing Best Practice*. Thomson Learning.

15. Kaplan, S. and Dawney, M. (2000) E-Hubs: The new B2B marketplaces. *Harvard Business Review* 78(3), 97–103.

16. Lindberg, R (2018) Robots are now everywhere, except in the productivity statistics. Available from www.bloomberg.com/news/articles/2018-04-10/robots-are-now-everywhere-except-in-the-productivity-statistics (accessed 9 June 2018).

17. Lindgren, J.H.E. (2003) *Marketing in Marketing Best Practice*. Thomson Learning.

18. Lindstrom, M. and Seybold, P. (2003) *BRAND Child*. Kogan Page.

19. Marshall, T. (2016) *Prisoners of Geography: Ten Maps That Explain Everything about the World*. Elliott and Thompson.

20. Moore, M. (2018) Palm oil lobby smears Iceland boss Richard Walker. *The Times*, 20 April.

21. Motamedi, S. and Choe, P. (2015) Smartphone information displays when reading news in Persian and English languages. *International Journal of Human-Computer Interaction* 31(6), 427–439.

22. Mulligan, G. (2015) Good prognosis: The rise of e-health in Africa. 17 March. *New African*. Available from http://newafricanmagazine.com/good-prognosis-rise-e-health-africa/ (accessed 11 June 2015).

23. Nykamp, M. (2001) *The Customer Differential*. AMACOM.

24. Ofek, E. and Wathieu, L. (2010) Are you ignoring trends that could shake up your business? *Harvard Business Review* 88(7/8), 124–131.

25. Our Africa (2015) Health. Available from www.our-africa.org/health (accessed 11 June 2015).

26. Richardson, N., James, J., & Kelley, N. (2015). *Customer-Centric Marketing: Supporting Sustainability in the Digital Age*. Kogan Page Publishers.

27. Ritter, T. and Walter, A. (2006) Matching high-tech and high-touch in supplier-customer relationships. *European Journal of Marketing* 40 (3–4), 292–310.

28. Rosling, H. (2018) *Factfulness: Ten Reasons We're Wrong About the World – And Why Things Are Better Than You Think*. Sceptre Books.

29. Sawand, A., Djahel, S., Zhang, Z. and Nait-Abdesselam, F. (2015) Toward energy-efficient and trustworthy eHealth monitoring system. *Communications China* 12(1), 46–65.

30. Snyder, D.P. (2005) Extra-Preneurship. *Futurist* 39(4), 47–53.

31. *South China Morning Post* Alibaba founder Jack Ma's 5 top tips for entrepreneurs, 22 November. Available from www.scmp.com/tech/leaders-founders/article/2121081/alibaba-founder-jack-mas-5-top-tips-entrepreneurs (accessed 22 April 2018).

32. Sweeney, M. (2018) Martin Sorrell's WPP reports worst year for growth since 2009, *The Guardian* 1 March. Available from www.theguardian.com/media/2018/mar/01/martin-sorrell-wpp-reports-worst-year-growth-since-2009 (accessed 23 April 2018).

33. Tay, V. (2018) Trouble brews on for WPP as Ford puts global creative account up for review, *Marketing*. Available at www.marketing-interactive.com/ford-global-creative-account-up-for-review-wpp-on-alert/ (accessed 23 April 2018).

34. Timmers, P. (1999) *Electronic Commerce Strategies and Models for Business to Business Trading*. Wiley.

# INTERNATIONAL MARKETING PLANNING: IMPLEMENTATION, CONTROL AND EVALUATION

## Introduction

In the previous two Directed Study Activity sections on planning, we explored the dimensions of analysis and strategy development. We now turn to the implementation of the plan through the application of the marketing mix covered in the chapters in Part III. In practice, of course, some of the content in previous chapters will be revisited because there are overlaps between strategy, development and implementation. This is especially true for B2B service organizations, where many decisions can be regarded as operational and market entry decisions are closely associated with distribution.

The starting point for implementation is planning the international marketing mix by completing the product and service plan and preparing communications, distribution and pricing plans. The marketing plan should explain how relationships with key partners can be built and managed within the supply chain, how customer relationships can be maintained and how technology can be used to facilitate the firm's international marketing plan implementation.

The success of the implementation plan is dependent on the planning ability, management capability, and motivation and effectiveness of the firm's staff. The global market environment is continuously changing, and competition from existing and new companies is intensifying. As we saw in DSA 2, organizations must critically review trends in the international market sector, identify growth areas, understand the actions of new and existing competitors and justify innovations to products and services that meet the needs of consumers. By continually researching and investigating these areas, businesses can compete successfully on an international basis – no matter

what challenges are faced. In the implementation stage, this means being able to quickly assess situations, develop innovative solutions, make strategic decisions when necessary and implement new plans.

Therefore, the management team(s) need to anticipate and plan for potential problems that might arise in managing the implementation stage. Of course, these problems may well originate in topics that were considered in the first two parts of this textbook. It is also necessary to establish appropriate performance standards and/or measurement techniques that can be used to maintain control over the marketing plan and the evaluation that will enable corrective action should the firm's performance deviate from the plan (as it surely will).

In this activity the focus is on developing the skills of decision making for a large international business; however, the principles are the same for small localized business units.

## Learning objectives

On completing this activity, you should be able to:

- Appreciate the opportunities for growth in an international business sector and how the external environment will influence strategic decisions
- Use appropriate concepts and an analysis of market factors to develop marketing mix implementation strategies
- Appreciate the benefits of developing better customer relationship management
- Identify methods to manage and control the business

# ISS World: servicing the world

**The scenario:** In the early days ISS World was made up of just 20 night-watchmen who provided security services for local businesses. At that time the company was named Copenhagen-Frederiksberg Night Watch (Kjøbenhavn-Frederiksberg Nattevagt). In 1934, Director Sørensen spotted an opportunity by observing that the night-watch team finished their security services at 4 a.m. and left the building, but employees did not arrive at the building until 8 a.m. During those four hours, he mused, would be the perfect time for security staff to clean the premises while keeping the building safe at the same time. This idea took off, and the Danish Cleaning Company (Det Danske Rengøringsselskab) was founded. The Danish Cleaning Company became known as a cleaning services company that provided a professional service for local businesses to provide improved spaces for employees to work in and customers to visit. Danish Cleaning Company grew and soon overtook security services regarding revenue and began to make handsome profits. Through identifying other opportunities, entering new overseas markets and building their portfolio through acquisitions, the Danish Cleaning Company changed its name to ISS. Today ISS World still has its head office in Denmark but now operates in 74 countries around the world and has offices in 46 of those countries. It does business in other countries such as Bulgaria, Kazakhstan, Nigeria and Vietnam where it does not have offices. Every employee of ISS World knows the company's vision, which is 'We are going to be the world's greatest service organisation'.

ISS World has developed over the years. It now wants to provide the world's greatest Cleaning Services (internal, external and technical) and Security Services (guarding, surveillance, security and safety). It also wants to be the greatest outsourcing company in four other areas, namely:

1   **Catering services** that include contract catering, vending services and catering at events.

2   **Property services** that include maintenance of a business's property and external surroundings. Additionally, ISS offers advice and guides environmental and energy solutions to provide safe workspaces.

3   **Support services** by providing reception staff, mail handling and call centre operators.

4   **Facility management services** to ensure that there is a productive environment that integrates people with processes and technology to provide a smooth end-to-end service.

Despite growth in all service areas, cleaning services provide ISS World with a substantial revenue stream.

Revenue by service demonstrates that around 50% of revenue comes from cleaning functions, 20% from property, 14% from catering services, 7% from support services, 7% from security services and 3% from facility management. The story is the same across ISS World's international portfolio, with cleaning services accounting for 53% of revenue in Continental Europe, 42% in Northern Europe, 51% in Asia and Pacific and 45% from the Americas.

It is interesting to see that contract cleaning services are the highest revenue earner for a multinational company such as ISS World, because people often think cleaning services are provided by unprofessional, poorly managed, small local operators that employ unskilled, part-time, casual, low-paid, unmotivated staff. ISS World is proof that cleaning services can be professional, profitable and have highly motivated employees.

## Market environment changes

ISS World has grown from strength to strength by identifying opportunities resulting from the changes in the macro- and micro-environment. ISS spotted opportunities to rejuvenate and restructure the cleaning business. ISS multiplied its business on the back of a move by both the private and public sectors, which began outsourcing support services and facilities management. Recently, ISS World bid and won a contract for Victorian State Government, Australia. Victorian State Government saw ISS World's track record with other large universities and educational institutions and appointed ISS to provide cleaning services to 214 schools in Western and North Eastern Melbourne. Not only that, but ISS are also providing cleaning services, support services and facilities management for Deutsche Telekom, Germany (launch date 4th quarter 2019). The contract with Deutsche Telekom is the single biggest contract in ISS World's history.

As stated earlier in this text the trend to outsource is growing, and because ISS is a world-class, high-quality, reliable and transparent service company its business is increasing in many areas because of the changing aspirations and needs of banks, hotels, event arenas, schools, hospitals and parks.

## The ISS competitive advantage and strategy

The continued growth of ISS World is partly due to its expertise in contract tendering and project management, but the key to its success is due to its investment in the workforce. ISS World invests heavily in the training of all staff, illustrated by the launch of its Leadership Competency Framework, the roll-out of its Key Account Manager Certification and the Service with a Human Touch training. ISS World prides itself on providing around 7 million hours of training per year for its workforce, not just to managers but to all staff to maintain quality, avoid accidents, improve their health and safety standards culture, maintain and develop relationships with business customers and ensure the most cost-effective processes are implemented. On top of that ISS likes to promote from within: moving people from the 'shop floor' to management positions. Along the way from the 'shop floor' to management positions, ISS appoints team leaders who have responsibility for profit and performance of individual cleaning contracts for large businesses as well as for small- and medium-sized enterprises. Not only does the team leader manage the profit and performance of the contract, they are also trained on how to motivate their local team. The local team, always made up of two or three people, no matter how small the contract, is called the 'Hit Squad'. Each member of the 'Hit Squad' is trained on cleaning and teamwork.

As shown in Chapter 1, more and more businesses want to play their part in being sustainable in markets in which they are operating. ISS World is no exception. Internally it cares for its workforce by creating a sense of purpose for all employees, building leadership capabilities, championing an equality and diversity agenda, and retaining staff through its corporate ethos. Similarly, it is striving to reduce its carbon footprint. Its commitment is illustrated at the offices of ISS Germany where the team's 'New Ways of Working' mantra means working in less space, using less energy, which means less resource consumption. Businesses who are also active in caring for the environment and reducing their carbon footprint will choose outsourcing businesses such as ISS World, because they have similar environmental values. By having a green/environmentally friendly culture, ISS has a competitive advantage over outsourcing businesses that do not.

## Growth strategies

ISS World sees growth opportunities in all regions of the world. These growth aspirations can be justified because the firm is offering a more innovative approach to cleaning at the service delivery level. It is a professional operator with considerable resources and can handle large complex contracts that will maintain standards and control across borders and cultures. ISS's business growth comes partly from winning new contracts such as Victorian State Government, Australia and Deutsche Telekom,

and from natural organic growth and repeat business. As with many organizations, once ISS World had reached saturation point in Denmark, it moved beyond the home market to the international market.

## Implementation

The critical factor for success for ISS – the main subject of your task – is developing an international marketing strategy. The solution is to recognize that success in international services starts by achieving excellent relationships at all levels throughout the business.

ISS strives to ensure the entire workforce provides a professional service from the board room to every employee at the local level in every country. It recognizes that each interaction between the cleaner, receptionist, call centre worker, security guard and maintenance personnel and its customers is vital to success. ISS calls the interaction between ISS personnel and its customers Touchpoints@ISS. Take, as an example, a fictitious customer journey through ISS World's Touchpoints@ISS, using a bank as their business customer. The first Touch Point occurs when a visitor arrives at the bank's head office. ISS World's Property Service will have ensured the visitor encounters a building and surrounding areas that are well maintained. TouchPoints@ISS two occurs when the visitor moves into the bank's head office and is greeted by ISS World security guards who guide them to the reception area where ISS Support staff meet them. During the day, the visitor encounters many TouchPoints@ISS: they may use vending machines and/or take lunch in the bank's restaurant; both facilities are operated through ISS World Catering Services. Throughout the day the visitor will enjoy a fresh, sanitary, orderly and welcoming environment, be that in the lobby, the lift, within toilet facilities or conference rooms, again serviced by ISS World's highest revenue by service – cleaning.

Employees or visitors in business premises may not wish to engage specifically with the maintenance, cleaning or reception staff; however, successful contact at each TouchPoints@ISS is essential. Therefore, successful delivery of the services is arguably more important than offering low prices for a service.

## Relationships

ISS World endeavours to form strong and lasting relationships with all businesses with which it has service contracts. New B2B relationships are with Bombardier and John Crane in North America, Royal Mail and Hitachi Rail in the United Kingdom, Heineken in the Netherlands and Jakarta Airport in Indonesia. B2B relationship management is vital as customers are often reluctant to change a service provider without good reason. B2B outsourcing contracts tend to last for three to five years. If the service provider delivers reliable, good service and the business receiving the service pays on time, then a good relationship is established. Good relationships lead to contacts being renewed. Clearly, Barclays Bank was impressed with the services ISS provided as it has recently announced a five-year extension to the partnership it has with ISS World. However, if there are complaints, the contract would be terminated very quickly and that news would spread rapidly through the industry damaging a business's reputation.

Excellent techniques, management systems and human resource processes are essential for dealing with people. However, B2B service expectations and service delivery, like B2C service expectations, are affected very much by cultural considerations. So this is often an important consideration in maintaining service delivery consistency.

One of the primary considerations in effective implementation and growth for ISS World is to acquire an existing business and with that the people that are currently employed or forming new partnerships. Either way ISS must understand the employment rights, health and safety laws and other legislation specific to the local country. Moreover, they often have to manage the different working conditions applied by different companies and the different cultures associated with each country. Take, for example, ISS forming a new relationship to supply catering for a major business's workforce. ISS World will research the cultural associations related to food. It will investigate the types of food the workforce eats, whether they prefer light or heavy meals during work hours, whether they take time over their meals or prefer 'grab and go' services. Further, ISS World will investigate which meats and fish are popular and if veganism is on the rise. Like all businesses, ISS espouses that a healthy workforce is a productive workforce, and so ISS takes great care in designing country and culture-specific foods whenever they form a new, or renew, a catering contract with a business, wherever they are in the world.

Finally, the monitoring and control of a sizeable people-based service industry are critical, as ISS has found to its cost. Failure to monitor and control its operations can lead to disastrous consequences. It was in the back office that problems occurred in ISS. In the mid-1990s poor control in the USA failed to spot accounting errors and this almost drove the firm into bankruptcy. ISS learnt from that and now aspires to be GREAT – yes in capital letters. To be GREAT, ISS states that it empowers people through great leadership and makes employees proud to work at ISS. It also ensures that its business model

is purposeful to guarantee customers (other businesses) receive a great experience, and, most importantly, it strives for excellence to be ahead of its competitors.

## References

ISS World (2017) *Corporate Responsibility Report 2017* www.responsibility.issworld.com/report2017/; ISS World (2017) *Group Annual Report* www.annualreport.issworld.com/2017/?page=2; ISS World (2018) www.issworld.com/; ISS World (2018) How ISS creates personalised food experiences www.youtube.com/channel/UCi_AhtsjNAqiNWyFlBBo_aA.

## The task

1   Critically evaluate the global marketing implementation strategy of ISS World paying particular attention to the changing nature of B2B buying by large domestic and global clients.

2   Choose one region of the world, and one of the services that ISS supplies, and develop a marketing strategy in outline. Focus on the external environment and the marketing mix implementation issues, including an assessment of the key brand, product, service and communications issues. Identify, too, the factors that will influence pricing.

3   Develop a relationship marketing approach that will build necessary partnerships with key customers and stakeholders to obtain long-term business.

4   Prepare a plan for the control, management and continuous improvement of the operations, including the organization structure, measures and processes that are required to achieve sustained success.

## Getting started

This section focuses on the B2B sector and a service business as well. You should use this case study not only to focus on the implementation issues of the strategy process but also to study in greater depth the particular issues involved in the B2B sector. ISS World provides cleaning services, security services, catering services, property services, support services and facility management services.

Clearly, the effective marketing of a people-based business requires an understanding of staff motivation and management, service expectations, customer relationship building and the cultural issues that underpin much of this.

Task 1 requires an analysis of the factors that have led to the growth in outsourcing in international markets, particularly in emerging markets over recent years and of the factors that will determine the nature of B2B outsourcing purchases in the future – and consequently how important relationship building with global customers will be in the future. By now you should have a good understanding of how you can access and analyze research material from libraries and online sources to complete this task. There is a huge amount of information and comment about ISS, outsourcing and ISS competitors (namely Ecolab Inc, Interserve plc, Lassila & Tikanoja plc, Rentokil Initial plc, ServiceMaster Global Holdings, Inc.) in the literature and business press to help you complete Tasks 2 and 3, but you must also include your own creative approaches. You require an understanding of the sector and how it differs in the markets around the world.

Customer satisfaction is dependent on the customers' perception of the brand but also the suitability of the product that understands the workforce, culture of the country and service expectations. Consequently, setting realistic customer expectations, motivating and training an international workforce, managing the supply chain effectively, providing quality services and managing a cost-effective business are all critical for success. Task 3 requires you to think about how you would organize and manage this on a global basis.

In completing the tasks you need to consider the issues highlighted in the following framework and shown in Table I.

## The way forward

Strategy development and planning is a continuous process. Having completed the tasks in this section, you will have gained a better understanding of the B2B market and the perceived value that the relationship between businesses is. You should now be well informed to revisit the strategy development process.

## Table I Key factors to consider in evaluating the implementation of the strategy

| The element of the plan | Some concepts, models and issues to be addressed |
| --- | --- |
| Environmental analysis | • Identify the global trends that have provided the opportunity for growth in the sector<br>• Analyze the nature of customer needs and the nature of competition in the sector<br>• Evaluate the firm's strategy and its regional focus |
| Marketing mix | • Building the corporate identity and managing the brand<br>• Product differentiation and the three service Ps<br>• Communication with business customers and other stakeholders<br>• Managing the delivery to achieve customer satisfaction<br>• Managing cost and the pricing strategy<br>• The use of technology |
| Relationship marketing | • The methods of identifying current and potentially high-value customers<br>• Knowledge and database management<br>• Customer relationship management |
| Control and management | • The organization and management structure using the 7S framework<br>• Internal communications with its own staff<br>• Financial and marketing measures and controls<br>• Performance management and improvement processes, including benchmarking, balanced scorecard and self-assessment and improvement<br>• Technology-enabled systems |

You should return to the Part I planning framework to review the current market environment for ISS as the basis for its ongoing strategy. The most important issue is to decide where and how the firm can further build its strong global position, using an assessment of the market environment, business customer demands and competitor activity. Given the fast growth of the outsourcing sector, you should review the firm's ambitions particularly in developing markets. You should then focus on the market factors in these countries and use the market information and research framework to identify further growth opportunities. You should also consider its more traditional markets: cleaning services as well as newer markets, such as contract catering, to assess the opportunities to increase market share. Finally, you might reassess the company's capability and expertise that will be expected to underpin its continued expansion.

You should review the firm's apparent vision and objectives from the material that is contained on its website from which you can re-evaluate and restate the firm's competitive advantage and assess how this informs the international positioning of ISS. Using the recent data available online you should assess the market entry methods used and the effectiveness of these methods in delivering the strategy.

## Checklist for success

Having completed the directed study activities you should think about how comprehensive your work is and whether you really have addressed the fundamental issues that could well make the difference between a failing and a successful strategy. To help you do this we have identified some of the issues you should consider. Clearly, you may not be able to answer these in detail because you will not have sufficient detail about the firm's operations, but you should have thought about how you would address the issues given access to the information.

Does the plan contain:

- Assumptions about the world economy and the environmental trends in the principal markets?
- Details of historical performance (sales, costs, profitability)?
- Forecasts of future performance based on (a) an extrapolation of the past, (b) alternative scenarios?
- Identified opportunities and threats?
- An analysis of the company strengths, weaknesses and future capabilities in comparison with the local and international competition?
- Long-term aims and objectives and the strategies to achieve them?
- One-year marketing objectives and individual strategies (for example, budgets, brand objectives and development of personnel)?
- Country-by-country forecasts and targets?
- Country-by-country plans for all marketing activities and coordination with other functions (for example, supply chain management)?
- An explanation of how country plans will be integrated regionally or globally if appropriate? It might be useful to comment on the current structure of the company.
- A summary of the critical factors for success?
- An assessment of the likely competitor response? If your objective is to increase market share in some markets, your competitors will not simply lie down and let you take their business without fighting back!
- A contingency component for when the unexpected happens and things do not go to plan?
- A control process for feedback, evaluation and taking corrective action?

# GLOSSARY

**7S framework**  Framework devised by consultants McKinsey & Co for analyzing how well the organization is positioned to deliver its objectives

**Acquisition**  A market entry strategy in which the firm invests in assets outside the home country

**Adaptation**  Flexible approach to marketing that aims to vary the marketing mix programmes to meet the local conditions in each country market

**Asian Free Trade Area (AFTA)**  As of 2015 the ASEAN members are Brunei Darussalam, Cambodia, Indonesia, Lao PDR, Malaysia, Myanmar, Philippines, Singapore, Thailand and Vietnam

**Association of South East Asian Nations (ASEAN)**  A free trade area of 580 million across Thailand, Indonesia, Singapore, Brunei, Malaysia, the Philippines, Vietnam, Myanmar, Cambodia and Laos

**Attitude**  A complex mental state involving beliefs and feelings and values and dispositions to act in certain ways

**Balance of payments**  A system of recording all of a country's economic transactions with the rest of the world over a period of one year

**Barrier to entry**  Real or perceived reason why a firm might be prevented from marketing its products and services in a new market

**Beliefs**  The psychological state in which an individual holds a proposition or premise to be true

**Born global**  A business who, from the very start, chooses its target market and sales outputs to be in several countries; most often with a drive to grow internationally, as opposed to expanding in its home market

**Brand piracy**  Naming a product in such a way that it confuses customers, or enables the pirate firm to sell forgeries and fake products

**Branding strategies**  The alternative approaches to applying names (or brands) to a product and groups of products to achieve the desired positioning

**Build to order**  When a product is scheduled and built in response to a specification and confirmed order received from a final customer

**Business-to-business marketing**  Marketing products and services to other organizations

**Business-to consumer-marketing**  Marketing products and services to people who will consume them

**Buyer–seller relationships**  Collective term for the categories of relationship between a buyer and seller. These can be categorized into transactional relationships, collaborative relationships, alliances and reciprocal relationships

**Category management**  Category management is a retailing concept in which the total range of products sold by a retailer is broken down into discrete groups of similar or related products; these groups are known as product categories

**Communications adaptation**  Marketing communication strategies that are flexible, allowing variation in the use of the mix between countries to meet local conditions

**Communications mix**  Often used interchangeably with promotions mix, the communications mix implies a broader range of uses of offline and online interactive tools

**Communications tools**  The range of tools a marketer can use, including personal selling, advertising, sales promotion, public relations, sponsorship and online media

**Comparative advantage**  The advantage a nation has by being able to produce products or services more efficiently and at lower cost than a competitor nation

**Comparative research**  Comparative research is a research methodology in the social sciences that aims to make comparisons across different countries or cultures

**Competitive advantage**  Competitive advantage is something which organizations provide to consumers to make them seem more interesting, better value for money, more engaged on social media or provide better offers than their competitors

**Consumer behaviour**  The behaviour of individuals when buying goods and services for their own use or for private consumption

**Contract manufacture**  Arrangement in which a subcontractor undertakes manufacturing (or service provision) under licence

**Control**  The management responsibility for measuring performance and taking corrective action when deviation from the standards set occurs, so that the goals of the organization are achieved

**Corporate identity**  The corporate personality demonstrated in branding and other communications to reflect the values and culture of the organization

**Countertrade**  Exchanging goods or services which are paid for, in whole or part, with other goods or services, rather than with money

**Country of origin effect**  The perceptions and attitudes that exist towards the products or brands on the basis of their country of origin, design or manufacture

**Cross-cultural**  Dealing with or comparing two or more cultures

**Cross-cultural research**  The conducting of a research project across a number of nations or culture groupings

**Cultural identity**  Cultural identity is the identity of a group or culture, or of an individual, as far as one is influenced by one's belonging to a group or culture

**Cultural paradoxes** A term used to describe the cultural sensitivities in a market where there is evidence both of the westernization of tastes and the assertion of ethnic, religious and cultural differences

**Cultural sensitivity** Cultural sensitivity is the quality of being aware and accepting of other cultures. This is important because what seems acceptable in some countries can be rude or derogatory in others

**Customer relationship management (CRM)** The process of storing and analyzing data relating to customers, to enable the organization to serve their needs efficiently and effectively

**Customer-led** Adopting marketing approaches that primarily focus on the needs and expectations of customers

**Customs** The overt forms of behaviour and significant events which symbolize the particularistic characteristics of a particular culture

**Data mining** A technique for searching large-scale databases for patterns; used mainly to find previously unknown correlations between variables that may be commercially useful

**Differentiated marketing** Strategy whereby a company attempts to appeal to two or more clearly defined market segments with a specific product and unique marketing strategy tailored to each separate segment

**Direct channels** Distribution channel in which a producer supplies or serves directly an ultimate user

**Direct marketing** Online or offline communication with potential consumers or business customers designed to generate a response, such as an order or request for more information

**Distribution channel structures** Path or 'pipeline' through which goods and services flow from vendor to consumer. A distribution channel may include several interconnected intermediaries such as wholesalers, distributors, agents, retailers

**Distributors** Firms that buy and stock products from a manufacturer before adding a margin and selling them to the final customers

**Doha Round** Commenced 2001, the name given to the current negotiations being undertaken by members of the WTO who are attempting to liberalize trading rules in a number of areas, including agricultural subsidies, textiles and clothing, services, technical barriers to trade, trade-related investments and rules of origin

**Domestic purchasing** International trade in which a foreign firm approaches a non-exporter, buys the product 'at the factory gate' and takes the responsibility for all aspects of exporting, without involvement from the seller

**Domestically delivered or developed niche services** Services that are marketed to international customers but delivered in the home country

**Dumping** When a manufacturer in one country exports a product to another country at a price which is either below the price it charges in its home market or is below its costs of production

**e-commerce** The exchange of goods, services and cash using the Internet

**Economic and Monetary Union** The creation of a single currency bloc within the European Union which began on 1 January 1999

**Economies of scale** Unit cost reductions which result from increasing total output

**Effective consumer response** Supply chain partnerships which work together towards making the retail sector more responsive to consumer demand and promote the removal of unnecessary costs from the supply chain

**Elastic demand** Demand for a product that changes substantially in response to small changes in price; when demand is elastic, a small decrease in price may substantially increase total revenues

**Electronic commerce** Exchange of goods and services using the Internet or other online network

**Electronic data interchange (EDI)** refers to the structured transmission of data between organizations by electronic means. It is used to transfer electronic documents from one computer system to another, i.e. from one trading partner to another trading partner

**Emerging economies** Emerging markets are nations with social or business activity in the process of rapid growth and industrialization

**Enabling technologies** The use of a variety of largely integrated technologies that facilitate fast and effective international marketing processes

**Enculturation** Enculturation is the process by which a person learns the requirements of the culture by which he or she is surrounded

**e-procurement** The use of the Internet or other online services to manage the purchasing and delivery of services and products

**Ethical challenges** Challenge of setting the ethical values in international marketing strategies and then driving those through long distribution channels across geographical markets with different ethical values

**Ethnocentric** Centred on a specific ethnic group, usually one's own

**European Union** An international organization of European countries formed after the Second World War to reduce trade barriers and increase cooperation among its members

**Eurozone** The eurozone, officially the euro area, is an economic and monetary union (EMU) of 19 European Union (EU) member states which have adopted the euro currency as their sole legal tender

**Exabyte** A measure of data storage space that is equivalent to about one billion gigabytes

**Exchange rate** Rate of exchange: the charge for exchanging currency of one country for currency of another

**Exchange Rate Mechanism (ERM)** The ERM was a system introduced by the European Community in March 1979, as part of the European Monetary System (EMS), to reduce exchange rate variability and achieve monetary stability in Europe, in preparation for economic and monetary union

**Exchange rate risk** The potential to lose money because of a change in the exchange rate

**Existing markets** Product/service markets where customers' demands are served from a number of suppliers and the infrastructure to support the market is established

**Export administration** The management of the processes that allow an export transaction to take place

**Export houses (also export management companies)** Specialist firms that act as the export department for a range of companies and take on the role and responsibilities that would normally be done by those companies

**Export marketing** Marketing of goods and/or services across national/political boundaries

**Export processing zone** Designated area or region where firms can import duty-free as long as the imports are used as inputs into the production of exports

**Exporting** Selling abroad products produced in the home country, typically without significant adaptation to foreign market needs

**Failures of communications** When the recipient does not receive the marketing messages as intended

**Fixed production cost** Costs of production that are fixed and unrelated to the volume of production

**Foreign currency** Any currency that is in use in a foreign country, but not in one's own

**Foreign market channels** Channels of distribution within countries outside a firm's domestic operations

**Franchising** A contractual arrangement whereby a parent company (the franchisor) allows another firm (the franchisee) to operate a business that it has developed in return for a fee, provided that it adheres to the stated policies and practices

**Function-specific hubs** Electronic marketplaces where buyers and sellers meet using the Internet to trade in business services, such as HR services or business process management

**Generic marketing strategies** Marketing strategies that can be applied to all market contexts, based on segmentation, targeting and positioning and underpinned by Porter's generic growth strategies (cost leadership, focus and differentiation)

**Geocentric** Having the earth as the centre

**Gigabyte** A measure of data storage space or disk space that is equivalent to about 1000 megabytes

**Global appeal** The attraction of certain products and services to a global customer segment

**Global brand** A brand that has a similar name, similar distinctive image and positioning around the world

**Global marketing** The process of conceptualizing and then conveying a final product or service worldwide with the hopes of reaching the international marketing community

**Global presence** Ensuring that the company has assets and operations located in all (major) country markets

**Global reach** The ability of the marketing efforts of the firm to connect with customers around the world, where appropriate using third parties

**Global segments** Through research and analysis global segments can be identified into homogeneous entities that are categorized by psychographic and behavioural similarities

**Global sourcing** The process of arranging goods and services to be supplied irrespective of geographic location

**Global System of Trade Preferences among developing countries (GSTP)** A trade agreement established in 1988 to encourage and increase trade with and between developing nations. The trade agreement is supported by the United Nations

**Global youth culture** Contemporary 15–24-year-olds combining local and international culture and identities through technology and social media

**Globalization** The process of progressing towards trading in all major regions and most country markets

**Grey marketing** The trade of a commodity through distribution channels which, while legal, are unofficial, unauthorized or unintended by the original manufacturer

**Gross national income** National income plus capital consumption allowance

**Gross national income per capita** The GNI per capita is the gross national income divided by the country's population, thus becoming the GNI per person living in the country

**Hard currency** A currency that is not likely to depreciate suddenly in value

**Heterogeneity** Because services are delivered and received by individual people the concept suggests that each interaction will be unique

**High context cultures** Cultures in which the context is at least as important as what is actually said

**Incipient markets** Markets where economic conditions suggest a market may develop but the market as yet does not exist

**Indirect channels** The selling and distribution of products to customers through intermediaries such as wholesalers, distributors, agents, dealers or retailers

**Indirect exporting** Market entry methods in which firms commit few resources to international marketing and largely rely on third parties to build their international business

**Individualism** The moral stance, political philosophy, ideology or social outlook that stresses the moral worth of the individual

**Industry-specific hubs** Electronic market places where buyers and sellers meet using the Internet to trade components and services required in particular industries, such as aerospace manufacture

**Inelastic demand** The demand that exists when price changes do not result in significant changes in the quantity of a product demanded

**Information technology** The organization's management process for creating, storing, exchanging and using information

**Inseparability** In services marketing, the service is created, delivered and consumed at the same point whereas in product marketing there is usually separation between manufacture and consumption

**Intangibility** Whereas products are physical entities, services are characterized by being intangible – they cannot be touched, smelled or seen

**Integrated supply chain** The optimization and control of the supply chain network of suppliers, factories, warehouses, distribution centres and retailers through which materials are acquired, transformed and delivered to the customer

**Interactive customer marketing** Ability to address an individual and the ability to gather and remember the response of that individual leading to the ability to address the individual once more in a way that takes into account his or her unique response

**Interactive shopping** Allows the consumer to play an active role in the selection and customization of his/her order

**Internal cost structures** Cost elements that correspond to the specific internal operations of a company

**International branding** A brand that is known in a region of the world or in a cluster of countries

**International Development Association (IDA)** An agency of the United Nations affiliated with the World Bank

**International manager** A member of staff with the responsibility of managing across country borders

**International marketing** The process of planning and conducting transactions across national borders to create exchanges that satisfy the objectives of individuals and organizations

**International Monetary Fund** A United Nations agency to promote trade by increasing the exchange stability of the major currencies

**International niche marketing** Marketing a differentiated product or service to different countries, usually to a single customer segment (a group of customers with a distinctive, common characteristic)

**International product life cycle** A concept that enables the firm to describe the stages (introduction, growth, maturity, decline) that its product portfolio has attained in different country markets

**International product offer** The bundle of benefits for international customers that are presented in the total product 'package'

**International product portfolio** The firm's chosen range of products and services that provide a complete and satisfactory offer to customers

**International trade** International trade is the exchange of capital, goods and services across international borders or territories. It refers to exports of goods and services by a firm to a foreign-based buyer (importer). In most countries, it represents a significant share of gross domestic product

**Internationalization** Pursuit of market opportunities outside the home country

**Internet** The network of computers that enable digital files, such as emails, to be sent

**Joint ventures** A market entry approach whereby two or more companies share ownership of a newly created firm

**Knowledge management** Strategies and practices used by organizations to identify, share and enable adoption of the insights and experiences that constitute knowledge

**Latent markets** A group of people who have been identified as potential consumers of a product that does not yet exist

**Learning curve** A learning curve is a line graph displaying opportunities across the x-axis and a measure of performance along the y-axis

**Least developed economies** The name given to countries which, according to the United Nations, exhibit the lowest indicators of socio-economic development, with the lowest human development index ratings of all countries in the world

**Legislation** The legal framework enacted by governing bodies that determines how business can be carried out. The Internet is subject to the laws of many governing bodies

**Licensing** A market entry strategy in which a firm makes assets, such as an image or know-how, available to another firm in exchange for royalties

**Logistics** The management of the flow of goods, information and other resources, including energy and people, between the point of origin and the point of consumption in order to meet the requirements of consumers

**Logistics or distribution strategy** Management's plan for moving products to intermediaries and final customers

**Low context cultures** Are those where people are more psychologically distant so that information needs to be explicit if members are to understand it

**Management contracts** Service projects undertaken by partner firms in conjunction with a supplier, typically of major infrastructure installations

**Marginal cost pricing** The outcome of perfectly competitive markets in which the price of each good is equal to its marginal cost

**Marginal costing** An accounting technique whereby the effect on costs of a small increment or decrease in output may be estimated. Assuming that the change in output does not affect the elements comprising fixed costs, the marginal cost will be the variable cost per unit of output

**Market access** The opportunity for firms to enter sectors from which they were previously barred

**Market concentrators** Typically smaller firms that focus their internationalization on a small number of geographic markets

**Market entry** The approach that a firm uses to pursue market opportunities outside its home market

**Market expanders** Typically larger firms that focus their internationalization on a large number of geographic markets

**Market involvement** The degree to which a firm commits resources to a specific market, enabling it to directly control its marketing activities, rather than rely on third parties

**Market-orientated pricing** Determining the initial price of a product by comparison with competitors' prices

**Market profile analysis** An analysis that draws a marketing profile of a country

**Market segmentation** A market segment is a sub-set of a market made up of people or organizations sharing one or more characteristics that cause them to demand similar products and/ or services based on qualities of those products, such as price or function

**Marketing information** A system in which marketing information is formally gathered, stored, analyzed and distributed to managers in accordance with their informational needs on a regular basis

**Marketing research** Research that gathers and analyzes information about the moving of goods or services from producer to consumer

**Mass customization** The use of flexible computer-aided manufacturing systems to produce custom output

**Mass customize** The use of flexible computer-aided manufacturing and service systems to produce output that is designed to meet the individual requirements of the customer

**Mercosur** Regional common southern market integrated by the full members Argentina, Brazil, Paraguay, Uruguay and Venezuela (Venezuela suspended in 2016)

**Micro-multinationals** Small- to medium-sized companies that invest time and effort in a constellation of different countries; enabled through the technological advances of the twenty-first century

**Movement of services** Businesses often employ other businesses to supply services. Traditionally, many service businesses had high street outlets or offices in business parks. More recently many organizations can provide their services online. Therefore, not only are businesses selling products online; there is also a movement of services online

**Multi-country study** A market research study that is carried out across a number of countries

**Multinational enterprise (MNE)** An international or transnational enterprise which has productive capacity in several countries

**Multimedia technology** The knowledge and use of tools, techniques, systems or methods of organization of media and/ or content that use a combination of different content forms

**Network** A collection of individuals that are willing to share information

**New product development (NPD)** The process of ensuring that new products and services are created to meet changing customer needs and replace those that are no longer satisfactory

**Next Eleven** The Next Eleven (or N11) are 11 countries identified as having the potential to become among the world's largest economies in the twenty-first century

**Non-tariff barriers** Trade barriers that restrict imports but are not in the usual form of a tariff

**Non-verbal communication** Gestures, body language, facial expression, sign language are all ways of communicating without the spoken word

**North American Free Trade Area (NAFTA)** Formed between Canada, Mexico and the USA

**Omnibus studies** An omnibus study is completed via a quantitative survey. The questions in the survey are provided by different companies, and the questions are often about different products and/or services

**Omnibus surveys** A survey covering a number of topics, usually for different clients. The samples tend to be nationally representative and composed of types of people for which there is a general demand

**Online auction** Participants are able to bid to purchase products and services using the Internet

**Online databases** An electronic collection of information

**Open market** A competitive market where buyers and sellers can operate without restrictions

**Organization structure** Explanation of how tasks are allocated, activities coordinated and staff supervised in the delivery of the organization's strategy

**Outsource** Obtaining supplies or services from another firm (typically in a lower cost country), rather than carrying out the work within the firm

**Pareto Law** Also known as the 80–20 rule, states that for many events, 80 per cent of the effects come from 20 per cent of the causes. In marketing, 80 per cent of the sales often come from 20 per cent of the customers

**Perception of risk** The subjective judgement that people make about the characteristics and severity of a risk

**Perishability** Services cannot be stored and, hence, if an opportunity for a sale is missed, then it is lost for ever

**Physical movement** Businesses often physically move their products, including physical movement of products from factories to warehouses or from warehouses to high-street stores

**Piggybacking** A market entry approach based on riding on the back of an already successful international marketer by persuading the firm to carry non-competing products

**Piracy** A contemporary security concern for shipping; annual cargo crime losses are estimated at US$30–50 billion internationally

**Polycentric** Having many centres, especially centres of authority or control

**Price coordination** The attempt to coordinate prices across dispersed geographical markets with the objective of achieving a consistent pricing policy across those markets

**Price standardization** Setting a standard, identical price in all markets, regardless of whether they are foreign or domestic

**Price transparency** The accessibility of information on the order flow for a particular stock, allowing knowledge of the quantities of stock being offered and the bids at the various price levels

**Primary data** Data observed or collected directly from first-hand experience

**Product and service differentiation** The process of distinguishing a product or service offering from competitive offerings to make it more attractive to a particular target market

**Product strategies** The approach adopted to selection and positioning of products and services, and the marketing support provided to satisfy customer needs

**Production costs** The cost-of-production theory of value is the theory that the price of an object or condition is determined by the sum of the cost of the resources that went into making it. The cost can compose any of the factors of production (including labour, capital or land) and taxation

**Promotional mix** The mix of communications tools used to persuade customers to buy and use products or services

**Pull strategy** Pull strategies involve promoting the product or service to the intended consumer, who will demand supplies from the intermediaries

**Purchasing power parity (PPP)** The situation where the exchange rate between two currencies represents the difference between the price levels in the two countries

**Push strategy** Push strategies involve promoting the product or service to intermediaries, who will then promote them to the final consumers

**Qualitative research** A set of research techniques in which data is obtained from a relatively small group of respondents and is not analyzed with statistical techniques

**Reciprocal trading** Trading in which the supplier also purchases products or services from the customer

**Relationship marketing** The creation of mutually beneficial long-term value through building customer relationships rather than relying on converting customers through advertising and sales promotions

**Research process** The ordered set of activities focused on the systematic collection of information using accepted methods of analysis as a basis for drawing conclusions and making recommendations

**Research question** Formed by researchers around which they centre their research project. Research questions are written after researchers have gathered sufficient secondary information to understand a subject area, what is already known about that subject area and how they would like to investigate the subject area further

**Risk and control** The necessary balance to be struck in entering new markets, which involves accepting risk of failure, set against committing sufficient resource in an attempt to exert control in the market and 'guarantee' success

**Secondary data** Data collected and recorded by another

**Self-reference criterion** The assumption that a product can successfully be sold abroad on the basis of its success in the home market

**Services** Intangible, largely experience-based economic activity

**Silent language** Non-verbal signals in a communication

**Single European Market** The complete integration of the economies of member states of the European Union

**Small- and medium-sized enterprises** Small (typically up to 50 employees) and medium (50 to 250 employees) firms that have a different approach and mindset to large multinational organizations

**Social and cultural factors** Customs, lifestyles and values that characterize society

**Social customer relationship management (SCRM)** A way of collecting data about a consumer based on their interactions with the brand on and offline, engagement in social media conversations and through purchasing records (online and high street). The data collected, when linked with customer relationship management (CRM) systems, will provide insight into customer profiles and behaviours which will be analyzed and improvements made to quality to enhance customer engagement

**Spoken language** Spoken language is a form of communication in which words are derived from a large vocabulary

**Stages of internationalization** An international marketing concept in which firms progress through a series of steps as they develop from a domestic to a global company. Each step has distinctive characteristics

**Standardization** Approach to marketing that aims to reduce marketing mix variation between countries and regions of the world

**Standardization of international marketing communications** Where possible, reducing variation in the use of the communications mix between different countries and regions

**Strategic alliance** A contractual arrangement whereby two or more firms form a partnership to exploit a market opportunity together, so that they reduce risk

**Supply chain** A group of firms that undertake support activities in the manufacture and supply of materials and components, conversion into finished goods and making them available to buyers

**Supply chain management** The management of a group of firms that contribute to the development, manufacture and delivery of a final product to maximize efficiency and effectiveness

**Tariff barriers** A government tax on imports or exports

**Terabyte** A measure of data storage space or disk space that is equivalent to about 1000 gigabytes

**Total distribution cost** The total cost incurred by an exporter in the distribution of merchandise internationally including transport, warehousing, inventory holding, order processing, documentation, taxes, packaging, etc.

**Trade deficit** A negative balance of trade

**Trading blocs** A trade bloc is a type of intergovernmental agreement, often part of a regional intergovernmental organization, where regional barriers to trade (tariffs and non-tariff barriers) are reduced or eliminated among the participating states

**Trading companies** Organizations involved in the exchange of products, services and cash that were particularly important in opening up new markets in underdeveloped countries

**Transactions** The exchange of items of value, including information, goods, services and money

**Transfer pricing** The price that is assumed to have been charged by one part of a company for products and services it provides to another part of the same company, in order to calculate each division's profit and loss separately

**Transnational segmentation** Entering foreign markets with a solid marketing plan that helps a company create a positive brand presence and resonates with residents of the foreign country

**Transnationality** The pursuit of opportunities in all parts of the world by integrating and coordinating sourcing of products and services from all parts of the world and serving multiple country markets across all world regions

**Values** Ideas about what is good, right, fair and just, that guide society to act and behave in certain ways

**Websites** Collections of related webpages containing images, videos or other digital material

**Wholly owned subsidiary** Independent business unit in a home or foreign location owned by a parent firm with headquarters in the home country

**World Bank** An international banking organization established to control the distribution of economic aid between member nations and to make loans to them in times of financial crisis

**World trade** The value of the trading of goods and services across the globe

**World Trade Organization (WTO)** The WTO deals with the rules of trade between nations at a global or near-global level

**World Wide Web** Global network of computers connecting the sites that supply a variety of data, audio and visual resources

**Zettabyte** A measure of data storage space that is equivalent to about 1000 exabytes

# CREDITS

# INDEX